The Reviewers Say ..

"*Core Web3D* is the most thorough explanation I have seen of how the Web3D Consortium is developing and promoting open standards to integrate 3D graphics into the very fabric of the Web. 3D is the next major media revolution, and the Web is going to be the vehicle through which it reaches deeply into our lives. Today we are laying the foundation for that revolution, with compelling new content and 3D-enabled sites appearing every day. This book is an insightful primer and manual for becoming part of Web3D's future."

—Neil Trevett
President
Web3D Consortium (web3d.org)

"3D graphics on the Web has arrived. *Core Web3D* is the only book of its kind, carefully prepared and tested for programmers who want to tap into the future of 3D today. Buy it, read it, and get to work!"

—Don Brutzman
Naval Postgraduate School
and Web3D Consortium

"This book is not just an interpretation of standards, but an authoritative exposition by the experts in the fields. After finishing this book, you will feel that you are routed to the InsightWeb3D node!"

—Euee S. Jang
MPEG-4 SNHC Group Chair

"A fabulous and timely tour de force covering VRML, Java 3D, X3D, and the soon all-important MPEG-4 3D scene description format. A must have."

—Sandy Ressler
Web3D Guide for About.com (web3d.about.com)

core

WEB3D

ISBN 0-13-085728-9

90000

9 780130 857286

PRENTICE HALL PTR
CORE SERIES

*Sun Microsystems Press titles

core
WEB3D

AARON E. WALSH
MIKAËL BOURGES-SÉVENIER

PH
PTR

Prentice Hall PTR
Upper Saddle River, NJ 07458
www.phptr.com

Library of Congress Cataloging-in-Publication Data

Walsh, Aaron E.
    Core Web 3D / Aaron Walsh, Mikaël Bourges-Sévenier.
        p.   cm.
    ISBN 0–13–085728–9
    1. Computer graphics. 2. Three-dimensional display systems. 3. Web sites—Design. I.
    Bourges-Sévenier, Mikaël. II. Title.

T385.W364 1999
006.6'93—dc21   99–046122

Production Editor: *Faye Gemmellaro*
Acquisitions Editor: *Tim Moore*
Editorial Assistant: *Julie Okulicz*
Development Editors: *Jim Markham, Ralph Moore*
Marketing Manager: *Bryan Gambrel*
Manufacturing Manager: *Maura Zaldivar*
Cover Designer: *Talar Agasyan*
Cover Design Direction: *Jerry Votta*
Art Director: *Gail Cocker-Bogusz*

© 2001 Prentice Hall PTR
Prentice-Hall, Inc.
Upper Saddle River, NJ 07458

Prentice Hall books are widely used by corporations and government agencies for training,
marketing, and resale. The publisher offers discounts on this book when ordered in bulk quantities.
For more information, contact
        Corporate Sales Department
        Prentice Hall PTR
        One Lake Street
        Upper Saddle River, NJ 07458
        Phone: 800-382-3419; FAX: 201-236-7141
        E-mail: corpsales@prenhall.com

Printed in the United States of America

10 9 8 7 6 5 4 3 2 1

ISBN 0-13-085728-9

Prentice-Hall International (UK) Limited, *London*
Prentice-Hall of Australia Pty. Limited, *Sydney*
Prentice-Hall Canada Inc., *Toronto*
Prentice-Hall Hispanoamericana, S.A., *Mexico*
Prentice-Hall of India Private Limited, *New Delhi*
Prentice-Hall of Japan, Inc., *Tokyo*
Pearson Education Asia Pte. Ltd.
Editora Prentice-Hall do Brasil, Ltda., *Rio de Janeiro*

Dedication

To my wife and family, with love.

Aaron E. Walsh

To my wife Shu-Ting for her support, without which I could not have pursued, much less completed, this endeavor.
To Riitta, for being my friend and for her support as well as advice.

Mikaël Bourges-Sévenier

Contents

PART 1:

Foreword

Dave Raggett
W3C HTML Architect on assignment from HP Labs

I first became aware of the seductive power of 3D computer models in 1980 when I was working at the University of Edinburgh on artificial intelligence. The papers by Whitted and Blinn included wonderful color plates of models of teapots, translucent glass, and surrealistic fruits. Computers clearly had the potential to make imagination tangible in a much more direct way than the written word or even movies and television.

Later I learned about the developing field of virtual reality (VR), but it seemed remote with its dependence on very powerful computers and expensive peripherals—something that only a privileged handful of people could play with.

By the early nineties I was working at HP Labs on hypertext ordering systems that converted sales manuals and other paperwork into interactive graphical displays. The project was canceled, but it gave me lots of ideas. I posted a wacky suggestion to the news group "alt.hypertext" for a collaborative skunk-works project on a global hypertext system; soon I was led to the work being done by Tim Berners-Lee and Robert Caillau at CERN and decided to work with them.

I met Tim on a flying visit to CERN in '92, and we talked and talked about ideas for the Web. I soon found myself spending my spare time writing code for browsers, servers, and firewall tunnels. My experience with the HP ordering system led me to write an Internet Draft for HTML+, an early attempt to define a richer model for Web hypertext. My experimental browser, Arena, was the first to support tables, text flow around images, and math. Arena was later transferred to CERN and used as the original test bed for developing style-sheet support for the Web.

NCSA's Mosaic browser—rugged, simple to use, and best of all free— helped to fuel the exponential explosion of the Web. Anyone with access to the Internet could download a browser and a server and within minutes have a Web site up and running! Graphics turned out to be very important, fueling people's creative impulses. Soon every company wanted a Web site of its own.

In the free-for-all that characterized the early development of the Web, rough consensus and running code held sway. Nonetheless, there were a lot of variations from one browser to the next. Every company thought it could introduce new tags of its own. Standardization efforts that started in the Internet Engineering Task Force (IETF) and were carried on by the World Wide Web Consortium have helped stave off the threat of fragmentation.

Standards are built with the hard work and willing cooperation of the parties involved. Sometimes standards cement existing practices, and sometimes they point the way forward. The high cost of maintaining existing code acts as a brake to the smooth adoption of standards. Standards moderate the excesses of the frontier spirit that has characterized the meteoric growth of the Web, and they provide stability to sustain further growth.

In early 1994, I turned my attention to the glittering promise of extending the Web to an interconnected 3D landscape that one could roam at will, to meet others for work, to buy and sell, or just out of curiosity. In part, this interest grew out of my frustration with remote working via telephone conferences, but my imagination had been fired by the new 3D games on PCs, especially "Doom."

Doom was essentially a tedious shoot-em-up game with a few puzzles to solve along the way. What was new was the intense immersive 3D experience you could enter using an ordinary PC. Doom showed that the necessary computing power was on hand and that it wasn't necessary to use the expensive helmets and gloves found in professional virtual reality systems.

It was easy to envisage the use of a 3D Web to bring to life historical scenes (e.g., medieval cities); to realize imaginary places that don't exist anywhere in the real world; to experience wildlife parks and undersea vistas; to visit places you could never normally go—the canyons on Mars, the international space station—or simply to get familiar with somewhere you are going to visit soon.

Around this time, tools appeared that exploited the power of fractals for building computer-generated natural landscapes—clouds, mountains, rivers, lakes, trees and forests, snow, rocks, and vegetation. These models took a long time to compute, but with increasing computer power (courtesy of Moore's law) and some sleight-of-hand, the opportunities looked grand!

Encouraged by my colleagues, I started work on a vision paper for the first international Web conference, to be held in CERN in the summer of 1994, and for the Internet Society Conference a few weeks later in Prague.

One of the sad things about the Internet is that you never have enough bandwidth. This actually got worse as more people started using modems from home. Unfortunately, 3D models involve large amounts of geometry data along with texture files. How, then, could 3D scenes, large enough to be interesting, be downloaded quickly enough to be worthwhile?

Bandwidth is increasing more slowly than processing power, which quadruples every three years, following Moore's law. The solution, I realized, was to avoid transferring such files whenever you could, instead transferring instructions which could be used to locally recreate the data needed by the rendering engine—in essence, to use local computer power to compensate for bandwidth limitations.

Perhaps a markup language could be used to describe models that in turn would be interpreted by scripts to create the 3D scenes? Thus was born the idea of VRML—an extensible virtual reality markup language.

The missing ingredient was an object-oriented scripting language for rendering the markup and adding behavior. Java and ECMAScript have since emerged, and I am now working with ECMA on improving ECMAScript's fit to this role. My "Spice" proposal covers a way to bind novel markup to object classes using style rules (http://www.w3.org/People/Raggett/Spice/).

Using these tools, skilled programmers would be able to define collections of object classes for interpreting matching markup. Less skilled programmers could tinker with the rendering and behavior via simple scripts and style sheets.

To get a feeling for what this means, you can imagine markup for creating a variety of buildings. The markup specifies parameters such as the number of floors, the color and type of wall claddings, the wallpaper in each room, etc. The markup could allow you to specify an optional floor plan if desired. A style sheet binds the tags to the code needed to interpret them. This code can then be downloaded as required. There is no need to standardize the tags, since their meaning is determined by the downloaded code used to interpret them.

The ease of Web-site construction has a critical impact on how many people are prepared to have a go. Most of us want practically instant gratification! Being able to use a text editor is much easier than having to struggle to learn a complex new tool. This observation motivated the idea of using simple markup and scripts.

Like many people, I have been attracted by the power of fractals to generate arbitrarily complex images from the simplest of rules. It occurred to me that this could be applied to synthetic virtual reality scenes other than naturalistic landscapes. One example that sprang to mind was the open-plan office cubicles familiar from every HP site. The cubicles are made from a small set of components and are populated with shelves, filing cabinets, whiteboards, desks, computers, and so on. A handful of rules could construct an infinite number of varying cubicles and interconnecting corridors.

Provided that the code used to generate the offices gave the same results on different machines, you could give each cubicle a unique identifier to inform the Web server what personal effects are present in each cubicle—for instance, what books are on the shelves, what is written on the whiteboard, and whose files are on the computer.

In essence, you can think in terms of a biological metaphor, where seeds are transported to be grown into plants. In fact, you only need to transfer the DNA, if the cellular machinery is already present. This approach can be applied to much more than the geometry of a 3D scene. For instance, think of "animals," and you get the idea of DNA determining behavior as well as form. Perhaps the virtual meeting places of the future will be much more "organic" than today's architecture!

Another issue is how to provide realism without excessive computational demands. To date, the computer-graphics community has focused on geometrical and lighting models to achieve realism. An alternative approach could draw upon artistic metaphors for rendering scenes. Paintings are not like photographs, and artists don't try to capture all details; rather, they aim to distill the essentials with a much smaller number of brush strokes. This is akin to symbolic representations of scenes. We may be able to apply this to VR. As an example, consider the difficulty in modeling the folds of cloth on your shirt as you move your arm around. Modeling this computationally is going to be very expensive, but perhaps a few rules can be used to draw in some creases when you move your arms.

I presented my ideas for VRML to a meeting I ran together with Tim Berners-Lee at the CERN Web conference for those interested in exploring the idea of a 3D Web. The meeting was packed—particularly so, on account of Mark Pesce's great talk on the vision he and Tony Parisi had for 3D hypertext. After the conference ended, the VRML mailing list was set up and was swamped by some 2,000 subscribers in a matter of weeks.

I didn't get to read Stephenson's *Snow Crash* and similar books until much later. Stephenson describes the "Metaverse," a virtual world that replicates many of the properties of the real world including zoning laws and urban sprawl. The "Metaverse" supports virtual presence for its participants, allowing them to congregate together, even though separated by thousands of miles in the real world.

For an effective virtual presence, it would be important to be able to see people's facial expressions in real time with a low latency, preferably as low as 100 milliseconds. Longer latencies would progressively worsen the experience. Computer games have shown that the latency is more important to the sense of engagement than the quality of the graphics!

If you try "pinging" different Web sites, you can see that such latencies are achievable across the Internet, at least within the same country. Perhaps we could use a video camera to capture just people's facial expressions and combine these with a 3D model of people's heads and the rest of their bodies? By a strange coincidence, I found out about some research in the University of Essex that seemed ideally suited to this purpose.

British Telecom had commissioned Adrian Clark to investigate ways to improve the quality of low-bitrate videotelephony. The existing standard smeared people's lip movements so much that lip reading was impossible. The solution was to develop software that incorporated a model of the human head, which it used to interpret the video signal and to provide the instructions for pasting the image data back onto a wireframe model at the receiver. This yielded a 3D model that you could rotate, even though the starting point was a regular 2D video camera.

Model-based coding techniques seem well suited for adoption for virtual presence, since they make it straightforward to create lifelike avatars with minimum bandwidth demands. For instance, head movements can be compressed into simple changes in coordinates. Further gains in bandwidth could be achieved at a cost in accuracy by a real-time characterization of facial gestures in terms of a composition of "identikit" stereotypes (e.g., shots of mouths which are open or closed, smiling or frowning). The face is then built up by blending the static model of the user's face and jaw with the stereotypes for the mouth, cheeks, eyes, and forehead.

Before we can construct the "Metaverse," we must solve a number of tough scaling problems. Rendering engines slow down as the size of the geometric model increases. A realistic model of a skyscaper can run into millions of polygons used to construct scores of rooms, corridors, foyers, etc. Now picture a city composed of thousands of buildings and the difficulty of the task becomes obvious.

Picture yourself inside a building. You see the room you are in, plus glimpses of others through doors, windows, and walkways. If for each room the geometric model identifies the visibility set of other rooms that can be seen from within it, then the rendering engine has an easy way to ignore the rooms that can't be seen. This technique can be combined with others. For things that are far away, a simple model will do. By representing objects at different levels of detail, the rendering engine can pick the level appropriate to the distance of the object and the total complexity of the scene. For outdoor views, the city "smog" can be used to shroud distant buildings, so that only nearby buildings need to be considered.

The information needed to construct the city could come from many different Web sites. If you are a frequent visitor, then the information can be cached locally, perhaps even in advance. There are many possibilities for doing this, ranging from background feeds to using a "standard" CD-ROM. Other challenges arise from the need to manage the information flows used to populate the city with people. Here again the notion of "visibility sets" proves helpful. Your computer needs to receive information only about the people you can see. The use of visibility sets allows servers to route real-time updates to the appropriate clients.

Solving these scaling problems will allow a cohesive 3D Web to appear. Individuals and companies will be able to set up Web sites that fit together to create buildings and cities that function collectively as an effective whole instead of isolated sites. Although I have mostly focused on immersive applications of 3D, there are many other opportunities—on Web pages devoted to mathematics, for instance, where the ability to animate polyhedra can make the topic more vivid and easier to grasp. On pages devoted to cars, 3D models offer potential customers a novel way to experience a new design before visiting a real showroom.

Sadly, my work on HTML and HTTP has left me little time for work on VRML. As you can read elsewhere in this book, the development of VRML has been focused on geometric modeling rather than the higher-level approach I envisaged in my paper. The acronym VRML was soon repositioned to mean "Virtual Reality Modeling Language" rather than markup language. I have been intrigued by the way the fates have brought matters back full circle, with work on Extensible 3D (X3D), VRML's successor, focusing on an XML-based markup solution for representing 3D scenes. The new emphasis on extensible markup, together with the success of Java and ECMAScript, suggests that the 3D Web is entering an exciting phase with wonderful opportunities for further work.

I would like thank Aaron Walsh and Mikaël Bourges-Sévenier for their great efforts in pulling this information together into *Core Web3D*, and I encourage readers to use this material to bring about the next generation of 3D for the Internet.

Foreword

Mark Pesce
Co-inventor, VRML

Worlds in the Web*

Before the Web, when virtual reality had barely escaped from the lab to make its way into Japanese department stores, real-time 3D meant half-million-dollar Silicon Graphics workstations running industrial-strength operating systems. Heady times—but only for a lucky few.

I wasn't one of them.

I read the articles—in *Scientific American*, the *Wall Street Journal*, and *Mondo 2000*—and got the concept immediately. Virtual reality meant the visualization of the imagination, an opportunity to take a peek at things that had only ever been touched—in poetry or art—but never truly realized, never made tangible.

After reading William Gibson's *Neuromancer* I found myself energized by his vision of *cyberspace*—the "consensual hallucination" which would become the communications playground of the twenty-first century. Working as a software engineer at Shiva, I knew something about communications; I was convinced that the networks that Gibson envisioned would soon spread ubiquitously across the world. But networking in 1990 felt more like a string between tin cans compared to the rich universe of Gibson's cyberspace. The networks were coming into place, but the interface to these networks remained light-years behind, an anachronistic opening to an undiscovered world.

Over the next few months, absolutely consumed, I began to think about how to tie the ever-expanding world of the Internet (which I had been working on for several years) into the imaginary worlds of virtual reality. My work at Shiva gave me an enormous background in networks, and my reading taught me lots about VR. On March 7, 1991, I had an insight which forever tied the two together in my mind.

In *Neuromancer*, Gibson wrote about the network and its visualization—cyberspace—as if they composed the twinned strands of DNA, each incomplete without the other. It seemed to me that the FTP sites which spanned the Internet—even in 1991—could be considered just as real as any of the "places" in Gibson's vision of the future, and—with a little work—it might be possible to make them as "real" as anything Gibson had described.

Shiva began as a Macintosh peripherals company, and most of the engineers used Macintoshes; when Spectrum Holobyte released *Spectre*, its enormously popular 3D networked video game, it became our passion; week after week we'd blast each other across the company network. *Spectre* ran just fine on underpowered Macs—now I knew for sure that all of those big computers and defense networks would soon be overrun by cheap machines connected through the Internet.

I could see the future—at least, I believed I could—and I couldn't think about anything else. In early 1992 I left Shiva to found Ono-Sendai (named after the company in *Neuromancer* that manufactured "cyberspace deck" portals into the infosphere) and set out to create an inexpensive VR system that could connect to the Internet and create a shared VR experience for game play, for education, for anything imaginable. That goal turned into a bigger task than any of us had imagined.

Ono-Sendai survived about eighteen months before it ran out of capital and collapsed. It did, however, put me in the right place, at the right time, to witness an almost insignificant event. I subscribed to a number of mailing lists, including one calling itself *FRINGEWARE*, dedicated to cutting-edge reports of the weird or unusual. Around June 1993 I began to see strange bits of computer effluvium show up in messages:

```
http://www.io.com/news/june/steve_jackson_vs_fbi.html
```

I had no real idea what this was, only that it was called a Uniform Resource Locator, or URL, or "earl," and that it referred to a document stored on something called the "World Wide Web." All of this meant nothing to me at the time, just an impenetrable bit of hacker-speak that I promptly ignored.

A month later I made my first visit to SIGGRAPH, the annual technical and trade show for the computer graphics industry. My friend Coco Conn had an area for SIGKIDS, bringing students from ages eight to eighteen in contact with the latest in technology. The SIGKIDS got an opportunity to play with the kinds of high-end computers they'd normally never see until they got into graduate school. While there, I walked over to a lonely Silicon Graphics workstation which seemed to display nothing more interesting than a text document. A few of the words in this document, underlined and in blue, seemed to hold some hidden meaning. I moved the mouse over them—it turned into a pointing finger—and I clicked.

And the whole world changed.

I had just traversed my first link on the World Wide Web, using a week-old browser known as *NCSA Mosaic*. It seemed entirely unimpressive at the time—the links went to pages with more text, and further links went to even more text—but I got the concept.

After SIGGRAPH, I returned home and loaded NSCA Mosaic onto my refurbished SPARCstation, loaded the NCSA WWW server software, logged onto the Internet, and—abracadabra!—my machine became Web site number 330 in a small but growing universe of hypertext. Every night, for two weeks, I came home from my consulting job and surfed the Web. And then I was done. I'd seen everything, gone everywhere, read every word on the Web—including a handful from a man named Tim Berners-Lee, half a world away in Geneva, who talked about future directions for the Web, including virtual reality.

It all clicked: I had bought the SPARCstation to finish my work on Internet protocols for virtual reality, but I had wondered what to put in this cyberspace once I'd finished the job. Tim gave me the answer: Make worlds in the Web. I'd gotten my marching orders. I had all the parts of the vision that would, just a few months later, become VRML.

Labyrinth

In December I received a phone call from Tony Parisi, with whom I'd previously had an acquaintance. I didn't know that Tony was a serious hacker in his own right or that his skills perfectly complemented my own.

On New Year's Day, 1994, as they moved into their new apartment, I gave Tony and his wife, Marina, an overview of my new ideas regarding VRML and cyberspace. Tony, interested, asked if there was any way he could help. "Absolutely," I agreed. "You want to work on this 3D browser for the Web?" He had already heard of the Web and said, sure, what the heck, let's do it.

Over tall, strong coffees at our favorite coffeehouse—Jumpin' Java—we sat and plotted the design. Tony was an expert in computer languages; he knew how to translate text into commands the computer could understand and execute. I knew how to connect the computers over the Internet, and—because of a gift of some software from a tiny company in London called Rendermorphics—we had a high-performance 3D graphics package to make the 3D worlds visible. We quickly sketched out a language that would create 3D spaces inside the Web. Tony took a few days to write the language parser; I took a few more to integrate it with the Web and tack it onto the Rendermorphics software. By early February we were finished. What we'd created wasn't much to look at; you could click on a link inside of Mosaic, then another window opened a "helper application" that displayed a 3D projection of a cube, which could be rotated and examined from any angle. Labyrinth was not very impressive, but it was a beginning.

Going Public

Tony thought the whole thing would end there—what else could you do with it? But I had greater plans, and I knew someone who would care about what we'd done. I fired off an email and told the inventor of the Web that we'd realized his goal of worlds within the Web, space in cyberspace. Within a few hours Tim had answered, congratulating us on our work and inviting us to present it at a conference he was planning for the Spring, at CERN, the gigantic European atom-smasher which was birthplace to the Web.

So, in May, Tony and I pooled our resources to send me to Geneva. The First International Conference on the World Wide Web, an incredible week-long festival for hypertext hackers, brought the entire community together for the first time. On the first afternoon of the conference fifteen people got together in a tiny meeting room to discuss virtual reality on the Web.

Tim was there. And so was Dave Raggett. Dave, who had been intimately involved in the creation of HTML, proposed that the Web needed a "virtual reality markup language" or VRML—and the name stuck. (Later, "markup" was changed to "modeling," which more accurately reflects the function of the language.) I offered the source code that Tony and I had developed to the Web community so that it could become a foundation for an extended exploration of cyberspace visualized.

In retrospect, that was one of the wisest decisions we could have made. It gave all of the loose efforts toward development of VR on the Web a specific focus, and it brought like-minded folks into our orbit—people like Brian Behlendorf, a 19-year-old setting up shop as the first Webmaster for *WIRED* magazine even while moonlighting as a co-founder of Organic Online, the first Web design firm. Brian offered to establish a Web site and www-vrml mailing list on *WIRED*'s servers, giving us a place to house a virtual community of VRML enthusiasts. Within a month two thousand people from around the world had joined www-vrml to discuss the requirements and possibilities of virtual reality on the Web.

In early July, Brian dragged me down to Silicon Graphics to meet up with two researchers, Rikk Carey and Gavin Bell, who had created their own 3D language, known as *Inventor*. Far more evolved than our own simple efforts, Inventor proved to be the foundation for VRML 1.0—so Brian is, in his own way, very much responsible for VRML.

Daniel's Story

Tony and I realized that we needed a project—a "killer app"—that could thrust VRML into public consciousness. Invited by Coco Conn to show our work at 1994's SIGKIDS, we began to cast about for a project that could do justice to our own work. We found it in the Holocaust Memorial Museum, recently opened in Washington, D.C. One of the tours through the museum—designed specifically for children—told "Daniel's Story," the sad tale of a young Jewish boy growing up in Nazi-era Berlin, then forcibly relocated to the Warsaw Ghetto, and, terminally, to Auschwitz. We used our simple VRML browser to create a model of Daniel's room in the ghetto. As in the real-world installation, Daniel's "notes"—fragments from his diary—tacked onto the walls, informed visitors of his daily struggle for survival.

With a lot of help from C. Scott Young—the first VRML modeler—and plenty of encouragement from the Museum, we finished the project just hours before SIGGRAPH opened its doors at the Orlando Convention Center. Ten hours a day, I sat and guided children through a story which many of them had only vaguely heard of. The kids got it immediately; I knew we'd struck a chord, at least with the younger set.

To my surprise, the media began to drop by. At that time, VR meant huge, expensive systems; in our modest booth we showed a full VR system running on an unadorned PC connected to the Internet. This, put simply, blew their minds. One prominent VR journalist confessed that this was the most impressive thing he'd seen at the show. A buzz began to develop.

The Big Bang: VRML 1.0 and 2.0

On Wednesday evening, SIGGRAPH attendees were invited to take part in the first VRML "birds-of-a-feather," where we got together to brainstorm about future directions for VRML. Rikk Carey put forward an exciting proposition: why not use Silicon Graphics' *Inventor* to make VRML industrial-strength? After a handshake deal, Gavin Bell began to work with Tony and me on the design of the VRML 1.0 specification, which we presented at the Second International Conference on the World Wide Web, just two months later!

The first versions of VRML were designed to emulate the Web of 1994. The only "interactivity" in the early Web came from clicking on links and going to new pages or VRML worlds. If this seems rather simplistic, it can be traced to the fact that HTML—the content of the Web—expressed the "look" of things, but not how they'd "play." To make the Web playful, you'd need a standard programming language, which could be written once and run anywhere, on any computer or operating system. Such a language did not exist in the world of 1994.

It was back to the drawing board for us; just after SIGGRAPH '95—where we saw VRML explode across the trade show floor—we secreted ourselves away with Rikk Carey, Gavin Bell, and a few others, a hand-picked crew with a mandate to create a next-generation VRML.

We didn't succeed. Too many good ideas competed for their place in the specification. What about JavaScript? What about Java? What about sound? What about event models? We decided that engineering by committee was a bad idea, so we threw the problem back to the VRML community, creating a set of recommendations and asking for proposals.

By January 1996, we'd received a dozen different specifications from companies like IBM, Microsoft, Sony, and Silicon Graphics. Each of them had merits, and each had shortcomings. We reviewed them, made some comments, then left it to the community to decide which proposal would become VRML 2.0. The Sony/Silicon Graphics proposal—"Moving Worlds"—which successfully integrated Java, JavaScript, and a sophisticated event model, became the basis for VRML 2.0. In May, VRML 2.0 browsers began to appear.

It was like the Big Bang; a legion of content developers began to show off their own imaginings, shared over the Web. Although by no means perfect,

VRML 2.0 provided a platform for a new kind of network visualization. It had taken a few years, but with companies like IBM and Microsoft promoting it, VRML now seemed poised to conquer the world.

VRML97, X3D, Java 3D, MPEG-4, and Beyond

By early 1998 it became clear that VRML, for all of its power, had some serious drawbacks. The VRML browsers required multimegabyte downloads, a big turn-off for Web surfers on slow modems; they ran slowly, at least for users conditioned to the lightning-fast worlds of *Quake* or *Tomb Raider*; and they didn't integrate very well with the Web environment.

Microsoft, which had sensed that 3D for the Web would be a very powerful tool for presentations and visualization, began work on a project called *Chrome*. Chrome differed from VRML in one very significant way; rather than conforming to the "scene-graph" structure of Inventor-like languages (like VRML 2.0), it belonged to the family of XML languages—giving it a closer relationship to the Web browser. Chrome looked a lot like HTML and could be dropped directly into a Web page, interacting with all of the elements on that page. Soon, it seemed, 3D would become an integral part of the Web environment.

Microsoft backed away from Chrome soon after they released it, but the idea had caught on, and the many companies involved in VRML work began to sketch an architecture they named "X3D," a combination of XML and VRML which would take the best ideas in Chrome and marry them to the existing base of VRML applications and content. In the year 2000 the wraps will be taken off X3D, and—finally—virtual reality will become synonymous with the Web.

In 1997 VRML 2.0 evolved into VRML97, an International Standards Organization (ISO) specification that guaranteed a worldwide standard for Web3D and pioneered the way for other forms of Web3D. Java 3D borrows heavily from VRML, MPEG-4/BIFS is directly based on VRML97, and X3D is the official successor to VRML97, due out in 2000.

It makes little difference which of these becomes *the* standard for Web3D; each may become a de facto standard—four standards for four universes. VRML works well as an interchange format for real-time 3D and is really designed as a modeling tool; Java 3D provides the low-level system control that graphics hackers demand; MPEG-4 delivers 3D over a variety of network connections and devices, from the Web to broadcast television; and X3D allows Web designers to drop 3D into their pages without concern for the plug-in architecture or client platform. These technologies complement each other far more than they compete, and none of them is likely to go away anytime soon.

Inside this book you'll find the technical treatises which underlie each of these different approaches toward Web3D. Sometimes they contradict, sometimes they run in perfect concordance; but, differences aside, each can give you the ability to articulate your own feelings, your own dreams, your own imagination. And that, in essence, is what this book is about, what Aaron Walsh and Mikaël Bourges-Sévenier have worked hard to bring you. Learn, and you'll speak a new language—unlike English or German or Japanese—but just as powerful in its ability to express what we are.

And that makes it something worth learning.

Visit www.CoreWeb3D.com/go/forward/ *to read an expanded version of this document, which includes Mark Pesce's view of the future of Web3D content.*

Foreword

Tony Parisi
Co-inventor, VRML

Outside the Tornado

After a long and often frustrating incubation period, Web3D technology is finally poised for mainstream market acceptance. To date, the development of markets based on Web3D products has been haltingly slow. While other technologies that comprise the fabric of today's Web have experienced explosive growth and become a routine part of daily life for tens of millions of people around the world, Web3D has languished on the sidelines. In hindsight the reasons are clear. In our haste to bring the promise of Gibsonian cyberspace to life, we neglected some basic market realities. As a result, 3D is still not broadly deployed on the Web, despite the expenditure of millions of dollars and countless man-hours of effort.

While this diagnosis is not a happy one, the prognosis is generally bright. Over the past five years we have learned valuable lessons which we apply going forward. Also, the world is more ready for us than it was five years ago, as bandwidth, processing power, and user sophistication converge to support a richer online experience. Web3D is on the sidelines today, but it is ready to enter the limelight. *Core Web3D* will give you what you need to participate in the long-awaited transformation of the computer infrastructure to a two-way, fully interactive rich-media communications medium.

Moore's Laws

Most computer technologists are familiar with semiconductor pioneer Gordon Moore's observation that computer power doubles every eighteen months, known as "Moore's Law." Perhaps not as many are familiar with the equally important industry trends identified by another Moore. Geoffrey Moore's seminal works on high-technology marketing, *Crossing the Chasm* and *Inside the Tornado,* describe a set of laws which govern the dynamics of emerging technology markets. While 3D graphics has been a beneficiary of the first Moore, with the awesome number-crunching that empowers 3D accelerator chips coming bundled with even the lowliest personal computer these days, Web3D technologies, most notably VRML, have been the victims of the second Moore's laws.

According to Geoffrey Moore, to establish a technology and lead the market with it, you must create a maelstrom of activity around solutions based on that technology (a "tornado"). Narrowly focused, custom-designed solutions eventually expand their scope to become general-purpose technologies. Personal computers are an example. First adopted in great numbers by corporations to boost productivity and cut costs, PCs today span the range from office productivity to graphic design to video games to Internet access. Databases are another example. Originally used to store vast quantities of financial data, database technology is now used in everything from astrophysics to cookbooks. According to Moore, most successful mass-market technologies follow this pattern of adoption: a nexus of custom solutions, low volumes, and premium prices spiraling upward into a storm of general usage, higher volumes, and more accessible prices.

Moore's Law governing this tornado effect says: *identify a "beachhead" application*—one which serves a specific need, for which customers will pay a premium because they can't get it anywhere else. In other words, find the customers who are feeling the most pain, serve their needs, help them outpace the competition, and they'll pay handsomely for it. If you are successful at this stage, you have revenue to support continuing your business as well as a customer testimonial to help spread the word. From there, expand beyond your beachhead. Broaden the scope of the technology to support other uses, eventually to the stage where you occupy an entire territory.

VRML never had a beachhead. Like Athena, it sprang from our collective mind fully grown. VRML was one of those *damn good ideas*: people do 3D; people do the Web. Why not put these two great tastes together? We assembled the great minds from the disciplines of graphics, networking, and languages. Our approach to the technology was sound, at least theoretically. We specified a general-purpose engine that could perform a range of 3D tasks over a network wire. The problem was, VRML didn't do any of these tasks particularly well, and most vendors didn't spend enough time with paying customers to determine exactly what they needed or which features were most important. As a result, professional developers drawn to VRML either tried to build businesses and failed, or were smart enough to stay out of the game in the first place. Throughout its five-year existence the Web3D industry built around VRML narrowly scraped out of economic nose dives more than once because nobody could provide needy customers with a specifically tailored solution. Fortunately, the technology community at the heart of VRML persevered during this period, continuing to refine the specification. VRML survives today as X3D: older, wiser, and poised for commercial deployment.

Moore also theorizes that the force that powers emerging market tornadoes is *discontinuous innovation*, or simply *discontinuity*. This refers to a technological innovation which enables functionality not previously possible in any other way. Graphical User Interfaces (GUIs) are an example of this. During their introduction in the mid-1980s the business community viewed GUIs as being sexy but of little value outside of niche applications. Today GUIs dominate as the human-computer interface, and nobody questions their utility. Many believe that 3D graphics represents the next wave of discontinuous innovation, and that some day the majority of human-computer interaction will take place in 3D. This is what motivated my own entry into the field in early 1994. 3D graphics hardware was on the way to becoming a commodity; I saw the opportunity to create software applications for this hardware that would demonstrate the benefits of a general-purpose 3D user interface.

Which brings us to another of Geoffrey Moore's laws: *Don't introduce a discontinuity inside another discontinuity*. VRML attempted to introduce 3D as a new paradigm at the same time that the world was undergoing the most sweeping technological change in history. 3D demands a change in thinking: from bitmaps to 3D objects; from tag-based authoring to modeling; from imperative, procedural programming to declarative, event-driven programming. While the masterminds behind VRML were building an elegant architecture to support a scalable online virtual universe, Web developers were busy learning how to Internet-enable their clunky old GUIs, author with angle brackets, and write programs all over again in a new language called Java. Meantime, Joe Six Pack was just learning about something called the "Internet." We built it, but they didn't come . . . there was something bigger happening right next door.

Starting the Tornado

Now is the time to start the Web3D tornado again. The world is recovering from the massive discontinuity that is the Internet and is ready for something new. Broadband networks and low-cost, 3D-capable computers are enabling a rich-media experience everywhere. Personal computers are on a convergence course with television, where the MTV generation has expectations of high-resolution, animated content that only 3D can fulfill. The stage is set. Now we only have two hurdles to jump: deployment and design.

Core Web3D introduces the applications in which developers should consider using Web-based 3D, including data visualization for analysis and presentation, product visualization for eCommerce sales and marketing, animation for advertising and entertainment, and multiuser collaborative design and engineering environments. For these applications, 3D brings more utility than 2D, more fun, or both. Work closely with paying customers to deliver beachhead applications, where 3D provides clear benefits in productivity or user experience. Work closely with Web3D technology suppliers to ensure that what they deliver meets your needs and the customer's.

Design is more challenging. Quality 3D applications are intrinsically harder to conceive and create, requiring the talent of an artist, the technique of an architect, and the discipline of a programmer. *Core Web3D* describes the tools of the trade, including enabling technologies such as VRML, X3D, Java 3D, and MPEG-4/BIFS, and authoring solutions ranging from beginner-level to professional. This valuable book points the way, but the hard work is up to you.

Preface

Welcome to *Core Web3D*, a programmer's introduction to 3D for the Internet. As a professional Web developer, you've probably heard about technologies such as VRML97, Java 3D, MPEG-4, and X3D. This book introduces you to each, in detail and from a programmer's perspective, so that you can weave any one (or all four) into your own Web sites.

If you've been waiting for the right opportunity to jump into Web3D, now is the time. For the first time in computer history, the major pieces of the puzzle are in shape to deliver interactive 3D to the average end user. Yesterday Web3D for the average computer user was impractical, if not entirely impossible. Today, for the first time ever, advances in key Web3D technologies, bandwidth, and sheer processing power give us the ability to deploy interactive 3D to our friends, users, and clients.

This book has been a long time in the making. Over six years, actually, as VRML emerged from concept in 1994 and re-emerges as X3D today. Until now, there was no market for *Core Web3D* simply because the infrastructure wasn't in place to deliver such content to the masses. Things have changed, and today's a different game entirely.

Just as images swept over the Web soon after text-only pages surfaced, followed by audio and video. 3D is now on fire. Major online retailers and entertainment sites have recently embraced Web3D as a strategic mechanism for attracting and holding onto customers, opening the floodgates that we've been battering at for years. By the year 2005 you won't be able to surf the Web without encountering 3D content anymore than you can surf today without bumping into audio and video: 3D is the natural progression of media for the Web. It is inescapable. Learn how to harness it.

The authors of *Core Web3D* are not passive observers in this revolution; we're on the front lines, every day. With no exception, each author and technical reviewer involved with this book is actively involved in the design, development, and advancement of Web3D technologies and standards. We share an unbridled passion for rich, interactive 3D experience delivered over the Internet and hope that our time in the R&D trenches and rides atop commercial Web3D ventures will be of value and interest to you as you lead the charge for Web3D on your own virtual ground.

Although we would have preferred to provide you with in-depth coverage of every Web3D technology now available, a physical limit to the number of pages we could use in this book puts a practical block on how much we would write about. It's impossible to cover everything. We choose, instead, to focus on four key Web3D technologies: VRML97, Java 3D, MPEG-4, and X3D. And, since it's not possible to cover these four technologies exhaustively in one book, we didn't try. Instead, *Core Web3D* is the lead book in a forthcoming series of Web3D books—*Core Java 3D*, *Core MPEG-4*, and *Core X3D* are soon to follow.

What you have in *Core Web3D* is a technical introduction, from a professional programmer's perspective, of each. In this book you'll learn how these four technologies are similar and how they differ. You'll program in each, as you explore the fundamental concepts and major features of each. And, finally, you'll learn how to customize existing Web3D content for your own purposes, so that you can get a jump on developing professional quality 3D for your own Web site. We hope you enjoy the ride as much as we do.

How This Book Is Organized

Core Web3D is organized into five major parts, each dedicated to a specific technology. Following is an overview of each part.

Part 1: Introduction

Although 3D for the Internet has been with us since 1994, when VRML 1.0 was first conceived, today we're finally seeing Web3D technologies flourish thanks to significant advances in technology, bandwidth, and desktop processing power. Part 1 takes a hard look at why Web3D in general, and VRML in particular, were impractical before today. Here you'll find an explanation of the term "Web3D" as used throughout this book and the key technologies discussed herein (specifically VRML97, Java 3D, MPEG-4/BIFS, and X3D).

The chapters in this part also provide an overview of the Web3D Consortium (http://www.web3d.org/) and its role in 3D standards for the Internet, as well as a gentle introduction to the basic concepts and jargon you'll encounter as you enter the 3rd Dimension in the chapters that follow.

Part 2: Virtual Reality Modeling Language

Virtual Reality Modeling Language (VRML) is the pioneer Web3D technology that burst onto the scene in 1994 and promised to immerse us in a 3D Internet. That didn't happen for a number of reasons, as Part 1 explains. In Part 2, you'll learn about VRML in detail as we trace its history from concept to realization and ultimately to international standardization (a.k.a. VRML97). Along the way you'll learn how to program in the VRML language and how to customize existing VRML content for your own purposes. You'll also learn about a new and exciting crop of visual content creation tools that allow you, the professional Web developer, to create exceptionally compelling VRML content using little more than your mouse and your imagination.

In Part 2 you'll learn how to weave VRML worlds into Web pages, how to reprogram existing VRML content to fit your needs, and how to construct virtual worlds and characters using visual authoring tools. The concepts and skills that you gain in this part of the book will serve you well in the remaining parts, as VRML is at the heart of all Web3D technologies discussed in this book.

Part 3: Java 3D

Java 3D is Sun's standard Java 2 platform extension ("optional package") for creating interactive 3D applets and applications. As a member of the Java Media family of Application Programming Interfaces (APIs), Java 3D delivers a suite of standard Java classes that programmers can use to construct a wide variety of 3D programs. Although Java 3D programs are written in Java, the Java 3D architecture has a great deal in common with the VRML technology that inspired it. The VRML programmer will find that VRML and Java 3D have a surprising kinship. Java 3D programs can, in fact, utilize VRML content, thus maximizing any investment that you make in VRML as you'll soon learn.

In Part 3 you'll explore in detail how VRML and Java 3D parallel one another, and where they diverge. You'll learn how to write Java 3D applets and applications, use VRML content in your Java 3D programs, and customize premade Java 3D content for your purposes. Because Java 3D is rooted in Java, the chapters in Part 3 assume that you're an experienced Java developer. If this is not the case, the first chapter in this part of the book lists a number of resources that you can turn to when learning Java for the first time.

Part 4: MPEG-4/BIFS

MPEG-4 is the fourth major version of the Motion Picture Experts Group (MPEG) standard, the previous versions of which (MPEG-1 and MPEG-2, in particular) are largely responsible for the audio and video invasion that we have experienced through our desktop computers and digital televisions. MPEG-4 is a toolkit of multimedia solutions that developers can use to deliver audio, video, 2D graphics, and 3D graphics over a variety of network and broadcast connections.

MPEG-4 Binary Format for Scenes, better known as MPEG-4/BIFS, is (as the name implies) a component of MPEG-4 that supports binary encoding and delivery of scenes. Although not restricted to 3D scenes, this book focuses on MPEG-4/BIFS in the context of Web3D. In Part 4 you'll learn about BIFS in great detail. Here you'll examine how BIFS works, how it was derived from VRML, how you can control and animate 3D scenes with BIFS commands, and how you can integrate existing VRML content with MPEG-4.

Part 5: X3D

Extensible 3D (X3D) began life as VRML Next Generation (VRML-NG), and today has grown into a new form of Web3D that promises to address many of the shortcomings of VRML97 while pushing the envelope in terms of real time 3D for the Internet. As a technology tied to the Extensible Markup Language (XML), X3D allows VRML content to be expressed in terms of XML. In addition, X3D is built around a componentized, extensible architecture that supports layering in new features and enhancements far beyond those found in VRML.

Although X3D is extremely exciting, it has one major downside: It's not available yet! Due to ship in the second half of 2000, the X3D development schedule didn't align precisely with the publication date of this book. At the time of this writing X3D was under constant development, meaning the X3D material in Part 5 of this book was under threat of being obsolete from the moment it was written.

To help reduce this potentially frustrating situation, Part 5 gives you an insider's look at the world of X3D rather than a programmer's view (simply because the programmer's view was constantly changing due to the pace at which X3D is being developed). Here you'll find the motivation behind X3D, including a candid look at the technical shortcomings of the VRML technology it was designed to surpass. In addition, you'll get an exclusive look at the various proposals submitted to the Web3D Consortium's X3D Task Group in 1999 for evaluation as potential X3D solutions, as well as an overview of one potential authoring solution known as X3D Markup Language (X3DML).

Conventions

Like all books in the Core series, *Core Web3D* adheres to a standard suite of production elements. Source code, for example, is set in a typeface different than that used in the main text. Following is a snippet of VRML source code to illustrate the style in which you'll be presented with such material:

```
#VRML V2.0 utf8

Background {
  skyColor 1 1 1          # create a bright white sky
}

Shape {
  appearance Appearance {
   material Material {}   # create a "lit" shape
  }
  geometry Box {}         # display a 3D box geometry
}
```

Likewise, special format and style elements are used to call your attention to important pieces of material such as sidebars, notes, warnings, and tips. The following warning icon, for example, illustrates what will appear anytime there is a crucial issue that you must be aware of:

Warning: X3D in Flux

At the time this book was written X3D was under constant change. As a result, the material in this book will be outdated as X3D emerges from development. As a Core Web3D reader, however, you're free to visit the Core Web3D book site at http://www.CoreWeb3D.com/ for updates and links to new X3D content.

About the CD-ROM

If you've been feverishly looking for the CD-ROM that came with this book you'll be relieved to find that no, you're not going mad: A CD-ROM is not included with *Core Web3D*. Instead, the source code listings, hyperlinks, and examples found in this book are available online, free of charge, through the *Core Web3D* web site at http://wwwCoreWeb3D.com/. This site was created for you, the *Core Web3D* reader and is updated regularly as important Web3D innovations occur (such as the emergence of X3D from the development process, or new versions of the Java 3D API are released by Sun, for example). Here you'll also find links to a wide variety of Web3D resources, including an online discussion group where you can share your thoughts, comments, and suggestions about *Core Web3D* with your fellow readers.

Tip: Core Web3D Site

Visit the Core Web3D *book site at* http://www.CoreWeb3D.com/ *for free electronic updates to this book, links to new and exciting Web3D technologies and events, and an invitation to join your fellow readers in an exclusive* Core Web3D *discussion group.*

Support Site

As a reader of *Core Web3D* you've undoubtedly noticed that we haven't included a CD-ROM with this book, and for good reason: It would be out of date by the time you read this welcome. Fixed media simply can't compete with the dynamic, ever-changing Web, and so we've created CoreWeb3D.com specifically to keep you plugged in to the exciting and rapidly advancing world of Internet-based 3D.

Visit CoreWeb3D.com for instant access to source code listings appearing in this book, links to tools and support resources, regularly updated links for each chapter (we've included printed URL summaries at the end of each chapter, although you'll probably find live online links more convenient), late-breaking news, errata, and other material that we think you'll find useful and interesting. CoreWeb3D.com also gives you one-click access to a special discussion group that connects you with fellow readers, so that you can share your thoughts, questions, and suggestions with like-minded professionals and us.

We hope that you enjoy *Core Web3D* as much as we enjoyed creating it for you; let us know what you think—we'll see you on CoreWeb3D.com!

-- Aaron and Mikaël

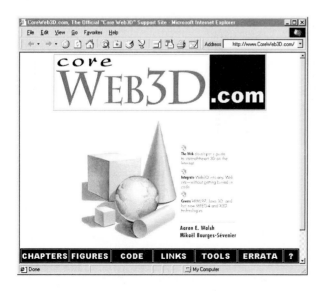

Acknowledgments

Core Web3D would not have been possible without many individual and group efforts. I would like to thank the entire Prentice Hall team that worked on this book. In particular, great thanks go to Tim Moore (the Prentice Hall VP who made this book possible by placing his bet on the Web3D horse early in the race); to Jim Markham (my development editor, who kept this title on track, as we galloped down the home stretch); to Ralph Moore (who took the reins as development editor when we first got out of the gate); and to Faye Gemmellaro (who rode every page that you now hold in your hands through the production process). And with special thanks to Barbara Mikolajczak, my coworker, who kept legal permissions in play while we ran the race. All Kentucky Derby analogies aside, I've enjoyed this ride thoroughly, and appreciate everyone taking it with me.

I would also like to thank my co-authors, who also took the ride and without whom Part 3 (Java 3D), Part 4 (MPEG-4/BIFS), and Part 5 (X3D) of this book would not have been possible. In this industry time is a precious resource, and each of these men carved out a substantial piece of their life to be involved with Core Web3D. Mikaël Bourges-Sévenier wrote the MPEG-4/BIFS part of this book solo, Bob Crispen and Len Bullard wrote the X3D material, and Bernie Roehl and Justin Couch wrote the bulk of the Java 3D material.

Acknowledgments

To our technical editors, Ken Martin, Doug Gehringer, and Bob Crispen (who wore two hats on this project), I would like to thank you all for not only reading early versions of our work, but for taking the time to give valuable feedback and suggestions along the way.

Finally, I would like to thank the entire Web3D community. Without you, there would be no such thing as Web3D, Core Web3D, or a Web3D Series. The writing I've done in 1999, and will do in 2000, is a result of your blood, sweat, and tears. In particular, I would like to thank several individuals who helped put Core Web3D to bed in one way or another, including Tim Berners-Lee, Dave Raggett, Mark Pesce, Tony Parisi, Don Brutzman, Dick Puk, Sandy Ressler, Gerardo Quintieri, Nicholas Quintieri, Holger Grahn, Eric Anschutz, Jim Stewartson, Steve Guynup, Bob Lipkin, and Dan Lipkin.

Aaron E. Walsh

I would like to thank all contributors to the MPEG-4 chapters for their pictures, their valuable comments and suggestions, their help, their support, and their patience: Peter van Beek, Riitta Väänänen, Jean-Claude Dufourd, Olivier Avaro, Touradj Ebrahimi, Eric Scheirer, Carsten Herpel, the MPEG-4 teams of iVast Inc., France Télécom Centre Commun d'Etudes de Télédiffusion et Télécommunications (CCETT), Ecole Nationale Supérieure des Télécommunications (ENST), and Centro Studi e Laboratori Telecomunicazioni (CSELT). My deepest gratitude to Ganesh Rajan, Homer Chen, and Patrick Kelly, who suffered through discussions of earlier versions of these chapters and provided useful suggestions to improve them.

Mikaël Bourges-Sévenier

Part 1

INTRODUCTION

WHY BOTHER?

Topics in This Chapter

- Why 3D was unable to reach the mass of Web users before today

- Unveiling key Web3D technologies (VRML, X3D, Java 3D, and MPEG-4/BIFS) and the Web3D Consortium

- An overview of yesterday's roadblocks: bandwidth, platform, and authoring-tool limitations

- Exploring how Web3D facilitates product and data visualization, eCommerce and business applications, entertainment, Web page enhancement, and news and advertisement enhancement

- A tour of the Web3D future by way of VRML sites available today

Chapter 1

3D is difficult. Extremely difficult. Thinking and working in three dimensions is natural for human beings; we do it every moment of every day. Our brains are wired for three dimensions because our world is made up of three dimensions: height, width, and depth. But "3D"—the field of computer science that deals expressly with creating, manipulating, and navigating *computer* content in three dimensions—is difficult. Extremely difficult.

It should come as no surprise, then, that Web3D—the distribution and navigation of 3D content over the World Wide Web—is also difficult. In fact, it's more technologically challenging than traditional 3D, owing to the high bandwidth required to smoothly deliver realistic 3D content through the Internet. And, once such content arrives at the desktop, an astonishing amount of computing power is required to interact with it. As a result, compelling Web3D content was practically impossible for the average end user to experience before today. Which raises the question: Why bother?

To understand the answer, you must first understand *what* Web3D actually is. The term "Web3D," as used throughout this book, didn't even exist before the end of 1998, even though many of the technologies it describes have been around in one form or another for several years. Web3D does not describe a specific technology, nor is it merely a way to deliver 3D content over the World Wide Web. Finally, Web3D is not solely about content that just *looks* 3D to the eye—a visual trick that any experienced graphics artist can produce with Adobe Photoshop by simply adding the appearance of depth to an image; Web3D goes much further than that.

So what's Web3D all about, and why should you care?

Unveiling Web3D

Web3D is not a specific technology for delivering 3D over the Internet, it's not a particular programming language used to develop 3D applications, and it's not a solitary file format for storing 3D content; Web3D is all of these things.

As Chapter 2, "Overview of Web3D," explains in great detail, Web3D is a general term used to describe protocols, languages, file formats, and other technologies that are used to deliver true, interactive 3D content over the World Wide Web. More specifically, Web3D is a group of standard technologies recommended by the Web3D Consortium for use in delivering 3D content over the Internet.

The Web3D Consortium, whose home on the Web can be seen in Figure 1-1, is a non-profit organization comprised of over 50 high-technology companies that provide technical and marketing expertise to advance the state of industry-wide standards for 3D Internet and broadcast applications. Through the Web3D Consortium, industry heavyweights such as Apple, IBM, Intel, Microsoft, Mitsubishi Electric, Oracle, Silicon Graphics, Sun, and Sony work together to design, develop, and promote a suite of open, interoperable, and standardized technologies known collectively as *Web3D*.

The Web3D Consortium began life several years ago as the VRML Consortium, a nonprofit organization focused exclusively on developing and promoting the Virtual Reality Modeling Language (VRML) as an Internet 3D standard. VMRL, when it burst onto the scene in 1994, was the only player in town when it came to openly developed Internet 3D. Developed in a collaborative manner, VRML became the first technology officially recognized by the International Organization for Standardization (ISO) as a standard for the encapsulation, delivery, and playback of 3D over the Internet.

VRML ignited the imagination, brought 3D to the Web, and ushered in a suite of VRML-inspired Internet 3D technologies that we know today as Web3D. VRML pioneered the way for Web3D technologies such as Extensible 3D (X3D), Java 3D, MPEG-4's Binary Format for Scenes

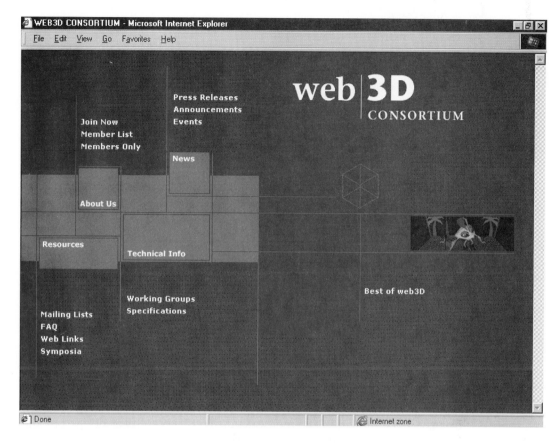

Figure 1-1 The Web3D Consortium (http://www.web3d.org/) is the center of the Web3D universe, where open, industrywide Internet 3D standards are designed, developed, and promoted.

(MPEG-4/BIFS), and other forms of Internet 3D. As the original Internet 3D standard, VRML is truly the center of gravity around which all other forms of Web3D orbit, as illustrated in Figure 1-2.

VRML has matured considerably over the years, owing largely to the efforts of the VRML Consortium and its members. These efforts paved the way for a variety of new Internet 3D technologies. As a result, in July of 1998, the VRML Consortium officially expanded its charter to embrace all standard Internet 3D technologies *and* promote interoperability with existing Web technologies such as Dynamic HTML (DHTML), Document Object Model (DOM), Extensible Markup Language (XML), and Motion Picture Experts Group level 4 (MPEG-4).

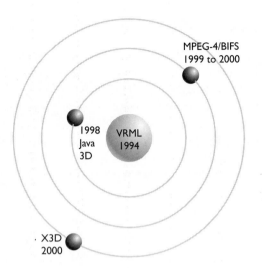

Figure 1-2   As the original Internet 3D standard, VRML is the center of gravity around which Web3D revolves.

In December of that same year the VRML Consortium was formally re-named the "Web3D Consortium" to reflect its broadened role, making "Web3D" a general term that describes a number of interoperable Internet 3D standards endorsed by the consortium. Today, Web3D as defined by the consortium includes VRML and the forthcoming X3D, both of which were developed within the consortium. Java 3D and MPEG-4/BIFS, on the other hand, have not yet been "blessed" by the Web3D Consortium, although they may be in the future. MPEG-4 has already been designated an ISO standard, while Sun has struggled to standardize Java (the parent technology of Java 3D) through the standards-setting group of the European Computer Manu-facturers Association (ECMA) as well as ISO.

In this book we'll cover Java 3D and MPEG-4/BIFS in addition to VRML and X3D, as the term *Web3D* is meant to expand in meaning over time to encompass those technologies that satisfy the goals of the Web3D Consor-tium. We believe these four technologies are key to Internet 3D.

While you may find the evolution of VRML, Web3D, and the Web3D Consortium interesting, it doesn't explain why you should bother with Web3D in the first place. After all, VRML has been around for years and it has yet to live up to the hype it generated when first introduced to the

Note: Web3D to Me

At the time of this writing Web3D *as defined by the Web3D Consortium includes only VRML and the forthcoming Extensible 3D (X3D, due in 2000). We'll refer to Java 3D and MPEG-4/BIFS as forms of Web3D, however, as they are both significant Internet 3D technologies and good candidates for "blessing" by the consortium. MPEG-4 has already achieved status as an international ISO standard, while Java is now under evaluation for approval as an ECMA standard.*

Internet community. It's true that VRML has progressed by leaps and bounds since those early days, and a variety of related Web3D technologies have also emerged that you can use together with VRML or independently, but even so, why bother?

Everything Changes with Web3D

The simple answer to why you should bother with Web3D is that, as of today, everything changes. At the time of this writing, the Web3D Consortium is just over a year old and in full blossom as it embraces an expanded charter that unifies an entire industry around a suite of open, interoperable technologies. By the end of the year 2000, all fundamental Web3D technologies and infrastructures will have matured to a point that makes Web-based 3D content relatively easy to create, deploy, and experience.

Before today, there was no such thing as Web3D. VRML was the only option when it came to open, standardized 3D on the Web. Unfortunately, major technological barriers sat between VRML and the average end user, effectively walling VRML off from the general public and making it the private domain of a relatively small community of researchers, educators, and 3D enthusiasts. These barriers, which can now be overcome, included:

- Bandwidth limitations
- Platform limitations
- Content authoring-tool limitations

These barriers didn't magically disappear. In fact, they didn't disappear at all; these are issues that still exist today. The magic, if you can call it that, is the way in which innovative technological solutions and the march of time have provided a way for VRML and other forms of Web3D to reach the average end user *despite* these challenges. While the barriers that originally prevented VRML from reaching the masses still exist today, we now know how to get around them. With this in mind, let's dig a little deeper into the fundamental challenges that prevented VRML from taking over the world before today, and see how the next generation of VRML and other Web3D technologies overcome these challenges.

Bandwidth Limitations

Web3D is delivered to end users primarily via the Internet. Exceptions exist, of course, because Web3D can also be delivered on fixed media such as CD-ROM, but it almost goes without saying that "Web" 3D is typically experienced over the World Wide Web. That means using a browser such as Netscape Navigator or Internet Explorer equipped with a plug-in (see "Platform Limitations," later in this chapter, to learn more about Web3D

Don't Believe the Hype

The first version of VRML was by no means perfect, and its lack of key features such as behavior modeling and animation capabilities undoubtedly contributed to its inability to live up to early hype. Although VRML 2.0 solved the shortcomings of VRML 1.0, it remained, practically speaking, out of reach of the general public until today, primarily because of bandwidth, platform, and authoring-tool limitations.

It's hard to recall any technology that has fully lived up to massive early hype. Java, for example, is only now emerging with deliverables that mesh with version 1.0 promises, while some technologies aren't so lucky and practically drown as a result of their own big splash (remember the Internet "Push" craze?). VRML, meanwhile, continues to gain momentum and grow in popularity, even as it shakes off the hangover of the early hype naturally associated with any technology that promises to bring "Virtual Reality" to the masses.

plug-ins). Web3D is challenged by bandwidth limitations in the same way that every single page on the Web is: If there's not enough bandwidth available to smoothly deliver content to the end user, the experience will be less than pleasant.

Bandwidth is always a concern when dealing with the Internet; there never seems to be enough of it to go around. When VRML was invented in mid 1990s, 14.4-Kbps modems were considered lightning fast. Even though VRML was designed from the very beginning to be bandwidth efficient, even modest 3D content created with the language could take several minutes to transmit over dial-up modems of that speed.

To complicate matters, the most compelling VRML scenes often contain both images and sounds, further straining meager network connections. As a result, it wasn't uncommon for end users connecting to the Internet from home to wait half an hour or more to experience complex VRML content as it sluggishly crawled from the server to the client over a modem connection. A high-speed network connection, typically available at the time only to higher education, research facilities, and big businesses, was often required to tap into the best VRML content. Sadly, the vast majority of Web surfers simply didn't have enough bandwidth to experience VRML in all its glory before now.

Today, bandwidth is becoming less and less of an issue, thanks to the proliferation of 56-Kbps dial-up modems, cable modems, and a variety of high-speed network connections to the home such as ISDN, DSL, and even satellite access. As the year 2000 unfolds, the home Internet access market is fast approaching network speeds that enable easy delivery of rich 3D content.

Today's high-speed Internet connections for the home greatly extend the reach of VRML and other forms of Web3D, especially when combined with bandwidth-conscious technologies such as *streaming, compression*, and *Universal Media* (see Figure 1-3). Streaming allows content to be delivered over the network incrementally, meaning the end user can experience Web3D as it comes over the wire, a little at a time, rather than having to wait for everything to arrive in full. Compression (particularly binary compression) allows Web3D scenes to be substantially reduced in size long before the download journey actually begins, saving precious bandwidth that would otherwise be consumed in the process. Powerful compression schemes used by MPEG-4/BIFS, for example, can produce tightly packed scene files that are twenty times smaller than the uncompressed originals.

Whereas both streaming and compression make efficient use of network bandwidth, Universal Media is a collection of locally resident media

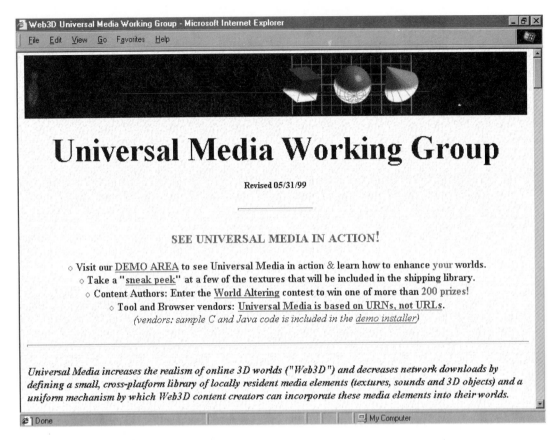

Figure 1-3   New technologies such as streaming, compression, and Universal Media allow media-rich Web3D to be delivered over slow network connections (http://www.web3d.org/WorkingGroups/).

elements (images, sounds, and objects) that allow media-rich Web3D content to be created without concern for bandwidth at all. Because Universal Media resides on the end user's hard drive, these media elements don't need to be downloaded over the network; only the Web3D scene is sent over the wire to the desktop, where it can be combined with media that are stored locally.

Thanks to these new technologies and low-cost, high-speed network connections, compelling, media-rich Web3D content can now be smoothly delivered. With bandwidth concerns considerably reduced, Web3D finally has an opportunity to invade the home and reach the masses. Making the trip from server to end user is only one leg of the journey, however; such content must actually be delivered into a hospitable computing environment in order to be executed. With this in mind, our focus now turns to the platform, another area that seriously challenged VRML in the past but is practically a nonissue today.

Platform Limitations

VRML was always intended for the masses; the technology was originally conceived as an Internet 3D standard that would allow the average Web surfer to become immersed in virtual reality content using little more than a Web browser. Unfortunately, complex 3D environments demanded much more than contemporary off-the-shelf consumer PCs and Web browsers could offer. The Web3D "platform"—the combination of hardware and software required to partake of immersive 3D content delivered over the Web—is substantial, to say the least.

VRML isn't native to the Web, nor are other forms of Web3D; a browser plug-in is required to actually handle such content. But a browser plug-in capable of dealing with Web3D isn't enough; the computer on which the Web browser and plug-in are run must also be up to the challenge. Until recently, only expensive, high-powered workstations were capable of gracefully

---

Platform Particulars

Although the term "platform" has historically meant the combination of an operating system (OS) and hardware that together provide an environment under which software applications may be run, such as the Windows OS combined with Intel-based computers, software-only platforms are now becoming mainstream.

The Java platform, for example, is a popular software-only platform that isn't bound to a specific hardware system. It is instead defined as the combination of a Virtual Machine (VM) interpreter and a standard Application Programming Interface (API), both of which are software implementations.

Together the Java VM and Java API provide a software runtime environment through which Java programs can run across a wide variety of hardware systems. Because it's not bound to a specific hardware system, Java provides developers with a more broadly defined notion of what a platform can be.

handling 3D content with which the user could interact. As a result, only a very small segment of the Internet community has had what amounted to an adequate Web3D platform.

Today, however, a Web3D platform has emerged for the average consumer. Personal computers now available for less than $1,000 can easily outperform high-end workstations that cost 10 times as much only a few years ago. Just as high-speed network connections have invaded the home, computers capable of handling the demands of Web3D have flooded the market. Practically every new personal computer sold since 1999 is up to the challenge, and the vast majority of PCs purchased by consumers today are overkill.

At the time of this writing, over 80 percent of all new computers sold come standard with either a 3D video board installed or a 3D chipset integrated directly with the motherboard or CPU. By late 2000, analysts predict that nearly every new computer will come equipped with a 3D video board, 3D chipset, or 3D-enhanced CPU designed specifically to handle complex 3D processing. Even the *least* expensive personal computers sold today are more powerful than the majority of special-purpose 3D visualization workstations coveted by scientists and researchers when VRML was brand spanking new.

While computers double in power every 18 months even as they plummet in price, following Moore's Law, the software side of the Web3D platform advances at an even more astonishing pace. The VRML specification is in its third major revision, giving it capabilities that are leaps and bounds above the original version introduced in 1994, while browser plug-ins required to handle VRML content have improved even more dramatically. Today's most popular VRML plug-ins are several orders of magnitude more sophisticated than those of just a few years ago, and, in keeping with the spirit of the Web itself, they're free!

The majority of personal computers sold today come preinstalled with a Web browser, and many come with a modern VRML plug-in as well. Not only are today's entry-level computers exceptionally powerful in terms of their ability to process 3D content, many also come equipped to handle at least one form of Web3D out of the box. A consumer who buys a system not already equipped with a Web3D plug-in can grab one off the Internet. Browser plug-ins for VRML and Java 3D are readily available on the Web for free, with those for X3D and MPEG-4 to follow, while the processing power needed to truly take advantage of the 3D content they deliver is being mass produced for sale at rock-bottom prices compared to what equivalent systems cost years ago.

Moore's Law

Gordon Moore's time-proven law asserts that the transistor capacity of microchips will double approximately every year and a half without a corresponding rise in production costs. Although Moore observed this fact in 1965, even before the dawn of the semiconductor age that he ushered in as founder of Intel in 1968, it remains true even today. Moore's Law helps to explain why computers roughly double in power and capacity every 18 months without a corresponding rise in price— and why a Web3D Platform the consumer market can comfortably afford is now at hand.

Without a doubt, a Web3D platform for the masses has arrived (see Figure 1-4). However, platform and bandwidth limitations weren't the only factors that prevented yesterday's VRML from sweeping the Web. A scarcity of low-cost, high-quality development tools also played a part. Without development tools that the novice Webmaster can comfortably afford and quickly master, VRML and other forms of Web3D remain the exclusive domain of software developers who can actually weave content at the code level.

Unfortunately, no form of Web3D is *easy* to code by hand; to create compelling 3D content with a language such as VRML or Java 3D requires experience, skill, and lots of patience. Fortunately, inexpensive visual development tools are now available that give everyone a shot at creating powerful Web3D content that can impress even the most experienced software developers.

Figure 1-4   The Web3D Platform has emerged today thanks to dramatic increases in personal computing horsepower and sophisticated, freely available browser plug-ins.

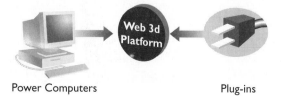

Power Computers   Plug-ins

Content Authoring-Tool Limitations

Only a few years ago, if you wanted to create VRML content, you actually had to know how to program in the VRML language. Although a number of authoring tools have been introduced with a splash since VRML first set sail in the high seas of Internet 3D, most weren't comprehensive enough to keep a typical Web developer's head above water. In the old days, you had to submerge yourself in the VRML programming language if you wanted to take advantage of everything the standard offers.

Today, however, powerful yet affordable Web3D content development tools abound. Over the years, VRML authoring tools have matured in step with the language itself; gone are the days when advanced programming was required to create complex, fully interactive Web3D content. To create sophisticated, interactive Web3D pages these days, you need only point and click using any of several visual authoring tools as depicted in Figure 1-5.

Shoring up the abundance of feature-rich, cost-effective VRML authoring tools that were available at the time this book went to print, powerful X3D, Java 3D, and MPEG-4 authoring tools will undoubtedly emerge in the coming years as well. By 2001 content developers will be able to pick and choose from a wide assortment of affordable, professional Web3D authoring products that will require little more than a mouse and imagination to operate. Visual VRML authoring tools that once cost hundreds of dollars, for example, have plummeted in price while increasing significantly in capability and can now be had for less than a month's supply of Starbuck's cappuccino. To add fuel to the fire,

Figure 1-5   Thanks to advances in affordable authoring tools, you can now create stunning Web3D content using little more than a mouse and your index finger (Nendo image courtesy of Nichimen Graphics, http://www.nichimen.com/).

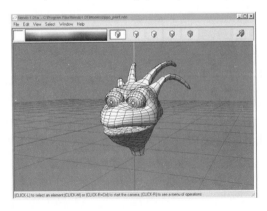

a new generation of exceptionally powerful and affordable 3D modeling tools such as Nichimen's Nendo modeler (see Figure 1-5) support VRML, making it easier than ever to become a Web3D content author.

Creating original Web3D content is now a snap thanks to widespread availability of affordable, powerful, and comprehensive VRML authoring tools, while other forms of Web3D will be just as easy to author with the imminent arrival of X3D, Java 3D, and MPEG-4 authoring tools. Where once the circle of proficient VRML developers numbered in the thousands, today's visual authoring tools can empower millions. Professional and novice Web developers of all stripes and colors can tap into the power of Web3D without actually learning the programming languages that lurk just beneath the surface. Artists, architects, sales people, business owners, musicians, and marketers represent just a fraction of the population that has a need for Web3D and can now create and publish it themselves.

Web3D is about to explode in popularity because the right tools are now making their way into eager and capable hands. In much the same way that images and sounds swarmed the Web once high-quality, low-cost graphics and audio editors became widely available, Web3D is now poised for liftoff thanks to a wealth of sophisticated authoring tools that are available to the general public for little or no cost.

Web3D in Action

Like nearly every important technology, Web3D will improve over time. Just as VRML has progressed by leaps and bounds since it was first conceived in 1994, the relatively new Java 3D and forthcoming X3D and MPEG-4/BIFS technologies will improve dramatically, while developers become more skilled at exploiting their already impressive capabilities. In just a handful of years, we'll all be able to interact with *Toy Story*-quality 3D delivered over the Internet and a variety of broadcast networks, allowing us to become fully immersed in realistic 3D worlds that aren't yet possible.

Although tomorrow promises to consume us in a three-dimensional cyberspace the likes of which Tim Berners-Lee, Dave Raggett, Mark Pesce, Tony Parisi, and legions of like-minded 3D aficionados only dream of, Web3D is already changing the way we interact with the Internet. Thanks to VRML, Web3D is changing the way we work, learn, and play this very moment. Right here, right now.

Note: Web3D Gallery

Links to the VRML examples described in the following text are available online through the Web3D Gallery (www.web3dgallery.com). The Web3D Gallery will also showcase compelling Java 3D, X3D, and MPEG-4/BIFS content as they push the envelope of online 3D even further.

In the sections that follow, we'll explore the many ways in which Web3D—by way of VRML—is already affecting the very concept of Web content and how we experience it. As you walk through these examples, you'll see that compelling, interactive 3D content is the low-hanging fruit of today's Web and is ripe for the picking. All you have to do is reach for it.

Product and Data Visualization

Product visualization and data visualization are two areas where three dimensions truly outshine two. Without Web3D, products and information on the Web are typically presented to the viewer in the form of 2D images, a paragraph or more of descriptive text, or a combination of both images and text. And while a photograph or illustration can go a long way towards accurately describing a product, especially when accompanied by a text description, traditional two-dimensional images and text lack the expressive power of Web3D.

Whereas images and text are static and can only be experienced from a single perspective, Web3D allows products to be visualized from whatever angle the end user desires and in many ways that images and text simply do not allow. The Nokia communicator seen in Figure 1-6, for example, is an example of Web3D product visualization designed to give the end user complete control over the viewing experience. Rather than merely looking at a photo or illustration of the combination cellular phone and personal digital assistant (PDA), or reading a description about it, Web3D gives us the ability to thoroughly examine it from any angle we'd like and actually give the device a test drive.

We can zoom in and inspect in great detail specific parts of the communicator, which sports a clam-shell design. When closed, the device looks much like any other cell phone, yet it flips open to reveal a small screen and

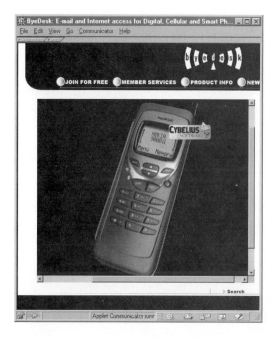

Figure 1-6   Product visualization gives us the power to interactively examine and even "test drive" goods such as this Nokia 9000 communicator device (http://www.cybelius.com/FrmVir.htm).

keyboard (seen in Figure 1-6). Merely clicking on this VRML model triggers a smooth, animated transition from phone to email system, making it immediately evident what the main features of this clever consumer device are. Further exploration reveals that this particular demonstration is more than eye candy; it actually supports email. Using my own computer keyboard I send an email message to anyone on the Internet by way of the VRML model, a simple but effective task that really drives home the fact that the Nokia 9000 communicator isn't merely a cellular phone.

Thanks to Web3D, we can also view our prospective purchases in a variety of configurations. Consider the piece of office furniture seen in Figure 1-7. Don't like the standard, drab steel surface of this desk? No problem; slap on a nice pine veneer instead. Pine isn't your bag, baby? Because this interactive experience is designed to let you build and customize a variety of furniture pieces, you can choose a number of different materials for your new desk (and even a different desk, or an entirely new piece of furniture for that matter). If

Figure 1-7   Product visualization can allow prospective buyers to interactively assemble and customize purchases, such as the style and material of this office desk (http://www.technicon.com/prod-show.htm).

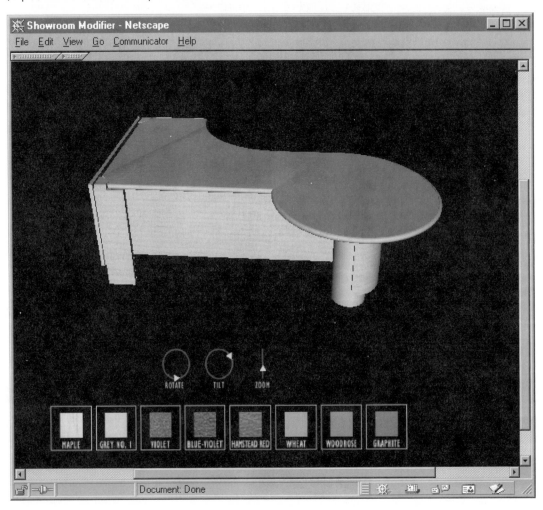

metal and steel don't appeal to you, how about a strange, rubbery surface material? This is Web3D, after all. There's no need to settle for anything less than your personalized desk, however outlandish your personal taste may be.

Suppose you're shopping the Web for a new bike, which you can assemble and customize courtesy of Web3D. Data visualization can be used to convey how much your bike will cost, the reliability and availability of each custom piece you select, how long it will take to assemble, and when it should reach you by mail. Information such as this would traditionally be displayed in text format, which can be difficult to digest. Using Web3D, however, data can be visualized and presented in a more palatable and understandable form than ever before.

Data visualization isn't new. Scientists have relied on it for years to help them make sense of extremely complex information sets such as global weather patterns, seismic activity, human gene mapping, and other types of highly sophisticated data that would be impossible to comprehend in raw form. Today, however, data visualization has escaped from research labs and found a new home on the Internet.

Web3D brings data visualization to the Web, where massive mountains of data grow even more massive with every passing minute. Data relating to Web surfing trends, user demographics, the medical industry, electronic commerce activity, and even the stock market is routinely collected through the Internet. Large volumes of complex data sets such as these are nearly impossible to make sense of without data visualization, yet can be easily understood when viewed as Web3D content. Figure 1-8, for example, displays medical and weather information in an intuitive 3D form that would be a nightmare to comprehend as raw data.

Visualized as Web3D content, complex data such as this is a snap to understand. You can interactively examine the innards of a human body constructed from very complex magnetic resonance imaging (MRI) scans (http://www.npac.syr.edu/projects/3Dvisiblehuman/). Likewise, the 3D weather model is an interactive 3D visualization of global weather data collected by satellites in orbit over the earth (http://vrml.gsfc.nasa.gov/). In both cases, Web3D makes it possible to intuitively comprehend and explore extremely complex information visually.

eCommerce and Business Applications

In recent years, the Web has become an astonishing conduit for commerce. Electronic commerce (eCommerce) and general business applications now account for the vast majority of Web development expenditures. After all,

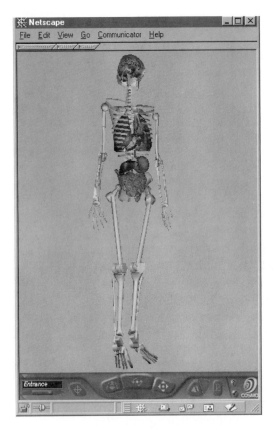

Figure 1-8   Data visualization can help make complex information such as medical data (left) or weather-pattern data (right) relatively easy to understand.

how many multimillion-dollar Web sites can you think of that *aren't* concerned with generating revenue in one form or another, or attracting and retaining customers? Not many, you'll probably agree.

As eCommerce and business applications continue to fuel the growth of the Web, while the cost to produce and maintain such sites skyrockets, the companies behind these efforts are understandably concerned with getting the highest possible return for their investment. Techniques and technologies such as personalization, cross-promotion, affinity programs, digital coupons, contests, and sweepstakes are among the mechanisms commonly employed by eCommerce and business sites to gain an edge or simply remain competitive.

Web3D is rapidly emerging as a powerful competitive tool for eCommerce and business sites, where product and data visualization can make all the difference to a surfer who needs a compelling reason to actually make a purchase (see the previous section for information about visualization). Web3D also increases the "stickiness" of Web sites, as interactive 3D content tends to suck surfers into an involved experience that lasts much longer than that of viewing static content such as text or images.

Web3D also allows very abstract concepts to be expressed in ways that promote business. Sun's Java House, for instance, is an example of visualization used to explain a concept rather than a product or data set. Seen in Figure 1-9, the Java House provides a Web3D tour of Sun's complex Java 2

Figure 1-9   Sun's Java House, built using a combination of Java 3D and VRML, is an interactive overview of the Java 2 Platform (http://www.sun.com/desktop/java3d/demos/javahouse.html).

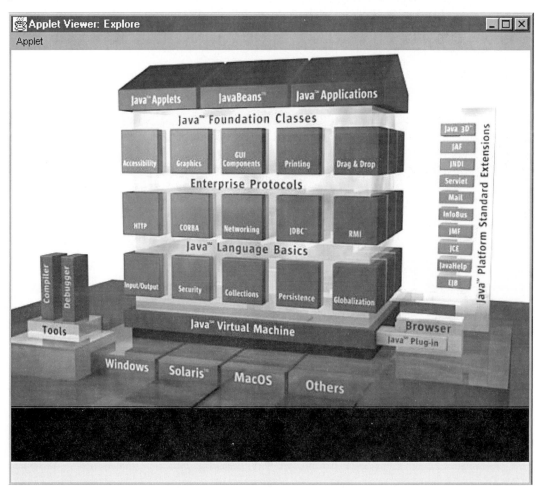

Platform. It helps people understand the relationships among the many technologies that make up the Java 2 Platform, which are rather difficult to understand by merely reading specifications and press releases. In this respect, Web3D contributes to Sun's business objective of promoting the complex Java 2 platform.

Figure 1-10 illustrates another area where Web3D can help businesses. Real estate agents and brokers often use the Web to display photographs and text descriptions of the buildings and homes they represent. Photographs and text, however, can go only so far and are often misleading. Web3D real estate, on the other hand, gives prospective clients a chance to actually walk through properties and examine them in detail. Architectural walk-throughs such as this can save both parties a great deal of time and frustration; buyers and sellers need not meet in person to visit properties that don't stand a good chance of selling.

Virtual real estate and product, data, and concept visualization are just the tip of the iceberg when it comes to exploiting Web3D for eCommerce and

Figure 1-10   Web3D real estate allows renters and owners to tour prospective properties from the comfort of their own home (http://www.planet9.com/).

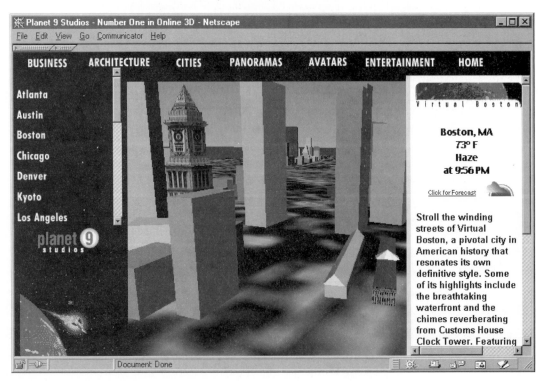

business gains. Advertisements, corporate identity, and product demos all lend themselves to Web3D content, whether fully immersive or merely animated. Simple animated logos and marketing presentations are less sophisticated forms of Web3D that are commonly used for business purposes, although they remain high-impact alternatives to the traditional photos and text found on most corporate Web sites. At the other end of the complexity spectrum, Web3D virtual sales agents can help close an online deal, while virtual customer-assistance agents can help customers solve problems around the clock.

Entertainment: Fun and Games

Entertainment is, without a doubt, the most common way in which people today are exposed to 3D. Computer and console games have infiltrated the home, bringing 3D to the masses. Today, 3D is all the rage in games played on personal computers and console gaming devices such as Nintendo, Sega Genesis, and Sony PlayStation. Best-selling games such as Quake, Tomb Raider, Super Mario 64, GoldenEye 007, Banjo Kazooie, Soul Reaver, and countless others push interactive 3D to the max in their quest for realism and smooth game play.

Likewise, many movies today take advantage of 3D in order to add a dash of realism to otherwise entirely fabricated characters, props, and locations. Box-office smashes *Toy Story, Antz,* and *A Bug's Life* were all created using sophisticated 3D technology developed exclusively for the movie industry. Although most movies aren't completely computer generated as these were, 3D technology nonetheless plays a major part in the production of nearly every movie made today. Almost every film that rolls out of Hollywood uses 3D technology in some way or another, so that anyone who has seen a movie in the past decade or so has been exposed to 3D whether they realize it or not.

Even though Web3D is many years away from being able to produce film-quality 3D for the Internet, today's crop of Web3D games and movie shorts deliver compelling Internet entertainment nonetheless. Figure 1-11, for example, shows an interactive game based on the *Lost in Space* television series and movie. As part of the promotional activity for the box-office movie released in 1998, Shout Interactive (http://www.shoutinteractive.com/) created this first-person shoot-'em-up using VRML. In the online game you become the robot, blasting your way through creepy mechanical spiders while desperately searching for a means to repair your damaged space craft.

Although the good folks at Shout have created a number of Web3D promotional pieces such as the *Lost in Space* game, they are perhaps best known for a series of VRML movies featuring "Jo" and "Oscar." Seen frozen in time

Figure 1-11   *Lost in Space* is an interactive Web3D game based on the movie and television series of the same name (http://dangerwillrobinson.lycos.com/vrml-s.html).

in Figure 1-12, Jo and Oscar dance the night away to a thumping Latin beat. Since they inhabit continuously looping, never-ending VRML animations, you don't actually have a chance to interact with Jo and Oscar. Instead, you simply sit back and watch the duo cut a rug on the dance floor, battle evil in the mean streets of their VRML world, and outrun gun-toting bad men.

Many other intriguing 3D characters live on the Web, courtesy of Web3D. Dilbert stepped into three dimensions long ago (http://www.unitedmedia.com/comics/dilbert/animations/), making him one of the first

3D Movie Magic

Because traditional movies aren't interactive, they really can't be compared to Web3D and the often-proprietary 3D technologies used to create console games, which put the user in the driver's seat. Movies are shot entirely from one viewpoint. When you watch a movie, you simply look at the frames of film as they speed by (giving the illusion of movement). You have no control over what point of view you see the movie from, nor can you navigate the contents of a movie; you can only watch what the director wants you to see.

The lack of interactivity in traditional movies is a benefit, actually, because it gives movie producers the ability to create 3D scenes of exceptionally high quality. Such scenes are extremely computer intensive and can take hours (and sometimes days) to render, even when the task is shared by a roomful of high-powered workstations. When rendering is complete, the individual frames of a scene are shot to film for your viewing pleasure.

The results can be mind-blowing, as *The Matrix* and *The Phantom Menace* have proved, although such movies are impossible to render in real time today. Nor can they be viewed over the Internet without substantial compression (and subsequent degradation of visual quality) due to the massive storage and bandwidth requirements of film. Each frame in a motion picture can require more than 50 megabytes of disk storage, meaning that every few seconds of film can easily consume over 1.5 gigabytes of storage when in uncompressed digital form.

Web3D movies, on the other hand, sacrifice quality for control. Although you can watch them from whatever viewpoint the movie's producers set for you, you can take control whenever you want. With Web3D, you can change perspective at will, watching the movie from the viewpoint of any character you choose. You can also interact with Web3D movies if they're designed with such participation in mind. Although they can't match the realism of motion pictures, they offer a level of interactivity that traditional movies can't touch.

Figure 1-12   Jo and Oscar dance the night away in Shout's MOD "Dance Party," one of several VRML movies featuring the duo (http://www.modvr.com).

traditional comic-strip characters to experience depth as well as height and width. Floops, meanwhile, is a strange-looking creature that has never known the flat world. Created to showcase the Cosmo line of VRML products, Floops began life as an interactive Web3D character and has appeared in 65 grin-evoking online episodes (http://www.cosmosoftware.com/galleries/floops).

Of course, games and cartoons aren't the only way in which Web3D weaves its way into the entertainment world. Take, for example, the NBC *Tonight Show* studio seen in Figure 1-13. Here an interactive VRML world is used to promote real-world broadcast entertainment. Thanks to Web3D, you can take a virtual tour of the Hollywood studio that Jay Leno calls home, seeing for yourself what it would be like to walk through the facility and take a seat as an audience member. If you are more interested in being a guest, nothing stops you from sauntering up to Jay's desk and taking a seat alongside the famously chinned host.

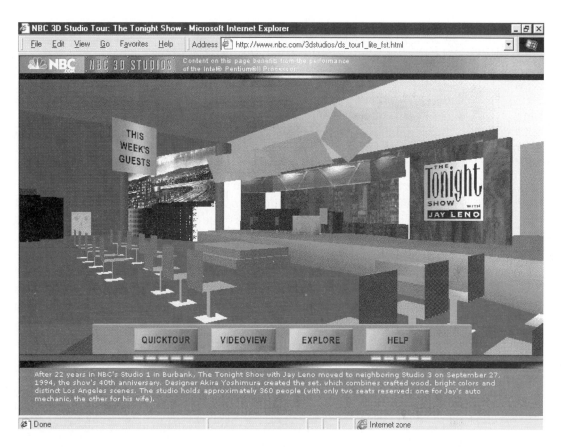

Figure 1-13 Take a Web3D tour of NBC's *Tonight Show* studio and view the stage from any seat in the house. Tickets not included (http://www.nbc.com/3dstudios/).

Web Page Enhancement

The most common form of 3D on the Web today is not interactive content, but 3D-style images. Animated GIF images often are used to further enhance the illusion of 3D, although many 3D images don't even go that far. Animated or not, these images merely enhance the visual appeal of Web pages, lending a "3D-ish" look to otherwise static content.

Web3D, by comparison, gives Web site developers a much bigger bang for their buck. For roughly the same amount of effort they can have truly interactive 3D content. And, because Web3D is extremely compact, a well-designed interactive world is often more bandwidth efficient than a series of animated images. In fact, some of the most striking VRML Web page effects consume less than 25 KB in disc space and download almost instantly over dial-up modems.

News and Advertisement Enhancement

Because it can convey valuable information about a story or product that video, audio, and text alone cannot, Web3D is an ideal technology to enhance both online news and advertisements. Today, in fact, traditional news and advertisements are commonly enhanced with traditional 3D.

3D simulations that help the audience to visualize what reporters are saying often accompany traditional news stories about topics such as weather patterns, medial breakthroughs, and traffic accidents. Likewise, traditional television advertisements frequently rely on 3D to bring products to life and to create compelling characters out of thin air that hawk goods without a hint of embarrassment. With traditional forms of news and advertisement becoming so dependent on 3D, online forms are bound to find the same value in Web3D.

For example, CNN embraced Web3D to bring an online story about the International Space Station to life (http://cnn.com/SPECIALS/multimedia/vrml/iss/). Although the space station is years from completion, CNN's VRML model gives anyone on the Web a chance to climb inside and take a virtual tour long before real-life astronauts will. Thanks to Web3D, this news story was greatly enhanced by an interactive model that people could actually play with and explore. Try to do that with television.

In a similar way, online advertisers, such as Volkswagen, tapped into the power of Web3D to add a new dimension to their products. When the new Beetle was introduced, a VRML model on Volkswagen's Web site allowed you to actually grab the car with your mouse and take it for a spin. You could step inside, close the doors, and ease the leather driver's seat back; you could even play with the steering wheel, windows, and glove box. This Web3D model, a fully interactive component of the online advertisement, allowed you to kick the tires without actually visiting a car dealer.

There are plenty more examples of how Web3D enhances online news and advertisements. It's no mistake that online news sites and advertisers are quickly tapping into interactive 3D as a way to enhance their content. They're already using 3D in the real world, after all, and with Web3D they get the added bonus of true interactivity.

Summary

Web3D, a relatively new term introduced by the Web3D Consortium (www.web3d.org) to describe all standard forms of Internet 3D endorsed by that organization, currently includes VRML and X3D. These technologies, together with Java 3D and MPEG-4/BIFS, comprise the subject matter of this book. Although the term is new, the practice of delivering interactive 3D content over the Web is not. Introduced in 1994, VRML pioneered the concept of 3D for the Web and is the international ISO standard that ushered in other forms of Web3D.

When it comes to interactive 3D content delivered over the Internet, today is the dawn of a new era. Web3D is prepared to invade the Internet, thanks to tremendous advances in bandwidth availability, platform processing power, and the recent maturation of comprehensive, cost-effective content authoring tools. In the past, each of these obstacles stood in the way of VRML's being deployed to the masses. Today they are fast becoming faded memories as "Web3D" comes of age.

Following is a complete list of URLs referenced in this chapter:

Web3D Consortium   http://www.web3d.org/

Web3D Consortium Working Groups   http://www.web3d.org/Working-Groups/

Web3D Gallery   http://www.web3dgallery.com/

Nichimen Graphics   http://www.nichimen.com/

Nokia 9000 Communicator   http://www.cybelius.com/FrmVir.htm

Furniture Customizer   http://www.technicon.com/prod-show.htm

3D Visible Human   http://www.npac.syr.edu/projects/3Dvisiblehuman/

NASA's "Earth in VRML"   http://vrml.gsfc.nasa.gov/

Java House   http://www.sun.com/desktop/java3d/demos/javahouse.html

Planet 9 Architectural Models   http://www.planet9.com/

Shout Interactive   http://www.shoutinteractive.com/

Floops   http://www.cosmosoftware.com/galleries/floops/

Lost in Space   http://dangerwillrobinson.lycos.com/vrml-s.html

Shout MOD   http://www.modvr.com/

Dilbert Comic Strip   http://www.unitedmedia.com/comics/dilbert/animations/

Tonight Show Studio   http://www.nbc.com/3dstudios/

International Space Station   http://cnn.com/SPECIALS/multimedia/vrml/iss/

OVERVIEW
OF WEB3D

Topics in This Chapter

- An overview of the Web3D Consortium, formerly the VRML Consortium, and the processes by which it develops Web3D technologies internally (such as VRML and X3D) and evaluates external 3D technologies (such as Java 3D and MPEG-4/BIFS) for possible "blessing" as Web3D technologies

- A walk-through of the evolution of VRML, which is today an international standard known as VRML97

- A discussion about Extensible 3D (X3D), the successor of VRML97 now under development by the Web3D Consortium and slated for delivery in the middle of 2000

- An introduction to Java 3D, Sun's 3D API for Java, released in December 1998

- An overview of MPEG-4/BIFS, a 3D scene encoding component of the MPEG-4 media encoding and delivery standard, due in 2000

Chapter 2

W eb3D is a general term used to describe a number of open, inter-operable Internet-based 3D technologies that have been endorsed by the Web3D Consortium. Although Web3D as such is relatively new, its roots can be traced as far back as 1994—the year VRML was first conceived.

This chapter will describe in detail the term "Web3D," as well as the role the Web3D Consortium plays in deciding what technologies actually comprise it. Here you'll find that Web3D as defined by the consortium today consists of VRML and the forthcoming Extensible 3D (X3D) technology. However, this book also considers Java 3D and MPEG-4/BIFS to be forms of Web3D, even though they haven't been "blessed" by the Web3D Consortium as official Web3D technologies at the time of this writing.

This book shows you how to weave the only forms of Web3D available today, VRML and Java 3D, into your own Web pages, and it also prepares you for a future filled with X3D and MPEG-4/BIFS. This chapter provides a gentle introduction to VRML, X3D, Java 3D, and MPEG-4/BIFS, while subsequent chapters cover each in more detail.

Web3D Consortium

The Web3D Consortium is a nonprofit organization that at the time of this writing consists of more than 50 leading high-technology companies, such as Apple, IBM, Intel, Microsoft, Oracle, Silicon Graphics, Sun, and Sony, just to name a few. Through the Web3D Consortium, whose home on the Web is seen in Figure 2-1, members work together to design, develop, and promote a suite of open, interoperable, and standardized technologies known collectively as *Web3D*.

The Web3D Consortium drew its first breath in December 1998. As a nonprofit organization whose charter is to establish a suite of compatible 3D

Figure 2-1   The Web3D Consortium (http://www.web3d.org/) brings industry leaders together to design, develop, and promote open, industrywide Web3D standards.

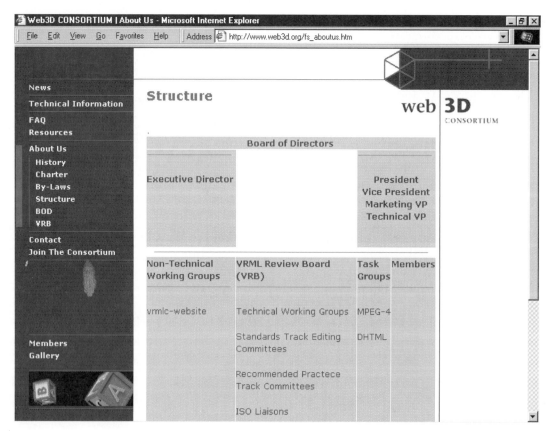

standards for the Internet, it is a direct outgrowth of the VRML Consortium, which was founded in 1996 to shepherd the development, evolution, and standardization of VRML alone.

Although the VRML Consortium was focused entirely on VRML in the early years, Java 3D and MPEG-4/BIFS eventually emerged as two powerful forms of Internet 3D that drew considerable attention. As a result, members of the VRML Consortium spent a great deal of time working with these new technologies, which, although competition to VRML, also complemented it in many ways. In addition to Java 3D and MPEG-4/BIFS, which were developed in an open, collaborative manner that fostered interoperability with VRML (as explained in the sections that follow), a number of nonstandard, proprietary 3D technologies have appeared in recent years as well.

Where once VRML was the only option when it came to Web-based 3D, by late 1998 several alternatives were available to choose from. Seeing a need to unite these various efforts, the VRML Consortium expanded its charter in July of 1998 to embrace a variety of Internet 3D technologies. Later that same year it officially adopted the name "Web3D Consortium" to reflect these new responsibilities.

Today the Web3D Consortium is responsible for evaluating multiple 3D technologies as potential Web3D standards, and it will only endorse those that pass through a formal evaluation process designed for such purposes (see the "Working and Task Groups" sidebar). Think of it as the Good Housekeeping Seal of Approval for Web-based 3D. The term "Web3D" as used by the Web3D Consortium describes only those technologies that the organization has fully evaluated and ratified as standards, which today include VRML and undoubtedly the forthcoming X3D technology now under development by the consortium.

Java 3D and MPEG-4/BIFS, meanwhile, have not yet been ratified by the Web3D Consortium and so aren't considered official forms of Web3D by that organization. Both, however, may become forms of Web3D, as both have ties to other standard-setting organizations. Java, for example, is now under consideration by the European Computer Manufacturers Association (ECMA) standards group. Standardization of Java, the parent technology that Java 3D is based on, moves Java 3D one step closer to possible standardization by the Web3D Consortium. MPEG-4 (the larger media framework of which BIFS is a part), on the other hand, has already been approved as an international standard by the International Organization for Standardization (ISO). That, plus the fact that BIFS—a 3D scene encoding component of MPEG-4—is based on VRML, makes MPEG-4/BIFS a particularly strong candidate for approval as a Web3D standard by the Web3D Consortium in the near future.

How Open Is Open?

The term "open" means different things to different developers, leading to inconsistency and ambiguity when it comes to defining the term. For the purposes of this discussion, *open* simply means nonproprietary in terms of how the technology is developed. Java3D, for example, was developed in a way that was not nearly as open as the process under which MPEG-4/BIFS was developed, yet we still consider both "open" when compared to completely proprietary forms of 3D. Java 3D was developed inside Sun Microsystems, the same company that developed Java itself, while MPEG-4/BIFS was developed by an international association known as the Motion Picture Experts Group (MPEG). Although Sun collaborated with a number of companies and individuals to develop Java 3D, it did so in a manner that wasn't as open as with the MPEG-4/BIFS process.

Sun was ultimately responsible for choosing every company and individual that contributed to the design and development of Java 3D, whereas every member of the MPEG group that wanted to could participate in the design and development of MPEG-4/BIFS. In spite of these differences in approach, neither technology was created behind completely closed doors in a traditional, proprietary way, and so it's fair to say that both Java 3D and MPEG-4/BIFS were developed in an open manner.

Despite the different degree of openness behind each development, both Java 3D and MPEG-4/BIFS are interoperable with VRML. By working closely with the Web3D Consortium (formerly the VRML Consortium), Sun Microsystems and the MPEG-4/BIFS group have achieved a level of VRML interoperability with their respective technologies that closed, proprietary development efforts typically do not.

In addition to standardizing Web3D technologies such as VRML and X3D (and possibly Java 3D and MPEG-4/BIFS in the future), the Web3D Consortium is also responsible for promoting interoperability between the technologies it standardizes as well as existing Web infrastructure technologies such as Dynamic HTML (DHTML), Document Object Model (DOM), and Extensible Markup Language (XML). Consequently, the Web3D Consortium works with organizations such as the World Wide Web Consortium (http://www.w3.org/) and the Internet Engineering Task Force (IEFT, located on the Web at http://www.ietf.org/) to ensure that the Web3D technologies are interoperable with those of other standards bodies (see Figure 2-2).

To achieve these substantial goals even as it continues to develop and improve the VRML technology around which it was originally formed, the

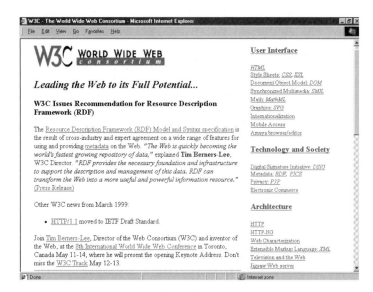

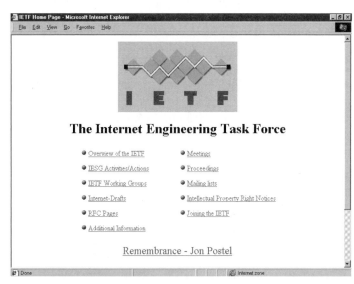

Figure 2-2   The Web3D Consortium works with organizations such as the World Wide Web Consortium (top) and the Internet Engineering Task Force (bottom) to ensure that Web3D standards are interoperable with those of other standards groups.

Working Groups and Task Groups

The bulk of activity within the Web3D Consortium happens within Working Groups and Task Groups, official technical committees that are chartered to solve specific technical issues. Any group or individual, even those who are not members of the Web3D Consortium, can start a Working Group. Such groups, however, are recognized by the Web3D Consortium only provisionally, pending approval after a formal proposal process.

Once approved by the Web3D Consortium, Working Groups follow a formal process designed to guide the work of group members as it progresses through stages. Along the way, the consortium's Technical Advisory Board (TAB) provides technical review and hands-on guidance for Working Group members. Many, although not all, Working Groups ultimately develop a *Standard* or *Recommended Practice* (RP) that is endorsed by the Web3D Consortium.

A Web3D Standard document describes a technology or process that Web3D product vendors must comply with, while a Recommended Practice document describes the preferred way in which a technology or process is implemented. The Universal Media Working Group, for example, is developing a Recommended Practice that Web3D browser and authoring-tool vendors can follow when it comes to implementing Universal Media. Vendors are not required to support Universal Media, however, because it is not a standard, simply a recommended way of supporting locally resident media.

Whereas Working Groups are self-forming, self-regulated, and self-directed, Task Groups are actually appointed by the Web3D Consortium Board of Directors (BoD) to tackle a specific issue or project that stems from marketing or political objectives established by the BoD. As such, the BoD takes a much more active role in Task Groups as compared to Working Groups; Task Groups are formed and driven from the top of the Web3D Consortium organization. The Extensible 3D (X3D) Task Group, for example, was established as such because the Web3D BoD saw this technology as critical to the evolution of VRML. For more information on both Working Groups and Task Groups, fire up your browser and visit: http://www.web3d.org/.

Web3D Consortium relies on time-tested Working Groups and Task Groups (see sidebar) as well as newly implemented internal processes designed to wring maximum efficiency out of the organization.

Web3D: A New Generation of 3D

Web3D ushers in a new generation of bandwidth-efficient 3D content that can be delivered to diverse computing platforms over the Internet. Today's Web3D technologies give developers the ability to create interactive Internet 3D content that can be run on a number of different platforms without regard for the low-level plumbing that actually renders the final results experienced by the end user.

In the past, 3D developers had to immerse themselves in low-level 3D graphics Application Programming Interfaces (APIs) such as OpenGL and Direct3D. Today, however, compelling, interactive 3D content can be created using high-level Web3D languages and APIs that effectively shield developers from the gory details of the platform (such as rendering engines, frame buffers, device drivers, video displays, and accelerator boards).

The high-level nature of today's Web3D technologies is achieved through the use of scene-graph data structures that help developers describe and encode objects and scenes in a hierarchical fashion that is better suited to 3D content than traditional programming techniques (see Figure 2-3). Thanks in large part to their use of scene-graph technology, VRML, Java 3D, X3D, and MPEG-4/BIFS free developers from low-level implementation details. As high-level languages and APIs expressed through scene-graphs, these Web3D technologies ease the programmer's burden while at the same time allowing content to run on numerous platforms via the Internet without extra effort on the developer's part. Taken together, these benefits define a new generation of 3D that is today realized by VRML, Java 3D, and the forthcoming MPEG-4/BIFS.

X3D, meanwhile, goes one step further, allowing 3D scenes to be constructed using the Extensible Markup Language (XML), effectively "exposing" the underlying scene-graph to Web markup tags that are similar in nature to HTML tags. This approach allows you to weave 3D content into Web pages in much the same way that you now weave images and text into pages using HTML. Unfortunately, X3D is still under development and won't be available until at least mid 2000.

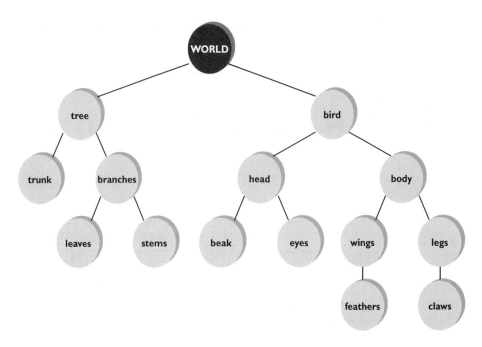

Figure 2-3   Web3D technologies utilize hierarchical scene-graphs as the fundamental datatype for the construction of 3D objects and scenes.

Virtual Reality Modeling Language (VRML)

VRML is, without a doubt, the granddaddy of Web3D. Conceived in 1994, and now undergoing a third major revision by the Web3D Consortium, VRML is a 3D content development language for the Internet. As a high-level language focused exclusively on 3D, VRML shields developers from gory, low-level implementation details while simultaneously supporting multiple platforms over the Internet.

VRML is a relatively simple language that is used to describe 3D objects and scenes, more commonly known as *worlds*. VRML worlds are nothing more than a series of VRML language commands that are typically stored in plain text files having the *.wrl* file extension, such as *shoppingmall.wrl* (*wrl* is short for *world*). As human-readable source code stored in plain ASCII text files, VRML worlds must be fully interpreted by a VRML browser plug-in (or standalone VRML browser) before they can actually be viewed and experienced by the end user. Paralleling the Hypertext Markup Language

(HTML) in this respect, the text-based nature of VRML makes it extremely accessible to a variety of computing platforms.

By far the most widely used form of Web3D on the Internet today, VRML was the first 3D content development language to achieve international standard status. It has provided much of the inspiration for more recent forms of Internet 3D. Although the original version of VRML was often criticized for its shortcomings, the technology has improved tremendously and can be categorized today into three major versions:

- VRML 1.0
- VRML 2.0, which served as the foundation for VRML97
- X3D (Extensible 3D, originally referred to as VRML Next Generation, or VRML-NG)

The sections that follow describe each version in relatively broad strokes, reserving details for Part II of this book. As the sections unfold, you'll learn how VRML evolved from a relatively simple 3D scene description language into today's dominant form of interactive Web3D, while the chapters that follow explore in detail how you can tap into the power of VRML yourself.

How VRML Came to Be

In 1994 Tim Berners-Lee, inventor of the Web and current director of the World Wide Web Consortium, invited Mark Pesce to participate in the first World Wide Web Conference hosted in Geneva that same year. Pesce and his partner Tony Parisi accepted the offer to present Labyrinth, a 3D user interface for the Internet the two had developed earlier in pursuit of their shared vision of an immersive, interactive cyberspace represented in three dimensions. Their concept of using the Web as a foundation on which immersive 3D worlds could be built fell on fertile ground at the conference, as did Labyrinth, effectively planting the seed from which VRML would later spring forth.

A number of conference attendees shared the vision of a 3D cyberspace described by Pesce, and, in fact, several developments similar to Labyrinth were already underway. During the conference, a Birds-of-a-Feather (BOF) gathering organized by Dave Raggett (one of the main developers behind HTML and other fundamental Web technologies) brought together individuals who shared a common interest in the budding concept, who agreed that a common language was needed that developers around the world could use to create interactive 3D content for the Internet.

After the conference an email list named "www-vrml" was established, through which development of the Virtual Reality Markup Language (VRML) began in earnest. The name "Virtual Reality *Markup* Language," coined by Raggett, intentionally paralleled the name of the tag-based *markup* language called Hypertext Markup Language (HTML). HTML was (and still is today) the language used to stitch together two-dimensional Web pages, whereas VRML was initially conceived as a markup language for describing three-dimensional Web content. It didn't take long before the 3D modeling aspects of the new language grew in importance, while its role as a markup language diminished. Eventually the word "Markup" was changed to "Modeling," resulting in the Virtual Reality *Modeling* Language that is better known today as VRML.

Note: "V-R-M-L" vs. "Vur-mull"

The acronym VRML can be pronounced in two ways. You can either spell it out one letter at a time ("V-R-M-L"), utter a strange phonetic chant ("Vur-mull"), or alternate between the two. Personally, I tend to use the former, although I've been known to slip into a Vur-mull chant from time to time.

VRML 1.0

The VRML list grew rapidly. Within a month over two thousand people from around the globe had formed a vital community of technologists, educators, content developers, Internet enthusiasts, 3D experts, and hackers. Using little more than email to exchange ideas, the group set out to define exactly what this new thing called "VRML" would really be.

In short order, the list members concluded that VRML would be a common language used to describe 3D scenes distributed over the Internet and therefore had to be 1) cross platform, 2) extensible, and 3) easily distributed over low-bandwidth connections such as dial-up modems. After carving out these tangible goals, the group then had to figure out how it would actually deliver on them in a timely manner.

Rather than start from scratch, list members decided to build on an existing technology called Open Inventor that Silicon Graphics Inc. (SGI) had developed several years earlier (see Figure 2-4). An ASCII text-file format used to describe 3D scenes, Open Inventor provided the VRML community with a solid framework on which to build their Internet 3D language. Open Inventor was ultimately selected over other 3D technologies because it offered a strong suite of 3D scene construction features and already had a strong presence in the traditional 3D community. In addition to offering a strong foundation language to build upon, the fact that Open Inventor

Figure 2-4   VRML is based on Open Inventor, an object-oriented toolkit for developing interactive 3D graphics applications produced by Silicon Graphics Inc. (http://www.sgi.com).

development tools were widely available across multiple platforms promised to give VRML a leg-up in that arena as well; with a little tweaking, existing Open Inventor products could also support VRML.

SGI's Open Inventor framework was proposed through a public Request For Proposals (RFP) process issued by the VRML community, meaning that any company or individual was free to submit a proposal to the group for consideration. Of the five submissions that were received, Open Inventor got the most www-vrml member votes as a suitable technology on which VRML could be built. SGI employees Rikk Carey and Gavin Bell then further refined the Open Inventor proposal in conjunction with Pesce, Parisi, and the entire VRML community.

The official VRML 1.0 specification emerged on May 26, 1995. As a subset of the Open Inventor feature set, but with new networking features, the VRML 1.0 specification described how Internet-based 3D scenes could be built with this new language. Using the VRML 1.0 specification as a guide, developers could now code 3D scenes in the VRML language, while tool vendors had all the details they needed to build products such as VRML plug-ins, standalone VRML browsers, and authoring tools. And build they did.

VRML worlds, tools, and plug-ins came out of the woodwork after the 1.0 specification was released. As an openly developed language backed by major industry players such as Microsoft and SGI, VRML 1.0 engulfed the World Wide Web in a blaze of 3D enthusiasm. For the first time ever, 3D content could be delivered over the Internet to any computer that had a VRML plug-in or standalone VRML browser (see Figure 2-5). Using VRML, entire 3D object and scene descriptions could be stored in simple text files for downloading and viewing across a wide variety of computer systems. Platform-independent 3D for the Web had arrived.

Although VRML 1.0 truly ushered in Web3D, it was just the first step in a long journey to virtual reality that we're still walking toward today. In fact, VRML 1.0 is extremely limited in its ability to create virtual worlds with realistic, interactive qualities. Being primarily a 3D-scene description language for the Internet, VRML 1.0 was extremely useful when it came to creating static 3D objects and scenes, but it simply did not allow for the immersive, realistic virtual worlds that the VRML community had envisioned. And for good reason; VRML 1.0 was created as a foundation language for Internet 3D, with the understanding that more advanced versions would be developed over time. As a result, work on VRML 2.0 began even as VRML 1.0 was being born.

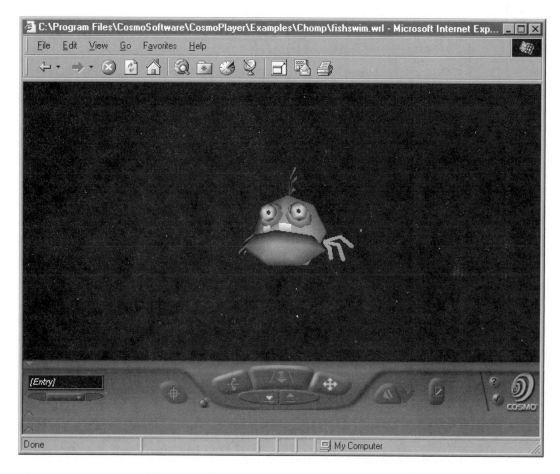

Figure 2-5   VRML worlds are stored in ASCII text files that are interpreted by Web browser plug-ins such as the Cosmo Player plug-in shown here. (http://www.cosmosoftware.com/)

VRML 2.0 and VRML97

Building on the initial success of VRML 1.0 and the open process by which it was developed, evolution of the language continued through the www-vrml list. The group considered adding a few minor improvements to the language, such as support for audio and animation, for a minor update dubbed VRML 1.1. In time, however, it became clear that the development community wanted more than just sound and animation in the next version of VRML, and so a major effort called VRML 2.0 was soon underway.

VRML Specifications

In the spirit through which VRML was born, every major VRML Specification is freely available online through the Web3D Consortium at:

   http://www.web3d.org/fs_specifications.htm

   Here you'll find the specification for VRML 1.0c as well. VRML 1.0c is a "clarification" version of the 1.0 specification that was released in early 1996, which better describes those portions of the original specification that were somewhat ambiguous. 1.0 and 1.0c are essentially the same specifications; the latter merely clarifies ambiguous material found in the former. When people today talk of the "1.0 specification," they are really referring to 1.0c, as it is the most current 1.0 specification.

Following essentially the same process through which VRML 1.0 was developed, a set of requirements for VRML 2.0 was crafted by members of the list and an open Request For Proposals was issued to the general public. As with the first version of the language, any company or individual was free to submit a proposal for VRML 2.0, which would be considered by the group provided it met the requirements they set forth.

The requirements for VRML 2.0 weren't insignificant, and they included enhancements such as support for interactivity, sound, and animation that the original language lacked. In addition, VRML 2.0 called for major improvements in the overall architecture of the language that would allow it to be used to create very complex 3D worlds. VRML 2.0's basic architecture requirements included:

- **Composability:** Allows the various objects and scenes that a world is composed of to be created independent of each other and stored in their own files. A VRML 2.0 shopping mall, for example, might consist of a variety of different objects (store fronts, shopping carts, shelves, products, check-out aisles, and so forth) that are created and stored independent of each other, yet can be assembled together as a virtual mall, thanks to composability.

- **Scalability:** Permits worlds of arbitrary sizes to be built with a viewing scale that can be altered dynamically. Thanks to scalability, we can zoom in and out of scenes at nearly any level of detail. For example, a VRML 2.0 forest might initially be viewed at close range, where every grain of sand on the forest ground is visible. A person viewing such a scene could pull back from the grains of sand to view the plants and shrubs above, and even further to see the forest treetops. One could continue retreating from the scene to see the earth itself, and further still until the galaxy itself is the scale at which the scene is viewed. After exploring the outer reaches of the universe, you could plunge back toward the earth, into the forest, past the treetops, and through the plants and shrubs until you were kissing that sweet soil once again.

- **Extensibility:** Gives developers the opportunity to extend the basic capabilities of the language as they see fit. As an extensible language, VRML 2.0 allows developers to implement features and capabilities that aren't actually in the 2.0 specification. Shared multiuser worlds, for example, are not supported by VRML 2.0. As a result, developers must extend the native capabilities of this version of the language if they wish to create shared worlds (see Chapter 4, "VRML Overview," for details).

The enhanced architecture and new features of VRML 2.0 were so significant that a special group called the VRML Architecture Board (VAG) was formed inside the VRML community to help guide the effort. In response to the VRML 2.0 Request For Proposals, companies such as Microsoft, SGI, Sony, and Sun submitted proposals, as did a number of institutions and individuals, each of which the VAG took into consideration.

Ultimately, the VRML community chose to back a proposal called "Moving Worlds," which the VAG formally recommended as the foundation on which VRML 2.0 would be built. Jointly developed by SGI and Sony, along with a number of individual contributors, Moving Worlds was a collaborative effort even during the proposal development stage. By joining forces rather than competing, the companies and individuals that submitted Moving Worlds had produced a winning proposal that would continue to develop under the VRML community's stewardship.

In late 1995, as the VRML 2.0 specification began to take shape, members of the VAG began actively working with the International Organization for Standardization (ISO) and the International Electrotechnical Commission

(IEC) in hopes of formally standardizing the language. Although the final draft of the VRML 2.0 specification was released in August 1996, standardizing the language through ISO/IEC would take another year.

In December 1997, more than a year after the VRML 2.0 specification was completed, ISO/IEC formally recognized VRML as an international standard. In keeping with ISO/IEC requirements, the VRML 2.0 specification document was modified to reflect the specific document formatting required of all ISO/IEC standards. Based on the VRML 2.0 specification, "VRML97" had arrived, complete with its own unique ISO/IEC designation (ISO/IEC 14772) to indicate that the language had passed through the demanding international standardization processes of both ISO and IEC (see Figure 2-6).

Figure 2-6   VRML97 is currently the only version of the language recognized by ISO/IEC as an international standard (http://www.web3d.org/fs_specifications.htm).

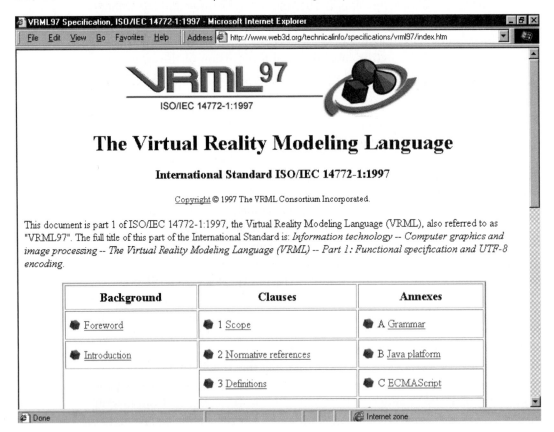

ISO and IEC

ISO and IEC are organizations dedicated to the development of international technology standards. ISO and IEC technical committees often collaborate with each other in the standardization of technologies in which they have a mutual interest, such as VRML. ISO and IEC technical committees typically collaborate with a number of international organizations, including governmental and nongovernmental organizations, in the development of ISO/IEC standards.

To learn more about ISO/IEC standards, visit ISO and IEC on the Web at http://www.iso.ch and http://www.iec.ch. To view the ISO/IEC specification document for VRML ("VRML97"), see the Web3D Consortium's VRML specification page located at http://www.web3d.org/fs_specifications.htm.

VRML 2.0 vs. VRML97

Technically speaking, there is practically no difference between the language described by the VRML 2.0 specification and that of the VRML97 specification. The difference that does exist is primarily in formatting and wording; VRML97 conforms to ISO/IEC document requirements while VRML 2.0 does not, and as such is a more thorough and comprehensive document. Because the two specifications share the same technical base, you'll often hear the terms "VRML 2.0" and "VRML97" used to describe what amounts to the same language. VRML97, however, is actually the most current specification document and is recognized as an international standard, whereas VRML 2.0 is not.

To avoid confusion, the Web3D Consortium has removed the VRML 2.0 specification from its Web site, making VRML97 the only specification to turn to if you have questions regarding this version of the language. Officially, the VRML 1.0 and VRML 2.0 specifications have been made obsolete by VRML97.

Today, VRML97 is the most current VRML language specification available. Although work on a new version originally called VRML Next Generation ("VRML NG," more commonly known as "X3D," as described in the section that follows) is well underway, VRML97 is the VRML specification endorsed by the Web3D Consortium. And, as of this writing, VRML97 is the only VRML specification recognized by ISO/IEC as an international standard.

Extensible 3D (X3D, Formerly Known as VRML-NG)

In 1998, the Web3D Consortium began to focus on an update to the VRML97 specification. This effort, originally known as VRML Next Generation (VRML NG), was eventually recast in early 1999 as "Extensible 3D" (X3D) because of its close relationship with the Extensible Markup Language (XML; see the "Extensible Markup Language (XML)" sidebar). At the time of this writing, development of X3D was well underway, with a draft specification and sample implementations delivered in late 1999 and a final, frozen specification due in the middle of the year 2000 along with at least two different open source code reference implementations (likely to be written using Java and C++, although other languages are also possible).

The overarching goal of X3D is "3D everywhere," or ubiquitous 3D. Whereas VRML97 is primarily experienced by users connected to the Internet with personal computers, X3D is being designed for a much broader audience. It is also targeted at low-cost consumer devices such as television set-top boxes, network computers, and other so-called "thin" devices that don't have the memory or hard-drive space of traditional computers. Although X3D will arrive first for personal computers attached to the Web, the consortium has clearly set its sights on the broader consumer market with this latest revision of VRML.

In keeping with its ambition of enabling 3D everywhere, X3D intends to simplify the authoring of such content in much the same way that HTML does for standard Web page content. Because it is tied to XML, you will be able to create and modify X3D using little more than XML tag sets; if you know how to code HTML by hand today, you're a scant step away from being able to author X3D content (see "Extensible Markup Language (XML)"). Although X3D authoring tools are expected to arrive soon after the technology becomes available in mid-2000, Web page authors will be able to dive in using nothing more than XML tags, a fact that greatly enhances the technology's ability to be used by non-programmers. Because it can be

Extensible Markup Language (XML)

Extensible Markup Language, better known as XML, is a very flexible markup language based on the same Standardized General Markup Language (SGML) from which HTML sprang forth many years ago. Both were developed by the World Wide Web Consortium. XML was designed to address many of the limitations of HTML. The most current version of HMTL, in fact, is now being redefined in terms of XML. By the time you read this, "XHTML" may have emerged from the World Wide Web Consortium as a replacement for HTML 4.0 and all future versions of HTML.

XML was designed as a solution for large-scale electronic publishing and is particularly adept at exchanging a wide variety of information among disparate sites. According to the World Wide Web Consortium, XML will enable international, media-independent publishing of electronic documents; allow industries to define platform-independent protocols used to exchange data (particularly data used in electronic commerce); deliver data to end-user agents in a form that allows these agents to automatically process the information without requiring user input; and allow end users to customize the way in which they view electronic documents. These are but a few of the many benefits that XML claims to deliver. Judging by the rate at which the Web development community is adopting this new technology, especially for electronic commerce purposes, it appears to be delivering on these promises.

To learn more about XML, visit the World Wide Web Consortium's XML home page at http://www.w3.org/XML/.

authored using markup tags, X3D will be accessible to a larger audience of authors (as opposed to VRML97, for example, for which, if you wish to create such content, you must either use a visual development tool or learn how to program in the language).

X3D design and development is taking place through the Web3D Consortium's X3D Task Group, a process being led by consortium director Don Brutzman (see Figure 2-7). As chairman of the X3D Task Group, Don steers this fast-paced effort with several key goals in mind:

- Backwards compatibility with the existing VRML97 standard, allowing X3D to tap into existing VRML97 content while also allowing authors of such content to continue using their existing skill set without fear that support for VRML97 will vanish when X3D hits the streets in the year 2000.

- Integration with the Extensible Markup Language (XML), allowing 3D content to be created and manipulated using XML tags. In other words, X3D allows VRML97 to be expressed through XML.

- Componentized functionality, which breaks the key areas of functionality into discrete components that can be loaded as needed at runtime. A lightweight "core" X3D component will be defined that

Figure 2-7   Extensible 3D (X3D) is the "next generation" of VRML currently under development by the Web3D Consortium (http://www.web3d.org/TaskGroups/x3d/).

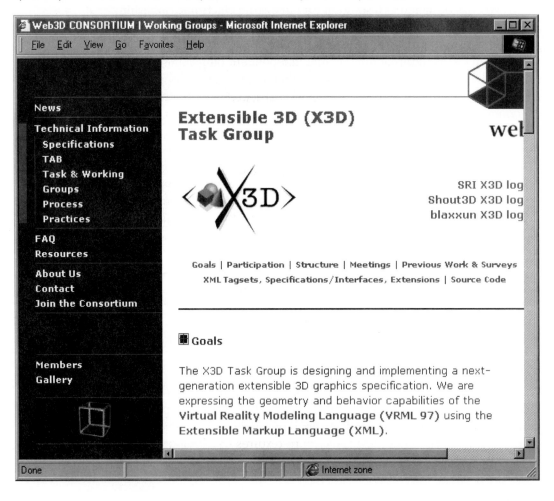

all vendors must comply with, while "extensions" to the core can be added as needed to further enhance the functionality of X3D. This approach stands in stark contrast with VRML97, for which product vendors were required to support the entire specification. As a result, VRML97 products have often been called "monolithic," as they had to take an all-or-nothing approach when it came to implementing the specification. If a product didn't support the entire functionality of the VRML97 specification, from soup to nuts, it could not claim to be VRML97 compliant. X3D, on the other hand, will require vendors to support a much less daunting core functionality, making it easier for them to support the technology.

- Conformance, consistency, and stability—these are three related areas where VRML97 has suffered in the past. In much the same way that Java's original "Write Once, Run Anywhere" promise fell short of the mark, VRML97 has also proven difficult to deploy consistently across a wide spectrum of computing systems. It is not uncommon for a complex VRML97 world to run flawlessly with a particular VRML browser plug-in, yet have problems or behave inconstantly when viewed in others (or, worse yet, crash). There are many reasons for such inconstancies, such as the monolithic approach that vendors must take when supporting the VRML97 specification (which leads to very complicated code) and the fact that reference implementations of VRML97 weren't developed in concert with the development of the specification itself. Solutions to these problems exist, however, and will be borne out during the development of X3D. Componentized functionality, for example (see above), makes life easier for vendors, especially when reference code is available that they can use to create their own products. Such code is being developed in tandem with the X3D design process, and the Web3D Consortium will make it freely available.

Although X3D is based on VRML97, it is not simply a new way of delivering VRML97 content. Instead, X3D will actually enhance VRML97 in many ways while also preserving backwards compatibility with the standard. X3D proposals are now on the table that describe technologies such as curved NURBS surfaces, a capability that VRML97 does not support. Likewise, multitexturing (the ability for two or more textures to be applied to a single object surface), a feature that VRML97 doesn't offer, is also under consideration by the X3D Task Group.

X3D Task Group

X3D is being developed through an open Task Group of the Web3D Consortium that anyone can join, even those who are not members of the consortium. Many of the companies and individuals involved with the development of previous versions of VRML are now involved with the X3D effort, as are a number of 3D experts that were not part of past VRML developments. For details, visit the X3D Task Group at http://www.web3d.org/TaskGroups/x3d/.

Whether these proposed technologies become part of the X3D "core" or are supported by "extensions" hasn't yet been determined, nor have such proposals been officially accepted by the X3D Task Group at the time that this chapter went to print. These and other enhancements are inevitable, however, as X3D is the next step in the evolution of VRML, and so it's only natural to expect that modern 3D features such as NURBS and multitexturing will eventually be supported by X3D. It's also a sure bet that X3D will integrate extremely well with other forms of media, such as 2D graphics, streaming audio, and streaming video, as it is being designed to enable a wide range of Web and broadcast applications.

Java 3D

Unlike VRML, which is an interpreted 3D content development language, Java 3D is a 3D extension to the popular Java programming language. As such, Java 3D allows developers to create comprehensive, platform-independent 3D applications for the desktop and Web-based applets that are executed by a Java Virtual Machine (JVM) residing on the client, as Figure 2-8 illustrates. VRML, on the other hand, is not a full-blown programming language in the way that Java3D combined with Java is.

Created by Sun Microsystems—the same company that created Java—in conjunction with SGI, Intel, and Apple Computer, Java 3D is a suite of Application Programming Interfaces (API) that developers can use to write standalone 3D applications or Web-based 3D applets. Software developers use the Java 3D API, which is analogous to a library of function calls or procedures, to write human-readable source code that must be compiled into platform-neutral bytecode before it can actually be run.

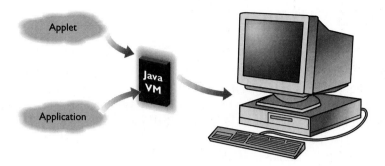

Figure 2-8   Java 3D applets and applications are comprised of Java bytecode that must pass through a Java Virtual Machine (JVM) interpreter before being executed.

Java bytecode is not human-readable source code, and so it doesn't have to be fully interpreted as VRML does. However, computers don't directly understand bytecode in the same way that they do binary machine code. Java bytecode is an intermediary form of code that must be interpreted by a JVM before it can be run. Falling somewhere between human-readable source code and binary machine code, Java bytecode files are more compact and efficient than text files containing human-readable code that must be fully interpreted, yet less efficient than native binary executables.

Java bytecode does enjoy a major advantage that machine code does not: platform independence. Platform-independent bytecode is the basis of Sun's "Write Once, Run Anywhere" claim for the Java language. As an intermediate form of code, bytecode isn't tied to a particular computing platform in the same way binary machine code is. Before it is actually executed on a specific type of computer, Java bytecode must first pass through a JVM that converts the intermediate bytecode into machine code the computer can then execute. Although it is ultimately converted into machine code at runtime, Java bytecode can be executed on any type of computer, so long as a JVM is present to perform the last step of translation to machine code.

Even though Java 3D bytecode must be interpreted by a JVM before it can be executed, just as VRML text files must be interpreted by a plug-in or standalone VRML browser, the Java bytecode format is much closer to machine code than the human-readable ASCII text contained in VRML files. As a result, Java 3D bytecode can be converted into machine code faster than VRML, giving it a performance advantage over VRML and other interpreted languages.

Java 3D and VRML: Similar, Yet Different

Although VRML and Java 3D differ in their approach to 3D content creation and delivery, both shield developers from low-level plumbing details. Java 3D is a high-level 3D API that allows programmers to develop comprehensive 3D programs without the complexity found in traditional 3D languages such as OpenGL and Direct3D, in much the same way that VRML spares developers from these gruesome details.

Java 3D also is similar to VRML in that it is a freely available technology that anyone with a Windows or Solaris operating system can use. (Java 3D for other platforms, such as the Macintosh, is expected in the future, once Java 3D takes hold.) In this respect, Sun's Java 3D API is analogous to the Web3D Consortium's VRML specifications; both are blueprints that developers can use to create 3D content and both are available for free over the Internet. Content developers don't have to plunk down a dime to use the Java 3D API, nor do they have to pay for the runtime environment that actually executes Java 3D bytecode: Sun's Java 3D APIs and JVMs are available free of charge through the official Java Web site (http://java.sun.com/).

In keeping with their many similarities, Java 3D can actually read VRML97 files, allowing Java 3D developers to take advantage of existing VRML content. Java 3D can read standard VRML97 files through a unique *loader* mechanism that gives Java 3D programs access to a wide variety of 3D file formats. Developed through a collaborative effort between Sun's Java 3D team and the Web3D Consortium, the VRML loader allows Java 3D applets and applications to tap into a vast quantity of VRML content and illustrates the close relationship the two technologies share. A number of Java 3D applets and applications use standard VRML files to store 3D object and scene descriptions, thanks to the ease with which Java 3D can read and render VRML content.

Despite their similarities, Java 3D and VMRL differ in many ways—perhaps most significantly in the scope of their capabilities as programming languages. VRML is a relatively simple 3D content development language, whereas Java 3D is a suite of 3D APIs that extend the comprehensive Java programming language.

As a standard extension to the Java platform, Java 3D programs can access all Java technologies and vice versa. Traditional Java applets and applications can be enhanced with 3D via the Java 3D API, while Java 3D applets and applications can tap into the wealth of Java APIs already available to every Java program. Java 3D programs, for example, can use Java's existing database APIs to interact with databases, or create custom graphical user interfaces through Java's windowing APIs, or use any of Java's existing network APIs.

Java3D Loaders

Java 3D loaders exist for a number of popular 3D formats in addition to VRML97, including Wavefront OBJ, AutoCAD Drawing Interchange File (DXF), Caligari trueSpace (COB), Lightwave Scene Format (LSF), Lightwave Object Format (LOF), and 3D-Studio (3DS), to name just a few. To find out more about the Java3D loader mechanism, or to locate a specific loader, turn to Part III of this book or fire up your Web browser and visit the official Java 3D site at http://www.sun.com/desktop/java3d/.

The Java 3D VRML loader was developed as a collaborative effort between Sun and the Web3D Consortium through the consortium's "Java 3D and VRML" Working Group. For details on the VRML loader, or more information on the relationship between VRML and Java 3D, visit the Working Group at http://www.web3d.org/WorkingGroups/vrml-java3d/.

Because Java 3D is so closely aligned with the Java platform, Java programs can tap into Java 3D features, while Java 3D has full access to the standard suite of Java APIs. Whereas Java 3D has a wide scope of programming capabilities, VRML is focused exclusively on encoding interactive 3D object and scene descriptions. As a result, the VRML file format is ideal for encapsulating 3D worlds for delivery over the Internet, while Java 3D lends itself to more comprehensive 3D application and applet development, thanks to its ties to the Java language.

Another major difference between Java 3D and VRML is found in their approach to storage and delivery. VRML is an interpreted, human-readable language that is stored in ASCII text files. Java 3D source code, on the other hand, is only human readable during the development stage; it must be compiled into a special byte code format before it can be deployed.

Compiled Java 3D files are not human readable, nor are they stored in the ASCII text format. As an extension to Java, Java 3D files are stored in the Java *class* format that is defined by Sun Microsystems (both Java and Java 3D class files have the *.class* extension, such as *shoppingmall.class*). Java and Java 3D class files are comprised of instructions in Java bytecode, an intermediate form of code that falls somewhere between human-readable source code and binary machine code that must be converted into machine code by a JVM before it can be executed, as discussed earlier.

Strike a Match

Although Java 3D was officially released to the public in December of 1998 and is several years younger than VRML, it boasts a strong heritage. Java itself was first unveiled by Sun Microsystems in 1995 and is the base on which Java 3D builds. As a standard Java extension, Java 3D fits hand-in-glove with its parent language.

Java 3D is designed to fully leverage the core Java technology as well as the considerable installed base of users and developers that Java has established over the years. With ties to a community of approximately 2,000,000 Java developers, access to a massive installed base of Java-savvy browsers (almost every Web browser used today has some level of Java built in) and compatibility with VRML, Java 3D is a powder keg of potential just waiting to explode.

Java Media Family

Java 3D is part of Sun's Java Media family. Java Media is a collection of media-oriented APIs that extend Java with advanced multimedia capabilities not found in the core Java APIs. As a member of the Java Media family, Java3D's siblings include:

- **Java 2D:** Extends Java's Abstract Windowing Toolkit (AWT) with advanced two-dimensional imaging capabilities that allow developers to draw with enhanced lines, colors, image transforms, and composites.

- **Java Advanced Imaging:** Supports a variety of image-processing techniques, such as scaling, cropping, warping, distorting, and image enhancement.

- **Java Media Framework:** Allows developers to create and use media players, media capture utilities, and media conferencing tools.

- **Java Shared Data Toolkit:** Supports interactive communications over a variety of networks, including collaborative whiteboards, multiuser chats, and shared document editing.

- **Java Sound:** Extends Java's basic sound-playing capabilities, with low-level audio features including audio mixing, audio capture, MIDI sequencing, and MIDI synthesis.

- **Java Speech:** Allows Java programs to support both speech recognition and speech synthesis.

- **Java Telephony:** Integrates telephones with computers, allowing programmatic control of telephones through Java.

In the same way that Java 3D has seamless access to the entire suite of core Java technologies (such as networking, database access, graphical user interface facilities, and so forth), and vice versa, Java 3D is also interoperable with the entire suite of Java Media APIs. Thanks to the close relationship that Java 3D shares with its parent and sibling technologies, as well as its ability to read and render standard VRML97 files, extremely powerful and complex Java 3D applets and applications can be built with a minimum of effort on the developer's part.

Note: Performance Boost

Java 3D supports hardware acceleration and other performance-enhancing features of the underlying platform, giving Java 3D programs a substantial performance boost when executed on systems equipped with such capabilities. In keeping with its high-level approach to 3D, the Java 3D API shields the developer from these low-level details; if performance can be enhanced by hardware acceleration, the Java runtime system will do so transparently without any coding effort on the developer's part.

MPEG-4

MPEG-4 is an integrated collection of multimedia technologies developed by the Motion Picture Experts Group (MPEG), the same organization that developed the Emmy Award-winning MPEG-1 and MPEG-2 standards. Both MPEG-1 and MPEG-2 have been extremely successful as two of the fundamental technologies that ushered in interactive video on CD-ROM and Digital Television, while the audio capabilities of MPEG-1 have been rocking the Internet music scene lately. MPEG-1 audio layer 3, better known as MP3, is among the most popular audio formats in use on the Web today and is one of many technological achievements of the MPEG development process.

Following in the footsteps of past MPEG development efforts, MPEG-4 has recently emerged as an international ISO/IEC standard after years of collaboration between hundreds of researchers and engineers from around the globe (ISO/IEC 14496; see the VRML discussion earlier in this chapter for details relating to ISO/IEC standards). Under development for over five years, MPEG-4 is only now seeing the light of day, yet promises to dramatically change the way we see, hear, and interact with multimedia.

MPEG-4, due to hit the world in the year 2000, is a comprehensive solution for encoding and delivering many different forms of media over a wide assortment of networks and computing platforms. As a cross-platform multimedia standard, MPEG-4 is a "global media solution" that supports audio, video, texture, 2D, and 3D content. With MPEG-4, these various forms of content can be delivered separately, much as MP3 audio is delivered independent of MPEG-1 video, or they can be integrated together to produce a rich multimedia experience.

Binary Format for Scenes (BIFS)

Binary Format for Scenes (BIFS) is a complete framework for encoding scene data in MPEG-4. BIFS allows MPEG-4 media to be mixed with 2D and 3D content. It also handles user interactivity with such content, and manages local and remote alterations of scene data over time. The BIFS layer of MPEG-4, better known as "MPEG-4/BIFS," was originally based on VRML 2.0 and is today built upon VRML97. (VRML 2.0 was a draft version of VRML that would eventually become an intentional ISO/IEC standard called VRML97, as described earlier.) Although VRML is the foundation on which MPEG-4/BIFS is built—making the process of encoding existing VRML worlds for use with MPEG-4 relatively easy—MPEG-4/BIFS also extends VRML in many ways to make it more suitable for use in broadcast applications.

Extending VRML

The Internet is only one of many delivery mechanisms supported by MPEG-4. Broadcast delivery systems, such as those used to deliver content to digital televisions and set-top boxes, are also supported by this technology. Because broadcast systems are fundamentally different from networks such as the Internet, VRML alone wouldn't suffice as the 3D content layer of MPEG-4. Thus, MPEG-4/BIFS extends the VRML97 standard in several key areas in order to accommodate many different forms of network and broadcast, including:

MPEG-4 Working Group

A Web3D Consortium MPEG-4 Task Group was formed just a short time before this book went to print, which complements the MPEG-4 Working Group that has been in existence for several years. For details on the MPEG-4 Task Group and Working Group, visit http://www.web3d.org/. To learn more about the MPEG-4/BIFS development now underway, or any other MPEG technology, visit the MPEG site at http://drogo.cselt.it/mpeg/ (see Figure 2-9).

Figure 2-9   Although MPEG-4/BIFS is based on VRML97, it also extends the VRML standard in many ways in order to accommodate a wide variety of delivery mechanisms and platforms (http://drogo.cselt.it/mpeg/).

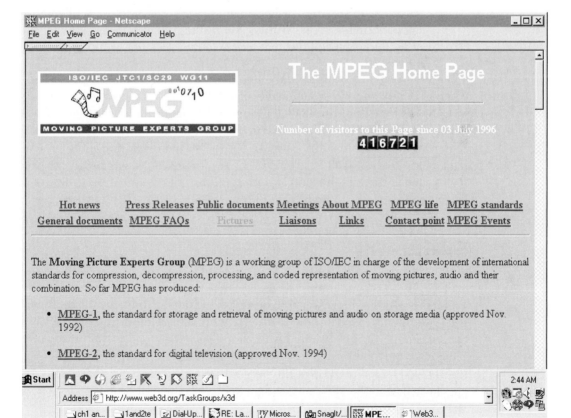

- **Binary Compression**: Compression is perhaps the most obvious area where BIFS enhances VRML. Indeed, the "Binary Format For Scenes" name itself describes a compressed binary format for 3D scenes. BIFS files are stored in compressed binary format, unlike VRML files that are typically stored in human-readable text format. (VRML files can also be compressed using the GZip utility, as described in the following chapters.) BIFS files are often 10 to 20 times smaller in size than their VRML equivalents, thanks to powerful compression techniques designed to optimize 3D content delivery.

- **Media Mixing**: Media integration is another area where BIFS extends standard VRML functionality. As one of many media components supported by MPEG-4, BIFS integrates extremely well with other media types. Rich media compositions of 3D, 2D, video, and audio are commonplace in MPEG-4 as a result of BIFS's ability to easily mix with other forms of media, something that isn't so easily achieved with VRML.

- **Audio Composition**: BIFS's audio composition features allow mixing of sound sources, synthesized sounds, special sound effects, and other audio capabilities that VRML alone does not support.

Although compression, media integration, and audio aren't the only areas where BIFS extends the functionality of VRML97, they're among the most significant. As Part IV of this book explains, BIFS builds on VRML a great deal, which in turn gives MPEG-4 access to a large reservoir of existing VRML content in a way similar to that of Java 3D (see the earlier discussion about Java 3D loaders for details). Conversely, VRML developers can access broadcast platforms such as digital television and set-top boxes, for example, by simply converting their standard VRML97 worlds into the MPEG-4/BIFS format.

Summary

Web3D is a general term used to describe a variety of Internet 3D technologies. The Web3D Consortium (formerly the VRML Consortium) is responsible for standardizing various forms of Internet 3D, and at the moment it recognizes only the Virtual Reality Modeling Language (VRML) and Extensible 3D (X3D) as Web3D. For the purposes of this book, however, we also discuss Java 3D and the 3D component of MPEG 4 (Binary Format for Scenes, or BIFS).

VRML was developed by the VRML Consortium, which eventually became the Web3D Consortium, and forms the basis of X3D. X3D was originally called VRML Next Generation (VRML NG), which was meant as a major update to the current VRML97 standard, although the name was changed to reflect its close relationship to the Extensible Markup Language (XML) recently introduced by the World Wide Web Consortium. Sun Microsystems is ultimately responsible for Java 3D, which is an extension to the standard Java platform. MPEG-4/BIFS is the scene framework component of MPEG-4, a comprehensive media encoding and delivery system developed by the same group that brought us MPEG-1 and MPEG-2.

VRML and Java 3D are both available at the time of this writing, while X3D and MPEG-4/BIFS remain under development. While preliminary developmental versions of both X3D and MPEG-4/BIFS were available at the time this book went to press, we won't really have a chance to weave these forms of Web3D into our Web pages until mid or late 2000. In the meantime, you can tap into the power of VRML and Java 3D today while anticipating the next wave of Internet 3D promised by tomorrow's X3D and MPEG-4/BIFS.

Following is a complete list of URLs referenced in this chapter:

Web3D Consortium (Web3DC)   http://www.web3d.org/

World Wide Web Consortium (W3C)   http://www.w3.org/

Internet Engineering Task Force (IEFT)   http://www.ietf.org/

Silicon Graphics Inc. (SGI)   http://www.sgi.com/

Cosmo Player   http://www.cosmosoftware.com

VRML Specifications   http://www.web3d.org/fs_specifications.htm

International Organization for Standardization (ISO)   http://www.iso.ch

XML   http://www.w3.org/XML

International Electrotechnical Commission (IEC)   http://www.iec.ch

X3D Task Group   http://www.web3d.org/TaskGroups/x3d/

Sun's Java Web site   http://java.sun.com/

Sun's Java 3D Web Site   http://www.sun.com/desktop/java3d/

Java 3D VRML Working Group   http://www.web3d.org/WorkingGroups/vrml-java3d/

MPEG site   http://drogo.cselt.it/mpeg/

Web3D Task Groups   http://www.web3d.org/TaskGroups/

Web3D Working Groups   http://www.web3d.org/WorkingGroups/

ENTERING THE THIRD DIMENSION

Topics in This Chapter

- An introduction to the human "stereo" visual system
- Using monocular depth cues to give the illusion of depth
- Projecting 3D data onto 2D surfaces
- Essential 3D concepts and jargon

Chapter 3

Although Web3D is relatively new, having only become practical for the everyday Internet user as of late 1998 (thanks to the maturation of enabling technologies described in Chapter 1, "Why Bother?"), the field of computerized 3D is decades old. And while 3D on the computer seems fairly modern, considering that it has only been in widespread use for the past dozen years or so, it is, in truth, simply one more step in the evolution of 3D that began thousands of years ago.

In this chapter I will describe how 3D "began" in the physical world when our primitive ancestors first focused their eyes in order to survive, found its way into the art world through eye-fooling techniques developed by Renaissance artists, and eventually entered the computer world courtesy of mathematics. In the sections that follow you will find that Web3D borrows heavily from 3D technologies that went before it, sharing many of the concepts, techniques, and terms common to the fields of art, mathematics, and traditional computer graphics.

This chapter sets the table for those that follow, giving you the implements that will let you consume the remainder of this book with ease. You will learn what the third dimension is, how it works, and why we need it. Along the way you will be introduced to the unique vocabulary of 3D, as we show you how the illusion of depth is projected onto flat, two-dimensional surfaces such as art canvases and computer screens, and how interactive 3D technologies allow you to *enter* the third dimension.

Consumed by 3D

3D is a specialized form of computer graphics that has evolved over a number of years and can't be completely covered in a single book, let alone one chapter. The purpose of this chapter is to give you a basic understanding of 3D in preparation for the chapters that follow. Because computer 3D is fascinating, you may soon find yourself consumed by the concept. If you're interested in learning more about 3D in general, visit the following Web page. Here you'll find a number of links to print and online resources related to 3D:

http://www.web3dgallery.com/3d/resources.html

Wired for 3D

From the dawn of time human beings have been wired for 3D. As predators, we have two eyes spaced slightly apart on the front of our head, allowing us to drink in the same visual scene from two slightly different angles. Our brain receives these two visual images, one from each eye, and combines them into a single three-dimensional picture having depth; we "see" in 3D because of our stereo, or binocular, visual system (see Figure 3-1).

Through a relatively large binocular field of vision we're able to quickly perceive the physical, three-dimensional world around us. Our eyes and brain work in unison to allow us to see opportunity and threats instantly, which must have been a particularly handy skill in primitive times when it was necessary to hunt for food and hide from enemies as a matter of survival. Although we no longer struggle to stay alive on a daily basis the way our ancestors did, our 3D vision nonetheless remains essential in our modern, everyday life.

Just as it was for our ancestors, the real world we live in today is made up of three-dimensional objects (animals, people, trees, rocks, and so forth) located in three-dimensional space. This means that the things around us have depth as well as height and width, and they can be located close to or far away from us as well as to our left or right, or above or below us, or even behind us. It is the dimension of depth that accounts for what we commonly call the third dimension, an ever-present aspect of our world that we take for granted because it is an inherent and natural part of daily life.

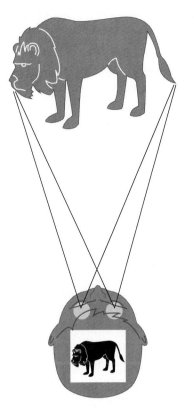

Figure 3-1 The human visual system is a stereo, or binocular, system that creates a single 3D image from two slightly different views of the same scene.

To reach out and pluck an apple off a tree, for example, requires a tremendous amount of 3D processing between your eyes and brain, even though you aren't conscious of what's going on. In order to successfully perform the task you must be able to judge exactly where the apple resides in 3D space and how large it is in all dimensions, in order to wrap your fingers around it. Furthermore, you must be able to instantaneously process any changes to the situation.

A breeze might come along and sway the apple to and fro, for instance, forcing you to dynamically recalculate an ever-changing location in 3D space. A strong wind can even blow your snack off the tree altogether, in which case you must track the apple's movement as it falls to the ground, where it bounces a few times and then rolls to a stop. Although it may seem trivial to follow the moving apple with your eyes, an astonishing amount of

Note: Eat or Be Eaten

The human visual system is similar to that of all predators. We have two eyes located at the top of our heads and slightly apart, giving each eye a slightly different view of the world. Our brain instantly and automatically resolves this retinal disparity *(also known as* parallax*), combining the images each eye delivers into a single three-dimensional picture, giving us binocular or* stereo *vision. Our binocular, predatory vision system is extremely well developed and is essential for hunting food that moves. Prey animals, on the other hand, have eyes located further apart, typically on each side of their head, which helps them "keep an eye out" for predators.*

3D processing is necessary to perform this simple, natural task. Imagine how much more your eyes and brain work when you trot across a street while avoiding oncoming traffic, or play a pickup game of basketball, or drive up to the takeout window of your favorite fast food joint for that matter.

Because we live in a three-dimensional world, our visual system automatically renders what we see in terms of 3D; we don't have to think about it, it just happens. We take 3D for granted nearly every waking moment of our lives. Representing the third dimension of depth on a flat, two-dimensional surface, such as an art canvas or computer screen, however, is a different story altogether.

3D on Canvas

The physical world around us is made of up three dimensions, but the same cannot be said for representations on the flat surface of an art canvas. Although our visual systems are highly developed and very sensitive to 3D information, artists did not commonly represent the third dimension on canvas until the Renaissance period. Whereas sculpting has always been a 3D art form since real-world materials used to create sculptures (typically clay) are inherently three-dimensional, applying paint to a flat canvas always produces two-dimensional art.

An artist cannot, for example, reach deep into a canvas and place a brush stroke of paint far away from the viewer, any more than he can apply paint in

Flat Surfaces and Monocular Depth Cues

In the real world our binocular vision is combined with single-eye, or monocular, depth cues to give us the full sense of the objects around us. However, on flat surfaces such as an art canvas, computer display, or photograph, only monocular depth cues are available to give us a sense of the third dimension.

mid-air to allow some brush strokes to appear closer to the viewer than others. Instead, every brush stroke is applied to a canvas on the same plane, where only the height and width vary. As a result, painting is by its very nature a two-dimensional art form.

Paintings created before the Renaissance are generally devoid of any sense of depth because of the physical limitations imposed by this two-dimensional medium. During the Renaissance period, however, artists such as Leonardo da Vinci developed and refined a number of visual techniques that could be used to give paintings the illusion of depth. Carefully examining the natural world around them, Renaissance artists found that they could trick the viewer's visual system by using a number of *monocular depth cues* found in our real world.

Monocular Depth Cues

Although we typically view the world around us using both eyes, which allows us to perceive the third dimension as described in the previous section, closing one eye does not result in a complete loss of depth. Try, for example, covering one eye while looking at a three-dimensional object such as the book you are now reading. Even though you will have lost the stereo vision that comes with two eyes, 3D objects do not suddenly appear flat and two dimensional when viewed with only one eye. However odd or unsettling it may seem at first to view the world with one eye, many people do in fact function quite well with only one, thanks to monocular depth cues.

Monocular depth cues are visual hints about the depth and location of objects that can be recognized with only one eye (hence the term *monocular depth cues*). Although they may have been used in the art world previously, the Renaissance period, and Leonardo da Vinci in particular, brought about an unprecedented sense of realism in art by applying six specific monocular depth cues, which are used even today. Our visual systems pick up on these depth cues without any conscious effort on our part, just as our eyes and brain give us stereo vision automatically. Artists, however, both traditional and computer based, go to great lengths to imitate the following monocular depth cues using paints and pixels:

- **Size Differences:** Objects that are further away from us appear smaller than objects that are closer. This is why a car coming down the block seems to get larger as it approaches, even though it never really changes in size. Likewise, if you look down along a line of telephone poles, those that are furthest away from you will look the smallest, even though they are actually the same physical size as every other pole in the line. These size differences are visual clues that help us determine how close or far objects are from us, and where they are positioned in relation to one another.

- **Occlusion:** Objects that are closer to us can block, or occlude, objects that are further away. This seems to place objects "in front" of others, which tells us about their relative position to one another. A person standing in front of a building, for example, will occlude a portion of that building, which is a visual hint that tells us the front-to-back order of the scene. Because the person occludes the building, we can safely assume that he or she is in front of the building.

- **Lighting and Shading:** When light strikes an object that has depth, the surface of the object that is hit directly by the light appears to be the brightest, while the sides are shaded progressively darker. The back side of the object, meanwhile, is the darkest because it receives the least amount of light. The light seems to pour over the object to create gradients of bright to dark; light is most intense at the point of impact and gradually becomes less intense on surface areas further from the light source. If you shine a flashlight on a pumpkin, for example, the area where the light hits the pumpkin directly will appear to be the brightest shade of orange, while the sides of the pumpkin gradually darken and so are seen as progressively darker shades of orange. The back of the pumpkin, meanwhile, is the darkest shade of orange or perhaps even appears brown, because very little light hits that surface. Light sources also are often used to calculate shadows for objects, which can add a great deal to the sense of realism of a 3D scene. In cases where real-time shadow calculations are restrictive, such as with interactive Web3D, 3D content developers can actually "create" fake shadows. (VRML and Java 3D, for example, don't support real-time shadow calculations, although experienced developers often create their own shadow effects in order to increase the realism of their content.)

- **Texture Density:** Real-world textures (such as the repeating tiles of a floor, shingles on a roof, or the stones in a wall) appear to become more dense the further away they are, which is a direct result of objects appearing smaller at greater distances (see Size Differences). If you are standing on a brick sidewalk, for example, the bricks beneath your feet form the texture of the walkway. The bricks directly under you appear to be larger and less densely packed than those that are further down the sidewalk. The brick texture seems to become even more densely packed with added distance, as the individual bricks that make up the texture appear smaller and closer together. Eventually the brick texture becomes so dense that you can't actually see the individual bricks, and instead see only their red color.

- **Linear Perspective:** Lines that are parallel to our line of sight, such as railroad tracks, appear to narrow as they recede, eventually converging at a point in the far distance known as the *vanishing point*. Although the Greeks discovered perspective almost a full millennium before the Renaissance, it was all but forgotten until artists such as Leonardo da Vinci and Albrecht Dürer used it to increase the realism of their artwork. The general concept of perspective in artwork actually combines linear perspective with size differences. Thus, in the case of railroad tracks, linear perspective is responsible for the tracks narrowing in the distance and eventually converging at a vanishing point on the horizon. Size differences, however, account for the railroad ties (the horizontal wooden beams between the tracks) appearing to become progressively shorter as they move further and further away from the viewer.

- **Atmospheric Perspective:** Objects that are close to us generally appear very sharp and detailed, while those in the distance are less detailed and often fuzzy. This difference in appearance is a result of light traveling through atmosphere; the further light travels, the more atmosphere it must pass through. Simply put, we "see" things as a result of our eyes receiving rays of light reflected by objects in our field of vision, which is the information our brain uses to form a picture of the physical world around us. Rays of light passing through the atmosphere scatter when they collide with tiny dust particles and microscopic molecules of water and gas on their journey to our eyes, which can make objects look fuzzy and less detailed when compared to nearby objects that reflect light in a more direct path. In addition, light rays that travel long distances are more likely to also become refracted by heated masses of air, further distorting the information that reaches our eyes (mirages are the result of light rays that have been greatly distorted by heat masses). As a result, distant objects appear to be fuzzy while those close to us are sharper. Objects in the distance also tend to have a blue or monochromatic appearance, while the colors of nearby objects are typically more vibrant and vivid. This is a result of blue light rays having a shorter wavelength than other colors in the light spectrum, causing blue rays to be more easily scattered by atmospheric conditions than other colors (which in turn casts a blue tone over objects in the distance).

By applying these real-world monocular depth cues to their artwork, Renaissance artists elevated drawing and painting to an entirely new level. Realistic-looking artwork that appeared to have the dimension of depth was finally possible, thanks to these innovative eye-fooling techniques. Flat, two-dimensional surfaces such as art canvases and cathedral walls came to life through the illusion of 3D, paving the way for forms of computer 3D that would come centuries later.

3D on the Computer

Computer 3D is a relatively new phenomenon. Computers were born in research labs in the middle of the twentieth century and have only become "personal" and commonplace in the past decade or so. To put an even finer point on it, computer-based 3D has emerged for the general population only in the past few years, thanks to powerful, low-cost desktop computers combined with mass-market 3D technologies such as Web3D (see Chapter 1, "Why Bother?" for details). However, even though more than five hundred years have passed since Renaissance artists first learned how to use monocular depth cues to give their art a sense of depth and realism, the same basic techniques are used in modern-day computer 3D.

Because the computer screen is a flat, two-dimensional surface, just as the art canvas is, the monocular depth-cue techniques that are effective in the art world are also effective in the computer world. The main difference, of course, is that paint is not physically applied to a computer screen. Instead, light illuminates picture elements, or pixels, of the computer screen, giving us what amounts to a digital canvas lit from behind.

Although the art canvas and our computer screens are similar in a few very important ways (both are flat, 2D surfaces used to display graphical representations of real or imaginary objects), they are more different than they are the same. The most significant difference lies in the fact that, at its heart, computer 3D is all about mathematics and number crunching. Three-dimensional computer content involves sophisticated mathematical manipulation of 3D data structures that represent objects and scenes having depth, which are ultimately projected onto a display device in a visual form the viewer can understand. Traditional art, however, is produced using real-world materials (such as chalk or paint) applied to a canvas by the hand of a human artist.

And while it is true that 3D computer content is also created by human artists using input devices similar to those employed by real-world artists (such as a mouse or stylus, which are the computer equivalent of a paint brush or pencil), the computer is an entirely different beast. Because the technology of computer 3D is so different, artists working in this field must learn an entirely new vocabulary and set of skills in order to master it.

Computer 3D Concepts and Jargon

Although computer-based 3D has become commonplace only in the past few years, it has been part of our high-technology landscape for several decades. 3D computer technology was hard at work long before the World Wide Web was even invented, transforming industries such as architecture, design, medicine, manufacturing, theoretical mathematics, and entertainment, to name just a few.

As a result of the marriage between computers and 3D, human beings have been able—for the first time in history—to create, manipulate, and explore three-dimensional structures without actually using real-world 3D materials such as clay, metal, or wood. Before computer 3D, for example, architects had no way of modeling buildings other than to create physical structures using real-world materials. Such physical models are time consuming and extensive to produce, as well as inflexible and quite constraining.

Virtual Reality

Computerized 3D can be said to be "nothing more than an illusion," since the results are commonly displayed on flat, two-dimensional displays and rely on monocular depth cues in order to trick our visual system into seeing a third dimension. Virtual Reality (VR), however, is somewhat different.

True VR is typically experienced with the aid of 3D eye goggles, where each eyepiece displays a slightly different version of the same image (each image makes use of monocular depth cues, as do all other forms of computer 3D). The viewer's brain will automatically combine these two images into a single stereoscopic 3D image, which is generally more realistic looking than 3D displayed on a traditional computer screen.

Although this VR approach to 3D is more like our own biological stereo vision system, it's still an illusion; the objects and scenes created for each eyepiece in a VR system are no more "real" than those created on a desktop computer (the viewer's eyes and brain receive computer-generated images in both cases). However, stereo vision is actually achieved as a result of each eye receiving a slightly different version of the same scene, which the brain then resolves into a single 3D image.

Altering the physical model of a building in response to a client's feedback, for instance, takes a good deal of time and money, whereas a computerized 3D model can be altered with relative ease and at less cost.

Computer 3D also allows us to rapidly visualize concepts that might otherwise be impractical or impossible to construct in the real world. Accurately visualizing the molecular makeup of a new drug and how it might interact with the chemistry of the human body, for example, is practically impossible without the aid of computer 3D. Medical companies today routinely use computer 3D to design and develop drugs and medical devices at a fraction of the cost of traditional research and development, while surgeons can now simulate complex surgical procedures on their desktop computer before physically walking into the operating room. Similarly, mathematicians often rely on computer 3D to visualize complex mathematical equations that might otherwise be impossible to understand.

Over the years computer 3D, like most computer technology, has evolved at a tremendous pace. Whereas the first 3D computer programs were merely the technological equivalent of simple drawing tools that could create simple 3D shapes, computer 3D technologies today are much more sophisticated and generally fall into three broadly defined categories:

- **Traditional 3D**, used to create 3D images and animation (sequences of images) that are viewed by the end user from a fixed perspective chosen by the artist.
- **Interactive 3D**, which allows the end user to navigate and explore three-dimensional scenes and the objects they contain from any viewpoint.
- **Immersive 3D**, which utilizes special input and output devices (such as video goggles and data gloves) to allow the end user to view and interact with 3D content in a way that closely resembles the real world.

Traditional 3D

Traditional 3D graphics programs create static computer art that has the illusion of depth using the monocular depth-cue techniques described earlier. These programs are the 3D analog to Adobe Photoshop, in that the images that they produce are just that: images. Unlike interactive and immersive 3D, which allow the end user to actually explore and manipulate three-dimensional objects positioned in 3D space, traditional computer 3D programs generate images that are viewed from a perspective chosen by the artist.

More sophisticated traditional 3D programs allow the artist to create animated image sequences, or movies, from a series of 3D images. However, just as with single static images the viewpoint is always predetermined by the artist creating the animation and can't be altered by the user. The best we can do is sit back and look at the image or animation produced by someone else; we're not able to interact with what we see.

However, despite a lack of interactivity, the content these programs create is usually of superior quality when compared to interactive and immersive forms of 3D. Because the viewpoint of traditional computer 3D is fixed (the angle of viewing does not change in response to user activity), the computer can spend a great deal of time drawing, or rendering, each image created by the artist long before it is displayed to the end user. Interactive and immersive 3D are dynamically rendered in real time; traditional 3D is pre-rendered before the user sees it. A single image can take hours or even days to render as the computer crunches away at 3D data, yeoman's work that can produce wonderfully realistic results.

Traditional 3D is often used in television and motion pictures, as these forms of entertainment don't require input from the viewer; we just sit back and watch. However, the data crunching required to produce even one full minute of broadcast-quality 3D animation would bring a desktop computer to its knees. Because of the massive amount of processing power needed to create 3D such as this, television and movie studios typically rely on rendering farms—large networks of powerful, interconnected 3D rendering workstations—to generate 3D images and animation.

The 3D programs used to create broadcast-quality 3D are high-end and extremely expensive (prices start in the thousands of dollars and can quickly move into tens or even hundreds of thousands) and are often custom developed. You won't find programs such as these on the shelf of your local computer superstore. Artists literally spend years becoming proficient with these complex and very specialized 3D programs, and their skills are in high demand.

At the opposite end of the spectrum are mass-market traditional 3D programs, such as those used by Web page authors to create simple Web page buttons, images, and animations that have a three-dimensional appearance. Like their higher-end brethren, these products produce 3D content that is always experienced from the viewpoint selected by the author; you can't explore or manipulate such content any more than you can a GIF or JPEG image.

The advantage of these tools is that they are inexpensive (some are available as freeware or shareware, while others cost upwards of a few hundred

Note: Computer-Generated Imagery (CGI)

Traditional 3D computer graphics used in the production of broadcast-quality 3D images and animation are often referred to as Computer-Generated Imagery (CGI). George Lucas employed a fleet of 3D artists to create the Star Wars *prequel,* Episode I: The Phantom Menace, *of which approximately 90% of the scenes contained computer-generated characters, backgrounds, or special effects. Some feature films, however, are completely computer generated.* Toy Story, Antz, *and* A Bug's Life, *for example, were created entirely inside the world of the computer.*

dollars), easy to use, and don't require massive computing power to render the final results; a standard desktop computer is plenty of horsepower. The trade-off, of course, is that the images and animation produced by such low-end products are nowhere near as realistic as those created by high-end 3D graphics programs. However, they're more than sufficient when it comes to spicing up a Web page or exploring the 3D side of computer graphics.

Filling the giant gap between low- and high-end products are mid-level traditional 3D graphics programs that are typically employed to create 3D artwork used in print (magazine advertisements and product packaging, for example) and nonbroadcast applications. Mid-level packages are also commonly used to create introduction sequences for low-budget television programs and movies, for example, or materials distributed on CD-ROM, such as animated "cut scenes" that appear between the interactive segments of video games.

Although not as cheap as mass-market 3D products, mid-range 3D graphics programs are affordable when compared to high-end 3D products, typically ranging in price from a few hundred to a few thousand dollars. Mid-level 3D graphics programs are also more complicated to learn and use compared to low-end products, although they are not nearly as complex as high-end systems. Because mid-level 3D programs are more sophisticated and expensive than low-end systems, they're most popular with graphics professionals who don't require specialized products such as those used in the production of broadcast-quality 3D.

Despite the fact that they range in price, complexity, and capability, these forms of traditional 3D share a common purpose: they produce 3D images or animation sequences that are experienced from the viewpoint of the artist, not the user. Traditional 3D content has been fully rendered by the time you view it, meaning you can only look at it. You simply can't interact with traditional 3D.

Interactive 3D

As the name implies, the term "interactive 3D" describes a form of three-dimensional content that you can interact with. Unlike traditional computer 3D, interactive 3D is not prerendered or limited to a specific viewpoint. Instead, it is rendered dynamically ("on the fly") in response to user activity, giving the end user *control* over what viewpoint he or she sees the scene from.

Panoramic 3D

In recent years panoramic 3D technology has emerged to straddle the ground between traditional and interactive 3D. Panoramic 3D consists of prerendered 3D artwork (or photographs) that depict a complete 360-degree scene. The individual images that make up the scene are joined together, or *stitched*, in such a way that the viewer appears to be positioned at the center of a circular scene or *image bubble.*

Imagine standing in the center of a hollow globe, the inside surface of which is covered with seamless images that together create a full 360-degree panoramic scene. Wherever you look you'll see a different portion of the scene.

Panoramic 3D give users the *feeling* that they are inside a 3D world that can be explored in any direction. Interaction with a panoramic 3D world is limited, however, as the images that make up the scene are pre-rendered and so prevent the user from moving about freely in all directions. Truly interactive 3D, on the other hand, is rendered on the fly as the user moves about, allowing for exploration in all directions as well as walking up to objects in a scene and examining them from any angle.

Interactive 3D comes in many forms. Web3D itself, as used in this book, is an umbrella term that covers several specific forms of interactive 3D, such as VRML, Java 3D, MPEG-4/BIFS, and X3D. Video games that use 3D technology are another form of interactive 3D, as are data-mining tools that display data in three dimensions instead of two. Likewise, many computerized Geographic Information Systems (GIS) take advantage of interactive 3D, as do many state-of-the-art network management tools, Computer Aided Design (CAD), and product manufacturing software packages.

The common theme that runs through these and all other forms of interactive 3D technologies is their ability to allow the end user to view a scene or visualize information from any perspective, not one predetermined by someone else. Interactive 3D also allows you to examine in detail those elements of a scene that you find interesting, just as you can walk up to objects in the real world and examine them from any angle.

Because interactive 3D is rendered on the fly in response to user activity, significant computing power is required to keep the display in sync with

Note: Restricting Interactive 3D

Authors of interactive 3D content can completely restrict the mobility and viewpoint of the end user if they desire, although they rarely do so, because severe restrictions defeat the purpose of interactive content. In general, content authors restrict user actions only when it makes sense in the context of a given scene.

A user might be restricted from walking in a certain direction if there is nothing in that direction to see, or prevented from walking through walls, for example. Similarly, users are often prevented from interacting with objects that they have no business touching (a pit bull guard dog, for example, might be off limits, while a French poodle could be approachable).

changes that occur in a scene as the result of a constantly changing viewpoint. In this sense interactive 3D is similar to our own visual system; in both cases what we see is computed real-time. Because computers powering most of today's interactive 3D pale in comparison to the computational capabilities of the human brain, however, interactive 3D as experienced by the general public is far from realistic.

However, thanks to advances in computing (see Chapter 1, "Why Bother?"), today's newly purchased home computers have the horsepower needed to deliver adequate interactive 3D. Using little more than a mouse or keyboard, users can interact with dynamically rendered 3D computer content delivered on fixed media, such as a floppy disk, CD-ROM, or DVD, or through networks. Web3D technologies, for example, typically deliver interactive 3D content via the Internet, yet can also deliver interactive 3D on fixed media (in the same way that standard HTML Web pages can be delivered over the Internet and on fixed media).

When experienced on a computer, interactive 3D content is generally displayed on a computer monitor and navigated with a mouse or keyboard. Console video game systems (such as the Sony Playstation) however, typically utilize a standard television screen for display purposes. Users of these systems don't require a mouse or keyboard to navigate and manipulate interactive 3D content, but instead use a specially designed controller device (similar to a joystick).

Although display and input devices used to experience various types of interactive 3D content may vary somewhat, in all cases the user remains in

Web3D Is Interactive 3D

Fundamentally, Web3D is a collection of 3D technologies designed specifically for distribution of interactive 3D content over the Internet. Although it's possible for various forms of Web3D to provide immersive 3D experiences (see "Immersive 3D"), the vast majority of people who experience Web3D do so using a standard desktop computer. In the future, however, immersive computer display devices may become commonplace, at which time Web3D technologies will be used to deliver immersive 3D content to the masses over the Internet.

visual contact with the real world throughout the experience. The average computer user, for example, typically sits about three feet away from the computer monitor, while console gamers often sit six or more feet away from the television display. Other forms of interactive 3D, such as information kiosks, also require the user to look at a video display situated some distance from the viewer's eyes.

In all cases, interactive 3D users are in constant visual contact with the real world around them through peripheral vision and eye or head movement (gazing away from the display, or turning their head). As a result, interactive 3D experiences don't give users the sense that they are actually *inside* the scene. Instead, they feel as if they are merely looking at computer-generated 3D imagery that they happen to control. They don't feel immersed in the experience.

Immersive 3D

Immersive 3D attempts to increase the realism of the 3D experience by walling off visual contact with the real world, essentially surrounding the viewer with computer-generated imagery. Both traditional 3D and interactive 3D are viewed within the context of the real world; people view these forms of 3D while also being able to see the world around them through peripheral vision or by moving their eyes or head. When you experience traditional 3D and interactive 3D, the experience doesn't envelop you.

Immersive 3D, on the other hand, heightens the experience by placing the viewer *inside* the display using special display technology such as video goggles (see "Immersive Display Devices"). Video goggles, which typically resemble the rather bulky masks worn by scuba divers and downhill skiers, are fitted with a pair of diminutive CRT or LCD displays positioned just a few inches away from the viewer's eyes. Each eyepiece displays a slightly different version of the same 3D image (meaning each eye sees a single scene from somewhat different viewpoints), which are then processed by the viewer's own visual system in the same way real-world scenes are. The viewer's brain combines the two disparate images into a single, three-dimensional scene.

Because immersive display devices such as video goggles cut the viewer off from the real world, users generally feel as if they've truly stepped into the computer display. They can't simply turn their head or look sideways to escape the computer-generated imagery; they must either close their eyes completely or remove the immersive display that has taken over their entire field of vision.

As with traditional 3D and interactive 3D, there are a number of different forms of immersive 3D. The most simplistic forms merely present traditional 3D images and animation through immersive display devices, enhancing the realism of that content by removing the distraction of the world around the viewer. More sophisticated forms combine interactive 3D with immersive display devices and 3D input and feedback devices, and are often called Virtual Reality (VR).

VR is a vague, loosely defined term that is used to describe a wide range of synthetic, computer-generated environments. In one sense, any form of interactive 3D can be considered VR, simply because users can participate directly with such computer content (an alternate reality that exists only within the computer, making it virtual compared to our real world). However, to many in the field of computer technology, myself included, a true VR experience is much more than merely interactive 3D.

Purists believe that true VR is a convincing alternative to the reality of the physical world we live in, and, as a result, is the ultimate, most sophisticated form of immersive 3D. True VR tricks more than just our eyes; it manipulates many more of our senses in order to make the experience seem real, and as such it can be considered *fully immersive 3D*. Surround-sound systems, for example, can dramatically increase the realism of 3D environments, while specialized input devices such as head-position-tracking devices and data gloves allow our bodies to become part of the VR experience to create more fully immersive experiences.

Head-position-tracking devices allow immersive 3D displays to be updated in sync with the user's head movement (looking up, for example, will automatically generate the appropriate display corresponding to such head movement). Data gloves, meanwhile, allow users to reach out and interact with the contents of a scene using their hands and fingers instead of a mouse. These types of 3D input devices can even be coupled with force-feedback output devices to further enhance the realism of a VR experience, allowing users to "feel" the objects that they handle in a virtual world.

Force-feedback devices can also stand on their own, acting only as output devices. The force-feedback vest, for example, is a wearable device that looks like a vest or perhaps a very thin life jacket. Most often used with immersive video games, it can produce the physical sensation of being struck on the torso, sides, or back in response to on-screen activity (such as a fist fight or gun play) without the unpleasant real-world side effect of internal bleeding.

Immersive 3D in general, and VR in particular, are the most specialized forms of 3D technology and therefore aren't yet commonplace. Because of the substantial computing power required, together with the high cost of immersive display devices (such as video goggles) and 3D input/output devices (such as data gloves and force-feedback vests), it will be years, perhaps even decades, before the average computer user partakes in any form of immersive 3D on a regular basis. Today, however, immersive 3D is making inroads in the entertainment world, particularly in high-end video-game arcades and theme-park rides, and also in professions that can justify the high costs and substantial computer-processing requirements.

The medical field, for example, has embraced immersive 3D (and even true VR) in an effort to reduce the risk associated with many complex surgical procedures. Surgeons can not only use immersive 3D to *practice* high-risk procedures (such as brain-tumor removal) in advance; today many can actually *conduct* such surgeries virtually through a computer rather than using their own hands.

Virtual surgery allows the surgeon to control various surgical implements (probes, scalpels, suction devices, and so forth) by manipulating 3D computer representations of these devices. Surgeons can guide these virtual devices through 3D data representations of the patient, such as a 3D tumor visualization created from Magnetic Resonance Imaging (MRI) scans of the patient's body. Traditional risk factors such as hand tremors of the surgeon can be eliminated altogether.

Today immersive 3D is generally limited to very high-end applications, such as specialty VR games available only at certain video-game arcades, expensive theme-park rides, engineering and simulation systems, and virtual surgery. It's only a matter of time, however, before the technology trickles down to the consumer. Already, immersive 3D displays and input/output devices are available for home computer users, although they are quite expensive (a good pair of video goggles starts at about $1,000, for example) and there isn't much consumer demand for such products quite yet.

However, just as color computer displays and laser-writer printers came down in price over time while also improving in quality, eventually immersive 3D technology will come to the masses. I suspect that it will be several years, and more likely a full decade or more, before the average computer consumer steps into immersive 3D with any regularity. That day, though, will surely come—and, when it does, today's interactive Web3D technologies will have paved the way for immersive 3D distributed over the Internet.

Immersive Display Devices

Video goggles, the least expensive and most common type of immersive display device, are sometimes called "video glasses," "stereo goggles," or "shutter glasses." Video goggles are a modern-day embodiment of the "Ultimate Display" developed in the late 1960s by Ivan Sutherland. This was a Head-Mounted-Display (HMD) viewing device containing small video screens that allowed the wearer to become immersed in computer content.

HMDs are generally more bulky than video goggles and, as a result of hardware tracking devices typically built into them, tend to resemble battle helmets. When equipped with position-tracking devices, HMDs can report back to the computer any movement in the viewer's head position, for which the visual display can be automatically updated (thus, the HMD itself becomes a 3D *input* device that captures head movement). When the viewer's head turns to the left, for example, the HMD eyepieces are automatically updated in sync with that movement, similar to what happens when you look around in the real world. Although HMDs equipped with head-position-tracking devices can provide a much more realistic immersive 3D experience, they are highly specialized and quite expensive compared to video goggles.

The days of the Ultimate Display have long since passed, but today's video goggles and HMDs are direct descendants of Sutherland's novel invention. As we enter the year 2000, entirely new forms of immersive display devices have emerged, such as the 3D projection systems and optical lasers.

3D projection systems do away with wearable display devices such as video goggles and HMDs and simply project 3D scenes onto real-world surfaces, such as screens or walls. Today's most advanced theme-park rides, for example, often use 3D projection systems to give participants the feeling that they're immersed in a fantasy world. As riders move along a closed track inside a theme-park building, various 3D scenes are projected onto screens or walls in sync with the moving car, giving riders the sense that they are part of the action as villains and heroes battle it out around them.

Similarly, CAVE Automatic Virtual Environments (or simply CAVE, which is a self-referential acronym) use 3D projection systems to provide unencumbered immersive experiences. A CAVE is a room whose walls are covered in rear-projected 3D scenes that are typically experienced in combination with video goggles and position-tracking devices. A CAVE can be occupied by more than one person at a time. Each person is free to move around the room, allowing for collaborative 3D environments and what's known as an unencumbered, or untethered, experience. However, typically the position of only one person in a CAVE is tracked, meaning each participant's view of the room isn't based on their individual viewpoint (unlike the real world).

A more radical approach to immersive 3D involves the use of optical lasers. Unlike display devices such as video goggles, HMDs, and projection systems, which deliver to the retina of the viewer's eye an image consisting essentially of reflected light rays, laser 3D systems use highly specialized laser beams to draw a 3D scene directly onto the viewer's retina. Such systems are very new and still in the experimental stages, yet hold great promise for the visually impaired. Because a laser excites the viewer's retina directly, such systems might one day provide computer-generated vision for the blind.

Note: Augmented and Enhanced Reality

Augmented, or enhanced, reality describes immersive 3D that is combined with real-world information. Virtual surgery, for example, often involves a combination of computer-generated 3D and real-world images. A 3D visualization of a brain tumor might be projected onto the real-world image of the patient's skull as he or she lies in the operating room. This would allow the surgeon to see a computer-generated 3D visualization superimposed on the patient's real-world body, making for an augmented, or enhanced, view of reality.

Sound

Although most people think of "3D" only in terms of the depth (the third dimension missing from 2D graphics), sound also plays an extremely important part in the 3D experience, as it enhances the realism of interactive 3D and immersive 3D content. And while traditional 3D images aren't usually associated with sound, traditional 3D animation (a series of 3D images) is often enhanced with sound in the postproduction stage.

Interactive and immersive forms of 3D, however, don't have a postproduction stage; these forms are experienced live, in real time. As a result, sound can't be added to them after the rendering, as is often the case with traditional 3D animation. Instead, sound is typically an inherent part of the interactive and immersive experience.

Audio can be used in interactive and immersive 3D environments as simple *ambient* sounds that seem to have no particular source, or they may be very sophisticated forms of *spatialized* sound.

Ambient sounds are sometimes called *background sounds* because they aren't tied to a particular location or element of a 3D scene; instead, they seem to be coming from all directions. No matter where you are in a scene, ambient sounds have the same volume and direction. Blowing wind, for instance, is a good example of ambient sound because you can't really pinpoint where it comes from. Likewise, background music tracks (such as those used in video games) are typically played as ambient sound because there is no need for them to be emitted from a specific location.

Spatialized sounds, on the other hand, are tied to a specific location, or *emitter*, in a 3D scene and, as such, are more like the sounds we typically hear in the real world. The sound of a chirping bird, for example, is tied to the bird itself. As you move closer to the bird, the chirping becomes louder; as you move away, it lessens. If you walk around the bird, the chirping will differ, depending on your position relative to the bird. If you stand with the bird to your right, for example, your right ear will hear more of the chirping than your left ear. If you reposition yourself so that the bird is on your left-hand side, your left ear will then hear more of the chirping than your right ear will.

Spatialized sounds are emitted from a sound source positioned somewhere in the 3D scene, meaning that what you hear from your computer speakers (or headphones) will change depending on your proximity and position relative to the source of the sound. As you move around, the sound produced by your speakers is based on how far you are from the sound source, and also the angle of your "virtual ears" to the sound source. Spatialized sound emitted from a trumpet in a 3D scene, for instance, is much louder when you stand directly in front of the trumpet than when you stand behind it.

Even though you may be the same distance from the trumpet in both cases, the volumes are different, because the sound waves emitted from the mouth of the trumpet hit your virtual ears directly when you stand in front. When you stand behind the trumpet, your virtual ears don't receive a direct blast of sound from the mouth of the trumpet, and so the tunes you hear aren't as loud. Similarly, spatialized sounds taper off, or *attenuate*, as you move further away from the source producing them. The further away you move from the trumpet, for example, the quieter it will sound.

Ambient and spatialized sound are used to enhance the realism of interactive and immersive 3D environments. While ambient sounds provide general background audio, spatialized sounds are often triggered by specific user activity and object behavior. Opening a wooden door to walk outside, for example, might trigger a creaking sound. Likewise, a car driving towards you might honk its horn if you are standing in the street when it is near, continuing to honk as it drives by until it's too far away to be heard. Meanwhile the ambient sound of rain might permeate the entire scene, filling the air with the soft music of raindrops to complement the visual treatment of a rainy evening.

Computer 3D Fundamentals

Although traditional, interactive, and immersive forms of 3D differ in their purpose and audience, at their core they are fundamentally the same: they're all forms of computer-generated three-dimensional graphics. Because all three stem from the same branch of computer science—3D computer graphics—they have many similarities beneath the surface.

Because the field of 3D computer graphics is the foundation on which various forms of computer 3D build, a number of concepts and techniques are common to traditional, interactive, and immersive 3D. The exact vocabulary used to describe these concepts and techniques may differ slightly from form to form and even from program to program, but the underlying fundamentals are surprisingly consistent.

Some 3D programs, for example, use the term "haze" to describe atmospheric perspective, while others use "fog" instead. These terms describe the same fundamental concept: computer-generated atmospheric perspective used to increase the realism of a 3D image or scene.

In this section you'll learn about the fundamental concepts and techniques common to traditional, interactive, and immersive forms of 3D. In the process you'll find that the field of 3D computer graphics has a vocabulary of its own, one quite different from the 2D graphics world that you may be familiar with. Learning the unique and sometimes confusing terminology of 3D, however, is essential to understanding Web3D and the chapters that follow, and so we press on.

Modeling and Rendering

3D computer graphics can be broken into two primary steps: *modeling* and *rendering*. Modeling involves creating three-dimensional objects and arranging, or composing, those objects into a scene (see "Objects and Scenes" in the following section), while rendering is the process by which such content is actually displayed to the viewer.

Modeling can be thought of as the process of creating the architectural blueprints for a 3D scene, where each object in the scene is associated with its own blueprint that describes what the object looks like and where it is positioned in 3D space.

The act of modeling creates models, just as the act of sculpting creates sculptures. A *model* is a representation of some object or concept that captures its essential elements. A model train, for example, represents a real-world locomotive but isn't actually a working train itself. Instead, the model captures the essence of the real-world train by mimicking its appearance and perhaps even its behavior (how it acts).

Although models can be hand-coded in 3D programming languages (such as OpenGL, VRML, and Java 3D, to name a few), more often than not they are generated with visual modeling tools designed specifically for creating and manipulating 3D content (see Figure 3–2). Such modeling tools allow the nonprogrammer to create sophisticated 3D content, in much the same way as visual Web page development tools allow nonprogrammers to produce sophisticated Web pages without requiring detailed knowledge of HTML.

Unlike HTML files, however, there is no single, universally accepted 3D file format, just as there is no single, universal bitmap image file format. Over the years a number of different 3D file formats have emerged, and today most modeling tools support at least half a dozen or more to allow models to be easily imported, exported, and exchanged with other programs. Popular 3D file formats include AutoCAD Drawing Interchange File, Caligari trueSpace (COB), Digital Exchange Format (DXF), Lightwave Object

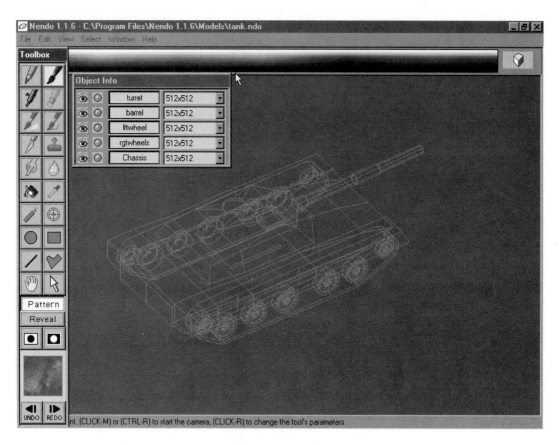

Figure 3-2   Visual 3D authoring tools such as Nendo can be used to create sophisticated models without the hassle of programming (Nendo image courtesy of Nichimen Graphics, http://www.nichimen.com).

Format (LOF), Lightwave Scene Format (LSF), Virtual Reality Modeling Language (VRML), Wavefront Object format (OBJ), 3D-Studio (3DS), and 3D Meta File (3DMF)—and there are many, many more.

Whereas modeling is generally considered the first step in creating 3D graphics, rendering is the last step; it involves the *rasterization* of 3D models. Rasterization is a rather fancy term that describes the simple concept of displaying an image on-screen based on the internal data the computer uses to represent that image (see Figure 3-3). Each pixel in a bitmap image (such as a GIF or JPEG image), for example, is stored in a computer file as a numeric value that describes a point location in 2D space (X, Y) and the color in which that point should be displayed. In order to display such a pixel to the

Geometric and Behavioral Modeling

Geometric modeling describes the process of creating objects based on geometry (shape or form). Behavioral modeling is used to define how objects behave (act or react). A geometric model of a car, for example, represents the shape and form of an automobile, while a car's behavior model defines what happens when you step inside and stomp on the gas pedal.

Geometric modeling can usually be broken down into six basic steps. First, the simplest parts of each object are created (in the case of a model car, for example, the simplest parts would be the wheels, bumpers, doors, hood, roof, windshield, and so forth). Next, these simple parts are composed into more complex objects (the car, in this example), after which surface and material properties such as color, texture, and reflectivity are specified (which control whether the car is red or blue, for example, and whether it is shiny or dull looking).

Objects are then positioned and oriented into a scene along with other objects (various car and urban objects might be arranged into parking-lot scene, for example), after which light sources are added. Finally, camera viewpoints are selected. After all of these steps have taken place, the model is ready to be rendered.

user, the computer must translate this numeric information into a point of light on the screen. The translation of image data into a visual representation that the user can actually see on the screen is known as the *rasterization process.*

The rasterization of 3D graphics is much more complex than that of bitmap images, however. The entire process, known as rendering, must take into account a great deal of information directly related to the third dimension of depth that 2D graphics lack. Whereas rendering a 2D bitmap image is a relatively straightforward process that involves translating numeric pixel values into on-screen points of light, 3D graphics rendering is considerably more complicated.

As the following sections describe, 3D graphics rendering involves the translation and projection of 3D model data onto a flat 2D surface plane. Like all computer data, 3D model data is stored in numeric form, although 3D models contain much more information than the simple numeric pixel

Figure 3-3   Rendering involves the rasterization of models, a process that ultimately draws pixels on the viewing device in order to visualize model data.

Raster Graphics

Raster graphics was invented by Xerox Palo Alto Research Center (Xerox PARC) in the early 1970s. Computer displays at the time were simplistic and similar in nature to pen plotters, as they were capable of tracing the outline of shapes with a beam of light (analogous to a plotter pen) but weren't proficient at filling these outlines in. Xerox PARC researchers devised a computer display that consisted of row after row of tiny phosphor spots that were lit from behind by a sweeping light beam.

These rows of phosphor spots were called *rasters*, a term borrowed from the mechanical press (the shelf holding a line of type in a mechanical press is a raster). The sweeping beam of light could turn phosphor spots on and off very quickly as it scanned each raster (row), one after another, allowing for shapes to be both outlined and filled. When the last raster was reached, the beam would repeat the process. Images created in this fashion became known as *raster graphics*, while the process of converting computer data into a light point on the screen is known as *rasterization* (also known as scan conversion or, more generally, rendering). Most computer screens used today are raster based, although the technology has progressed considerably since the early days at Xerox PARC.

values used to represent 2D bitmap images. 3D models typically contain information about geometry (an object's form, or shape), location and orientation in 3D space, surface properties (such as color, texture, and reflectivity), and light sources, all of which are taken into account during the rendering process. In addition, interactive and immersive 3D models often describe the *behavior* of an object, which defines how the object acts and reacts in relation to the world and events around it.

All of these things, and more, can be contained in a 3D model, which the renderer must graphically display on screen. Such detail doesn't come for free, however, and requires much more processing on the computer's part during the rendering process when compared to 2D graphics. In order to digest this bounty of information, 3D rendering takes place in a series of steps or stages, much like an assembly line (see Figure 3-4).

The various steps that a model progresses through during the rendering process are collectively known as the *graphics pipeline* or *rendering pipeline*. At each stage the results are rendered into a *framebuffer*, which is an allotment of off-screen computer memory that stores the image as it develops. When the model has been fully rendered, meaning that the last stage in the pipeline has been completed, the contents of the off-screen framebuffer are transferred to on-screen memory so that the user can actually see the results.

Models can be rendered in a variety of ways, allowing for a great diversity in the visual appeal of a fully rendered scene. *Ray tracing* is among the most sophisticated of all rendering techniques, as this process literally calculates the precise path that rays of light follow as they bounce about a scene and interact with various objects. Extremely realistic results are produced with ray tracing, as light reflection, refraction, and even shadows are calculated during the rendering process, although the computational requirements are staggering. Ray tracing is typically restricted to traditional 3D, as light-ray calculations for extremely complicated scenes often require overnight processing by one or more computers.

Figure 3-4   The rendering process is actually a series of steps that a model progresses through before its internal data can be visualized on-screen.

Other forms of rendering, such as *radiosity rendering*, can also produce high-quality results with equal or less computational effort. Radiosity rendering is quite useful in calculating the results of diffuse light bounced between reflective surfaces. The term *radiosity* refers to a light source that is reflected off objects in a 3D scene, making the light appear to be coming from all directions rather than a specific source, an effect sometimes referred to as *indirect* or *ambient* light.

If time permits, ray tracing and radiosity rendering might both be used, perhaps along with other rendering techniques (each being applied in a separate rendering "pass" that builds upon the results of the previous passes).

Because traditional 3D images and animation don't require real-time processing, they can be rendered over an extended period by more than one computer, or by so-called "rendering farms" as described earlier, and so can take advantage of sophisticated, photorealistic rendering techniques such as ray tracing and radiosity rendering. Interactive and immersive forms of 3D, however, are rendered in real time in response to user input and events (such as user movement and the passage of time) that continually alter the on-screen appearance of a scene; this places practical limitations on the rendering process.

Owing to their continual real-time rendering requirements, interactive and immersive forms of 3D use faster, less sophisticated rendering techniques that produce less visually realistic results than traditional 3D (light reflections and shadows, for example, are often omitted altogether or simply approximated). Calculated rendering-quality trade-offs are made in order to engage the user in a unique and compelling experience that traditional 3D simply can't deliver.

Flat rendering, for example, is a very fast technique that applies a single color to flat polygonal surfaces at the expense of realism. Other relatively fast rendering techniques, such as Gouraud shading and Phong shading, produce more realistic results. Gouraud rendering (introduced by Henri Gouraud in 1971) calculates the color intensity at the corner point, or *vertex*, of each polygon used to represent the surface of an object. These values are then used to average the shading applied across the entire polygon surface, meaning that pixel colors are interpolated based on vertex values, which results in a continuous, smooth transition of surface color. (Banding can be an issue, however, when tonal values change dramatically across polygon borders.) Although Gouraud rendering is a more realistic alternative than flat rendering, it takes more time and isn't perfect; it can't render texture maps (images) applied to an object surface, nor can it create shadows.

Phong rendering was introduced by Phong Bui Tuong two years after Gouraud shading was first proposed. Like Gouraud rendering, it is an interpolated rendering technique, although values of reflected light are calculated for each pixel. As a result, Phong rendering can produce even

Rendering Engines

The component of a 3D-software program that is responsible for rendering three-dimensional model data is known as the *rendering engine*, or simply the *renderer*. Many 3D products use third-party rendering engines, rather than reinvent the rendering wheel themselves. Licensing a third-party renderer allows developers to focus their energy on other aspects of their program, such as the user interface or networking, rather than becoming bogged down with rendering details. Some rendering engines, in fact, are actually standalone software products (especially those used to create traditional 3D images and animation for film and video).

In all cases, from extremely sophisticated photorealistic techniques to simplistic real-time approaches, the rendering process takes into account three main aspects of a 3D model: geometry (shape or form), surface materials and properties (such as color and texture), and lighting (the effect that light sources have on a model). Generally speaking, the more time a renderer can spend on each aspect of a model, the more realistic the final scene will appear.

During the rendering process, the rendering engine must decide which parts of an object or scene are visible and which ones are "hidden" from view. A technique known as *hidden-surface removal* is used to determine what parts of an object are hidden, while *culling* describes the general process of eliminating entire objects from rendering. Imagine, for example, that you are looking at a 3D box shape head-on. In this case the back face of the box shape shouldn't actually be visible to you until you rotate the box or walk behind it. As a result, the renderer can hide this surface from you (a technique also known as *back-face culling*) until you need to see it. The box, however, may also obscure another shape entirely. If a cone sits behind the box, for instance, the cone can be culled entirely from the scene; only when you reposition the viewpoint in such a way that the cone becomes visible does the rendering engine actually need to display it on screen.

smoother surface appearances as well as shiny surface highlights (commonly refered to as *specular reflection*). The Phong technique can also be used to calculate texture map effects on surface pixels, and, in some implementations, it can render shadows. Although more computationally expensive than Gouraud rendering, this technique isn't nearly as demanding as either ray tracing or radiosity rendering.

Objects and Scenes

3D modeling involves creating 3D objects and arranging them into a 3D space commonly known as a *scene* (3D space is also called a "world" or "universe"; see "Scene Management" later in this chapter for details). Once modeled, objects and scenes can then be rendered as described in the previous section.

The appearance and behavior of objects in a scene ultimately account for our final experience in viewing or interacting with a 3D work, just as the appearance and behavior of actors, actresses, and props determine the experience of a theatrical performance. In terms of their geometrical appearance, the Web3D objects that you'll encounter typically fall into one of three very general categories:

- **Primitive objects**, such as boxes, cones, cylinders, and spheres, are the fundamental building blocks of 3D computer graphics (see Figure 3-5). Primitive objects are the simplest 3D shapes that a 3D program can represent, as they cannot be reduced or decomposed into subsidiary shapes. Primitive objects are often used as the basis for more complex shapes. A human body, for example, can be represented quite easily with primitive objects (a sphere for the head, inverted cone for the thorax, a box for the pelvis, thin cylinders for arms and legs, and so forth). The resulting form, however, is far from realistic. As a result, primitives are often combined with machined and freeform objects to create more realistic looking shapes.

- **Complex objects** is a general term applied to objects that are more sophisticated than primitives. Complex objects come in many forms, such as machined and freeform objects. They can be created by combining primitive shapes together in a meaningful way, such as using spheres to construct a snowman object. They can also be constructed using other geometric shapes, such as points, lines, grids, polygons, and curves (see Figure 3-6). Often, complex objects are created using

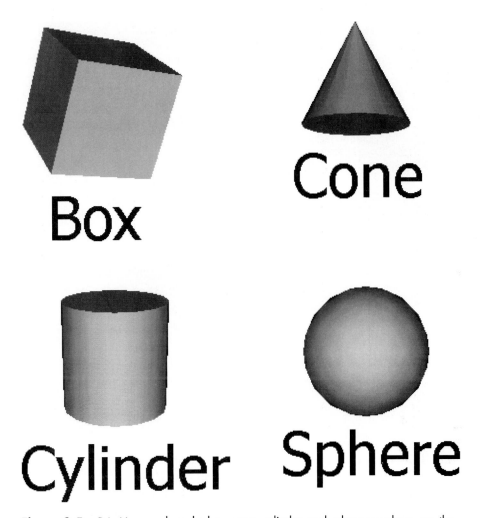

Figure 3-5   Primitives, such as the box, cone, cylinder, and sphere seen here, are the simplest predefined shapes that a 3D program understands.

a combination of primitives and geometrical shapes (the eyes of a human head object, for example, might be created using sphere primitives, while the rest of the head object could be defined by lines and polygons). Because the term *complex object* is so general, it is often used to describe any object other than a primitive. In this sense there are really only two types of objects, primitive and complex.

Figure 3-6   Complex objects such as these can't be represented using only primitive shapes and so are typically created using primitives, lines, faces, grids, and other 3D shapes (http://www.parallelgraphics.com/).

- **Machined objects**, such as extruded and lathed shapes, resemble items produced by these processes in the real world (see Figure 3-7). Noodles, moldings, baseball bats, desk lamps, vases, and pottery are all examples of machined objects created through an extrusion or lathe process. Although machined objects such as these are more complicated for computers to represent and render, they lend a sense of realism to 3D scenes that primitive objects simply cannot provide. Machined objects are created by *sweeping* a 2D shape known as a *cross section* or *profile* through space, a process similar in many ways to creating a bubble by sweeping a wand covered with soapy water through the air. Extruded shapes are created by sweeping the profile in a straight or curved path, a process much like that of squeezing cake frosting out of a tube that has a special nozzle attachment, such as a star shape (analogous to the profile or cross

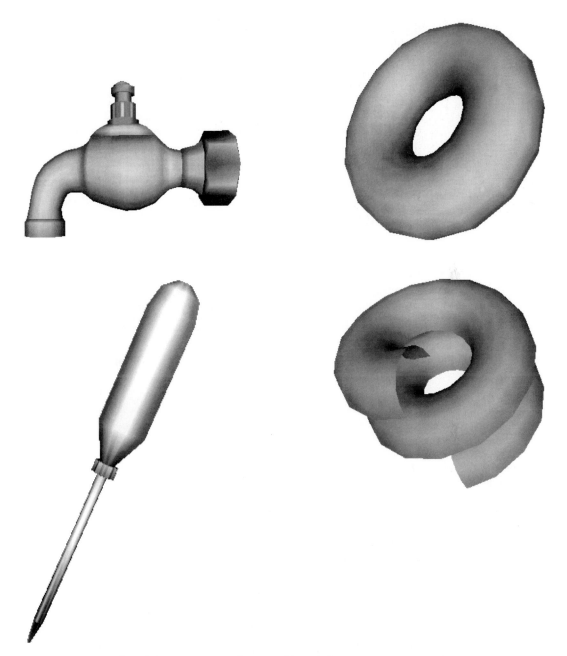

Figure 3-7 Machined shapes are typically created by a lathe or extrusion process, producing 3D objects that resemble those created in this way in the real world.

section of a 3D extrusion). Lathed shapes, on the other hand, are the result of sweeping a profile along an object that revolves around an axis, much like a pottery wheel or real-world lathe. In both cases the 2D profile that defines the resulting shape can be dynamically resized and even reshaped during the process, allowing for a variety of appearances. A 3D baseball bat, for example, is a lathed object for which the circular profile changes size during the process, making the bat thicker in some areas and thinner in others while always maintaining a symmetrical appearance. A 3D spaghetti noodle, on the other hand, is an example of an extruded shape created by sweeping a small circular profile along a winding path. Because the circular profile never changes in size or shape, the resulting noodle is always the same diameter, although it twists and turns because of the path this profile sweeps.

- **Freeform objects** resemble shapes found in the natural world, such as water, fire, flower petals, terrain, landscapes, and other forms that are simply too complicated to represent using primitive or machined objects (see Figure 3-8). Many manmade objects, such as cloth, also fall into the freeform category because they are not easily constructed using an extrusion or lathe process. Freeform objects are generally complex, irregular shapes that require more computing effort to model and render than do primitive and machined objects.

Figure 3-8   Freeform objects often resemble shapes found in the natural world, such as water and terrain (http://www.web3dgallery.com/people/gq/).

Freeform objects are typically produced as the result of mathematical algorithms or procedures (such as fractal generators, growth simulators, and particle systems), allowing for a programmatic, or procedural, approach to modeling and rendering.

Note: Creating Objects

Objects can be created in a variety of ways. Some programmers hand-code their objects, while others use modeling tools that allow for point-and-click object creation. In other cases, models are created using special 3D digitization devices that actually sample real-world items and convert the results into 3D model data.

Points, Lines, Polygons, and Curves

Although 3D objects can be seen on-screen during the modeling process and upon rendering, at heart they are really nothing more than numbers that represent points, lines, polygons, and curves in 3D space (typically defined in terms of X, Y, and Z axes, as seen in Figure 3-9). Just as bitmap images are merely files full of numbers that must be translated into on-screen pixels (a process known as rasterization; see "Modeling and Rendering"), 3D object files are also filled with numeric information that must be translated and projected onto a display device in order to be visualized.

Objects are defined as points in 3D space, which are connected by lines to form polygons or curves. These points are known as *vertex points*, or *vertices*, which is a mathematical term used to describe an arbitrary point in space. Each point, or *vertex*, used to represent a 3D object is actually a three-

Note: Procedural Objects

Objects can also be described dynamically by functions, or procedures. Procedural objects, however, aren't as commonplace as those represented using points, lines, polygons, and curves. Because polygonal meshes are well known, and the rendering of such objects is relatively simple, this approach to 3D representation has become ubiquitous over the years.

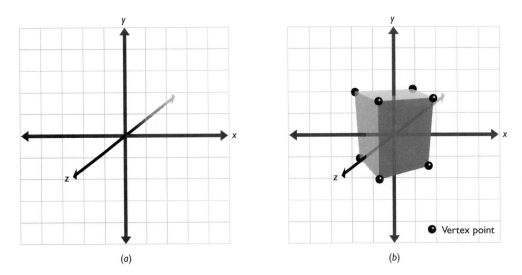

(a)   (b)

Figure 3-9   A vertex is a point in 3D space that corresponds to a given 3D coordinate
(X, Y, and Z).

dimensional coordinate value that describes a location relative to three axes: X (width), Y (height), and Z (depth), as Figure 3-9 illustrates.

Vertices are the fundamental data values underlying all 3D objects and can be considered the low-level internal building blocks of 3D computer graphics. Although unimpressive individually, collections of vertex points can be used to define lines, curves, edges, facets, polygons, polyhedrons, and virtually all other structures used to represent 3D objects and scenes.

Two vertices (two unique coordinate values) can specify the beginning and end points of a line, for example, while multiple lines (defined by groups of vertices) can be joined together to form polygons. Multiple polygons, then, can be assembled together to form shapes, or objects (see the "Polygons" section that follows). Likewise, vertex points can be used to define curves, which can also be combined together into 3D objects (see "Curves"). Depending on the particular 3D technology in question, shapes are represented using either polygons or curves, or even a combination of the two.

Web3D objects are typically represented on-screen using polygons because of their relative simplicity and the fact that polygonal technology has been widely used in the 3D graphics industry for years (and, as a result, polygonal formulas and algorithms abound). Curve-based 3D-object representation, however, is somewhat more complex and has generally been reserved for traditional forms of 3D, although curve technology has recently

Vector Graphics

In graphics terminology the word *vector* refers to a line with a given direction, meaning that a vector is obtained from two points (a start point and an end point). The term *vector graphics* is sometimes used to describe graphics technologies that define images using mathematical definitions (such as PostScript image definitions that are interpreted by output devices such as laser printers), as opposed to *bitmap graphics* technologies that define images using a collection of raw pixel values (such as bitmap JPEG or GIF images).

3D technologies can be thought of as combining both vector and bitmap graphics. Fundamentally, 3D graphics involves the description of object geometry (shape or form) and appearance (color, texture, surface properties, and so forth). Interactive and immersive forms of 3D tend to take into account object behavior as well, which describes how an object acts. While certain aspects of objects' appearance can be represented in bitmap form (textures and color, for example), most characteristics of 3D objects are captured in mathematical formulas and descriptions that more closely resemble vector graphics.

begun to make inroads into interactive and immersive forms of 3D as well as Web3D. Behind both polygons and curves are humble vertex points that form the backbone of all 3D objects.

Polygons

Polygons are commonly used in the representation of on-screen objects because they are well known in the field of 3D graphics and relatively easy to render, whereas curves are more complex. Polygons are closed 2D shapes comprised of straight lines (which in turn are defined by vertex points) that do not intersect. 2D rectangles, triangles, and quadrilaterals, for example, are all polygons. Although a single polygon doesn't do much to represent a 3D object, a number of interconnected, variously sized polygons can quite literally paint a different picture altogether.

The surface of most 3D shapes can be represented as a *polygonal mesh*, which is a grid of connected polygons (a *polyhedron* is a closed polygonal mesh). A polygonal mesh is similar, in a sense, to a latticework of interwoven strings, such as a fish net. Each polygon in a mesh is known as a *face*. Faces give

Surface Properties

In addition to geometry, or form, objects typically have associated surface properties such as color, reflectivity, transparency, and texture maps (images that are applied to the surface of a shape). During the rendering process, these properties are combined with properties of the scene (such as light sources or atmospheric fog settings) to determine what an object will look like when displayed on the screen.

Although you'll hear us talk about object surfaces a great deal throughout this book, as these are what we actually see when Web3D content is rendered, some specialized forms of 3D are actually concerned with the *insides* of objects. Specifically, volumetric forms of 3D ("volume 3D") focus on the internal representation of objects as much as, if not more than, object surfaces. Volume 3D as applied to the medical field, for example, can tell doctors what's inside a 3D model of the human body, which is generally more important to a surgeon than the model surface. Web3D, in contrast, is concerned with the outer surface of shapes—the insides are generally considered to be hollow.

polygonal objects a faceted appearance when they are viewed without being fully rendered (imagine wrapping a fish net around an object), as seen in Figure 3-10. When an object is rendered, however, each face of the polygonal mesh is painted with the object's corresponding surface properties, which usually hides the individual polygons to reveal the overall shape of the object itself.

Some rendering techniques, however, don't completely hide the faces of polygonal mesh models. In particular, interactive and immersive forms of 3D typically rely on very fast rendering techniques that aren't able to hide an object's polygon mesh entirely. If you look closely at a VRML primitive sphere, for example, you will be able to make out the faces of the polygonal mesh used to represent these shapes. Likewise, many traditional 3D modeling programs rely on quick-and-dirty rendering techniques in order to allow the artist to create and manipulate objects in real time (reserving high-quality rendering for final production).

Wireframe rendering is often used during the modeling process, omitting color, lighting, and shading altogether in favor of raw speed. A wireframe view of an object is merely a series of connected lines, revealing every polygon in the mesh (see Figure 3-11). Because the surface properties of each

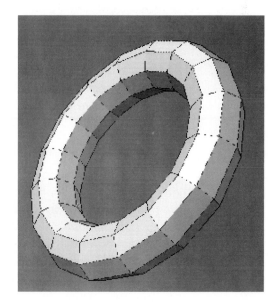

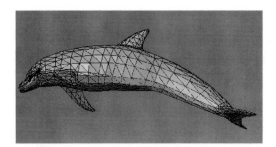

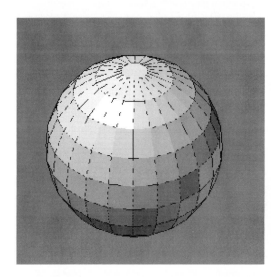

Figure 3-10 Polygonal meshes are made up of connected polygons, or faces, which give objects a faceted appearance when they're viewed before being fully rendered.

polygon in the mesh are not calculated and rendered on screen, wireframe rendering is exceptionally fast, and so it is useful in the design and development stages of modeling.

Although polygons are great at representing flat surfaces, such as the sides of a box or the walls of a building, they aren't so good when it comes to

Note: Surface Patches

The individual polygons that comprise a polygonal mesh are sometimes re-ferred to as patches, *or surface patches. These terms, however, are more commonly used to describe areas defined by parametric-curve algorithms (such as B-spline and NURBS algorithms).*

smooth, curved surfaces such as the natural curves and bends in the human body (e.g., elbows, shoulders, and knees). In order to create curved surfaces using polygons, the polygonal mesh faces must be quite small and plentiful; smaller polygons are used to create more finely detailed shapes. Unfortunately, a large number of very small polygons are consumed in the construction of smooth, curved shapes, which means extra work for the rendering engine. Because it is faster and easier to render a few big polygons than it is to render lots of tiny ones, objects and scenes rendered in real time often skimp on the number of polygons for performance reasons.

As a result, real-time polygon-based technologies (such as most forms of Web3D) tend to produce blocky objects when compared to non-real-time 3D technologies and those that support true curves. Traditional forms of 3D, for instance, are usually adept at creating smooth, organic shapes as a result

Figure 3-11   Wireframe rendering reveals every polygon face in a polygonal mesh.

Polygon Budget

The number of polygons used to construct an individual object or entire scene is called the *polygon count*. Simple Web3D objects and scenes can be constructed with very low polygon counts (a primitive box, for example, has six sides and so requires only six polygons to represent it), although there is no restriction on polygon count. In your Web travels, you'll eventually come upon VRML objects constructed from hundreds and even thousands of polygons. These objects, however, require a great deal of computing resources to render, and can bring a modest desktop computer to its knees.

The number of polygons that a computer can comfortably handle at any given time is known as a *polygon budget*. Experienced 3D modelers are well aware of the polygon budget for the systems their work will be deployed on, and they do their best not to exceed this limit. Interactive and immersive forms of 3D targeted at standard desktop users have the most restrictive polygon budgets because of the real-time nature of these technologies (typical desktop computers and console gaming devices support on-screen polygon counts in the low tens of thousands and can even approach upwards of 50,000 on-screen polygons). Traditional forms of 3D, however, have very high polygon budgets because of non-real-time approaches to rendering (it's not uncommon for traditional 3D images to be constructed using hundreds of thousands, and often millions, of polygons).

It should be noted that polygon count is only one of many factors that affect rendering performance. Texture mapping, lighting and shading, and even sounds, for example, all contribute to overall system requirements for a given object or scene.

of their ability to handle a huge number of polygons and also because of their support for true curves. As desktop-computer technology becomes more powerful, however, real-time 3D technologies are seeing a corresponding rise in the number of polygons used to represent individual objects and entire scenes (see "Polygon Budget"). It's also interesting to note that curves have recently become a popular topic of discussion in the Web3D community, and it's very likely that the same form of curve technology will be directly supported by future forms of Web3D (such as X3D).

Curves

Although polygons can be used to approximate curved surfaces, they tend to fall short of the mark when compared to the shapes created by a special class of curves used in computer graphics known as *splines*. Whereas polygons are a series of connected straight lines that do not intersect (such as triangles), splines are defined by points in space that control how a line is drawn.

The points used to define splines are commonly known as *control points*, which are used in the mathematical curve-generation process. Some types of splines are drawn as line segments that pass through each control point, while others come close to the control points but never actually pass through them. A specific form of spline known as the B-spline, for example, can pass through control points, or merely use them to influence the curvatures of line segments. Catmull-Rom splines, on the other hand, actually pass through all of the supplied control points .

B-splines of a particular form known as Non-Uniform Rational B-splines (NURBS) are often used in 3D graphics today. NURBS are constructed from control points for which extra parameter information may be supplied, and they are particularly useful in creating arced and elliptical shapes.

Scene Management

Although 3D objects can be interesting in their own right, they're generally destined to live in 3D space along with other objects. This space, when populated with objects, is commonly known as a scene, world, or universe. The main advantage of a 3D scene is that new viewpoints can be selected as needed, for which new renderings can be produced. As you walk through an interactive Web3D scene, for example, your perspective of the objects around you changes dynamically. Similarly, traditional 3D artists can position and reposition objects to their hearts' content, rendering anew each time. (Contrast this approach with 2D graphics, in which a change in object location or viewing angle typically involves substantial rework of the image on the artist's part.)

In order to accommodate an ever-changing viewpoint, 3D products must manage various aspects of the scene so that the rendering engine will know what must be drawn on-screen and what is hidden from view. Imagine, for example, that you're walking through an interactive 3D city. Such a scene might ultimately contain a number of skyscrapers, store fronts, apartment buildings, cars, taxi cabs, trains, and people. However, you don't view everything at once. Instead, as you move about the scene you'll see only those

Object Representation

Although it may be tempting to think of objects in 3D scenes as being represented using either polygons *or* curves, in practice they're often used together. VRML, for example, does not support NURBS directly, although some VRML browsers (such as blaxxun Contact and Parallel-Graphics Cortona) have extended the language to add support for objects created with these types of curves. Thus, VRML's traditional polygonal mesh objects can coexist with curved objects defined by NURBS. (Curves can also be used to describe the path that polygonal objects take when animated—a smooth animation path can be calculated using a mathematical curve formula, which the polygonal model might follow during the animation.)

However, polygonal meshes (also known as *polygonal nets*) and curves aren't the only ways in which 3D objects are represented; they're just two of the more common methods (with polygonal meshes being the most popular). A variety of other methods exist, including bicubic parametric patch nets that describe curved quadrilateral meshes and volumetric representation techniques such as Constructive Solid Geometry (CSG). For the purposes of this book, however, you need concern yourself only with polygonal meshes and, to some extent, curves.

things that are in your field of vision. Those that aren't don't need to be drawn on-screen, but they must somehow be kept track of so that, when the time comes, they can appear.

Turning your head to the left, for example, will reveal an entirely different aspect of the scene than if you were to look to the right. Likewise, as you move forward in a scene, those objects that you walk past are no longer rendered on-screen, yet they must be available immediately if you were to turn around (at which point a completely different view of the objects would be rendered—the back view).

The concept of a virtual *camera* is typically used to construct a view of a 3D scene. Positioning a virtual camera in 3D space can be compared to pointing a real-world Polaroid camera at something in our physical world and then clicking the button to take a snapshot; whatever the camera's lens captures is rendered (see Figure 3-12). With interactive 3D, the camera is often continually moving in sync with the viewer (it can be said that the *camera* is

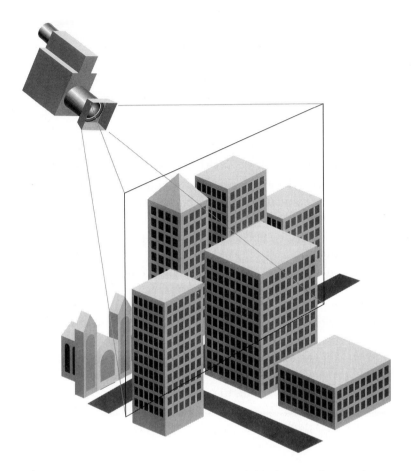

Figure 3-12   Scene elements that are in the field of vision of a virtual camera are rendered to the display.

bound to the user's viewpoint); in such cases a better analogy might be a home movie camera, or camcorder. In both cases, objects captured by the camera lens appear larger as the distance between the camera and the object decreases, while those further away appear smaller. Similarly, the angle at which the camera is positioned relative to objects controls how the object will look. (Pointing the camera up at a skyscraper, for example, will result in a very different rendering than if you shoot the building head-on or from above, because the angle and position of the camera are different in each case.)

Although the notion of a camera can help us conceptualize what information gets projected onto our computer screens and what is omitted, it's also important to realize that there is some serious number crunching going on behind the scenes, both literally and figuratively. In order to manage all of the information inherent in a 3D scene, special data structures known as *scene graphs* are often employed (all of the forms of Web3D discussed in this book, in fact, take advantage of scene-graph technology to construct, store, and manage 3D scene information).

Scene graphs are hierarchical treelike data structures (see Figure 3-13) that describe an entire 3D scene and typically contain the geometric representation of objects as well as their appearance (such as color, surface properties, and textures). In addition, scene graphs commonly include related information, such as camera location and light sources. Because the information in a scene graph is organized spatially (meaning that objects are arranged in the data structure according to their actual position in the scene; their spatial relationship is reflected in the data structure), scene graphs allow common traversals to take place very quickly.

Figure 3-13 Scene graphs are hierarchical treelike data structures often used to organize and manage 3D scenes.

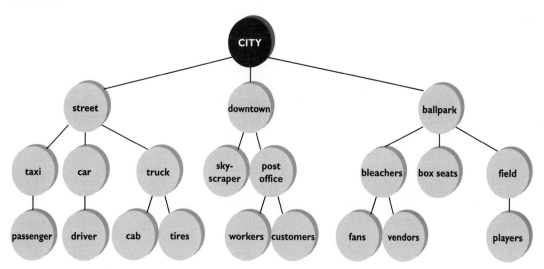

A "draw" traversal, for example, can quickly determine what objects in the scene graph are actually visible on-screen, allowing this information to be sent to the rendering engine as needed. A "collision" traversal, meanwhile, can decide whether or not the viewer has collided with an object in the scene (such as a wall). These and other common traversals are very efficient, thanks to the way in which scene-graph data structures are organized, making such structures ideal for many 3D scene-management tasks.

Scene graphs also help shield programmers from the gory details of low-level 3D Application Programming Interfaces (APIs) such as OpenGL or Direct3D. Instead of focusing on complex 3D rendering issues, programmers can focus on *what* to render, not *how* to render it. In this respect, 3D programmers can "program to a scene graph" instead of a specific API, much as Java programmers can write cross-platform code without dealing with specific system-level APIs.

Summary

Computer 3D graphics is a specialized form of computer graphics that has evolved considerably over the years. Although human beings are wired for 3D, thanks to our highly evolved vision system, computer screens are flat, 2D surfaces. As a result, 3D data must be projected onto computer screens in a way that produces the illusion of depth. To create this illusion, computer 3D programs commonly employ monocular depth cues introduced and refined by Renaissance artists (such as size differences, occlusion, lighting and shading, texture density, linear perspective, and atmospheric perspective).

3D computer graphics can be broken into two primary steps: *modeling* and *rendering*. Modeling involves creating three-dimensional objects and arranging them into a scene (also commonly referred to as a world or universe), while rendering is the process by which such content is actually displayed on-screen to the viewer. 3D coordinate values (X, Y, Z), or vertices, can be used to define points, lines, polygons, and curves used in the construction of objects, although a variety of other object-construction techniques are also used.

Objects are typically represented internally by three-dimensional coordinate values that describe a location relative to three axes that together constitute 3D "space": X (width), Y (height), and Z (depth). Objects and their associated properties (such as colors, textures, reflectivity, transparency, and so forth) are often stored in a treelike hierarchical data structure known as a scene graph along with related scene information (e.g, light sources and camera positions). Scene graphs give programmers a convenient mechanism for managing 3D scene information and help to shield them from underlying system details.

Following is a complete list of URLs referenced in this chapter:

Online 3D Resources   http://www.web3dgallery.com/3d/resources.html
Nichimen Graphics   http://www.nichimen.com
ParallelGraphics   http://www.parallelgraphics.com
Gerardo Quintieri   http://www.web3dgallery.com/people/gq/

Part 2

VIRTUAL REALITY MODELING LANGUAGE

VRML OVERVIEW

Topics in This Chapter

- How the VRML97 standard evolved from VRML 1.0 and VRML 2.0
- The importance of the www-vrml email list
- VRML MIME types and file headers
- Why VRML helper applications and plug-ins are considered VRML "browsers"
- VRML objects, scenes, and worlds
- Basic VRML file structure

Chapter 4

The Virtual Reality Modeling Language, more commonly referred to as VRML, is the original and most popular form of Web3D. As a 3D scene description language and file format that together allow encoding and encapsulation of 3D content for the Internet, VRML pioneered the concept of Web3D years before the term *Web3D* itself emerged to describe such technologies.

This chapter will give you a general overview of VRML. Here you will learn where VRML came from, what versions are available and under development, and the basic jargon used to describe common aspects of the technology. You'll also explore the innards of a simple VRML file in preparation for learning in later chapters how to customize existing VRML content using the VRML programming language.

History

VRML was developed through an open, collaborative effort that was sparked in 1994 by the first international World Wide Web Conference, held in Geneva, Switzerland. Conference organizer Tim Berners-Lee, father of the Web and current director of the World Wide Web Consortium, invited Mark

Pesce to describe the vision he and Tony Parisi had of an immersive, interactive 3D cyberspace. Their vision was presented to attendees of a Birds-of-a-Feather (BOF) gathering at the conference, which was spearheaded by Dave Raggett (the individual largely responsible for driving the development of HTML at the World Wide Web Consortium). During the presentation, Pesce demonstrated Labyrinth, a prototype 3D interface for the then-new World Wide Web that he and Parisi had developed, as proof of their shared vision.

As it turned out, Pesce and Parisi weren't the only ones dreaming of a 3D cyberspace. During a BOF session following his presentation, Pesce discussed the future of Web-based 3D with a number of like-minded Internet developers and 3D enthusiasts. At the time, Hypertext Markup Language (HTML) was the sole standard for encoding Web content. Although ideal as a glue language for creating Web pages composed of 2D content such as text and images, HTML lacked support for the third dimension, and so was useless as a 3D content development language. The BOF flock agreed that a new, common language was needed in order to bring 3D to the Web.

Thus, the concept of a Virtual Reality *Markup* Language, a term coined by Ragget based on his own vision of a 3D Internet, was born. Although originally intended to be a 3D analog to HTML, VRML had a short life as a markup language. Following the conference, *Wired* magazine's Brian Behlendorf established a "www-vrml" email discussion list, consisting of those who had attended the BOF gathering, through which the budding VRML concept would continue to take shape. Word of the list spread across the Internet like wildfire, and within one month over 2,000 people would join in the email discussions.

Although the concept of VRML was fairly new, demand for 3D on the Web was surprisingly strong. What had started as a small discussion group following the World Wide Web Conference quickly blossomed into a large, vital, and vocal community. Throngs of people around the globe joined the list to talk, shout, and scream about their view of what VRML should ultimately be. It soon became clear that the language being developed through www-vrml was far more comprehensive than a simple tag-based markup language such as HTML. Eventually, to emphasize 3D modeling over markup capabilities, the name was changed to the Virtual Reality *Modeling* Language. The VRML acronym would stick.

VRML was originally conceived as a common language that developers could use to create immersive 3D environments for the Internet, yet www-vrml participants quickly realized that such an ambitious goal might never

Joining the www-vrml Mailing List

The www-vrml email list remains a flourishing community to this day. Over 2,000 members discuss VRML and other forms of Web3D through the list, which bubbles with daily activity. Here you'll find the original developers of VRML 1.0 and 2.0, as well as those now working on the next major release known as Extensible 3D (X3D). In addition, scores of VRML authors and users use the www-vrml list as their main feed for VRML and related Web3D information.

This is a list worth joining if you are a Web developer and want to take your VRML skills to the limit. Interesting VRML tips and advice flow through it regularly. It's also a community in which you can feel comfortable asking just about any type of VRML question at any level, from newbie to rocket scientist.

To join, simply send email to **majordomo@web3d.org**. Leave the subject line blank and type the following as the message body:
subscribe www-vrml

That's it. A moment or two after sending your request you'll receive an authorization message from majordomo@web3d.org asking you to confirm the subscription. To do so, merely copy and paste the authorization confirmation password you're given into a new email message and send it back to majordomo@web3d.org. That's all it takes to join www-vrml. In a few minutes you'll be a member of the teeming VRML community.

see the light of day. Virtual Reality (VR), after all, is extremely complex and remains elusive even today. Creating a programming language that can adequately encode realistic representations of our real world is an immense challenge. Moreover, the processing requirements of Virtual Reality are so massive that even today's most powerful desktop computers aren't up to the task. In addition, immersive Virtual Reality content is most often experienced with the assistance of special devices such as 3D video goggles and data feedback gloves, equipment that very few Web surfers have access to (see Figure 4-1).

Even though VRML was created with the intention of ultimately bringing Virtual Reality to the Web, www-vrml list members were aware that their work would have to start off less ambitiously and grow more powerful over

Figure 4-1 Virtual Reality requires immense computer processing power and is typically experienced with the assistance of highly specialized 3D glasses and data gloves that help immerse the viewer in realistic, interactive content (image courtesy of NASA; http://ccf.arc.nasa.gov/dx/basket/storiesetc/VR.html).

time if it were ever to reach that goal. As a result, VRML began life as a relatively simple and easy-to-learn programming language used to create 3D content for the Internet. Today, as VRML enters its third major revision, true Virtual Reality isn't yet practical, given the state of consumer computing power and viewing or input devices (have you ever bought a computer off the shelf that came with a pair of 3D goggles or data gloves?). As a result, VRML has progressed over the years mainly in terms of its ability to deliver, over the Web, relatively basic interactive 3D content that users navigate using their mouse.

Instead of tackling immersive Virtual Reality head-on, the www-vrml community decided through consensus that the first version of VRML would merely support encoding and encapsulation of 3D objects and scenes for delivery over the Web. These capabilities alone, however, represented a major step forward for Web content. VRML objects and scenes wouldn't be pre-rendered, as was most Web content at the time, but would instead be geometric 3D models rendered on the fly as the user navigated through them.

Unlike 2D content, such as text, images, and movies, for which the viewpoint is frozen, VRML objects and scenes are viewable from any angle. You are forced to see 2D content from the perspective of the person who creates these materials, but you're free to choose the perspective from which you view VRML. As you navigate through VRML content, your computer constantly recalculates your position in relation to the objects around you and dynamically renders the scene accordingly; you're in control of the viewpoint as you explore VRML worlds.

Although this sounds simplistic today, such a technology didn't exist back then; a standard 3D language for the Internet was a radical concept in 1994. To be blunt, the Web itself was radical at that time, and it was capable only of 2D. VRML promised to liberate the Web from the constraints of 2D, an offer that proved to be seductive for anyone with an interest in the Internet; Web masters, programmers, content authors, and end users anxiously awaited the arrival of VRML 1.0.

VRML 1.0

Although the www-vrml community decided to develop VRML over time and through a series of releases, it certainly had its work cut out for it with version 1.0. The group decided that the first version of VRML would strive to achieve, at a minimum, the following three design goals:

1. **Cross platform:** As a programming language for the Web, VRML was expected to be fully cross platform in the same way as HTML. Platform-dependent features were not allowed into VRML, allowing it to operate independently of any specific type of computer. 3D content created with VRML would be accessible to users of consumer-oriented systems such as Windows and Macintosh just as readily as to users of high-end scientific workstations running operating systems that the general public was hardly aware of, such as IRIX and Solaris.

2. **Extensible:** Since VRML 1.0 couldn't possibly be everything to everybody, the group decided that the language had to accommodate browser and tool vendors who might wish to extend its default capabilities. By being extensible, VRML 1.0 wouldn't be overly rigid; vendors could add proprietary features that the language didn't initially support or might never support.

3. **Bandwidth conservative:** At the time that VRML 1.0 was being developed, the vast majority of end users connecting to the Internet from homes and small businesses did so over painfully slow dial-up modems, limited to a top speed of 14.4 Kbps. As a result, it was decided that VRML 1.0 had to be distributable over such low-bandwidth connections. The group could have decided just as easily to position VRML as a technology for use exclusively with high-speed connections, in anticipation of a broadband Internet that is only today beginning to emerge, yet it decided to make VRML available to everyone from the very beginning.

In addition to these three main goals, which clearly positioned VRML as a foundation language for 3D for the masses, the group even took into consideration the hardware on which such content would be run. At the time, Pentium CPUs were just beginning to roll off the Intel assembly line and into consumer computers. The year 1994 was awash in Intel 386 and 486 processors, hardly the speed demons shipping today, a reality that strongly influenced the www-vrml group. Rather than limiting VRML to fast workstations of the time, www-vrml members decided that their work should be enjoyed by the average person. In the same way that VRML was targeted at Web surfers having low-bandwidth connections to the Internet, it was also positioned by the group as a technology that could run on the low-powered personal computers that most people owned at the time.

After deciding on these and other design goals for VRML, the group further embraced the spirit of the Internet by issuing an open Request For Proposals (RFP) in 1994. Rather than building VRML 1.0 privately, members of the www-vrml community decided to open up the development process entirely. An open RFP allowed any person or company to submit a proposal that www-vrml would consider as a basis for building VRML 1.0. The group received and reviewed five proposal submissions:

- Cyberspace Developer's Kit, submitted by Autodesk, Inc.
- Labyrinth, submitted by Pesce and Parisi

The Web3D Platform

Although VRML 1.0 was targeted at relatively low-powered computers connected to the Internet over slow dial-up modems—ambitious design goals that the language did, in fact, achieve—a good deal of the most compelling VRML content contains media elements that place heavy demands on network connections and processing power. VRML scenes enhanced with images, movies, and sounds strain bandwidth as well as computer processors, effectively putting such content off limits to those with modest network connections and less capable personal computers.

Today, however, a Web3D Platform for the masses has truly emerged. As Chapter 1, "Why Bother?" explains in more detail, a growing number of end users today have access to both the bandwidth and computing power necessary to smoothly experience media-laden VRML scenes.

- Manchester Scene Description Language, submitted by Manchester University
- OOGL, submitted by the University of Minnesota
- Open Inventor, submitted by Silicon Graphics, Inc. (SGI)

After reviewing each proposal, a process that generated heated discussions, www-vrml members voted for their favorite by sending private email to the list moderator. The list membership was approximately 2,000 users at the time; of these, several hundred voted for their favorite proposal. The Open Inventor proposal submitted by Silicon Graphics, Inc. (SGI) edged out OOGL by a small margin, and the other three proposals by large margins.

Through this fast, informal, and open process, the www-vrml community decided that VRML would build on the existing Open Inventor technology that had been developed years earlier by SGI. Led by Rikk Carey and Paul Strauss, the Open Inventor project began at SGI in 1989 as a commercial effort to bring 3D graphics into mainstream computing circles. As a cross-platform, 3D computer-graphics application framework coupled with a file format designed expressly for the purpose of interchanging 3D content among a variety of computing environments, Open Inventor proved to be an ideal base on which to build VRML.

Open Inventor also had a strong presence in the traditional 3D community that proved attractive to the budding VRML community. Existing Open Inventor development tools were widely available on a number of different computing platforms, which translated into a large installed base of products and users that VRML could tap into. Existing Open Inventor products, it was thought, could be modified to support VRML with a modicum of effort, effectively giving VRML a giant boost in terms of product availability and developer support. Naturally, access to Open Inventor's products and developers appealed to the upstart VRML community in the same way as did the core technology itself; there existed a number of compelling reasons to vote in favor of Open Inventor.

The Open Inventor proposal became the working document from which the VRML 1.0 specification was produced. In order to convert the proposal into a specification, however, a great deal of additional work and editing had to be done. SGI's Gavin Bell spearheaded the effort. He, along with Pesce, Parisi, Carey, and a number of other contributors, succeeded in converting the proposal into a first-draft specification that was presented at the second International World Wide Web Conference in Chicago in October 1994.

VRML 1.0 would officially emerge several months later as a formal specification, released to the general public in April 1995. Based on a subset of Open Inventor that was enhanced to support networking, VRML 1.0 was an interpreted language whose main features included:

- The ability for Web surfers to interactively explore and examine VRML content residing on the Internet.
- Support for standard 3D objects such as cubes, spheres, and cones.
- Support for arbitrary, complex objects.
- The ability to wrap textures around objects ("texture mapping").
- Support for *lights*, allowing developers to alter the appearance of their VRML content using light sources and shading techniques.
- Support for *cameras*, allowing objects and scenes to be viewed from any perspective, or *viewpoint*.
- Support for URL hyperlinks, allowing VRML objects to be linked to Web pages or other VRML scenes.
- The ability for developers to define and reuse objects, allowing for efficiency of code and ease of programming.

As an interpreted, human-readable language, VRML 1.0 content was written in ASCII text format and stored in files having the .wrl extension (.wrl is short for *world*—see the "Essential VRML Jargon" section later in this

VRML 1.0 vs. 1.0c

The most current VRML 1.0 specification is actually called VRML 1.0c. VRML 1.0c is a clarification version of the original 1.0 specification, more clearly describing portions of the 1.0 specification that tended to cause confusion among developers. Functionally speaking, 1.0 and 1.0c are the same, although 1.0c is better written than the original specification. Whenever you hear people talk about the "1.0 specification," they are actually referring to 1.0c document, even though they may not realize it.

Every major VRML specification is freely available online through the Web3D Consortium at:

http://www.web3d.org/fs_specifications.htm

chapter for more details about VRML worlds and files). Just as Web developers could create HTML pages with nothing more than a text editor, provided they understood the fundamental tag commands of this language, a basic understanding of the VRML 1.0 specification and a text editor were the only things needed to create 3D content for the Web. The resulting .wrl files could then be stitched into Web pages and uploaded to the Internet, and anyone with access to a VRML-savvy browser could experience them.

Reaction to VRML 1.0 was positive and powerful, especially from the commercial world. In the spring of 1995 SGI released WebSpace Navigator, the world's first VRML browser. Later that same year Intervista (a VRML company founded by Tony Parisi) released its WorldView VRML browser plug-in, while Paper released a VRML browser plug-in called WebFX. Together these products would prove vital to the nascent VRML 1.0 effort; browser availability was an essential factor behind the language's early success. In the summer of 1995 Microsoft licensed Intervista's WorldView plug-in, which the software giant then bundled with Internet Explorer. This landmark event would later prompt Netscape to purchase the Paper company, whose WebFX product was integrated into Netscape Navigator's own VRML-inspired technology called Live3D.

The Internet was soon infected with the promise of VRML, as the buzz surrounding 3D for the Web grew louder and more persistent with every passing day. VRML 1.0, however, could not completely satisfy the world's growing hunger for interactive Web 3D. Although reasonably complex 3D scenes could be created with the language, Web surfers couldn't actually interact with VRML

VRML MIME Types and File Headers

VRML 1.0 files were initially associated with the following Multipurpose Internet Mail Extension (MIME) type, which was used to tell Web browsers that the contents they contained should be handed over to a VRML plug-in or helper application for processing:

x-world/x-vrml

MIME types such as this begin with "x" to indicate that the type is an *extension* to standard MIME types, as VRML 1.0 was when it first emerged. (New, temporary, or experimental MIME types begin with "x".) In time, however, VRML became an officially accepted form of MIME content, for which the following MIME type is now used:

model/world

When a VRML-savvy program begins processing a VRML file, it first tests the header line to determine the exact version and format of VRML commands found inside the file. The first line of every VRML 1.0 file begins with the following header:

#VRML V1.0 ascii

VRML programs rely on the header to identify the version of the VRML specification the code complies with (1.0, in this case) as well as the character set in which the language is encoded (such as ASCII text, which all VRML 1.0 files comply with). VRML 2.0 and VRML97 files contain a different header, **#VRML V2.0 utf8**, and are usually associated with the official **model/world** MIME type.

Be sure to set the appropriate VRML MIME type for your Web server, depending on the version of VRML that you end up serving, or ask your server administration to do so. If you do not, browsers will not be able to decode the VRML files that come across the wire, and these files will appear to the end user as gibberish. (Although you should take care to serve up only current VRML content, some servers use both **x-world/x-vrml** and **model/world** MIME types in order to accommodate all forms of VRML.) MIME types are described in detail in the IETF Request For Comment (RFC) documents 1521 and 1522, which are available on the Web at http://www.ietf.org/rfc.html. For more details about VRML file headers and formats see the VRML Files section that appears later in this chapter.

1.0 content. VRML 1.0 merely provided a mechanism for representing static 3D content that surfers could walk through and explore, and not much more.

Fundamentally, VRML 1.0 lacked animation capabilities as well as the ability to create 3D content that responded to user presence and input. As a result, the "M" in VRML 1.0 could just as easily stand for *Museum* as it does for *Modeling*, because this version of the language can create only lifeless 3D content that can be seen but not touched. This limitation of VRML 1.0, however, was not an oversight. VRML progresses over time and in stages, with version 1.0 being the very first, and least capable, release of the language. In order to experience truly interactive Web 3D, the world would have to wait for VRML 2.0.

VRML 2.0 and VRML97

Work on the second major version of VRML was well underway even as the Web community embraced the new VRML 1.0 specification. VRML 2.0 would emerge from the www-vrml community a little more than one year after the VRML 1.0 specification was finalized, solving the animation and dynamic 3D content limitations of the original technology. Following a development path similar to that of the original VRML 1.0 specification, VRML 2.0 would ultimately become the foundation of an international Web3D standard known as VRML97.

In the summer of 1995 several members of the www-vrml list formed the VRML Architecture Group (VAG) with a mission to guide the evolution of the VRML 1.0 specification. A small, technically oriented group comprised of ten individuals, including Pesce and Parisi, the VAG set out to design the VRML 2.0 specification in cooperation with the larger www-vrml community. Although the VAG initially intended to develop the VRML 2.0 specification itself along with feedback from www-vrml, the group eventually decided to issue an open RFP for VRML 2.0 in the same way that one had been issued for VRML 1.0.

Toward the end of 1995, the VAG began working with the International Organization for Standardization (ISO) in hopes of making VRML a formal standard for Internet-based 3D. Although ISO was developing its own 3D metafile format through a joint relationship with the International Electrotechnical Commission (IEC), the widely supported VRML 1.0 specification had been developed in an open fashion that appealed to the standards community. Based on the success of VRML 1.0 and the promise of VRML 2.0, the ISO/IEC group decided to collaborate with the VAG and pursue standardization of VRML.

VRML 1.1: Canceled Flight

VRML 1.1, a relatively minor enhancement to VRML 1.0, was considered the next logical step in the evolution of the technology. However, it never gained enough momentum within www-vrml to achieve liftoff. The basic animation and sound capabilities that VRML 1.1 was to deliver were simply not a sufficient improvement to the language to satisfy most developers and users of VRML 1.0. As a result, VRML 1.1 was permanently grounded in favor of the more substantive VRML 2.0 effort.

As the relationship between the VAG and ISO/IEC took root, activity on the www-vrml list continued to grow. In January of 1996 the VAG officially issued an open RFP for VRML 2.0, to which any organization or individual could respond. By February 2, the submission deadline, six proposals had been received:

- Active VRML, submitted by Microsoft
- HoloWeb, submitted by Sun Microsystems
- Moving Worlds, submitted as a collaborative effort between Sony, SGI, Mitra, and SDSC
- Out of This World, submitted by Apple Computer, Inc.
- Dynamic Worlds, submitted by the German National Research Center for Information Technology, et al.
- Reactive Virtual Environments, submitted by IBM Japan

Each of the six submissions proposed a unique solution for the next generation of VRML, the details of which were dissected, discussed, and absorbed by the VRML community though the www-vrml list. The VAG had established a six-week public review process, a time frame that allowed members of the community to dig into the guts of each submission before voting. When it came time to vote, www-vrml members were asked to rate each proposal in terms of its suitability as a solution for VRML 2.0 and also to name their favorite proposal.

Nearly 200 members of the community cast their votes, the majority of whom supported the Moving Worlds proposal created as a collaborative effort among Sony, SGI, Mitra, and SDSC (see below, "The Motivation Behind Moving Worlds"). After the votes were tallied, the VAG announced Moving Worlds as the clear winner. With a 92% suitability rating and 74% favored proposal rating, Moving Worlds was unanimously endorsed by the VAG as the basis for VRML 2.0. However, just as with VRML 1.0, plenty of work was required to turn the Moving Worlds proposal into an official VRML 2.0 specification.

The Motivation behind Moving Worlds

Moving Worlds was the most popular VRML 2.0 proposal as a result of its technical merit as well as the collaborative process by which it was developed. In August of 1995, almost half a year before the formal RFP for VRML 2.0 was issued, Sony had proposed its own Extended VRML (E-VRML) technology as the basis for VRML 2.0. Sony's E-VRML was an extension to VRML 1.0 that added *behaviors* to the original language in order to allow users to interact with VRML content. By adding behavior scripts and events to VRML 1.0, E-VRML allowed elements of a VRML scene to change based on user activity. Unlike static content created with VRML 1.0, E-VRML scenes were alive and could dynamically react to things the user was doing.

For example, you could explore an E-VRML building where doors would swing open when clicked or windows could be opened and closed if desired. Likewise, you could pick up and examine in detail and from any angle the various objects in the scene, such as a vase or lamp. Although such capabilities sound quite simple, VRML 1.0 didn't support interactive content. In VRML 1.0, you could see the door, windows, and objects in the building but not interact with them. E-VRML scenes bristled with a sense of realism that VRML 1.0 lacked.

In addition to interactive behaviors, E-VRML supported the concept of shared multiuser scenes. By allowing events in a scene to be distributed among multiple users, E-VRML allowed authors to develop shared 3D environments that further mimicked the real world. Suppose, for instance, that half a dozen people decided to explore the same house. If one person decided to open a window, that person and everyone else in the room would see the window open. If another person decided to close the window, everyone would receive a copy of that event and so would see the window close. By sharing events in this way, E-VRML supported shared multiuser scenes that were much more lifelike than possible with VRML 1.0.

As it turned out, Sony's early E-VRML proposal for VRML 2.0 was similar in nature to a proposal being developed by Mitra. A member of the VAG, Mitra (who goes only by the name Mitra, making him the single-name standout of the VRML community) had several years of experience with shared multiuser technology and had also been involved with the development of VRML 1.0. Rather than compete, the Sony E-VRML team and Mitra decided to combine their respective proposals into a single united proposal.

In addition to his proposal, Mitra brought members of the San Diego Supercomputing Center (SDSC) into the mix. Sony, Mitra, and SDSC shared a common vision of VRML 2.0, and 3D cyberspace in general, and by November of 1995 the three had produced a joint proposal that formed the basis of Moving Worlds. That same month, Silicon Graphics, Inc. (SGI) would become the fourth major contributor to the effort.

SGI had developed technology that complemented the combined work of Sony, Mitra, and SDSC. As the company that developed Open Inventor, the foundation on which VRML 1.0 was built, SGI naturally had intentions of proposing its own technology for VRML 2.0. It quickly became apparent, however, that the VRML community would benefit a great deal more if SGI collaborated with Sony, Mitra, and SDSC rather than compete. And so, in December of 1995 the four joined forces and agreed to combine their respective proposals into one body of work they called *Moving Worlds*.

Moving Worlds was formally presented to the VRML community that same month at the VRML95 conference in San Diego, California. Demonstrations created with E-VRML gave conference attendees tangible examples of the potential for Moving Worlds. A few months later the Moving Worlds proposal was officially submitted to the VAG in response to the VRML 2.0 RFP that had been issued in January 1996.

Unlike many of the proposals it would compete against, most of which advocated a substantial departure from the current VRML 1.0 technology, Moving Worlds was a solution that preserved and extended the VRML 1.0 approach to Web3D. In addition, Moving Worlds had already received a great deal of exposure in the VRML community by the time it was submitted for consideration. The joint proposal had been continually hammered on and refined by many members of the www-vrml list throughout its development, resulting in an extremely well-crafted document that captured the collective vision that many in the community shared for VRML 2.0.

From Moving Worlds to VRML 2.0

Converting the Moving Worlds proposal into a VRML 2.0 specification took place in the open over the www-vrml mailing list. Led by SGI employees Rikk Carey, Gavin Bell, and Chris Marrin, it proved to be a massive effort. At the same time, discussions between the VAG and ISO/IEC continued, as standardization of VRML moved closer to reality. In June of 1996, Carey flew to Kyoto, Japan, to attend an ISO/IEC meeting on behalf of the VAG, dur-ing which the groups would formalize the steps necessary to standardize VRML 2.0.

During that meeting a formal Cooperative Agreement was drawn up to describe the process that the VAG and ISO/IEC would follow in transforming the forthcoming VRML 2.0 specification into an official international ISO/IEC standard. Both parties agreed that the VRML 2.0 specification would serve as the basis for ISO/IEC standardization, and that alterations to that specification would not be made unless absolutely necessary. It was also agreed upon that both groups would distribute the same common document at various stages of the standardization process, ensuring that the VRML and ISO/IEC communities would literally be on the "same page" as the specification and standard progressed. In addition, the groups agreed that the final VRML standard would be published on the Web in HTML format, something the ISO/IEC had never done with an international standard before.

As part of the Cooperative Agreement between the VAG and ISO/IEC, each group appointed an editor for its respective portion of the work. Carey was appointed by the VAG, Richard Puk by the ISO/IEC. Together the two would produce a single document to serve both as the VRML 2.0 specification and as an ISO/IEC standards draft. Co-editors Carey and Puk, with considerable input from members of the VRML and international standards communities, completed the final VRML 2.0 specification within two months of their appointment.

The final VRML 2.0 specification was released to the public at Siggraph in August of 1996. During the conference VRML 2.0 was declared to be complete, meaning that content authors and tool developers could base their work on the frozen specification without fear that it would change in the future. Meanwhile, the VRML 2.0 specification document would become the working draft used by ISO/IEC as the foundation for their work.

Several hundred comments related to VRML 2.0 as an international standard were generated by the ISO/IEC communities between August and December of 1996. Although a number of these comments were technical, the

VRML 2.0 Triggers Formation of VRML Consortium

During the August 1996 Siggraph conference at which the final VRML 2.0 specification was released, members of the VRML community met to discuss the formation of a consortium around the increasingly popular technology. At the time, only the VAG existed, consisting of ten self-selected individuals from the www-vrml list who didn't necessarily represent the interests of the larger VRML community. As VRML continued to grow in popularity, a number of companies expressed concern that no central organization existed through which they could effect change of the technology.

When members of www-vrml formed the VAG, they understood that an organization such as a consortium of companies might ultimately be necessary in order for VRML to continue growing through industry support. At the time, however, a consortium was considered premature and so the VAG consciously deferred forming such an organization until their work on VRML 2.0 was complete.

Concurrent with the public release of VRML 2.0 in August of 1996, the VAG and other members of the VRML community formed the Consortium Working Group (CWG), through which the VRML Consortium would officially emerge in December of that same year. As a nonprofit organization initially chartered to promote VRML alone, the VRML Consortium expanded its charter in 1998 to embrace all forms of Web3D and eventually adopted the name *Web3D Consortium* to reflect this new role (see Chapter 2, "Overview of Web3D").

vast majority proved to be editorial in nature and simply pointed out areas of the specification that were vague or unclear and needed to be clarified. As a result, the technical changes required to convert the VRML 2.0 specification into an international standard were few compared to the editorial changes that were necessary.

The VRML 2.0 specification was completely converted into an ISO/IEC-compliant document in the year that followed and was formally recognized in December of 1997 as an international standard for Internet-based 3D. VRML97, officially designated as ISO/IEC standard 14772–1:1997, had arrived, making VRML 2.0 and VRML 1.0 obsolete. Although the VRML 2.0 specification and the VRML97 standard are nearly 100% compatible in terms of the technology they describe, they are very different documents. To this day, many people incorrectly assume that VRML 2.0 is the most current version of VRML, even though the VRML97 standard is actually more recent.

Note: VRML97

The intense collaboration between the VRML and ISO/IEC communities resulted in two records that stand even today. The VRML97 standard was produced within 18 months, a surprisingly brief time when compared to other standards efforts, setting a time-to-standardization record. In addition, VRML97 was published on the Web in the HTML format, making it the first international standard ever published in HTML. The VRML97 specification is still available online today through the Web3D Consortium at: http://www.web3d.org/fs_specifications.htm.

As a result of their close relationship, VRML 2.0 and VRML97 are sometimes referred to as *VRML2/97*, a concatenation of the two terms that reflects their kinship. Although it's tempting to use this hybrid name when referring in general to the second generation of the language, we'll use the term *VRML97* from this point on, because it emphasizes that the VRML 2.0 specification has been made obsolete by the VRML97 international standards. Besides all of the features found in VRML 1.0, VRML97 supports several very important enhancements that allow developers to create animated and interactive 3D content for the Internet:

- **Sensors** allow VRML objects and scenes to *sense* and respond to the passing of time and user activity. Time sensors, for example, can be used to animate objects after a specific period of time has elapsed, while touch sensors allow VRML programmers to craft content that reacts to mouse clicks, movement, and dragging (such as buttons, doorbells, television remote controls, light switches, and other objects that respond to *touch* input). Proximity sensors, on the other hand, can detect when the user moves within a certain distance of an object in a scene and can be used to create distance-sensitive content such as automatic revolving doors, barking guard dogs, and security alarms that respond to user presence.

- **Switches** allow VRML programmers to instantly toggle between related shapes in a scene. A VRML adventure game, for example, might use switches to toggle between the various positions and animations of each creature you encounter in your travels. That puppy standing at the gates of hell might appear harmless until you approach it, at which point it could switch into a hideous attacking beast with three heads and knives for teeth. Likewise, the sun could turn into a moon as evening sets in, or the soft, fluffy clouds might transform into thundering rain clouds in the blink of an eye, all courtesy of switches.

- **Background colors and images** add another level of realism to VRML by giving scenes what amounts to a horizon. When you walk around your neighborhood in the real world, for instance, what you see behind the trees and houses is a *background* of sky (unless you live in a city, where the buildings that you see often have a background of additional buildings). The sky appears far off on the horizon and acts as a backdrop to everything you see; without it your real world would seem quite unreal. In VRML, background colors and images can be used to lend a similar visual effect to virtual scenes. A light shade of blue, for example, might be used as the background for a ocean scene, while factory-building silhouettes might be the background for a virtual city. As in the real world, you could walk forever and never actually bump into VRML backgrounds; they always appear far off in the distance to give scenes a realism and perspective they would otherwise lack.

- **Animated textures** allow the image map applied to a object to be dynamically moved or altered in such a way that the object seems "alive." Texture transformations can alter the application of the texture image over time, or they can even be movies that literally play on the surface of the shape to which they are applied (ideal when it comes to creating a television set or drive-in theater, for example). Rippling water on the surface of a pond or stream, rolling clouds, flickering fire, and similar effects can be created courtesy of VRML's support for animated textures.

- **Sounds** further increase the realism of VRML scenes by bringing them to life with content that we can hear, not just see. VRML97 supports three formats of audio: WAV (.wav) files, Musical Instrument Digital Interface (MIDI) files, and MPEG-1 movie sounds. In addition to merely playing sounds at a consistent volume, they can also be *spatialized*, a feature of VRML that allows sound sources to be positioned within a scene in a way that mimics the real world. As you approach the sound source, it continues to get louder until it is playing at maximum volume. If you move away, the volume lessens, softening as you retreat from the source, and eventually stops playing if you move away far enough. Similarly, the sounds coming out of your speakers change volume depending on where you are in relation to the source. If you are facing a source located slightly to your right, for example, the volume coming from your right speaker will be stronger than that of the left speaker. As you move directly in front of the source, the volume in both speakers becomes equal, and it becomes stronger in the left speaker if you position yourself so that the source is on your left. In addition to controlling various aspects of spatialized audio, VRML authors can control playback rate (a feature known as *pitch shifting*) and intensity of volume. They also can start, stop, and loop sounds in response to user activity or the passing of time.

- **Extrusions** allow a variety of twisting, turning shapes to be created. VRML extrusions are based on a popular real-world manufacturing process. Products such as wire, steel beams, and moldings are made by forcing molten materials (usually metal, aluminum, or plastic) through a heat-resistant plate that has a certain shape cut into it. The material cools as it passes through the hole in the plate, emerging on the other side as a shaped strand of hardened material. A simpler form of extrusion is used when pasta is created, where the shape of the hole through which the pasta is forced dictates the resulting shape of the noodle. VRML's extrusion feature allows developers to create a variety of shapes such as spirals, tubes, and tori by defining a *cross section* through which their imaginary material will pass (the equivalent of a real-world hole). In addition the developer defines a path, or *spine*, that the material will follow on its way through the cross section. The spine and the shape of the cross section together determine the form that emerges, and both can be dynamically altered as the shape is produced. Extrusion is a popular technique often used to generate virtual snakes, screws, slides, donuts, noodles, and a variety of more complicated objects.

- **Scripts** allow VRML to be extended and enhanced by programming languages such as Java and JavaScript. VRML is, first and foremost, a programming language used to create 3D content. It is not, however, a full-featured programming language and so falls short of the computational and data-processing capabilities of other languages. As a result, VRML97 introduced the notion of scripting, a powerful feature that allows it to tap into external programs created by other languages. A VRML game, for example, might rely on externally defined scripts to handle complex computations such as artificial intelligence of monsters, or interaction with databases to save the state of each player. A multiuser VRML meeting space, on the other hand, might use scripting to keep track of each participant's actions, since VRML97 itself doesn't inherently support multiuser worlds.

- **Prototypes** allow developers to create custom objects and behaviors and reuse them as needed. Like scripts, prototypes give developers a way to extend the base capabilities of the language. Prototypes are used to define and encapsulate custom VRML nodes (the fundamental building blocks of VRML files, as described in the following chapters), which can then be reused in other VRML scenes without a major recoding effort. A VRML programmer might, for example, spend a great deal of time developing an animated 3D-charting object for a particular scene. If such an object were created as a prototype that was stored in its own VRML file, it could be quickly and easily added to any number of other VRML scenes. VRML prototypes are often used to create entire libraries of reusable objects.

Although these aren't the only features supported by VRML97, they are among the most significant in terms of creating sophisticated 3D content for the Internet. These and other capabilities address many shortcoming of version 1.0 and put the second generation of the VRML language leaps and bounds ahead of the original. Meanwhile, a new generation of the technology

Note: X3D—The Next Generation of VRML

At the time of this writing, the next generation of VRML beyond VRML97 was under development by the Web3D Consortium. This new version of VRML began life in 1998 as "VRML Next Generation" (VRML NG) but was recast in 1999 as "Extensible 3D" (X3D), owing to its close relationship with the Extensible Markup Language (XML). XML is a very different beast than VRML97 and is covered separately in Part V of this book.

is now under development by the Web3D Consortium that promises to push the envelope of Web3D to the very edge.

Essential VRML Jargon

Like most programming languages, VRML is rife with unique terms, concepts, and principles. Fortunately, you don't actually need to program in VRML in order to weave existing VRML content into your own Web site; you need only to skim the surface from the perspective of a Web developer rather than dive deeply into it as a programmer would.

Most of the time, of course, simply using existing VRML content as is isn't enough. You'll want to customize premade VRML objects and scenes to suit your tastes and needs, rather than settle for what you're handed, buy, or get free on the Internet. You can use visual authoring tools or learn the basics of the programming language, both of which are described in the chapters that follow. In either case, you'll need to know the basic terminology and principles of VRML, which is what this section and the next chapter are all about.

Following is the essential VRML jargon that you must know in order to make sense of the technology as a Web developer, assuming that you'll also want to customize existing content for your own purposes. You'll also find the terms, concepts, and principles described in this section and following chapters essential if you plan on creating your own VRML content from scratch, as Chapter 10, "Creating New VRML Worlds," explains.

VRML Browsers

Standard Web browsers such as Internet Explorer and Netscape Navigator don't have a clue when it comes to VRML. Unlike native Web content that they can display directly, such as text or images stored in the GIF and JPEG formats, VRML came along several years after the Web itself was invented. For this reason, and because VRML is very complicated content compared to text and images, traditional Web browsers must rely on helper applications and plug-ins.

VRML helper applications are full-fledged programs that are sublaunched by the Web browser, while plug-ins display VRML content within the context of the browser itself. Both are considered to be *VRML browsers*, which is a generic term used to describe programs that can handle Web-based VRML content.

By far the most popular form of VRML browser is the plug-in, primarily because plug-ins display VRML seamlessly within a Web page. VRML helper applications, on the other hand, run outside of the Web browser and are generally less popular, as they tend to disrupt the Web surfing experience. Due to their overwhelming popularity, this book will focus exclusively on plug-ins as a solution for processing VRML content.

VRML Plug-ins

VRML is stored in plain text files, much as Web pages are (see the earlier VRML 1.0 discussion, or skip ahead to the VRML Files section to learn more about the VRML file format). When a Web browser encounters a VRML file, however, it doesn't try to process it directly but instead hands it over for processing to an installed VRML plug-in (see Appendix A, "VRML Browsers"). The plug-in will interpret the VRML programming commands contained in the file. The plug-in parses the file, rendering the 3D contents it describes directly into the Web browser window while also handling user interaction and navigation of the resulting scene.

You can weave VRML content directly into your Web pages using HTML tags such as the <EMBED> tag shown in the following Web page snippet:

```
<HTML>
<HEAD>
   <TITLE>Simple VRML Demo</TITLE>
</HEAD>
<BODY>

<EMBED SRC="demo.wrl" WIDTH=300 HEIGHT=250>

</BODY>
</HTML>
```

As Chapter 6, "Weaving VRML into Web Pages," explains in great detail, you can also use the <OBJECT> tag, although the <EMBED> tag predates it and is more often used by Web page developers when it comes to adding VRML content to HTML pages. Using such HTML tags, VRML can be displayed in any rectangular portion of a Web page that you desire; it can consume all or just a small portion of it, as you see fit (see Figure 4-2). You can also place VRML alongside other types of content (such as text, images, sounds, and movies), a common technique used to create rich multimedia Web pages.

In most cases, VRML plug-ins appear along with a set of special navigation and examination controls that allow the user to explore the scene (see Figure 4-2). In some situations, however, these controls are hidden from the user, as seen in Figure 4-3. VRML animations (sometimes called VRML "movies"), for example, are often displayed without navigation and examination controls, because animation doesn't typically engage the user in the way that other forms of VRML do (such as an interactive building walk-through, games, or data visualization). Visibility of plug-in controls is a feature of VRML, yet it can be controlled through HTML as well. (See Chapter 6,

Figure 4-2   VRML plug-ins display their results in a rectangular portion of the Web browser window, the exact location and dimensions of which can be controlled using simple HTML commands (http://www.ryanosure.com/).

Figure 4-3   VRML plug-in navigation and examination controls are often hidden from view when not needed, as with the animation seen here; you can control this feature through the VRML language or HTML.

"Weaving VRML into Web Pages," to learn how to show or hide these controls in your own pages.)

Due to the complexity of VRML content, VRML browser plug-ins are by no means trivial. They are, in fact, extremely complicated software programs, usually consuming several megabytes of disk space when installed and a fair amount of RAM when in use. A VRML plug-in comes as part of the full installation of the latest versions of both Netscape Navigator and Internet Explorer, but users have to manually download and install their own plug-in when using a partial installation or earlier versions of the Web browsers. Therefore, you should consider adding a link to your VRML-enhanced pages that directs visitors to a Web page that tells them how to install a VRML plug-in (see Appendix A, "VRML Browsers").

Objects, Scenes, and Worlds

VRML content is often expressed in terms of *objects* and *scenes*. Generally speaking, VRML scenes, more commonly known as *worlds*, are compositions in 3D space that contain one or more objects. Objects, in turn, are the

Sniffing for VRML Plug-ins

You can use a simple client-side *sniffer* script in your VRML-enhanced pages to test incoming browsers for the presence of a VRML plug-in, automatically directing those without one to a Web page describing how they can go about installing one. You can also determine the exact version of the user's VRML plug-in to ensure that it is capable of handling the VRML content in your pages. Due to incompatibilities between the two major versions of the language, VRML plug-ins created specifically for VRML 1.0 content cannot handle VRML97, nor are all VRML97 browsers capable of handling VRML 1.0 (most are, but it's not guaranteed). Thanks to sniffer scripts, you can create VRML-enhanced Web pages that are capable of accommodating a wide variety of end-user configurations, a useful technique that's discussed in detail in Chapter 6, "Weaving VRML into Web Pages."

discrete items that populate a world and contribute to its character, look, and feel (see Figure 4-4). Using the navigation and examination controls provided by our VRML plug-in, we can walk through worlds and examine the objects they contain, much as we stroll through the real world around us and examine those objects we find interesting (see Appendix A, "VRML Browsers," for details).

A VRML park, for example, might be populated with objects such as trees, shrubs, flowers, fountains, people, dogs, birds, and squirrels. Using your mouse, you can navigate through the virtual world and examine at your leisure each of the objects it contains. You can walk up to a tree and take a close look at the knotted bark image wrapped around its trunk, peer up at the leaves and limbs swaying in the sky above, or look down at the roots that hug the ground below your feet. After thoroughly examining the tree, you can walk over to the nearest flowerbed and count each yellow petal you see, share your lunch with the hungry birds and squirrels, and even dive into the water fountain if you feel the urge.

You can do these things because a VRML developer took the time to assemble these objects into a single park scene. When taken on their own, these objects aren't necessarily related to a park. Flowers, for instance, can also be found in a greenhouse or flower shop, while trees are just as common in a forest as they are your back yard. VRML authors are responsible for

Figure 4-4   VRML worlds (left) are populated with one or more objects (right) that, when taken together, give scenes a sense of character, look, and feel (http://angels.kiasma.fng.fi).

creating each of these objects, which can then be assembled into a single scene, whether it is a park, a zoo, or any other virtual world.

It is interesting to note that almost every VRML object that you encounter can be deconstructed to reveal a combination of more simple objects. A tree, for example, can be broken apart into the various objects that make up its trunk, limbs, and leaves. Not surprisingly, each of these can be even further decomposed. A tree trunk might be composed of a cylinder that has an image of bark wrapped around it, while limbs are easily represented by a series of connected cylinders that have yet a different type of bark wrapped around them. Each leaf, on the other hand, could be constructed as a series of points that, when connected, have a fanlike appearance resembling a real-world leaf.

The fact that primitive objects often serve as building blocks for more complicated ones, as the sidebar Primitive Objects explains, gives the term

Note: Bandwidth Bottleneck

All of the objects a VRML scene contains must be downloaded and handed over to the VRML browser for processing before the scene can be experienced (that is, the entire VRML scene must be downloaded from the Web before it can be viewed or explored by the end user). Neither VRML 1.0 nor VRML97 accommodates streaming or incremental downloading of individual objects, although X3D may. Extremely large or complicated VRML worlds can be very time consuming to download, so they are often compressed to conserve bandwidth and disk space, as described in the "VRML Files" section that follows.

object a fairly loose definition. An object can be very simple, such as a cone or box, or extremely complicated, such as a house or space shuttle, yet in all cases it is something that can be placed in a VRML scene. Objects of all levels of complexity can be assembled into a single scene. Consider a beach scene, for example. The sun in the sky might be little more than a yellow sphere, while the beach chair is a much more complicated object residing in the same world.

VRML objects, no matter how simple or complex they may be, are stored inside text files as a series of human-readable VRML programming commands. A VRML file can contain the code for a single object or a number of different objects. VRML scenes, or worlds, are also stored in text files and can contain their own internally defined objects or reference those contained

Primitive Objects

Complex objects can be progressively decomposed until the fundamental shapes they are built upon are revealed. A tree trunk, for example, is ultimately built upon a simple cylinder shape. VRML offers four fundamental objects— box, cone, cylinder, and sphere—from which a variety of more complicated objects may be created. These low-level building blocks, known as *primitive objects*, are discussed in more detail in Chapter 5, "VRML Fundamentals."

in external files. In all cases, however, VRML objects and scenes created are ultimately stored in text files (which may then be compressed using the GZip utility, as described below).

VRML Files

VRML files are nothing more than plain ASCII text files that contain the programming commands used to describe 3D content. Although a VRML file can contain the source code for a single object, the most compelling VRML files usually contain entire scenes, or worlds, that are comprised of a wide variety of objects (comprehensive worlds, after all, are usually more interesting to explore than a single object).

Whether they contain one object or an entire world, VRML files normally end in the .wrl extension (short for *world*), although other extensions are often used in cases where the file contents have been compressed (see the sidebar "VRML File Extensions and Compression" for details).

Listing 4.1 shows the source code for a simple 3D object known as a cone primitive, which is stored in a VRML file that I've named *mycone.wrl*. Although this code isn't much to look at (nor is the shape it defines very exciting, as you can see from Figure 4-5), studying this listing will help you become familiar with the general structure of VRML files. Consider each line of code, beginning with the very first one.

Listing 4.1   "mycone.wrl"

```
#VRML V2.0 utf8

# This is an example of a very simple
# Shape node that uses the primitive
# Cone object for geometry (form).

Shape {

  appearance Appearance {
    material Material {
      diffuseColor 0 1 0    # R G B (this cone is pure green)
    }
  }

  geometry Cone { }
}
```

Figure 4-5   A primitive cone shape, the result of VRML code found in Listing 4.1.

Header Lines

The first line of every VRML file, known as the *header line*, is used to tell the VRML browser what version of the language the source code is written in, as well as the encoding format applied to each character in the file. The code in Listing 4.1 uses the standard header line found in all VRML 2.0 and VRML97 files, **#VRML V2.0 utf8**, while VRML 1.0 files rely on an entirely different header line (**#VRML V1.0 ascii**, as described in the sidebar "VRML MIME Types and File Headers," earlier in this chapter).

The first portion of the header line in this example is #**VRML v2.0**, which in human terms means something akin to "this file contains code that's in compliance with the second major version of the VRML language." Following this self-explanatory portion of the header, however, is a slightly more confusing string: **uft8**.

UTF8 describes the character encoding of this file. Although VRML 1.0 header lines describe a plain ASCII character set, VRML 2.0 and VRML 97 use the UTF8 International Standard that describes a text encoding scheme used to format multibyte characters. UTF is short for "Universal Character Set Transform Format" (UTF is short for UCS Transform Format, UCS for Universal Character Set). UTF8 is similar to Unicode (both are based on the International Standard ISO 10646–1:1993), as it supports a wide variety of languages and special character sets such as English, Russian, Spanish, French, Japanese, Chinese, German, and many more. As a result, programmers can write code in their native language and character set.

Because ASCII is a subset of UTF8, you don't need anything more than your traditional keyboard and a text editor to write VRML code. Everything you type is actually a UTF8 character. Simply start typing, and save your results in plain text format having the file extension `.wrl`. There's nothing to it.

Comments

Following the VRML header line are three comment lines, as indicated by the pound sign (#) preceding the text. VRML comments merely document source code for the benefit of human beings who have to read the code. VRML browsers completely ignore comments.

VRML comments include the pound sign and everything to the right of it up to the end of line. This allows code and comments to be mixed together, as the following line illustrates:

```
diffuseColor 0 1 0    # R G B  (this cone is pure green)
```

In this example, the code `diffuseColor 0 1 0` is followed by a fairly terse comment that documents the role that each integer value plays (Red, Green, Blue). This comment also explains that the current `diffuseColor` settings produce a pure green cone. Even though this line of text doesn't begin with a comment, VRML browsers are smart enough to scan through each line looking for comment identifiers (#). Every piece of text from that point on until the end of the line is ignored.

File Body

Every line of text that follows the required header line is considered to be part of the VRML *file body*, which is comprised of source code that defines 3D objects and scenes together with any comments that document the code. The majority of source code in a VRML file is used to create and manage *nodes*, which are self-contained bodies of code that can support both state and behavior (which together describe how an object looks and acts).

As the following chapter describes in detail, nodes are the fundamental VRML programming unit, analogous to objects in object-oriented languages such as C++ and Java, or functions and procedures in procedural languages such as C or Pascal. In Listing 4.1, a series of VRML source code lines is used to define a `Shape` node. This particular `Shape` node, in turn, uses a `Cone` node for its geometry, or form.

The `Shape` node in this example also defines an `Appearance` node, which itself contains a `Material` node. The `Material` node describes the surface properties of the shape we're building. Inside the `Material` node a field

VRML File Extensions and Compression

VRML files typically end in the .wrl extension (scene.wrl), which is short for *world*, although you'll also encounter VRML files that end in .gz or .wrz (scene.wrl.gz, or scene.wrz), indicating that they've been compressed with the GNU Zip ("GZip") utility. Files compressed with GZip ("GZipped" files) are much smaller than the equivalent file stored in plain text format, which conserves server hard drive space and reduces download time.

Compression can easily cut disk space requirements and download times by more than two-thirds for large VRML files and is more often applied to big, complex VRML files than those that are small to begin with. Although you can view the source code for standard, uncompressed VRML files, you cannot view the source code of compressed VRML files unless you first decompress them (otherwise you'll see nothing but garbled text).

Although most of the GZipped worlds you'll encounter will have either the .gz or .wrz file extension, sometimes you'll encounter compressed files that actually have the .wrl extension. Because some older browsers have difficulty handling files with the .gz and .wrz extensions, Web developers often use the original .wrl file extension for their compressed worlds.

If you are interested in viewing the source code of GZipped files, you'll be happy to know that most of today's popular compression utilities support the GZip format. The venerable WinZip program (http://www.winzip.com/), for example, can decompress GZipped files, provided that they have the .gz file extension (WinZip does not handle GZipped files that have the .wrl or .wrz extension). In addition, the GNU Zip utility is available free of charge on the Internet through the Free Software Foundation (http://www.gnu.org/). Simply FTP into the following GZip site:

ftp://www.gnu.org/gnu/gzip/

See Chapter 6, "Weaving VRML into Web Pages," to learn how to use GZip with your own VRML content.

Inlining

VRML *inlining* is a popular technique that allows different parts of a VRML world to be stored in separate files. It is similar in nature to composing HTML Web pages from a variety of images, sounds, and movies that are stored in their own files. As you'll learn in Chapter 10, "Creating New VRML Worlds," inlined files can contain individual objects or entire scenes.

A VRML airport, for example, might be composed by inlining a number of different files. The main world might consist of merely the runways, while the control tower, airplanes, baggage trucks, and all other pieces of the complete scene can be added through inlining.

Inlining facilitates code maintenance and encourages code reuse. It is often used to build libraries of VRML objects and scenes that can be used over and over again in a variety of worlds. In addition, inlining makes Web-based VRML worlds more responsive, as most browsers display skeletal outline structures as a placeholder for inlined content that has not yet been downloaded. Rather than being forced to wait until inlined files are completely loaded over the network, users are free to roam around the world while downloading goes on in the background. The skeletal outlines are replaced by content as the user moves around the scene.

called `diffuseColor` is set with a series of values that describe the color green. Although it's difficult to make sense of exactly what's going on here, in the end we wind up with a green 3D cone (see Figure 4-5).

In just a few lines of code, I've described a three-dimensional cone object that can be examined from any angle. In addition, this 3D cone can be grabbed, tilted, turned, and spun in any direction. Because VRML is all about 3D, the body of this file is mercifully short despite the richness of the object it describes. As a programmer, I can continue to build upon this simple example or else use a technique known as inlining to bring additional content into this scene (see the sidebar "Inlining").

Shape nodes are only one of the many types of nodes supported by VRML, as the following chapters explain in more detail. Nodes allow programmers to combine a number of different shapes to make more complex objects, and they can also be used to create interactive scenes containing a variety of objects. In supporting the creation of more complex content such as this, VRML employs a unique programming model known as a scene graph, a topic we'll tackle in the next chapter.

Summary

The Virtual Reality Modeling Language (VRML) was developed through an open, collaborative effort that was kick-started during the first international World Wide Web Conference in Geneva, Switzerland, in 1994. Following the conference, a "www-vrml" mailing list was established, through which VRML was developed with the help of input from thousands of people from around the globe. The first official version, VRML 1.0, emerged in 1995 and was based on SGI's Open Inventor technology.

VRML 1.0 was limited to static 3D scenes and lacked animation and interactive capabilities. VRML 2.0 (based on the Moving World proposal jointly developed by Sony, SGI, Mitra, and SDSC) solved these problems when it was released to the public in late 1996, and it served as the basis of the ISO/IEC International Standard 14772–1:1997, more commonly known as VRML97. VRML97 made VRML 2.0 obsolete, and today it is the current version of VRML available. However, a new VRML technology called Extensible 3D (X3D, formerly known as VRML Next Generation) is now under development and slated for delivery in 2000. X3D and all other forms of VRML technology are developed and promoted by the Web3D Consortium (formerly the VRML Consortium), a nonprofit organization comprised of more than 50 high-technology companies committed to the continued advancement of 3D for the Internet.

VRML scenes, or worlds, can be populated with simple or complex objects. VRML worlds, and the objects they contain, are defined by human-readable source code stored in plain ASCII text files that have the .wrl extension (.wrl is short for world). The source code contained in VRML files consists of nodes that are arranged into a scene-graph data structure.

Following is a complete list of URLs referenced in this chapter:

IETF Request For Comment (RFC) files   http://www.ietf.org/rfc.html

VRML specifications   http://www.web3d.org/fs_specifications.htm

Ryanosure   http://www.ryanosure.com/

Conversations with Angels   http://angels.kiasma.fng.fi/

WinZip   http://www.winzip.com/

Free Software Foundation   http://www.gnu.org/

GZip   ftp://www.gnu.org/gnu/gzip/

VRML
FUNDAMENTALS

Topics in This Chapter

- An overview of VRML scene graphs

- Writing and formatting VRML code

- Learning to read the VRML97 specification

- Exploring VRML nodes, fields, events, and data types

- Routing events from one node to another

- Defining object shape, geometry, and appearance

- Understanding the difference between primitive and complex objects

- Creating a text shape

- Walking around VRML's 3D coordinate system

Chapter 5

In the previous chapter (Chapter 4, "VRML Overview") you learned about the history of VRML and the basic structure of VRML files. In this chapter you'll actually explore the innards of VRML files as you learn the fundamentals of the language in preparation for the chapters that follow. Here you'll learn about the scene graph data structure used by VRML programmers to represent 3D objects and scenes, and you'll even construct your own scene graphs as you write VRML code that makes use of the basic building blocks of every world.

Scene Graphs

VRML content is developed using a *scene graph* programming model that was first popularized by Open Inventor (the SGI technology that VRML is built upon). Source code in a VRML file is organized into a scene graph data structure that holds each object description for a world and also describes the relationships that objects have with one another. Technically speaking, the VRML scene-graph structure is known as a *directed acyclic graph* (DAG) which means that a node in the directed parent-child relationship cannot be its own parent. In more general terms, a scene graph is simply a special type of

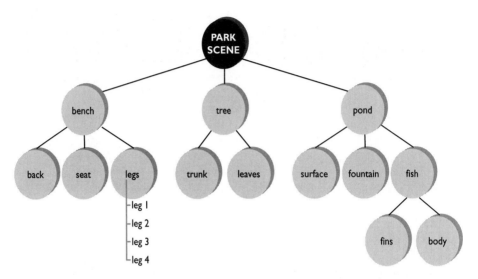

Figure 5-1   VRML file contents are arranged according to hierarchical scene graph data structures to describe the relationship that objects in a world have to one another.

data organization method used to describe 3D scenes, the objects they contain, and the characteristics of each object such as shape, size, color, and position in the scene.

When represented visually (Figure 5-1), scene graphs have the appearance of an upside-down tree, or, more accurately, the roots of a tree. Scene graphs also resemble the class hierarchies often used to visually express the parent-child relationship of objects in object-oriented programming languages such as Java or C++, although they shouldn't be confused with such hierarchies. Whereas object hierarchies represent the inheritance relationships among objects in a system, scene graphs are essentially special-purpose data structures used to construct 3D scenes and objects and, as such, represent the relationships that objects in a scene have with one another.

Scene graphs allow VRML developers to create 3D content at a very high level of abstraction, meaning they can create 3D objects and scenes without having to deal directly with the low-level details of the platform or rendering process. Thanks to the high-level nature of scene graph technology, authors can instead focus on *what* to render instead of *how* to render. The gory low-level rendering details are left to the VRML browser, which interprets the scene graph data structures stored in VRML files and displays the results on screen for the end user to enjoy.

Figure 5-2 Both scenes and objects can be described using a scene graph. The chair object in this figure, for example, is represented by a relatively simple scene graph, while an entire kitchen scene would require a much more complex scene graph.

Nodes

Scene graphs are created using programming elements called *nodes*. The VRML equivalent to Java and C++ classes, nodes are used to implement shapes, sounds, lights, animation paths, viewpoints, and other aspects of objects and entire worlds. VRML developers can construct scene graphs using any of the 54 different types of nodes that are built into the current version of the language, and they are free to create their own nodes from scratch in order to implement features that are not already built into VRML.

Parent nodes in a scene graph are responsible for managing the *child nodes* beneath them, while child nodes may in fact have children of their own. This nested relationship of nodes containing nodes can continue indefinitely, giving scene graphs a hierarchical root-like appearance as illustrated in Figure 5-1. To help make this concept more concrete, consider the scene graph of an object such as the chair in Figure 5-2.

It doesn't take much to decompose a common kitchen chair into three basic structures: legs, seat, and a back. Each of these structures can be broken down even further, at which point the raw building materials become apparent:

cylindrical dowels (legs), a flat board (seat), and rectangular pieces of wood (back). Although these raw materials don't amount to much on their own, they are grouped together into the basic structures (legs, seat, and back) that can then be further assembled into a kitchen chair. A corresponding scene graph shown in Figure 5-3 illustrates the hierarchical relationship that these individual pieces of building material (children nodes) and grouped materials (parent nodes) have when viewed in the context of a kitchen chair.

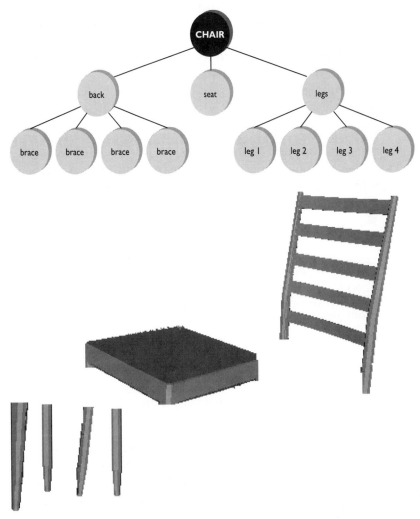

Figure 5-3   The various building materials used to create this chair must be arranged in a very specific way to actually produce a chair object, as depicted by this chair scene graph.

Nodes are referred to by names that begin with a capital letter, such as Shape, Cone, Point, Group and Transform. Inside each node are one or more *fields*, which the programmer manipulates in order to control the node's appearance or behavior. In the next section, we'll show you how to read VRML97 node definitions in order to find out what fields a particular node contains and the legal values it may be set to. For now, however, you can simply assume that nodes contain fields that you can set and manipulate.

The following three lines of code, for example, specify a Sphere node having a radius of 5 meters (numbers used to measure size and distance in VRML always correspond to meters, as explained later in the "Coordinate Systems" section). Here we've specified the Sphere node and set its *radius* field to 5:

```
Sphere {
  radius 5
}
```

When specifying nodes in VRML code, a pair of opening and closing curly braces ({ }) surround the fields that a node contains. Even in cases where no fields are actually specified for a node, the opening and closing braces are still supplied:

```
Sphere {}
```

In this example no fields are specified, and so the default field settings of the Sphere node are used. In order to conserve space and to make this code easier to read, we've placed the empty opening and closing parenthesis on the same line as the node name itself. Nothing, however, stops you from placing each on its own line as follows:

```
Sphere {
}
```

Note: Reserved Words

The following keywords are reserved by VRML. They cannot be used as node or field names, nor can they be used as prototype names (prototypes allow VRML developers to create their own custom nodes, as Chapter 10, "Creating New VRML Worlds," explains):

```
DEF, EXTERNPROTO, FALSE, IS, NULL, PROTO, ROUTE, TO,
TRUE, USE, eventIn, eventOut, exposedField, field.
```

VRML browsers don't care how you format your nodes, as long as they contain valid information. Provided the name of the node is spelled correctly and the fields that you specify inside the opening and closing parenthesis are valid for that node (and are set to legal values, as the next section explains), the browser couldn't care less. The following code used to describe a Cone node, for example, is entirely acceptable to the VRML browser:

```
Cone {bottomRadius 3 height 5}
```

Many visual VRML content development tools, in fact, produce code such as the above because they're not concerned with the readability of the .wrl files they create. However, when it comes to hand-coding your own nodes using a text editor, as you'll do in this chapter and those that follow, I'd recommend using a simple format such as the following to help you actually understand what you're writing:

```
Cone {
  bottomRadius 3
  height 5
}
```

In this example each field appears on its own line, indented two spaces in from the node name. The values for each field appear two spaces after their respective field name, although you might take it a step further and align the field values using tabs or additional spaces for further readability:

```
Cone {
  bottomRadius  3
  height        5
}
```

Of course, simply typing node and field names into a text file won't actually result in a VRML world unless you've successfully combined these nodes and fields into something meaningful. The snippets of code that you've just looked at, for example, don't do anything on their own; they must be rolled into a VRML file that contains an appropriate header line (#VRML V2.0 utf8) and file body as described in the previous chapter. Following, for example, is the bare minimum code needed to create a VRML world file based on the Cone node described earlier:

```
#VRML V2.0 utf8

Shape {
```

```
      geometry Cone {
        bottomRadius      3
        height            5
      }

   }
```

In this example we've used a Cone node as the geometry, or form, of a
Shape node. Nodes are commonly supplied to fields of other nodes, which is
similar to setting a variable equal to the address of a function or procedure in
a language such as C or Pascal (or assigning an object to a variable in Java or
C++). Here, the Shape node's *geometry* field is set to a Cone node, meaning
we've nested the Cone node inside of the Shape node. The only reason that
we can do this is because the Shape node is defined by the VRML97 specification as having a *geometry* field that can be set to geometric nodes such as
Cone (see "Shapes, Geometry, and Appearance" for details), allowing us to
construct a very simple world with the following structure:

```
   Node1 {
     fieldName Node2 {
        ...Node2 fields set here...
     }
   }
```

This, however, is an absolutely trivial example of a VRML world. Yes, you
can store this source code into a text file that has the .wrl file extension (such
as *mycone.wrl*) and then load it directly in a VRML browser. You might even
go so far as to weave the file into an HTML Web page using the <EMBED>
tag, through which you can specify the height and width of the world as displayed by the VRML browser (see Chapter 6, "Weaving VRML into Web
Pages," for details):

```
   <HTML>
   <HEAD>
      <TITLE>My VRML Cone</TITLE>
   </HEAD>
   <BODY>

   <EMBED SRC= "mycone.wrl" WIDTH=300 HEIGHT=300>

   </BODY>
   </HTML>
```

At the end of the day, however, we've done nothing more than create a 3D shape in the form of a cone, and you've taken me at my word that this will work. To prove it to yourself, give it a shot: fire up your text editor and then type in the previous code listing and store the results as a plain ASCII text file named *mycone.wrl*. Open *mycone.wrl* directly using a VRML browser (see Appendix A, "VRML Browsers," if you haven't already installed one) or by way of an HTML file and the <EMBED> tag as shown above. Either way, your VRML browser will chew through the source code in the VRML file and display the corresponding cone shape for you to play with—assuming that there are no typing errors and the code is in fact stored in a plain ASCII file having the .wrl file extension.

This is all well and good, but something vital is missing. True, this is the first step towards learning how to create more sophisticated worlds or customize existing VRML content, but at this stage you really don't know *how* we came to understand that the Shape node would accept a Cone node. How did we know that a field in the Shape node could be set to a Cone node, and how did we know that this field was named *geometry*? What about the Cone node itself; how did we know the name and function of the fields that we've used with this node? Furthermore, how did we know that the Cone node has these fields to begin with; are there more? Finally, how did we know what we could and could not place in the field of each node?

These are all legitimate questions that have yet to be answered. In truth, this simple example is missing a few key lines of code that would allow this Cone to be rendered using 3D lighting and shading. Specifically, the Shape node's *appearance* field is missing, which in turn contains a *material* field. The following listing, for example, creates a cone having a 3D appeal the previous example lacks:

```
#VRML V2.0 utf8

Shape {

  appearance Appearance {
    material Material { }
  }

  geometry Cone {
    bottomRadius 3
    height       5
  }
}
```

By omitting the Shape node's *appearance* field altogether, the cone is rendered "unlit," meaning it lacks the lighting and shading that would otherwise make it look like a 3D object. How would you have known that the Shape node's *appearance* field controls this aspect of 3D shapes, and what do you set it to?

What you're missing at this point is a formal definition of the many nodes offered by VRML97, which is detailed information described by the VRML97 specification. Aside from a description of each node and its function, the VRML97 specification defines every field that a node contains. It's now time to get a little closer to nodes by taking a look at how the VRML97 specification defines them, specifically the fields they contain.

Note: Visual Authoring Tools

To code compelling VRML content from scratch takes significant effort and lots of patience, which is why we recommend using visual authoring tools described in Chapter 10, "Creating New VRML Worlds." Such tools, however, don't spare you from having to become familiar with the various types of nodes supported by VRML97 as well as the fields each contains. Just as you often have to know how to tweak HTML code in order to get the most out of visual Web-page development tools, the best VRML developers have a deep knowledge of the VRML97 specification that complements their skill with visual VRML authoring tools.

Note: VRML97 Specification

The VRML97 specification is available in HTML form through the Web3D Consortium. You can browse the specification online or, better yet, download it to your computer for local browsing. Take a moment to download the VRML97 specification now, as it makes an ideal companion to the material that follows:

```
http://www.web3d.org/fs_specifications.htm
```

Grouping Nodes

Grouping nodes are nodes that can contain and manage other nodes. They are considered parent nodes, while the children nodes they contain may be grouping nodes with children of their own. Nesting of grouping nodes can continue indefinitely, and, when graphically depicted, takes the form of an upside-down tree or tree roots that reveal the hierarchical relationship among the nodes defined in a VRML file (see "Scene Graphs").

VRML shapes can be grouped together to make more complex shapes, courtesy of grouping nodes, in much the same way that many of today's graphics programs (such as Illustrator, Draw, and Freehand) allow drawing shapes to be grouped together. A number of slightly different-sized VRML spheres, for example, can be grouped together into a more complicated shape resembling a bunch of grapes. A stem can be created by adding a thin brown cylinder to the top of the group.

The resulting grape bunch, complete with stem, can be treated as a single object that can be placed in a world and examined accordingly—meaning a user can pick up the entire bunch of grapes by the stem and turn them around. If it weren't for grouping nodes, the stem wouldn't actually be attached to the grapes, nor would each grape be attached to the other, meaning the stem would come off the grape bunch when moved and the grapes themselves would fall to the floor.

VRML97 grouping nodes include Anchor, Billboard, Collision, Group, Inline, LOD (Level of Detail), Switch, and Transform. The Anchor node gives VRML content hyperlinking capabilities similar to HTML's own <A HREF> tag; it is discussed in more detail in the next chapter (Chapter 6, "Weaving VRML into Web Pages"). The Transform node is covered in Chapter 7, "Customizing Location, Size, and Orientation," as this is the node used to move, resize, and reposition VRML objects. The Group node is a general grouping node and is used later in this chapter to illustrate the concept of routing events (see "Routes").

Every node supported by the current version of VRML, including grouping nodes, is precisely defined in the VRML97 specification. Links to these and all other VRML97 nodes can be found in Appendix B "VRML97 Resources." In addition, the entire VRML97 specification is available online through the Web3D Consortium (http://www.web3d.org/). It is a vital document that many developers regard as the "VRML bible" because it contains all the information they need to program in this language.

Fields

Every node contains one or more *fields* that are used to define and control properties such as size, color, and location in 3D space. The spherical shape in Figure 5-4, for example, was created using VRML's primitive Sphere node (see "Primitive Objects" later in this chapter). As explained previously, the Sphere node contains a *radius* field that is used to define the size of rendered spherical objects, such as the one seen here.

Following is the formal definition of the Sphere node, as defined by the VRML97 specification, in which the radius field is described as a floating-point number that is set to 1 by default:

```
Sphere {
    field  SFFloat  radius  1      # (0, ∞)
}
```

Programmers rely on definitions such as this to know exactly what fields a node supports, the types of data each field accepts, and the default values a field is set to. This information tells programmers what they can and cannot do with a node, in much the same way that the variables and methods of a Java class define what can be done with those programming units. Node field definitions are presented in the remainder of this book (as well as the VRML97 specification) using the following syntax:

class_specifier data_type   field_name default range

The class specifier is used to classify node fields into one of four possible types: field, exposedField, eventIn, and eventOut. At the moment we're

Figure 5-4   Spheres such as this are typically created using VRML's built-in Sphere node, one of four primitive object nodes supported by the language (see "Primitive Objects" for more details about Box, Cone, Cylinder, and Sphere nodes).

dealing with the field class of node fields, because that's the only type of field found in the Sphere node definition. Later, we'll explore exposedField, eventIn, and eventOut fields. Following the class specifier is a data type that describes the format of data that can be placed into a field (integers, strings, floating-point numbers, and so forth). The name of the field is next, after which the default value of the field is specified. Finally, the legal range of values that can be stored in the field are listed in comment form. With this in mind, consider again the Sphere node's field definition:

```
class_specifier   data_type   field_name  default  range
field             SFFloat     radius       1        0 to ∞
```

As you can see, the Sphere node definition contains only one field, the field named *radius*. The Sphere *radius* field can be set to a floating-point number as indicated by the *SFFloat* data type (see the sidebar "Field Data Types: SF vs. MF"), the default value for which is 1. This means that the default radius for every sphere created in VRML is 1, which corresponds to one meter (size values in VRML are expressed in terms of meters, as the section "Coordinate Systems" explains later). Finally, the legal values that can be supplied for the radius field range from zero (0) to infinity (∞), meaning any numbers other than negative ones are valid.

Each type of node contains fields that are unique to it. A Cone node, for example, doesn't contain the *radius* field that the Sphere node does because cones don't have a need for this particular field. Instead, cones require an entirely different set of fields, including a special *bottomRadius* field that controls the size of the bottom of such shapes. The following snippet of code lists the formal definition for VRML's built-in Cone node, which is quite different in terms of the fields it supports when compared to the Sphere node:

```
Cone {
    field  SFFloat  bottomRadius  1      # (0, ∞)
    field  SFFloat  height        2      # (0, ∞)
    field  SFBool   side          TRUE
    field  SFBool   bottom        TRUE
}
```

Cone nodes consist of a *bottomRadius* field that is used to set the size of cone bases, as well as a *height* field that is used to determine the height of cones when measured from base to peak. In addition, Cone nodes contain visibility fields *side* and *bottom* that are used to control whether or not the sides and base of the rendered cone are visible to the viewer (a funnel or party hat can be created from a cone by hiding its base, for example). Both

Field Data Types: SF vs. MF

Node-field data types can either be single value or multiple value, as indicated by the presence of SF (Single-value Field) or MF (Multiple-value Field) immediately before the actual data type. Fields that are listed as SF data types, such as SFFloat, can contain only one value (a SFFloat field, for example, can only hold a single floating-point value), while MF data types, such as MFFloat, can accept an array of values.

Unlike SF data types, values supplied to MF data types are enclosed in square brackets, where each value is separated from the others with a comma or whitespace (VRML actually considers commas to be the same as whitespace). In cases where only one value is supplied to an MF data type field, the brackets may be omitted. The following examples illustrate legal settings for an MFFloat field named *length*:

```
length 5.25      # only one value supplied, so no need for
                   brackets
length [5.25]    # one value with brackets length [5.25,]
# one value, with brackets and a comma
length [5.25, 456, 1]   # multiple values separated by
                          comma
length [5.25  456  1]   # multiple values separated by
                          spaces
```

VRML supports a number of data types, including Bool (true/false Boolean values), Float (32-bit floating-point values), Int32 (32-bit signed integer values), String (one or more characters surrounded by quotes), and many more. Following are examples of several of the data types support by VRML that are used throughout the remainder of this chapter and those that follow, while Appendix B, "VRML97 Resources," contains links to a comprehensive listing of all data types supported by the language:

Data type	*Specifies*	*Examples*
Bool	Boolean values.	TRUE, FALSE
Float	Single-precision floating-point numbers.	5, 3.141, 12.5e-3
Int32	32-bit integer numbers.	10, -5, 230
Node	A VRML node.	Shape, Cone, Box
String	A sequence of characters.	"hi", "GOODBYE"

the *side* and *bottom* fields accept Boolean true/false values, as opposed to the floating-point integer values required by the *bottomRadius* and *height* fields.

Because each Cone node field has a default value, as all VRML node fields do, it is possible to create these shapes using little more than the name of the node itself. In fact, that's exactly what the following VRML code does:

```
#VRML V2.0 utf8

Shape {
   geometry Cone {}
}
```

In this example, a Shape node uses the default Cone node for its geometry, or form, resulting in a 3D cone object that measures two full meters from tip to base and has a bottom radius of one meter. Of course, defaults

Scripting

VRML's Script node is a general-purpose extension mechanism developers can use to add custom functionality to a world. Script nodes don't have any special capabilities, yet they can be loaded with executable script programs ("scripts") written in languages such as Java or JavaScript. Scripts are typically written to calculate complex object animation paths, provide characters in a world with artificial intelligence, maintain the state of multiple concurrent users to facilitate multiuser worlds, support complex user interaction through custom user interfaces, and encode capabilities that aren't possible using VRML's other built-in nodes.

VRML also supports advanced scripting through what's known as the External Authoring Interface (EAI), which allows programs outside of the VRML world to control aspects of the world (such as a Java applet woven into the same page as a VRML world). Where the Script node is considered an *internal* form of scripting, as the code in such nodes is a formal part of the world, EAI gives the developer *external* hooks into a VRML world. For more details about VRML scripting, visit http://www.web3dgallery.com/vrml/scripting/.

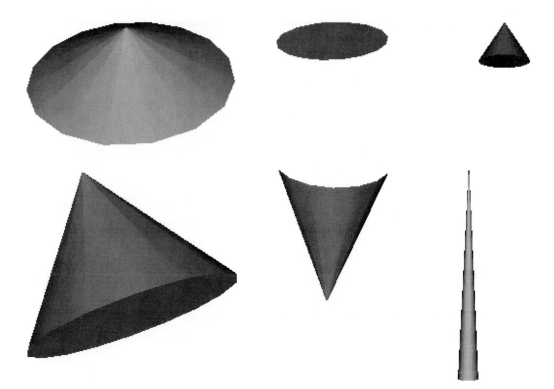

Figure 5-5   The shape and size of primitive cone objects is controlled through the four Cone node fields (*bottomRadius, height, side, and bottom*).

are just the beginning: the real power in fields lies in their ability to give programmers control over node attributes. Figure 5-5 shows several different cone shapes created by setting Cone node fields to various values.

Sphere and Cone are just two of the many nodes supported by VRML; yet, owing to their simplicity, they are among the most useful to study when learning about fields. However, fields aren't the only thing nodes can contain. A number of nodes also support a special type of field known as an *exposedField.* Unlike standard fields, exposedFields can be set and manipulated by scripts (hence the name exposedField, indicating that their functionality is *exposed* in ways that normal fields are not) and are closely tied to events.

Field Types

VRML fields can be classified into one of four types: *field, exposedField, eventIn,* and *eventOut*. Both field and exposedField are used to set attributes of a node (color, size, position, and so forth), while eventIn and eventOut are used to control the dispatching and handling of events (mouse activity, proximity sensors, passage of time, and so forth).

While fields are considered private node members, exposedFields are public node members that can be accessed through scripts and are more closely associated with events than regular fields are. Following is an overview of each class of field supported by VRML:

Field Class	*Description*
eventIn	An event *received* by the node; other nodes can set this field.
eventOut	An event *sent* by the node; other nodes can receive values from this field, but not set them.
exposedField	A *public* member of the node; other nodes are free to set this field and also receive them.
field	A *private* member of the node; no access to other nodes.

Events

Event support is the single most significant advantage that VRML97 has over VRML 1.0, and, in fact, is the primary reason that truly interactive content can be created with VRML97 where the original version of the language was limited to static objects and scenes. Thanks to events, VRML97 content can respond to user activity (such as mouse movement and mouse clicks), user presence (entering or leaving an area, or being within a certain proximity to an item), or the passing of time.

Events allow objects to have and express behavior, allowing for more realistic and lifelike virtual experiences. A VRML lion, for example, could be programmed to respond to user presence by standing up and roaring. If you don't back off within five seconds it might roar again, or slowly begin walking towards you with jaws agape. And, if you were crazy enough to try it, you'd quickly realize that waving your mouse at the beast provokes a savage attack in which you're ripped to bits (and possibly bytes).

This behavior is possible because the events the user generates trigger activity in the lion, which, when explained in slightly more technical terms, means that the various fields used to represent the complex lion node actually change in response to mouse, presence, and time events. By dynamically changing the values of node fields in response to events, the rendered object which that node (or group of nodes) represents will appear to change: it exhibits behavior.

The *eventIn* and *eventOut* fields of a node are used to receive and send events, although not every node supports events, and those that do don't always support both sending and receiving of events. The Cone node described earlier, for example, doesn't support events itself. Nowhere in the Cone node definition will you find *eventIn* or *eventOut* fields. As a result, cones can't create events, nor can an event be sent directly to a cone.

Instead, event handling for cones is done through an event-aware parent node that actually supports events. The parent node of a cone, for example, can receive an event saying something to the effect of "the user has just moved the mouse over the cone" that it might be programmed to react to. In response to such an event the parent might, for example, transform the child Cone node it contains in such a way that the cone actually begins spinning end over end.

Although this is an overly simplified description, the point is that some nodes handle events directly, while many do not and so must rely on other nodes in order to respond to events. Those nodes that support events directly do so through the *eventIn* and *eventOut* fields. The *eventIn* field is used to receive events, while *eventOut* can be considered the conduit through which the events generated by a node are sent. An *exposedField*, meanwhile, allows both sending and receiving of events.

All fields of type *exposedField* have an *eventIn* and *eventOut* implicitly associated with them (by implicit we mean that they're part of the node, although you won't see such fields listed in the formal node definition). The name of the corresponding *eventIn* is preceded with "set_" while the *eventOut* has a "_changed" suffix. An *exposedField* named *color*, for example, would automatically have an associated *eventIn* named *set_color* as well as an *eventOut* named *color_changed*. As a result, the single *exposedField* provides a mechanism for both sending and receiving events.

When an *eventIn* is received by an *exposedField*, the field value is immediately changed and the scene is updated as necessary to reflect the change. An *eventOut* is automatically generated with the value of the new field value, allowing the change of state to be communicated with other nodes.

Note: Events and Sensors

Events are a mechanism for passing data back and forth among nodes, since they can be routed from one node to another as explained in the next section. Events don't just happen; they are generated by such things as the passage of time or user activity. To trap and handle such events, VRML programmers use sensors as described in Chapter 4, "VRML Overview." In the following section we'll use a TouchSensor node to respond to mouse movement, as it is one of the easiest sensors to understand. VRML offers a variety of other sensor nodes, however. CylinderSensor, PlaneSensor, ProximitySensor, SphereSensor, TimeSensor, and VisibilitySensor are each described through links found in Appendix B, "VRML97 Resources."

Routes

Conceptually, events can be compared to the input and output jacks of traditional audio equipment, such as a stereo system and loudspeakers. A stereo, for example, has both input and output jacks (the equivalent to a node's *eventIn* and *eventOut* fields), while speakers generally have only input jacks (*eventIn*). To hook up a sound system, all you have to do is use audio cable to connect the output of the stereo to the input of the speakers.

You might, however, also want to connect a CD player to your stereo, and so would use an additional segment of audio cable to connect the output jack of the CD player to the input jack of the stereo. This allows the audio generated by your CD player to be passed through the stereo and into the speakers.

VRML events work in a very similar way. Some nodes generate events, some receive events, and some do both (while some don't support events at all, and must rely on other nodes to do the work for them as described earlier). And, much like the wiring that connects the various components in a stereo system, VRML allows developers to connect *eventOut* and *eventIn* fields using *routes*. A *route* connects the *eventOut* field of a node to an *eventIn* of a different node and can be considered the wiring used to connect event generators to event receivers, as illustrated in Figure 5-6.

In order to support event wiring, VRML offers a special command called ROUTE, which allows the programmer to wire together events between nodes. Following is the syntax of the ROUTE command:

```
ROUTE nodeA.eventOutName TO nodeB.eventInName
```

R O U T E

eventOut   eventIn

Figure 5-6 Routes wire together the *eventOut* field of one node with the *eventIn* field of another, allowing nodes to communicate and exchange information based on user activity, presence, or the passing of time.

This command essentially says "when an eventOut of this name is generated by node A, send it to the eventIn of this name found in node B." Listing 5.1, for example, uses a ROUTE statement that looks something like this:

```
ROUTE nodeA.isOver TO nodeB.set_on
```

Although this isn't the exact line of code actually appearing in Listing 5.1, the concept is similar: node A's *isOver* eventOut is routed to node B's implicitly defined *set_on eventIn*. If you inspect the code, however, you'll see that the precise ROUTE statement is:

```
ROUTE TS.isOver TO DL.set_on
```

What's going on? If you scan through the code of Listing 5.1, you'll see that it contains both a TouchSensor and a DirectionalLight node. The TouchSensor node is used to track "touch" activity such as mouse clicks and movement, and so it contains a Boolean *eventOut* field called $isOver$, as you can see from the following VRML97 specification definition:

```
TouchSensor {
   exposedField SFBool  enabled    TRUE
   eventOut     SFVec3f hitNormal_changed
   eventOut     SFVec3f hitPoint_changed
   eventOut     SFVec2f hitTexCoord_changed
   eventOut     SFBool  isActive
   eventOut     SFBool  isOver
   eventOut     SFTime  touchTime
}
```

The $isOver$ event is generated whenever the user moves the mouse over any geometry nodes contained within the same grouping node in which a TouchSensor appears. As an SFBool data type, this event can have either a TRUE or FALSE value. By reading the following VRML97 specification description of the TouchSensor node, we know that the value of *isOver* is TRUE when the mouse moves over the cone:

The isOver eventOut reflects the state of the pointing device with regard to whether it is pointing towards the TouchSensor node's geometry or not. When the pointing device changes state from a position such that its bearing does not intersect any of the TouchSensor node's geometry to one in which it does intersect geometry, an isOver TRUE event is generated. When the pointing device moves from a position such that its bearing intersects geometry to one in which it no longer intersects the geometry, or some other geometry is obstructing the Touch-Sensor node's geometry, an isOver FALSE event is generated. These events are generated only when the pointing device has moved and changed 'over' state. Events are not generated if the geometry itself is animating and moving underneath the pointing device.

Although this is a bit difficult to digest in one pass, it's what we needed to know (you won't find the specification to be exhilarating reading by any stretch of the imagination; it's solid, practically sterile documentation). Because the TouchSensor and cone are both children of the same Group node, the `isOver` TRUE event will be generated by the sensor any time you move your mouse over the cone. With this in mind, let us actually trigger some type of visual feedback when the event occurs by incorporating a light source node in the code (by way of the DirectionalLight node discussed in Chapter 9, "Customizing Light, Background, Fog, and Sound").

When this event is generated, we'll shine a red light on the cone. To make this happen, we need to route the sensor's `isOver` event to the Directional-Light node. Consider what would happen, however, if you simply referred to each node by its proper name in the ROUTE statement:

```
ROUTE TouchSensor.isOver TO DirectionalLight.set_on
```

Although this seems just fine with the current example, imagine if this scene contained more than one DirectionalLight node. Which node would the `isOver` event be sent to? To avoid such confusion, a special construct called DEF is used to give each node a unique name of your choosing. DEF, which stands for *define*, must be applied to both the *eventOut* node and the *eventIn* node of a route, meaning both TouchSensor and DirectionalLight nodes get a unique name that is then referred to in the ROUTE command.

You can think of DEF as a means of assigning identifiers to nodes that you can then use to reference the node as needed later, much like a variable name. DEF, in fact, has a corresponding USE construct that is vital to VRML's ability to reuse objects and avoid duplicating code (see Chapter 8, "Customizing Object Color and Texture," for details). Listing 5.1 defines very terse names for the TouchSensor and DirectionalLight nodes, "TS" and "DL" (the abbreviations of the formal node name), although you could just as easily have selected more descriptive names, as the following snippet illustrates:

```
DEF MovementSensor TouchSensor {}
DEF RedLight DirectionalLight {}

ROUTE MovementSensor.isOver TO RedLight.set_on
```

For the sake of brevity, however, and to avoid possible confusion between DEF names and the formal node names, Listing 5.1 distinguishes very clearly which is which by assigning each node a name based on the initials of the node itself. Following this listing is the formal VRML97 specification definition of the Group, TouchSensor, and DirectionalLight nodes used in this code (see Appendix B, "VRML97 Resources," for an overview of the fields in each node).

Listing 5.1   touch.wrl

```
#VRML V2.0 utf8

Group {

  children [

    Shape {
        appearance Appearance {
          material Material { }
        }
        geometry Cone { }
    }


    DEF TS TouchSensor { }     # define the sensor "TS"

    DEF DL DirectionalLight { # define the light "DL"
        color 1 0 0
        on FALSE
    }

  ]

  ROUTE TS.isOver TO DL.set_on
}
```

Upon inspecting the node definitions that follow, you'll no doubt notice that the DirectionalLight node doesn't actually contain an *eventIn* field called *set_on*. Instead, *on* is the closest field name that you'll find in this node, although it's of a field type *exposedField*, not *eventIn*. Because fields of type *exposedField* implicitly have a corresponding *eventIn* and *eventOut* as described earlier, the DirectionalLight node's *on* field automatically has a corresponding *eventIn* named *set_on* and *eventOut* named *on_changed*.

Knowing this, we were able to route the Boolean *eventOut* generated by the sensor to the implicit *set_on* eventIn of the light. Because the *on* field is defined as being a Boolean value, this is a legal route: the TRUE value of the *eventOut* is accepted by the implicitly defined *set_on* Boolean *eventIn*. You can opt, however, to omit the "set_" portion of the *eventIn* name, as the VRML routing system is smart enough to pass the event to the proper field, meaning the following ROUTE statement would also have done the trick:

```
ROUTE TS.isOver TO DL.on
```

Note: Matching Event Types

The data types of the eventOut *and* eventIn *used in a ROUTE statement must match, as they do in this case (both are SFBool values). You can't, for example, route an MFFloat* eventOut *to an SFBool* eventIn.

Event Fanning

A single *eventOut* can be routed to multiple *eventIn* fields, allowing one event to be handled by multiple objects (a technique known as *fan-out*). The *eventOut* of a light switch, for example, could be connected to the *eventIn* of every light source in a room (ceiling lights, floor lamps, wall sconces, and so forth). When the light switch is flicked to the "on" position, all the lights in the room will receive the event and turn on in response to it.

Similarly, a single *eventIn* can be wired to many different *eventOut* fields (the *fan-in* technique). A floor lamp, for example, can be wired not only to the light switch, but also to its own switch on the base of the lamp, a sound-activated clapper device, and even a proximity sensor that turns the light on when someone walks into the room. This example of event fan-in allows a single light to respond to multiple "on" events, each generated by a unique object.

```
Group {
  eventIn       MFNode   addChildren
  eventIn       MFNode   removeChildren
  exposedField MFNode   children       []
  field         SFVec3f bboxCenter     0  0  0      # (-∞,∞)
  field         SFVec3f bboxSize       -1 -1 -1 # (0, ∞) or -
1,-1,-1
}


TouchSensor {
  exposedField SFBool  enabled    TRUE
  eventOut       SFVec3f hitNormal_changed
  eventOut       SFVec3f hitPoint_changed
  eventOut       SFVec2f hitTexCoord_changed
  eventOut       SFBool  isActive
  eventOut       SFBool  isOver
  eventOut       SFTime  touchTime
}


DirectionalLight {
  exposedField SFFloat ambientIntensity  0       # [0,1]
  exposedField SFColor color             1 1 1   # [0,1]
  exposedField SFVec3f direction         0 0 -1  # (-∞,∞)
  exposedField SFFloat intensity         1       # [0,1]
  exposedField SFBool  on                TRUE
}
```

Shapes, Geometry, and Appearance

Most of the 3D objects that appear in VRML worlds are the result of Shape nodes at work. Shape nodes are used to render objects based on two key attributes: geometry and appearance. Geometry gives a shape form (such as a box, spiral, or pyramid form), while a shape's appearance describes surface attributes such as color, lighting, and texture. Every Shape node has *geometry* and *appearance* fields, which together determine how an object looks.

The source code that is found earlier in the "Nodes" section shows the basic Shape node in action, for which the formal definition is:

```
Shape {
   exposedField SFNode appearance NULL
   exposedField SFNode geometry   NULL
}
```

As you might have guessed, both the *appearance* and *geometry* fields of
the Shape node are, in fact, nodes in their own right. As a result, the Shape
node is a parent to both appearance and geometry child nodes, which accounts for the code appearing in the "Nodes" section. In that example a
shape was created based on the geometry of a primitive Cone node, while its
appearance was defined by an Appearance node, which in turn contains a
Material node.

The same is true for the source code in Listing 5.2. The code in this listing
is a slight variation on the shape code you've already seen. In this example,
however, a primitive Box node is used for geometry. And, instead of green,
the color of this object is red. As with the previous cone example, the Shape
node *appearance* field is set to an Appearance node. The Appearance node,
in turn, contains a Material node. By setting the *diffuseColor* field of the Material node to red, the color of the shape itself is set to red. The result is the
red, 3D box seen in Figure 5-7.

Listing 5.2   redBox.wrl

```
#VRML V2.0 utf8

# This is an example of a very simple
# Shape node that uses the primitive
# Box object for geometry (form).

Shape {
  appearance Appearance {
    material Material {
      diffuseColor 1 0 0   # R G B (this shape is pure red)
    }
  }
  geometry Box { }           # this shape is the form of a box
}
```

Keep in mind that *geometry* and *appearance* are merely field names of the
Shape node, while the term *Appearance node* refers to an actual node. Thus,
the *appearance* field of a Shape node can be set to an Appearance node, one
of the many built-in VRML nodes. Following is the structure of the Appearance node as defined by the VRML97 specification:

Figure 5-7 A primitive box shape, the result of VRML code found in Listing 5.2.

```
Appearance {
    exposedField SFNode material           NULL
    exposedField SFNode texture            NULL
    exposedField SFNode textureTransform NULL
}
```

As you can see, the Appearance node can contain its own nodes (each of which has NULL for a default value, meaning nothing is actually associated with these fields; the programmer must explicitly set NULL fields). This is, in fact, exactly what's going on in Listing 5.2; the Appearance node's *material* field is declared to use a Material node, which is yet another formal VRML node (remember, the field name and node names are two different things). The result is a nesting of nodes 3 levels deep, with Shape at the top, Appearance in the middle, and Material at the bottom (Shape → Appearance → Material), which creates the simple scene graph in Figure 5-8.

Figure 5-8 Even simple VRML scenes, such as the one created in Listing 5.2, are arranged into a scene graph structure.

Chock Full of Nodes

VRML97 nodes used to describe shapes and geometry include Box, Cone, Coordinate, Cylinder, ElevationGrid, Extrusion, IndexedFaceSet, IndexedLineSet, Normal, PointSet, Shape, Sphere, and Text. To alter the appearance of shapes, VRML97 offers a number of appearance-related nodes, such as Appearance, Color, FontStyle, ImageTexture, Material, MovieTexture, PixelTexture, TextureCoordinate, and Texture-Transform. Some of these nodes are discussed here, while others are explained in more detail in the following chapters. Appendix B, "VRML97 Resources," provides links that describe every VRML97 node. For a comprehensive overview of each node, you can also turn to the VRML97 specification available through the Web3D Consortium (http://www.web3d.org/).

```
Material {
    exposedField SFFloat ambientIntensity  0.2          # [0,1]
    exposedField SFColor diffuseColor       0.8 0.8 0.8 # [0,1]
    exposedField SFColor emissiveColor      0 0 0        # [0,1]
    exposedField SFFloat shininess          0.2          # [0,1]
    exposedField SFColor specularColor      0 0 0        # [0,1]
    exposedField SFFloat transparency       0            # [0,1]
}
```

We could just as easily have used the Appearance node's *texture* and *textureTransform* fields to wrap an image around the cone geometry, which is a powerful technique known as *texture mapping* that can radically alter the appearance of a shape. In Chapter 8, "Customizing Object Color and Texture," you'll learn how to use texture maps and the Material node to dramatically alter the surface appearance of shapes. For now it's simply enough to realize that Shape nodes contain *appearance* and *geometry* fields, each of which can contain its own nodes, which can in turn contain other nodes, leading to the hierarchical nature of scene graphs as described earlier.

Primitive Objects

VRML offers four fundamental geometric nodes that can stand on their own or be combined to form even more complex objects. Box, Cone, Cylinder, and Sphere nodes are built directly into VRML, allowing developers to quickly and easily add these 3D objects to their scenes (see Figure 5-9).

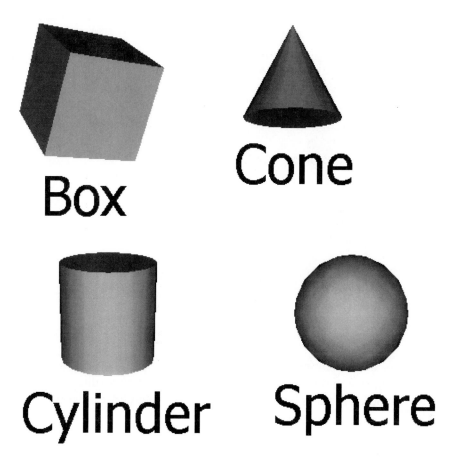

Figure 5-9   The shapes seen here were created using VRML's four primitive object nodes: Box, Cone, Cylinder, and Sphere.

You've seen the VRML97 specification definition for the Cone and Sphere nodes, and now it's time to introduce you to the Box and Cylinder nodes:

```
Box {
  field     SFVec3f size  2 2 2    # (0, ∞)
}

Cylinder {
  field     SFBool     bottom  TRUE
  field     SFFloat    height  2        # (0, ∞)
  field     SFFloat    radius  1        # (0, ∞)
  field     SFBool     side    TRUE
  field     SFBool     top     TRUE
}
```

Figure 5-10 This VRML snowman was created using nothing more than primitive spheres and cones.

Developers are encouraged to use primitive objects, as they are built into the VRML language and easily rendered by browsers. As a result, you'll find that boxes, cones, cylinders, and spheres populate many of the worlds you explore.

Of course, a world full of nothing but primitive objects usually isn't much to stand up and cheer about, which is why these forms are often combined to create more complex shapes such as the snowman seen in Figure 5-10. Although it's comprised of little more than spheres and cones, the obvious

Note: Default Object Positioning

Primitive objects are, by default, placed in the center of a scene unless an exact location in 3D space is specified by the developer. The center of a 3D scene is known as the origin and is located at the intersection of the world coordinate system's X, Y, and Z axes. By default, primitive objects are located at 0,0,0 (the origin coordinates). A Transform node is used to move objects into a position other than the origin. See "Coordinate Systems" later in this chapter to learn more about VRML's 3D coordinate system, the world coordinate system, and the Transform node.

result of combining a few primitive objects, this snowman is considerably more interesting to look at and play with than these objects on their own.

Complex Objects

Although primitive objects can be combined to create more complicated objects, such as the snowman described above, VRML isn't limited to these simple geometric shapes. The language also supports arbitrary shapes that can be created through vastly more complex nodes such as ElevationGrid, Extrusion, IndexedFaceSet, IndexedLineSet, and PointSet.

The ElevationGrid node is commonly used to create terrain grids, such as the mountain range and valley seen in Figure 5-11. This node allows VRML developers to construct rectangular grids comprised of variously spaced rows and columns, where each point of the grid can be controlled independently of the others. Peaks and valleys are created by supplying height values for grid points, which results in elevated or depressed grid areas that have the appearance of natural terrain often seen in the real world.

The Extrusion node creates machined objects by sweeping a 2D shape, or cross section, along a 3D path, or spine (as described in Chapter 3, "Entering the Third Dimension"). Similar in concept to creating a bubble by waving a soap-covered wand through the air, the Extrusion node is particularly useful in constructing twisting, turning shapes such as slides, screws, spirals, donuts, and similar geometric forms. Because the shape of the cross section can be dynamically altered as it sweeps along its course, the Extrusion node can also be used to create complex objects such as those in Figure 5-12.

The IndexedFaceSet node is used to create arbitrarily complex shapes comprised of polygon faces, such as triangles and quadrilaterals (see Chapter 3, "Entering the Third Dimension," for details). Arguably the most complicated VRML97 node, IndexedFaceSet is perhaps the most capable when it comes to constructing sophisticated objects. The Volkswagen Beetle seen in Figure 5-13, for example, was created entirely of IndexedFaceSet nodes. Likewise, the geometry of the praying mantis (see Figure 5-13) is defined using nothing more than polygonal faces courtesy of the IndexedFaceSet node.

In addition to the complex objects that may be created with the Elevation-Grid, Extrusion, and IndexedFaceSet nodes, VRML97 also supports line and point shapes. Using the IndexedLineSet and PointSet nodes, developers can create shapes comprised of lines and points as illustrated in Figure 5-14 and 5-15.

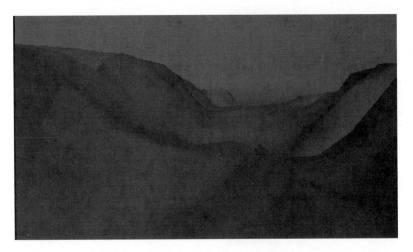

Figure 5-11   The ElevationGrid node is typically used to create terrain grids, such as this mountain range (http://www.irony.com/igmmte/) and valley (http://pandora.mts-inc.com/~rhian/).

Figure 5-12 The Extrusion node creates shapes by sweeping a 2D cross section along a path in 3D space. The wheels of this car and most of the parts of this jet were created using the Extrusion node (http://www.cybelius.com/ and http://vrml.environs.com/ivan/).

Figure 5-13   The IndexedFaceSet node constructs shapes using polygonal faces, such as triangles and quadrilaterals. This Volkswagen Beetle (courtesy of USWeb/CKS and Shout Interactive) and praying mantis were created entirely of IndexedFaceSet nodes (see http://www.ento.vt.edu/~sharov/3d/3dinsect.html).

Figure 5-14 The IndexedLineSet node allows developers to construct line-based shapes, such as this conceptual architectural structure (http://www.construct.net/worlds/behaviors/) and the strings of this Irish harp (http://www.geometrek.com/vrml/objects.html).

Figure 5-15   The PointSet node is used to create shapes comprised of points, such as the star burst and star field seen here.

Text Objects

Along with primitive and complex objects, VRML also supports text objects. VRML text objects are rendered flat on the screen, meaning you can't see them when viewed from the side (see Figure 5-16). VRML's built-in Text node is used to display one or more lines of text in a scene, the definition for which is:

```
Text {
  exposedField MFString   string       []
  exposedField SFNode     fontStyle    NULL
  exposedField MFFloat    length       []      # [0, ∞)
  exposedField SFFloat    maxExtent    0.0     # [0, ∞)
}
```

You'll learn more about the Text node in Chapter 8, "Customizing Object Color and Texture," although the node is worth considering now if only to familiarize yourself with MF data types. Node fields can hold one or more values, as the "Field Data Types: SF vs. MF" sidebar found in the earlier "Fields" section explains. Those that hold a single value are called Single-value Field (SF) data types, while those that accept more than one value are known as Multiple-value Field (MF) data types.

Both the *fontStyle* and *maxExtent* Text node fields are SF data types, meaning these fields can be set to a single value. The *fontStyle* field accepts a single node (a FontStyle node) that describes the font face and size in which the text will be displayed, while *maxExtent* accepts a single floating-point integer that sets the maximum width the text is allowed when rendered. If the rendered text is longer than *maxExtent* specifies, it will be squeezed into the width described by this field (the text is displayed normally if shorter than the allotted size).

The *string* and *length* fields, on the other hand, are MF data types, meaning they accept an array of values. "MF" precedes the actual data type accepted by these fields, which is the most obvious tip-off that they're multivalue fields. You might also have noticed that the default value for both of these fields is a set of opening and closing braces, [], which indicates an array data structure in VRML (and many other languages, such as C, C++, and Java).

Because it is an array, more than one line of text can be supplied to the Text node's *string* field. Likewise, one or more floating-point integers can be passed to the *length* field, which is used to control the width of each line of text supplied in the *string* field. This allows each line of text to have its own unique width setting; if the line of text is longer than the width it is allotted, it will be squeezed into that space. If it is shorter than the assigned width, the

Figure 5-16   Text in VRML is rendered flat on the screen, making it invisible when viewed from the side.

text will be stretched to fill up the space. The *length* field, in essence, gives VRML authors typesetting control over the text appearing in their worlds.

Listing 5.3 contains the source code used to create two strings of text ("HELLO" and "WORLD!") in a VRML world. In this example the default *length* and *maxExtent* Text node field settings are used, although the *fontStyle* field is set to a FontStyle node in which the style and size of the text font are defined.

Listing 5.3   "text.wrl"

```
#VRML V2.0 utf8

# This is an example of a Shape node that
# uses the Text node for geometry (form).

Shape {

   appearance Appearance {
```

(Listing 5.3 continues on page 184)

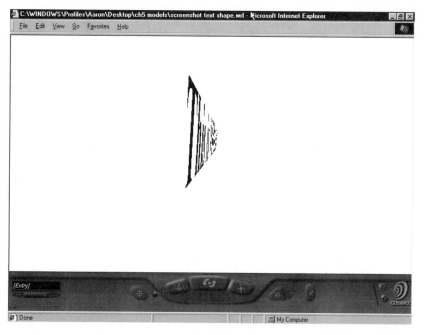

Figure 5-16   Continued

```
      material Material { }
    }

    geometry Text {
      fontStyle FontStyle {
        style "BOLD"
        size 4
      }
      string ["HELLO", "WORLD!"]
    }

  }
```

Coordinate Systems

VRML uses a 3D Cartesian coordinate system to describe the exact location of objects residing in 3D space. VRML's 3D coordinate system is an extension of the flat, two-dimensional Cartesian coordinate system that you were taught in math class in school.

As Chapter 3, "Working in the Third Dimension," explains, a 2D Cartesian coordinate system is expressed in terms of a horizontal X axis and a vertical Y axis that intersect at a location known as the *origin*. Coordinates in the system are given as a pair of X and Y values in the form x,y (such as 5,9 or 12,8) that together pinpoint an exact location in the system relative to the origin located in the center at 0,0.

The X axis is labeled with numbers that increase in value from left to right, while the Y axis is labeled with numbers that increase in value from bottom to top. Positive X values appear to the right of the origin, while negative X values fall to the left of the origin. Similarly, positive Y values appear above the origin, while negative values fall below the origin. Thus the coordinate 5,–2 describes a point that is located exactly five units to the right of the origin and two units below it, as illustrated in Figure 5-17.

VRML's 3D Cartesian coordinate system extends the flat 2D Cartesian coordinate system to include an axis that measures depth. The Z axis, illustrated in Figure 5-18, intersects with the X and Y axes at the origin and is used to position objects either close to or far away from the viewer of the scene, giving objects a sense of depth. The Z axis is labeled with numbers that increase in value from back to front, where positive Z values appear in front of the origin and negative numbers fall behind the origin.

Unlike a 2D coordinate system, which requires only an X and a Y value to locate a point in two-dimensional space, the 3D coordinate system used by VRML requires three values to define a point in three-dimensional space: X,

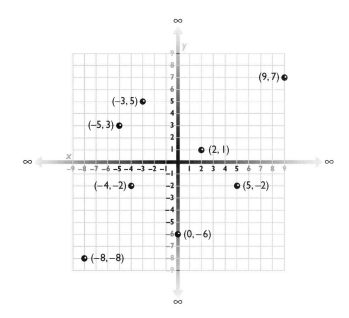

Figure 5-17 The exact location of any point on a 2D Cartesian coordinate system can be defined by a pair of X-axis and Y-axis coordinate values supplied in the form x,y.

Y, and Z, which are expressed as a 3D coordinate in the form x,y,z (such as 5,3,10 or 8,3,1). X and Y values define a point on these axes, moving it further to the left and right (X) or up and down (Y) just as in a 2D coordinate system, while Z values define the front-to-back position of the point relative to the origin located at 0,0,0.

Consider the scenario when a 3D world is viewed "straight-on," with the origin located in the center of the scene, the X axis running horizontally to the left and right, and the Y axis running up and down in the vertical direction as seen in Figure 5-18. In this case, the Z axis runs from front to back, meaning a point with a high positive Z value is closer to the viewer than points with low or negative Z values. A point defined by 3D coordinates 5,3,-8 is located eight units behind the origin, for example, placing it further away from the viewer than a point defined with the coordinates 5,3,10 (which is 10 units in front of the origin, and therefore closer to the viewer).

However, because VRML is an interactive form of 3D, scenes are almost never viewed exclusively from straight-on as I've just described. We're free to move about and explore scenes from any viewpoint that we'd like, which in turn alters the orientation of the X, Y, and Z axes in relation to our constantly changing position in the world. You might, for example, start out looking at a scene straight-on, but quickly run down the Z axis and turn around to view the scene from "behind" the origin. As a result, the point defined by the 3D coordinate 5,3,-8 would actually be closer to you than the point located at 5,3,10.

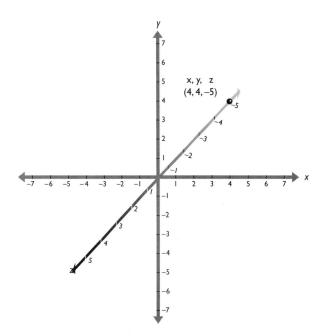

Figure 5-18 The exact location of any point on a 3D Cartesian coordinate system can be defined as a set of x,y,z numbers, where z defines a position on the Z axis (the depth axis).

Similarly, you might decide to walk over and straddle the X axis while facing the origin. In this case, the X axis now becomes the "depth" axis that runs toward and away from you, while the Z axis now runs to your left and right. Likewise, you might decide to fly up and look down at items from above, further scrambling your sense of exactly where the X, Y, and Z axes reside in relation to your ever-changing viewpoint. As the viewer of a scene, you really don't care; you're free to explore in all directions without concern for the coordinate system.

When you create VRML content, however, or customize existing VRML content as described in the following chapters, you will become intimate with the 3D coordinate system described here. In Chapter 7, "Customizing Location, Size, and Orientation," for example, you'll spend a good deal of your time dealing with 3D coordinates in order to place and position VRML objects in 3D space, rearranging and repositioning objects in the scene as you see fit.

Note: SFVec3f and MFVec3f

VRML's 3D coordinates are typically passed to fields in the form of three floating-point numbers as defined by VRML's SFVec3f and MFVec3f data types ("Vec3" stands for "three-dimensional vector," while "f" stands for "floating-point number"). The Box node's size *field, for example, is defined as a SFVec3f data type. As a result, you must supply three different floating-point numbers to this field, each separated by a space, that together determine how large the resulting box object is along each of the 3D coordinate axes (x,y,z).*

Measuring Units

The real-world value that a coordinate system's *unit* of measurement corresponds to varies from system to system. The coordinate system of a city map, for example, is different from that of a country map. A unit in a city map might represent one mile, while a country map unit could easily represent several hundred miles. A coordinate system used to describe the location of transistors on a circuit board, on the other hand, is measured in microns, not miles.

VRML numbers related to location or size are a measure of meters, where one unit corresponds exactly to one meter. The default Sphere node radius, for example, is exactly one meter. Similarly, a default cone is two meters high and has a base radius of one meter. Objects such as these reside in 3D space that is also measured in terms of meters. Thus, meters are the *scale* of measurement used by VRML to describe size and distance.

Numeric values are also used in VRML to describe angles, time, and colors. These numbers each correspond to a different unit of measurement, as described by the following table:

Category	*Unit*
Linear distance	Meters
Angles	Radians
Time	Seconds
Color	RGB (Red, Green, Blue in form [0.,1.], [0.,1.], [0., 1.])

The 3D coordinate system of a scene is known as the *world coordinate system* and may be different from the coordinate system of individual objects in the scene. This is especially true of inlined objects, as they are often created independent of the scenes in which they appear (see the"VRML files" discussion in Chapter 4, "VRML Overview," for more information about inlined objects).

Because any number of coordinate systems may be used in a single VRML scene, developers often translate objects from one coordinate system into another. The coordinate system of a kitchen chair object, for example, would be translated into the world coordinate system of an entire kitchen scene for proper placement and scale. Likewise, an inlined refrigerator would also require coordinate transformation. Coordinate transformation is accomplished using the Transform node, a versatile grouping node that is also used to scale, rotate, move, and animate objects in a scene (you'll use the Transform node in Chapter 7 "Customizing Location, Size, and Orientation").

```
Transform {
  eventIn       MFNode       addChildren
  eventIn       MFNode       removeChildren
  exposedField SFVec3f      center          0 0 0    # (-∞,∞)
  exposedField MFNode       children        []
  exposedField SFRotation   rotation        0 0 1 0 # [-1,1],(- ∞, ∞)
  exposedField SFVec3f      scale           1 1 1    # (0, ∞)
  exposedField SFRotation   scaleOrientation 0 0 1 0 # [-1,1],(- ∞, ∞)
  exposedField SFVec3f      translation     0 0 0    # (-∞,∞)
  field         SFVec3f      bboxCenter      0 0 0    # (-∞,∞)
  field         SFVec3f      bboxSize        -1 -1 -1 # (0, ∞) or -1,-1,-1,
}
```

Summary

Scene graphs are created using nodes. Nodes are the fundamental VRML programming unit and contain data and event fields that define both state and behavior (VRML nodes are analogous to classes used in object-oriented languages such as C++ and Java). VRML97 has nearly 60 different built-in nodes that developers can use to construct interactive and animated 3D content.

VRML nodes are used to create both primitive and complex objects. VRML supports four primitive objects—boxes, cones, cylinders, and spheres—that can be used to form more complicated objects (a snowman can be constructed using a series of progressively larger spheres, for example). Complex, arbitrary shapes are also supported by VRML, allowing developers to create shapes that are more natural and organic compared to those created with primitives.

VRML objects are positioned in three-dimensional space according to a 3D coordinate system that has X, Y, and Z axes, the unit of measurement for which corresponds to meters. VRML objects can have their own coordinate system or may share the same coordinate system of the scene they're in. The top-level scene coordinate system is known as the world coordinate system. By default, objects are placed at the origin of the world coordinate system. Because VRML supports any number of coordinate systems, developers use the Transform node to translate coordinate systems and also to scale, rotate, move, and animate objects.

Following is a complete list of URLs referenced in this chapter:

Web3D Consortium   http://www.web3d.org/

VRML97 Specification   http://www.web3d.org/fs_specifications.htm

Web3D Gallery VRML Scripting   http://www.web3dgallery.com/vrml/scripting/

ElevationGrid terrain, first example   http://www.irony.com/igmmte/

ElevationGrid terrain, second example   http://pandora.mts-inc.com/~rhian/

Extrusion car example   http://www.cybelius.com/

Extrusion jet example   http://vrml.environs.com/ivan/

IndexedFaceSet mantis   http://www.ento.vt.edu/~sharov/3d/3dinsect.html

IndexedLineSet conceptual architecture   http://www.construct.net/worlds/behaviors/

IndexedLineSet harp   http://www.geometrek.com/vrml/objects.html

WEAVING VRML INTO WEB PAGES

Topics in This Chapter

- Controlling the dimensions of your VRML content
- Creating JavaScript popup windows
- Embedding VRML into HTML with <EMBED> and <OBJECT>
- Compressing VRML files
- Sniffing for VRML browsers
- Related VRML nodes

Chapter 6

In this chapter you'll learn how to weave VRML content into Web pages. Specifically, you'll learn how to use JavaScript popup windows to control the dimensions of your VRML worlds when they are loaded directly by the Web browser. You'll also learn how to use the EMBED and OBJECT elements to seamlessly integrate VRML with HTML. Along the way you'll find that a freely available utility known as GZip can be used to greatly reduce the overall size of your worlds, saving precious download time and improving the overall experience for the end user.

In addition you'll find out how to use JavaScript code to write "sniffer" scripts that can determine what VRML browser plugin, if any, visitors to your site are using. This simple but effective technique can increase the appeal of your VRML-enabled Web pages by allowing you to immediately identify and assist those users who are not properly equipped to view your content. Finally, you'll learn about various VRML nodes that allow you to add author and copyright notices, hyperlinks, viewpoints and navigation controls to your worlds, which can further increase the appeal of your 3D pages.

Note

The source code appearing in this chapter (and all other chapters of this book) is available on the Web at http://www.CoreWeb3D.com/.

Direct Access

In much the same way that image and sound files can be accessed directly or as part of an HTML page, VRML worlds can be accessed directly through the Web rather than being woven into HTML pages. Loading the following Uniform Resource Locator (URL) into your VRML-enabled Web browser, for example, will load the seaside.wrl world directly; it will be displayed on its own, as seen in Figure 6-1, not as part of an HTML Web page:

http://www.web3dgallery.com/vrml/seaside/seaside.wrl

Although this is the easiest way to make your VRML worlds available to surfers, as it requires only uploading .wrl files to the Web, it is also among the worst ways to deliver VRML content, as it gives you no control whatso-ever over the viewing experience. You have no control over the height and

Figure 6-1   VRML worlds consume the entire Web browser window when viewed directly. Because end users are free to resize the browser window, which in turn alters the horizontal and vertical dimensions of the world, you have no control over the viewing experience (Seaside world courtesy of Gerardo Quintieri, http://www.web3dgallery.com/people/gq/).

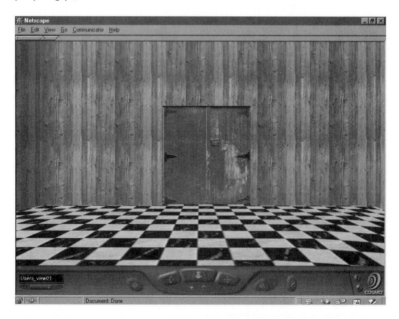

width dimensions of the browser window in which the world is displayed, nor can you be certain that the browser is actually "VRML-savvy" (capable of displaying VRML content).

In most cases you'll want to embed your VRML files directly into a Web page, or at least control the size of the Web browser window in which the file is opened, for several purposes. The first is for performance in cases where a VRML world is processor intensive, requiring significant computing power to view or navigate. Because larger display areas require more memory and processing effort to render, the end user's viewing and navigation of complex worlds can slow to a crawl if the browser window in which they are opened is too large. Figure 6-1, for instance, shows the seaside.wrl VRML file displayed at full screen. In such large dimensions this texture-heavy world becomes quite sluggish as the rendering engine struggles to refresh the onscreen image in response to continual user interaction.

You can produce a much smoother rendering of such worlds by limiting the size of the browser window in which they are viewed. Using JavaScript, you can dynamically "pop open" a new browser window having a height and width that you specify, and you can even prevent the user from resizing the window as seen in Figure 6-2. The JavaScript `window.open()` command gives you a great deal of control over the properties of the browser window in which your VRML files are viewed (see "JavaScript Popup Windows").

Alternately, you can weave VRML worlds directly into HTML Web pages using the <EMBED> or <OBJECT> elements described later in this chapter (see "Embedding VRML into HTML"). In doing so you specify a portion of the page in which the embedded world will be displayed, as illustrated in Figure 6-3, much as you might an image file or video clip, thereby controlling the height and width of the world when ultimately viewed by the end user.

Regardless of which approach you take, end users must first open a standard HTML Web page before they can get to your VRML world. In the case of JavaScript popup windows, the Web page acts as a launch pad for the new popup window whose dimensions you control, while the embedding approach allows you to place VRML content directly alongside other Web-page content. In any case, you have an opportunity to test, or "sniff," the end user's Web browser for the presence of a VRML browser plug-in. You can intercept those without VRML-savvy browsers and direct them to an appropriate installation site (see "Sniffers").

Figure 6-2   Using JavaScript, you can create a popup window of the exact size that you'd like for your VRML worlds.

Figure 6-3   You can weave your VRML worlds into a specific portion of a standard Web page using either the <EMBED> or <OBJECT> HTML elements.

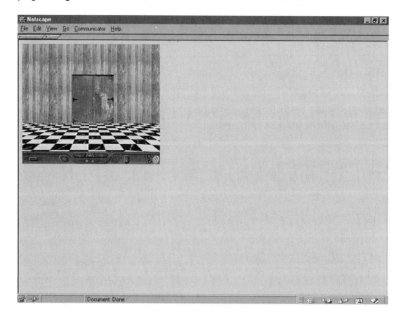

VRML Authoring Tools

Many of today's VRML authoring tools take care of weaving worlds into Web pages for you. CYBELIUS ShowMore! (http://www.cybelius .com), for example, is a VRML tool created for Web developers and designers who wish to customize existing VRML worlds and integrate the results into HTML Web pages. ShowMore! is integrated with Microsoft's FrontPage Web page authoring product and allows you to seamlessly stitch worlds into Web pages with this popular HTML authoring tool. Cosmo PageFX (http://www.cosmosoftware.com), on the other hand, is a standalone VRML authoring tool that automatically generates HTML Web pages along with the VRML special effects this product creates.

ShowMore! and PageFX are just a few of the VRML authoring tools that can help you weave worlds into Web pages. (To learn more about VRML authoring tools, see Chapter 10, "Creating New VRML Worlds.") However, just as it pays to understand the raw HTML code produced by Web-page generators such as Netscape Composer and Microsoft FrontPage, it's also a good idea to understand what goes on behind the scenes when it comes to integrating VRML and HTML files. When you know how to weave VRML into Web pages manually, as explained in this chapter, you'll have complete control over the end-user experience, even if the authoring tool that you're using isn't up to the challenge.

Note: UPPERCASE Elements

In the following sections we'll introduce you to a number of HTML tags, or elements, such as SCRIPT, EMBED, and OBJECT. We'll type such elements (and the attributes they support) in uppercase letters in order to make the text and code easier for you to read. You are, of course, free to use lowercase characters when it comes to coding these HTML elements in your own pages, since case doesn't matter for these items as far as Web browsers are considered.

JavaScript Popup Windows

VRML files can be displayed inside of popup windows that are dynamically created from within a standard HTML Web page. Because the size of the popup window determines the dimensions of the VRML file loading directly into it, and the window's size is specified at the time it is created, you can control the dimensions of the VRML world loaded into it. Unfortunately, HTML doesn't inherently support popup windows, and so you must turn to a client-side scripting language such as JavaScript if you wish to display VRML content using this technique. (Alternately, you can weave your VRML worlds directly into the fabric of HTML pages using the EMBED or OBJECT elements described later in this chapter.)

JavaScript, as you're probably well aware, is a popular Web-page scripting language developed by Netscape Communications Corp., in cooperation with Sun Microsystems, and introduced with version 2 of Netscape Navigator. JavaScript is sometimes thought of as a "lightweight" alternative to Java, although in truth the two are more different than they are similar.

Java is a robust software-development platform built around the Java programming language that is similar in many ways to C and C++. Java source-code files are compiled into a cross-platform bytecode format that must be run through a Java runtime environment (JRE) before it can be executed. Although Web-page applets and standalone desktop applications are the most popular forms of Java programs, the technology is also commonly used to produce other types of software, such as JavaBeans components and server-side executables known as servlets.

JavaScript, by comparison, is a fully interpreted, text-based scripting language that you type directly into HTML Web pages. (It is very similar to VRML in this sense, as both are interpreted languages.) JavaScript code, or "scripts," aren't compiled, and so remain fully human readable, just as HTML code does. The only tool you need in order to add JavaScript to a Web page is a text editor such as the Windows Notepad or Macintosh SimpleText program.

JavaScript is much more closely aligned with Web pages than Java is, and it gives you the ability to access and manipulate the contents of HTML documents in ways that Java applets simply cannot. Java applets, in contrast, are a form of executable Web content that simply see Web pages as a delivery vehicle, and as such have limited access to the pages in which they are embedded. JavaScript, however, is designed specifically with Web page scripting in mind; its very intention is to give you programmatic control over various aspects of Web pages.

Client and Server-Side JavaScript

Although JavaScript is used primarily as a client-side Web-page scripting language, it can also be executed on the server (so called "server-side" JavaScript) as an alternative to Common Gateway Interface (CGI) programs typically written in Perl. We're concerned here, however, only with using very simple client-side JavaScript code to help deliver VRML worlds to the end user. To learn more about server-side JavaScript, visit Netscape's JavaScript development site at http://developer.netscape.com/library/documentation/javascript.html.

JavaScript is arguably the most popular and widely supported client-side scripting language (see "Client and Server Side JavaScript"). Microsoft, however, has developed an alternative to JavaScript called JScript, which is supported by Internet Explorer. JavaScript and JScript are similar in many ways, although they are by no means 100% compatible. The simple JavaScript code that we'll show you in this section will run in script-capable versions of Netscape Navigator and Internet Explorer, but the more complicated JavaScript features aren't necessarily compatible with JScript, nor are some of the newer features recently introduced to the language. Conversely, many features of JScript aren't supported by JavaScript, which can lead to problems if you intend to create more comprehensive cross-browser scripts than those introduced here (see "JavaScript vs. JScript").

JavaScript vs. JScript

Although Netscape's JavaScript and Microsoft's JScript are similar, they aren't 100% compatible. To make matters more complicated, different versions of each language are available, and features introduced with more current versions of the languages won't be recognized by older browsers. Netscape Navigator 2, for example, supports only JavaScript 1.0, while Navigator 3 supports both JavaScript 1.1 and JavaScript 1.0. Navigator releases 4 to 4.05, however, support JavaScript 1.2, JavaScript 1.1, and JavaScript 1.0, while more recent releases (Navigator 4.06 to 4.7) support these versions as well as JavaScript 1.3.

Similarly, Microsoft's most current release of Internet Explorer supports a more complete suite of JScript than earlier versions. Internet Explorer 5, for example, supports JScript 5, which is not entirely compatible with the current release of JavaScript. Although the simple JavaScript 1.0 window commands used in this section will run just fine in current and earlier versions of both Navigator and Internet Explorer, the same cannot be said for more complex or recent features of the language.

As a result, be sure to consult the official documentation for both languages should you want to create more sophisticated cross-browser scripts than those shown here. Netscape's JavaScript development guide is available on the Web at http://developer.netscape.com/library/documentation/javascript.html, while the address http://msdnmicrosoft.com/scripting/jscript/default.htm gives access to Microsoft's JScript documentation.

Thankfully, Netscape's JavaScript and Microsoft's JScript have been partially standardized under a relatively recent standard, ECMA-262, more commonly known as ECMAScript. (ECMA refers to the European Computer Manufacturers Asociation.) Both companies learned something from the early days of HTML, when it seemed that a new HTML tag would appear in one browser at breakfast time, be copied by the other browser by lunch, and disappear from both by dinner. Microsoft and Netscape have chosen to narrow the area of conflict in lightweight scripting by arriving at a commonly accepted core standard to which both browser makers have pledged (eventual) support.

If you want your scripts to work on present and future versions of both browsers, you should keep handy a copy of ECMA-262 (which is available for free download at http://www.ecma.ch/stand/ecma-262.htm). Although ECMAScript isn't as comprehensive as either JavaScript or JScript, using it will ensure that you're using standardized scripting commands.

The VRML97 specification, in fact, avoids scripting-language wars by simply referencing ECMA-262. As a result, many VRML browsers support scripts only if they are in compliance with ECMA-262. The following rule of thumb is helpful if you intend to construct scripts for use with VRML:

If the script appears inside an HTML Web page: Use ECMA-262 plus the browser-specific classes and features that are supported by the most popular Web browsers.

If the script appears directly inside a VRML file (such as a Script node): Use only ECMA-262.

Fortunately, the smidgen of JavaScript that you need to add to your Web page in order to open a new window for your VRML world is very simple and is supported by both Netscape Navigator and Internet Explorer. Specifically, you'll use the JavaScript 1.0 `open()` method, which is a command that you'll send to the Web page "window" object in the following form:

```
window.open(url, name, features...);
```

This line of JavaScript code tells the Web browser to create a new window inside which the content pointed to by the *url* parameter will be displayed (a VRML world in our case). The URL that you supply to the `open()` method can be either *absolute* or *relative*, just as with URLs supplied to the standard HTML HREF and SRC elements (see "Absolute and Relative URLs").

The *name* parameter gives the newly created window an identity that you can refer to from within other JavaScript code or as the TARGET attribute in the standard HTML A, AREA, BASE, and FORM elements. This allows you to exert further control over the window once it has been created, such

Absolute and Relative URLs

Absolute URLs are fully qualified Web addresses that include a protocol scheme (such as "http" or "ftp"), host computer, and directory/file path. The following, for example, are absolute URLs:

http://www.web3d.org/
http://www.web3d.org/WorkingGroups/media/index.html
ftp://www.gnu.org/gnu/gzip/
http://www.web3dgallery.com/vrml/seaside/

Relative URLs, on the other hand, are partial addresses that specify an item located relative to the Web page in which the address appears. Following are examples of relative URLs:

index.html
WorkingGroups/
WorkingGroups/media/index.html
gnu/gzip/
vrml/seaside/seaside.wrl
seaside.wrl

as displaying various content in it based on user activity that takes place in the *parent* window from which the *child* popup was opened. We'll only set the name parameter to a legal value, however, and won't bother to actually use it (although you're free to do so, should the urge strike you).

Following the *url* and *name* parameters are "feature" parameters that determine how the new window will appear to the end user. The two most important for our purposes are *height* and *width* (see Table 6.1). The *height* and *width* feature parameters together specify the size of the new window, which is precisely what you need when it comes to controlling the horizontal and vertical dimensions of your VRML world when viewed by the end user, as described earlier.

In addition to *height* and *width*, many other JavaScript `window.open()` features are available as you can see looking at Table 6.1. This table lists the parameters that correspond to window features such as toolbar buttons (back, forward, refresh, stop, and so forth), scroll bars, and a status bar, for example. Although we'll use these features later, for the moment *height* and *width* are the only ones that you need to concern yourself with.

To use the JavaScript `window.open()` command, you must first wrap it inside a function definition. JavaScript functions are declared using the

| Table 6.1 | JavaScript window.open() features |
| | usage: window.open(url, name, features...); |

Feature Parameter Name	*Legal Values*	*Description*
alwaysLowered	yes/no *or* 1/0	Specifies whether or not the window will always be below other windows.[*]
alwaysRaised	yes/no *or* 1/0	Specifies whether or not the window will always be above other windows.[*]
dependent	yes/no *or* 1/0	Specifies whether or not the window will be the child of the window that opened it (if so, the child will close when the parent is closed).[**]

Feature Parameter Name	Legal Values	Description
directories	yes/no *or* 1/0	Specifies whether or not the browser directory buttons should be displayed.
height	*integer number*	Specifies the window height (in pixels).
hotkeys	yes/no *or* 1/0	Specifies whether or not hotkeys (control keys) should be enabled.**
innerHeight	*integer number*	Specifies the content area height (in pixels).**
innerWidth	*integer number*	Specifies the content area width (in pixels).**
location	yes/no *or* 1/0	Specifies whether or not the location area should be displayed.
menubar	yes/no *or* 1/0	Specifies whether or not the menu bar should be displayed.
outerHeight	*integer number*	Specifies the outside window height (in pixels).**
outerWidth	*integer number*	Specifies the outside window width (in pixels).**
resizable	yes/no *or* 1/0	Specifies whether or not the user can resize the window.
screenX	*integer number*	Specifies the location of the left side of the window (in pixels).**
screenY	*integer number*	Specifies the location of the top of the window (in pixels).**
scrollbars	yes/no *or* 1/0	Specifies whether or not scrollbars will be displayed if needed.
status	yes/no *or* 1/0	Specifies whether or not the status area will be displayed.
titlebar	yes/no *or* 1/0	Specifies whether or not the title bar will be displayed.*
toolbar	yes/no *or* 1/0	Specifies whether or not the toolbar will be displayed (back, forward, refresh, stop, home, etc.)
width	*integer number*	Specifies the window width (in pixels).
z-lock	yes/no *or* 1/0	Specifies whether or not the window can be raised or lowered.*

*Available only with signed JavaScript 1.2 (or higher) scripts

**JavaScript 1.2 or higher

JavaScript `function` keyword, which is immediately followed by a function name and a pair of parenthesis ( ) that contain the parameters, if any, that will be passed to the function when it is called. The code that actually makes up the body of the function appears inside a pair of curly braces { }, where each line of code is delimited with a semicolon. The entire function is then placed inside a SCRIPT element (see "The Script Element"), as the following example illustrates:

```
<SCRIPT LANGUAGE="JavaScript">
<!--
function openWorld(){

window.open("seaside.wrl","seaside","width=400,height=300");
}
//-->
</SCRIPT>
```

With only 7 lines of code we have constructed a JavaScript function named "openWorld," the core of which is the `open()` method complete with parameters. In this particular case the `open()` method is sent to the `window` object to create a new browser window that is 400 pixels wide and 300 pixels high, inside which the "seaside.wrl" VRML file will be loaded. The name of the window is set to "seaside," although we have no cause to reference it once created and so could just as easily have set it to something nonsensical, such as "cheese."

We'll build on this JavaScript function shortly, but all you really need to know now is that this is a self-contained body of code that, once woven into your Web page, can be called, or invoked, as needed (see "The Script Element"). You can call this function when the user clicks on standard HTML buttons and hyperlinks by explicitly referencing the function by name in response to the JavaScript `onClick` event that corresponds to such activity as follows:

```
onClick="openWorld()"
```

Warning: Feature Lists

When supplying feature parameters to the JavaScript `open()` *method you should be careful not to include spaces, tabs, carriage returns, or any other "white space" between parameters, because some JavaScript interpreters may not properly parse parameters separated by white space.*

The SCRIPT Element

JavaScript code is typically wrapped inside a SCRIPT element that hides the code from Web browsers using HTML comments <!-- and //--> in order to prevent the code from being treated like standard HTML. Web browsers that don't understand JavaScript (and those in which scripting has been disabled by the user) will ignore the code altogether. Script-savvy browsers, on the other hand, know how to deal with JavaScript code falling between these comments:

```
<SCRIPT LANGUAGE="JavaScript">
<!--
    ...SCRIPT CODE GOES HERE...
//-->
</SCRIPT>
```

Typically, code contained inside a SCRIPT element is executed as the browser loads it. Any output the code generates is dynamically inserted into the HTML document at the place it is found inside the SCRIPT element, allowing HTML pages to be dynamically constructed using scripting code. Functions, however, are treated differently.

JavaScript functions, such as the openWorld() function we create in the next section, are self-contained bodies of code that can be called into action when needed. In this respect JavaScript functions are analogous to functions, procedures, routines, and methods used in other programming languages. As you'll soon see, the JavaScript openWorld() function is called when the user clicks on a button or hyperlink, at which point it springs into action to create a new popup window, inside of which a VRML world is loaded.

If you wish to use version-specific JavaScript features, such as those offered by JavaScript 1.1 or JavaScript 1.2, you can prevent older browsers from "breaking" by specifying the version of code appearing in the SCRIPT element. If a browser doesn't support the version of code specified, it will ignore the code entirely. Following, for example, are SCRIPT elements corresponding to JavaScript 1.1 and 1.2, and one specifically for JScript:

```
<SCRIPT LANGUAGE="JavaScript1.1">
<SCRIPT LANGUAGE="JavaScript1.2">
<SCRIPT LANGUAGE="JScript">
```

(continued)

At one time <SCRIPT LANGUAGE="JavaScript"> meant that a Web browser that supported JScript but not JavaScript wouldn't touch the function, <SCRIPT LANGUAGE="JScript"> meant JScript but not JavaScript, while <SCRIPT LANGUAGE="javascript"> meant it was OK for the Web browser to try to use either. Today, however, all major Web browsers do their best to interpret scripts regardless of the LANGUAGE attribute (while being guided by the version number if one appears in the element). If you have a number of people with older browsers visiting your site, you may prefer to use "javascript."

The SCRIPT element has a corresponding NOSCRIPT element that is used to present information to Web browsers that don't support client-side scripting (or those in which scripting is disabled). You can follow your SCRIPT elements with NOSCRIPT to give users direct access to VRML worlds, without the benefit of a popup window:

```
<NOSCRIPT>

 <p> If you had a JavaScript-savvy browser, the following
world would open in a popup window… <a href="seaside
.wrl">Open Seaside Directly</a></p>

 </NOSCRIPT>
```

FORM Buttons

Once you've created a JavaScript function such as openWorld(), you must actually "hook it up." The following HTML FORM button, for example, is configured to call openWorld() when clicked by simply specifying the function name in response to the onClick event (onClick is not standard HTML and is understood only by JavaScript-aware browsers):

```
<form>
  <input type="button" value="Open Seaside Window"
  onClick="openWorld()">
</form>
```

Listing 6.1 lists the code for a simple HTML page that contains both the openWorld() JavaScript function and a button that responds to mouse clicks by calling this function. The function is defined in the HEAD section of the Web page, falling just before the closing </HEAD> element (JavaScript

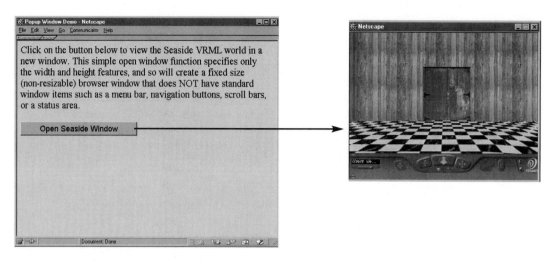

Figure 6-4   The FORM button appearing on the parent Web page (left) is configured to call the `open-World()` JavaScript function in response to an `onClick` event, resulting in a new, bare-boned child popup window (right).

functions should always be defined in the HEAD of an HMTL document), while the button is created by placing the above snippet of FORM code in the BODY section of the page. Figure 6-4 shows the page displayed in a Web browser and the resulting popup window generated by the JavaScript code. When the button on this page is clicked, the `openWorld()` function is called and the `window.open()` code is invoked, resulting in the no-frills window you see here.

Listing 6.1   popup.html

```
<html>

<head>
<title>Popup Window Demo</title>

<SCRIPT LANGUAGE="JavaScript">
<!--
function openWorld(){
  window.open("seaside.wrl","seaside","width=400,height=300");
}
//-->
</SCRIPT>
```

```
</head>

<body>

<p>Click on the button below to view the Seaside VRML world
in a new window. This simple open-window function specifies
only the width and height features and so will create a
fixed-size (nonresizable) browser window that does NOT have
standard window items such as a menu bar, navigation buttons,
scroll bars, or a status area.</p>

<form>
  <input type="button" value="Open Seaside Window"
  onClick="openWorld()">
</form>

</body>
</html>
```

Tip: Place JavaScript Functions in HEAD

JavaScript functions are defined in the HEAD section of Web pages and typically appear just before the closing </HEAD> element. Although you can place your JavaScript functions elsewhere, placing functions in the document HEAD forces them to load before other elements in a page, making the functions immediately visible to other portions of your page. Users with itchy fingers, therefore, can click on your onClick-enabled links before the entire page has finished loading and still invoke the function.

Functions defined in the document HEAD are considered global to the page and so can be called from multiple places (from various links and buttons in the page, for instance). Finally, placing your JavaScript functions in the HEAD section lends to more readable code; your functions are always at the very top of the page, so that you don't have to hunt for them when reading the source code of your pages.

While this window may look ideal at first blush, it's actually lacking a very important feature, namely the status bar! Because *height* and *width* are the only feature parameters supplied to the JavaScript `window.open()` method, the status area typically used to convey important browser information is missing from this particular window. As a result, end users will have no idea what's going on as the browser loads the seaside.wrl file, and they may close the window if a long delay exists after the window is created and before the world is actually displayed.

With very small VRML files the lack of status area really isn't a major concern, because such worlds are downloaded and displayed in a relatively short span of time. Larger files, however, can take several minutes or more to transfer over dial-up modem network connections, in which case the end users won't have the luxury of a status area telling them about the download in progress. Because the VRML97 standard doesn't include streaming, the entire world file must be loaded by the browser before it can be rendered. Fortunately, simply adding a status feature parameter to the `window. open()` call can eliminate such problems, as Listing 6.2 illustrates (see Figure 6-5).

Listing 6.2   popupStatus.html

```
<html>

<head>
<title>Popup Window with Status Area Demo</title>
<SCRIPT LANGUAGE="JavaScript">
<!--
function openWorld(){

window.open("seaside.wrl","seaside","status=yes,width=400,height=300");
}
//-->
</SCRIPT>

</head>

<body>

<p>Click on the button below to view the Seaside VRML
world in a new window. This open-window function specifies
only the width, height, and status features, creating
a bare-bones, resizable browser window that does have
a status area.</p>
```

```
<form>
  <input type="button" value="Open Seaside Window"
   onClick="openWorld()">
</form>

</body>
</html>
```

You'll notice that we've supplied the status feature parameter appearing in Listing 6.2 with a setting of "yes," which means that the status area should indeed be part of the popup window that this code creates. However, as you can see from Table 6.1, we might alternately have supplied the number "1" instead. For that matter, we could also have supplied just the *name* of the status feature parameter itself to indicate that this feature should be used (see "Window Defaults" later in this chapter). As far as the JavaScript interpreter is concerned, the following three lines of code are functionally equivalent:

```
window.open(url,name,"status=yes,width=400,height=300");
window.open(url,name,"status=1,width=400,height=300");
window.open(url,name,"status,width=400,height=300");
```

Figure 6-5   A status area is added to the bottom of the popup window as a result of supplying the status feature parameter to the `window.open()` call.

Tip: Netscape Navigator 2

Due to a bug in Netscape Navigator 2, a single call to the JavaScript `open()` *method may be ignored. To support Navigator 2 users you can call the* `open()` *method twice. Use a "sniffer" script as described later in this chapter to detect Navigator 2 browsers if you wish to avoid this redundancy when users visit your pages equipped with a more current browser (there's no need to call open twice unless Navigator 2 is used).*

Window Defaults

By default, JavaScript popup windows are not resizable, so that the end user won't be able to adjust the horizontal or vertical dimensions of the window unless you include the resizable feature parameter in your call to `window.open()`. In other words, the default resizable feature parameter setting is "no" or "0". The same is true for other features that accept "yes/no" or "1/0" values; they're all "no" by default. When you omit a feature parameter when calling `window.open()`, the new popup will be created without that particular feature.

You've seen this already when dealing with the status area; a status area won't be included in the popup window unless you add the status feature parameter to the `window.open()` call, as we've done in previous code listings. You don't have to explicitly set this parameter to "yes" as we've done, however; the mere presence of a feature parameter name is enough, as described earlier. The following `openWorld()` function, for example, creates a resizable window that has a status area, directory buttons, a menu bar, and even a tool bar. The resulting popup window, seen in Figure 6-6, is feature-packed compared to previous examples:

```
<SCRIPT LANGUAGE="JavaScript">

<!--
function openWorld(){
  window.open("seaside.wrl","seaside",
  "resizable,status,directories,menubar,toolbar,
   width=400,height=300");
}
//-->

</SCRIPT>
```

Figure 6-6   This feature-packed window is a result of including the resizable, status, directories, menubar, and toolbar feature parameters to `window.open()`.

Warning: Beware of White Space

We've included carriage returns in this call to `window.open()` *out of necessity, because it won't fit on a single printed line in this book. You should type this command into your Web page as one long line of code, however, because some JavaScript interpreters may have trouble parsing the parameter list if it includes white space (spaces, carriage returns, or tabs).*

Variable Window Settings

Although you might be content to specify one size for your JavaScript popup window, as seen in Listings 6.1 and 6.2, with just a bit more effort you can give your end users a choice. Listing 6.3, for example, specifies variable height and width parameters, allowing users to choose the window size that's best for their particular setup. Those with low-end systems can open Seaside in a small window, while those with more powerful computers can open the world in larger windows.

This freedom of choice is accomplished by adding two variables to the `openWorld()` function, one each for *width* and *height*. These custom function parameters vary in value depending on the FORM button clicked. When the "small" FORM button is clicked, a width value of 300 and a height of 200 is passed to `openWorld()`, while the "medium" button passes a *width* value of 400 and a height value of 300 to the `openWorld()` function. Clicking on the "large" button, meanwhile, results in the biggest popup window of all, measuring 600 pixels wide and 500 pixels high.

Note: Dynamically Concatenating Strings

The height and width values passed into the `openWorld()` *function as parameters are dynamically stitched into the body of the* `window.open()` *call using the JavaScript "+" concatenation operator as follows:*

```
function openWorld(w, h) {
  window.open("seaside.wrl","seaside", "status,width=" + w +
",height=" + h);
}
```

Listing 6.3   popupSizeChoice.html

```
<html>

<head>
<title>Choose Popup Size Demo</title>

<SCRIPT LANGUAGE="JavaScript">

<!--
function openWorld(w, h){
  window.open("seaside.wrl","seaside",
            "status,width=" + w + ",height=" + h);
}
//-->

</SCRIPT>

</head>

<body>


<p>Click on one of the buttons below to view the Seaside
VRML world in a new window.</p>
```

```
<form>
  <input type="button" value="Open SMALL Window"
    onClick="openWorld(300,200)">
</form>

<form>
  <input type="button" value="Open MEDIUM Window"
    onClick="openWorld(400,300)">
</form>

<form>
  <input type="button" value="Open LARGE Window"
    onClick="openWorld(600,500)">
</form>

</body>
</html>
```

In each of the previous examples a simple JavaScript function is used to open a world called Seaside (specified with the relative URL "seaside.wrl"). Although you can modify the URL portion of this script to specify your own VRML files, a more flexible `openWorld()` function such as the one found in Listing 6.4 is particularly useful in cases where you have a number of different worlds to weave into Web pages, or you would like to give users the option of viewing a variety of worlds from a single Web page.

To make the `window.open()` function more flexible, Listing 6.4 adds two new custom parameters to the function: *url* and *name*. Upon receiving these parameters, `window.open()` passes them to the `window.open()` command, just as with the *height* (h) and *width* (w) settings introduced in Listing 6.3, allowing the contents and name of the popup window to be dynamically specified as well.

Although the new `window.open()` function call is straightforward, calling it in response to the onClick event is now a little more complicated. Unlike the integer *height* and *width* parameters, *url* and *name* are actually strings, and so each must be enclosed in single quotes as follows:

```
onClick="openWorld('seaside.wrl','seaside',400,300)">
```

Although this can be confusing at first, simply keep in mind that the function call itself is surrounded with double quotes, while each string parameter (*url* and *name*, in this case) is surrounding with single quotes. By forcing you to mix single and double quotes in this fashion, the JavaScript interpreter is able to distinguish between the function call itself and any string parameters it may contain. Alternately, you can reverse the order of quotes, placing the entire function call inside single quotes and each parameter inside double quotes (either approach works just fine).

As you can see in Listing 6.4, the newly modified `openWorld()` function can now be used to handle a variety of VRML worlds regardless of their location. In this example we've created three different FORM buttons on the same Web page, each associated with a unique VRML file. The first two worlds, Seaside and Dance Party, are each specified using a relative URL, while the last world, Conversations with Angles, is specified using an absolute URL. As with previous examples, we supply a name for the window as required by the `window.open()` call, although we don't actually bother to use it as a reference to the newly created popup window.

Note: Function Declarations

You'll notice that we didn't bother to declare that the url and name parameters passed to `openWorld()` are actually string data types, nor did we specify that w and h are integer parameters. This is one of the conveniences offered by JavaScript; function parameter types are not declared. For that matter, neither are return types. Because JavaScript supports dynamic typing, you're spared the hassle of declaring data types for function parameters, variables, and return types.

Listing 6.4   popupWorldChoices.html

```html
<html>

<head>
<title>Choose World Demo</title>

<SCRIPT LANGUAGE="JavaScript">
<!--
function openWorld(url, name, w, h){
  window.open(url,name,"status,width=" + w + ",height=" + h);
}
//-->
</SCRIPT>

</head>
```

```
<body>


<p>Click on one of the buttons below to view a VRML
world in a new window.</p>

<form>
  <input type="button" value="Seaside"
  onClick="openWorld('seaside.wrl','Seaside',400,300)">
</form>

<form>
  <input type="button" value="Dance Party"
  onClick="openWorld('shout/dance.wrl','Dance',400,400)">
</form>

<form>
  <input type="button" value="Conversations With Angels"
  onClick=

"openWorld('http://web3dgallery.com/go/cwa/','cwa',600,500)">
</form>

</body>
</html>
```

Hyperlinks

In addition to creating popup windows in response to FORM buttons, as the previous section explains, you can also weave JavaScript function calls into standard text and image hyperlinks. Listing 6.5, for example, illustrates how to call openWorld() when the user selects a standard text hyperlink created with the HTML HREF element (see Figure 6-7), an action that produces the same onClick event generated by FORM buttons. You can easily extend this code to include image hyperlinks by adding an HTML IMG element immediately following the HREF element as follows:

```
<a href="aboutSeaside.html"
  onClick="openWorld('seaside.wrl','Seaside',400,300)">
<img src="seaside.jpg"></a>
```

In both cases the openWorld() function is called in response to the onClick event, which in turn creates a popup window as described in the previous section. However, unlike the FORM button examples that you saw earlier, these hyperlinks are "live," meaning that the URL supplied to the HREF element will be loaded in the parent window, as seen in Figure 6-8. This is particularly helpful if you'd like to provide information about the VRML world displayed in the newly created child popup window, as we've done in these examples by supplying standard HTML files to the HREF element, although you're free to disable this default "link following" behavior.

If your page has been loaded into a Web browser that supports JavaScript 1.1 or later, you can disable link following as shown in Listing 6.6. To do so, simply ensure that the openWorld() function returns **false** when called, and also wrap your function calls inside the parenthesis of "return( )" as shown in Listing 6.6. This will disable link following in version 1.1 of JavaScript and higher, meaning that the parent window won't bother to load the URL you supply to the HREF element.

Tip: File Not Found

*Although you can disable link following in JavaScript 1.1 and higher by returning **false** when openWorld() is called, older JavaScript 1.0 browsers (namely the original JavaScript-savvy versions of Navigator and Internet Explorer) will attempt to load the URL you supply to the HREF element. Rather than greet such users with a "link not found" error, you should always supply a valid URL to HREF. You can, for example, supply the URL of the parent window itself, which will result in the parent window's simply reloading itself when the hyperlink is selected in older Web browsers.*

Figure 6-7 JavaScript functions can be called in response to the user's selecting standard HREF text hyperlinks, such as those shown here, and even image hyperlinks created with the IMG element.

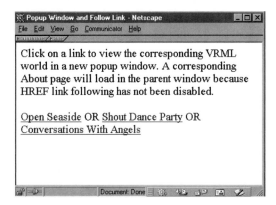

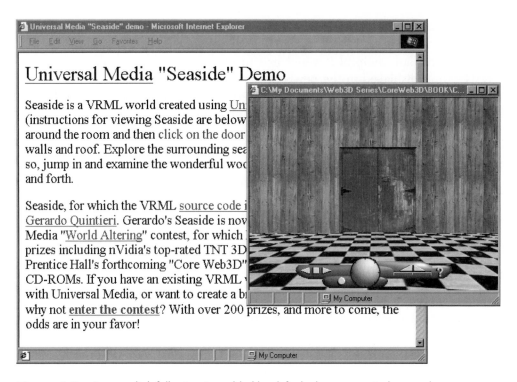

Figure 6-8   Because link following is enabled by default, the parent window can be used to provide information about the world that appears in its child popup widow.

Listing 6.5   popupFollowLink.html

```html
<html>

<head>
<title>Popup Window and Follow Link</title>

<SCRIPT LANGUAGE="JavaScript">
<!--
function openWorld(url, name, w, h){
  window.open(url,name,"status,width=" + w + ",height=" +
h);
}
//-->
</SCRIPT>
```

```
</head>
<body>


<p>Click on a link to view the corresponding VRML world in a
new popup window. A corresponding About page will load in the
parent window because HREF link following has not been dis-
abled.</p>

<a href="aboutSeaside.html"
 onClick="openWorld('seaside.wrl','Seaside',400,300)">
 Open Seaside</a>

OR

<a href="DanceParty.html"
 onClick="openWorld('shout/mod/dance.wrl','Dance',400,400)">
 Shout Dance Party</a>

OR

<a href="http://web3dgallery.com/go/cwa/about.html"
 onClick=

"openWorld('http://web3dgallery.com/go/cwa/','cwa',600,500)">
 Conversations With Angels</a>


</body>
</html>
```

Tip: Netscape's JavaScript Command Line

You can open a JavaScript "command line" within Netscape by opening the following URL in that browser:

javascript:

Through the command-line interface you can type in JavaScript commands that will be executed immediately, allowing you to quickly test code without the need for an HTML file.

Listing 6.6   popupFollowLinkDisabled.html

```html
<html>
<head>
<title>Popup Window, but DON'T Follow Link</title>
<SCRIPT LANGUAGE="JavaScript">
<!--
function openWorld(url, name, w, h){
  window.open(url,name,"status,width=" + w + ",height=" + h);
  return false; // return false to prevent link following
}
//-->
</SCRIPT>
</head>
<body>

<p>Click on a link to view the corresponding VRML world in a new win-
dow. NOTE that each function call is surrounded by a return(..) call,
and that the function has been modified to return false. As a result,
the hyperlink will not be followed by the main browser window when the
new window is created.</p>

<a href="seaside.wrl"
 onClick="return(openWorld('seaside.wrl','Seaside',400,300))">
 Open Seaside</a>

OR

<a href="shout/mod/dance.wrl"
 onClick="return(openWorld('shout/mod/dance.wrl','Dance',400,400))">
 Shout Dance Party</a>

OR

<a href="http://web3dgallery.com/go/cwa/about.html"
 onClick=
 "return(openWorld('http://web3dgallery.com/go/cwa/','cwa',600,500))">
 Conversations With Angels</a>
</body>
</html>
```

Note: External JavaScript Files

The SCRIPT element supports an optional SRC attribute that accepts a URL, which is used to reference JavaScript files stored external to the Web page (on a Web server, for example). By convention, JavaScript files are stored in pure text format with a .js file extension. The following SCRIPT element takes advantage of the SRC attribute by supplying a relative URL leading to a JavaScript file containing the `openWorld()` *function:*

```
<SCRIPT LANGUAGE="JavaScript" SRC="myscripts/openWindow.js">
```

You should keep in mind, however, that original JavaScript-savvy browsers (such as Navigator 2) didn't know how to deal with the SRC attribute, and so this technique is best used only in cases where you're certain that end users are equipped with a modern Web browser.

Embedding VRML into HTML

Although JavaScript popup windows are quite useful when it comes to constraining the viewing dimensions of your VRML worlds, as the previous section explains, they're not always practical. Sooner or later you'll want to weave VRML content directly into the fabric of a Web page in order to allow other forms of content, such as text and images, to appear alongside your 3D material. Fortunately, integrating VRML and HTML is a snap thanks to two HTML tags, EMBED and OBJECT, known more formally as HTML *elements* (tags and elements are interchangeable terms, although we'll primarily use the latter throughout the remainder of this chapter).

Unfortunately, you'll have to use both EMBED and OBJECT if you'd like to support the widest possible spectrum of Web browsers out there. Netscape, as you'll soon learn, uses the EMBED element, while Internet Explorer prefers OBJECT. In the sections that follow, you'll learn how to use both elements in your own Web pages and also how to combine the two in a nested fashion in order to support both Navigator and Internet Explorer browsers.

Tip: HTML Authoring Tools

*Many HTML authoring tools support both the EMBED and OBJECT elements, meaning that you can use standard Web-page authoring products to stitch VRML into your HTML pages. Microsoft's FrontPage authoring tool, for example, supports both through its **View** → **Other Components** menu. When you choose "PlugIn" from the FrontPage **View** → **Other Components** menu, you'll be presented with a dialog box through which you can select your VRML file and set corresponding EMBED element attributes described in the next section. Similarly, if you select "ActiveX Control" from this menu, you can construct an OBJECT element for any installed component using little more than your mouse.*

<EMBED>

VRML files are most commonly woven into the fabric of Web pages using the EMBED element, which is a nonstandard HTML element introduced years ago by Netscape Communications Corp. (which has since been acquired by America Online) when Navigator 2.0 was released. Microsoft eventually added EMBED support to Internet Explorer, starting with Explorer 3, opting instead to focus on the OBJECT element described later in this chapter (in order to support the widest range of browsers you can nest EMBED inside of OBJECT, a technique that we'll explain when discussing the OBJECT element).

The EMBED element, as the name implies, is used to embed into Web pages information that must be handled by a plug-in. Video files, streaming audio, and VRML worlds are but a few of the types of nonstandard information that Web browsers can't process directly and so get handed off to a plug-in via an EMBED element (or OBJECT, as described later). The appropriate plug-in is chosen based on the MIME type of the file containing the information to process, which the browser typically determines using the file's extension (such as .wrl, which corresponds to the **model/world** MIME type, as explained in Chapter 4, "VRML Overview").

The formal definition of the EMBED element is quite complex, as you can see from Table 6.2. Fortunately, you only need to use the EMBED element's SRC, HEIGHT, and WIDTH attributes to stitch a VRML file into your Web page. The following EMBED configuration, for example, will display the Seaside VRML file in a rectangular portion of the Web page that is 300 pixels high and 400 pixels wide:

Table 6.2	The EMBED Element
	usage: `<EMBED SRC="location" HEIGHT=# WIDTH=#`
	`attributes>`

Attribute	*Description*
SRC="location"	Location of the plug-in data file using a URL. The MIME type of the file (typically based on the file extension, such as .wrl) determines which plug-in is loaded to handle this EMBED tag. You must include either the SRC attribute or the TYPE attribute in an EMBED tag.
HEIGHT="height"	Height of the area to be occupied by the plug-in. The units are determined by the UNITS attribute. The default is pixels.
WIDTH="width"	Width of the area to be occupied by the plug-in. The output from the embedded file is scaled to fit the specified height and width. The units are determined by the UNITS attribute. The default is pixels.
TYPE="MIMEtype"	MIME type of the EMBED tag, which in turn determines which plug-in to load. Use the TYPE attribute for a plug-in that requires no data. For a visible plug-in, you must include both the WIDTH and HEIGHT attributes if you use TYPE; no default values are used.
PLUGINSPAGE= "instrURL"	URL that contains the instructions for installing the plug-in if it is not already installed.
PLUGINURL= "pluginURL"	URL of a Java Archive (JAR) file. The default plug-in invokes the JAR Installation Manager (JIM) with this JAR file URL rather than loading the URL into a window.
	Note: PLUGINURL takes precedence over PLUGINSPAGE. It is recommended that you use PLUGINURL rather than PLUGINSPAGE. (Supported by Navigator 4.0.)
ALIGN=	Specifies the alignment for the embedded plug-in:
"BOTTOM"	BOTTOM aligns text to the bottom (the default).
"LEFT"	LEFT aligns text flush left.

Attribute	*Description*
"RIGHT" "TOP"	RIGHT aligns text flush right. TOP aligns text to the top.
BORDER="borderWidth"	Size, in pixels, of the border around the plug-in.
FRAMEBORDER="NO"	Specifies that the plug-in has no border.
UNITS="units"	Measurement units used by the HEIGHT and WIDTH attributes. The value can either be pixels (the default) or en (which specifies half the point size).
HIDDEN= "TRUE" "FALSE"	Specifies whether the plug-in is visible on the page. The default is FALSE.
HSPACE="horizMargin"	Margin, in pixels, between the left and right edges of the plug-in and surrounding content (the "horizontal space").
VSPACE="vertMargin"	Margin, in pixels, between the top and bottom edges of the applet and surrounding content. (the "vertical space").
NAME="pluginName"	Name of the plug-in (the name can be used by JavaScript to discover the plug-in, as described in the "Sniffing for Browsers" section later in this chapter).
PALETTE= "FOREGROUND" "BACKGROUND"	This attribute is relevant only on the Windows platform, for which a value of FOREGROUND makes the plug-in use the foreground palette. Conversely, a value of BACKGROUND makes the plug-in use the background palette, which is the default.

Tip: Navigation Controls

VRML browsers are not consistent when it comes to displaying navigation controls in a world so small that the controls become impractical to use. The blaxxun Contact browser, for example, simply hides the navigation controls altogether in such cases. Cosmo Player, on the other hand, will shrink the navigation controls as much as possible, after which they are actually cut off and therefore not usable. In cases where your VRML world size is particularly small (anything under 150 pixels high or wide), you should consider disabling the navigation controls, either via an <EMBED> element attribute or directly in the VRML world's NavigationInfo node as described later in this chapter.

```
<EMBED SRC="seaside.wrl" HEIGHT="300" WIDTH="400">
```

The URL supplied to the SRC attribute in this particular example is relative, meaning that the seaside.wrl file is located relative to the Web page in which this EMBED element appears (the VRML and HTML files are assumed to be in the same folder in this example). You can, however, also supply an absolute URL to SRC, as the following example illustrates:

```
<EMBED
 SRC="http://www.web3dgallery.com/vrml/seaside/seaside.wrl"
 HEIGHT="300" WIDTH="400">
```

In both cases we've constructed an EMBED element that gives browsers enough information to fetch the Seaside VRML world and display it in a specifically sized area of the Web page (later you'll see how to use the ALIGN attribute to control the flow of text around an embedded world). Upon seeing these EMBED elements, a Web browser will retrieve the VRML world specified by the SRC attribute and then hand it over to the appropriate plug-in. If the user doesn't have a VRML plug-in installed, the browser will prompt the user to install one.

You should also be aware that not all attributes of EMBED apply to every plug-in. The BORDER attribute, for example, is typically ignored when the EMBED element references a VRML world. Likewise, PALETTE has no effect, because VRML plug-ins handle color internally and so have no need for this attribute. However, you'll often find yourself using general layout attributes such as ALIGN, VSPACE, and HSPACE to control how your worlds appear in the Web page, and so the next sections discuss these in more detail. In addition, plug-ins can support their own custom attributes, a feature of the EMBED element that VRML browsers often take advantage of as you'll soon see (see "Custom Browser Attributes").

Warning: Double Quotes

You'll notice that in supplying information to the EMBED element attributes great care was taken to wrap each piece of data inside a pair of double quotes (" "). If you were to use single quotes instead, the browser might have problems parsing the information you provide. As a result, you should always surround EMBED element attribute data with double quotes, even if the urge to use single quotes sneaks up on you.

Tip: Filling Pages and Frames

In cases where you'd like to fill an entire Web page or frame with a VRML world, you can supply "100%" as the EMBED element's width and height as follows:

```
<EMBED SRC="seaside.wrl" WIDTH=100% HEIGHT=100%>
```

<NOEMBED>

Although the EMBED element has been around almost as long as the Web itself, some browsers aren't equipped to handle it or plug-ins at all. Handheld computing devices (such as the Palm Pilot), for instance, usually aren't sophisticated enough to process much of the rich media flowing around the Web today, even with the help of a browser plug-in. When a browser can't deal with the EMBED element at all, it will simply skip over it.

If you wish to inform such users that they're missing out on something worthwhile (possibly to entice them to return later when connected to the Web using a more capable system), you can follow every EMBED element that you construct with a corresponding NOEMBED element. The NOEM-BED element is ignored entirely by those browsers that can handle the EMBED element, giving you a convenient mechanism for communicating with users who can't see your plug-in enhanced Web pages, as the following example illustrates:

Tip

Although it is not required, you can supply alternate text before a closing </EMBED> tag. Alternate EMBED element text is similar in nature to alternate text supplied before a closing </APPLET> element used with Java applets. This text is ignored by browsers that support plug-ins via the EMBED element, yet will be displayed by those that can't handle EMBED:

```
<EMBED SRC="seaside.wrl" HEIGHT="300" WIDTH="400">
Your browser does not support the embed tag!
</EMBED>
```

```
<EMBED SRC="seaside.wrl" HEIGHT="300" WIDTH="400">
<NOEMBED>Sorry, but your Web browser does not support plug-
ins! Please return when you're equipped to handle the killer
3D you're now missing.</NOEMBED>
```

Controlling Alignment with ALIGN

Although you need only supply SRC, HEIGHT, and WIDTH attributes in order to construct a valid EMBED element, chances are pretty good that you'll also want to include the ALIGN attribute in order to control the placement of your VRML world in relation to the text around it. Similar in nature to the ALIGN attribute used with the IMG element, which controls the placement of images with respect to the line of text in which they appear, the EMBED element ALIGN attribute can be set to "LEFT," "RIGHT," "TOP," or "BOTTOM" (see Table 6.3).

Table 6.3   EMBED Element ALIGN Attribute

Attribute	*Description*
ALIGN=	Specifies the alignment for the embedded plug-in:
"BOTTOM"	BOTTOM aligns text to the bottom (the default).
"LEFT"	LEFT aligns text flush left.
"RIGHT"	RIGHT aligns text flush right.
"TOP"	TOP aligns text to the top.

Note: Although not included in Netscape's definition of the EMBED tag, today's most current browsers can also accept ALIGN attribute values of "MIDDLE," "ABSBOTTOM," "ABSMIDDLE," and "BASE-LINE."

By default, text appearing around an EMBED element is aligned to the text's bottom baseline as Figure 6-9 illustrates. The HTML code for this image is found in Listing 6.7, where the EMBED element could alternately have specified a setting of ALIGN="BOTTOM" as follows:

```
<EMBED SRC="seaside.wrl" WIDTH="200" HEIGHT="200"
ALIGN="BOTTOM">
```

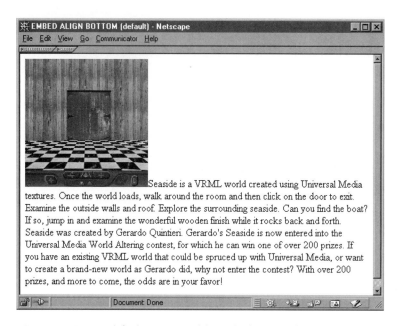

Figure 6-9   By default, VRML worlds stitched into Web pages using the EMBED element are aligned with the baseline of the text in which they appear (the equivalent of ALIGN="BOTTOM").

Listing 6.7   embedAlignDefault.html

```
<html>

<head>
<title>EMBED ALIGN default (BOTTOM)</title>
</head>

<body>

<p><EMBED SRC="seaside.wrl" WIDTH="200" HEIGHT="200">Seaside
is a VRML world created using Universal Media textures. Once
the world loads, walk around the room and then click on the
door to exit. Examine the outside walls and roof. Explore the
surrounding seaside. Can you find the boat? If so, jump in
and examine the wonderful wooden finish while it rocks back
and forth. Seaside was created by Gerardo Quintieri. Ger-
ardo's Seaside is now entered into the Universal Media World
Altering contest, for which he can win one of over 200
prizes. If you have an existing VRML world that could be
```

```
spruced up with Universal Media, or want to create a brand-
new world as Gerardo did, why not enter the contest? With
over 200 prizes, and more to come, the odds are in your
favor!</p>

</body>
</html>
```

If you're wondering why a bottom alignment such as this doesn't position the top of the VRML world with the text baseline, think about how the IMG element handles bottom alignment. In both cases the elements are considered to be *character-level* elements, meaning that an image or embedded world is positioned in a line of text as if it were actually a character itself. If the image or world is too big to fit on the line as the other characters do, as is the case with every VRML world including those seen here, it will push the text out of place in order to accommodate the added width or height. In this respect you can think of your VRML worlds as being extremely large characters, such as the "S" appearing in the following paragraph:

Seaside is a VRML world created using Universal Media textures. Once the world loads, walk around the room and then click on the door to exit. Examine the outside walls and roof. Explore the surrounding seaside. Can you find the boat? If so, jump in and examine the wonderful wooden finish while it rocks back and forth. Seaside was created by Gerardo Quintieri. Gerardo's Seaside is now entered into the Universal Media World Altering contest, for which he can win one of over 200 prizes. If you have an existing VRML world that could be spruced up with Universal Media, or want to create a brand-new world as Gerardo did, why not enter the contest? With over 200 prizes, and more to come, the odds are in your favor!

In the above example, text appears only *after* the leading "S", just as text follows the VRML world found in Listing 6.7 (see Figure 6-9). If the large element appeared in the middle of the paragraph, however, it would push the text above it out of the way, as the following paragraph and Figure 6-10 illustrate (for which the corresponding code is found in Listing 6.8).

Seaside is a VRML world created using Universal Media textures. Once the world loads, walk around the room and then click on the door to exit. Examine the outside walls and roof. Explore the surrounding seaside. Can you find the boat? If so, jump in and examine the wonderful wooden finish while it rocks back and forth. **S**easide was created by Gerardo Quintieri. Gerardo's Seaside is now entered into the Universal Media World Altering contest, for which he can win one of over 200 prizes. If you have an existing VRML world that could be spruced up with Universal Media, or want to create a brand-new world as Gerardo did, why not enter the contest? With over 200 prizes, and more to come, the odds are in your favor!

You'll notice that the flow of text appearing in Figure 6-10 is awkward, to say the least, because the text appearing before the EMBED element is pushed out of the way to make room for the VRML world. A simple HTML BR element (commonly known as the "break" tag), however, can be placed immediately before the EMBED element to force the world (and the text

Figure 6-10   EMBED is a character-level element, which is why this bottom-aligned VRML world pushes out the text around it (ALIGN="BOTTOM" is equivalent to omitting the ALIGN attribute altogether).

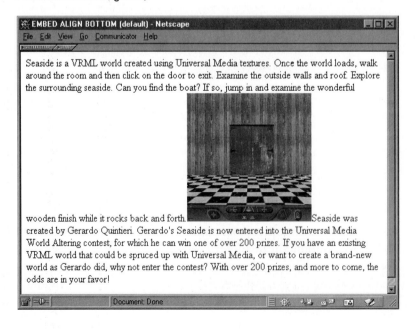

Listing 6.8   embedAlignBottom.html

```html
<html>

<head>
<title>EMBED ALIGN BOTTOM (default)</title>
</head>

<body>

<p>Seaside is a VRML world created using Universal Media tex-
tures. Once the world loads, walk around the room and then
click on the door to exit. Examine the outside walls and
roof. Explore the surrounding seaside. Can you find the boat?
If so, jump in and examine the wonderful wooden finish while
it rocks back and forth.<EMBED SRC="seaside.wrl" WIDTH="200"
HEIGHT="200" ALIGN="BOTTOM">Seaside was created by Gerardo
Quintieri. Gerardo's Seaside is now entered into the Univer-
sal Media World Altering contest, for which he can win one of
over 200 prizes. If you have an existing VRML world that
could be spruced up with Universal Media, or want to create a
brand-new world as Gerardo did, why not enter the contest?
With over 200 prizes, and more to come, the odds are in your
favor!</p>

</body>
</html>
```

---

that follows it) onto its own line, as seen in Figure 6-11. The following snippet of code contains the BR element used to cleanly separate the text appearing before and after the VRML world in Figure 6-11:

```
...Can you find the boat? If so, jump in and examine
the wonderful wooden finish while it rocks back
and forth.<BR><EMBED SRC="seaside.wrl" WIDTH="200"
HEIGHT="200" ALIGN="BOTTOM">Seaside was created by
Gerardo Quintieri...
```

Although "BOTTOM" is the default EMBED alignment, you're free to
set the ALIGN attribute of the element to "TOP," "LEFT," and "RIGHT" in
order to position your world accordingly. Figure 6-12 illustrates a setting of
ALIGN="TOP", which results in the top of the world being aligned with the
top of the text around it. As with the default bottom alignment, the text is actually pushed out in order to accommodate the larger world. Figure 6-13, on

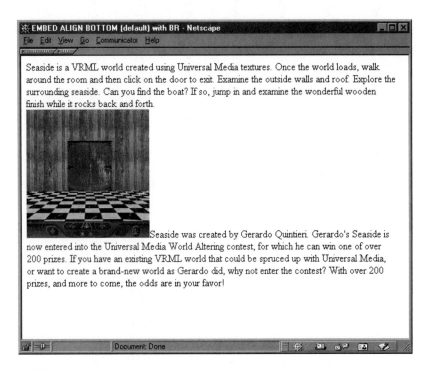

Figure 6-11   The BR element was used to force a line break before the bottom-aligned VRML world is displayed, which places the world on its own line.

the other hand, was produced with a setting of ALIGN="LEFT", while Figure 6-14 uses ALIGN="RIGHT".

In cases where ALIGN="LEFT" or ALIGN="RIGHT", the text following the EMBED tag automatically flows around the image, as seen in Figures 6-13 and 6-14. You can, however, use the BR element combined with a CLEAR attribute in order to override the flow of text. Following are three variations on the BR CLEAR attribute:

```
<BR CLEAR="LEFT">
<BR CLEAR="RIGHT">
<BR CLEAR="ALL">
```

The first BR element example shown above can be placed after a left-aligned EMBED element, which will result in the VRML world appearing on its own line. Similarly, you might place the second example following a right-aligned EMBED element in order to place such a world on its own line. Alternately, you can always clear both the left and right margins by simply clearing "all," as the last example illustrates.

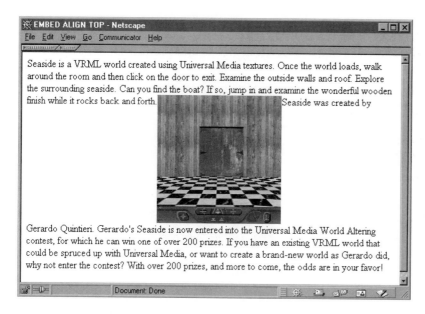

Figure 6-12   The EMBED element in this example was configured with ALIGN="TOP", aligning the top of the VRML world with the top of the text in which the element appears.

Figure 6-13   The EMBED element in this example was configured with ALIGN="LEFT", aligning the VRML world to the left of the page, around which the text automatically flows.

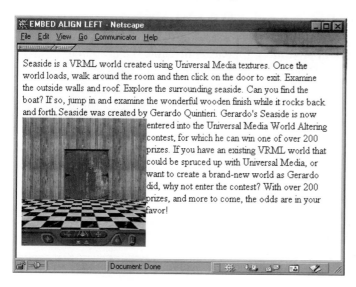

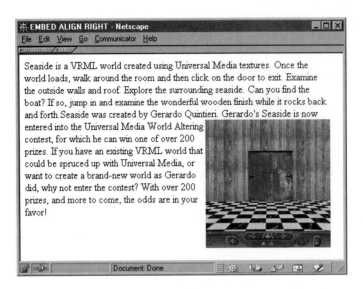

The window shows a Netscape browser titled "EMBED ALIGN RIGHT - Netscape" with the text:

> Seaside is a VRML world created using Universal Media textures. Once the world loads, walk around the room and then click on the door to exit. Examine the outside walls and roof. Explore the surrounding seaside. Can you find the boat? If so, jump in and examine the wonderful wooden finish while it rocks back and forth. Seaside was created by Gerardo Quintieri. Gerardo's Seaside is now entered into the Universal Media World Altering contest, for which he can win one of over 200 prizes. If you have an existing VRML world that could be spruced up with Universal Media, or want to create a brand-new world as Gerardo did, why not enter the contest? With over 200 prizes, and more to come, the odds are in your favor!

Figure 6-14   The EMBED element in this example was configured with ALIGN="RIGHT", aligning the VRML world to the right of the page, around which the text automatically flows.

ALIGN "MIDDLE," "ABSBOTTOM," "ABSMIDDLE," and "BASELINE"

The EMBED element attributes appearing in Table 6.2 are documented at Netscape's DevEdge site (http://developer.netscape.com/) and are supported by Navigator 2.0 to 4.0. If you're familiar with the IMG element ALIGN attribute, however, you'll notice that the EMBED ALIGN attribute appearing here does not include "MIDDLE." You can middle-align VRML worlds in modern Web browsers by simply setting ALIGN to "MIDDLE" as follows:

```
<EMBED SRC="xyz.wrl" WIDTH="200" HEIGHT="200" ALIGN=
"MIDDLE">
```

Current versions of Navigator and Internet Explorer will also accept ALIGN values of "ABSBOTTOM," "ABSMIDDLE," and "BASELINE."

Controlling Space with VSPACE and HSPACE

In addition to controlling the general alignment of your VRML worlds through the ALIGN attribute, the EMBED tag offers two attributes that you can use to specify the amount of horizontal and vertical space appearing around your worlds (also known as the "gutter" space around a plug-in). The HSPACE attribute is used to specify the amount of space, measured in pixels, falling between the left and right edges of your VRML world and the content that surrounds it (such as text). VSPACE, on the other hand, is used to specify the amount of space between the top and bottom of the world (see Table 6.4).

By default, there is almost no space between the plug-in area and the content surrounding it (refer to previous figures to see how small this space is by default). If you want a little elbow room around your VRML worlds, however, feel free to use HSPACE to specify an amount of horizontal space or VSPACE to specify vertical space. Not surprisingly, you can also use both attributes at the same time, as Figure 6-15 illustrates. In this example a relatively wide berth of 25 pixels was specified for both horizontal and vertical space using the following EMBED element:

```
<EMBED SRC="seaside.wrl" ALIGN="LEFT" HSPACE="25"
VSPACE="25" WIDTH="200" HEIGHT="200">
```

Table 6.4   EMBED Element HSPACE and VSPACE Attributes

Attribute	*Description*
HSPACE="horizMargin"	Specifies a margin, in pixels, between the left and right edges of the plug-in and surrounding content (the "horizontal space").
VSPACE="vertMargin"	Specifies a margin, in pixels, between the top and bottom edges of the applet and surrounding content (the "vertical space").

Note: Although Netscape Navigator supports EMBED HSPACE and VSPACE attributes, Microsoft's Internet Explorer does not and instead ignores them. You should use the OBJECT tag's ALIGN attributes of the same name when it comes to supporting Internet Explorer (see "<OBJECT>" later in this chapter).

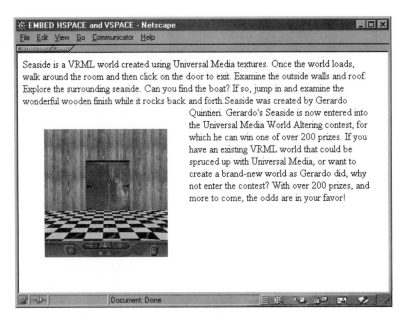

Seaside is a VRML world created using Universal Media textures. Once the world loads, walk around the room and then click on the door to exit. Examine the outside walls and roof. Explore the surrounding seaside. Can you find the boat? If so, jump in and examine the wonderful wooden finish while it rocks back and forth. Seaside was created by Gerardo Quintieri. Gerardo's Seaside is now entered into the Universal Media World Altering contest, for which he can win one of over 200 prizes. If you have an existing VRML world that could be spruced up with Universal Media, or want to create a brand-new world as Gerardo did, why not enter the contest? With over 200 prizes, and more to come, the odds are in your favor!

Figure 6-15   The EMBED element in this example was configured with VSPACE and HSPACE both set to 25, giving this world a little elbow room with respect to the text around it.

Warning: Internet Explorer

Internet Explorer ignores the EMBED element HSPACE and VSPACE attributes. In order to support both Navigator and Internet Explorer you should nest your EMBED elements inside corresponding OBJECT elements, as described later (see "<OBJECT>").

Custom Plug-in Attributes

Although EMBED offers a number of "pre-made" attributes, such as ALIGN, HSPACE, and VSPACE, this element gains its real power when combined with custom plug-in attributes. Depending on the plug-in that you're using, you may have a number of different attributes to choose from. Consider, for example, the custom EMBED attributes listed in Table 6.5.

Table 6.5 lists the EMBED attributes supported by Microsoft's VRML 2.0 Viewer plug-in, which is based on version 2.0 of Intervista's WorldView plug-in. As a result, Microsoft's VRML 2.0 Viewer and WorldView 2.0 support the same custom EMBED attributes. You'll notice that each of these custom plug-in attribute names begins with "VRML_", for which there is also a corresponding "SGI_" attribute. This is a reflection of the browser's support for a suite of EMBED attributes originally introduced by Silicon Graphics, Inc. (SGI), although the equivalent "VRML_" attributes are more commonly used today.

For good measure, we've also tossed into this table two custom attributes supported by WorldView 2.1, VRML_DITHERING and VRML_FULL-COLOR, for which there is no "SGI_" equivalent, as these attributes were introduced by Intervista along with the most current version of their browser. For a detailed summary of custom EMBED attributes supported by other VRML browsers (such as Cosmo Player, blaxxun Contact, and ParallelGraphics Cortona), see Appendix A, "VRML Browsers").

Table 6.5   Microsoft's VRML 2.0 Viewer, WorldView 2.0 and 2.1 <EMBED> Attributes
usage: <EMBED ... *attribute="value"*>

Attribute	Value	Description
VRML_DASHBOARD (or SGI_DASHBOARD)	TRUE	Turns on horizontal and vertical toolbars
	FALSE	Turns off horizontal and vertical toolbars
VRML_IMAGEQUALITY (or SGI_IMAGEQUALITY)	BEST	Sets image quality to "Smooth"
	SMOOTH	Sets image quality to "Flat"
	SMOOTHEST	Sets image quality to "Wireframe"
VRML_POPMENU (or SGI_POPMENU)	TRUE	Enables right mouse button menu.
	FALSE	Disables right mouse button menu.
VRML_SPLASHSCREEN (or SGI_SPLASHSCREEN)	TRUE	Displays splash screen at startup
	FALSE	Prevents splash screen from appearing at startup

WorldView 2.1 supports all of the above, plus the following:

Attribute	Value	Description
VRML_ DITHERING	TRUE	Turns on dithering
	FALSE	Turns off dithering
VRML_FULLCOLOR	TRUE	Turns on Full Color mode
	FALSE	Turns off Full Color mode

Shifting Sands

Intervista (http://www.intervista.com/) was one of the first VRML development firms to hit the Web with a VRML plug-in. Founded by Tony Parisi, Intervista produced the WorldView line of VRML browsers (plug-ins) for Navigator and Internet Explorer. Subsequently, WorldView 2.0 became the VRML browser around which Microsoft developed its own "VRML 2.0 Viewer" plug-in for Internet Explorer (http://www.microsoft.com/vrml/).

In time, Intervista, along with a number of popular VRML companies (such as Cosmo Software, the SGI spin-out that produced the Cosmo Player plug-in and a variety of VRML authoring tools such as Cosmo Worlds and PageFX), were acquired by Platinum Technology (http://www.platinum.com/). Platinum, a large enterprise application developer, had intentions of using VRML for a variety of business visualization technologies (such as enterprise database visualization, 3D presentation graphics, and so forth).

In the middle of 1999, however, Computer Associates (http://www.cai.com/) acquired Platinum in a multibillion-dollar transaction. As this book went to print, WorldView, Cosmo Player, and a number of other VRML products owned by Platinum were in the process of being absorbed by Computer Associates, whose intentions with regard to these products had yet to be publicly announced. To learn more about WorldView, Cosmo Player, and other VRML browsers, see Appendix A, "VRML Browsers."

When a plug-in doesn't support a specific custom EMBED attribute that you supply, it will simply ignore that attribute altogether. Listing 6.9, for example, uses the EMBED element to weave a primitive sphere shape into a Web page (the sphere.wrl world file is defined in Listing 6.10). This particular EMBED element specifies both the VRML_DASHBOARD and VRML_IMAGEQUALITY attributes seen in Table 6.5, which tells the plug-in to hide its VRML controls (commonly known as the "dashboard") and render the image in wireframe mode.

If these attributes were omitted from EMBED altogether, the VRML browser's dashboard controls would be displayed by default, and the sphere would be rendered using default 3D lighting and shading as seen in Figure 6-16. By setting VRML_DASHBOARD="FALSE" and VRML_IMAGE-QUALITY="SMOOTHEST", however, as we've done in Listing 6.9, Microsoft's VRML 2.0 Viewer and WorldView browsers hide the dashboard and render the world accordingly, as seen in Figure 6-17.

Note: Dashboards

Every VRML browser has a unique look and feel for its dashboard; there is no standard user interface for these VRML controls, although practically every browser supports the "VRML_DASHBOARD" custom attribute found in Table 6.5. To see examples of various dashboard interfaces, as well as the custom plug-in attributes supported by a number of popular VRML browsers, turn to Appendix A, "VRML Browsers." Later in this chapter you'll see how the NavigationInfo node can be used to control various properties of the dashboard, such as whether the controls are preset to walk around a world or examine the objects it contains.

Figure 6-16   This sphere shape is rendered as a 3D object by default, with the VRML controls visible.

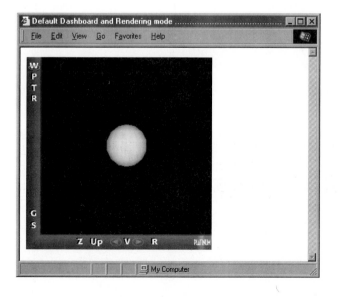

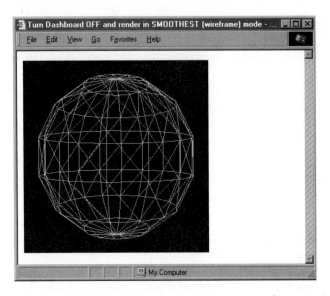

Figure 6-17   The sphere is now rendered in wireframe mode and the VRML controls are hidden, thanks to custom EMBED element attributes VRML_DASHBOARD and VRML_IMAGEQUALITY.

Listing 6.9   embedCustomAttributes.html

```
<html>

<head>
<title>Custom EMBED Attributes</title>
</head>

<body>

<EMBED SRC="sphere.wrl" WIDTH="400" HEIGHT="400"
 VRML_DASHBOARD="FALSE" VRML_IMAGEQUALITY="SMOOTHEST">

</body>
</html>
```

Listing 6.10   sphere.wrl

```
#VRML V2.0 utf8

Shape {
  appearance Appearance {
    material Material { }
  }
  geometry Sphere { }
}
```

Plug-in Support

The custom EMBED attributes supported by today's most popular VRML plug-ins can be found in Appendix A, "VRML Browsers." You can also turn to the VRML development area for each vendor if you'd like more detailed technical information, such as a comprehensive description of proprietary features, bug reports, and authoring advice. Following are links to the developer's area for several popular VRML plug-ins:

Contact (blaxxun): http://www.blaxxun.com/developer/

Cortona (ParallelGraphics): http://www.parallelgraphics.com/htm/en/ prod/

Cosmo Player (Cosmo): http://www.cosmosoftware.com/developer/

VRML 2.0 Viewer (Microsoft): http://www.microsoft.com/vrml/toolbar/

WorldView (Intervista): http://www.intervista.com/support/

For links to other VRML plug-ins, you can visit the following sites:

About Web3D:
   http://web3d.about.com/

VRML Works:
   http://home.hiwaay.net/~crispen/vrmlworks/

Web3D Gallery:
   http://www.web3dgallery.com/vrml/plugins/

Although VRML_DASHBOARD and VRML_IMAGEQUALITY are supported by Microsoft and Intervista VRML browsers, others aren't guaranteed to honor these EMBED attributes. Cosmo Player, Contact, and Cortona, for example, both will honor the VRML_DASHBOARD attribute but ignore VRML_IMAGEQUALITY entirely, as these browsers don't have a setting that corresponds to this attribute.

<OBJECT>

The OBJECT element was introduced by the World Wide Web Consortium in response to the many nonstandard elements such as EMBED, APPLET, and DYNASRC that cropped up in the early days of the Web in order to facilitate the integration of non-standard content with HTML. Rather than throwing its support behind competitor Netscape's EMBED element, Microsoft decided that Internet Explorer would instead support the OBJECT element.

In time, however, both browsers eventually came to support EMBED *and* OBJECT, meaning you can't add both elements to your page unless you nest EMBED inside of OBJECT. If you don't nest in this way, and instead include standalone versions of both elements, users with a current version of Navigator or Internet Explorer will actually load two separate instances of your VRML world (see "Nesting Elements" later in this section for details on how to avoid dueling tags).

OBJECT is an all-purpose element designed to accommodate a wide variety of multimedia content. Images, sounds, movies, applets, and VRML

Note: OBJECT on the Move

The World Wide Web Consortium (http://www.w3c.org) designed the OBJECT element to be a standard HTML mechanism for embedding multimedia content into Web pages (in HTML 4.0, OBJECT actually supersedes IMG). Although OBJECT can be used as a replacement for IMG, APPLET, EMBED, and other types of content embedding element, it will be a very, very long time before these tags disappear, because so many Web developers have come to rely on them. In addition, a tremendous number of pages out there are full of nonstandard elements that would "break" if future browsers decided not to support them (imagine a Web browser that doesn't support the APPLET element, for example).

In fact, while the traditional wisdom once was "use OBJECT for Microsoft Internet Explorer and EMBED for Netscape Navigator," one recent release of Internet Explorer handles EMBED elements without a problem, yet misbehaves when it encounters OBJECT elements!

worlds are a few of the types of content that can be woven into Web pages using OBJECT, which accounts for this element being one of the most complex you'll ever see. Table 6.6 summarizes the various attributes of the OBJECT element, although you'll only need to know about a few of these to integrate VRML into your Web pages.

Specifically, you'll need to use DATA, WIDTH, and HEIGHT within an opening OBJECT element, which is terminated by a closing OBJECT element, as the following example illustrates:

```
<OBJECT DATA="seaside.wrl" WIDTH="300" HEIGHT="300">
</OBJECT>
```

The DATA attribute is analogous to the SRC attribute of the EMBED tag, as it accepts a URL that points to the data to load (which in this case is a VRML world named seaside.wrl, located in the same folder as the Web page itself). Similarly, the OBJECT element's WIDTH and HEIGHT attributes are equivalent to those of the same name used by the EMBED element. In this respect, the above OBJECT element is equivalent to the following EMBED element:

```
<EMBED SRC="seaside.wrl" WIDTH="300" HEIGHT="300">
</EMBED>
```

Although you might be tempted to include both fully constructed elements in your Web pages in an effort to support both Navigator and Internet Explorer, you should be aware that current versions of each browser support both OBJECT *and* EMBED. If you weave both into your Web pages as stand-alone elements, each tag will be loaded, and you'll have two versions of the same world displayed in your page! To avoid this potential disaster, you can nest your EMBED elements inside corresponding OBJECT elements, as the next section explains.

Tip: Specifying MIME Types

In addition to specifying a VRML world using the OBJECT element's DATA attribute, you can also include MIME type information about that world via the TYPE attribute. (Browsers can use this added information to determine whether or not they can actually handle the type of content specified by DATA before they attempt to download the file.)

Following is an example OBJECT element fortified with VRML's "model/vrml" MIME type information:

```
<OBJECT TYPE="model/vrml" DATA="sphere.wrl" WIDTH="300"
HEIGHT="300">
</OBJECT>
```

Table 6.6	The OBJECT Element
	usage: <OBJECT DATA="location" HEIGHT=# WIDTH=# attributes>

Attribute	*Description*
ACCESSKEY="key"	Accelerator key for the object, where "key" is a string of characters that represents a key on an alphanumeric keyboard (object receives focus when the user presses the ALT and accelerator keys simultaneously).
ALIGN= "ABSBOTTOM" "ABSMIDDLE" "BASELINE" "BOTTOM" "LEFT" "MIDDLE" "RIGHT" "TEXTTOP" "TOP"	Alignment of the object in relation to the text around it: ABSBOTTOM aligns the object bottom with the absolute bottom of the surrounding text (the baseline of the text minus the height of the largest descender in the text). ABSMIDDLE aligns the middle of the object with the absolute middle of the surrounding text (the midpoint between the absolute bottom and text top of the surrounding text). BASELINE aligns the object bottom with the baseline of the surrounding text. BOTTOM aligns the object bottom with the bottom of the surrounding text (the baseline minus the standard height of a descender in the text). LEFT aligns the object to the left of the surrounding text (all preceding text and any text that follows flows to the right of the object). MIDDLE aligns the object middle with the surrounding text. RIGHT aligns the object to the right of the surrounding text (any text that follows flows to the left of the object). TEXTTOP aligns the object top with the absolute top of the surrounding text (the baseline plus the height of the largest ascender in the text). TOP aligns the top of the object with the top of the text (the baseline plus the standard height of an ascender in the text).

Attribute	*Description*
CLASS="classname"	Class of the object, where classname is a string that specifies the class (or a style rule).
CLASSID="id"	Class identifier for the object, where id is a string that specifies the object's class identifier. The class identifier format for registered Microsoft ActiveX Controls is: "clsid:XXXXXXXX-XXXX-XXXX-XXXX-XXXXXXXXXXXX".
CODE="url"	URL of the file containing the compiled Java class, where url is a string that represents the URL pointing to the file.
CODEBASE= "url[#version=a,b,c,d]"	URL of the component. The url string can optionally be appended with: #version=a,b,c,d, to specify a specific version number of the component (if the client computer already has a newer version installed, no download occurs).
CODETYPE="media-type"	Internet media type, or MIME type, for the code associated with the object.
DATA="url"	URL that references the data of the object.
DATAFLD="colname"	Specifies a field of a given data source (as specified by the dataSrc property) to bind to the specified object, where colname is a string that represents the field name.
DATASRC="#ID"	Specifies the source of the data for data binding, where ID is a string that represents the identifier of the data source.
HEIGHT="n"	Height of the object, where n is a string that represents an integer value corresponding to the height of the object in pixels. Alternately, n can represent a percentage integer (an integer value followed by the % symbol) that specifies the height of the object as a percentage of the height of its parent (75%, for example, specifies an object that is two-thirds the height of the browser window in which it appears). See WIDTH.
ID="value"	String identifying the <OBJECT>, where value is any alphanumeric string that begins with a letter.
LANG="language"	Language to use, where language is a string that specifies an ISO standard language abbreviation (the parser uses this property to determine how

Attribute	*Description*
	to display language-specific choices for items such as quotations and numbers).
LANGUAGE="script"	Language in which the current script is written (i.e., JScript, JavaScript, VBScript, VBS, or any other supported scripting language).
NAME="name"	Specifies the name of the control, bookmark, or application.
STYLE="css1-properties"	Specifies an inline style for the object.
TABINDEX="n"	Specifies the index within the tab selection order of the object, where n is a nonnegative integer that represents the tab index (to remove the object from the tab selection order, use –1).
TITLE="text"	Specifies a "ToolTip" for the object (the ToolTip text appears when the user hovers the mouse over the object).
TYPE="MIME-type"	MIME type of the object (note that when no CLASSID attribute is specified for an object, the TYPE property is used to retrieve the class identifier for the object).
WIDTH="n"	Specifies the width of the object, where n is a string that represents an integer value corresponding to the width of the object in pixels. Alternately, n can represent a percentage integer (an integer value followed by the % symbol) that specifies the width of the object as a percentage of the width of its parent (75%, for example, specifies an object that is two-thirds the width of the browser window in which it appears). See HEIGHT.

Nesting Elements

Because current versions of Navigator and Internet Explorer support both OBJECT and EMBED, you must take care to nest the latter inside the former to avoid loading two separate instances of your VRML worlds. Such nesting is possible because the OBJECT element was specifically designed to accommodate other HTML elements nested inside it for purposes of backward compatibility. If a Web browser supports OBJECT, it will use that element and skip over any nested elements it contains. Alternately, if a Web browser does not understand OBJECT, it will ignore this element and proceed to the next element it finds.

With this in mind, consider Listing 6.11. Here you'll see that the Seaside world used in previous examples has been specified with both an EMBED and OBJECT element, with the EMBED element nested inside of the OBJECT tag as follows:

```
<OBJECT DATA="seaside.wrl" WIDTH="300" HEIGHT="300">
  <EMBED SRC="seaside.wrl" WIDTH="300" HEIGHT="300"></EMBED>
</OBJECT>
```

When this Web page is encountered by a Web browser that understands OBJECT, the world pointed to by the OBJECT element's DATA attribute is loaded and the EMBED tag is ignored altogether. Those browsers that don't support OBJECT, however, will skip over it and instead load the world specified by the EMBED element. Although both elements specify the same world in this example, you could, of course, specify a different world for each element if you wanted to (although doing so would result in an inconsistent page when viewed across a wide variety of browsers).

You can, in fact, nest more than one element inside of OBJECT, allowing Web browsers to effectively "walk through" each until it encounters an element that it can actually handle. The following snippet of code follows the nested EMBED element with an IMG element, allowing browsers that don't support either OBJECT or EMBED to show a JPEG image of the world at the very least:

```
<OBJECT DATA="seaside.wrl" WIDTH="300" HEIGHT="300">
  <EMBED SRC="seaside.wrl" WIDTH="300" HEIGHT="300"></EMBED>
  <IMG SRC="seaside.jpg" WIDTH="300" HEIGHT="300">
</OBJECT>
```

Listing 6.11   nesting.html

```
<html>

<head>
<title>Nesting EMBED in OBJECT</title>
</head>

<body>
<p>
<OBJECT DATA="seaside.wrl" WIDTH="300" HEIGHT="300">
<EMBED SRC="seaside.wrl" WIDTH="300" HEIGHT="300"></EMBED>
</OBJECT>Seaside is a VRML world created using Universal Media
textures. Once the world loads, walk around the room and then
```

```
click on the door to exit. Examine the outside walls and
roof. Explore the surrounding seaside. Can you find the boat?
If so, jump in and examine the wonderful wooden finish while
it rocks back and forth. Seaside was created by Gerardo Quin-
tieri. Gerardo's Seaside is now entered into the Universal
Media World Altering contest, for which he can win one of
over 200 prizes. If you have an existing VRML world that
could be spruced up with Universal Media, or want to create a
brand-new world as Gerardo did, why not enter the contest?
With over 200 prizes, and more to come, the odds are in your
favor!</p>

</body>
</html>
```

Forcing a Specific Plug-in

The OBJECT element supports an interesting attribute called CLASSID, which can be used to force Internet Explorer to load a specific VRML browser plug-in rather than rely on the default plug-in associated with a world file. (Multiple VRML browsers can be installed on a system, although only one can be the default used by Internet Explorer to view VRML content.) Because VRML browsers running in the Windows environment are actually ActiveX controls, the CLASSID attribute can be used to supply the unique class identifier for a specific registered control (see Table 6.7 for a list of common VRML browser class identifiers). If the control specified by CLASSID is installed, Internet Explorer will load it instead of the default.

Listing 6.12, for example, forces Internet Explorer to use the blaxxun Contact VRML browser control if it is installed, while Listing 6.13 specifies the ParallelGraphics Cortona browser instead. You'll notice in each listing that a new element named PARAM is present immediately following the opening OBJECT element. The PARAM element is a companion to OBJECT and is used to pass information to the plug-in in NAME-VALUE pairs (similar in nature to PARAM elements used to pass parameters to Java applets).

In these examples we've used PARAM to pass a relative URL pointing to the VRML file to be loaded, which is why you don't see a DATA attribute in the opening OBJECT element. Although we actually recommend including a DATA attribute even when using custom PARAM elements, as the "Browser Incompatibilities" warning explains, we've omitted DATA in these particular examples to illustrate how different browsers can use different

PARAM names to carry out the same task. Whereas blaxxun Contact supports a PARAM named "World," for instance, the Cortona browser created by ParallelGraphics requires a "Scene" PARAM instead. As the next section explains, you have to ensure that the correct PARAM names and values are supplied in your OBJECT elements; otherwise, the plug-in won't receive the information you're trying to pass to it.

Warning: Browser Incompatibilities

You should only use the OBJECT element's CLASSID attribute with Internet Explorer, as Navigator does not yet support this attribute. When Navigator encounters an OBJECT tag with a CLASSID attribute, it will typically display an alert claiming that the plug-in has not been installed (even if the plug-in has been installed) or simply display a blank area where the plug-in should appear). Use a bit of sniffer script to ensure that you use this attribute only with Internet Explorer, as explained in the "Sniffers" section (the CLASSID attribute is typically used in conjunction with sniffer scripts, since it's not supported by all browsers).

In cases where you do use the OBJECT element (regardless of whether or not you use the CLASSID attribute), be sure to specify your VRML world file using the DATA attribute even when you also supply the world location as a PARAM (such as <PARAM NAME="World" VALUE="seaside.wrl"> or <PARAM NAME="Scene" VALUE="seaside.wrl">). Some browsers don't read the world location when supplied as a PARAM, relying instead on the DATA attribute's being set to the URL of your world (there's no harm in supplying both).

Table 6.7   VRML Browser ActiveX Control Class IDs
usage: <OBJECT CLASSID="clsid:XXXXXXXX...">...>

VRML Browser	*CLASSID*
blaxxun Contact	"clsid:4B6E3013-6E45-11D0-9309-0020AFE05CC8"
Cosmo Player	"clsid:06646724-bcf3-11d0-9518-00c04fc2dd79"
Intervista WorldView	"clsid:B0D7D800-4EBF-11D0-9490-00A02494D8A5"
Microsoft VRML Viewer	"clsid:90A7533D-88FE-11D0-9DBE-0000C0411FC3"
ParallelGraphics Cortona	"clsid:86A88967-7A20-11D2-8EDA-00600818EDB1"

Listing 6.12   forceContact.html

```
<html>

<head>
<title>Force blaxxun Contact</title>
</head>

<body>

<OBJECT CLASSID="clsid:4B6E3013-6E45-11D0-9309-0020AFE05CC8"
 WIDTH="300" HEIGHT="300">

<PARAM NAME="World" VALUE="seaside.wrl">
</OBJECT>

</body>
</html>
```

Listing 6.13   forceCortona.html

```
<html>

<head>
<title>Force ParallelGraphics Cortona</title>
</head>

<body>

<OBJECT CLASSID="clsid:86A88967-7A20-11D2-8EDA-00600818EDB1"
  WIDTH="300" HEIGHT="300">

<PARAM NAME="Scene" VALUE="seaside.wrl">
</OBJECT>

</body>
</html>
```

OBJECT Parameters

Whereas the EMBED element supports custom attributes (see "Custom Plug-in Attributes"), the OBJECT element has an associated PARAM element for such purposes. Much like the PARAM element used to pass parameter information to Java applets, you supply custom plug-in information (such as the location of the VRML world to load, dashboard visibility, rendering quality, and so forth) in NAME/VALUE pairs, as illustrated previously in Listings 6.12 and 6.13. In those examples the OBJECT element's DATA attribute was omitted in favor of a custom PARAM unique to each browser.

Similarly, Listing 6.14 uses a number of PARAM elements to control the VRML browser's appearance. Here we've specified that the dashboard should be hidden and that the right mouse button popup menu should be disabled. We've also specified the "smoothest" possible rendering, which is wireframe mode according to Intervista Worldview and Microsoft VRML 2.0 Viewer browsers, as you learned earlier in the "Custom Plug-in Attributes" discussion.

Of course, not all VRML browsers support these parameters. Fortunately, those parameters that aren't understood by a browser are simply ignored. As a result, you can add your "dream" parameters without concern for breaking those browsers that don't support them (see Appendix A, "VRML Browsers," for details on parameters supported by a number of popular VRML browsers).

Listing 6.14   objectPARAM.html

```
<html>

<head>
<title>Object PARAM elements</title>
</head>

<body>

<OBJECT DATA="sphere.wrl" WIDTH="400" HEIGHT="400">
<PARAM NAME="VRML_DASHBOARD" VALUE="FALSE">
<PARAM NAME="VRML_POPMENU" VALUE="FALSE">
<PARAM NAME="VRML_IMAGEQUALITY" VALUE="SMOOTHEST">
</OBJECT>
</body>

</html>
```

Tip: Using DATA as a Backup

When constructing OBJECT elements that are not targeted at a specific VRML browser (i.e., when the CLASSID is not specified), be sure to supply the URL to your VRML file using the DATA attribute, which is the OBJECT element's general mechanism for supplying this information to a plug-in. Because VRML browsers vary in the PARAM they expect for such purposes, you have to either support all of them (such as <PARAM NAME="World" VALUE="sphere.wrl">, <PARAM NAME="Scene" VALUE="sphere.wrl"> and others) or use a sniffer script to aid in the construction of an appropriate OBJECT element. You can also include a properly specified DATA attribute as a backup to PARAM settings (it's fine to include multiple PARAM settings and a DATA attribute, as plug-ins will load the first they can handle and ignore the others). Refer to Appendix A, "VRML Browsers," to learn more about the PARAM elements supported by popular VRML browsers.

Compressing VRML Files

Before uploading your VRML files to the Web, you should seriously consider first compressing them in order to conserve as much bandwidth as possible. Although VRML text files are quite small on their own when compared to traditional 3D files, you can generally reduce them in size by half or more by applying GNU Zip compression. GNU Zip, more commonly known as GZip, uses Lempel-Ziv compression (LZ77) to reduce files in size. It is made freely available through the Free Software Foundation at the following sites:

```
http://www.gnu.org/
ftp://www.gnu.org/gnu/gzip/
ftp://prep.ai.mit.edu/pub/gnu/
```

GZip is a command-line utility available for UNIX, VMS, and Windows systems. It is executed at a command prompt, such as the Windows

Binary Compression

VRML does not inherently support binary compression, although GZip can be used to reduce the size of VRML text files. GZip utilizes the well-known Lempel-Ziv LZ77 compression scheme, an algorithm in which the amount of compression achieved is directly related to the size of the file being compressed and the distribution of common substrings it contains. Text files such a VRML worlds are typically reduced 60–70% using GZip, although this technique isn't nearly as efficient as some binary compression schemes.

Other forms of Web3D, however, do support binary compression of scene geometry (geometric scene data, which does not include media such as textures and sound files). Java 3D and MPEG-4/BIFS, for example, both offer binary compression of scene data (BIFS actually stands for Binary Format for Scenes and is an extremely powerful compression scheme that can reduce scene data by as much as 20 times). At the time of this writing X3D was still under development, and specifics regarding X3D compression were not yet available.

MS-DOS prompt seen in Figure 6-18. You must, therefore, be comfortable issuing command-line instructions in order to use this utility. (Windows users will find an introduction to the MS-DOS command line in the online Core Web3D chapter called "Installing Java 3D" located at http://www. core web3D.com/java 3d/install/.)

Although GZip is based on the same compression algorithm used by a number of popular Zip archive utilities, such as PKZip and WinZip, GZip is designed to compress only one file at a time (whereas standard Zip utilities can compress multiple files at once and place them into a single archive). As a result, you must compress each of your VRML files individually. To do so, simply type the name of the GZip utility at the command line, followed by the full name of the VRML file you'd like to compress (where ">" indicates the command-line prompt, and Seaside.wrl is assumed to reside in the same folder as the GZip program):

```
>  gzip Seaside.wrl
```

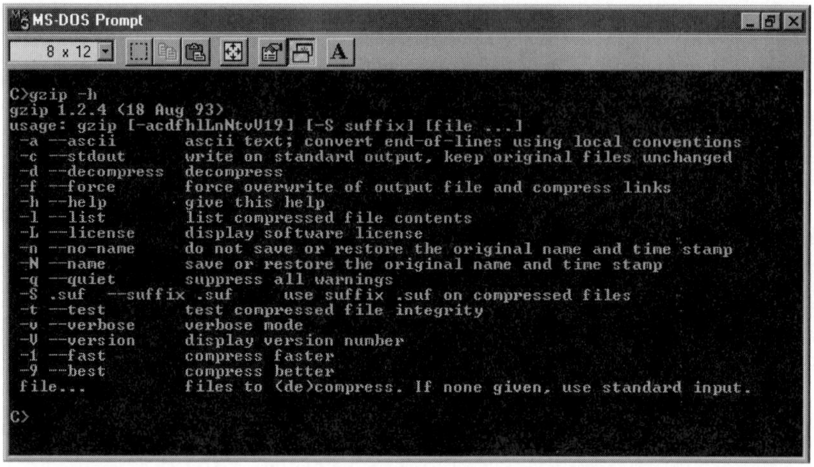

Figure 6-18   GZip is a command-line utility, meaning it does not offer a graphical user interface. GZip is instead executed at a system prompt, such as the Windows MS-DOS prompt shown here.

Upon compressing a VRML file, GZip will change the file's extension to .wrz to indicate that it has been successfully GZip compressed (or "GZipped"). If successful, the utility will display a notice on the command line regarding the name of your newly GZipped file (an error message is displayed if compression wasn't successful). In this particular example, the following line of text was output to the MS-DOS command prompt after Seaside.wrl was compresssed:

```
>   gzip: Seaside.wrl compressed to Seaside.wrz
```

To decompress a GZip-compressed VRML world, you can execute GZip along with the file name and the -d option (the "decompress" flag) as follows:

```
>   gzip Seaside.wrz -d
```

After decompressing your world, GZip will remove the .z portion of the file extension. In the above example, the resulting file will simply be named "Seaside.wr". If you wanted your operating system to be able to identify this freshly decompressed file as a VRML world, you would actually have to change the .wr file extension to .wrl.

Weaving .wrz Files into Web Pages

Every modern VRML browser understands and supports GZipped files. As a result, you can weave .wrz files into Web pages just as easily as you can .wrl files. Because some older browsers had difficulty recognizing .wrz files, however, you'll often come across GZipped worlds that have the .wrl extension.

Fortunately, the .wrz file extension is widely supported by today's VRML browsers and tools so that you no longer have to worry about converting the file extension to .wrl unless you want to. Some visual authoring tools will, in fact, automatically GZip-compress your worlds when you save them as a file having the .wrz extension, while others offer GZip compression as a "Save" option. In the event that you don't explicitly specify the .wrz file extension for your world, however, such authoring tools may simply store GZip-compressed files using the .wrl extension. ParallelGraphic's Internet Scene Builder product, for example, offers GZip as an option when you save VRML files and stores the results in .wrl files regardless of whether or not you actually apply compression (http://www.parallelgraphics.com/).

.gz File Extensions

The default GZip file extension is .gz, meaning that this extension will be given to files that don't already have an extension. If you fed the GZip utility a file named "Seaside", for example, it would be compressed and saved in a file named "Seaside.gz". In cases where a file already has an extension, such as .wrl, the last character is converted to a z (.wrl is renamed to .wrz, for example).

When surfing the Web, you'll occasionally encounter VRML worlds having the both the .wrl and .gz file extensions, such as Seaside.wrl.gz. While many browsers will recognize such files as being GZip-compressed VRML worlds, the .wrz extension is more commonly used and therefore recommended when it comes to choosing a file extension for your own compressed worlds.

Beyond GZip Compression

GZip compression isn't the only way to reduce the size of your VRML files. Before you are even ready to GZip a VRML world, chances are pretty good that you can trim a sizable amount of fat off it using optimizer tools. Optimizer tools can help reduce the size of your VRML text files by stripping away the unnecessarily precise floating-point numbers that many visual authoring tools generate automatically. The floating-point number 3.1415926, for example, can often be reduced to 3.142, 3.14, or even 3.1 or 3 without noticeably altering the look or behavior of the object or scene. And while it doesn't seem like much when considering only one number, shaving a handful of digits off hundreds or even thousands of numbers can result in a considerable reduction in file size.

In addition to optimizing files in this way, a number of polygon-reduction tools are also available that can help eliminate unnecessary or wasteful object representation. In many cases you'll find that objects in your worlds can be represented with far fewer polygons than currently used without drastically changing the overall look of your scene. This can further reduce the size of your files before they are run through GZip.

To get your hands on a few of the more popular VRML optimization tools, visit http://www.web3dgallery.com/vrml/tools/.

Sniffers

Although a number of VRML browsers are freely available today, you can't be certain that everyone visiting your VRML-enhanced pages will actually have one installed. Fortunately, Web browsers are smart enough to inform those without a VRML browser that they won't be able to view the contents of an associated EMBED or OBJECT tag unless they install a corresponding plug-in. Novice users, however, won't necessarily know what to do when such a notice appears.

A more helpful approach involves "sniffing" the end user's Web browser for the presence of a VRML plug-in, allowing you to direct those without one to a page of your own that describes in more detail the installation process they must go through. Typically, these so-called "sniffers" are client-side scripts written in the JavaScript language, although other scripting languages (such as VBScript) are also capable of interrogating Web browsers.

In addition to easing novice visitors into VRML content, sniffers are also used in cases where a VRML file must be viewed with a specific Web browser or VRML plug-in. Some VRML worlds, for example, take advantage of custom, nonstandard features offered only by a particular VRML browser. Other worlds may simply look better when viewed in a particular VRML browser due to rendering differences.

Sniffer scripts are constructed using the JavaScript `navigator` object, which contains vital information about the Web browser in which the script is executed (see Table 6.8). Two properties of the `navigator` object are vital to most sniffer scripts. The `navigator.appName` property contains the name of the Web browser, while the `navigator.plugins` property is an array that contains the name of each installed plug-in in by Internet Explorer Netscape Navigator environments (the `plugins` property is not supported).

Listing 6.15, for instance, contains the source code for an HTML Web page and a simple JavaScript sniffer. The script in this example probes both the `navigator.appName` and `navigator.plugins` properties to learn about the end user's configuration. The `navigator.appName` property is first tested to determine if the Web browser in use is Netscape Navigator. If so, the `navigator.plugins` is then tested for Cosmo Player version 2.1.1. If this particular VRML browser is detected, an EMBED tag is dynamically generated with a call to the `document.write()` method (see "The Document Object"). If not, the `document.write()` method is used to display an error message to the end user and to provide a link to a "help" page.

Note: The Document Object

The JavaScript `document` *object contains information about the current Web page ("document"). The* `document` *object also supports a "write" method, used to send output to the Web page. The* `document.write()` *method is typically used to dynamically construct HTML code for a Web page. For more details, visit Netscape's JavaScript development site at http://developer.netscape.com/library/documentation/javascript.html.*

Listing 6.15	sniffNavigatorCosmo.html

```html
<html>

<head>
<title>Sniff Navigator and Cosmo</title>
</head>
```

```
<body>

<SCRIPT LANGUAGE=JavaScript1.1>
<!--
  if (navigator.appName == 'Netscape') {
    if (navigator.plugins["Cosmo Player 2.1.1 from PLATINUM
                           technology, inc."])
      document.write('<EMBED SRC="sphere.wrl" WIDTH=400
                     HEIGHT=400>');
    else {
      document.write("Sorry. Cosmo Player 2.1.1 required");
      document.write("<a href='help.html'>Click for help!</a>");
    }
  }

  if (navigator.appName == 'Microsoft Internet Explorer') {
   document.write("Internet Explorer detected.");
   document.write("This VRML world requires Navigator and
                  Cosmo Player 2.1.1");
   document.write("<a href='help.html'>Click for help!</a>");
  }

//-->
</SCRIPT>

<NOSCRIPT>
  JavaScript 1.1 must be enabled in order for this sniffer
  to execute properly.
</NOSCRIPT>

</body>
</html>
```

Table 6.8   JavaScript Navigator Object Properties
usage: navigator.propertyName

Property Name	JavaScript	Description
appCodeName	1.0	Contains the "code name" of the Web browser. Both Navigator

Property Name	JavaScript	Description
		and Internet Explorer have the code name "mozilla."
appName	1.0	Contains the name of the Web browser ("Navigator" or "Microsoft Internet Explorer").
appVersion	1.0	Contains the operating system and release version number.
language	1.2	Contains the Web browser language translation (will contain "en" for English browsers).
mimeTypes	1.1	Contains an array of MIME type objects that the Web browser supports through plug-ins or helper applications.
platform	1.2	Contains the type of machine the Web browser is compiled for (will contain "Win32" Windows NT, 95, and 98, for example)
plugins	1.1	Contains an array of plug-in objects corresponding to those plug-ins installed for the Web browser.
userAgent	1.0	Contains a user agent string sent to the server by the Web browser as part of the HTTP request header.

In cases where you don't need to sniff for a specific VRML browser, you can perform a more general VRML test using the `navigator.mimeTypes` property. The `navigator.mimeTypes` property contains an array of MIME types supported by installed plug-ins and helper applications. As Listing 6.16 illustrates, you can test this property to determine if Navigator has a plug-in or application installed that can handle the VRML "`model/vrml`" MIME type.

Unfortunately, the `navigator.plugins` and `navigator.mimeTypes` properties are available only in JavaScript 1.1 and higher. As a result, they're not available in Navigator 2 or *any* version of Internet Explorer (see "Warning: Browser Incompatibilities"). Because these properties aren't available in all browsers, you must take care to shield incompatible browsers from script that tests the properties. You can do so by specifying your scripts as

JavaScript 1.1 and also by testing the `navigator.appName` property to ensure that you're working with Netscape Navigator or a compatible browser, as shown in Listing 6.15 and Listing 6.16.

Warning: Browser Incompatibilities

The JavaScript `navigator.plugins` *and* `navigator.mime Types` *property are available in Navigator 3 and higher. Navigator 2 does not support these properties, nor does Internet Explorer. As a result, you should set the* LANGUAGE *attribute of your* SCRIPT *elements to* JavaScript1.1 *so that Navigator 2 will ignore the script entirely, and also test the* `navigator.appName` *property to ensure that you're actually working with Navigator (see Listings 6.15 and 6.16 for details).*

Alternately, you can test for a specific browser name and version by using a combination of `navigator.appName` *and* `navigator.appVersion`. *Keep in mind, however, that some browsers "spoof" Navigator (such as Opera and WebTV), so you'll have to do additional tests if your VRML world is strictly for Navigator. For more details, see Netscape's "Ultimate JavaScript Client Sniffer" at http://developer.netscape.com/docs/examples/javascript/browser_type.html.*

Listing 16.16   sniffMIME.html

```
<html>

<head>
<title>Sniff MIME </title>
</head>

<body>

<SCRIPT LANGUAGE=JavaScript1.1>
<!—

  if (navigator.appName == 'Netscape') {
   if (navigator.mimeTypes["model/vrml"])
    document.write('<EMBED SRC="sphere.wrl" WIDTH=400 HEIGHT=400>');
```

```
  else {
    document.write("Sorry, this browser isn't VRML-savvy.");
    document.write("<a href='help.html'>Click for help!</a>");
    }
  }

  if (navigator.appName == 'Microsoft Internet Explorer') {
    document.write("Internet Explorer detected. Sorry, but");
    document.write("Navigator and a VRML plug-in required");
    document.write("<a href='help.html'>Click for help!</a>");
    }

//-->
</SCRIPT>

<NOSCRIPT>
JavaScript must be enabled in order to sniff for MIME types.
</NOSCRIPT>

</body>
</html>
```

Sniffers that handle both Navigator and Internet Explorer are very complex due to Internet Explorer's lack of support for the `navigator.plugins` and `navigator.mimeTypes` properties. Listing 6.17, for example, contains the complete source code of Robert Lipman's popular VRML Browser Detector ("VBDetector") script, which sniffs Navigator *and* Internet Explorer for VRML browsers. In order to accommodate both Navigator and Internet Explorer, this code uses a combination of JavaScript and Microsoft's Visual Basic script (VBScript).

When Navigator (or a compatible browser, such as Opera, http://www.opera.com/) is used, the entire sniffing process is carried out using pure JavaScript code. In this case the `navigator.plugins` array is iterated over, allowing all installed VRML browsers to be detected. When Internet Explorer is encountered, however, the JavaScript code dynamically constructs VBScript code that tests only for specific VRML browsers (Contact, Cortona, Cosmo Player, VRML 2.0 Viewer, Viscape Universal, and WorldView). Because Internet Explorer doesn't support `navigator.plugins`, this VBScript code takes an entirely different approach to sniffing; it actually constructs an OBJECT tag for each VRML browser and then probes the

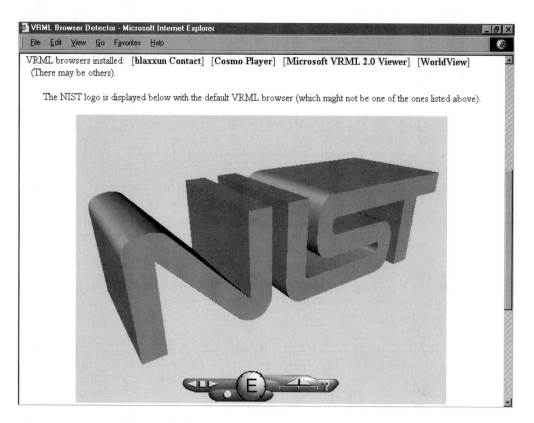

Figure 6-19   VBDetector sniffs for VRML browsers in both Navigator and Internet Explorer (http://cic.nist.gov/vrml/vbdetect.html).

properties of these tags to determine if the given VRML browser is physically installed.

In both cases VBDetector displays the full name of each VRML browser it finds, then constructs an EMBED tag for the specified VRML world (nist.wrl in this example, as seen in Figure 6-19), although a relative or absolute URL pointing to any world can be used. If a VRML browser can't be found, the sniffer script will instead display a snippet of "no VRML browser found" explanatory text to the user.

To make your VRML-enabled Web pages friendlier, you can modify VBDetector's "No VRML browser found" code so that the user is presented with a direct hyperlink to a VRML browser download page. Better yet, you can link the users to a page on your site that explains what VRML is and tells them how to install a VRML browser. In either case you'll need to write a hyperlink to the Web page when a VRML browser can't be found. The following snippet of JavaScript, for example, can be substituted for the current error message code used in the Navigator portion of VBDetector:

```
if (ok) {
 document.write('No VRML browser detected.');
 document.write('<a href="help.html">Click for help!</a>');

}
```

In order to provide the same functionality in Internet Explorer, you'll need to modify the VBScript portion of the sniffer so that the last *vbtxt* variable assignment contains a hyperlink as follows:

```
' vbtxt = vbtxt + "<a href=""help.html""> No VRML browser de-
tected. Click for help!</a>"\n'+
' End If\n'+
' document.write(vbtxt)\n'+
```

Tip: Sniffing Specific VRML Browsers

Improbable as it may seem, the version of VBDetector seen in Listing 6.17 is actually considered simple—there's a more complicated version of the script available online at http://cic.nist.gov/vrml/vbdetect.html. Here you'll find the full source code for Robert's standard and "simple" versions of VB-Detector, both of which you're free to download and use in your own pages.

Although the standard version of VBDetector sniffs for the most current version of Cosmo Player (2.1.1 at the time of this writing), you can modify it to look for a specific version of any VRML browser. In addition, the standard version of VBDetector alerts the users if they're using an outdated Web browser.

Listing 6.17　vrmlBrowserDetector.html

```
<SCRIPT LANGUAGE=JavaScript>
<!--

// VRML Browser Detector (August 4, 1999)
// http://cic.nist.gov/vrml/vbsimple.html
```

```
// Robert Lipman
// National Institute of Standards and Technology (NIST)
// Building and Fire Research Laboratory
// Computer Integrated Construction Group
// 100 Bureau Drive, Stop 8630
// Gaithersburg, Maryland  20899-8630

// robert.lipman@nist.gov
// http://cic.nist.gov/lipman/


// check for VRML browser within Navigator (or compatible Web browser)
// first test to see if Internet Explorer is being used. If it is,
// this block of code is NOT executed:

  var appname = navigator.appName;
  var vbenabled = '';
  var ok = 1;

  if (appname != 'Microsoft Internet Explorer') {
    var nplugin = navigator.plugins.length;
    if (nplugin >= 0) {
     for (i = 0; i < nplugin; i++) {
      var plugin = navigator.plugins[i];
      var nmimetype = plugin.length;
      for (j = 0; j < nmimetype; j++) {
       mimetype = plugin[j];
       enabledPlugin = mimetype.enabledPlugin;
       mimetypeSuffix = mimetype.suffixes.toLowerCase();
       if (mimetype.type.indexOf('vrml') != -1 &&
        mimetypeSuffix.indexOf('wrl') != -1) {
       if (enabledPlugin && (enabledPlugin.name == plugin.name)) {
         vbenabled = plugin.name;
         if (ok) {
          document.write('VRML browser: <B>' + vbenabled + '</B><P>');
          document.write('<EMBED SRC="nist.wrl" WIDTH=600 HEIGHT=450>');
          ok = 0;
         }
        }
       }
      }
     }
    }
    if (ok) {
      document.write('No VRML browser detected.');
```

```
      }
    }

// check for VRML browser with Microsoft Internet Explorer
// credit goes to J. Fairley:
//   http://www.megsinet.com/~jfairley/vrmlcheck.htm

if (appname == 'Microsoft Internet Explorer') {
  document.write('<OBJECT ID=cplay width=0 height=0\n'+
    'classid="clsid:06646724-bcf3-11d0-9518-00c04fc2dd79"></OBJECT>');

  document.write('<OBJECT ID=mvrml width=0 height=0\n'+
    'classid="clsid:90A7533D-88FE-11D0-9DBE-0000C0411FC3"></OBJECT>');

  document.write('<OBJECT ID=wview width=0 height=0\n'+
    'classid="clsid:B0D7D800-4EBF-11D0-9490-00A02494D8A5"></OBJECT>');

  document.write('<OBJECT ID=viscp width=0 height=0\n'+
    'classid="clsid:1b487523-BEC2-11CF-BF9E-0020AF998FF5"></OBJECT>');

  document.write('<OBJECT ID=blaxn width=0 height=0\n'+
    'classid="clsid:4B6E3013-6E45-11D0-9309-0020AFE05CC8"></OBJECT>');

  document.write('<OBJECT ID=corto width=0 height=0\n'+
    'classid="clsid:86A88967-7A20-11D2-8EDA-00600818EDB1"></OBJECT>');

    document.write('<SCRIPT LANGUAGE=VBScript>On Error Resume Next\n'+
      'Dim wviewInstalled\n'+
      'Dim mvrmlInstalled\n'+
      'Dim cplayInstalled\n'+
      'Dim viscpInstalled\n'+
      'Dim blaxnInstalled\n'+
      'Dim cortoInstalled\n'+
      'Dim vbtxt\n'+
      'Dim vbspace\n'+
      'Dim nvrml\n'+
      'Dim src\n'+

      'wviewInstalled = False\n'+
      'mvrmlInstalled = False\n'+
      'cplayInstalled = False\n'+
      'viscpInstalled = False\n'+
      'blaxnInstalled = False\n'+
      'cortoInstalled = False\n'+
      'vbtxt = ""\n'+
```

```
'vbspace = "    "\n'+
'nvrml = 0\n'+

'src=cplay.src\n'+
'If Not Err = 0 Then\n'+
'  Err.clear\n'+
'Else\n'+
'  cplayInstalled = True\n'+
'  nvrml = nvrml + 1\n'+
'End If\n'+

'src = mvrml.World\n'+
'If Not Err = 0 Then\n'+
'  Err.clear\n'+
'Else\n'+
'  mvrmlInstalled = True\n'+
'  nvrml = nvrml + 1\n'+
'End If\n'+

'src = wview.World\n'+
'If Not Err = 0 Then\n'+
'  Err.clear\n'+
'Else\n'+
'  wviewInstalled = True\n'+
'  nvrml = nvrml + 1\n'+
'End If\n'+

'src = viscp.World\n'+
'If Not Err = 0 Then\n'+
'  Err.clear\n'+
'Else\n'+
'  viscpInstalled = True\n'+
'  nvrml = nvrml + 1\n'+
'End If\n'+

'src = blaxn.World\n'+
'If Not Err = 0 Then\n'+
'  Err.clear\n'+
'Else\n'+
'  blaxnInstalled = True\n'+
'  nvrml = nvrml + 1\n'+
'End If\n'+

'src = corto.src\n'+
'If Not Err = 0 Then\n'+
```

```
        '   Err.clear\n'+
       'Else\n'+
        '   cortoInstalled = True\n'+
        '   nvrml = nvrml + 1\n'+
       'End If\n'+

       'If (nvrml > 0) Then\n'+
        '   vbtxt = vbtxt + "VRML browsers installed:"\n'+
        '   If (blaxnInstalled)  Then\n'+
        '      vbtxt = vbtxt + vbspace + "[<B>blaxxun Contact</B>]"\n'+
        '      End If\n'+
        '   If (cortoInstalled)  Then\n'+
        '      vbtxt = vbtxt + vbspace + "[<B>Cortona</B>]"\n'+
        '      End If\n'+
        '   If (cplayInstalled)  Then\n'+
        '      vbtxt = vbtxt + vbspace + "[<B>Cosmo Player</B>]"\n'+
        '      End If\n'+
        '   If (mvrmlInstalled)  Then\n'+
        '      vbtxt = vbtxt+vbspace+"[<B>MS VRML 2.0 Viewer</B>]"\n'+
        '      End If\n'+
        '   If (viscpInstalled)  Then\n'+
        '      vbtxt = vbtxt + vbspace + "[<B>Viscape Universal</B>]"\n'+
        '      End If\n'+
        '   If (wviewInstalled)  Then\n'+
        '      vbtxt = vbtxt + vbspace + "[<B>WorldView</B>]"\n'+
        '      End If\n'+
        '   vbtxt = vbtxt + vbspace + "(There may be others)."\n'+
        '   vbtxt=vbtxt+"<P><EMBED SRC=""nist.wrl"" WIDTH=600 HEIGHT=450>"\n'+
       'Else\n'+
        '   vbtxt = vbtxt + "No VRML browser detected."\n'+
       'End If\n'+
       'document.write(vbtxt)\n'+
       'Set vrml = Nothing\n'+
     '<\/SCRIPT>');
   }

//-->
</SCRIPT>

<NOSCRIPT>
JavaScript must be enabled in the web browser for the VRML browser detector
to work.
</NOSCRIPT>
```

Tip

A number of complex sniffer scripts are freely available on the Web in addition to VBDetector. Visit the Web3D Gallery at http://www.web3dgallery. com/vrml/sniffers/ for details.

Related VRML Nodes

When weaving VRML content into Web pages, there are a number of related VRML nodes that you might consider adding to your world. If these nodes are already present, you can customize them to suit your needs. In the sections that follow, we'll explain the essential fields of these nodes, leaving the VRML97 specification to explain them in full detail. Alternately, you can turn to Appendix B, "VRML97 Resources" for links to materials that explain these and other VRML nodes in greater detail.

WorldInfo

VRML's WorldInfo node allows you to embed documentation information directly into your world. As a documentation node, WorldInfo has no effect whatsoever on the appearance or behavior of a world. It is used, however, to give your world an official title (a name) and is also particularly useful for adding author and copyright information to your worlds. Following is the VRML97 specification definition of the WorldInfo node:

```
WorldInfo {
    field MFString info   []
    field SFString title  ""
}
```

The *title* field is typically used to assign a name, or title, to a world in the form of a single string. The *info* field, on the other hand, can accept one or more strings and is often used to store related world information such as the author's name, copyrights, and a basic description of the world. Because VRML browsers are under no obligation to provide a way for end users to view WorldInfo node information, some ignore this node altogether. Others, however, respect this node and can display the information you supply should the user choose to view it (see Figure 6-20).

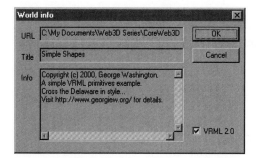

Figure 6-20 Although VRML browsers are under no obligation to display WorldInfo data, some browsers will show this information if requested by the user. blaxxun Contact, for example, displays WorldInfo data in a popup window as shown here.

Although the information you supply to the WorldInfo node isn't always available to the end user, you should use it any time you publish proprietary VRML content to the Web. At the very least you should supply author information and a copyright notice in the WorldInfo node, allowing this information to "travel" with your world should others be tempted to use it without permission. In addition, you can include descriptive information about your world in the form of comments, as seen in Listing 6.18.

Like any other VRML node, the WorldInfo fields you use don't have to be supplied in the order they appear in the VRML97 specification. Listing 6.19, for example, reverses the order of the WorldInfo fields. In addition, the World-Info node in Listing 6.19 appears as the child of a Transform node. The World-Info can appear either at the top level of a VRML file, as shown in Listing 6.18, or as the child of another node (such as the Transform node, as seen in Listing 6.19). See Chapter 7, "Customizing Location, Size, and Orientation," to learn about child nodes in general, and the Transform node in particular.

Listing 6.18   WorldInfo.wrl

```
#VRML V2.0 utf8

# Primitive VRML shapes. The Sphere and Cylinder are
# translated (moved) from their default position in
# the scene using the Transform node. The Cone remains
# at the default location — the origin at (0,0,0).

WorldInfo {
  info  [
```

```
        "Copyright (c) 2000, George Washington.",
        "A simple VRML primitives example.",
        "Cross the Delaware in style...",
        "Visit http://www.georgew.org/ for details."
      ]
  title "Simple Shapes"
}

Shape {
  appearance Appearance {
    material Material { }
  }
  geometry Cone { }
}

Transform {
  translation -3 0 0   # x y z   (move down X axis)
  children [
      Shape {
        appearance Appearance {
        material Material { }
      }
      geometry Sphere { }
      }
  ]
}

Transform {
  translation 3 0 0    # x y z   (move up X axis)
  children [
      Shape {
        appearance Appearance {
        material Material { }
      }
      geometry Cylinder { }
      }
  ]
}
```

Listing 6.19   WorldInfo2.wrl

```
#VRML V2.0 utf8

Shape {
  appearance Appearance {
    material Material { }
  }
  geometry Cone { }
}

Transform {
  translation -3 0 0   # x y z   (move down X axis)
  children [
      WorldInfo {
         title "Simple Shapes"
         info [
            "Copyright (c) 2000, George Washington.",
            "A simple VRML primitives example.",
            "Cross the Delaware in style...",
            "Visit http://www.georgew.org/ for details."
         ]
      }

      Shape {
        appearance Appearance {
        material Material { }
      }
      geometry Sphere { }
      }
  ]
}

Transform {
  translation 3 0 0   # x y z   (move up X axis)
  children [
      Shape {
        appearance Appearance {
        material Material { }
      }
      geometry Cylinder { }
      }
  ]
}
```

Anchor Node

Like HTML, VRML supports hyperlinks. The Anchor node, in fact, is VRML's analog to the HTML anchor <A> element:

```
Anchor {
    eventIn      MFNode    addChildren
    eventIn      MFNode    removeChildren
    exposedField MFNode    children        []
    exposedField SFString  description     ""
    exposedField MFString  parameter       []
    exposedField MFString  url             []
    field        SFVec3f   bboxCenter      0 0 0      #(-∞,∞)
    field        SFVec3f   bboxSize        -1 -1 -1   #(0,∞) or -1,-1,-1
}
```

As a grouping node, the Anchor node can contain children (see Chapter 7, "Customizing Location, Size, and Orientation," to learn about grouping nodes and children). The children that it contains are associated with a URL supplied in the *url* field. Upon selecting the child of an Anchor, the world is replaced with the page pointed to by the URL. In other words, when users click on an Anchor-enabled object they are presented with whatever the *url* field points to (assuming you've supplied a valid URL to this field).

Like all VRML *url* fields, the Anchor node's *url* field can contain more than one string (see Chapter 8, "Customizing Color and Texture," for details). In cases where you'd like to provide the end user with some information about the link, you can supply a string to the corresponding *description* field. You should be aware, however, that not all browsers display *description* field information to the end user when the mouse is moved over an associated Anchor node child.

Most VRML browsers, however, will change the appearance of the mouse pointer when it is moved over the child of an Anchor. Figure 6-21, for example, shows the mouse as displayed by blaxxun Contact when the pointer is moved over an Anchor node child. The code for this world can be found in Listing 6.20. Here a primitive cone shape has been made the child of an Anchor node, while the other shapes in the world are constructed and displayed using the Transform node. As a result, the cone shape is the only one that has a hyperlink associated with it. In Listing 6.21, however, each of the shapes used in this world is made a child of the same Anchor node (meaning they all share the same URL).

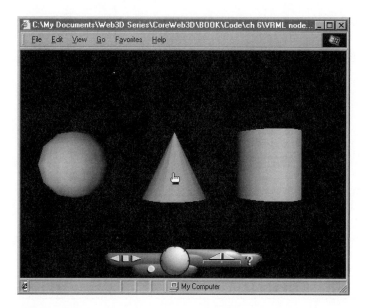

Figure 6-21   VRML browsers typically change the appearance of the mouse when it moves over the child of an Anchor node to visually indicate that the object is a hyperlink that can be "clicked."

Listing 6.20   Anchor.wrl

```
#VRML V2.0 utf8

Anchor {
  url "http://www.georgew.org/"
  description "George Washington's Web site"
  children [
    Shape {
      appearance Appearance {
      material Material { }
      }
    geometry Cone { }
    }
  ]
}

Transform {
  translation -3 0 0   # x y z  (move down X axis)
  children [
      Shape {
        appearance Appearance {
```

```
      material Material { }
    }
    geometry Sphere { }
    }
  ]
}


Transform {
  translation 3 0 0    # x y z   (move up X axis)
  children [
      Shape {
        appearance Appearance {
        material Material { }
      }
      geometry Cylinder { }
      }
  ]
}
```

Listing 6.21   Anchor2.wrl

```
#VRML V2.0 utf8

Anchor {
  url "http://www.georgew.org/"
  description "George Washington's Web site"
  children [
    Shape {
      appearance Appearance {
      material Material { }
      }
    geometry Cone { }
    }

    Transform {
      translation -3 0 0    # x y z   (move down X axis)
      children [
          Shape {
            appearance Appearance {
            material Material { }
          }
          geometry Sphere { }
          }
      ]
    }
```

```
Transform {
  translation 3 0 0    # x y z   (move up X axis)
  children [
      Shape {
         appearance Appearance {
         material Material { }
      }
      geometry Cylinder { }
      }
  ]
}

]
}
```

Anchor Features

The Anchor node's *parameter* field is used to pass information to a VRML browser in the form of "keyword=value" pairs. Many browsers, for example, allow you to specify a link "target" that will force the hyperlink to a specific part of an HTML document (such as a frame). For example:

```
Anchor {
  parameter [ "target=name_of_frame" ]
     ...
}
```

Anchor nodes can also be used to bind the end user's initial view to a specific Viewpoint node (see the "Viewpoint" node discussion later in this chapter for details on user views). To do so, you supply a URL to the *url* field that ends with "#ViewpointName" (where "ViewpointName" is the name of a Viewpoint node in a VRML file). When the following Cone shape is selected, for example, the Anchor will load the specified world and bind the user's initial view to the Viewpoint node named "FrontDoor" found in that world:

```
Anchor {
  url "http://www.xyz.org/worlds/house.wrl#FrontDoor"
  children  Shape {
     geometry Cone {}
  }
}
```

Viewpoint

A *viewpoint* is a point in 3D space where a virtual camera can be positioned. Using the Viewpoint node, you can specify one or more positions in a scene that users can quickly jump to using the navigation features of their VRML browser. Following is the VRML97 specification definition of the Viewpoint node:

```
Viewpoint {
    eventIn       SFBool       set_bind
    exposedField SFFloat      fieldOfView      0.785398   # (0, π)
    exposedField SFBool       jump             TRUE
    exposedField SFRotation orientation        0 0 1 0    # [-1,1], (-∞, ∞)
    exposedField SFVec3f      position          0 0 10    # (-∞,∞)
    field         SFString     description      ""
    eventOut      SFTime       bindTime
    eventOut      SFBool       isBound
}
```

VRML browsers display viewpoints by name, allowing end users to choose from those available for any given world. The world seen in Figure 6-22, for example, contains four different Viewpoint nodes that the user can choose from ("Inside," "Outside," "Boat," and "Seashore"). These unique names are supplied to the node's *description* field in the form of a single string. When a given viewpoint is selected, the browser takes the user to the 3D point described by the *position* and *orientation* fields of the corresponding Viewpoint node (see Chapter 7, "Customizing Location, Size, and Orientation," to learn more about position and orientation of objects).

The *fieldOfView* field, meanwhile, defines the angle of the viewpoint in radians (see Chapter 7 for details on radians). The default *fieldOfView* value creates a field of view similar to that of the human eye. Values less than the default of 0.785398 create smaller, more tightly focused fields of view, while larger values create wider fields of view. If you can imagine looking at the world through a camera lens, large *fieldOfView* values would be the equivalent of looking through a camera equipped with a wide-angle lens. Small *fieldOfView* values, on the other hand, create a view similar to that of a telephoto lens.

Figure 6-23 shows the viewpoint corresponding to this world's "Outside" Viewpoint node. Figure 6-24, however, is associated with the "Inside" view-

Viewpoint Tours

Viewpoint nodes are often used to construct guided tours of a world. Guided tours, more commonly know as *viewpoint tours*, move the user from viewpoint to viewpoint without any interaction on the users' part (they're effectively "taken for a ride" around the various viewpoints in the world). Instead of jumping directly to each viewpoint, the camera is animated between each stop on the tour.

point, which also happens to be the default viewpoint for this world. The first Viewpoint node that appears in a VRML world is considered the default or initial viewpoint, defining the first view the user has when entering a world.

Figure 6-22 Users can jump to any of the predefined world viewpoints, which are defined by Viewpoint nodes. The interface for choosing viewpoints differs from browser to browser. Many, like the blaxxun Contact browser shown here, present viewpoints in a popup list available from a menu that appears when the user right-clicks on a world.

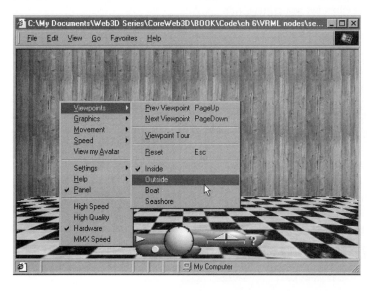

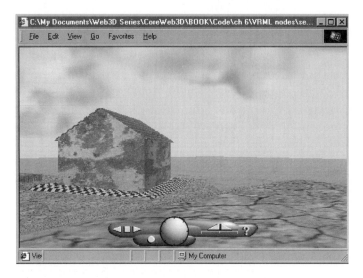

Figure 6-23   This world's "Outside" viewpoint brings users to a 3D point outside of the home in which their journey begins.

Figure 6-24   The "Inside" viewpoint for this world is also its default viewpoint; this is where users are taken when the world first loads.

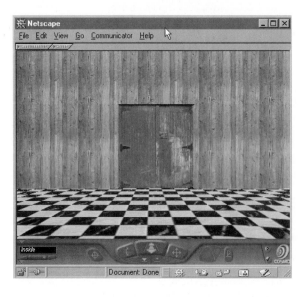

Although it's possible to construct viewpoints by hand, it's much easier to use a visual development tool. Then you can simply navigate to a point in your world using your mouse and "set" it as a viewpoint. Many visual development tools let you create and position virtual cameras in 3D space, each of which defines a unique viewpoint for a world. See Chapter 10, "Creating New VRML Worlds," to learn more about visual development tools.

NavigationInfo

VRML's NavigationInfo node encapsulates information about the viewer's physical characteristics, expressed in terms of an avatar, as well as aspects of the current viewing model (see Figures 6–25 and 6–26). With interactive forms of 3D such as VRML, Java 3D, MEPG-4/BIFS, and X3D, "avatar" is a general term used to describe a virtual representation of a human being. In other words, the avatar represents you, the viewer, residing inside a virtual world.

Multi-user VRML worlds, such as those supported by blaxxun Contact and ParallelGraphics Cortona (see Appendix A for details), allow your avatar to be seen by other visitors. You might, for example, choose a flashy avatar, such as a unicorn or wizard, when playing a multi-user game. When participating in a business-oriented world, such as a collaborative staff meeting, you might choose a somewhat more conservative avatar, such as a human-like creature ("humanoid"), or perhaps even a briefcase if you're particularly uptight.

Although the VRML97 standard does not support multi-user worlds directly (shared multi-user worlds are a non-standard feature supported only by specialty browsers such as Contact and Cortona), it does utilize avatar information for traditional (single-user) VRML worlds. Specifically, VRML97's NavigationInfo node is focused entirely on how the user's avatar moves around, or navigates, in a virtual environment. To this end you can use the NavigationInfo node's avatarSize field to customize the size of the user's avatar for purposes of collision detection and terrain following, as the VRML97 Specification definition indicates:

```
NavigationInfo {
  eventIn       SFBool   set_bind
  exposedField MFFloat  avatarSize      [0.25, 1.6, 0.75] # [0,∞)
  exposedField SFBool   headlight       TRUE
  exposedField SFFloat  speed           1.0               # [0,∞)
  exposedField MFString type            ["WALK", "ANY"]
  exposedField SFFloat  visibilityLimit 0.0               # [0, ∞)
  eventOut      SFBool   isBound
}
```

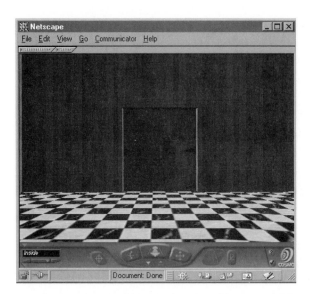

Figure 6-25   The VRML browser's built-in headlight can be disabled (turned off) by setting the NavigationInfo node's *headlight* field to FALSE. In this world the headlight has been disabled, making the scene darker as a result (compared with Figure 6-26).

By default, VRML avatars are shaped like a cylinder that is 1.6 meters tall with a radius of 0.25 meters. The "eyes" of the avatar are located on top of the cylinder, and correspond to the view that you see in your VRML browser (you see the virtual world through the eyes of your cylinder-shaped avatar). Your avatar, by default, is able to step over objects that are up to 0.75 meters high. To customize these settings, you can alter the corresponding *avatarSize* field, which accepts three floating-point numbers in the range of zero to infinity.

The first *avatarSize* field value controls what amounts to the avatar's girth, which is used to determine how much distance can exist between the avatar and an object in the scene before a collision is detected. Not all geometry in a scene is "collidable," however, and therefore a collision detection is only signaled when the avatar bumps into collidable geometry (as specified by a Collision node). A stone wall, for example, is a good candidate for collidable geometry, while a waterfall is not. An avatar, therefore, might be able to walk through a waterfall but not through a stone wall, depending on the design of the world in question.

The second *avatarSize* field value specifies a height above the terrain underfoot, at which the VRML browser maintains the viewer's viewpoint.

Figure 6-26   By default, the VRML browser's built-in headlight is enabled (on and shining light into the scene from the user's viewpoint). By setting the NavigationInfo node's *headlight* field to TRUE, programmers can enable an otherwise disabled headlight (see Figure 6-25).

Simply put, this field determines how high off the ground the viewpoint is set. This value is approximately the distance between the avatar's eyes and its feet (i.e., roughly the distance between the top and bottom of the cylinder shape).

The third *avatarSize* field value specifies the height of the tallest object that the viewer can step over. Conceptually, this value specifies how high the avatar can lift its legs. Suppose, for example, that an avatar encounters a virtual staircase where each stair is half a meter high. Assuming a default avatar height setting of 0.75 meters, viewers could easily ascend the staircase. If the stairs were 1 meter high, however, the default avatar could not climb them. Either the scale of the staircase would have to be changed to create shorter steps, or the *avatarSize* height field would have to be increased to a height of 1 or more meters. Note that the transformation hierarchy of the currently bound Viewpoint node scales *avatarSize*, while translations and rotations have no effect on this field (see Chapter 7, "Customizing Location, Size, and Orientation" to learn more about translation and orientation).

Whereas the NavigationInfo node's *avatarSize* field specifies physical characteristics about the viewer's avatar, the *speed* field is used to control how fast the avatar moves initially. With a default setting of 1.0, *speed* allows the avatar to move about a scene at the rate of 1 meter per second. When in "EXAMINE" mode (as opposed to "WALK" or "FLY"), the *speed* field determines the rate at which the user can examine objects when moving them side to side, spinning them around, or zooming in and out.

Although most VRML browsers provide end users with a simple mechanism for changing this rate (pressing the space key in blaxxun Contact, for example, increases navigation speed on the fly), you can set the initial pace of your avatar using the *speed* field. This setting can have a dramatic impact on your worlds, because the speed of your avatar can greatly affect the overall navigation experience. A beach scene, for example, would do well to use the default 1.0 *speed* setting, although a solar system model would be much more effective and enjoyable if the user could travel thousands of miles in a single second. Imagine the pain and suffering viewers would endure if forced to fly between distant planets at the rate of 1 meter per second!

The NavigationInfo node's type field is used to specify the mode in which viewer's navigate, or move about, a scene. Common types of navigation are "WALK", "FLY," and "EXAMINE." The "WALK" and "FLY" navigation modes are similar in that they allow you to explore a virtual world in a manner consistent with that of the real world. When walking, your avatar remains firmly on the ground as it follows the terrain underfoot ("terrain following"), whereas flying removes the effect of gravity altogether. In both cases you're allowed to move about the scene at will. Examination mode, on the other hand, presents the viewer with an interface designed for close inspection of objects. By setting the NavigationInfo node's *type* field, to "EXAMINE," for example, users are treated to an interface that allows them to pick an object up, turn it around, and zoom in and out to get a view from various distances.

By setting the NavigationInfo node's *type* field, you can set the initial navigation mode for your worlds. Keep in mind, however, that VRML browsers give the user the option of changing modes at runtime as they explore a world (assuming "ANY" appears in the *type* field array). By default, VRML worlds are set to the "WALK" navigation type. You'll also notice that the *type* field is a multi-value string datatype (MFString), into which you can stuff more than one navigation type. If a browser isn't able to handle the first type specified, it will skip to the next one in the array and use that if it can. If not, the browser will try the next type in the array (if one exists). It will continue in this fashion until it finds a type that it can support, and it will resort to the interface of its choosing if a valid type is not supplied.

Note: Navigation Types

Although VRML browsers can support custom navigation types, the VRML97 Specification requires all browsers to support at least five navigation types: "ANY," "WALK," "EXAMINE," "FLY," and "NONE." The "ANY" navigation type gives browsers the latitude to choose the navigation interface that best suits the current world, and it gives browsers the option of allowing the user to change navigation types dynamically at run time. The blaxxun Contact browser, for example, allows users to right-click anywhere in a world and choose a navigation type from the popup menu that appears.

When a navigation type of "NONE" is specified, the user is prevented from navigating the world using standard controls. In this case navigation controls are hidden from view, and the user is forced to experience the world using navigation controls created by the author (such as a custom heads-up display). Often, alternate navigation controls are not provided in cases where "NONE" is specified. Animated VRML movies, for example, are typically experienced with the navigation type as "NONE," because movement and examination controls usually don't apply to such content. The viewer just sits back and watches the animated movie unfold.

By default, a VRML browser "headlight" illuminates objects that populate VRML worlds. As you'll learn in Chapter 8 and 9, the default headlight acts like a DirectionalLight node bound to the current viewpoint: Anywhere the avatar goes, so goes the headlight. In this sense the headlight can be thought of as flashlight, or miner's hat, attached to the head of the avatar. By default this light is on, although setting the NavigationInfo node's *headlight* field to FALSE will turn it off.

Objects in a scene that exist beyond the distance specified by the current NavigationInfo *visibilityLimit* field may not be rendered, regardless of whether or not the headlight is on. This field gives the VRML browser an opportunity to optimize rendering performance by clipping objects beyond *visibilityLimit* out of the rendering process. In more simplistic terms, the *visibilityLimit* field specifies how far an avatar can see. Anything beyond the specified distance is not rendered and is therefore considered to be out of view. By default, avatars can see infinitely in all directions because a *visibilityLimit* value of 0.0 specifies an infinite visibility limit. Values higher than 0.0, however, create a finite visibility limit measured in meters (this field must be set to a value greater than or equal to zero).

The NavigationInfo Stack

VRML's NavigationInfo node is a bindable node (for details on bindable nodes see the VRML97 Specification section 4.6.10, "Bindable children nodes"). In other words, a stack data structure exists that can contain one or more NavigationInfo nodes (more than one NavigationInfo node can be added to a single VRML world). The NavigationInfo node on top of the stack is said to be the currently bound, or current, NavigationInfo node. The current NavigationInfo node is treated as a child of the current Viewpoint node (irrespective of where these nodes actually reside in the VRML file), so that changes to the current Viewpoint node are reflected in the corresponding NavigationInfo node. Specifically, the current NavigationInfo node is re-parented to the current Viewpoint anytime there is a change to the Viewpoint. Conversely, anytime the current NavigationInfo node changes, the VRML browser will re-parent it to the new Viewpoint node.

As a stack data structure, the NavigationInfo stack supports what amounts to push and pop operations by way of the set_bind eventIn of the NavigationInfo node. VRML browsers create the navigation interface for a world based on the fields of the currently bound NavigationInfo node. Thus, the NavigationInfo stack is a convenient mechanism that can be used to dynamically alter the user interface controls of a world at runtime. Whenever a value of TRUE is sent to set_bind, the corresponding NavigationInfo node is pushed on top of the stack. This binds the NavigationInfo node, which is automatically re-parented under the currently bound Viewpoint node. Sending FALSE to set_bind pops the NavigationInfo node off the stack (for which a corresponding is-Bound FALSE event is generated), which pops the next NavigationInfo node in the stack to the top, where it becomes the current NavigationInfo node.

Summary

VRML worlds can be loaded directly into a Web browser or, when you want to control the dimensions of your content, into a JavaScript popup window. Alternately, VRML worlds can be woven into HTML Web pages using the EMBED and OBJECT elements. Introduced by Netscape, EMBED is a nonstandard element that has been around longer than OBJECT and, as such, is the more popular of the two techniques.

Although originally supported only by Netscape Navigator, EMBED is now supported by Internet Explorer as well. Internet Explorer also supports the OBJECT element, which was created by the World Wide Web Consortium as a standard, all-purpose object-embedding mechanism to replace EMBED and similar non-standard elements.

"Sniffer" scripts can be used to determine if a user is properly equipped to view your VRML pages. Unfortunately, Internet Explorer doesn't support the same JavaScript methods as Netscape Navigator. As a result, you must use two different "sniffer" techniques to support both browsers.

Before publishing your world to the Web, you should consider adding author and copyright information to it using VRML's WorldInfo node. Using the Anchor node, you can add hyperlinks to your VRML worlds. You can also give users one or more pre-defined views of your world using the Viewpoint node and control various aspects of Navigation using the NavigationInfo node.

Regardless of how you choose to display your VRML files to the end user, you can greatly enhance the experience by first compressing the files with GZip. The GZip utility, available on the Web free of charge, can reduce the size of most VRML worlds by two-thirds or more. GZip-compressed worlds consume less disk space and consequently take less time to download, making for a more enjoyable end-user experience.

Following is a complete list of URLs referenced in this chapter:

Core Web3D online   http://www.CoreWeb3D.com/

Seaside World   http://www.web3dgallery.com/vrml/seaside/

Gerardo Quintieri   http://www.web3dgallery.com/people/gq/

Cybelius ShowMore!   http://www.cybelius.com/

Cosmo PageFX   http://www.cosmosoftware.com/

Netscape JavaScript   http://developer.netscape.com/library/documentation/javascript.html

Microsoft JScript   http://msdn.microsoft.com/scripting/jscript/default.htm

ECMA-262   http://www.ecma.ch/stand/ecma-262.htm

Conversations With Angels   http://www.web3dgallery.com/go/cwa/

Netscape DevEdge   http://developer.netscape.com/

Intervista   http://www.intervista.com/

Microsoft VRML 2.0 Viewer   http://www.microsoft.com/vrml/

Platinum Technology   http://www.platinum.com/

blaxxun Contact developer   http://www.blaxxun.com/developer/

ParallelGraphics Cortona developer   http://www.parallelgraphics.com/htm/en/prod/

Cosmo Player developer   http://www.cosmosoftware.com/developer/

Microsoft VRML 2.0 Viewer developer   http://www.microsoft.com/vrml/toolbar/

Intervista WorldView developer   http://www.intervista.com/support/

About Web3D   http://web3d.about.com/

VRMLworks   http://home.hiwaay.net/~crispen/vrmlworks/

Web3D Gallery plug-ins   http://www.web3dgallery.com/vrml/plugins/

The World Wide Web Consortium   http://www.w3c.org

GZip   http://www.gnu.org/
        ftp://www.gnu.org/gnu/gzip/
        ftp://prep.ai.mit.edu/pub/gnu/

Installing Java 3D   http://www.CoreWeb3D.com/java3d/install/

ParallelGraphics   http://www.parallelgraphics.com/

VRML optimization tools   http://www.web3dgallery.com/vrml/tools/

Ultimate JavaScript Client Sniffer   http://developer.netscape.com/docs/
examples/javascript/browser_type.html

VRML browser detector   http://cic.nist.gov/vrml/vbdetect.html

Opera Web browser   http://www.opera.com/

VRML sniffers   http://www.web3dgallery.com/vrml/sniffers/

CUSTOMIZING LOCATION, SIZE, AND ORIENTATION

Topics in This Chapter

- Introducing the Transform grouping node

- Using the Transform node's *translation* field to move objects

- Using the Transform node's *scale* field to change the size of objects

- Using the Transform node's *rotation* field to alter the orientation of objects

- Nesting Transform nodes to create objects that are easily managed as a single unit

Chapter 7

Chances are pretty good that at some time or another you're going to get your hands on VRML content that you're not entirely happy with. Whether you purchase VRML files from a 3D vendor, download samples from the Internet free of charge, or are fortunate enough to have a friend or colleague create content for you, eventually you'll want to change some aspects of what you end up with.

Perhaps some of the objects in a scene aren't positioned exactly where you'd like them, or maybe their shape, size, or color doesn't appeal to you. Similarly, a world's background, sky, or ground might look unrealistic, and so you might want to replace it with a photographic image. Finally, the world might be acoustically lacking, and so it's up to you to add a background sound track and a few audio sources to make it as easy on the ears as it is on the eyes.

Fortunately, you don't have to be a full-blown VRML programmer to correct all of these things and more. As long as you have existing content to work with, you can customize it. Simply open your less-than-satisfactory VRML file with any standard text editor and begin sifting through the various nodes in the scene graph it contains. (See Chapter 4, "VRML Overview," to learn about VRML files, and Chapter 5, "VRML Fundamentals," for details about nodes and scene graphs.) When you see a node that controls some aspect of the scene that you'd like to customize, tweak it, save it, then open

Garbled VRML Files

Some VRML files are compressed with GNU Zip ("GZip") to conserve both bandwidth and disk space. Compressed files are not readable by human beings, and when opened for editing appear to be garbled text. To customize such files, they must first be decompressed using the GZip utility (or any other compression program that understands the GZip format). Refer to Chapter 6, "Weaving VRML into Web Pages," for details on how to compress and decompress VRML files.

the file in your VRML browser. Repeat the basic process of tweaking nodes, saving your changes, and reloading the browser until everything looks and sounds good to you.

Of course, knowing what nodes to look for and how to tweak them is more than half the battle. Most of the VRML files you'll come across are packed full of nodes, and making sense of them is no easy feat if you're new to the language. In this chapter you'll see how to customize your worlds using the Transform grouping node to move, resize, and rotate VRML objects. This will allow you to reposition, grow, or shrink any object that a world contains, making you, in a sense, the virtual stage director of a 3D production.

Moving, Scaling, and Rotating

One of the first things you may want to do with an existing VRML world is change the position, size, or angle of objects it contains. You might, for example, find that an object is too far away from the viewer and therefore difficult to see. It would be helpful to move the object closer or enlarge it (perhaps doubling or tripling in size). Likewise, you might find that objects in a scene are not oriented to your liking, which you can easily fix by rotating them to a different angle.

Objects in a VRML scene can be moved, scaled (resized), and rotated using the versatile Transform node. Entire scenes, in fact, can be moved, scaled, and rotated using this node, provided you take the time to understand the various fields it offers.

The Transform Node

The term *transformation* refers to a mathematical operation that is applied to one or more values of a 3D coordinate (X, Y, Z). Because all 3D objects are fundamentally a collection of 3D coordinates, as explained in Chapter 3, "Entering the Third Dimension," objects can be dramatically altered by mathematically transforming the matrix of coordinates they are comprised of.

Position and size transformations can be applied to VRML objects through the Transform node. This means that objects contained in a Transform node can be moved, resized, and even rotated with very little effort as long as you know how to operate the various fields of the node. As you can see from the following VRML97 specification definition, the Transform node has its fair share of fields:

```
Transform {
    eventIn       MFNode      addChildren
    eventIn       MFNode      removeChildren
    exposedField  SFVec3f     center          0 0 0    # (-∞,∞)
    exposedField  MFNode      children        []
    exposedField  SFRotation  rotation        0 0 1 0  # [-1,1], (-∞, ∞)
    exposedField  SFVec3f     scale           1 1 1    # (0, ∞)
    exposedField  SFRotation  scaleOrientation 0 0 1 0 # [-1,1], (-∞, ∞)
    exposedField  SFVec3f     translation     0 0 0    # (-∞,∞)
    field         SFVec3f     bboxCenter      0 0 0    # (-∞,∞)
    field         SFVec3f     bboxSize        -1 -1 -1 # (0, ∞) or -1,-1,-1
}
```

VRML's Transform node is a grouping node that can contain one or more children, something you might have guessed upon seeing the three MFNode fields in this definition. Children of Transform nodes are typically Shape nodes, Group nodes, and other Transform nodes. Transform node operations (transformations related to position, scale, and size) are applied to each of the children the node contains, allowing transformations to be applied to a number of VRML objects at once.

A Transform node might, for instance, include all the shapes necessary to create a human form such as the one seen in Figure 7-1. In this example, the head, torso, arms, and legs are all children of the same Transform node, meaning that this human body can be manipulated as a single unit rather than as a bunch of different shapes. To stand this woman on her head, you

Managing Children and Helping Browsers

Transform node children can be added and removed manually using the *children* field, as you'll see later in this chapter. They can also be added or removed dynamically in response to events, which is why the *addChildren* and *removeChildren* fields are defined as eventIn types (see Chapter 5, "VRML Fundamentals," to learn more about events).

The *bboxCenter* and *bboxSize* fields are used to tell the VRML browser about the children contained in a Transform node, although these two fields are not absolutely necessary. When used, *bboxSize* defines an imaginary box inside of which all the children of the node could fit, which tells the browser how much 3D space the children of a Transform node occupy. The *bboxCenter* field tells the browser where the center of the box is in 3D space. Together these two fields allow the browser to prepare itself to handle the children of a given Transform node, which is more efficient than forcing the browser to calculate this information on its own (which is what it will do if *bboxCenter* and *bboxSize* are not used).

In precreated worlds, most of the difficult work has already been done for you; the children have already been created, and the bounding box (if any) has been calculated. As a result, *translation*, *scale*, and *rotation* are the only fields of the Transform node that you really have to concern yourself with when customizing existing VRML content. And these you have to bother with only if you want to change the position, size, or orientation of objects in the scene. If you do change any of the properties of an object, you'll have to recalculate the *bboxCenter* and *bboxSize* fields if they've already been set (or, alternately, remove them entirely to force the browser to calculate these fields).

would simply set the *rotation* field of the Transform node accordingly; each child in the node would then have that rotation transformation applied to it, meaning that the entire human form would rotate as a result.

You are not forced to manipulate all children of a Transform node as one unit, however. There are plenty of times when you might actually want to alter the position or size of a specific child node independently of the other children contained in a Transform. To make a person wave goodbye, for

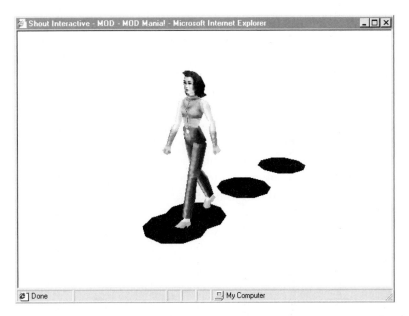

Figure 7-1   The head, torso, arms, and legs of this person are grouped together as children of a Transform node. Operations applied to a Transform are applied to each child, allowing this human form to be moved, scaled, or rotated as a single unit. (http://www.shoutinteractive.com/)

instance, you need only to control a single arm and hand. Likewise, walking requires only the movement of legs, not the entire body. And to turn a head or nod doesn't mean the entire body should also be moved. In each of these cases, you could get away with transforming only specific children of the main Transform node, not all of them.

Transform Nesting

Because Transform nodes can contain other Transform nodes, children can be controlled individually as well as a whole unit. This assumes that a child has its own Transform node, however. If the human form in this example weren't constructed with Transform nodes governing the legs, arms, and head, you wouldn't have the ability to directly control each of these shapes independently of the others (see "Nesting Transform Nodes" later in this chapter for more information).

Coordinate Systems

Technically speaking, each Transform node has its own coordinate system that is used to position the children it contains relative to the node's parent coordinate system. (For more details about coordinates, refer to Chapter 3, "Entering the Third Dimension," and Chapter 5, "VRML Fundamentals.") Because Transform nodes can contain other Transform nodes, the coordinate system of a child Transform node is relative to the coordinate system of its parent. If a Transform node is not a child of another node, however, its coordinate system is then relative to the top-level coordinate system of the VRML file itself, also known as the *world coordinate system* (see Figure 7-2).

Figure 7-2   The world coordinate system is the top-level coordinate system of every VRML file. Local coordinate systems created by the Transform node are positioned relative to the origin (X = 0, Y = 0, Z = 0) of their parent's coordinate system, which is often, but not always, the world coordinate system.

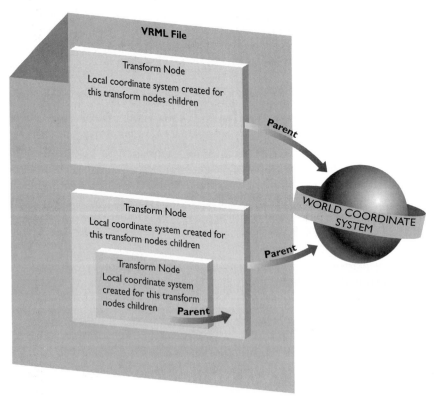

Note: Text Shapes

Text shapes (shape nodes whose geometry is specified by a Text node) are flat, two-sided string objects. Unlike other VRML shapes, they aren't placed into a world with their center at the origin of the coordinate system by default. Instead, text shapes are placed, by default, into a world on the X axis with the lower left edge of the first character positioned at the location Y = 0. Subsequent characters appear one after another along the positive X axis. In other words, when viewed head-on, Text shapes start at the Y = 0 position and run to the right along the X axis. Other VRML shapes, however, are positioned by default with their center at the coordinate-system origin (0, 0, 0). Text nodes can contain a FontStyle node, allowing you to control various characteristics, including font face, style, size, spacing, direction of character flow, and justification (see Appendix B, "VRML Resources").

When a new shape is created without a Transform and placed into a scene, it is positioned, by default, with its center at the *origin* of the world coordinate system (the origin of any coordinate system is the point where its X, Y, and Z axes intersect, corresponding to the 3D coordinate 0, 0, 0). That is, default shapes have the same coordinate system as the scene itself and are placed with their center at the origin of the world. This is true for all shapes; every shape that you create uses the world coordinate system by default unless you create the shape as a child of a Transform node (in which case the Transform node creates a new "local" coordinate system for the children it contains).

Suppose that you create a shape for each of the VRML primitive objects and place them all into the same scene. Your box, cone, cylinder, and sphere overlap each other because they are all placed at the origin of the world by default. In order to move them elsewhere, you must use the Transform node. Specifically, you have to use the *translation* field of the Transform node to position objects relative to the world coordinate system.

Translation

By default, VRML shapes are placed into a scene at the origin (0, 0, 0) of the top-level world coordinate system. As a result, objects will cluster around the scene origin unless a transformation is used to move them elsewhere.

The *translation* field of the Transform node does just that, allowing you to position objects in 3D space:

```
exposedField SFVec3f    translation    0 0 0    # (-∞,∞)
```

The Transform node's *translation* field is an exposedField, meaning that you can set it directly (see Listing 7–1) or it can be changed by an event (through the implied set_translation eventIn, which in turn generates an implied translation_changed eventOut event, as explained in Chapter 5, "VRML Fundamentals"). Because the *translation* field is a SFVec3f data type, it accepts three floating-point values that correspond directly to the X, Y, Z values of a 3D coordinate (see Chapter 5). The values that you supply for this field define a 3D point relative to the origin (0, 0, 0) around which the Transform node's children will be rendered, allowing you to move all the children of the node to any point in a scene that you'd like.

The 3D coordinate that you supply to *translation* measures the distance and direction to move away from the origin of the Transform node's parent coordinate system. By default, the *translation* field is set to 0 0 0, meaning that no movement will take place, because these values essentially say "Move zero units away from the parent coordinate system for all three axes." However, it's a snap to specify a new coordinate for this field and actually move objects around in 3D space. The following, for example, specifies a point that is three units above the Y axis (remember, axis values supplied to the *translation* field are in the form of a 3D coordinate "X Y Z"):

```
translation    0 3 0    # x y z
```

This simple line of code will move the children contained in this Transform node three units above the Y axis of the node's parent coordinate system. If this system is the world, then the objects it contains will be moved up three units on the Y axis relative to the world coordinate system. However, if this node is the child of another Transform node (which is possible because Transform nodes can be nested, as you'll see later in this chapter), the movement takes place relative to the coordinate system of the parent node.

So just how does a shape become the child of a Transform node? By using the *children* field, as you might have suspected. The *children* field can accept one or more nodes, as indicated by the array brackets [ ], meaning that you can place one or more shapes inside of this field. Because the Transform node can contain children, it is considered a grouping node, as explained in Chapter 5, "VRML Fundamentals." To see how the Transform node's *children* and *translation* fields work, consider the source code in Listings 7.1 and 7.2.

The code in Listing 7.1 creates two shapes: a default cone and cylinder, both of which use the world coordinate system for positioning, and both of which are placed at the origin of this system. Neither of these shapes is contained in a Transform node, so they are destined to overlap on screen when rendered by the VRML browser. The cone is rendered first, followed by the cylinder. Because they are positioned around the same point (the origin) in the same coordinate system (the world coordinate system), the cylinder is drawn on top of the cone; the cone is completely obscured by the cylinder, as seen in Figure 7-3.

Figure 7-3 Default shapes are positioned at the origin (0 0 0) of the world coordinate system, and, as a result, will overlap. The cone in this example is completely obscured by the cylinder that is drawn on top of it, because both shapes are rendered at the same coordinate.

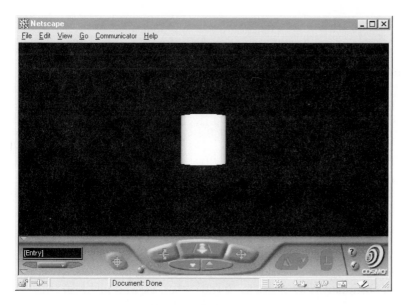

Listing 7.1   Defaults.wrl

```
#VRML V2.0 utf8

# This is an example of two primitive shapes, one
# cone and one cylinder. These shapes are placed
# by default at the origin (0,0,0) of the world
# coordinate system, and overlap as a result.


Shape {
  appearance Appearance {
    material Material {
      diffuseColor 0 1 0    # R G B (this shape is green)
    }
  }
  geometry Cone { }
}


Shape {
  appearance Appearance {
    material Material {
      diffuseColor 1 1 1    # R G B (this shape is white)
    }
  }
  geometry Cylinder { }
}
```

A simple Transform node is all that's needed to remedy the situation. List-ing 7–2 contains a variation on the previous example, placing into a Trans-form node the entire Shape node used to create the cone. The code for the cone shape is nestled comfortably between the opening and closing brackets [ ] of the *children* field, making it a child of this Transform node:

```
Transform {
  translation 2 0 0    # x y z
  children [
        # the entire Shape node goes here
  ]
}
```

The *translation* field of this Transform node specifies that the cone will be moved two units along the positive X axis (2 0 0), which places it to the right of the world coordinate system origin (0 0 0) when viewed head-on (that is, when viewed with the X axis running horizontally, the Y axis running verti-

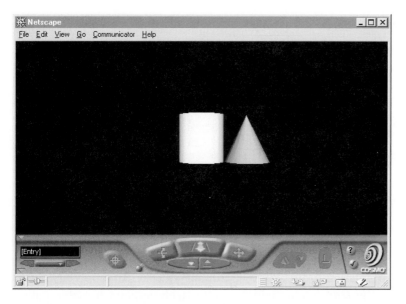

Figure 7-4   The cone shape is now a child of the Transform node, allowing it to be moved independently of the cylinder. Here, the cone is moved two units along the X axis by supplying the value "2 0 0" to the Transform node's *translation* field, which positions it to the right of the cylinder that once obscured it from view.

cally, and the Z axis running from front to back). This small but significant transformation moves the cone out from under the cylinder that once obscured it and into the open where the viewer can see it (see Figure 7-4).

Listing 7.2   Translated.wrl

```
#VRML V2.0 utf8

# This is an example of two primitive shapes,
# one cone and one cylinder. The cone is placed at
# a specific position in the world coordinate
# system using the Transform node.

Transform {
  translation 2 0 0        # x y z   (move +2 units on X axis)
  children [
      Shape {
        appearance Appearance {
          material Material {
            diffuseColor 0 1 0 # R G B (this shape is green)
          }
        }
```

```
      geometry Cone { }
    }
  ]
}


Shape {
  appearance Appearance {
    material Material {
      diffuseColor 1 1 1   # R G B (this shape is white)
    }
  }
  geometry Cylinder { }
}
```

In this example, the Transform node creates a new coordinate system for its children, known as the children's *local coordinate system*, which is then transformed in relation to the world coordinate system. By supplying a value of "2 0 0" to the *translation* field I've effectively applied a mathematical transformation to the cone's local coordinate system, causing this object to be displayed around a point two units to the right along the positive direction of the X axis of the world coordinate system origin (0 0 0).

I could just as easily have moved the cone to the left by supplying a negative value to the *translation* field. I might also have moved the cone along the Y axis, placing it above or below the origin, or even along the Z axis to position it closer to the viewer or farther away, giving the scene a sense of depth. You can, in fact, move along all three axes at once if you so desire. Following are just a few variations for the *translation* field in Listing 7.2, each accompanied by a screen shot of the rendered scene:

```
translation -6  0  0   # move down 6 units on X axis
                       # relative to origin (see Figure 7-5)


translation  0  3  0   # move 3 units up Y axis
                       # relative to origin (see Figure 7-6)

translation  0 -2  0   # move 2 units down Y axis
                       # relative to origin (see Figure 7-7)

translation  2  0  6   # move up 2 units on X axis,
                       # and 6 units up on Z axis
                       # relative to origin (see Figure 7-8)

translation  2  0 -6   # move up 2 units on X axis,
                       # and 6 units down Z axis
                       # relative to origin (see Figure 7-9)
```

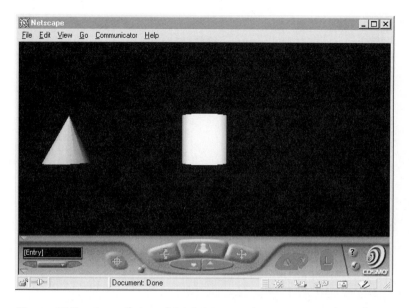

Figure 7-5 A translation of "-6 0 0" moves the cone 6 units down the X axis, positioning it to the left of the world coordinate system origin where the cylinder resides by default.

Figure 7-6 A translation of "0 3 0" moves the cone 3 units up the Y axis, positioning it above the world coordinate system origin where the cylinder resides by default.

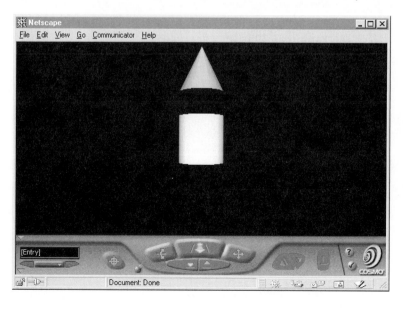

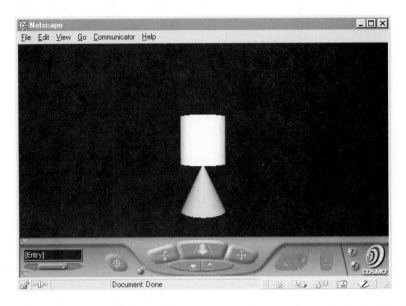

Figure 7-7   A translation of "0 -2 0" moves the cone 2 units down the Y axis, positioning it below the world coordinate system origin where the cylinder resides by default.

Figure 7-8   A translation of "2 0 6" moves the cone 2 units up the X axis and 6 units up the Z axis, positioning the cone to the right and in front of the world coordinate system origin where the cylinder resides by default.

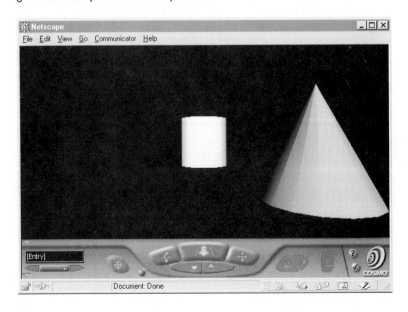

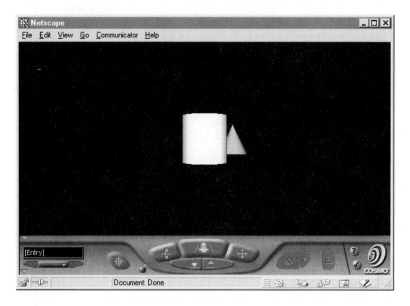

Figure 7-9   A translation of "2 0 -6" moves the cone 2 units up the X axis and 6 units down the Z axis, positioning the cone to the right and in back of the world coordinate system origin where the cylinder resides by default.

In each of these examples only one child—the cone shape—is added to the Transform node. Because this node is a grouping node, however, more than one child can be added to the *children* field. You might, for example, place the cylinder shape under control of the same Transform, like so:

```
Transform {
  translation 2 0 0   # x y z
  children [

    Shape {
      appearance Appearance {
        material Material {
          diffuseColor 0 1 0 # R G B (this shape is green)
        }
      }
      geometry Cone { }
    }

    Shape {
      appearance Appearance {
```

```
      material Material {
        diffuseColor 1 1 1 # R G B (this shape is white)
      }
    }
    geometry Cylinder { }
  }
]
}
```

In this example, the entire cylinder Shape node is included immediately after the cone Shape node, placing it between the opening and closing brackets [ ] of the *children* field. By placing both shapes' definitions here, they both become children of the same Transform node. Unfortunately, we now have the same overlap situation that occurred earlier when each shape was added to the default world coordinate system. Because they both exist within the Transform node's own coordinate system, the cone and cylinder will be moved together to whatever point the *translation* field specifies; they are both positioned at (2 0 0) relative to the world coordinate system, meaning that the cylinder will obscure the cone as before.

In order to include both shapes under the same transform with any degree of usefulness, at least one of them should have its own Transform node. By wrapping the cylinder Shape node in its own Transform node, for example, the cylinder can be moved independently of the cone, yet both can be moved together relative to one another. Transform nesting such as this allows shapes to be controlled individually or as a whole (controlling a waving hand on the human form described earlier, for instance). Later in this chapter I'll show you how to identify and modify nested Transform nodes (see "Nesting

Tip: Bracketing MF Values

You can supply one or more values to the Transform node's children field because it is declared as being a Multivalue Field data type ("MF" data type; see Chapter 5, "VRML Fundamentals"). If you supply only one value to an MF field, you needn't include the opening and closing brackets [ ] around that value, although it's a good idea to do so anyway. Including array brackets around MF field values makes it easier to keep track of where the field ends. It also makes it easy to add another value to the field should you need to do so later (as I've done here by placing the cylinder shape beneath the cone shape).

Transform Nodes"), at which point you'll see how nesting transformations can effect object scaling and rotation, two topics worth tackling now.

Scaling and Rotation

Besides controlling the position of objects residing in 3D space, the Transform node lets you change the size of its children as well as their orientation in the world. The Transform node's *scale* field is used to change the dimensions of each child (see Figures 7-10, 7-11 and 7-12), while *rotation* alters the orientation of each child (see Figure 7-13). Following are the formal VRML97 specification definitions for both of these fields:

```
exposedField SFVec3f      scale      1 1 1   # (0, ∞)
exposedField SFRotation   rotation   0 0 1 0 # [-1,1],(-∞, ∞)
```

Note: Scale Factors

Scaling is a multiplication transformation. The values that you supply to the Transform node's scale field are known as scale factors *because they perform multiplication transformations of the local coordinate system (relative to the node's parent coordinate system). The scale factor that you supply for each axis (X, Y, and Z) is multiplied with the corresponding coordinate system's axis, which results in the coordinate system being transformed in that direction.*

Scale factors above 1 increase a dimension, while scale factors below 1 shrink it (a scale factor of 1 does nothing, because 1 multiplied by any number is always that same number). A scale factor of 2 doubles the size of a shape along the given axis, while a scale factor of .5 reduces it to half. To grow or shrink a shape in one direction, you merely supply a scale factor for the axis that you want to alter and leave the others at 1. Set the Transform node's scale field to (2 1 1), for instance, if you wish to double the size of a shape along the X axis only.

To grow or shrink a shape non-uniformly in each dimension, you can supply a different scale factor for each axis. Set scale to (2 .5 3), for example, to double a shape's size along the X axis while reducing it by half on the Y axis and tripling it along the Z axis. To grow or shrink objects uniformly in all directions, you would supply the same value to each axis, such as (2 2 2) to double a shape in size across all dimensions, or (.5 .5 .5) to shrink all dimensions by half.

Figure 7-10   The original dance scene, with all body parts in their proper scale (1 1 1) (http://www.shoutinteractive.com/).

Figure 7-11   The male character's head is first scaled by 3x in all dimensions (X Y Z) by setting the *scale* of the Transform node parent containing this object to (3 3 3).

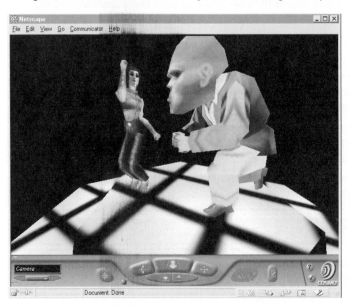

Figure 7-12   The same head is then reduced to three-fourths of its normal size by using a scale factor of (.75 .75 .75).

Figure 7-13   The original dance scene in Figure 7-10 has been rotated, allowing it to be viewed from the top rather than the side (http://www.shoutinteractive.com/).

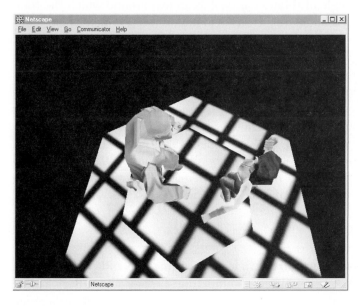

The *scale* field is similar to the *translation* field in that it is also an SFVec3f data type, meaning that it accepts three floating-point values. (Like *translation*, *scale* is also an exposedField that can be set directly or through an event.) Each of the three floating-point values passed to the *scale* field can range from zero (0) to infinity (∞), and, just as with *translation*, each corresponds to an axis in a coordinate system (X, Y, and Z).

By default, the *scale* field is set to (1 1 1), meaning that the children nodes are displayed at their normal size across the X, Y, and Z axes. Numbers above one increase dimensions on a given axis, while numbers less than one decrease size on the given axis. To double the size of children objects uniformly across all axes, for example, you would set the Transform node's *scale* field to (2 2 2). Conversely, setting the *scale* field to (.5 .5 .5) will reduce the size of each child's dimensions by half.

Figures 7-10, 7-11, and 7-12 illustrate the dramatic effect that scaling can have on a scene. The two dancers shown in Figure 7-10 are displayed at their default (1 1 1) scale. In Figure 7-11, the male dancer's head is tripled in size across all dimensions by setting the *scale* field of the Transform node containing this object to (3 3 3). Figure 7-12 then shows the male's head shrunk to 75% of its normal size by setting the *scale* field to (.75 .75 .75). The rest of the scene remains unchanged, since we alter only the Transform node that controls the male head object.

In comparison to the *scale* field, the Transform node's *rotation* field is slightly more complicated. This field takes an SFRotation data type that is used to specify an angle of rotation as well as an axis around which the rotation will take place. Although the Transform node's *rotation* field is more difficult to master than *scale*, it gives you a great degree of control over how objects and even entire scenes are oriented in 3D space. Rotation is responsible for the bird's-eye view of the dance scene shown in Figure 7-13. This scene is normally viewed from the angle seen in Figure 7-10. Thanks to the *rotation* field, however, it's possible to customize the viewing angle of this entire scene and any of the objects in it.

In order to customize VRML worlds through scaling and rotation, you'll need to dig a little deeper into the Transform node's *scale* and *rotation* fields. We'll begin by examining the *scale* field, which is relatively straightforward, after which you'll explore the inner workings of the more complicated *rotation* field.

The *scale* Field

To see the *scale* field in action, take a look at Listings 7.3 and 7.4. These two source code listings give you what amounts to a "before" and "after" look at scaling. The first one doesn't use the *scale* field at all; it just positions a green cone directly above a white cylinder by setting the *translation* field of the cone's Transform node to (0 2 0). This moves the cone two units up on the Y axis, putting it directly above the center of the world coordinate system origin and the cylinder positioned there by default. Neither of these shapes has been scaled, and so they fit perfectly together based on their default dimensions. The result, seen in Figure 7-14, looks something like the nose of a rocket or the tip of a big crayon.

Listing 7.3   BeforeScale.wrl

```
#VRML V2.0 utf8

Transform {
  translation 0 2 0    # x y z (move up 2 units on Y axis)
  children [
      Shape {
        appearance Appearance {
          material Material {
            diffuseColor 0 1 0 # R G B (this shape is green)
          }
        }
        geometry Cone { }
      }
  ]
}
Shape {
  appearance Appearance {
    material Material {
      diffuseColor 1 1 1    # R G B (this shape is white)
    }
  }
  geometry Cylinder { }
}
```

Listing 7.4 is a slight variation on Listing 7.3. Here the *scale* field of the cone's Transform node is set to (5 1 1). As a result, the cone is stretched to five times its normal size along the X axis, while its dimensions along the Y and Z axes remain unchanged. Scaling the cone in this way gives it a shape similar to a beach umbrella viewed head-on (Figure 7-15). Because the cone is scaled only along the X axis, however, viewing it from a slightly different angle reveals that it is quite narrow along the Y access and so is not uniform in appearance on all sides (see Figure 7-16).

Listing 7.4   AfterScale.wrl

```
#VRML V2.0 utf8

Transform {
   translation 0 2 0      # x y z
   scale 5 1 1            # x y z
   children [
      Shape {
        appearance Appearance {
        material Material {
           diffuseColor 0 1 0   # R G B (this shape is green)
        }
      }
      geometry Cone { }
      }
   ]
}

Shape {
   appearance Appearance {
     material Material {
        diffuseColor 1 1 1   # R G B (this shape is white)
     }
   }
   geometry Cylinder { }
}
```

Because a cone is the only shape contained in the Transform node found in Listing 7.4, only the cone is scaled. The cylinder shape is defined outside of the Transform node, leaving it untouched. Any number of Transform nodes can be used in a single VRML file, however, and in complicated worlds you'll find plenty of them. Each shape or group of shapes can be wrapped inside its own Transform node, and very often they are nested together as described earlier. To understand why nesting Transform nodes is necessary, consider the code in Listing 7.5.

Listing 7.5 adds a new Transform node specifically for the cylinder shape, giving this VRML file a total of two Transform nodes (one for the cone and one for the cylinder). In this example both shapes are resized using the same scale settings (5 1 1), resulting in the boatlike object seen in Figure 7-17. Of course, as children of different Transform nodes, the cone and cylinder can also be scaled independently of each other.

Naming Nodes with DEF

In many precreated VRML worlds you'll notice that nodes are given a name using the DEF construct described in Chapter 5, "VRML Fundamentals," which can save you time when it comes to locating the specific part of a scene that you wish to customize. Following, for example, are the names given to the Transform nodes that define the heads of Oscar and Jo, the two animated dancers seen in this section (keep in mind that DEF can be applied to any node, not just Transform nodes):

```
DEF Os_Head-ROOT Transform { ... }

DEF Jo_Head-ROOT Transform { ... }
```

Because the developers of this VRML animation choose self-explanatory names for the Transform nodes used to control each character's head, it didn't take me too long to find these structures and begin experimenting with the fields they contained. Had these nodes not been named with DEF, I would have had to examine every node in the file in detail in order to find what I was looking for. However, thanks to DEF, I was off and customizing in less than a minute (the "Head" portion of the DEF name was the biggest tip-off that I had found what I was looking for).

I started by altering the size of Oscar's head to give him the appearance of a gigantic melon, and then moved Jo's head far away from her neck to give her an out-of-body experience. After I finished customizing the Transform node for each head, I searched through the VRML file to see where else "Os_Head-ROOT" and "Jo_Head-ROOT" appeared.

As it turns out, "Os_Head-ROOT" and "Jo_Head-ROOT" are used at the end of the VRML file to reference each character's head during event routing, meaning that the heads are dynamically altered throughout the animation in response to events. Specifically, OrientationInterpolator and PositionInterpolator nodes are used to animate these characters based on the passing of time (OrientationInterpolator nodes contain a list of key rotations, while PositionInterpolator nodes list key positions used in VRML animation; see Appendix B, "VRML Resources").

In fact, each major body part has its own DEF name and corresponding suite of interpolators, events, and routes, as the heads aren't the only part of this VRML scene that are animated. To see for yourself, visit the MOD Dance Party at http://www.modvr.com/ and view the source code for any of the various Oscar and Jo worlds (you'll have to first decompress these files with a GZip tool; see Chapter 6, "Weaving VRML into Web Pages").

To learn more about using DEF with events and routes, see Chapter 5, "VRML Fundamentals." In Chapter 8, "Customizing Object Color and Texture," you'll see how DEF and USE together allow VRML programmers to reuse code.

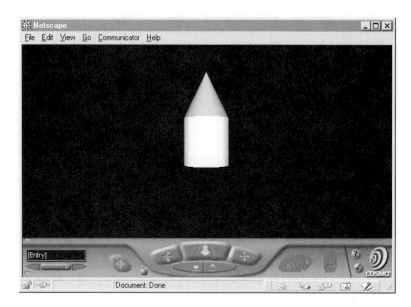

Figure 7-14   The cone and cylinder shapes in this figure are displayed at their default dimensions. The cone has been moved 2 units above the cylinder by setting the *translation* field to (0 2 0) but has not yet been scaled.

Figure 7-15   As a result of setting the Transform node's *scale* field to (5 1 1) the cone is increased in size by 5 times along the X axis, yet remains unchanged along the Y and Z axes. The cylinder also remains unchanged, as it is outside the cone's Transform node.

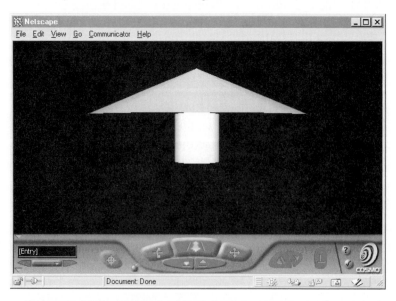

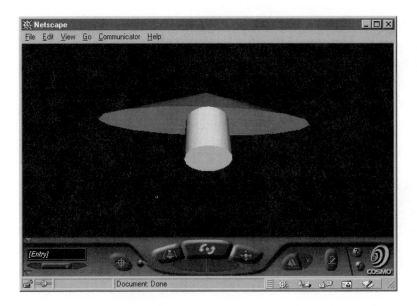

Figure 7-16   The (5 1 1) scaling applied to the cone shape is more obvious when viewed from the bottom. From this perspective you can clearly see that the cone has been stretched significantly along the X axis, but not at all along the Y axis (nor has it been changed along the Z axis, although it's difficult to tell from this angle).

Listing 7.5   TwoTransforms.wrl

```
#VRML V2.0 utf8

Transform {
  translation 0 2 0       # x y z
  scale 5 1 1             # x y z
  children [
      Shape {
        appearance Appearance {
          material Material {
            diffuseColor 0 1 0 # R G B (this shape is green)
          }
        }
        geometry Cone { }
      }
  ]
}

Transform {
  scale 5 1 1             # x y z
```

(Listing 7.5 continued on p. 313)

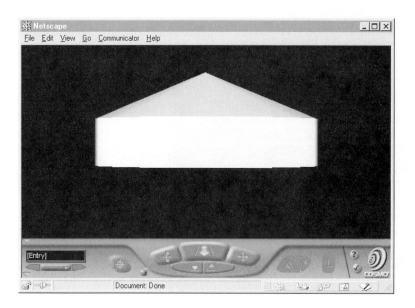

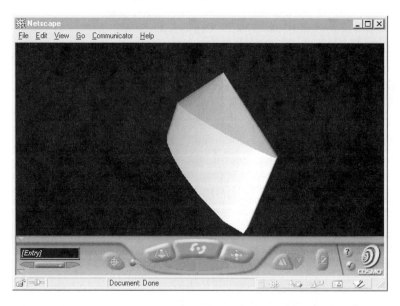

Figure 7-17   The cone and cylinder are children of different Transform nodes, allowing independent scaling of these shapes. Here both shapes are scaled to the same dimensions, producing an object that looks something like a boat.

```
children [
    Shape {
        appearance Appearance {
          material Material {
            diffuseColor 1 1 1 # R G B (this shape is white)
          }
        }
        geometry Cylinder { }
    }
  ]
}
```

Placing the cone and cylinder under the control of different Transform nodes allows each shape to be moved, resized, and rotated independently of the others. The pine tree seen in Figures 7-18 and 7-19, for example, is a direct result of having the cone and cylinder in separate Transform nodes with their own transformation fields.

Figure 7-18   This pine tree is the result of two different Transform nodes. One Transform node contains the cone "tree top," the other contains the cylinder "trunk."

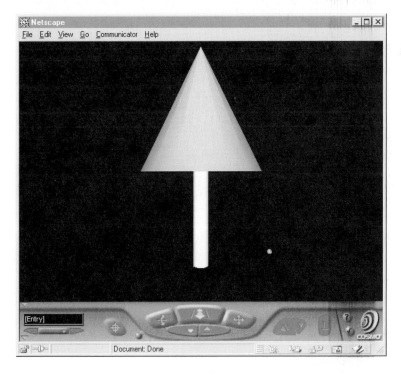

Listing 7.6 contains the VRML source code used to create the pine-tree object in Figures 7-18 and 7-19. In this example, the cone is uniformly doubled in size along all axes (2 2 2) to create a pointed treetop. The cylinder, meanwhile, is scaled down to one-quarter its original size along both the X and Z axes and increased in length on the Y axis (.25 1.5 .25) to create the appearance of a thin tree trunk. The elongated cylinder is then moved one and a half units under the origin by setting the *translation* field of that shape's Transform node to (0 –1.5 0). The result is a pine-tree object. Or is it?

Listing 7.6 PineTree.wrl

```
#VRML V2.0 utf8

Transform {
  translation 0 2 0      # x y z
  scale 2 2 2            # x y z
  children [
      Shape {
        appearance Appearance {
          material Material {
            diffuseColor 0 1 0 # R G B (this shape is green)
          }
        }
        geometry Cone { }
      }
  ]
}

Transform {
  translation 0 -1.5 0      # x y z
  scale .25 1.5 .25         # x y z
  children [
      Shape {
        appearance Appearance {
          material Material {
            diffuseColor 1 1 1 # R G B (this shape is white)
          }
        }
        geometry Cylinder { }
      }
  ]
}
```

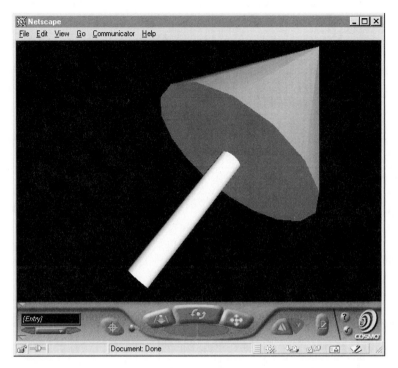

Figure 7-19　When we view it from beneath, we see that this pine tree is symmetrical in shape along the X and Y axes as a result of uniform scaling in these directions.

Because the cone and cylinder in Listing 7.6 are under the control of two different Transform nodes, these shapes are easily manipulated independently of each other. They are not, however, grouped together as one manageable unit. As a result, they can't really be considered an "object." The cone and cylinder have been transformed in a way that only makes them appear to be a pine tree, but they're really two separate shapes that have nothing to do with each other. This becomes especially apparent when the shapes are rotated independently of one another using the *rotation* field of their respective Transform nodes, as you'll soon see.

The *rotation* Field

The Transform node's *rotation* field is used to alter the orientation of shapes in 3D space. Objects and entire scenes can be rotated using this field, for which the following definition appears in the VRML97 specification:

```
exposedField SFRotation  rotation   0 0 1 0 # [-1,1],(-∞, ∞)
```

As an exposedField, *rotation* can be set directly or through an event. It is similar in this respect to the Transform node's *translation* and *scale* fields, which are also exposed (see Chapter 5, "VRML Fundamentals," for details about field types). The *rotation* field, however, is an SFRotation data type, whereas *translation* and *scale* are both SFVec3f data types.

VRML's SFRotation data type is comprised of four floating-point values (one more than SFVec3f accepts), which together define an axis of rotation and the angle of rotation around that axis. SFRotation can conceptually be thought of as an SFVec3f data type plus an additional floating-point number.

The first three floating-point values of an SFRotation data type represent the axis around which the rotation will take place (0 1 0, for example, which specifies the Y axis). Each of these values can range from negative 1 to positive 1, as indicated by the field definition comment [-1, 1]. The fourth SFRotation floating-point value represents the angle of rotation measured in

---

The *center* and *scaleOrientation* Fields

The Transform node's *center* and *scaleOrientation* fields can give you additional control when rotating and scaling objects, although you probably won't find these fields useful until you've mastered the basics of *scale* and *rotation*.

The *center* field is used to change the point around which an object is scaled. By default, the origin (0 0 0) of the coordinate system is that point. You can, however, scale objects around any arbitrary point by setting the Transform node's *center* field to something other than its default value. The *center* field can also be used in combination with the *rotation* field, allowing objects to rotate around an arbitrary point rather than their own geometric center (see "The *rotation* Field").

Like the *rotation* field, *scaleOrientation* is an SFRotation data type for which you supply a rotation axis and angle. Unlike rotation, however, the *scaleOrientation* is used to rotate the coordinate system by a specified amount before the scale operation takes place, after which the rotation is undone (after the scale operation, the inverse scale orientation operation is applied). Thus, the *scaleOrientation* field allows you to temporarily orient a coordinate system before scaling takes place.

Note: SFRotation vs. MFRotation

VRML supports both Single-value Field (SF) and Multi-value Field (MF) rotation data types (SFRotation and MFRotation, respectively). The Transform node's rotation field is an SFRotation data type, meaning that the values you supply to it are used for only one rotation. MFRotation data types, on the other hand, can accept an array of rotation values (VRML's built-in Extrusion and OrientationInterpolator nodes both contain MFRotation fields).

radians (see "Radians vs. Degrees" later in this section) and can range from negative infinity to positive infinity (-∞,∞).

To help make sense of the *rotation* field, consider the following setting:

```
rotation    0 1 0 3.14
```

In this example, I've specified a *rotation axis* of (0 1 0) and an angle of rotation of 3.14 radians. What this says, in essence, is "rotate 3.14 radians around the Y axis, relative to the origin." Of course, this still doesn't make much sense unless you've dealt with rotation in 3D before, and so perhaps an analogy is in order.

Imagine that you're spinning a basketball on your index finger; your index finger points straight up and the ball sits on top of it. Now imagine that an invisible line runs out of the tip of your finger and through the basketball. This is the rotation axis around which the ball spins (see Figure 7-20). Because your finger is pointing straight up, this particular rotation axis runs along the Y axis of a 3D coordinate system. To represent this axis using the SFRotation data type required by the Transform node's *rotation* field, you would supply the following three values (forget for a moment the fourth value, which specifies an angle of rotation):

```
rotation 0 1 0
```

The values (0 1 0) indicate that the rotation should take place around the Y axis, while the values (1 0 0) would specify a rotation around the X axis. Similarly, the values (0 0 1) mean that the rotation should occur around the Z axis. To rotate, for example, a rotisserie chicken, you might supply a rotation axis of (1 0 0) to indicate that it should rotate around the horizontal axis as it cooks.

Although there is really more going on than meets the eye when it comes to specifying a rotation axis (see "The Rotation Axis"), to get started with 3D rotations in VRML all you have do is specify which axis the rotation should revolve around (X, Y, or Z) along with an angle of rotation. These two pieces of information are all you need to orient VRML objects in 3D space.

Note: The Rotation Axis

There is more going on than meets the eye when you supply X, Y, and Z axis values to the rotation field. The first three floating-point values that you supply to the rotation field form a 3D coordinate in the local coordinate system, which is then compared against the origin (0 0 0) of the Transform node's parent coordinate system to determine the final axis of rotation. An imaginary line is drawn from the origin to the 3D point that you specify in the form of three floating-point values. The direction of the imaginary line running from the origin to your point determines the rotation axis. The fourth value that you supply to rotation specifies either a positive or negative rotation angle, measured in radians.

If you supply X, Y, Z values of (1 0 0) to the rotation field, for example, that point falls to the right of the origin (0 0 0) on the X axis. The imaginary line connecting these two points, therefore, runs along the X axis, making the X axis the rotation axis. You could use a higher number, such as (5 0 0), but it wouldn't matter because the direction is the same; your rotation will occur around the X axis in either case.

The last floating-point value of an SFRotation data type determines the angle of rotation. This value is measured in radians, not degrees, as you might have expected. Although degrees are relatively easy for humans to understand, radians are easier for computers to process, so we're forced to deal with the angle of rotation in terms of radians. Fortunately, converting between radians and degrees isn't all that difficult if you have the formula (see the sidebar entitled "Radians vs. Degrees," later in this chapter).

With this in mind, consider the following snippet of code:

```
Transform {
    rotation 1 0 0 3.142    # x y z  angle

    children [
      Shape {
        appearance Appearance {
```

```
        material Material {
           diffuseColor 1 1 1
        }
      }
    geometry Cone { }
    }
  ]
}
```

In this example, a primitive cone shape is rotated around the X axis at an angle of 180 degrees (3.142 radians). The result is not dramatic, but it does flip the cone completely upside down, as seen in Figure 7-21. The cone is upside down because the 180-degree rotation took place around the X axis (imagine a line running through the cone horizontally; this is the axis about which the cone is rotated).

Rotating the cone around the Z axis would produce almost the same effect, but only because all sides of the cone look the same (they're all white in this example, so you can't tell what side of the cone is actually facing you). If the rotation took place around the Y axis, however, the cone wouldn't appear

Figure 7-20 The rotation axis can be thought of as an invisible line or string that runs through an object, around which the rotation takes place.

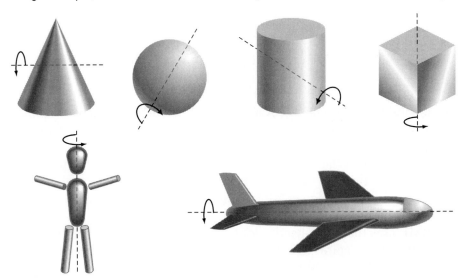

Note: Rotation and Scale Centers and the center Field

By default, shapes are constructed around the origin of their parent's coordinate system. As a result, their natural center is (0 0 0), which is also the point around which rotation will occur (a point known as the rotation center*). Although you can use the Transform node's* translation *field to move a shape away from its default location in a scene, it will still rotate around its own center point. Often, however, we need to rotate objects around a different point. To rotate the hand of a human form, for example, it makes more sense to rotate around a point on the hand itself (such as the wrist) than to rotate relative to the origin of the entire arm shape (which might be the elbow, for example).*

Using the Transform node's center *field, you can specify a 3D coordinate to be used as the rotation center around which objects will be rotated (the* center *field is used to specify a translation offset from the origin of the local coordinate system). The* center *field can also be used to change the point around which an object is scaled. When you scale a shape using the Transform node's* scale *field, the shape's coordinate system expands or contracts based on the values you supply, yet the center point remains the same. You can, however, specify a different scale center by setting the Transform node's* center *field when using the* scale *field (see the earlier section, "The* scale *Field," to learn how to scale objects).*

to move at all (it would be rotated, but you wouldn't be able to tell because all sides of the cone look the same).

In this example, the cone started out in its default position (tip up, base down) and rotated around the X axis in the direction of the viewer (tip moving forward, base moving backward). It continued until it had rotated 180 degrees from its start position, at which point it came to rest. Although the direction in which the rotation takes place doesn't make any difference in this example—the cone will come to rest upside down as long as it's rotated on the X axis for 180 degrees—it is an important factor to consider when orienting objects.

VRML uses the "right-hand rule" to determine the direction of rotations, as illustrated in Figure 7-22. You can also use the right-hand rule to figure

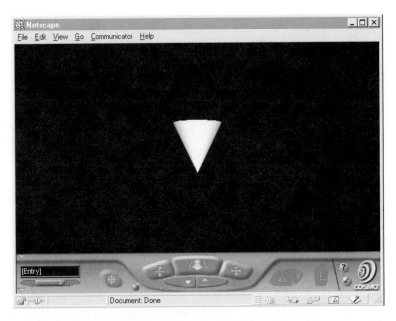

Figure 7-21 This cone is rotated 180 degrees (3.14 radians) around the X axis (1 0 0), which flips it upside down.

Figure 7-22 VRML uses the "right-hand rule" to determine the direction in which to rotate objects.

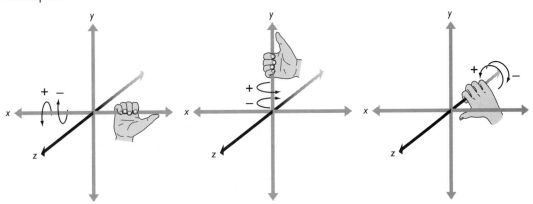

Radians vs. Degrees

Although degrees are generally easier for people to deal with than radians, computers prefer radians when calculating angles. Fortunately, the formula for converting from degrees to radians isn't terribly difficult:

```
radians = degrees / 180 * 3.142
```

To convert 45 degrees into radians, for example, divide 45 by 180 and then multiply the result by 3.142. The answer, .785, is the number of radians in 45 degrees. To convert radians to degrees, the formula is applied in reverse:

```
degrees = radians / 3.142 * 180
```

Following are a few of the more common angles you'll use in VRML, expressed in both degrees and radians:

DEGREES	RADIANS
0	0.000
10	0.175
45	0.785
90	1.571
180	3.142
270	4.712
360	6.283

out the direction your rotations will take. Imagine grabbing with your right hand the axis about which you wish to rotate an object (the X axis, in this example). With your right hand open and your palm facing you, first position the axis in the middle of your palm (this means you have to slip your hand behind the X axis, as if to pull it toward you). Make certain that your thumb is pointing in the positive direction of the axis (your thumb should point right, since you're grabbing the X axis).

Now, close your fingers around the axis. The direction in which your fingers curl is the one in which objects will be rotated when you supply positive values as the rotation angle (toward you, in this case). Objects will rotate in the opposite direction of your fingers when you supply negative values for rotation angles. You can use this technique to determine positive and negative rotation angles for all axes, not just the X axis.

To make the right-hand rule more concrete, suppose you modify the snippet of code that rotates the cone 180 degrees. Instead, rotate it only 45 degrees (.785 radians):

```
Transform {
    rotation 1 0 0 .785     # x y z  angle (rotate forward)

    children [
      Shape {
        appearance Appearance {
          material Material {
            diffuseColor 1 1 1
          }
        }
      geometry Cone { }
      }
    ]
}
```

Now the cone will rotate a small distance toward the viewer, as seen in Figure 7-23. It still rotates around the X axis, but not enough to flip it upside down, making it easier to see the direction of rotation. To rotate the cone in the opposite direction (away from the viewer; see Figure 7-23), just supply a negative rotation angle such as this:

```
rotation 1 0 0 -.785     # x y z  angle  (rotate away)
```

Now it's time to rotate the pine tree that was created earlier. You might recall that I said it really wasn't an object, because the cone and cylinder are separate shapes that act independently of one another. I went on to say that because the cone and cylinder weren't grouped together, the pine tree they resembled couldn't be treated as a single unit. This fact becomes painfully obvious when I try to rotate the tree.

Without thinking too much about the issue of rotation, I simply set both the cone and the cylinder Transform nodes to rotate exactly the same

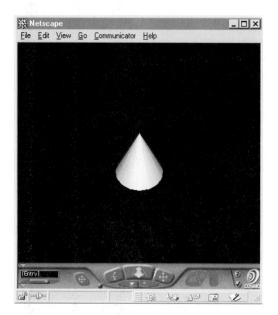 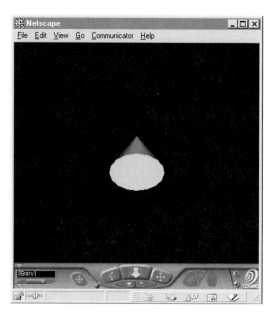

Figure 7-23   Following the right-hand rule, positive rotation angles rotate the cone to-ward the viewer along the X axis (left), while negative rotation angles rotate it away from the viewer (right).

amount: 45 degrees (.785 radians) around the Z axis, the code for which is found in Listing 7.7. This might seem like exactly the thing to do, but it isn't. Because the cone and cylinder shapes are contained in different Transform nodes, through which a different scale and translation are applied to each, rotating these shapes in tandem isn't as easy as it might seem at first. Instead of rotating together as a pine tree, the cone and cylinder rotate independently of each other, as seen in Figure 7-24.

Listing 7.7   PineTreeRotate.wrl

```
#VRML V2.0 utf8

Transform {
   translation 0 2 0      # x y z
   scale 2 2 2            # x y z
   rotation 0 0 1 .785     # x y z, angle
   children [
       Shape {
          appearance Appearance {
             material Material {
```

```
            diffuseColor 0 1 0 # R G B (this shape is green)
          }
        }
      geometry Cone { }
      }
   ]
}


Transform {
   translation 0 -1.5 0     # x y z
   scale .25 1.5 .25      # x y z
   rotation 0 0 1 .785       # x y z, angle

   children [
      Shape {
        appearance Appearance {
          material Material {
            diffuseColor 1 1 1 # R G B (this shape is white)
          }
        }
        geometry Cylinder { }
      }
   ]
}
```

Although it might be possible to muddle around in each Transform node until I hit the magic *rotation* values for each shape (which would likely require the use of the *center* field as well), that's far too much work. I might be able to figure out a solution to this particular rotation dilemma, but what happens when I want to rotate the tree around a different axis? I would have to go through the same process, meaning I'd lose my mind long before I figured out all of the *rotation* values necessary to move my pine tree around as a single unit. Instead of bothering with individual Transform nodes, I should instead nest the Transform node of each shape under a single parent Transform.

Nesting Transform Nodes

Transform nodes can be the children of other Transform nodes, a nesting capability that allows each child node to be under the direct control of its immediate parent while also being grouped together as a single unit. Listing 7.8 illustrates a very simple, one-level nesting of Transform nodes. Here the cone and cylinder shapes are both children of the same Transform node, yet each also is contained in its own unique Transform node.

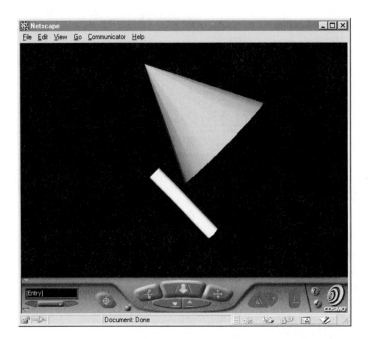

Figure 7-24   Because the cone and cylinder are in their own Transform nodes, they're rotated independently of one another even when supplied with exactly the same rotation values. To rotate these shapes as a single unit, they must be under the same Transform node.

I can now control the position, scaling, and rotation of these shapes as a single unit. Rotating the top-level Transform node 45 degrees (.785 radians) around the Z axis, for example, results in the entire "pine tree" shape being rotated, as seen in Figure 7-25. The *rotation* field of the top-level Transform node is set to (0 0 1 .785), which instructs this node to rotate the coordinate systems of the children it contains relative to one another. The cone and cylinder are each rotated accordingly, allowing them to be controlled as one object through their parent.

Listing 7.8   PineTreeNestedTransforms.wrl

```
#VRML V2.0 utf8

Transform {
   rotation 0 0 1 .785     # x y z, angle
   children [

      # make the cone shape a child of the root Transform,
      # but give the cone a Transform of its own so that it
```

```
# can be controlled independently of any other child:

Transform {
  translation 0 2 0      # x y z
  scale 2 2 2            # x y z
  children [
      Shape {
        appearance Appearance {
          material Material {
             diffuseColor 0 1 0 # R G B (green)
          }
        }
        geometry Cone { }
      }
    ]
}


# now make the cylinder shape a child of the root
# Transform as well, and also place the cylinder
# in its own Transform so that it can be controlled
# independently of other children:

Transform {
  translation 0 -1.5 0    # x y z
  scale .25 1.5 .25       # x y z

  children [
      Shape {
        appearance Appearance {
          material Material {
             diffuseColor 1 1 1   # R G B (white)
          }
        }
        geometry Cylinder { }
      }
    ]
}

  ]
}
```

I'm also free to alter each shape independently of the other. This is possible because each shape is under the immediate control of its own Transform node, through which they can be individually translated, scaled, and rotated. Indeed, the translation and scaling applied to each shape are still the same; the cone looks like the top of a pine tree while the cylinder is elongated to look like a trunk. The only difference is that both are now under the control of a single Transform node, allowing them to truly become a pine tree object instead of the separate shapes they were in the previous section.

In this example the Transform nodes are nested only one level deep. In many of the VRML files you'll encounter, however, nesting is often much deeper. A human-body object, for example, might be under the control of a top-level Transform node, inside of which a number of Transform nodes might be nested. The head, torso, arms, and legs can each be controlled by a unique Transform node, which would allow these body parts to be manipulated and moved independently of one another.

The Transform nodes of these body parts would likely contain their own child Transform nodes as well, each of which might also contain additional Transform nodes. Such a deep nesting of Transform nodes allows developers to control, as needed, either specific parts of a detailed structure or the entire structure as a whole. In a VRML human arm, for example, it would allow independent movement and rotation of the upper arm, forearm, hands, and fingers. Thanks to nested Transform nodes, the index finger on a human hand can

Figure 7-25   By nesting the cone and cylinder under the same Transform node, these shapes are now grouped together and can be rotated as a single unit through the top-level Transform node, or independently of one another through their own Transform node.

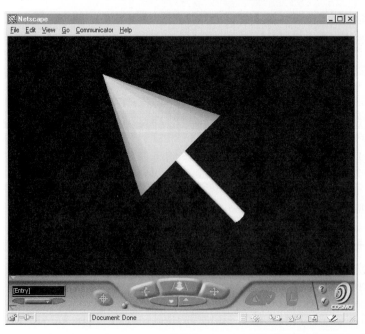

be pointed forward without requiring every other finger to also point forward. Likewise, a hand can be waved on its own without waving the entire arm to which it is attached. This behavior, exactly what you'd expect from a human arm, is a result of nesting Transform nodes within Transform nodes.

Summary

By default, VRML shapes are built around the origin (0 0 0) of the top-level co-ordinate system known as the *world coordinate system*. In order to move a shape elsewhere in the scene, the shape must be created as a child of a Trans-form grouping node. It can then be positioned anywhere in the scene using that node's *translation* field. Children of a Transform node can be also be re-sized (either uniformly in all directions or along any given axis) using the node's *scale* field, while the node's *rotation* field is used to orient children in 3D space.

The Transform node creates a new coordinate system for its children, known as the children's *local coordinate system*, which is relative to the coor-dinate system in which the Transform node itself is defined. In other words, children of a Transform node reside in a coordinate system that is relative to the parent coordinate system of the Transform node.

In this chapter, the world coordinate system has been the parent coordinate system of most Transform node examples, although it's possible to nest Trans-form nodes inside one another as well. In doing so, complex objects can be cre-ated that can be managed as a single unit through the top-most Transform node, while also allowing each child (and the sub-parts it is made of) to be ma-nipulated independently through its own parent Transform nodes.

Following is a complete list of URLs referenced in this chapter:

Shout Interactive   http://www.shoutinteractive.com/
Oscar and Jo   http://www.modvr.com/
Web3D Consortium   http://www.web3d.org/

CUSTOMIZING COLOR AND TEXTURE

Topics in This Chapter

- Customizing the color of shapes using the Appearance and Material nodes
- Mixing red, green, and blue (RGB) light to create custom colors
- Creating dull, shiny, glowing, and transparent surfaces
- Wrapping images around shapes ("texture mapping") using the Texture node
- Texture mapping with images, movies, and raw pixel data
- Using the TextureTransform node to control texture mapping

Chapter 8

In Chapter 7, "Customizing Location, Size, and Orientation," you learned how to customize VRML content using the Transform node to position objects in a scene, change the size of objects, and even rotate objects in 3D space. Moving, sizing, and orienting shapes, however, is just the beginning when it comes to customizing VRML worlds.

You can also customize various visual aspects of your worlds with very little effort if you're familiar with the basic nodes that control how objects appear to the viewer of a scene. In this chapter, we'll see how to use VRML's Appearance and Material nodes to change the color and texture of shapes, attributes that can greatly enhance the visual appeal of your Web3D pages in exchange for a modest amount of your time.

Appearance and Material

As you may recall from Chapter 5, "VRML Fundamentals," the objects that populate VRML worlds are created using the Shape node. VRML's built-in Shape node allows developers to specify the form, or geometry, of a shape independent from its appearance. Because every shape's geometry and appearance are divided into two distinct bodies of code, you can easily alter the way a shape *looks* without touching the code that defines the form of the shape. Also, you can quickly customize the color and texture of every object in a scene no matter how complicated the form of the object. Customizing the appearance of simple, primitive objects (such as cones and spheres) follows the same basic steps that are required for more sophisticated objects (such as elevated grid shapes, indexed face shapes, or even text). Once you can customize the appearance of one type of object, you're well on your way to doing so for every type.

To customize the color or texture of a VRML object, however simple or complex, you will alter the *appearance* field of the object's Shape node:

```
Shape {
  exposedField SFNode appearance NULL
  exposedField SFNode geometry   NULL
}
```

The *appearance* field is typically associated with an Appearance node:

```
Appearance {
  exposedField SFNode material        NULL
  exposedField SFNode texture         NULL
  exposedField SFNode textureTransform NULL
}
```

It is through the Appearance node that you will customize a shape's surface properties, specifically color and texture, as well as reflectivity and transparency. A shape's color is set using the *material* field, while its texture is set using the *texture* and *textureTransform* fields. Later in this chapter, you'll learn how to apply textures to shapes. First, however, it's worth getting to know the *material* field, as you'll likely customize the color of shapes more often than you will their texture. (Also, it's much easier to understand textures once you know about color, especially when it comes to combining textures and colors.)

Material Colors

The Appearance node's *material* field is typically associated with a Material node. It is inside the Material node that the color of a shape is defined. The Material node is full of fields that you can use to specify flat

Note: Outside the Appearance Node

The Appearance node isn't the only way to customize the way a shape looks, just the easiest. You can, for example, customize the color of IndexedFaceSet, IndexedLineSet, and PointSet shapes using the color fields that are built into these nodes (see Appendix B, "VRML Resources"). You can also change the appearance of shapes using lights, as described later in this chapter (see "Lighting and Shading"), and even using fog, as described in Chapter 9, "Customizing Light, Background, Fog, and Sound."

In this chapter you will learn how to set the overall color of shapes using the Appearance node. At times, however, you'll want even more control when it comes to coloring shapes. To learn about advanced color control in VRML, visit the following area of the Web3D Gallery: http://www.web3dgallery.com/vrml/color/.

colors, glowing colors, shining colors, and the transparency or opacity of a shape.

Using Material node fields, you can create an infinite number of colors and appearances for your VRML objects. If you've ever found yourself getting carried away with HTML Web page colors, wait until you get a crack at coloring 3D objects. It can be addictive, because the possibilities are truly endless. Not only can you create any color that can be displayed by a computer monitor, but you can also color shapes in a way that makes them appear to be made of real-world materials such as metal or plastic. Once you begin experimenting with the Material node, it'll be a long, long time before you get a solid night's sleep.

Note: Field and Node Names

VRML field names often correspond to node names, making it easier to remember what type of node you place in a field. The Shape node's appearance field, for example, is associated with an Appearance node. Likewise, the Appearance node's material field is associated with a Material node.

Following is the VRML97 specification definition for the Material node:

```
Material {
  exposedField SFFloat ambientIntensity  0.2          # [0,1]
  exposedField SFColor diffuseColor       0.8 0.8 0.8 # [0,1]
  exposedField SFColor emissiveColor      0 0 0       # [0,1]
  exposedField SFFloat shininess          0.2         # [0,1]
  exposedField SFColor specularColor      0 0 0       # [0,1]
  exposedField SFFloat transparency       0           # [0,1]
}
```

In previous chapters I've used the Material node's *diffuseColor* field to create shapes that are either pure red, pure green, or pure blue. The following snippet of code, for example, creates a pure green cone shape (see Figure 8-1) by turning the green component of the *diffuseColor* field on while leaving the red and blue color components off (0 1 0). Although I haven't discussed VRML color in detail until now, this code should nonetheless be familiar to you, as it illustrates the basic structure of the Shape node (if it is not, refer to Chapter 5, "VRML Fundamentals"):

```
#VRML V2.0 utf8

Shape {
  appearance Appearance {
    material Material {
      diffuseColor 0 1 0  # R G B  (pure green)
    }
  }
  geometry Cone { }
}
```

Figure 8-1   This shape's Material node *diffuseColor* field is set to pure green (0 1 0). The shape's cone geometry is rendered in pure green as a result.

In this example a Shape node is created that uses a primitive cone as its form (geometry). As described earlier, the Shape node's *appearance* field is set to a corresponding Appearance node. The Appearance node, in turn, contains a *material* field that is set to a corresponding Material node. Finally, the Material node's *diffuseColor* field is set to (0 1 0), which specifies a pure green color. As a result, the cone shape is rendered in the color green.

The Material node's *diffuseColor* field is an exposedField, as are all Material node fields. This means that it can be set directly, as I've done in this code, or by an event (see Chapter 5, "VRML Fundamentals" for details about node fields). The *diffuseColor* field is a SFColor datatype based on the RGB (Red Green Blue) color model; each of the three floating-point numbers that the field accepts correspond to the amount of red (R), green (G), and blue (B) light that are mixed together to produce the actual color. The first floating-point number of an SFColor datatype corresponds to the color red, the second to green, and the third to blue.

The amount, or intensity, of each RGB component ranges from 0 to 1. A setting of 0 indicates that no light of that color will be used, while a setting of 1 specifies that 100% of that light color should be used. A setting between 0 and 1, such as .75, indicates that a portion of color should be used (75%, in the case of .75). Thus, setting the *diffuseColor* field to (0 1 0) creates a bright green color, because the green color component is set to 100%, while absolutely no red or blue light is used. We could have created a green color half as bright by simply specifying half as much green light (0 .5 0).

Note: Material Node Field Definitions

Every field of the Material node accepts one or more floating-point numbers that can range from 0.0 to 1.0. Fields that are of type SFFloat accept a single floating-point number, while those that are used to create color (diffuseColor, emissiveColor, and specularColor) are defined as being SFColor datatypes. SFColor fields accept a single color value expressed as three floating-point numbers (one each for red, green, and blue light values, as described in this section).

Every field of the Material node is also defined as an exposedField type, meaning it can be set directly, as in these examples, or in response to an event, as described in Chapter 5, "VRML Fundamentals."

By mixing different amounts of red, green, and blue light you can create any color that your computer screen is capable of displaying. In previous chapters we've created shapes that are rendered in pure red (1 0 0), pure green (0 1 0), or pure blue (0 0 1), although you can also create colors by mixing these color components together. The following code, for example, creates a pure yellow cone by mixing together equal amounts of red and green, while omitting blue altogether (see Figure 8-2):

```
#VRML V2.0 utf8

Shape {
  appearance Appearance {
    material Material {
      diffuseColor 1 1 0   # R G B   (pure yellow)
    }
  }
  geometry Cone { }
}
```

Mixing color components together at 100% intensity—as I've done here to create bright yellow—allows you to create only a limited number of colors, however. Mixing pure amounts of red, green, or blue cannot create the color brown, for instance. Instead, as Figure 8-3 illustrates, you must mix red, green, and blue together at various *intensities* to create colors such as brown, purple, aqua, gray, and others (see the sidebar "Common RGB Colors").

Following is an example of a brown cylinder created by mixing various intensities of red, green, and blue light together in the *diffuseColor* field:

```
#VRML V2.0 utf8

Shape {
```

Figure 8-2   This yellow cone was created by mixing both red and green light at 100%, while omitting blue altogether (1 1 0).

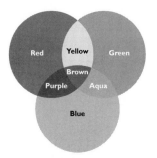

Figure 8-3 Only a small number of colors can be created by mixing various combinations of red, green, and blue light at 100%. Most colors are a combination of various intensities of each color component.

Common RGB Colors

The RGB color model allows you to create a wide variety of colors by mixing together different amounts of red, green, and blue light. Several of the Material node's fields accept SFColor values, based on the RGB color model (Material's *diffuseColor*, *emissiveColor*, and *specularColor* fields require SFColor values).

To create a color using the SFColor datatype (or MFColor, which accepts an array of SFColor values), supply three floating-point numbers that correspond to red, green, and blue light values (the first value corresponds to red, the second to green, and the third to blue). Each must be in the range of 0 to 1, where 0 indicates that no amount of the given color component is used and 1 indicates full intensity for that color. A value between 0 and 1 indicates that a portion of that color should be used. Following are a few of the many possible colors you can create using VRML's RGB color model:

```
R    G    B    # RESULTING COLOR    R    G    B    # RESULTING COLOR
1    0    0    # all red            0    .75  0    # light green
0    1    0    # all green          0    .25  0    # dark green
0    0    1    # all blue           0    0    .75  # light blue
                                    0    0    .25  # dark blue
1    1    0    # yellow
0    1    1    # cyan
1    0    1    # magenta            .50  .50  .50  # gray
                                    .75  .75  .75  # light gray
0    0    0    # all black
1    1    1    # all white          .25  .25  .25  # dark gray
                                    .8   0    .8   # purple
.75  0    0    # light red          0    .8   .8   # aqua
.25  0    0    # dark red           .3   .15  .05  # brown
```

```
   appearance Appearance {
     material Material {
       diffuseColor .3 .15 .05 # R G B  (brown)
     }
   }
  geometry Cylinder { }
}
```

Lighting and Shading

In each of the earlier example source code listings, as well as those in previous chapters, the shapes I've created have been lighted and shaded so that they appear three-dimensional. VRML browsers take great care to apply color to objects using lighting and shading techniques that create the illusion of depth, a rendering technique that actually tricks our brain into thinking that we're looking at 3D objects. In truth, however, everything that you see on your computer screen is actually two-dimensional, because the display is a flat surface that has no depth (see Chapter 3, "Entering the Third Dimension," for more details). VRML browsers make you *think* that the objects you see have depth, when in fact they are no more three dimensional than standard 2D bitmap images.

The blue cone in Figure 8-4, for instance, appears to be three-dimensional only because the VRML browser has done than render it as a flat triangular surface. Instead, the browser uses lighting and shading to make it seem as if a source of light is directly in front of the cone. The cone is rendered bright blue on the front surface (as if light were striking the front of the cone), while the sides are rendered in progressively darker shades of blue (evoking the sense of shadows cast on an object with depth). In this way the

Figure 8-4   Through lighting and shading, this cone appears to be three dimensional even though it is actually a two-dimensional graphics image displayed on the flat surface of a computer monitor.

Reusing Appearances with DEF/USE

VRML nodes can be reused, thanks to a mechanism known as DEF/USE (short for "define and use"). As you may recall from Chapter 5, "VRML Fundamentals," the DEF keyword is used to assign a name to a node. In order to give an Appearance node a name, for example, you would supply the DEF keyword followed by the name you'd like to use immediately before the formal node name and description:

```
Shape {
appearance DEF GOLD Appearance {
    material Material {
        diffuseColor      .25 .15 .00
        specularColor     .75 .70 .60
        shininess  .20
    }
  }
geometry Cone { }
}
```

After defining a node name with DEF, you can reuse that node later in your VRML file. To reuse the gold appearance defined above, for example, you would simply follow the *appearance* field of any Shape node with "USE GOLD" as follows:

```
Shape {
  appearance USE GOLD
  geometry Box { }
}
```

By using DEF/USE in this way, you can save yourself a lot of typing and also increase the readability and overall efficiency of your scenes (the original node is reused each time the USE keyword is applied, eliminating redundant code and processing). Because DEF/USE can be applied to any node, not just the Appearance node, this code-reuse mechanism will appear throughout many of the VRML worlds that you encounter. For a listing of the legal characters that can be included in a DEF name, refer to the VRML97 specification (see Appendix B, "VRML Resources").

Figure 8-5   Without lighting and shading this cone appears to be a flat, two-dimensional object.

lighting and shading of the cone object give it a 3D appearance even though it is actually a two-dimensional shape displayed on a two-dimensional computer monitor; your eyes and brain only think they see a 3D cone.

Without lighting and shading, VRML shapes would not appear to be 3D, a startling reality that you can prove to yourself by removing the *appearance* field from any Shape node (see "Default Lighting and Shading"). Likewise, if you remove every source of light from a VRML scene, the objects in it will appear two dimensional, as Figure 8-5 illustrates. In this example, the cone is rendered without taking into account a light source, and so no shading is needed. As a result, this cone is displayed in a single, uniform shade of blue and so appears to be a flat object instead of the elegant 3D shape we're accustomed to.

The Default Headlight

The direction from which a light source strikes an object, together with the intensity of the light, greatly affects how that object appears to the viewer. By default, VRML browsers have a *headlight* light source that is positioned to strike objects head-on, as if worn on the head of the viewer. Much like a miner's light, the headlight moves in sync with the viewer so that it always strikes objects from the user's viewpoint, as illustrated in Figure 8-6.

Although all VRML browsers include a default headlight to help illuminate objects in a scene, users aren't obligated to use it. The viewer is free to turn the headlight off or on at will, which toggles the lighting and shading of objects based on this light source. When the headlight is off, objects will

Figure 8-6   The headlight of a VRML browser always shines on objects from the viewpoint of the user. Turning the headlight off will eliminate 3D lighting and shading unless another light source is present in the scene.

appear flat and two-dimensional, as seen in Figure 8-5, unless another light source is present (see "Headlight Blackout").

Direct and Ambient Lighting

VRML shapes are rendered based on the sum of every light source that strikes them, a calculation that includes both direct and ambient light sources. *Direct light* travels in a straight line from a light source to the object being illuminated, while *ambient light* is the scattered, randomly reflected light bounced around a scene as the result of direct lighting. Calculation of the amount of ambient light in a scene is based on the number of direct light sources and is a rough approximation of how light is reflected off objects in the real world (see "Toward Consistent Rendering").

VRML supports three different direct light source nodes: Directional-Light, PointLight, and SpotLight. These nodes are used to cast direct light

Note: Default Lighting and Shading

Shapes created without the benefit of a Material node are displayed as pure white, with no lighting or shading whatsoever, making them appear to be flat two-dimensional objects. A Shape node is considered to be "unlit," meaning it is not lighted, if either the node's appearance field is NULL or the material field in the Appearance node is NULL. By default the Shape node's appearance field is NULL, and so is the material field of the Appearance node, meaning that shapes are not lit or shaded by default.

Lighting and shading do not affect every geometric form, however. Specifically, VRML's IndexedLineSet and PointSet nodes are not lit or shaded as other geometry nodes are (e.g., primitive Box, Cone, Cylinder, and Sphere nodes and more complex nodes such as ElevationGrid, Extrusion, and IndexedFaceSet). To create shapes, the IndexedLineSet node uses lines, while PointSet uses points. As a result, the shapes these nodes create are simply colored and cannot be lit or shaded in the way that most other geometric nodes are (nor can textures be applied to these nodes, as the "Textures" section explains later in this chapter).

onto objects and scenes, which in turn offers another way to customize the appearance of your VRML content. DirectionalLight, PointLight, and Spot-Light nodes may be used alone or in combination to illuminate worlds, as described in Chapter 9, "Customizing Light, Background, Fog, and Sound." These nodes, together with the default headlight (which acts like a DirectionalLight node), contribute to the amount of ambient light in a scene.

The Material node's *ambientIntensity* field is used to control how much or how little ambient light is reflected by the surface of a shape. (Note, however, that some browsers ignore this field altogether, as explained in the sidebar "Toward Consistent Rendering.") As a SFFloat datatype ranging from 0 to 1, the *ambientIntensity* field is set to 0.2 by default. The value of this field is multiplied by the value of the *diffuseColor* field, which results in the minimum color used to render the surface of a shape. When calculated in the presence of ambient light, values closer to 1 result in brighter base shape colors, while values closer to 0 result in darker base colors:

```
exposedField SFFloat ambientIntensity  0.2     # [0,1]
```

Warning: Headlight Blackout

VRML browsers differ in how they respond to the headlight being disabled. Some, such as WorldView, continue to render objects as flat, two-dimensional shapes by eliminating the 3D lighting and shading that the headlight produces when striking an object. A blue cone displayed against a black background, for example, would appear to lose its 3D appearance when the headlight is turned off. It would still be visible against the black background, however, as a two-dimensional flat-blue cone (the color blue would stand out against the black background).

Other browsers, such as Platinum's CosmoPlayer, go even further when the headlight is off and actually remove every trace of light that the head-light produces. In this case, objects that appear in a scene against a black background will seem to disappear, just as objects in the real world disappear when viewed at night unless there is a light source to illuminate them.

If you are concerned that objects may disappear when viewed without a headlight, you can add a light source yourself using any one of VRML's three light nodes (DirectionalLight, PointLight, or SpotLight) as described in Chapter 9, "Customizing Light, Background, Fog, and Sound." Alternately, you can change the default black background used by VRML. To do so, simply add a VRML Background node to the top level of your VRML file (or the top-level grouping node) and specify a color other than black for the skyColor (see Listing 8–1 later in this chapter, or turn to the next chapter for more details):

```
Background {
  skyColor 0 0 .5    # R G B (medium blue background)
    }
```

Diffuse Colors

The *diffuseColor* field is perhaps the most popular of all Material node fields, as it can be used to create colors that you might consider "normal" when compared to glowing, shining, or transparent colors. When used alone, the *diffuseColor* field creates flat, matte colors such as those used to color shapes

Toward Consistent Rendering

Because VRML is an interactive 3D technology, it is not precise about lighting and reflection in the way that traditional 3D modeling products are. VRML content is constantly recalculated and rerendered in response to user activity, meaning that realistic lighting and reflection effects aren't practical, given the processing power of today's desktop systems. Instead, VRML browsers do their best to *approximate* real-world lighting and reflection.

VRML browsers follow a suite of coloring and lighting formulas in order to render reasonably realistic worlds in real time. If you're interested in these mathematical formulas, refer to the VRML97 specification, which is available online through the Web3D Consortium (http://www.web3d.org). VRML97 specification section 4.14, "Lighting Model," lists the equations used by browsers to simulate the real-world properties of light striking a surface. Likewise, the "Node Reference" section of the VRML97 specification (section 6) details how browsers should render each shape supported by the language.

Due to differences in implementation, however, browsers are not perfectly consistent in the way they render content (some browsers ignore the *ambientIntensity* field altogether, for instance, while others use this field). Lighting, color, and textures of a VRML scene, for example, will look somewhat different when rendered by CosmoPlayer as compared to WorldView, Cortona, or Contact, even when viewed on the same computer system. Similarly, worlds viewed on the Windows platform differ in appearance from those viewed on the Macintosh or UNIX platforms. As a result, if you wish to present users with content that is consistent from platform to platform, you must be careful to test your VRML worlds across a variety of browsers and system configurations when customizing these and other attributes.

For assistance in crafting consistent content in the face of today's somewhat inconsistent VRML browsers, you should consider joining the www-vrml mailing list as described in Chapter 4, "VRML Overview." The www-vrml list, comprised of over two thousand VRML users, is the place to turn when you've hit a wall regarding just about any VRML-related question, including rendering issues.

Alternately, you can craft VRML content with a specific VRML browser in mind (in much the same way you can create HTML pages specifically for Netscape Navigator or Internet Explorer Web browsers). If you do so, however, be sure to alert those visiting your pages as to the VRML browser required (see Chapter 6, "Weaving VRML into Web Pages," for details on how to use VRML browser "sniffer" scripts for such purposes).

in previous examples, although it can also be combined with other Material node fields to create glossy and transparent colors (see "Shiny Surfaces" and "Transparency" for details).

The *diffuseColor* field creates colors based on *diffuse reflection*, a term used to describe light that bounces off objects in random directions. Because light rays that strike a diffuse reflection surface are reflected in random directions, objects colored only with the *diffuseColor* field have a soft, consistent overall look; there are no bright or shiny spots.

Specular reflection, on the other hand, bounces light off objects in a much more predictable manner, creating shiny reflective spots such as the sparkle of a diamond ring or the twinkling of sun off a car's hood on a bright summer day. The *shininess* and *specularColor* fields of the Material node create reflective color spots on the surface of shapes, while the *diffuseColor* field creates colors that are flat or dull by comparison. Often, however, these fields are used together; the *diffuseColor* field sets the base color for an object, while the *specularColor* field specifies the color of reflective spots and the *shininess* field controls how large or small these spots are (see "Shiny Surfaces" for details).

The exposed *diffuseColor* field is an SFColor datatype, which is based on the RGB color model described earlier (see "Material Colors"). As a result the *diffuseColor* field accepts three floating-point numbers that together define how much red, blue, and green light are mixed together to produce the

---

Note: Diffuse and Specular Reflection

VRML attempts to approximate the way light bounces off surfaces in our real world by incorporating two forms of light reflection into the mathematical calculations that result in the lighting and shading of objects: diffuse reflection and specular reflection.

Diffuse reflection bounces light off objects in random directions, resulting in a soft, uniform lighting, while specular reflection is much more mathematically precise and so produces lighting effects such as highlights, glints, light spots, sparkling and twinkling when applied to shiny surfaces (see "Shiny Surfaces").

Shapes colored with the diffuseColor field reflect all light sources based on the angle of the object in relation to each light source. If a shape is directly facing a light source, for example, the shape will reflect a great deal more light than if positioned at an angle to the light.

actual color a shape is rendered in. By default this field is set to create a color that is almost completely white (.8 .8 .8):

```
exposedField SFColor diffuseColor        0.8 0.8 0.8 # [0,1]
```

Although the *diffuseColor* field can be combined with other Material node fields to create interesting effects (such as *specularColor* to produce shiny surfaces or *transparency* to create objects that are see-through), it is often used alone to create solid colors as shown in Listing 8.1. In this example, the pine-tree object that was created in the previous chapter is colored using nothing more than the *diffuseColor* field. The cone "treetop" is a dark green (0 .25 0), while the cylinder "trunk" is a shade of brown (.3 .15 .05).

Because it is difficult to see these colors when displayed against VRML's default black background (see Figure 8-7), the scene background color has

Figure 8-7   The dark green and brown colors of this tree are created using only the *diffuseColor* field of the Material node. These colors, however, are difficult to see against the default black background.

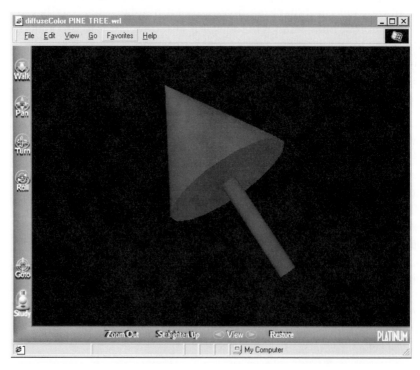

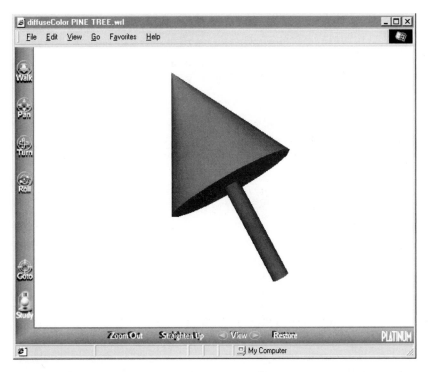

Figure 8-8   The dark green and brown colors of this tree are much easier to see against the white background of this scene, which was created by setting the *skyColor* field of this VRML file's Background node to (1 1 1).

been changed to pure white (by adding a Background node to the top level of this file as described earlier in "Headlight Blackout"). The final, colored tree is shown in Figure 8-8, where it clearly stands out against the white background. (Visit www.coreweb3d.com for this and all other source code listings in this book.)

Listing 8.1   PineTreeColored.wrl

```
#VRML V2.0 utf8

Background {
  skyColor 1 1 1   # R G B (white background)
}

Group {
  children [

      # first create the cone "tree top" shape, and
```

```
# give it a dark green color:

Transform {
  translation 0 2 0      # x y z
  scale 2 2 2            # x y z
  children [
      Shape {
        appearance Appearance {
          material Material {
            diffuseColor 0 .25 0  # (dark green)
          }
        }
        geometry Cone { }
      }
    ]
}
# now create the cylinder "tree trunk" and color
# it brown:

Transform {
  translation 0 -1.5 0     # x y z
  scale .25 1.5 .25        # x y z

  children [
      Shape {
        appearance Appearance {
          material Material {
            diffuseColor .3 .15 .05   # R G B (brown)
          }
        }
        geometry Cylinder { }
      }
    ]
}

  ]
}
```

Shiny Surfaces

Although the Material node's *diffuseColor* field is used to create soft, relatively dull colors, you'll often come across VRML objects that appear to have shiny, glossy surfaces such as metal and plastic. Shiny shape surfaces are

Group vs. Transform

The code in Listing 8.1 uses VRML's Group node to manage children nodes (cone and cylinder shape nodes, in this case). In the previous chapter (Chapter 7, "Customizing Location, Size, and Orientation"), the same pine-tree shape was created using a Transform node. Because they can contain children, both the Group node and Transform node are considered *grouping nodes*, and both are used to create compound objects that can be manipulated as a single unit (see Chapter 7, "Customizing Location, Size, and Orientation," for details on the Transform node).

In the previous chapter, we created a pine-tree object by grouping the cone and cylinder shapes together under a top-level Transform node. Using various Transform node fields, we were able to move, scale, and rotate the entire pine-tree structure as a single object. In Listing 8.1, however, I've replaced the top-level Transform node with a Group node, which does not have transformation capabilities. As a result, the pine tree you see here (Figures 8-7 and 8-8) was tipped at an angle manually, using a mouse and the rotate controls of my VRML browser. Had I instead used a Transform node to group these shapes, the tree could have been tipped in VRML code, using that node's *rotation* field as explained in the previous chapter.

created in VRML by combining the *diffuseColor* field with the Material node's *specularColor* and *shininess* fields:

```
exposedField SFColor specularColor    0 0 0      # [0,1]
exposedField SFFloat shininess        0.2        # [0,1]
```

The *specularColor* field is used to alter the surface properties of a shape based on *specular reflection*. This term describes light that reflects off surfaces in a predicable, mathematically precise way, resulting in highlights such as gleams, sparkles, twinkles, and glints. These highlights appear when rays of light strike the surface of an object and are reflected in a very specific direction, as opposed to the random directions in which diffuse reflection bounces light off objects (resulting in uniform lighting that creates soft, dull colors as described in the previous section).

In the real world, specular reflection highlights occur principally as a result of two main factors: the surface color of an object and the color of light that strikes the object. The two colors combine to form a third color—the color of light that is actually reflected by the object. The chrome bumper of a car, for example, gleams bright white when hit by rays of white light, while the car's red hood reflects the same white light as a red-colored highlight. Similarly, a blue glass bottle reflects light in a very different way than does a red glass bottle, both of them producing specular highlights that look different from those created by a green glass bottle. And, because plastic has surface properties altogether different from those of metal or glass, plastic materials reflect light yet a different way.

Although surface color and light color are the two main factors that combine to form specular highlights in the real world, VRML doesn't attempt to calculate specular highlights in this way for performance reasons (such calculations are time intensive and impractical for interactive 3D, given today's desktop computing power). Instead, VRML allows you to specify the color of specular reflection highlights explicitly through the Material node's *specularColor* field. The color that you supply to this field is used for specular highlighting, meaning that surface color and light color aren't actually taken into account. To create white glints on a VRML chrome bumper, for example, you supply a white value such as (1 1 1) to the *specularColor* field. Likewise, to create realistic-looking specular reflections on a bar of gold you set *specularColor* to a gold or yellow color.

The Material node's *shininess* field, on the other hand, defines the size of specular highlights. The floating-point values accepted by the *shininess* field can range from 0 to 1, where low values create small, focused highlights, and high values create larger specular highlights. Small specular highlights give surfaces a shinier appearance, while large ones produce duller surfaces.

To understand the affect that the *shininess* field has on specular reflection, study Figure 8-9 while considering the code of Listing 8.2. The series of VRML dolphins seen in Figure 8-9 were created using various *specularColor* and *shininess* field settings (see Listing 8.2). For reference, the first dolphin was created using a *diffuseColor* field setting of (.25 .25 .25) and has no specular reflection applied to it at all. As a result, this dolphin is a flat shade of gray.

The second dolphin in the series keeps the same *diffuseColor* field setting (.25 .25 .25) but is given large gray specular highlights by setting the *specularColor* field to (.7 .7 .7) and *shininess* to 1 (the maximum amount this field will accept). As a result, this dolphin has a relatively small shiny area immediately below its top dorsal fin. Although it seems counterintuitive, keep in mind

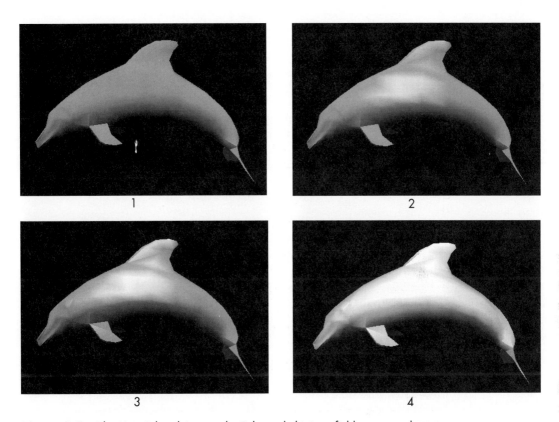

Figure 8-9   The Material node's *specularColor* and *shininess* fields were used to create a variety of "shiny" appearances based on the drab reference dolphin (top image) created using only the *diffuseColor* field.

that large *shininess* field values distribute specular highlights over a large area, resulting in duller, less shiny surfaces, such as the back of this dolphin.

By comparison, the third and fourth dolphins in the series look much glossier. However, the value of the *shininess* field is the only thing that is changed to achieve this look. The third image was created with a *shininess* field setting of .5, which results in a moderately shiny dolphin, while the fourth image was created with the default *shininess* field value of .2 to create a small, focused specular reflection highlight area that results in the shiniest dolphin of all.

Listing 8.2

```
# The following Material node settings were used to create
# the four different dolphin appearances seen in Figure 8-9
```

```
# 1st dolphin (no specular highlights)
# this dolphin is a dull, flat shade of gray:
material Material {
  diffuseColor .25 .25 .25 # dark gray base color
}

# 2nd dolphin (light gray specular highlight, maximum size)
# this dolphin has a shiny area below the dorsal fin:
material Material {
  diffuseColor .25 .25 .25 # dark gray base color
  specularColor .7 .7 .7   # light gray highlights
  shininess 1 # very large highlight area
}

# 3rd dolphin (light gray specular highlight, moderate size)
# the entire back of this dolphin is shiny:
material Material {
  diffuseColor .25 .25 .25 # dark gray base color
  specularColor .7 .7 .7   # light gray highlights
  shininess .5 # moderate sized highlight area
}

# 4th dolphin (light gray specular highlight, small size)
# this is the most shiny of all dolphins:
material Material {
  diffuseColor .25 .25 .25 # dark gray base color
  specularColor .7 .7 .7   # light gray highlights
  shininess .2 # small, focused highlight area
}
```

Because I've selected a dark shade of gray as the base color (*diffuseColor*) for these dolphins, which is then combined with light gray specular reflection highlights (*specularColor* and *shininess*), the overall appearance is quite similar to that of a real-life dolphin. And, not coincidentally, you don't miss much by looking at these printed pages. What you see in these grayscale prints is reasonably close to what you'd see in a VRML browser, because I've used a combination of gray colors and gray highlights. Although it's impossible to really drink in the beauty of specular highlights in print, shades of gray do a decent job in conveying their purpose.

Of course, gray isn't a terribly exciting color. To see these dolphins rendered in more lively colors, turn to the color insert in the middle of this book. Here you will see dolphins that appear to be created from a metallic red alloy, brass, gold, aluminum, and plastic, as well as a ghostly dolphin

Metal, Plastic, and Glass Surfaces

By combining the Material node's *diffuseColor*, *specularColor*, and *shininess* fields in various ways you can create metallic, plastic, and glass surfaces. The following snippet of code, for example, creates a red metal alloy appearance by setting the *specularColor* field to red (1 0 0) while leaving the base color dark gray (.25 .25 .25):

```
# Red metallic alloy (gray base color, red specular
# color):
material Material {
   diffuseColor .25 .25 .25 # dark gray base color
   specularColor 1 0 0    # solid red highlights
   shininess 1 # very large highlight area
}
```

Because of the dark gray base color defined by this Material node, the large red specular highlights take on a strange reflective coloring similar to that of a metal alloy. To create a somewhat less ephemeral coloring you can change the base color to dark red, making for a more solid red metal appearance:

```
# Red metal (dark red base color, small red specular
# highlights)
material Material {
   diffuseColor .25 0 0 # dark red base color
   specularColor 1 0 0    # solid red highlights
   shininess .2 # very small highlight area
}
```

Following are just a few of the surfaces that can be created by combining various *diffuseColor*, *specularColor*, and *shininess* settings. Visit http://www.web3dgallery.com/vrml/color/ to see these and others in action:

Surface	diffuseColor	specularColor	shininess
Aluminum	.37 .37 .37	.89 .89 .89	.13
Blue Plastic	.20 .20 .70	.85 .85 .85	.15
Copper	.30 .10 .00	.75 .30 .00	.08
Gold	.49 .34 0.0	.89 .79 0.0	.13
Red Alloy	.34 0.0 0.34	.84 0.0 0.0	.12
Black Onyx	0.0 0.0 0.0	.72 .72 .72	.18

created using transparent colors (see "Transparency" later in this chapter). By specifying different base colors and various specular settings, I was able to create a variety of interesting appearances for the VRML dolphin rendered only in gray here.

Glowing Colors

Whereas the Material node's *diffuseColor* field is used to create relatively dull, matte colors that appear to be painted onto the surface of a shape (which may be combined with the *specularColor* and *shininess* fields to create glossy surfaces), the *emissiveColor* field produces glowing colors that seem to emanate from within the shape itself. The *diffuseColor* field would be used to color a light bulb that has not been lit up, and the *emissiveColor* field is much more appropriate to color a light bulb that is actually on; light appears to be emitted from within the bulb, making it glow yellow.

The *emissiveColor* field has nearly the same definition as the *diffuseColor* and *specularColor* fields, the only difference being the name of the field and the default settings. All are exposedField types that can be set directly or through an event, and each is a SFColor datatype that accepts three floating-point numbers to describe color as a mixture of red, green, and blue light. As with *diffuseColor* and *specularColor*, the legal range for the *emissiveColor* field SFColor values is 0 to 1. With *emissiveColor*, however, 0 is used to specify no glowing light for a given color, while 1 specifies the highest possible amount (see "Material Colors" for details on RGB color components). By default, the *emissiveColor* field emits no glow whatsoever, because each of the color components is set to 0:

```
exposedField SFColor emissiveColor    0 0 0      # [0,1]
```

To appreciate the difference between flat colors created with the *diffuseColor* field and glowing colors created using *emissiveColor*, consider the yellow spheres in Figure 8-10. The sphere on the left was colored through a *diffuseColor* field setting of (1 1 0), resulting in a relatively dull-looking 3D object, while the sphere on the right was created by setting the Material node's *emissiveColor* field to the same (1 1 0) value. If the difference in the overall appearance of these two shapes is obvious when viewed as a pair of grayscale images, it's downright dramatic in color (as the color insert in the middle of this book will attest).

Figure 8-10   The yellow sphere on the left was created using a *diffuseColor* field setting of (1 1 0), while the glowing yellow sphere on the right was created by setting the *emissive-Color* field to the same (1 1 0) value.

Despite the considerable difference in the visual appeal of these two images, only a single line of code was required. Following are the snippets of code used to create these two very different yellow spheres:

```
# create a yellow sphere using the diffuseColor field:
Shape {
  appearance Appearance {
    material Material {
       diffuseColor 1 1 0    # R G B  (flat, matte yellow)
    }
  }
 geometry Sphere { }
}


# create a GLOWING yellow sphere using
# the emissiveColor field:
Shape {
  appearance Appearance {
    material Material {
       emissiveColor 1 1 0    # R G B  (glow yellow)
    }
  }
 geometry Sphere { }
}
```

Glowing colors are often used to create shapes that seem to have their own internal light source, such as light bulbs, fireflies, the sun and stars, drums of radioactive waste, and other objects that emit light. Glowing shapes

Figure 8-11   This pine tree is now easily seen against VRML's default black background, because the green cone "treetop" and brown cylinder "trunk" have been defined as emissive colors that glow.

are generally easier to see against dark background colors than those created with flat or shiny colors. The pine tree created in the previous section, for example, was very difficult to see against, VRML's default black background, because the flat, diffuse colors used to create the tree top and tree trunk were also quite dark. Had these shapes been created with glowing colors by using the *emissiveColor* field, however, they would be seen easily, as Figure 8-11 illustrates.

Transparency

Using the Material node's *transparency* field, you can create clear, see-through shapes through which light can travel. VRML windows, eyeglasses, beer mugs, insect wings, and a variety of other objects take on an added sense of realism when rendered with some degree of transparency, as they more closely approximate their real-world counterparts. Rather than reflecting or absorbing all the light they are exposed to, transparent shapes allow some amount of light to pass through them, as determined by the value of the *transparency* field.

As an exposedField that accepts floating-point numbers in the range of 0 to 1, *transparency* has nearly the same definition as the *shiniess* field. The *shininess* field, however, is set to (.2) by default, whereas the *transparency*

Note: Glowing Shapes Aren't Light Sources

Shapes that are colored with the emissiveColor field appear to emit light from within, to glow. The light emitted by a glowing shape does not illuminate objects around it, however. A flashlight created using the emissiveColor field will not, for example, light up the scene in which it resides. Nor will a glowing sun actually cast light into the world it is part of.

As a result, either the VRML browser's built-in headlight must be turned on, or alternate light sources must be added to a scene in order to create the desired lighting effect. See "Lighting and Shading" for details on default headlights and light sources, and Chapter 9, "Customizing Light, Background, Fog, and Sound," to learn how to create light sources.

field is set to 0 by default. As a result, shapes are entirely opaque (solid; not see-through) by default:

```
exposedField SFFloat transparency      0          # [0,1]
```

To create a transparent shape, simply set the *transparency* field of the shape's Material node to something other than 0. Values closer to 1 introduce more transparency to a shape by allowing more light through it, while a value of 1 creates shapes that are completely transparent (making them invisible). The dolphin seen in Figure 8-12, for example, has a ghostly appearance, because the *transparency* field of this shape's Material node is very high (.8). Conversely, the dolphins you saw earlier (Figure 8-9) are entirely opaque, because the *transparency* field wasn't used at all, meaning that the default value (0) was applied when these shapes were rendered.

Likewise, the leftmost cone in Figure 8-13 is completely opaque by default, and so obscures a large portion of the cylinder positioned behind it. By setting the cone's *transparency* field to something other than 0, however, light is allowed to pass through this shape. As a result, the cone appears ghostlike, allowing the entire cylinder shape behind it to be seen (Figure 8-13). The source code to produce this simple transparency example is found in Listing 8.3 (a Transform node is used to position the cone shape 4 units forward on the Z axis; see Chapter 7, "Customizing Location, Size, and Orientation," for Transform node details).

Figure 8-12   Thanks to a high *transparency* field setting (.8), this dolphin has a ghostly, see-through appearance.

Listing 8.3

```
#VRML V2.0 utf8

# Position a cone in front of a cylinder. Use transparency
# to allow viewers to "see through" the cone.

Transform {
  translation 0 0 4    # x y z
```

Figure 8-13   Shapes are completely opaque by default (left), yet can be set to various levels of transparency by setting the Material node's *transparency* field to something other than 0 (right).

```
   children [
      Shape {
        appearance Appearance {
        material Material {
          diffuseColor 0 1 0    # R G B (green)
          transparency .75
        }
      }
      geometry Cone { }
      }
   ]
}

Shape {
   appearance Appearance {
     material Material {
       diffuseColor 1 1 1    # R G B (white)
     }
   }
   geometry Cylinder { }
}
```

VRML browsers use different rendering techniques when it comes to creating transparent shapes, as illustrated in Figure 8-14. CosmoPlayer, for example, uses mathematical calculations to blend the pixels of transparent shapes with underlying pixels, which results in a very realistic transparency effect. WorldView, on the other hand, renders transparent shapes using a screening technique in which a dithered screen mesh (similar in appearance

Figure 8-14 VRML browsers differ in their approach to rendering transparent shapes. Some browsers use color blending (left), while others employ screen mesh overlays (right).

to a screen door or window screen) is overlaid on the transparent shape. In this case the values you supply to the *transparency* field control how large or small the "holes" in the screen mesh grid are, which in turn dictates the degree to which shapes behind the screen can be seen. High values create large holes in the screen (resulting in more transparency), while low values create smaller holes (less transparency). Although screening is less computationally complex than color blending, putting less strain on computer processors, the results are not as realistic.

Textures

In addition to altering the color of VRML shapes, you can also wrap flat, two-dimensional images around their surface to further customize appearances. When used in this way, images are usually referred to as *textures,* because they can give objects the appearance of surface variations, or texture, such as the ribbing of a corduroy fabric or the rough bark of a tree trunk. A shape covered with an image of wood grain, for example, appears to have a wooden texture that a solid brown color created with the *diffuseColor* field simply cannot convey. Likewise, wrapping the same shape with an image of cloth gives it a very different texture, which is quite different again from the texture a marble image lends to an object, as illustrated in Figure 8-15.

Because textures are bitmap images that are applied, or *mapped,* to the surface of VRML shapes, they can give objects a much more detailed appearance than is possible using the color fields of the Material node. As a result, texture mapping—the act of mapping flat, two-dimensional images to 3D shapes—is often used to enhance the realism of objects and scenes. Although VRML textures are typically stored in bitmap image formats such as JPEG, PNG, or GIF files, they can also be stored in the MPEG1 movie

Warning: Transparent Texture Images

Although you can use the Material node's transparency field with shapes that are texture mapped by an image (see "Textures" in the following section), be aware that not all browsers will render the texture as a transparent image. Instead, you should use transparency within the image itself. VRML supports texture maps that have transparent pixels, which you can use in the place of the Material node's transparency field.

Figure 8-15   Wrapping different images around a shape can dramatically alter the texture it appears to have (images freely available at http://www.web3d.org/Working Groups/media/).

format. Such textures are known as *movie textures* and are used to play a series of images on the surface of a VRML shape. Thus, both images and movies can be used as VRML *texture maps* (see "Texture Maps, Images, and Movies").

VRML's powerful texture-mapping features can give you amazing control over the appearance of objects and worlds. You can greatly enhance premade objects and scenes by simply applying textures to them, or altering the textures they come with, as illustrated in Figures 8-16 and 8-17. In both examples you see a VRML scene that is first rendered using only RGB colors specified through the Material node's *diffuseColor* field, followed by the same scene enhanced with photorealistic textures. The difference in realism is dramatic, to say the least.

You can wrap textures around any VRML shape except those created with the PointSet and IndexedLineSet nodes (see the following "Applying Textures to Shapes" section for details). Primitive and compound shapes created

Note: Texture Maps, Images, and Movies

Texture mapping describes the process of covering the surface of a 3D shape with a 2D bitmap image, such as a JPEG, PNG, or GIF image. In texture mapping, each pixel of a 2D image is applied, or mapped, to a corresponding point on the surface of a 3D shape. The image used in texture mapping is commonly referred to as a texture map (or simply "map"), which is applied to a shape's surface according to a mapping algorithm.

In addition to image textures, VRML also supports movie textures. These are images stored in a movie format that can be applied to a shape in the same way that a single image is. With movies, however, mapping isn't static; every image, or frame, of a movie can be mapped one after another onto the surface of a shape. A movie can, in effect, play on the surface of a VRML shape. Each frame of a movie is considered to be a unique texture map, meaning that a movie comprised of 100 video frames can be thought of as a file containing 100 different texture maps that are applied to a shape in sequence.

VRML texture images are specified through the ImageTexture node and can be in the JPEG, PNG, or GIF format. VRML texture movies, on the other hand, are specified through the MovieTexture node, which supports only the MPEG1 movie format (see "Image Textures" and "Movie Textures" later in this chapter for details).

with the Box, Cone, Cylinder, and Sphere nodes are fair game, as well as more complex shapes created using the Extrusion, ElevationGrid, IndexedFaceSet, and Text nodes. You can also apply textures to the sky, background, and even the ground of a world using the Background node (see Chapter 9, "Customizing Light, Background, Fog, and Sound"), allowing you to customize nearly every aspect of your scenes with images.

You can, in fact, get completely carried away with texture mapping if you're not careful. But be warned: too many textures can be worse than none at all! Because wrapping an image around a shape is far more complicated than simply coloring a shape, texture mapping requires a lot more computing horsepower than coloring objects using the Material node fields. Not only are textures more difficult to process, they can consume a great deal of disk space and bandwidth, which is why so many of the online worlds you

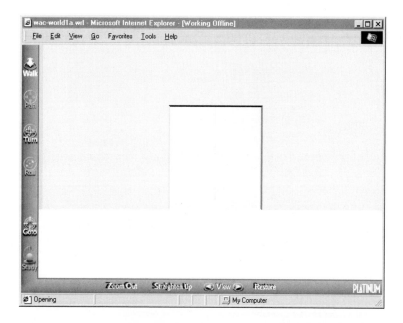

Figure 8-16   This scene is first rendered only with colors (top), then enhanced with textures (bottom) to create realistic wooden walls, a marble floor, and a barn door (http://www.web3dgallery.com/people/gq/).

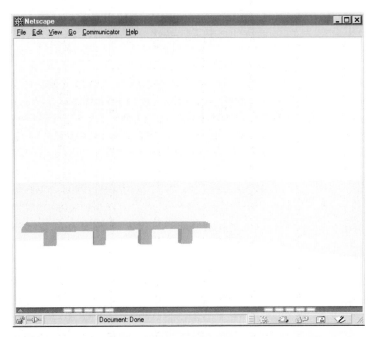

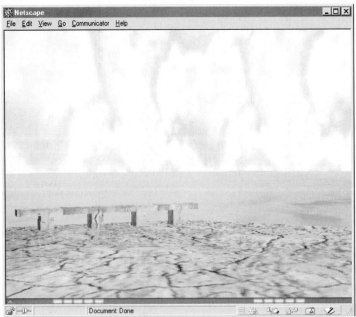

Figure 8-17 This coastal scene is first rendered only using colors (top), then again with textures (bottom). The difference is dramatic because of the detail that images can provide when compared to colors (http://www.web3dgallery.com/people/gq/).

encounter use textures sparingly. When used in moderation, however, textures can really blow the socks off an otherwise ho-hum world.

Applying Textures to Shapes

Customizing VRML objects with textures is similar in concept to customizing the color of an object; in order to do so, you must first become familiar with the various nodes and fields that control the mapping of textures onto shapes. As with colors, textures are applied to objects using the *appearance* field of the Shape node:

Warning: Texture Overload

Be careful not to add too many textures to a single scene, and be sure to test across a range of computers to ensure that your texture-mapped worlds won't bog down when run on low or modestly powered systems. Also take care to consider those users who access your worlds over dial-up modems, as they're likely to become frustrated waiting for textures to come across the wire if you've used too many.

To overcome this problem, you can use the freely available Universal Media textures developed by the Web3D Consortium (http://www.web3d .org/WorkingGroups/media/). Universal Media textures are professionally developed texture maps that are preinstalled on the user's hard drive, and so don't have to be downloaded over the network by a VRML browser in order to appear in your worlds. They load instantly, even though they are extremely high-quality images that would otherwise require a substantial amount of time to download.

The Universal Media Working Group, which I chair (accounting for my fondness of the notion), is responsible for developing the Universal Media system through the Web3D Consortium. Unfortunately, Universal Media is very new (it will officially ship around the time this book hits the shelves), and so very few VRML browsers actually support this system as of today. However, because the working group decided to utilize multiple-texture URLs as explained in this section, standard VRML browsers can also take advantage of Universal Media. For more details, visit: http://www.web3d .org/WorkingGroups/media/.

```
Shape {
  exposedField SFNode appearance NULL
  exposedField SFNode geometry   NULL
}
```

You may recall from the previous color discussion that the Shape node's *appearance* field is, in turn, associated with an Appearance node. However, instead of using the *material* field of the Appearance node as you do with colors, you specify and control textures using the *texture* and *textureTransform* fields:

```
Appearance {
  exposedField SFNode material         NULL
  exposedField SFNode texture          NULL
  exposedField SFNode textureTransform NULL
}
```

While the *texture* field is used to specify a texture map that will be applied to the surface of a shape, the *textureTransform* field can be used to alter a texture before it is actually applied to the shape. This gives you a great degree of control over how textures are mapped to the surface of an object, allowing you to rotate, scale, and translate textures as you'll learn later in this chapter; however, you don't have to use the *textureTransform* field at all. You can, and often will, use the *texture* field by itself.

By default, the *texture* field is NULL, meaning that shapes have no texturing applied to them unless you set this field to a valid node type. The following three texture nodes are supported by VRML:

- **ImageTexture,** which is used to create texture maps from bitmap image files stored in the JPEG, PNG, or GIF format (although the VRML97 specification only requires VRML browsers to support the JPEG and PNG image formats, most also support the GIF image format).

Tip: Combining Textures with Material

Textures can be combined with various Material node fields to create a variety of interesting texture maps, as described throughout this section.

- **MovieTexture,** which is used to create texture maps from movie files stored in the MPEG1 format. Both the MPEG1-Systems and MPEG1-Video versions of MPEG1 are supported (the former encodes both video and audio, the latter only video).

- **PixelTexture,** which is used to create texture maps from an array of pixel values that are typed directly into the node itself. PixelTexture texture maps are created using pixel data stored within the VRML file in which the shape itself is defined (as opposed to creating texture maps based on external image files, as is the case of texture maps created with both the ImageTexture and MovieTexture nodes).

To use one of these three texture node fields, you simply set the Appearance node's *texture* field accordingly. To map a JPEG image onto a cone, for example, you would use an ImageTexture node as follows:

```
Shape {
   appearance Appearance {
     material Material { }
     texture ImageTexture {
       url "checkerboard.jpg"
     }
   }
   geometry Cone { }
}
```

In this case, a texture map is created from the JPEG image file named "checkerboard.jpg," which is then mapped onto the surface of the cone geometry of this Shape node (see Figure 8-18). Because I'm mapping a texture around this shape and have no need for coloring, the Material node isn't used at all; I simply left the Material node's opening and closing braces empty { } without bothering to set any fields. I could have omitted the *material* field altogether, in which case shape would be considered "unlit," meaning it would be rendered without the benefit of 3D lighting and shading (see "Color vs. Grayscale Textures").

Of course, simply adding an ImageTexture node alone didn't result in this cone being texture mapped. I had to actually specify the name and location of the image file to use as a texture map, which I did through the node's *url* field. If I weren't aware of the ImageTexture node's *url* field, and how to use

Color vs. Grayscale Textures

VRML browsers ignore the Material node's *diffuseColor* field when you use textures that contain color; the texture's own colors override any color specified by the *diffuseColor* field. The Material node's other fields, however, may still be used, allowing you to create shiny, transparent, or glowing textures using the *specularColor*, *transparency*, and *emissiveColor* fields (not all browsers render transparent textures created with the *transparency* field, however, and so you should instead use transparent pixels in the texture image itself).

Textures that contain only grayscale pixels, however, do not override the Material node's *diffuseColor* field. Instead, grayscale images are treated as "intensity maps" rather than texture maps. The value of each grayscale pixel stored in an intensity map is multiplied by the value of the Material node's *diffuseColor* field before being applied to a shape, which alters the brightness or darkness of colors across the surface of a shape. Intensity maps are typically used to cover shapes with colored patterns that vary in brightness and darkness (see the "Texture Types, Color Components, and Transparency Values" sidebar in the "Image Textures" section later in this chapter).

In cases where the Appearance node's *material* field has not been specified (meaning that it has been omitted from the Shape node code), a textured shape—whether color or grayscale—is rendered "unlit" and without 3D lighting or shading. As a result, textured shapes created without a *material* field are rendered using flat shading and do not have a 3D appearance (see "Lighting and Shading," earlier in this chapter). You can avoid flat rendering of your shapes by setting the *material* field to an empty Material node as follows:

```
material Material { }
```

it, I would not have been able to create the checker board texture map from the "checkerboard.jpg" JPEG image. Just as you must know how each of the fields in the Material node works in order to customize object colors, you must also understand the innards of VRML's three texture nodes in order to customize the textural appearance of objects.

Before diving into the particulars of VRML's ImageTexture, PixelTexture, and MovieTexture nodes, you should first understand the way in which

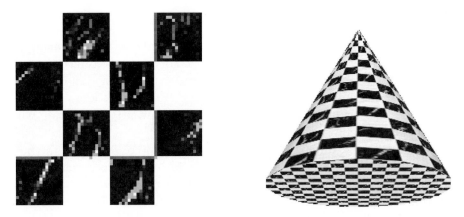

Figure 8-18 A JPEG image (left) has been defined as a texture map through VRML's ImageTexture node, allowing it to be applied to the surface of a cone (right).

texture maps created from these nodes are actually applied to shapes. As I mentioned earlier, you can use the Shape node's *textureTransform* field to alter the way in which browsers apply texture maps to the surface of an object. In many cases, however, you may be content to rely on VRML's default mapping scheme, which varies depending on the geometry of a shape.

The geometry, or form, of a shape determines how a texture is applied to it, meaning that each geometric node supported by VRML is texture mapped in a way that best suits that form. Cones are texture mapped differently than boxes, for example, while text shapes are mapped using an altogether different scheme. Following is a brief overview of the default mapping for each of VRML's geometric nodes. In each case, the image seen in Figure 8-19 is used as a texture map.

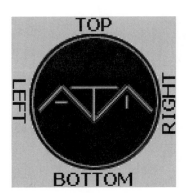

Figure 8-19 This test image is used as a texture map throughout the following sections to help you visualize the default mapping of VRML's geometric nodes.

Boxes

Shapes created with VRML's primitive Box node are default texture mapped in a way that places the complete texture on each of the box's six faces (boxes have four sides, a top, and a bottom). The texture map is applied rightside up to the front, back, left and right sides of the box. If you look at any of these faces of the box head-on (with the box top facing upward), the texture will appear to be perfectly oriented as seen in Figure 8-20.

In addition, the texture map is applied right-side up to the top of the box as well as the bottom. As a result, the texture will seem perfectly oriented if you look down at the top of the box from above, or tilt the top of the box toward you without otherwise reorienting the shape. Likewise, the bottom texture appears perfectly oriented if you look upward at the bottom of the box from below, or tilt the box so that the bottom faces you.

Cones

Shapes created using VRML's primitive Cone node are default texture mapped in a way that wraps the texture around the body of the cone while also applying the texture to the bottom of the cone. The left edge of the texture is affixed to the back of the cone, while the remainder of the texture is wrapped counterclockwise (when viewed from above) once around the cone body, stretching and squeezing the texture as needed. Pixels at the top of the

Figure 8-20   Texture maps are applied rightside up to each face of a box. The image on the left shows the texture as applied to the front of the box, while that on the right shows the left, top, and front of the box (this box was rotated to the right and down, allowing these three faces to be seen at once).

cone are squeezed together, while those close to the base may be stretched in the mapping process. The right edge of the texture ultimately meets the left edge in the back of the cone to form a vertical seam (see Figure 8-21).

The cone bottom is "capped" using a circular cutout of the texture map. The cap is cut out of the lower left-hand corner of the image and applied to the cone bottom so that it appears rightside up when viewed from the bottom looking up, or when the cone bottom is tilted toward you without otherwise reorienting the shape (see Figure 8-21).

Cylinders

Shapes created using VRML's primitive Cylinder node are default texture mapped much as cone shapes are (see "Cones"). Cylinders have both a circular top and circular bottom, however, whereas cones have a circular bottom and a pointed top. As a result, texture mapping of cylinders is somewhat more straightforward (there is no need to pinch or squeeze pixels together at the top, because a cylinder doesn't come to a point in the way that a cone does).

Figure 8-21   Cone texture maps are wrapped around the cone body so that the left and right texture edges form a seam in the back (top images). Pixels at the top of the cone are squeezed together, while the bottom is "capped" with a circle cut from the texture (bottom images).

The texture is wrapped once around the cylinder body (the horizontal diameter of the cylinder) in a counterclockwise direction when viewed from above. As with cones, the left edge of the texture is affixed to the back while the remainder of the texture is wrapped once around the cylinder body. The right edge of the texture meets the left edge in the back to form a vertical seam (see Figure 8-22).

Both the top and bottom of the cone are "capped" using a circular image cut from the texture's lower left-hand corner. The top texture cap appears rightside up when the cylinder is viewed from above or when tilted forward so that the top faces you. Likewise, the cylinder's bottom texture cap appears right-side up when the cylinder is viewed from below or when it is tilted so that the bottom faces you (see Figure 8-22).

Spheres

Shapes created using VRML's Sphere node are texture mapped by wrapping the texture once around the horizontal diameter of the sphere. As with cone and cylinders, the left edge of the texture is affixed to the back while the remainder of the texture is wrapped counterclockwise (when viewed from the top) once around the body of the shape. The right edge of the texture meets the left edge at the back of the sphere, where a vertical seam is formed (see Figure 8-23). Both the top and bottom portions of the texture map are pinched, or squeezed, to a single point as seen in Figure 8-23.

Text

Shapes created using VRML's Text node are default texture mapped by scaling the texture in both the horizontal and vertical directions so that it can cover the entire surface area of a text shape. You can think of the characters

Figure 8-22   The cylinder body is wrapped once by a texture, with the texture's left and right edges forming a seam at the back, while a circular "cap" is applied to both top and bottom.

Figure 8-23　Sphere textures are wrapped once around the horizontal diameter starting at the back, where the left and right edges form a vertical seam, while the top and bottom portions of the texture are squeezed to a point.

in a text shape as being cookie cutters, pressed into the texture "dough" that has been rolled out along the horizontal and vertical dimensions so that it is large enough to accommodate every letter (see Figures 8-24 and 8-25).

The origin of the texture is the same as that of the first string of text. If more than one string of text is supplied, as shown in Figure 8-26, the texture is scaled as needed to accommodate every string.

Face Sets

Shapes created using VRML's IndexedFaceSet node are among the most complicated to texture map because of the many polygonal faces that such shapes can be made of (see Chapter 5, "VRML Fundamentals"). Because of their complexity, face set shapes are usually texture mapped based on custom TextureTransform node settings rather than the default mapping scheme (see "Transforming Textures" later in this chapter).

The default texture mapping of face set shapes is based on the shape's local coordinate-system bounding box. The VRML browser determines the shape's two largest dimensions, which form the plane onto which the texture is projected. The texture's horizontal axis is mapped to the largest dimension, while the shape's vertical dimension is mapped to its second largest

Figure 8-24   Text textures are scaled both horizontally and vertically as needed in order to fit the dimensions of a text shape. The text string is then "stamped" into the texture.

dimension. If two or three of the shape's bounding-box dimensions are the same (equal), the mapping will take place along the X, Y, or Z dimension of the shape (in that order).

Figure 8-27 illustrates the default mapping of a texture to a box created with the IndexedFaceSet node.

Elevation Grids

Shapes created using VRML's ElevationGrid node are default texture mapped by laying the texture directly on the grid; the texture's left edge is aligned with the left edge of the grid, while its right edge is aligned with the grid's right edge. Similarly, the texture's top edge is aligned with the grid top (the first row of grid coordinates), while its bottom is aligned with the grid bottom (the last row of grid coordinates).

By default, the texture is placed on the grid upside down, as seen in Figure 8-28. To map a grid texture rightside up, you can use any graphics program (such as Adobe PhotoShop) to flip the texture image both horizontally and vertically so that it appears rightside up when mapped. Alternately, you can use the ElevationGrid node's *texCoord* field to specify per-vertex texture coordinates for the shape (see Appendix B, "VRML Resources," to learn more about the structure of the ElevationGrid node).

Extrusions

Shapes created using VRML's Extrusion node are default texture mapped based on the cross section and spine of the shape; the texture is wrapped once around the horizontal dimension of the cross section and appears once on the shape's spine. In both cases the texture is stretched or squeezed as

Figure 8-25   The larger a string of text is, the more a texture will be scaled.

Figure 8-26 If more than one string of text is created for a text shape, as shown here, the texture will be scaled accordingly in order to cover every character in each string.

needed to accommodate the dimensions of the extruded shape, as seen in Figure 8-29.

The texture's left edge is aligned with the cross section's first coordinate, while its right edge is aligned with the last coordinate of the cross section. Similarly, the texture's bottom edge is aligned with first spine coordinate of the extruded shape's first cross section, while its top edge is aligned with the last spine coordinate of shape's last cross section. If the extruded shape has either an end cap or beginning cap, the texture is stretched along the cap's

Figure 8-27 A box created with IndexedFaceSet, with all sides equal in size. By default, the texture map is projected onto the front face of the box (top left) and appears in reverse on the back face (top right). The edges of the texture map are smeared along the box side faces during the projection (bottom).

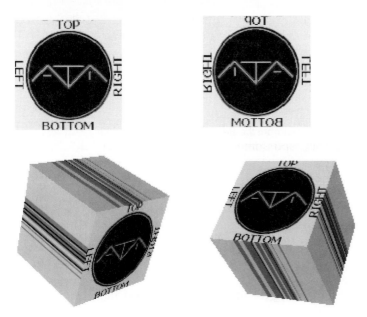

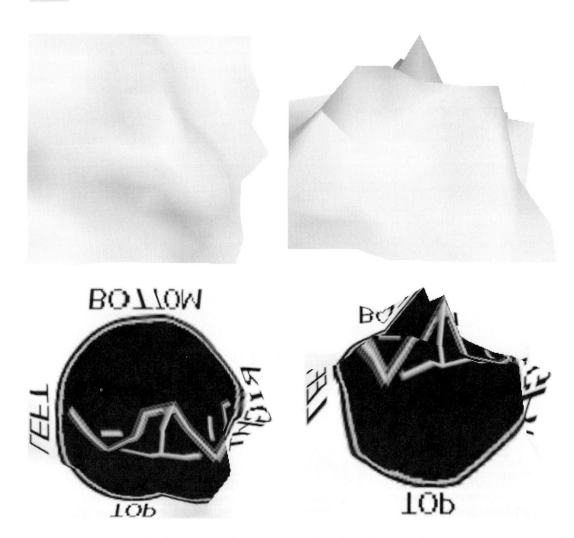

Figure 8-28   A simple elevation grid shape seen from the side and above before texturing (top) and after texturing (bottom). By default, textures are mapped upside down onto elevation grids.

largest dimension (X or Y). The texture's horizontal axis is aligned with the X axis of the cap cross section, while its vertical axis is aligned with the Z axis of the cap's cross section (see Figure 8-29).

Image Textures

VRML's ImageTexture node is used to create texture maps from image files, such as JPEG, PNG, and GIF images:

Figure 8-29 Although similar in appearance to a primitive cylinder shape, texturing reveals that this extrusion's top cap (the lower left image) faces in the opposite direction to the top cap of primitive cylinder shapes. The bottom cap (lower right) has the same orientation, however.

Point and Line Set Shapes

Textures cannot be applied to shapes created with either the PointSet or IndexedLineSet nodes because these shapes don't actually have a structure around which an image can be wrapped. The PointSet node is used to create shapes out of points, which have no height or width. Similarly, the IndexedLineSet node is used to create shapes out of lines, which are not thick enough to wrap a texture around. Because they aren't capable of being texture mapped, the PointSet or Indexed LineSet nodes ignore textures altogether.

```
ImageTexture {
  exposedField MFString url      []
  field        SFBool   repeatS TRUE
  field        SFBool   repeatT TRUE
}
```

Image files are supplied to the ImageTexture node through the exposed *url* field, which can be set directly or through an event (see Chapter 5, "VRML Fundamentals," for details on exposedField and events). As the *url* field name implies, the image files you specify are in the form of a Uniform Resource Locator (URL), which may be either absolute or relative. Following is an example of a cone shape texture-mapped using a JPEG image located relative to the VRML file in which this node is found:

```
Shape {
  appearance Appearance {
    material Material { }
    texture ImageTexture {
      url "redbricks.jpg"
    }
  }
  geometry Cone { }
}
```

The ImageTexture node's *repeatS* and *repeatT* fields accept a single TRUE/FALSE Boolean value that indicates whether or not the texture should be repeated in the given direction when mapped to a shape. As you'll learn in detail in the "Transforming Textures" section later in this chapter, textures are defined in a two-dimensional coordinate system that consists of an S and T axis. A texture's S axis runs along the bottom edge of the image, while T is a vertical axis that runs along the left edge.

Thus, the *repeatS* and *repeatT* fields determine how a texture is applied to a shape in the S and T directions, respectively. By default, both the *repeatS* and *repeatT* fields are TRUE, meaning that textures are repeated in both the S and T directions when applied to the surface of a shape. A FALSE value, on the other hand, will prevent a texture from being repeated in the given direction (the texture coordinate is *clamped* for that direction).

In order to fully understand the *repeatS* and *repeatT* fields and their relation to the S and T coordinate system that textures reside in, we need a more detailed discussion of texture coordinates. Because such a discussion is lengthy, and also much more fruitful when covered in parallel with the Appearance node's *textureTransform* field (for which VRML offers a corresponding TextureTransform node), the "Transforming Textures" section found later in this chapter covers texture coordinates and transforms at the same time.

Absolute and Relative URLs

The ImageTexture node's *url* field might remind you of the HTML <IMG> tag, which can also accept absolute or relative URLs that specify the location of an image. In both cases, absolute URLs are fully qualified addresses, meaning they begin with a protocol scheme identifier (such as "http://" or "file://"), followed by the location of the image. The following, for example, is an absolute URL used to identify an image stored on the Web3D Consortium's host computer (web3d.org):

```
http://www.web3d.org/images/logo.jpg
```

Relative URLs, on the other hand, are partial addresses (such as images/logo.jpg, or perhaps simply logo.jpg) that are used to specify objects that are located *relative* to the document in which they appear. A VRML file located at the root level of the Web3D Consortium's host computer, for example, would itself have the absolute URL address of http://www.web3d.org. Inside this VRML file the following relative URL might appear:

```
images/logo.jpg
```

Because the VRML browser knows the location of the file in which this relative URL appears, it can find the file pointed to by this partial address. The absolute URL of the VRML file (http://www.web3d.org/) is concatenated with the relative URL (images/logo.jpg) to form a fully qualified absolute URL: (http://www.web3d.org/images/logo.jpg) The browser can then use this address to fetch the image (see "Resolving URLs").

Similar to the HTML <IMG> tag, images are supplied to the ImageTexture node *url* field in the form of a URL string enclosed in double quotes, as the following code snippet illustrates:

```
texture ImageTexture {
  url "logo.jpg"
}
```

In this example, a relative URL is used, meaning that the JPEG file named "logo.jpg" is expected to be located relative to the VRML file in which this ImageTexture node is found. In this particular case, the relative URL doesn't specify a directory in which the object is located, and so the browser will assume that "logo.jpg" is located inside the same directory that the VRML file itself resides in. You can, of course, use relative URLs to

---

Resolving URLs

Browsers must *resolve* URLs in order to fetch, or retrieve, the objects they point to (such as images). To resolve a URL, the browser first breaks the URL string into its most significant pieces (protocol scheme, host, path, and object name). Using this information, it can then retrieve the exact object pointed to by the URL, which, in the case of network-resident files, involves interaction with a Web server. File-based URLs, however, are fetched from the local system and so don't require interaction with a Web server (absolute file-based URLs begin with the *file:* protocol scheme, while relative URLs are considered file-based when they point to a local file instead of one residing on the network).

The portion of a browser that resolves URLs is known as the *resolver.* Many VRML browsers rely on the resolver of the Web browser in which they operate to resolve URLs that appear in VRML files. Because their URL resolver requirements is the same as that for Web browsers, VRML browser vendors typically hook into the Web browser's resolver to do the work for them rather than reinvent the wheel.

specify images that reside in directories other than the one in which the VRML file is located, as the following code sample illustrates. In this case, the JPEG file resides inside an "images" folder that is relative to the VRML file in which this code appears:

```
texture ImageTexture {
  url "images/logo.jpg"
}
```

Absolute URLs, on the other hand, are fully qualified and so take the guessing game out of where the file is expected to be located. The first example below creates an image texture using an absolute URL that points to a JPEG image residing on the Web, while the second example uses a locally resident GIF image specified by an absolute file URL:

```
texture ImageTexture {
  url "http://www.web3d.org/images/logo.jpg"
}
```

```
texture ImageTexture {
  url "file:///C:/images/logo.gif"
}
```

Multiple URLs

Although the HTML <IMG> tag and VRML's ImageTexture node are very similar in terms of URL usage, there is one major difference: VRML supports multiple URLs, while HTML does not. You're free, of course, to supply a single URL string to the ImageTexture node's *url* field, as I've done

---

Note: Absolute and Relative URLs

For more information about absolute and relative URLs, refer to the following Internet Engineering Task Force (IETF) Request For Comment (RFC) documents:

```
(RFC 1738; Uniform Resource Locator)
   http://www.ietf.org/rfc/rfc1738.txt
(RFC 1808; Relative Uniform Resource Locator)
   http://www.ietf.org/rfc/rfc1808.txt
```

in the previous examples, but you can also supply up to 10 URL strings at once, because this field is defined as a MFString datatype. As you may recall from Chapter 5, "VRML Fundamentals," "MF" datatypes are multiple-value, meaning they can accept an array of values (as opposed to "SF" datatypes, which are single-value).

Actually, *every* VRML node field that accepts URL values is defined as a MFString datatype, not just the ImageTexture node's *url* field. Because MF-String is a multiple-value datatype, you can supply more than one string to such fields. Simply ensure that each string falls between the opening and closing array brackets [ ] required by multiple-value datatypes, and separate each with a comma as I've done here with the ImageTexture node *url* field:

```
texture ImageTexture {
  url [
      "logo1.jpg",
      "logo2.jpg",
      "logo3.jpg",
      "logo4.jpg",
      "logo5.jpg"
  ]
}
```

Multiple URLs are prioritized from high to low in the order listed. In this example, "logo1.jpg" is the highest-priority URL and "logo5.jpg" is the lowest, while the URLs falling between these two are prioritized accordingly ("logo2.jpg" has a higher priority than "logo3.jpg," for example, but is lower in priority than "logo1.jpg"). VRML browsers attempt to resolve URLs in order of precedence, from high to low, and will use the first resolvable one for texture mapping.

If, for instance, the browser can successfully resolve the "logo1.jpg" URL string supplied first in this example, that image will be used to create the texture map, and the others will be ignored. If "logo1.jpg" cannot be resolved, however, the browser will then attempt to resolve "logo2.jpg" and use that image if available. If not, the browser will continue down the list in order of priority until an image can be found or there are no more URLs to resolve (in which case the shape is rendered without texture mapping).

Because VRML browsers resolve multiple URLs in the order you supply them, you can create very robust worlds by mirroring textures across a number of different Web servers. If the browser can't load a texture stored on one server, it will try the others in the order you specify. The following ImageTexture node, for example, specifies that the browser should first try to

Tip: Coding Multiple URLs

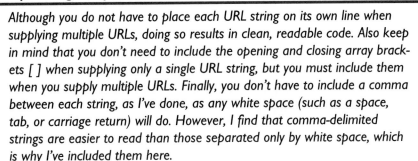

Although you do not have to place each URL string on its own line when supplying multiple URLs, doing so results in clean, readable code. Also keep in mind that you don't need to include the opening and closing array brackets [ ] when supplying only a single URL string, but you must include them when you supply multiple URLs. Finally, you don't have to include a comma between each string, as I've done, as any white space (such as a space, tab, or carriage return) will do. However, I find that comma-delimited strings are easier to read than those separated only by white space, which is why I've included them here.

use the image located in the same directory as the world file itself. Should this fail, for any reason, the browser then attempts to load the image from alternate servers in the order that I've supplied them in the *url* field:

```
texture ImageTexture {
   url [
       "redbricks.jpg",
       "http://www.web3d.org/images/redbricks.jpg",
       "http://www.web3d.net/images/redbricks.jpg",
       "http://www.vrml.org/images/redbricks.jpg"
   ]
}
```

A similar technique can be used to supply texture images in a variety of formats, ensuring that every VRML browser has an opportunity to load the highest-quality image it can handle. Imagine, for example, that you want to create a texture map using an image of your company's color text logo, for which the sharpness of each letter is more important than a full range of colors. In this imaginary example, assume that PNG is the most appropriate format because it supports up to 48 bits of color and uses a lossless compression scheme that won't degrade the sharp edges of text. GIF, then, might be the next best format (even through it supports only 8 bits of color) because it, too, uses a lossless compression scheme that preserves the edges of the text. JPEG, however, might be your least preferred format because it employs a lossy compression scheme that tends to do a poor job with text (see "Image Formats" below for more details on these formats).

Although you might be tempted to simply use the PNG format and be done with it, suppose that this particular VRML world is destined to appear on your company's home page and so must be viewable by as many visitors as possible. Because some older VRML browsers don't support the PNG format, the PNG-only approach might alienate a portion of your potential audience (see "Image Formats" below for more details). However, thanks to VRML's support for multiple URLs, you can accommodate browsers of all levels, as the following snippet of code illustrates:

```
texture ImageTexture {
  url [
       "logo.png",   # first try the high-quality PNG
       "logo.gif",   # if PNG fails, try the GIF image
       "logo.jpg"    # use JPEG if both PNG and GIF fail
  ]
}
```

Image Formats

The VRML97 specification requires browsers to support both the JPEG and PNG image formats for use with the ImageTexture node. As a result, VRML browsers that do not allow texture maps to be created from these image formats are considered to be "out of compliance" with the VRML97 specification. VRML browsers are not required, however, to support the GIF format in order to be compliant with the VRML97 specification. The specification *recommends* that browser's support GIF images but doesn't mandate support for this format, giving browser vendors latitude when it comes to accommodating GIF images.

Warning: URL Overload

Although the VRML97 Specification requires that browsers need support only up to 10 strings for MFString fields, some browsers support many more. Because VRML URL fields are all defined as MFString datatypes, you may be tempted to store as many URL strings in these fields as your browser can handle. However, to ensure that your VRML files are in full compliance with the VRML97 Specification, and therefore run across the full spectrum of VRML browsers, don't supply more than 10 strings to a single MFString field (including URL fields).

Although not required, most VRML browsers do in fact support the GIF format, because it is arguably the most popular image format used on the Web today. In fact, every major VRML browser shipping today supports JPEG, PNG, and GIF images, and many support additional nonrequired formats such as BMP, RAS, and TAG. You should not, however, use image formats other then JPEG, PNG, and GIF if you expect to create VRML content that is accessible across a wide spectrum of browsers. These three formats are supported by the majority of today's browsers, and they are all you'll need when it comes to creating custom textures for your worlds.

Both PNG and GIF support pixel transparency, although JPEG does not. The transparent pixels of an image override the Material node's *transparency* field, allowing you to create texture-mapped shapes that are see-through in areas (see Figure 8-30). Objects such as plants and trees are often mapped with photorealistic images that contain transparent pixels in strategic areas to allow the viewer to see through spaces between branches and leaves, for example (Figure 8-31).

Following is a general overview of the JPEG, PNG, and GIF image formats, along with a discussion of the transparency capabilities that each supports:

- JPEG, short for Joint Photographer's Experts Group, was developed by an international committee of imaging experts (like VRML, JPEG

Tip: Accommodating Older Browsers

Although most of today's modern VRML browsers support JPEG, PNG, and GIF images, many older browsers don't. Some older browsers support only JPEG and GIF images, for example, as PNG was a relatively new image format when the second major version of VRML was released (as a result, many of the first "VRML 2.0" browsers to hit the Web didn't support PNG). To accommodate those with older browsers, you can use multiple URLs to supply the ImageTexture node with images in each of these three formats, as described in the previous section. Alternately, you can use "sniffer" scripts as described in Chapter 6, "Weaving VRML into Web Pages," to alert users with older browsers that they may not be able to enjoy the full experience of your texture-mapped worlds.

Figure 8-30   The top sphere is texture mapped with an image that contains no transparency, while the bottom sphere is mapped with the same basic image in which all of the black pixels have been specified as transparent.

Figure 8-31   Tree objects are often mapped with photorealistic images containing areas of transparency that allow the viewer to "see through" spaces between branches and leaves (http://www.planet9.com).

is an ISO/IEC international standard; ISO/IEC 10918–1:1994, http://www.jpeg.org). Interestingly, JPEG isn't actually an image format at all. Instead, it is a suite of compression techniques that are especially good at reducing the size of full-color images such as digitized photographs, highly detailed electronic artwork, and paintings, and other images that have a large number of colors and subtle color gradations. Because JPEG can efficiently compress images that contain up to 24 bits of data per pixel (a bit depth that allows for up to 16.7 million colors), it has become the de facto standard for compressing photorealistic images used in Web pages. However, although JPEG is an excellent choice for rich color images that contain smooth gradations and color blends, it is particularly poor at compressing type (text) and line art, while both PNG and GIF excel at these forms of compression.

Files compressed with JPEG are typically stored in a format known as the JPEG File Interchange Format (JFIF), although JPEG-compressed image data can also be stored in other formats (Apple QuickTime, for example, uses JPEG compression). Normally, however, JPEG compressed data is stored in JFIF files that have either the .jpg or .jpeg extension (the .jfif extension is also common on UNIX systems, while Macintosh systems use the "JPEG" file type to identify JPEG images regardless of file extension). As a result of their close association, just about everyone considers the JFIF file format and JPEG compression to be one and the same even though they are not. For the purposes of this discussion and throughout this entire book, rather than confuse the issue by becoming mired in the distinction between JPEG compression and the associated JFIF file type, we will simply use the term JPEG to describe both the compression scheme and file format.

Unlike PNG or GIF, JPEG employs a *lossy* compression scheme that actually results in pixel data being lost in the process (hence the term *lossy*). The more an image is compressed with JPEG, the more pixel data will be lost, which can result in visual artifacts such as blurring or pixelization in certain parts of the image. In exchange for lost pixel data, however, JPEG gives us excellent image compression that can dramatically reduce image file sizes. And, in many cases, it's difficult (if not entirely impossible) to see that image data has in fact been lost during the compression process.

Unfortunately, JPEG does not support transparency at all, meaning you'll have to rely on either PNG or GIF images if you need to create transparent pixels in your texture maps.

- PNG, which stands for Portable Network Graphics, was developed by a consortium of graphics developers largely in response to the high demand for an image file format designed specifically for the Web. The PNG specification (http://www.w3.org/TR/REC-png-multi.html) describes the innards of this very powerful and flexible file format, which many believe will eventually obsolete both JPEG and GIF images. As a modern "network" graphic format, PNG was designed to speed image data across the wire without sacrificing image quality. Like GIF, PNG is a lossless compression format that perfectly preserves pixel data and image quality (it does not create the visual artifacts that highly compressed JPEG images often exhibit).

PNG is excellent when it comes to compressing type and line art, an area where JPEG falls flat. Because PNG supports a variety of color models, it is adept at compressing a variety of image forms; PNG can deftly handle full-color photographs, continuous-tone images and those with subtle color gradations, text, and line art. PNG supports full-color mode (both 24 and 48 bits per pixel), grayscale mode (1, 2, 4, 8, and 16 bits per pixel), and indexed color modes (1, 2, 4, and 8 bits per pixel), meaning that it can use different color models to accommodate a wide variety of image types.

PNG is very efficient and typically compresses images better than GIF (if you save the same image in both PNG and GIF formats, the PNG image will likely take up less disk space). PNG is not, however, quite as efficient as JPEG, because it is based on lossless compression that does not discard pixel data. As a result, an image is usually somewhat larger when compressed with PNG than when compressed with JPEG.

Unlike JPEG and GIF, however, PNG has a wonderful transparency system. The PNG format uses *alpha channels*, which allow for various levels of pixel transparency. Whereas GIF supports a simple form of transparency that allows you to specify transparent pixels, which often produces jagged edges around transparency areas, PNG alpha channels give you the equivalent of selection or layer masks (such as those found in Adobe Photoshop) to produce transparency gradations. As a result, PNG transparency areas can be much smoother than those created with GIF transparency. (Unfortunately, not all VRML browsers are adept at handling PNG transparency gradations, so you should take care to test such images using a variety of browsers before deploying your PNG-enhanced worlds.)

PNG images are typically stored in files having the .png file extension. Macintosh systems, however, identify PNG images using the "PNGf" file type.

- GIF, short for Graphics Interchange Format, was invented in the mid 1980s by CompuServe Information Service, a popular bulletin board system (BBS) that predated the Web. CompuServe developed the GIF file format to allow its users to efficiently exchange images over slow dial-up modems of the time. Due to its affinity for networks, GIF was a natural fit for the Web that was born years later.

Because the GIF image format was developed by a company, however, rather than in the open environment in which both JPEG and PNG were developed, product vendors that support GIF images are subject to licensing fees. Shortly after GIF images became commonplace on the Web, Unisys began to enforce the intellectual property rights that it had as owner of the Compuserve GIF patent, an act that hastened the development of the more sophisticated PNG format. For this reason, the VRML97 specification only *recommends* that browser vendors support the GIF format; it isn't a requirement for compliance in the way that JPEG and PNG formats are.

Many VRML browsers support GIF, however, as it remains a wildly popular format for the Web despite the license fees that Unisys can impose. GIF files are stored in an indexed color mode that is limited to 8 bits of data per pixel (256 colors), which places an upper limit on file sizes from the onset. Because of GIF's limited color support and the manner in which it compresses image data, this format is best suited for text, line art, and images created with a relatively small palate of colors (PNG and JPEG are better equipped to handle full-color images).

Like PNG, the GIF format uses a lossless compression scheme that preserves pixel data and image quality, although PNG is somewhat more efficient than GIF (which should come as no surprise when you consider that PNG was created as a more capable alternative to GIF).

And, also like PNG, GIF supports transparency, although only in the "GIF89a" version. GIF89a offers a particularly simple form of transparency when compared to that of PNG, as it allows you to specify one or more colors that will be treated as transparent when the image is rendered. Unlike PNG, GIF89a doesn't support alpha channels and so tends to create transparent areas that are jagged around the edges (as opposed to the smooth gradient edges possible with PNG transparency).

In addition to its support for transparency, GIF89a also supports simple animation, a feature that neither JPEG nor PNG offer. Although some VRML browsers can properly render animated GIF89a images, most can't, and so in cases where you require moving textures you should instead use the MovieTexture node (alternately you use the TextureTransform node to

Texture Types, Color Components, and Transparency Values

JPEG, PNG, and GIF images are composed of numeric values that define the color of each pixel in the image. Every pixel in a full-color JPEG image, for example, is typically represented using three 8-bit integer values, one each for the red, green, and blue components that are mixed together to produce color. Full-color JPEG images are considered *three-component* images because each pixel is represented by three different 8-bit integers. By comparison, grayscale images (intensity maps) are one-component images because each pixel is represented using a single 8-bit integer.

VRML supports texture maps created from one to four component images, where the number of components describes the type of map produced:

    one-component = grayscale intensity maps
    two-component = grayscale intensity maps + alpha value
    three-component = full-color RGB texture maps
    four-component = full-color RGB texture maps + alpha value

Because images typically store pixel components as 8-bit integers, each component of a pixel can be represented using whole numbers in the range 0 to 255. VRML browsers, however, work with colors represented as floating-point values in the range 0.0 to 1.0, and so must convert these whole numbers into their corresponding floating-point values. To do this, VRML browsers typically divide each pixel component value by 255.0 (bitwise division is also used).

The same is true for images that use alpha values to specify the transparency level of a pixel. Similar to color components, transparency alpha values are usually stored as 8-bit values, giving them a whole number range of 0 to 255 (where 0 represents complete transparency for the given pixel and 255 represents complete opacity, while numbers in between represent various transparency levels). VRML browsers must convert alpha values into floating-point numbers in the range 1.0 to 0.0 (the reverse range of color components), and do so by dividing the whole-number alpha value by 255.0, the result of which is subtracted from 1 ($1.0 - alpha/255.0$).

animate textures created with the ImageTexture node, as explained later in this chapter).

GIF images are typically stored in files having the .gif file extension. Macintosh systems, however, identify GIF images using the "GIFf" file type.

Size Considerations

Image size is one of the most important factors to take into consideration when customizing your worlds with textures. The larger a texture is, in terms of both bit depth and physical dimensions, the longer it will take to download over the Internet, and the harder the end-user computer systems will have to work to apply it to the surface of a shape. Like Web pages, VRML worlds can quite easily become bogged down with too many images.

In general, you should reduce the bit depth of VRML textures as much as possible, just as with images that are used in standard Web pages. Texture size, however, is a somewhat more complicated issue that is directly related to the rendering engine of VRML browsers. Naturally, smaller textures are easier to render, although the horizontal and vertical dimensions of a texture can impact system performance more than you might realize.

Rendering engines used by VRML browsers typically work most efficiently with textures that are smaller than 256 pixels in both dimensions, so, whenever possible, you should limit your textures to a maximum size of 256 pixels in the horizontal and vertical directions (height and width, represented as "256x256"). In many cases, however, 128x128 is the actual upper limit for texture sizes. As a result, textures larger than 128x128 are often resized to 128x128 when rendered by some systems, even though others can render larger textures as-is. To ensure that the majority of VRML browsers can render your textures directly and without scaling, strive for dimensions of 128x128 or smaller.

You should be careful, however, not to create textures that are too small. Although unnecessarily large textures put undue strain on both the rendering engine and network connections, textures that are too small can also cause problems: The visual impact of your world can suffer terribly. A texture too small to cover the surface of an object may be stretched in both the horizontal and vertical dimensions to the point where the image takes on a distorted or grainy appearance, a condition known as *pixelization*.

Worlds that suffer from texture pixelization are often more unpleasant to view than those having no textures at all. You'd do well, then, to craft custom textures at sizes appropriate for the objects to which they'll be applied. An increase in your world's efficiency shouldn't come at the expense of its overall appearance. If, for example, an object in your world truly looks best when wrapped in a 128x128 texture, you shouldn't bother trying to reduce the texture size dramatically (say, to 32x32) to improve download time or rendering efficiency.

Instead, you should methodically reduce texture sizes one step at a time based on *power-of-two* dimensions (256, 128, 64, 32, 16, 8, 4, and 2). The first step down from 128x128, for example, would be 64x64. If your object still looks good at this size, try stepping down another level (to 32x32, in this case). Continue, one step at a time, until you reach a size that no longer looks acceptable; then return to the previous size. In general you'll find that textures will continue to look good when reduced one or two steps down from their ideal dimensions, although three or four steps usually causes too much pixelization (unless the texture is tiled across the shape's surface, in which case it won't be stretched).

You'll notice that I've only recommended square dimensions for your textures, which is not a mistake. Although rendering engines will accept images of rectangular sizes, such as 256x128, they're more efficient when dealing with square images. Furthermore, renderers are usually most efficient when handed textures with square dimensions that are a power of two, such as 4x4, 8x8, 16x16, 32x32, 64x64, 128x128, and 256x256. Some rendering engines actually require that textures be square, power-of-two dimensions, and they will scale what you give them in either direction as needed in order to satisfy these requirements.

In order to create the most efficient texture maps, use square images in power-of-two sizes measuring 128x128 or less (always avoid odd sizes such as 121x123, which place undue strain on the rendering engine when scaled). To ensure the best possible compression rate while preserving image quality,

Tip: Texture Tiling

VRML texture maps can be tiled (repeated end-to-end) when applied to shapes in much the same way that standard background images are repeated over and over in order to cover the entire area of a Web page. By tiling a texture during the mapping process, you can cover the surface of a shape that would otherwise be too large for the texture alone, thereby avoiding the need for scaling that leads to unsightly pixelization. For details, see "Transforming Textures," later in this chapter.

take the time to reduce bit depth using a graphics program (such as Adobe Photoshop) as much as you can before saving your image in a compressed format. Also, be certain to store your textures in the file format that is most appropriate for the type of image content they contain, as described in the preceding "Image Formats" section. Finally, limit the total number of textures that you use in a world, as too many can bring slow and modest computers to a crawl, even though they run smooth as silk on fast or accelerated systems.

Movie Textures

Whereas the ImageTexture node allows you to texture map shapes using image files, VRML's MovieTexture node is used to play movies on the surface of a shape. Movie textures are essentially the same as those created with images. RGB colors in a movie texture override the Material node's *diffuseColor* field; grayscale values in a movie texture are treated as intensity maps; and movie textures can contain transparent pixels, in which case the Material node's *transparency* field is ignored (see "Image Textures" for details).

Tip: Magic Numbers

The total number of textures that a world can contain and still be accessible to a wide audience via the Web depends on many factors. The size and bit depth of each image play an important role, but these are by no means the only factors to consider. Quality of image compression, the number and complexity of objects to which textures are mapped, and even the size of the window in which the scene is viewed all play a part in determining the system requirements of a given world.

The only way to be certain that your textured worlds will be accessible to the masses is to routinely test your work across a wide spectrum of computer systems, VRML browser configurations, and network connections. Even if you don't have access to such resources, you should, at the very least, test your worlds on a low-powered system connected to the Web using a dial-up modem. Personally I've found a stock 160-MHz Pentium laptop equipped with a 56-Kbps modem to be adequate for such purposes; it represents what I consider to be the entry-level system for viewing texture-enhanced worlds.

The VRML97 specification requires VRML browsers to support movie textures supplied in the form of MPEG1-Systems (audio and video) and MPEG1-Video (video only) formats, although many browsers support additional nonrequired movie formats, such as Real Video, QuickTime, and AVI. In order to create movie textures that are supported across a full range of VRML browsers, you should only supply MPEG1-Systems and MPEG1-Video to the MovieTexture node.

Like the ImageTexture node, the MovieTexture node is supplied to the *texture* field of a shape's Appearance node. And, as with the ImageTexture node, you don't have to do much more than set the MovieTexture node's *url*

Warning: Clogged Pipes and Extra Overhead

Motion Picture Experts Groups version 1 (MPEG1) is an international media compression and transmission standard (ISO/IEC 11172–1:1993) designed specifically for media stored on devices such as CD-ROM and hard drives; it was not meant for playing video over the Internet! MPEG1 files are quite large compared to today's streaming media formats, and so they aren't the ideal format for use with Web-based VRML worlds (although MPEG1 is fine for worlds delivered on fixed media such as CD-ROM and DVD). If you absolutely must use movies in your Web-based worlds, be careful to use very short video clips in relatively small dimensions (no larger than 128x128 if possible) to reduce bandwidth requirements. Alternately, you can tailor your content for a specific browser if you wish to use movie formats that are not required by the VRML97 specification (see Chapter 6, "Weaving VRML into Web Pages," to learn how to create sniffer scripts for such purposes).

Also keep in mind that movies take additional processing power, as they must be decoded in order to extract the video frames contained therein. Although it's convenient to think of movies as nothing more than a bunch of individual images bundled together into a single file, the truth is that most movie formats (including MPEG1) actually encode image frames in a much more sophisticated and complex way. MPEG1, for example, uses a differential encoding approach that stores complete images only every few frames, while in-between frames are encoded as the "difference" between complete frames. Because of the reconstruction necessary to create a full suite of frames from the differential data stored between complete frames, MPEG1 movies require a fair amount of processing power to decode for playback.

field to a valid URL string that will resolve to a movie file. URLs are handled by the MovieTexture node in exactly the same way as the ImageTexture node: URLs can be either absolute or relative, and you can supply more than one because this field is defined as a MFString datatype (see "Image Textures" for details). The following snippet of code uses a single relative URL to specify an MPEG movie named "flipper.mpg" for texture mapping:

```
Shape {
  appearance  Appearance {
    material Material { }

    texture  MovieTexture {
      url  "flipper.mpg"
    }
  }
  geometry  Box { }
}
```

By default, each frame of the movie will "play" on the surface of the box, one after another, until the last frame is reached, at which point the movie will stop playing (movies do not automatically repeat, or loop, unless you specify that they do so, using the *loop* field). Each frame of the movie is treated as a unique texture map, while the movie file is treated as a container for multiple images. One after another the images in the movie file are applied to the shape's surface, using the same mapping scheme utilized with texture maps created by the ImageTexture and PixelTexture nodes (see the earlier "Applying Textures to Shapes" discussion for mapping details). In the case of the box, the movie texture appears on each of the six faces, as seen in Figure 8-32.

Although this simple example gets the job done, there's much more to the MovieTexture node than the *url* field:

```
MovieTexture {
    exposedField SFBool    loop              FALSE
    exposedField SFFloat   speed             1.0       # (-∞,∞)
    exposedField SFTime    startTime         0         # (-∞,∞)
    exposedField SFTime    stopTime          0         # (-∞,∞)
    exposedField MFString  url               []
    field        SFBool    repeatS           TRUE
    field        SFBool    repeatT           TRUE
    eventOut     SFTime    duration_changed
    eventOut     SFBool    isActive
}
```

Figure 8-32 Movie textures are mapped to shapes in the same way that image and pixel textures are, although movies can contain multiple textures that are "played" one after another on a shape's surface.

Like the ImageTexture node (and also the PixelTexture node that we'll explore in a moment), the MovieTexture node contains two fields that control the tiling, or repeating, of textures during the mapping process. By default, the *repeatS* and *repeatT* fields are set to the Boolean TRUE value, meaning that movie texture maps repeat in both the horizontal and vertical directions, while a value of FALSE will clamp the texture in the given direction (see "Transforming Textures" for details).

New to the MovieTexture node, however, are fields related to the playback of time-based media. Whereas image and pixel textures are static, movie textures are dynamic. MovieTexture, therefore, has a number of fields that are unique to this node. The exposed *loop* field, for example, is used to control whether or not a movie will repeat itself ("loop") after the last frame is played. By default, movies do not loop; they stop when the last frame of the movie has been reached (when a movie stops playing, the current frame remains texture mapped on the shape). In order to begin playing again from the first frame, you can set the Boolean *loop* field to TRUE:

```
Shape {
  appearance  Appearance {
    material Material { }

    texture  MovieTexture {
      url  "flipper.mpg"
      loop  TRUE
    }
  }
  geometry  Box { }
}
```

The exposed *speed* field controls the rate and direction at which the movie plays. By default, this floating-point field is set to 1, which means the movie plays forward at normal speed. Values between 0 and 1 slow the movie down, while 0 stops a movie from playing altogether, in which case the first frame is used for texture mapping. Speed values greater than 1 increase the rate at which a movie plays, while negative values will actually play a movie backward (in reverse; beware that some browsers don't support movies that play backward, in which case the negative *speed* values are ignored).

A *speed* setting of 2, for instance, plays the movie twice as fast as it normally would, while a setting of 3 will play it three times as fast. Because *speed* accepts floating-point numbers, however, you can also change the playback rate to fractional times. In the following example the *speed* field has been set to 2.5, specifying that the movie should play on the surface of the box shape two and a half times as fast as normal. Because the *loop* field is set, this movie will start playing again from the beginning, once the last frame has been texture mapped to the object:

```
Shape {
   appearance  Appearance {
     material Material { }

     texture   MovieTexture {
        url   "flipper.mpg"
        loop   TRUE
        speed 2.5
     }
   }
   geometry   Box { }
}
```

In this example, the movie will begin playing immediately after it is loaded, and it will loop indefinitely, because both the *startTime* and *stopTime* fields are the same value by default (both are set to 0 by default). The exposed *startTime* field is a measurement of time in seconds and is used to control when the movie starts playing, which, by default, is immediately; the default setting of 0 indicates that no time (0 seconds) should pass before the movie begins to play. The corresponding exposed *stopTime* field, meanwhile, is used to control the time at which a movie will stop playing. By default, both of these fields are set to 0. As a result, movies start playing immediately and stop playing after every frame of the movie has been texture mapped to the shape. In this example, however, the *loop* field has been set to TRUE, forcing the movie to repeat itself.

Although *startTime* and *stopTime* seem relatively straightforward at first blush, these fields are somewhat more complicated than you might imagine. Because they both represent a measurement of absolute time, not relative time, they can be confusing to work with at first. Both *startTime* and *stopTime* are SFTime fields, meaning that they are used to store the amount of time, in seconds, that has elapsed since 12 midnight, Greenwich Mean Time (GMT), January 1, 1970. As a result, you can't, for example, set *startTime* to "5" in hopes of postponing the movie play time by five seconds after your world loads, any more than you can set *stopTime* to "60" and expect the movie to stop playing after a minute has elapsed.

StartTime and *stopTime* are generally used in combination with VRML sensor nodes, such as ProximitySensor, TouchSensor, and TimeSensor, as described in the sidebar "Passing SFTime." Fortunately, *startTime* and *stopTime* can also be set manually without a great degree of effort, because very simple values can also be used to control the behavior of movie playback. If you set *stopTime* to –1, for instance, and leave *startTime* at its default setting of 0, the movie will loop forever, assuming you've also set the MovieTexture node's *loop* field to TRUE. This occurs because the VRML97 specification requires browsers to play movies forever if *startTime* and *stopTime* are equal (the case with both defaults set to 0) or when *stopTime* is less than *startTime* (which is the case when *stopTime* is -1 and *startTime* hasn't been set).

The MovieTexture node's *duration_changed* and *isActive* fields are both outgoing events, as indicated by the eventOut datatype (see Chapter 5, "VRML Fundamentals," for details). Generally you will not deal with either of these fields directly, as the VRML browser is responsible for managing their state. A *duration_changed* event is generated once the browser has loaded a movie and determined its duration (the duration of a movie is measured in seconds based on the number of frames it contains and is entirely independent of the *speed* field). If the browser can't determine the duration of a movie, which can be the case during a long download or if the file is damaged, the *duration_changed* field is set to –1.

Similarly, the browser generates *isActive* events in response to the state of the movie. A movie is considered inactive until its start time has been reached, at which point the movie becomes active and will start playing. While a movie is inactive, its first frame is used as the shape's texture map, unless the *speed* value is negative. A negative *speed* value indicates that the movie should play in reverse (assuming the browser supports such behavior,

Passing SFTime

The SFTime datatype accepts floating-point numbers that represent the number of seconds that have elapsed since January 1, 1970, 00:00:00 GMT (Greenwich Mean Time). Generally you'll never have to calculate such time values yourself, as many of VRML's built-in nodes use SFTime fields to automatically generate timestamp values.

A ProximitySensor node, for example, can be used to trigger the playing of a MovieTexture node by sending it a valid start time in response to users walking within a specified distance of the object for which the movie is a texture. Likewise, a VRML television might be created by texture mapping a movie onto the face of a rectangular shape, for which a "power on" button could be created using a TouchSensor node.

Clicking the "on" button would invoke the TouchSensor, which in turn could be used to route the current time (a valid SFTime value) to the *startTime* field of the television's MovieTexture node. In response, the movie would begin playing and the television would appear to have been turned on. To turn the movie off, a corresponding "power off" button could be created to send the current time to the MovieTexture node's *stopTime* field, which would tell the movie to stop playing at that very moment. For details on events and routing, see Chapter 5, "VRML Fundamentals." To learn more about sensor nodes such as Proximity-Sensor and TouchSensor, see Appendix B, "VRML Resources."

---

although not all do), in which case the last frame of the movie is used for texture mapping during an inactive state. As soon as its start time is reached, the movie becomes active and starts playing. In response, the *isActive* event field is set to TRUE, indicating that the movie is now active. When the movie stops playing (if it reaches the last frame and has not been set to loop, for example), the *isActive* event field is set to FALSE to indicate that it has entered an inactive state.

Pixel Textures

Unlike movie and image textures created using image date stored in an external file, pixel textures are created from data that is actually encoded directly *into* the VRML file itself. Using the PixelTexture node, you can create

Note: Movie Sounds

Although MovieTexture nodes are generally used to enhance the visual appeal of an object through texture mapping, they can also be used to add audio to a scene. MovieTexture nodes that contain movies with sound can act as the source for a Sound node, as described in Chapter 9, "Customizing Light, Background, Fog, and Sound."

texture maps from raw image data supplied directly through the node's *image* field:

```
PixelTexture {
   exposedField SFImage   image     0 0 0
   field        SFBool    repeatS   TRUE
   field        SFBool    repeatT   TRUE
}
```

As an exposed field of the SFImage datatype, *image* can be set by an event (typically a script) or manually. Encoding pixel data by hand is tedious and time consuming, however, so it's unlikely that you'll embrace the Pixel-Texture node when first customizing your worlds, especially when image textures are so much easier to create using a graphics tool such as Adobe Photoshop. As you become more experienced with VRML, you may find that pixel textures are a useful alternative to image and movie textures, because they are very fast and efficient and can be created dynamically to produce what amount to procedural textures.

Generally speaking, pixel textures are quite small (typically 16x16 or less) and often less detailed than their image and movie counterparts, as they are

Note: Procedural Textures

Although VRML doesn't support procedural texture files (files that contain code to create a texture programmatically, as opposed to image data), pixel textures can be created on the fly using scripts. Because a script can generate pixel-texture images programmatically, VRML developers can use the PixelTexture node to create the equivalent of procedural textures.

primarily used to create intensity maps and very simple texture maps. Because they are encoded directly into the body of VRML files, pixel textures load quickly; there is no associated network connection overhead, as there is no external file to load. Instead, VRML browsers can decode pixel-texture data as soon as the world file itself has been loaded.

However, because pixel data is stored as plain ASCII text, compression cannot be applied to the image data (other than GZip compression of the entire VRML file, as described in Chapter 6, "Weaving VRML into Web Pages"). As a result, pixel textures can actually take up more space than the equivalent image stored in a compressed format such as JPEG, PNG, or GIF.

The PixelTexture node's *image* field is used to store the raw pixel data from which a pixel texture is created. It is made up of three values, each set to 0 by default (0 0 0). The first two values of the *image* field specify the height and width of the pixel texture, while the third is used to describe the raw pixel data that will follow this field (the third value specifies the number of color components each pixel contains, after which an array of raw pixel values is supplied). Following is the basic structure of the *image* field (and all other SFImage fields):

```
image <width> <height> <component count> <pixel values>
```

The number of components a pixel texture contains is specified as an 8-bit byte, for which the values in Table 8.1 are valid.

To create an "empty" RGB color pixel map that is 1 pixel high and 2 pixels wide, therefore, you would use the following PixelTexture settings:

```
texture  PixelTexture {
  image  2 1 3
}
```

Table 8.1   Valid Component Values for Pixel Textures

0	Specifies that texturing is disabled
1	Specifies that grayscale-intensity map data will follow
2	Specifies that grayscale-intensity map data with alpha transparency values will follow
3	Specifies that RGB-color texture data will follow
4	Specifies that RGB-color texture data with alpha transparency values will follow

Of course, a texture with no pixel data isn't really a texture at all. In order to complete the PixelTexture node, raw data must follow the third *image*-field value that decribes each of the pixels in the texture. Pixel values can have up to 256 different intensity levels and are typically represented in hexadecimal format in the range 0x00 to 0xFF (the equivalent of 0 to 256 when represented as a decimal value), where 0x00 represents the least value of intensity and 0xFF highest possible value.

In the earlier example, I created an "empty" RGB-color pixel map. I would then be required to supply pixel data for each of the red, green, and blue color components of this 3-component image. Because each color component can be represented with a hexadecimal value in the range 0x00 to 0xFF (no intensity to full intensity), I can create an RGB pixel by supplying hexadecimal intensity values for red, green, and blue components (in that order).

To create a pure red RGB color pixel using hexadecimal representation, fox example, I would specify full intensity for the pixel's red component and no intensity whatsoever for the green and blue components, or 0xFF0000. The first byte of this hexadecimal value sets the intensity for red (0xFF), the second sets the blue intensity (0x00), and the third sets the green intensity (0x00). Because the red color component is set to full intensity (0xFF), and the blue and green color components are set to the least intensity (none, or 0x00), the hexadecimal value 0xFF0000 creates a pure red pixel (see the earlier RGB color discussion to learn more about color components).

Similarly, a pure green 3-component color would be represented in hexadecimal as 0x00FF00, indicating that red and blue are "off" while green is "on" at 100%. The hexadecimal value 0x0000FF, however, represents a pure blue 3-component RGB color, because red and green are set to 0x00, while blue is specified at 0xFF to indicate full intensity.

A 4-component pixel value uses an additional byte to specify the pixel's transparency. The hexadecimal value 0x00FF0080, for example, creates a partially transparent green pixel. The last byte of a pixel containing transparency is known as the alpha opacity byte, where 0x00 specifies a completely transparent pixel (invisible) and 0xFF specifies a pixel that is opaque (not transparent at all). The hexadecimal value 0x00FF00FF, therefore, would result in a solid green pixel, because the alpha opacity value is set to 0xFF, while 0x00FF0000 would result in an invisible green pixel.

The first raw hexadecimal pixel value that you provide to the *image* field defines the pixel in the lower left-hand corner of the texture map, while subsequent values specify pixels from left to right and bottom to top. This means that the bottom row of pixels is specified first, starting from left to right. The next row follows, again from left to right, until the pixel in the map is

Note: Unsigned Numbers

Values used to represent pixels in the PixelTexture node are treated as unsigned numbers.

completely defined (thus, the last pixel value you supply defines the pixel in the upper right-hand corner of the map).

The following snippet of code defines an RGB texture map (3 components) that is two pixels wide and one pixel high. The first value supplied is 0xFF0000, meaning that the pixel in the lower left-hand corner is red. The next pixel is set to green (0x00FF00), and, because it's the last pixel in the map, it's considered to be in the upper right-hand corner of the image, even though the image is only one pixel high:

```
#VRML V2.0 utf8

Shape {
   appearance Appearance {
     material Material { }
     texture PixelTexture {
        image 2 1 3 0xFF0000 0x00FF00
     }
   }
   geometry Cone { }
}
```

Transforming Textures

Although VRML's default mapping of textures to geometric surfaces may suit your needs, at times you'll find that you need more control over the way in which a texture is applied to a shape. Fortunately, VRML gives you two special-purpose nodes for such purposes. The easiest to use is the TextureTransform node, as it lets you transform textures prior to mapping, using fields that are similar in nature to those of the Transform node that you learned about in Chapter 7, "Customizing Location, Size, and Orientation." Following is the VRML97 specification definition of the TextureTransform node:

Warning: PixelTexture Inconsistency

Be certain to exercise extreme caution should you decide to construct texture maps from scratch using the PixelTexture node. This is one node in particular that many VRML browsers seem to have a very difficult time handling consistently, and so your best-laid plans can be blown out of the water if you don't test your code in a variety of browsers. What looks smashing in one browser might appear altogether different in another. For this reason, and because constructing textures from raw pixel data is more than just a bit challenging, you should consider using the ImageTexture node instead.

```
TextureTransform {
    exposedField SFVec2f center        0 0      #  (-∞,∞)
    exposedField SFFloat rotation      0        #  (-∞,∞)
    exposedField SFVec2f scale         1 1      #  (-∞,∞)
    exposedField SFVec2f translation 0 0        #  (-∞,∞)
}
```

Like the Transform node, the TextureTransform node is all about transformations; using TextureTransform you can rotate, scale, and position textures to alter how they are mapped to a shape. Unlike the Transform node, which operates on 3D coordinates, however, the transformations that you specify through a TextureTransform operate on 2D coordinates of a texture. As you may recall from the previous sections, textures are measured in terms of S and T coordinates expressed as (S,T). The S coordinate describes a texture's horizontal direction, while the T coordinate describes its vertical direction, as seen in Figure 8-33.

In Figure 8-33 you can see that the origin of the texture coordinate system is located at the lower left-hand corner of the texture. The S coordinate ranges from 0.0 at the origin and extends to 1.0 at the far right edge of the texture image. Similarly, the T coordinate ranges from 0.0 at the origin and extends up to the top of the texture image at 1.0. Interestingly, the S and T coordinates are in no way related to the size of the texture image itself; they always range from 0.0 to 1.0 no matter how large or small the texture is, allowing you to specify a location on a texture irrespective of the texture's actual size. A texture coordinate of (.5, .5), for instance, will always fall at the exact center of the texture regardless of the texture image's size, while a

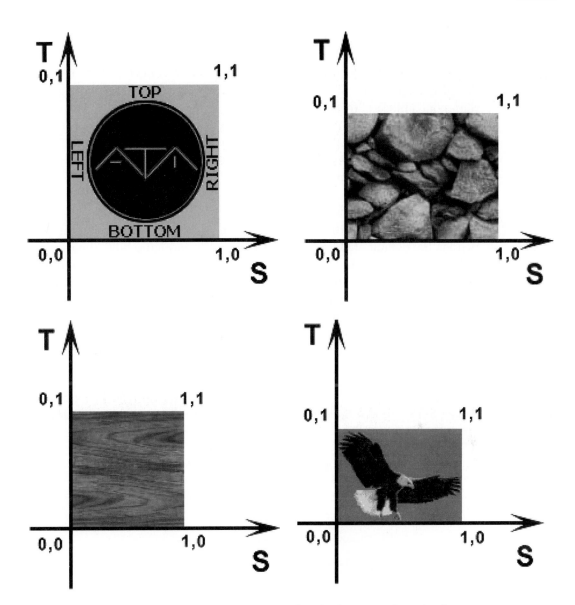

Figure 8-33   VRML's texture coordinate system is described in terms of S and T directions, where S corresponds to the horizontal direction and T to the vertical direction. Each coordinate ranges from 0.0 to 1.0, regardless of the actual size of the texture image.

texture coordinate of (1, 1) always specifies the upper right-hand corner of the texture, as illustrated in Figure 8-34.

When using the TextureTransform node, it's often convenient to think of the process in terms of describing a texture "cutter" that will be used to stamp out a piece of texture "fabric" that will then be mapped to a shape. To continue the analogy, think of the texture as a bolt of fabric that repeats end to end (like the pattern on a sheet, or wallpaper). The TextureTransform node fields, in turn, allow you to specify the size and shape of a cutter that will be stamped into the bolt of repeating fabric, as illustrated in Figure 8-35.

If you set the *scale* field to (2 2) for example, the texture-cutter shape is twice as large as normal in both directions, meaning that it can stamp out more fabric than the default of (1 1) allows. As you can see in Figure 8-36, the result is that the texture used in the mapping process is a smaller, tiled version of the original. To actually use the TextureTransform node, you need only set it in the corresponding *textureTransform* field of the Appearance node, as seen in Listing 8.4, which provides the code used to produce this image.

Figure 8-34   Because S,T texture coordinates range from 0.0 to 1.0 irrespective of texture image size, you're able to specify a point on the texture without regard for its true horizontal and vertical dimensions.

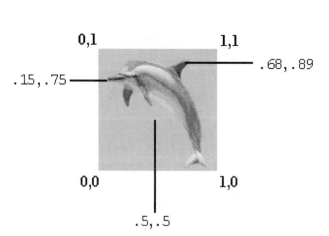

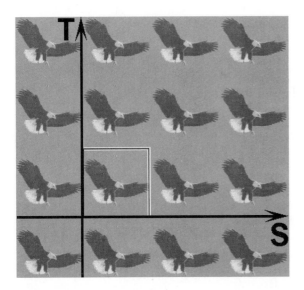

Figure 8-35   When using the TextureTransform node, you actually define the size and shape of a "cutter" used to stamp out a piece of texture from a repeating bolt of "fabric."

Listing 8.4   TextureTransform.wrl

```
#VRML V2.0 utf8

Shape {
  appearance Appearance {
  material Material {   }
    texture ImageTexture {
      url "testPattern.gif"
    }

  textureTransform TextureTransform {
    scale 2 2
  }
  }
  geometry Sphere { }
}
```

Because you can alter the size, shape, and orientation of the texture cutter, it's possible to include multiple texture maps on a single image, as illustrated by Figure 8-37. Here you see two images, one each for Oscar and Joe

scale 1 1   scale 2 2   scale 4 4

Figure 8-36   Scaling the cutter up in size means that it can stamp out more fabric, resulting in a smaller, tiled texture map.

(the two VRML dancers shown earlier in this chapter). Each image contains a number of texture maps used to alter the surface of these characters, from their hair and face right on down to their shoes. Thanks to elaborate use of rotation and translation texture transformations, a single image is used to "stamp out" the many different texture maps needed (see Figures 8-38 and 8-39). Because only one image is used for each character, the result is an

Learning More about TextureTransform

To learn more about the TextureTransform node, see Appendix B, "VRML Resources." In addition, you can turn to the Web3DGallery when you're ready to dig into the guts of the TextureTransform and TextureCoordinate nodes:

http://www.web3dgallery.com/vrml/textures/

Figure 8-37   Multiple texture maps can be stamped out of a single image, a technique that some VRML authors use to reduce download times.

rotation 1.57   rotation -1.57   rotation 3.14

Figure 8-38   The TextureTransform node's rotation field can be used to reorient the texture cutter about the default S, T origin (0,0), while the center field can be used to specify an alternate rotation center.

overall decrease in download time—the VRML browser has to download only one image for each character, which is more efficient than downloading multiple images (see "Learning More about TextureTransform" to find out exactly how this is accomplished).

Note: The TextureCoordinate Node

Both the IndexedFaceSet node and ElevationGrid node have a field called texCoord, *for which you can supply a TextureCoordinate node that contains a list of* s,t *coordinate values. The TextureCoordinate's point field can contain an infinite number of 2D texture coordinates used to control the mapping of textures to vertices of IndexedFaceSet node and ElevationGrid node:*

```
TextureCoordinate {
  exposedField MFVec2f point   []      # (-∞,∞)
}
```

The TextureCoordinate node gives you very fine control over how a texture is applied to IndexedFaceSet and ElevationGrid surfaces, and so it requires a detailed understanding of these geometric nodes. Because such a discussion is beyond the scope of this book, you can turn to the Web3D Gallery to learn more about texture transforms and coordinates.

http://www.web3dgallery.com/vrml/textures/

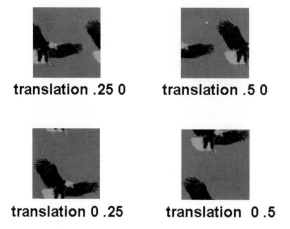

translation .25 0   translation .5 0

translation 0 .25   translation 0 .5

Figure 8-39   The TextureTransform node's translation field can be used to move the texture cutter about the S and T axes, allowing you to stamp out different parts of the rolled-out texture for use as a texture map.

Summary

VRML's Shape node separates appearance and geometry, allowing the color and texture of a shape to be defined independent of its form. By setting the *appearance* field of the Shape node to a corresponding Appearance node, you can specify surface colors and properties (such as texture, reflectivity, and transparency) for a shape. Such appearances can be reused through VRML's DEF/USE construct, meaning you can save yourself the hassle of copying and pasting code while also increasing the overall readability and efficiency of a scene.

The Appearance node contains a *material* field, which in turn is set to a Material node. The Material node is full of fields related to color and surface properties, with which you can create dull, shiny, glowing, and even transparent shapes of any color. By mixing various levels of red, green, and blue (RGB) light, you can create any color that your computer monitor is capable of displaying.

The Appearance node also contains two fields related to texture mapping, *texture* and *textureTransform,* which are used to wrap images around shapes for further visual appeal. These images can either replace color settings or augment them. The *texture* field can be set to one of three nodes: ImageTexture, MovieTexture, and PixelTexture. The ImageTexture node is used to create a texture map from an image stored in JPEG, PNG, or GIF format, while the MovieTexture node is used to play MPEG1 movies on the surface of the shape. Both ImageTexture and MovieTexture are used to create texture maps from files that reside outside the VRML file, whereas the Pixel-Texture is used to create an image map using raw pixel data that is encoded directly into the VRML file itself.

VRML uses a default mapping scheme to apply textures to geometric nodes, which varies from node to node (the Box node default is different from the Cone default, for example). Using the TextureTransform and TextureCoordinate nodes, you can customize the way in which textures are applied to VRML shapes. Because detailed coverage of these nodes is beyond the scope of this book, supplementary Core Web3D material dedicated to transforming texture is available online, should you want to delve into this topic after you've become familiar with default texture mapping: (http://www.web3dgallery.com/vrml/textures/).

Following is a complete list of URLs referenced in this chapter:

Web3D Gallery Color Links   http://www.web3dgallery.com/vrml/color/

Web3D Consortium   http://www.web3d.org/

Web3D gallery VRML Color   http://www.web3dgallery.com/vrml/color/

Gerardo Quintieri   http://www.web3dgallery.com/people/gq/

Universal Media   http://www.web3d.org/WorkingGroups/media/

Uniform Resource Locators (URLs)   http://www.ietf.org/rfc/rfc1738.txt

Relative URLs   http://www.ietf.org/rfc/rfc1808.txt

Planet9   http://www.planet9.com/

JPEG   http://www.jpeg.org/

PNG   http://www.w3.org/TR/REC-png-multi.html

VRML Texture Mapping   http://www.web3dgallery.com/vrml/textures/

CUSTOMIZING LIGHT, BACKGROUND, FOG, AND SOUND

Topics in This Chapter

- Going beyond the default browser headlight with the DirectionalLight node, PointLight node, and SpotLight node
- Creating sky, ground, and panoramic backgrounds with the Background node
- Creating the effect of atmospheric perspective (fog or haze) using the Fog node
- Adding ambient and spatialized audio to your world with the Sound node

Chapter 9

In previous chapters you've manipulated various settings of specific node fields in order to customize properties such as object location, orientation, and appearances. In this chapter, however, you'll learn how to customize more general properties that can affect an entire scene. Here you'll learn how to control the overall lighting of your worlds, in addition to the sky, ground, and backdrop elements of scenes. You'll also learn how to introduce and control the atmospheric effect of fog (haze, or, as Leonardo da Vinci called it, "atmospheric perspective"—Chapter 3, "Entering the Third Dimension"), as well as sound.

Lights

In addition to the default headlight that VRML browsers automatically provide (see Chapter 8, "Customizing Color and Texture"), VRML offers three specific types of light nodes that authors can use to illuminate their worlds: DirectionalLight, PointLight, and SpotLight. Together these light nodes give content authors a means to simulate three common light sources found in our real world, namely directional lights, point lights, and spotlights.

Directional light sources are positioned infinitely far away from a scene. As a result, the light rays cast by a directional light are parallel and travel in the same direction. In the real world, light rays cast by the sun originate so far away that they are practically parallel when they reach the earth. Because our planet is awash in parallel rays of light that travel mostly in the same direction, we can consider the sun a directional light source.

In truth, however, like a light bulb, the sun is actually a point light source. Point lights emanate rays in a radial pattern in all directions, illuminating objects all around them.

Spotlights, on the other hand, cast light in a specific direction. Spotlights used to light an actor on stage in a theater production, for example, emanate light in the direction in which they are aimed. The light rays travel in a "light cone," which can be tightly focused to shine light on a specific area, or widened to illuminate a larger area. Adjustable flashlights or penlights are also good examples of spotlight sources, as these real-world devices shine light in a specific direction. By adjusting them you can change the size of the light cone, allowing you to shine light on larger or smaller areas.

In the real world, light doesn't shine on forever. It begins to drop off noticeably after traveling over a certain distance (the range of a flashlight, for example, is about 25 feet). VRML's PointLight and SpotLight nodes support this phenomenon, known as *light attenuation*. Using the *radius* and *attenuation* fields of these nodes, you can create attenuated light sources whose illumination effect gradually weakens over distance, just as we experience in the real world.

The DirectionalLight node, however, creates light sources that are considered to be infinitely far away. These light sources have no specific location in a 3D scene, and the light they cast can't be attenuated. Because it does not support attenuation, the DirectionalLight node doesn't offer the *radius* and *attenuation* fields found in both PointLight and SpotLight.

Like all VRML light-node fields, the *radius* and *attenuation* fields of the PointLight and SpotLight are exposed. As a result, you can control the attenuation of these VRML light sources by directly setting *radius* and *attenuation*. Alternately, these fields can be dynamically altered through an event. Likewise, you can set any other VRML light-node field directly or through an event. (See Chapter 5, "VRML Fundamentals," for details on events and exposed fields.)

Calculating Lighting Effects

VRML browsers calculate the effect that all light sources, including the default headlight, have on a scene; shape nodes in a scene are illuminated as the sum result of all light sources that affect them. Browsers take into account the intensity of light sources, the direction in which they shine (and whether or not shape faces are struck by these rays), the color of light sources and the color and appearance of the surfaces they strike (VRML light sources can shine colored light), as well as the amount of *ambient light* in the scene.

Ambient light, as you learned in Chapter 8, "Customizing Color and Texture," is illumination created as the result of scattered light that is reflected off objects in random directions when struck by direct light sources. *Direct light*, in contrast, illuminates objects by shining light rays in a straight path from the source. A spotlight in the real world, for example, is a direct light source that shines light in a straight line. When these light rays strike an object, however, some are reflected in random directions, producing ambient light that illuminates objects outside the light cone.

For performance reasons, VRML browsers grossly approximate light sources found in the real world. Each VRML light node has an *ambientIntensity* field that is used to specify the amount of ambient light generated by the node. The ambient intensity of every light source in a scene contributes to the overall lighting effect for the scene. Scenes with a large amount of ambient light are bright and exhibit a high degree of contrast, while those with smaller amounts of ambient light are darker by comparison.

In the sections that follow we'll illustrate the effect that each VRML light node has when shone on the grid of spheres created in Listing 9.2. Figure 9-1, for example, shows the effect that the default browser headlight has when turned on in the presence of these spheres (the end user can turn the browser headlight on or off at will; see Chapter 8, "Customizing Color and Texture"). The code found in Listing 9.1 inlines the sphere world created in Listing 9.2, allowing each world to reside in its own VRML file. This is the same technique used in the following sections, meaning that the `sphereColumns.wrl` world defined in Listing 9.2 is reused in each light-node example below (see Chapter 10, "Creating New VRML Worlds," for details on inlining).

Listing 9.1   defaultHeadLight.wrl

```
#VRML V2.0 utf8

NavigationInfo {
  headlight TRUE
}

Inline {
  url "sphereColumns.wrl"
}
```

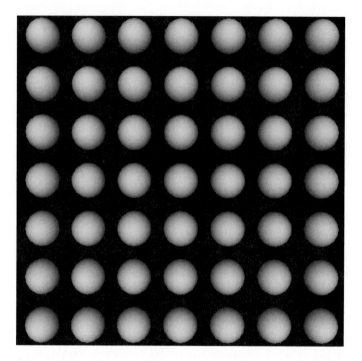

Figure 9-1   This grid of spheres is illuminated using only the default browser headlight, which acts like a directional light source bound to the user's viewpoint.

Listing 9.2   sphereColumns.wrl

```
#VRML V2.0 utf8

DEF SphereColumn Group {
  children [
    DEF OneSphere Shape {
      appearance Appearance {
        material Material {}
      }
      geometry Sphere {radius .75}
    }
    Transform { translation 0 6 0 children USE OneSphere }
    Transform { translation 0 4 0 children USE OneSphere }
    Transform { translation 0 2 0 children USE OneSphere }
    Transform { translation 0 -2 0 children USE OneSphere }
    Transform { translation 0 -4 0 children USE OneSphere }
    Transform { translation 0 -6 0 children USE OneSphere }
```

```
   ]
}

Transform { translation -6 0 0 children USE SphereColumn }
Transform { translation -4 0 0 children USE SphereColumn }
Transform { translation -2 0 0 children USE SphereColumn }
Transform { translation 2 0 0 children USE SphereColumn }
Transform { translation 4 0 0 children USE SphereColumn }
Transform { translation 4 0 0 children USE SphereColumn }
Transform { translation 6 0 0 children USE SphereColumn }
```

Light Limits—8 is Enough!

Lights don't come for free; the rendering engine must calculate the effects that every light source has on objects in a scene, which can be costly in terms of processing power. Many browsers, in fact, will simply ignore some light sources in cases where you have too many (a consequence of the underlying rendering engine and graphics hardware being unable to keep up).

As a result you should be sparing when it comes to lights, attempting always to limit your scenes to no more than 8 light sources whenever possible (a rule-of-thumb number that includes the default headlight, which is actually a DirectionalLight node bound to the user's viewpoint). Many VRML browser rendering engines are built atop OpenGL. Because most OpenGL implementations have a limit of 8 active lights at any given time, VRML worlds are also limited to 8 active lights. Although most of today's graphics boards can handle more than 8 light sources at once, many rendering systems often can't, and so you should try to keep in mind that when it comes to lights, "eight is enough!"

DirectionalLight

The DirectionalLight node is the simplest of the three types of lights supported by VRML. The definition of DirectionalLight found in the VRML97 specification is fairly crisp and easy to understand when compared to the PointLight and SpotLight nodes, as you can see here:

```
DirectionalLight {
    exposedField SFFloat ambientIntensity   0       # [0,1]
    exposedField SFColor color               1 1 1   # [0,1]
    exposedField SFVec3f direction           0 0 -1  # (-∞,∞)
    exposedField SFFloat intensity           1       # [0,1]
    exposedField SFBool  on                  TRUE
}
```

Unlike PointLight and SpotLight nodes, light cast by the DirectionalLight node is not controlled by radius or attenuation settings, and so these fields are not present in this node as they are in PointLight and SpotLight. Instead, light rays created using a DirectionalLight node are cast only on children of the grouping node in which this node is included, such as a Transform or Group node, and any descendants they may contain. Similar to our sun, the parallel light rays generated by a DirectionalLight node shine on objects from what is considered to be an infinite distance away, meaning that this light source has no specific location in a scene as PointLight and SpotLight do.

As the node name implies, light emitted from a DirectionalLight node travels in a specific direction, a setting that you can control through node's *direction* field, as we'll explain in a moment. Because light created by this node is aimed at objects from infinitely far away, the light rays are parallel and all travel in the same direction, as seen in Figure 9-2.

Warning: Browser Variances

Some VRML browsers don't restrict the lighting effects of the Directional-Light node to the group in which it is placed; as a result, this node will light all shapes in a world regardless of where you place it. To create lighting effects that are consistent across a wide range of browsers you should place your entire scene inside a top-level Group node, making all lights in the scene children of the group. This will result in lights that affect the entire scene, regardless of whether or not a browser properly scopes light sources.

The DirectionalLight node can either be "on" or "off," a setting that's controlled by the node's SFBool *on* field. When the *on* field is TRUE (the default for this field), the light that this node creates is considered to be "on" and will therefore shine on objects in the group in which the node appears (assuming that the browser properly scopes light sources, otherwise the

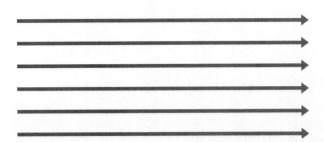

Figure 9-2 Light rays created by a DirectionalLight node are parallel and travel in the same direction.

scene is illuminated; see "Browser Variances"). When the *on* field is FALSE, however, the light is considered to be "off" and as a result will not illuminate the shapes around it.

The brightness of the light generated by the DirectionalLight node is controlled by the SFFloat *intensity* field, which is set to shine at full power (1.0) by default. Settings of less than 1.0 will result in a less intense light source, while a value of 0.0 specifies that the node should produce no light at all.

The *ambientIntensity* field, on the other hand, specifies the intensity of the ambient light emitted from this light source, which is used to calculate the degree to which ambient light affects the overall appearance of objects that it lights up. This field is combined with ambient lighting effects produced by other light sources in the scene, which together determine how much ambient light is in the scene. Large amounts of ambient light in a scene result in a brighter overall appearance, while lower amounts result in darker worlds. A sunny beach scene lit in the middle of the afternoon has a high amount of ambient light, for example, while an evening stroll on the beach has much less ambient light (see Chapter 8, "Customizing Color and Texture," to learn more about ambient light).

By default, the color of light cast by all VRML light nodes, including DirectionalLight, is white. Using the *color* field, however, you can shine light of any color onto objects, which can dramatically alter the visual appearance of your worlds. An underwater scene, for example, would appear more realistic if tinted in blue light, while a sunset on the high plains would be better lit in an orange or perhaps even purple color. Because the *color* field is an SF-Color data type, the three floating-point values that you supply to it specify red, blue, and green (RGB) color components that are mixed together to produce the actual color of light emitted by this source. Mixing color in this way should seem familiar to you, as it's exactly the same method you used to set the various Material node color fields in Chapter 8, "Customizing Color and Texture."

The DirectionalLight node's *direction* field will also be familiar to you, as it's an SFVec3f data type used to specify the direction in which the light rays generated by this node will travel, which is specified in a manner similar to that of the rotation axes that you encountered in Chapter 7, "Customizing Location, Size, and Orientation." As with a rotation axis, the 3D coordinate (X Y Z) that you supply to the *direction* field defines a point that is compared with the origin (0 0 0) of the current coordinate system. Unlike a rotation axis, however, you don't need to specify an angle of rotation when it comes to creating a light direction. Instead, you need only specify a point in 3D space.

An imaginary line is drawn from the origin to the point specified by *direction*, which in turn defines the direction in which the parallel light rays will travel when generated by this light source. If, for example, you set the *direction* field to (1 0 0), the light rays will shine along the positive X axis (imagine a line drawn from 0 0 0 to 1 0 0, which represents the light direction). Similarly, you can shine light up the Y axis by setting *direction* to (0 1 0). You can even supply values for X, Y, and Z to aim light diagonally, such as (1 1 1) to shine light at 45 degrees in the positive direction of each axis. By default, DirectionalLight node light rays are aimed along the negative Z axis (0 0 –1).

Keeping the default field settings of the DirectionalLight node in mind, consider Listing 9.3. Here we've simply used the NavigationInfo node to turn the default headlight off, replacing the light it generates with a default DirectionalLight node. The result, seen in Figure 9-3, is indistinguishable from the browser's default headlight figure (Figure 9-1) because the browser headlight is, in fact, treated like a directional light source that has the special property of being bound to the user's viewpoint (see Chapter 8, "Customizing Color and Texture," to learn more about the default headlight).

In Listing 9.4, however, we've reduced the intensity of the light cast by the DirectionalLight node and also aimed it in the positive direction of the Y axis. As a result, the spheres are lit by dimmer parallel light rays approaching from a different angle altogether, as seen in Figure 9-4. The code in Listing 9.5, on the other hand, explicitly sets the light intensity back to its 100% default, yet aims the light at a 45-degree angle along all axes, as Figure 9-5 illustrates.

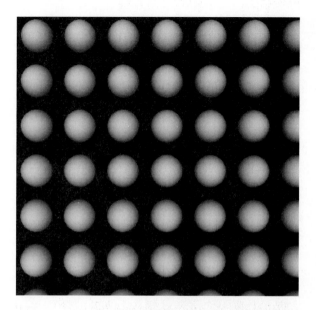

Figure 9-3   The default DirectionalLight node casts very intense parallel rays of light along the negative Z axis.

Figure 9-4   These spheres are hit with less intense parallel light rays (`intensity .75`) traveling along the positive Y axis (`direction 0 1 0`).

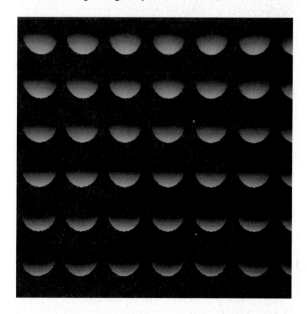

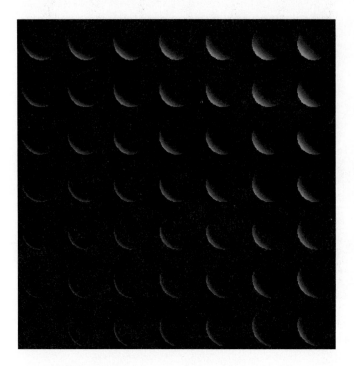

Figure 9-5   The spheres are struck once again at full intensity (`intensity 1`), but this time from a diagonal 45-degree angle (`direction 1 1 1`).

Listing 9.3   DirectionalLight-default.wrl

```
#VRML V2.0 utf8

NavigationInfo {
  headlight FALSE
}
Group {
  children [
    DirectionalLight {}

  Inline {
    url "sphereColumns.wrl"
  }
  ]
}
```

Listing 9.4   DirectionalLight-Y.wrl

```
#VRML V2.0 utf8

NavigationInfo {
  headlight FALSE
}
Group {
  children [
    DirectionalLight {
      direction 0 1 0    # aim in the positive Y direction
      intensity .75      # make 2/3rds as intense as default
    }

  Inline {
    url "sphereColumns.wrl"
  }
 ]
}
```

Listing 9.5   DirectionalLight-XYZ.wrl

```
#VRML V2.0 utf8

NavigationInfo {
  headlight FALSE
}

Group {
  children [
    DirectionalLight {
      direction 1 1 1    # aim in the positive X,Y,Z
      intensity 1.0      # full intensity
    }

  Inline {
    url "sphereColumns.wrl"
  }
 ]
}
```

PointLight

The PointLight node is used to create a light source that radiates lights in all directions from a single point, much as a light bulb does in the real world (see Figure 9-6). Because the light created by the PointLight node emanates in all directions, this node has no need for a specific direction field as the DirectionalLight node does. The PointLight node does, however, contain several fields that the DirectionalLight node does not in order to give you control over radiating light sources. Although the PointLight node contains *ambientIntensity*, *color*, *intensity*, and *on* fields just as the DirectionalLight node does (see the above discussion of DirectionalLight for details), you'll notice from the following VRML97 specification definition that the Point-Light node also contains *attenuation*, *location*, and *radius* fields:

```
PointLight {
  exposedField SFFloat ambientIntensity  0        # [0,1]
  exposedField SFVec3f attenuation        1 0 0    # [0,∞)
  exposedField SFColor color              1 1 1    # [0,1]
  exposedField SFFloat intensity          1        # [0,1]
  exposedField SFVec3f location           0 0 0    # (-∞,∞)
  exposedField SFBool  on                 TRUE
  exposedField SFFloat radius             100      # [0, ∞)
}
```

Figure 9-6   Light created with the PointLight node radiates outward in all directions from a single point.

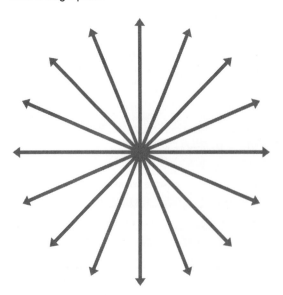

Note

A light source can be placed inside the Transform node, allowing you to change its position and orientation in 3D space just as you would a shape. For details on the Transform node see Chapter 7, "Customizing Location, Size, and Orientation."

Unlike light sources created with the DirectionalLight node, which have no specific location, as such light sources emanate from infinitely far away, lights created with the PointLight node are actually placed somewhere in a world. By default, this "somewhere" is the origin of the coordinate system, although you can set the *location* field of a PointLight node to any 3D point in your world.

Warning

Because of VRML browser rendering variances, and depending on the underlying graphics subsystem, the radius field may be ignored altogether for both PointLight and SpotLight nodes. When running Cosmo Player atop OpenGL, for example, the radius field is ignored and, as a result, PointLight and SpotLight nodes illuminate the entire scene. To create VRML content that is consistent across a wide range of systems, avoid attenuated light sources whenever possible (i.e., don't specify attenuate and radius settings for worlds that you intend to be viewed on a wide variety of VRML browser configurations).

The PointLight node will light up objects within a specified radius of the node's location in a scene, which is 100 meters by default (remember that all units of measurement for distance in VRML are expressed in terms of meters, as Chapter 7, "Customizing Location, Size, and Orientation," explains). You can, however, set the node's *radius* field to something other than the default of 100 if you'd like to increase or decrease the "reach" of a PointLight.

Also, this node contains an *attenuation* field that is used to control the brightness of the light as it travels outward from its location in 3D space (as defined by the *location* field) to the edges of the spherical shape defined by the *radius* field. To help visualize the relationship between the *location, radius,* and *attenuation* settings, imagine placing a tiny light bulb inside the center of a beachball. The light is brightest at the center of the ball, where the bulb's *location* is (0 0 0) in terms of the 3D coordinate system of the ball. As light emanates from the bulb, it becomes weaker and less bright. By the time light rays reach the inner walls of the ball (a distance specified by the *radius* field) they may lose power and therefore can't shine beyond this distance.

On the other hand, the light bulb might be strong enough to radiate light over the entire distance without any noticeable drop-off in brightness. Using the SFVec3f *attenuation* field, you can control to what extent, if any, the light's illumination falls off over distance, based on the following attenuation factor (where *r* is a measure of distance from the light source to the surface being illuminated):

```
1/max(attenuation1 + attenuation2 × r + attenuation3 × r², 1)
```

The first *attenuation* field value (attenuation1) specifies whether or not the light has a constant brightness. The second value supplied to this field (attenuation2) controls how the light brightness falls off as it travels from the source (which defines a linear attenuation), and the third value determines how the light source falls off in terms of the square of the distance it travels (exponential attenuation). By default, there is no attenuation with light created by the PointLight node (the default attenuation setting of 1 0 0 is equivalent to 0 0 0 as far as VRML browsers are concerned).

Note

Not all browsers support the full range of values that you can supply to the attenuation field (some approximate attenuation settings, while others ignore the field altogether).

Figure 9-7 illustrates the default PointLight node in action as it applies to our grid of spheres, for which the corresponding source code is found in Listing 9.6. The light source is placed at the origin of the coordinate system (0 0 0) by default, from which it radiates outward at the highest possible intensity (`intensity 1`), illuminating shapes within a 100-meter radius (`radius 100`). Because all of the sphere shapes are within this distance, they're all illuminated by the light source.

Listing 9.7, however, restricts the light radius to 5 meters, a much smaller distance that the outermost spheres are actually beyond. As a result, the light doesn't reach those spheres beyond 5 meters from the origin, as seen in Figure 9-8. Of course, you're free to move the light source to any point in the coordinate system, as we've done in Listing 9.8. Here the center of the light is placed in the lower right-hand corner of the scene by setting the location field accordingly (`location 3 -3 0`), producing the effect seen in Figure 9-9.

Figure 9-7   By default, PointLight node light sources are positioned at the origin of the coordinate system (0 0 0) and radiate outward in all directions at full intensity (and at a continuous attenuation, with no fall-off) for a radius of 100 meters. Every sphere in the grid is reached as a result. (See Listing 9.6.)

Figure 9-8   Using the PointLight node's *radius* field you can restrict the distance that the light rays will travel. The outermost spheres in this figure aren't touched by the PointLight node light rays, because the node's *radius* field is 5 meters (`radius 5`). (See Listing 9.7.)

Figure 9-9   The center of the PointLight node in this example has been moved to the lower right-hand corner of the scene by setting the *location* field (`location 3 -3 0`). (See Listing 9.8.)

Figure 9-10   The light created by the PointLight node in this example falls off linearly as it radiates outward and over the 8-meter radius (`radius 8`), thanks to the *attenuation* field (`attenuation 1 .15 0`). (See Listing 9.9.)

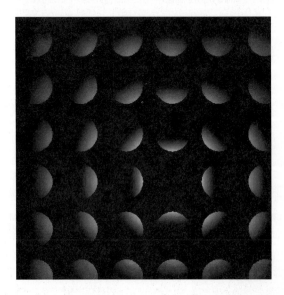

In all of these cases, however, the default continuous attenuation of the PointLight node applies, because we haven't bothered to specify an alternative setting. The light radiating from each point in these examples, therefore, is continuous—there is no fall-off as the light travels over distance. You can, however, use the *attenuation* field to control light fall-off as seen in Listing 9.9. In this example a linear attenuation is specified (attenuation 1 .15 0), the result of which is seen in Figure 9-10.

Listing 9.6   PointLight-default.wrl

```
#VRML V2.0 utf8

NavigationInfo {
  headlight FALSE
}

Group {
  children [
    PointLight {
    }

  Inline {
    url "sphereColumns.wrl"
  }
 ]
}
```

Listing 9.7   PointLight-radius.wrl

```
#VRML V2.0 utf8

NavigationInfo {
  headlight FALSE
}

Group {
  children [
    PointLight {
      radius   5
    }
```

```
Inline {
    url "sphereColumns.wrl"
  }
 ]
}
```

Listing 9.8   PointLight-location.wrl

```
#VRML V2.0 utf8

NavigationInfo {
  headlight FALSE
}

Group {
  children [
    PointLight {
      location 3 -3 0     # move to lower right-hand corner
    }

  Inline {
    url "sphereColumns.wrl"
  }
 ]
}
```

Listing 9.9   PointLight-attenuation.wrl

```
#VRML V2.0 utf8

NavigationInfo {
  headlight FALSE
}

Group {
  children [
    PointLight {
      radius    8
      attenuation 1 .15 0     # drop off linearly
    }

  Inline {
    url "sphereColumns.wrl"
```

```
      }
    ]
}
```

SpotLight

The most complicated (and processor intensive) of all VRML light nodes is
the SpotLight node, which is similar in many ways to the PointLight node.
Like the PointLight node, the SpotLight node creates a light source that radiates outward from a central point. However, unlike lights created with the
PointLight node, those created with the SpotLight node cast light in a cone
shape, as illustrated in Figure 9-11.

The SpotLight node has all of the same fields as the PointLight node, including three additional fields (*beamWidth, cutOffAngle,* and *direction*), as
you can see from the following specification definition:

```
SpotLight {
  exposedField SFFloat ambientIntensity  0          # [0,1]
  exposedField SFVec3f attenuation       1 0 0      # [0, ∞)
  exposedField SFFloat beamWidth         1.570796   # (0,π/2]
  exposedField SFColor color             1 1 1      # [0,1]
  exposedField SFFloat cutOffAngle       0.785398   # (0,π/2]
  exposedField SFVec3f direction         0 0 -1     # (−∞,∞)
  exposedField SFFloat intensity         1          # [0,1]
  exposedField SFVec3f location          0 0 0      # (−∞,∞)
  exposedField SFBool  on                TRUE
  exposedField SFFloat radius            100        # [0, ∞)
}
```

Figure 9-11   Light created with the SpotLight node radiates outward in a conical shape
from a single point. This is commonly known as a "light cone."

The *location* field specifies a point in 3D space that represents the tip of the light cone created with this node, while the *direction* field controls the direction in which light rays travel as they pass from this point over the *radius* of the cone (the *direction* field specifies the direction of the light's central axis in terms of the local coordinate system, as seen in Figure 9-12). See the DirectionalLight node for more details on the *direction* field, and the PointLight node to learn more about the *radius* field.

The "outer" solid angle of the light cone is controlled by the *cutOffAngle* field, which is a value expressed in terms of radians (see Chapter 7, "Customizing Location, Size, and Orientation," to learn more about radians and angles). As you can see from Figure 9-12, the *cutOffAngle* is measured from the centerline of the light cone and controls the "spread" of the light (light won't shine beyond the outer edge of the cone, which is defined by the *cutOffAngle* field). By default, the cut off angle of the light cone is 45 degrees (cutOffAngle 0.785398), which can accept a range of values from 0 to 90 degrees (0 to $\pi/2$ radians, or 1.571 radians as Chapter 7 explains). Smaller *cutOffAngle* values will create a tighter light cone, while larger values result in a larger spread of light.

The *beamWidth* field is used to define an "inner" solid angle located within the light cone, inside of which the light eminates at full intensity. Light cast beyond this inner angle defined by *beamWidth* starts to fall off in intensity based on the following specification equations (where "angle" is the angle between the SpotLight's direction vector and the vector from the SpotLight location to the point to be illuminated):

```
if (angle >= cutOffAngle):
  multiplier = 0
else if (angle <= beamWidth):
  multiplier = 1
else:
  multiplier = (angle-cutOffAngle)/(beamWidth-cutOffAngle)

intensity(angle) = SpotLight.intensity × multiplier
```

As with the *cutOffAngle* field, values supplied to *beamWidth* must be in the range of 0 to 90 degrees (0 to $\pi/2$ radians, or 1.571 radians, as Chapter 7 explains). By default, however, the solid angle defined by *beamWidth* is 90 degrees (beamWidth 1.570796), which produces a smaller "inner" cone

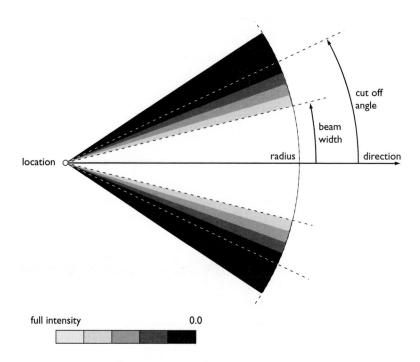

full intensity   0.0

Figure 9-12 Light sources created with the SpotLight node shine in a conical pattern. Light will not illuminate objects beyond the "outer" cone defined by the *cutOffAngle*, where *beamWidth* defines an "inner" cone beyond which light begins to drop off.

within the larger "outer" cone created by the *cutOffAngle* field, as you can see from Figure 9-12. In cases where the value of the *beamWidth* field is greater than that of the *cutOffAngle* field, the light source will emit at full intensity within the entire "outer" solid angle defined by *cutOffAngle* (i.e., *beamWidth* is considered to be equal to the value of *cutOffAngle* in such cases).

Listing 9.10 shows the illumination effect that a default SpotLight has when aimed in the positive Y direction of our sphere grid, as seen in Figure 9-13. Listing 9.11, on the other hand, creates a tighter cone by setting the *cutOffAngle* field to 20 degrees (`cutOffAngle .349`), the result of which is seen in Figure 9-14.

Listing 9.10   SpotLight-Y.wrl

```
#VRML V2.0 utf8

NavigationInfo {
  headlight FALSE
}

Group {
  children [
    SpotLight {
      direction   0 1 0 # shine in the positive Y direction
    }

  Inline {
    url "sphereColumns.wrl"
  }
 ]
}
```

Listing 9.11   SpotLight-cutoffangle.wrl

```
#VRML V2.0 utf8

NavigationInfo {
  headlight FALSE
}

Group {
  children [
    SpotLight {
      cutOffAngle .349  # reduce outer cone to 20 degrees
      direction   0 1 0 # shine in the positive Y direction
    }

  Inline {
    url "sphereColumns.wrl"
  }
 ]
}
```

Figure 9-13   The default "outer" light cone created by the SpotLight node is 45 degrees (`cutOffAngle 0.785398`). The light cone in this example is aimed at the positive Y axis (`direction 0 1 0`), which illuminates our spheres from below when viewed head-on. (See Listing 9.10.)

Figure 9-14   The "outer" light cone created here is only 20 degrees (`cutOffAngle .349`), which creates a tighter, more focused light source. (See Listing 9.11.)

Tip: Dealing with Browser Variances

Subtle but important variances in how VRML browsers handle lighting can often explain why some worlds look smashing in one browser and shabby in another. Some browsers, for example, properly scope DirectionalLight nodes, while others do not. In addition, some browsers ignore the attenuation and radius fields found in the PointLight and SpotLight nodes, while others respect them.

To create worlds that are less prone to browser variances you should do your best not to rely on attenuated light sources. In addition, you can create lighting effects that are consistent across a wide range of browsers by placing your entire scene inside a top-level Group node, making all lights in the scene a children of the group. This will result in lights that illuminate the entire scene, regardless of whether or not a browser properly scopes light sources.

Sky, Ground, and Backgrounds

In the real world, we're accustomed to an outside environment in which a sky is above us and ground is below our feet. In addition, a panoramic backdrop seems to be lurking far off in the horizon, behind objects in the foreground. If you're standing in the middle of the lone prairie, for example, a distant mountain range set against a blue sky might be that backdrop. When in Times Square, however, buildings form the background against which everything else appears.

VRML worlds, too, can benefit from sky, ground, and backdrops. Using VRML's Background node you can mimic the outside environment of our real world, creating sky, ground, and panoramic backgrounds. In addition to giving your virtual worlds a greater sense of realism, these elements also assist the user in navigation. Because the laws of physics that govern our physical world don't apply in the virtual world, it's quite easy to get turned upside down when exploring a VRML scene. A sky, ground, or background image, however, can give disoriented users an immediate sense of up and down, providing them with the visual cues they need to reorient themselves.

Conceptually, VRML backgrounds (the combination of sky, ground, and a panoramic background) can be thought of as a box sitting inside two spheres, as illustrated in Figure 9-15. The box, upon each face of which a different image may be placed, represents the panoramic background. Outside the box is the ground sphere, which is actually just a half sphere that surrounds the bottom of the box. The sky sphere, in turn, encloses both the partial ground sphere and the background box inside of it.

Your VRML world is positioned inside the box. The user, in turn, is positioned by default at the center of the box (the center of your world), as illustrated by Figure 9-16. This means that by default, the top pole of the sky is directly above the user's head, the ground is below and extends in all directions, while the panoramic background is far off on the horizon. As in the real world, the user can walk toward these scene elements, but can never actually reach them. Because they're considered to be infinitely far away, the user can never actually touch the sky or background. Similarly, the ground beneath the user's feet extends infinitely in all directions, meaning the edge of the world is never within reach.

The Background node can appear at the top level of a VRML file, or it may be made the child of a grouping node (most of the time you'll simply

Figure 9-15 The Background node is used to create a backdrop of sky and ground colors, as well as panoramic background images. The sky can be conceptualized as an infinitely large sphere surrounding the VRML world, inside of which is a partial ground sphere. An imaginary box sits inside both of these spheres, enclosing your world, the faces of which are used to display background images.

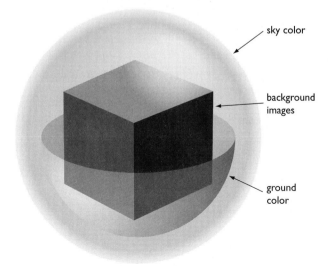

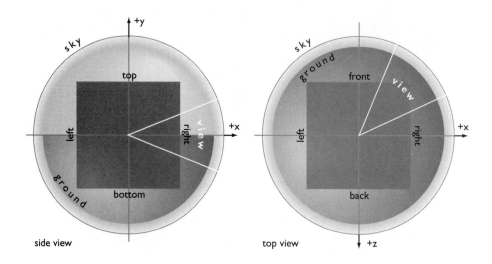

Figure 9-16   The viewer sits at the center of the backdrop. On the left is a side view of the backdrop, while the right image illustrates the top view of the backdrop.

place it at the top level). As you can see from the following VRML97 specification definition, the Background node is full of fields, although you're under no obligation to use them all. Instead you can use only those that correspond the background elements that you'd like to implement, as subsequent sections explain:

```
Background {
    eventIn       SFBool    set_bind
    exposedField MFFloat   groundAngle    []          # [0,π/2]
    exposedField MFColor   groundColor    []          # [0,1]
    exposedField MFString  backUrl        []
    exposedField MFString  bottomUrl      []
    exposedField MFString  frontUrl       []
    exposedField MFString  leftUrl        []
    exposedField MFString  rightUrl       []
    exposedField MFString  topUrl         []
    exposedField MFFloat   skyAngle       []          # [0,π]
    exposedField MFColor   skyColor       0 0 0       # [0,1]
    eventOut      SFBool    isBound
}
```

Note

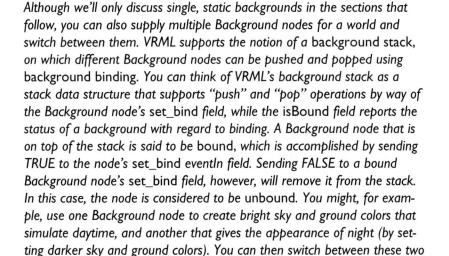

Although we'll only discuss single, static backgrounds in the sections that follow, you can also supply multiple Background nodes for a world and switch between them. VRML supports the notion of a background stack, on which different Background nodes can be pushed and popped using background binding. You can think of VRML's background stack as a stack data structure that supports "push" and "pop" operations by way of the Background node's set_bind field, while the isBound field reports the status of a background with regard to binding. A Background node that is on top of the stack is said to be bound, *which is accomplished by sending TRUE to the node's set_bind eventIn field. Sending FALSE to a bound Background node's set_bind field, however, will remove it from the stack. In this case, the node is considered to be* unbound. *You might, for example, use one Background node to create bright sky and ground colors that simulate daytime, and another that gives the appearance of night (by setting darker sky and ground colors). You can then switch between these two nodes whenever you'd like, effectively changing the scene from day to night as needed. Sky, ground, and background images can also be animated. Background animation is a popular but sophisticated technique that truly brings worlds to life by simulating what we experience in our real world. To learn how to use multiple and animated backgrounds visit the Web3D Gallery at http://www.web3dgallery.com/vrml/background/.*

Sky Colors

A VRML sky can be thought of as a sphere that surrounds the world in which the viewer is located at the center, as illustrated earlier in Figure 9-15 (the sky sphere is further from the viewer than the ground sphere, so that the ground will appear in front of the sky in cases where the two overlap). Using the Background node's *skyColor* and *skyAngle* fields, you can control the color of the sky, as the following partial node definition implies:

```
Background {
  exposedField MFFloat   skyAngle    []       # [0,π]
  exposedField MFColor   skyColor    0 0 0    # [0,1]
}
```

The *skyColor* field can be used alone to specify a single RGB color, as Listing 9.12 illustrates. Here the color of the sky has been defined as pure

---

Listing 9.12   Background-skycolor.wrl

```
#VRML V2.0 utf8

Background {
  skyColor 1 1 1    # a white sky
}

NavigationInfo {
  headlight FALSE
}

Group {
  children [
    DirectionalLight { }

  Inline {
    url "sphereColumns.wrl"
  }
  ]
}
```

---

white (`skyColor 1 1 1`), which allows the spheres in this world to be seen better than with the default black sky color defined by this field (see Figure 9-17). Alternately, the *skyColor* field can be combined with the *skyAngle* field to create transitions of color for the sky (concentric circles of color are drawn around the sphere, which you can reference with *skyAngle* values). The sky in Figure 9-18, for example, transitions from the color white at the very top of the sky (the top pole of the sky sphere, or zenith, that is directly above the viewer, specified by a *skyAngle* of 0) to dark blue at the bottom.

Note

Sky and ground colors are specified using three floating-point numbers that correspond to the amount of Red, Green, and Blue (RGB) light mixed together to produce the actual color that appears on screen. See Chapter 8, "Customizing Color and Texture," for details on specifying RGB colors.

In order to create such color gradients, you supply multiple RGB *sky-Color* values as well as corresponding *skyAngle* values (which are a measure of radians; see Chapter 7, "Customizing Location, Size, and Orientation," for

Coloring the Sky

The values that you supply to the *skyAngle* field specify angles from the sky sphere top, or zenith, which is directly above the viewer and implicitly defined to be 0 radians. The natural horizon is specified at 90 degrees ($\pi/2$, or 1.571, radians), while the nadir (the bottom sky sphere pole located directly below the viewer) is at 180 degrees (π, or 3.14159265, radians). Values that you supply to *skyAngle* field must therefore increase, indicating a progression from 0 to 3.14159 radians (top to bottom).

Although you can supply color values and angles all the way down to the nadir, if you do not do so the last color value that you supply to *skyColor* will be used to color the sphere from the last *skyAngle* value to the nadir. The dark blue color (0 0 .5) appearing in Listing 9.13, for instance, is used to color the lower part of the sky sphere because the last *skyAngle* value that we supplied fell short of the nadir. As a result, dark blue is used to color from the horizon (`skyAngle 1.571`) to the bottom sky-sphere pole.

Figure 9-17 A pure white sky (`skyColor 1 1 1`) makes it easier to see these spheres.

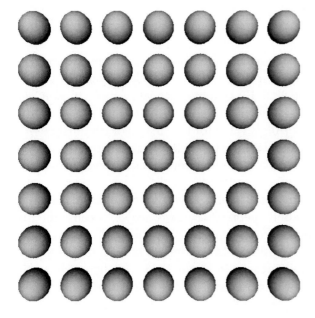

Figure 9-18   A more realistic sky is created using a combination of *skyColor* and *skyAngle*, which allows for smooth color transitions such as the transition from white at the top of the world, to bright blue (middle), and finally to dark blue (bottom).

details on converting angles to radians). The colors that you specify are transitioned between for each corresponding angle, which produces a smooth gradation of sky colors. The first RGB value that you supply to *skyColor* specifies a color that automatically corresponds to the top of the sky, so that you don't have to specify a *skyAngle* value for the first color (the first color is always assumed to be associated with the top of the sky sphere).

For every subsequent *skyColor* value that you specify, however, you will also supply a *skyAngle* value, meaning that you'll always have one more *sky-Color* value than you will *skyAngle* values. If you specify 3 RGB values to *skyColor*, for example, you'll only specify 2 *skyAngle* angles, because the first color automatically corresponds to the top of the sky sphere. The sky created in Listing 9.13, for example, transitions from white to blue, and blue to dark blue, which produces the gradient seen in Figure 9-18. This figure shows the top of the sky sphere, toward which we've turned our virtual head upward (as a result the spheres are no longer in view; they're below the current viewpoint in this figure). Table 9.1 shows the mapping between *skyColor* values and *skyAngle* values that this code produces.

Listing 9.13 Background-skyangle.wrl

```
#VRML V2.0 utf8

Background {
   skyColor [1 1 1,      # white at top point (0 degrees)
             0 0 1,      # blue at 45 degrees
             0 0 .5]     # dark blue at 90 degrees

   skyAngle [0.785,      # 45 degrees
             1.571]      # 90 degrees

}

NavigationInfo {
   headlight FALSE
}

Group {
   children [
     DirectionalLight { }

   Inline {
     url "sphereColumns.wrl"
   }
  ]
}
```

Table 9.1 *skyColor* and *skyAngle* mappings from Listing 9.13

Color	*skyColor*	*skyAngle*
white	1 1 1	*top pole (0 degrees; 0 radians)*
blue	0 0 1	.785 (45 degrees)
dark blue	0 0 .5	1.571 (90 degrees)

Ground Colors

In addition to creating sky colors as described in the previous section, you can also create colors for the ground. A green ground color, for example, might be used in a park scene, while a sandy brown ground color would be more appropriate for a beach scene. Like sky colors, the RGB colors values that you specify for *groundColor* correspond to angles of a ground sphere, as the following snippet of the Background-node definition indicates:

```
Background {
  exposedField MFFloat   groundAngle  []      # [0,π/2]
  exposedField MFColor   groundColor  []      # [0,1]
}
```

Ground angles, however, are mapped to a partial sphere that rests inside and at the bottom of the sky sphere, as you saw earlier in Figure 9-15. The first value that you supply to the *groundColor* field automatically defines the color of the ground at the very bottom of ground sphere, which is directly below the viewer and specified at 0.0 radians (0 degrees). As with sky colors, you don't supply this initial *groundAngle* value; it's implicitly supplied, meaning that you supply angle values for all ground colors other than the first one (and, as a result, you'll always have one more *groundColor* value than you will *groundAngle* values).

The *groundAngle* values that you do supply specify angles from the ground-sphere bottom (also known as the nadir), which define concentric circles of color that are drawn. And, as with sky colors, RGB ground-color values are used to create color gradients, as seen in Figure 9-19. This image, created with the code found in Listing 9.14, has sky and ground coloring. The sky color is a gradient from dark blue to white, starting at the top of the sky sphere, while the ground color transitions from white at the bottom of the ground sphere to black on the ground-sphere horizon (90 degrees, or 1.571 radians). The color values and angle mappings for the ground color in this example are found in Table 9.2.

Note

The values that you supply to groundAngle cannot decrease in value. If the last groundAngle that you supply is less than the horizon located at 90 degrees (π/2, or 1.571, radians), the area between it and the equator of the scene is considered to be nonexistent.

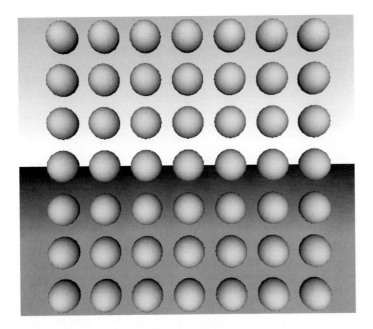

Figure 9-19 This world now has sky *and* ground coloring. The sky transitions from dark blue to white (starting at the top of the sky sphere), while the ground transitions from white to black (starting at the bottom of the ground sphere), creating a horizon line off in the far distance. (See Listing 9.14.)

Listing 9.14   Background-ground.wrl

```
#VRML V2.0 utf8

Background {
  skyColor [0 0 .5,  # dark blue at sky top (0 degrees)
            0 0 1,   # blue at sky sphere 45 degrees
            1 1 1]   # white at sky sphere 90 degrees
  skyAngle [0.785,   # 45 degrees
            1.571]   # 90 degrees

  groundColor [1 1 1,    # white at ground bottom (0 degrees)
               .5 .5 .5, # gray at ground sphere 80 degrees
               0 0 0]    # black at ground horizon 90 degrees

  groundAngle [1.396,    # 80 degrees
               1.571]    # 90 degrees

}
```

```
NavigationInfo {
  headlight FALSE
}

Group {
  children [
    DirectionalLight { }

  Inline {
    url "sphereColumns.wrl"
  }
  ]
}
```

Table 9.2	groundColor and groundAngle mappings from Listing 9.14

Color	groundColor	groundAngle	
white	1 1 1	*bottom pole (0 degrees; 0 radians)*	
gray	.5 .5 .5	1.396	(80 degrees)
black	0 0 0	1.571	(90 degrees)

Panoramic Background Images

Whereas the sky and ground fields of the Background node allow you to color these areas of your VRML worlds with solid colors and color gradients, the URL fields of this node give you the ability to create a panoramic series of background images. As you can see from the following partial definition, the Background node can accept image URLs corresponding to the top, bottom, left, right, front, and back faces of an imaginary box that encloses the VRML world (refer to Figure 9-15):

```
Background {
  exposedField MFString backUrl      []
  exposedField MFString bottomUrl    []
  exposedField MFString frontUrl     []
  exposedField MFString leftUrl      []
  exposedField MFString rightUrl     []
  exposedField MFString topUrl       []
}
```

Although you can create worlds that utilize all six background images, you can use any number of them as you see fit (or none at all). You might, for example, omit the top and bottom background images—as many VRML authors do—in order to allow the sky and ground colors to show through. As Figures 9-15 and 9-16 illustrated earlier, the imaginary background image box that surrounds every VRML world actually sits *inside* both the sky and background spheres; when you omit a background image (or use a background image that has transparent pixels), these colored spheres can be seen. To block the sky and ground out entirely, then, you could supply all six background images (assuming each image is entirely opaque with no transparent areas).

Note

All URL fields in VRML are multivalue, meaning that you can supply more than one image URL to each field. The browser will use the first image it can fetch, skipping over any URLs that it can't resolve. You can therefore reference various types of images in your background image fields, as browsers will skip over those they can't load. (Browsers are required to support both PNG and JPEG format images, and almost all support the GIF format image as well, although GIF support is not required for VRML97 specification compliance.)

As with texture maps, background images consume more network bandwidth and processing power than a simply colored world. As a result, you should take care to test your image-laden worlds on a variety of systems and network connections. See Chapter 8, "Customizing Color and Texture," to learn more about the multiple URLs and image formats supported by VRML, and to get advice about choosing image format, sizes, and resolutions.

Background images are individually mapped to their corresponding cube face. When the front, back, right, and left faces of the cube are viewed from the origin while looking down the negative Z axis (with the Y axis running in the up direction), the images (specified by the *frontUrl*, *backUrl*, *rightUrl*, and *leftUrl* fields, respectively) are mapped to these faces using the same orientation as if they were displayed normally in 2D (facing forward, with the top of the image at the top of the box face).

When the top face of the cube is viewed from the origin while looking up along the positive Y axis (with the positive Z axis in the up direction), the image specified by the *topUrl* field is also mapped to the top face using the same orientation as if it were displayed normally in 2D. Similarly, when the bottom face of the box is viewed from the origin along the negative Y axis (with the negative Z axis in the up direction), the image specified by the *bottomUrl* field is mapped to the bottom face using the same orientation as if the image were displayed normally in 2D.

The code found in Listing 9.15 is used to create a world in which all cube faces except the top and bottom are mapped, for which the corresponding images can be seen in Figure 9-20. When laid side-by-side in the order they're specified, these images are seamless; there are no visible seams from the transition of one image to another, which creates the effect of a realistic panorama surrounding the world. Because the top and bottom images have been omitted from this particular Background node, the sky and ground colors in this world are visible (the sky and ground colors are black by default, although we could have created colors for each, as the previous sections describe). As a result, the spheres seen in Figure 9-21 now appear to float in front of a backdrop of clouds when viewed in these directions.

Listing 9.15 Background-images.wrl

```
#VRML V2.0 utf8

Background {
  frontUrl     "cloudySkyFront.JPG"
  backUrl      "cloudySkyBack.JPG"
  leftUrl      "cloudySkyLeft.JPG"
  rightUrl     "cloudySkyRight.JPG"
}

NavigationInfo {
  headlight FALSE
}

Group {
  children [
    DirectionalLight { }

  Inline {
    url "sphereColumns.wrl"
  }
  ]
}
```

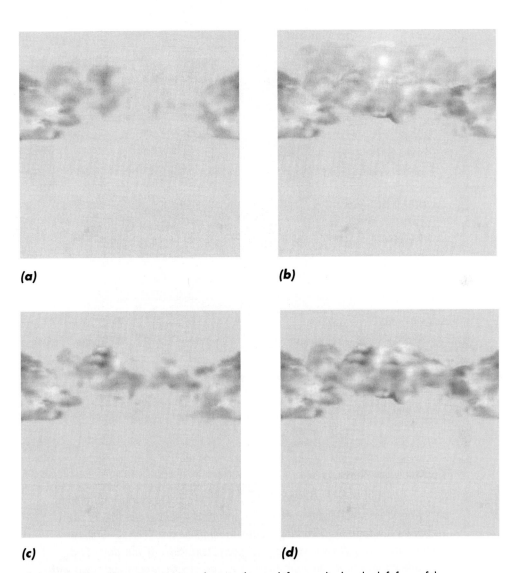

(a)   *(b)*

(c)   *(d)*

Figure 9-20 The image (a) seen here in the top left is applied to the left face of the backdrop cube, while the image (b) seen in the top right is applied to the cube's right face. Similarly, the bottom left image (c) is applied to the front face of the cube, and image (d) on the bottom right is applied to the back face of the cube.

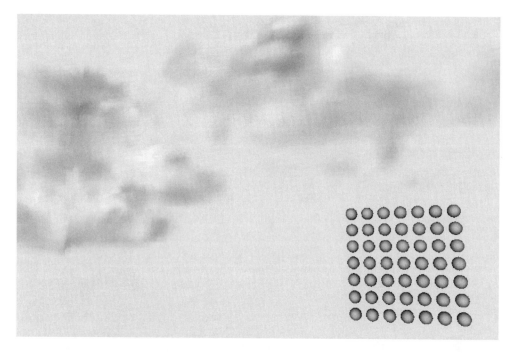

Figure 9-21   The spheres in this image now appear to float above a cloudy panoramic backdrop.

Tip: Universal Media

To get your hands on a variety of freely available, professionally developed background images, visit the Web3D Consortium's Universal Media site (http://www.web3d.org/WorkingGroups/media/) or the Web3D Gallery Texture area (http://www.web3dgallery.com/textures/). If you don't find premade images that suit your needs, you can always create your own with a graphics tool such as SkyPaint (http://www.skypaint.com/). Created by Rikk Carey and Gavin Bell—two major forces behind the design and development of VRML—SkyPaint allows you to create custom panoramic images for a variety of 3D technologies (including VRML). Visit the VRML Tools area of the Web3D Gallery (http://www.web3dgallery.com/) for links to SkyPaint and other VRML authoring tools.

Fog

VRML's Fog node can be used to add the atmospheric effect of fog, or haze, to virtual worlds. In our real world, as you may recall from Chapter 3, "Entering the Third Dimension," objects in the distance are fuzzy and less vibrant in color than those closer to us. This is the result of an atmospheric effect that Leonardo da Vinci dubbed *atmospheric perspective*, which today we know is caused by light waves being scattered and distorted by molecules of water and dust in the air (as well as heated masses of air). The further light waves must travel to reach our eye, the more scattered they'll become, obscuring our view of objects in the distance.

To approximate the real-world atmospheric effect of fog or haze, VRML's Fog node gives us the ability to specify the color, type, and thickness of fog in our virtual worlds. The first world seen in Figure 9-20, for example, is cloaked in fog that is light blue in color. As a result, the entire beach scene is cast in a bluish tint that gives this isolated world a very specific mood. In particular, the sandbar in the far distance seems ephemeral and very far away. In contrast, the same world rendered without the effect of fog seems stark and unrealistic (see Figure 9-22). To view this complex seaside world and examine the source code used to create it, visit the Web3D Consortium's Universal Media site at http://www.web3d.org/WorkingGroups/media/.

By default, VRML worlds do not have fog. To add this effect to a world, you simply insert a Fog node at the top level of the VRML file (or as the child of a grouping node) and set its fields accordingly. Following is the VRML97 specification definition of the Fog node:

```
Fog {
    exposedField SFColor   color           1 1 1      # [0,1]
    exposedField SFString  fogType         "LINEAR"
    exposedField SFFloat   visibilityRange 0          # [0,∞)
    eventIn      SFBool    set_bind
    eventOut     SFBool    isBound
}
```

The default color of fog is white (color 1 1 1). However, as an SFColor data type you can specify any RGB color for your fog through the *color* field (see Chapter 8, "Customizing Color and Texture," for details on RGB colors). Fog thickness is controlled by the *fogType* field, which can be set to one of two values: "LINEAR" or "EXPONENTIAL." By default, fog is linear; it increases in thickness linearly as distance from the viewer increases.

(a)

(b)

Figure 9-22   Beach scene (a) is blanketed in a thick, light blue fog. As a result, the entire world is tinted blue, and objects in the distance (such as the sandbar) are hazy. Beach scene (b), on the other hand, has no fog at all, making for a stark and synthetic-looking world that lacks the realism of scene (a).

Exponential fog, on the other hand, increases in thickness over distance as an exponential function, making for thicker fog effects.

The Fog node's *visibilityRange* field specifies the distance at which objects become completely obscured by fog, meaning that they're no longer visible. A *visibilityRange* field setting of 5, for example, means that objects further than five meters from the viewer are cloaked entirely in fog (*visibilityRange* field values are measured in terms of the current coordinate system). Small *visibilityRange* settings create fog that thickens quickly, while larger settings produce fog that gradually thickens over distance. The beach scene in Figure 9-22, for example, sets the Fog node's *visibilityRange* to 200 to create fog that gradually thickens over 200 meters.

Although fog will gradually wash out shapes in the distance, eventually obscuring them once the *visibilityRange* setting is reached, it has no effect whatsoever on background images created with the Background node (see "Sky, Ground, and Backgrounds"). Instead, background images remain unchanged by fog settings, so you should take care to design them with the overall effect of your world in mind. The seaside world in Figure 9-22, for example, uses a series of blue-tinted, wispy cloud images (see Figure 9-20) that complement the following Fog node employed by this scene:

```
Fog {
   color 0.6588 0.7451 0.7765    # light blue color
   fogType "LINEAR"              # default thickness
   visibilityRange 200          # 200 meter visibility range
}
```

Listings 9.16 and 9.17 contain the code for a variation on the sphere examples you've seen previously. Here, however, a line of spheres is created that extends away from the viewer (in the direction of the –Z axis). Because no fog is applied to this world, all of the spheres in it are easily seen (Figure 9-23). Figure 9-24, on the other hand, where a Fog node has been introduced to this world, looks quite different. Listing 9.17 contains the complete code for the newly fogged world seen in Figure 9-24, which is accomplished with the following Fog node:

```
Fog {
   color 1 1 1             # white color
   fogType "LINEAR"        # default thickness
   visibilityRange 30  # 30 meter visibility range
}
```

Although we've explicitly set the *color* and *fogType* fields in this example, we could have omitted them entirely, because they are nothing more than

Multiple Fog Nodes

Like the Background node, VRML supports multiple Fog nodes, so that you can supply more than one Fog node for a world and switch between them as needed. VRML supports the notion of a *fog stack*, on which different Fog nodes can be pushed and popped using *fog binding*.

The fog stack can be thought of as a stack data structure supporting "push" and "pop" operations by way of the Fog node's *set_bind* field, while the *isBound* field reports the status of node binding. A Fog node on top of the stack is said to be *bound*, which is accomplished by sending TRUE to the node's *set_bind* eventIn field. Sending FALSE to a bound Fog node's *set_bind* field removes it from the stack, making it *unbound*.

Binding Fog nodes allows you to create multiple fog effects for a single world. A world viewed in the early morning, for example, might have a large amount of fog, which can burn off gradually throughout the day. To learn how to use multiple Fog nodes, visit the Web3D Gallery at http://www.web3dgallery.com/vrml/fog/.

default settings. Thus, the following Fog node is functionally equivalent to the one above:

```
Fog {
   visibilityRange 30
}
```

Figure 9-25, however, illustrates the effect of setting the *fogType* field to "EXPONENTIAL" in order to create a thicker fog. Although the *color* and *visibilityRange* fields remain unchanged, the world itself looks quite different from that of Figure 9-24. Figure 9-26 shows the fog effect taken one step further. Here the fog is colored bright red (`color 1 0 0`). As a result, each sphere is tinted red.

Listing 9.16   Fog-OFF.wrl

```
#VRML V2.0 utf8

Group {
  children [
```

```
Background {
  skyColor 1 1 1
}

DEF OneSphere Shape {
  appearance Appearance {
    material Material {}
  }
  geometry Sphere {radius .5}
}
Transform { translation 0 1 -4 children USE OneSphere }
Transform { translation 0 2 -6 children USE OneSphere }
Transform { translation 0 3 -8 children USE OneSphere }
Transform { translation 0 4 -10 children USE OneSphere}
Transform { translation 0 5 -12 children USE OneSphere}
Transform { translation 0 6 -14 children USE OneSphere}
Transform { translation 0 7 -16 children USE OneSphere}
Transform { translation 0 8 -18 children USE OneSphere}
Transform { translation 0 9 -20 children USE OneSphere}
Transform { translation 0 10 -22 children USE OneSphere}
Transform { translation 0 11 -24 children USE OneSphere}
]

}
```

Figure 9-23 Fog has not been applied to this scene, making the spheres in the distance as easy to see as those in the foreground. (See Listing 9.16.)

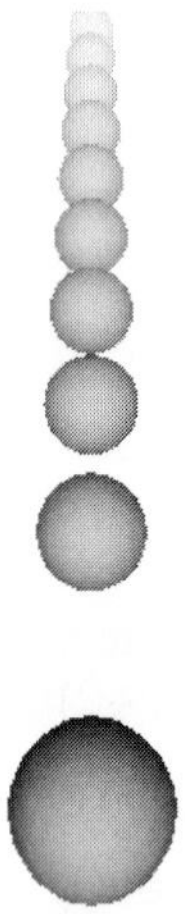

Figure 9-24   White, linear fog has been introduced to this scene. With a visibility range of 30 meters, spheres in the far distance are barely visible, owing to the fog effect. (See Listing 9.17.)

Listing 9.17   Fog-ON.wrl

```
#VRML V2.0 utf8

Group {
  children [
    Background {
      skyColor 1 1 1
    }
```

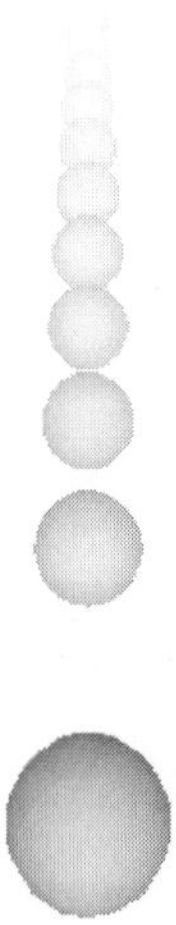

Figure 9-25   A thicker fog is produced simply by using an exponential fog type instead of the default linear fog type (fogType "EXPONENTIAL").

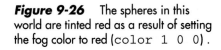

Figure 9-26   The spheres in this world are tinted red as a result of setting the fog color to red (color 1 0 0).

```
Fog {
  color 1 1 1         # white color
  fogType "LINEAR"    # default thickness
  visibilityRange 30  # 30 meter visibility range
}
DEF OneSphere Shape {
  appearance Appearance {
    material Material {}
  }
  geometry Sphere {radius .5}
}
Transform { translation 0 1 -4 children USE OneSphere }
Transform { translation 0 2 -6 children USE OneSphere }
Transform { translation 0 3 -8 children USE OneSphere }
Transform { translation 0 4 -10 children USE OneSphere}
Transform { translation 0 5 -12 children USE OneSphere}
Transform { translation 0 6 -14 children USE OneSphere}
Transform { translation 0 7 -16 children USE OneSphere}
Transform { translation 0 8 -18 children USE OneSphere}
Transform { translation 0 9 -20 children USE OneSphere}
Transform { translation 0 10 -22 children USE OneSphere}
Transform { translation 0 11 -24 children USE OneSphere}
  ]
}
```

Warning

Although most modern VRML browsers are capable of creating realistic fog effects, some aren't as adept. Cortona, for example, uses color blending to create wonderfully realistic fog effects. WorldView, on the other hand, uses a rendering technique that results in less appealing fog.

Sounds

VRML, like most other forms of interactive 3D, is capable of introducing sound into otherwise silent worlds. To do so, you must combine a *sound emitter* with a *sound source*. A VRML sound emitter is analogous to a real-world stereo speaker, as it is the element in a scene that actually outputs (plays) sound. A sound source, on the other hand, is a file that contains the audio signals that the emitter plays.

VRML's Sound node specifies a sound emitter that can be combined with a sound source created by either the AudioClip node or the MovieTexture node. The Sound node is combined with an AudioClip node to produce sounds from waveform (WAV) or Musical Instrument Digital Interface (MIDI) files. To create sounds from an MPEG-1 Systems movie (MPEG movie), however, the Sound node is combined with a MovieTexture node.

Tip

A number of audio files are available free of charge on the Web. For links to free sounds visit the Web3D Gallery at http://www.web3dgallery.com/sounds/.

Ambient and Spatialized Sounds

You can create both *ambient* and *spatialized* sounds for your scenes by combining the Sound node with either an AudioClip node or a MovieTexture node. Ambient sounds, you may recall from Chapter 3, "Entering the Third Dimension," and Chapter 4, "VRML Overview," have no specific

Streaming Audio and Video

VRML97 specifies that browser vendors must support WAV, MIDI, and MPEG-1 Systems sound sources. Some VRML browsers, however, also support streaming audio formats. Version 2 of Cortona, for example, can play streaming sound sources stored in the RealAudio format. Cortona 2 can also play streaming movies stored in the RealVideo format, allowing you to create media-rich worlds that are accessible over slow network connections (see http://www.real.com/ to learn more about RealAudio and RealVideo, and http://www.parallelgraphics.com/ to learn about Cortona).

Because streaming audio and video is not covered in the VRML97 standard, however, such worlds are nonstandard and browser specific. You should always provide users with installation instructions in cases where your VRML content takes advantage of nonstandard features that require a specific browser.

location in a scene and so seem to emanate from all around. Howling wind, the din of city traffic, and background music, for example, are typically created as ambient sounds because they don't emit from a specific point in a world.

Note

Not all browsers support spatialized sounds, nor are all end-user systems capable of the digital signal processing necessary to produce them even where the browser supports them.

Spatialized sounds, on the other hand, seem to emit from an exact location in 3D space. Spatialized sounds are produced by digital signal-processing (DSP) techniques that dynamically alter playback properties of the sound in response to the users' proximity to the sound emitter as well as their position relative to it. Sound emitted from a foghorn, for example, is loudest when the user stands directly in front of the horn. Volume decreases as the user moves away from the horn, until she is so far away that the sound it generates can't be heard at all.

Similarly, spatialized sounds pan from left to right as the user changes position relative to the emitter. When you stand directly in front of a spatialized foghorn, for example, the sound it emits will be output equally to your computer's left and right audio speakers (or headphones). If you position yourself in the scene so that the horn is on your right, the sound will then play louder through your right speaker and softer through the left one. Likewise, placing the horn to your left will result in a higher volume for your left speaker, corresponding to your left ear.

Note

Sounds can be made the children of grouping nodes and are therefore affected by Transform node transformations. A chirping sound might be created as the child of a group that defines an animated, flying bird, for example. As the bird flits about the scene, the spatialized sound seems to move with it.

Sound Node

A sound emitter outputs, or emits, sound signals that are stored in a sound source file. Using VRML's Sound node you can add any number of sound emitters to a world, each of which can be associated with a different sound source:

```
Sound {
    exposedField SFVec3f  direction   0 0 1   # (-∞,∞)
    exposedField SFFloat   intensity   1       # [0,1]
    exposedField SFVec3f  location    0 0 0   # (-∞,∞)
    exposedField SFFloat   maxBack     10      # [0,∞)
    exposedField SFFloat   maxFront    10      # [0,∞)
    exposedField SFFloat   minBack     1       # [0,∞)
    exposedField SFFloat   minFront    1       # [0,∞)
    exposedField SFFloat   priority    0       # [0,1]
    exposedField SFNode    source      NULL
    field        SFBool    spatialize  TRUE
}
```

VRML's Sound node specifies the spatial presentation of sound in a scene. The sound is located at a point in the local coordinate system, as specified by the *location* field, and is emitted in an elliptical pattern defined by an inner and outer ellipsoid. As Figure 9-27 illustrates, these ellipsoids are oriented in a direction that is specified by the *direction* field.

When standing outside of the outer ellipsoid you'll be so far away from the sound emitter that it will be inaudible. However, if you move into the inner ellipsoid, the sound will play at full volume because you'll be in the immediate vicinity of the sound. As you move from the outer ellipsoid to the inner ellipsoid, the sound's volume is attenuated accordingly (see Figure 9-27).

Using the *maxBack*, *maxFront*, *minBack*, and *minFront* fields you can modify the shape of the inner and outer ellipsoids. As Figure 9-28 illustrates, the inner ellipsoid is known as the *minimum ellipsoid* while the outer one is called the *maximum ellipsoid*. The *minBack* and *minFront* fields specify the size of the sound's minimum ellipsoid, while *maxBack* and *maxFront* control the size of its maximum ellipsoid.

The *minFront* field specifies the distance from the sound's location (as specified by the *location* field) to the front of the minimum ellipsoid, while *minBack* specifies the distance from the sound to the back of the minimum ellipsoid. Similarly, *maxFront* specifies the distance from the sound location to the front of the maximum ellipsoid, while *maxBack* specifies the distance from the sound to the back of the maximum ellipsoid. These fields are a measure of distance in the current coordinate system and are parallel to the direction in which the sound is aimed (see Figure 9-28).

A Sound node is associated with a sound source by setting the node's *source* field to an AudioClip node or MovieTexture node (these nodes are discussed in more detail later). The Sound node's exposed *source* field is an SFNode data type that you can set manually or through an event, meaning that sound sources can be changed dynamically over time or in response to user activity. (See Chapter 5, "VRML Fundamentals," to learn about events.)

Typically, however, you'll manually specify sound sources as shown in Listing 9.18. Here we've created a sound emitter that is associated with an Audio-Clip, through which a WAV file is specified. In cases where no source is specified (or the source can't be located), the Sound node will not emit sound.

Much like a real-world stereo speaker, sound emitters are positioned at an exact 3D point in a VRML scene. This point is specified through the Sound node's *location* field. As an SFVec3f data type, the *location* field accepts three floating-point numbers that correspond to the X Y Z axes. Together, the X Y Z values supplied to *location* comprise a 3D coordinate in the local coordinate system (see Chapter 7, "Customizing Location, Size, and Orientation," for details on specifying 3D coordinates). In cases where *location* isn't specified, the emitter is placed at the origin (0 0 0) of the Sound node's local coordinate system by default.

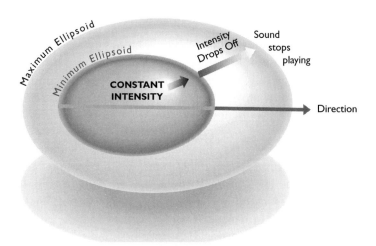

Figure 9-27   The Sound node specifies a sound emitter that emits sound in an elliptical pattern as defined by two ellipsoids. The inner *minimum ellipsoid* defines an area in which the sound plays at full volume, while the outer *maximum ellipsoid* defines a perimeter outside of which no sound can be heard. Sound volume drops off as the user moves from the inner minimum ellipsoid toward the edge of the outer maximum ellipsoid.

In addition to having a location in 3D space, sound emitters can also be aimed in a specific direction. The Sound node's *direction* field specifies the aim direction for an emitter, which is similar in nature to specifying the direction in which a light shines (see "DirectionalLight"). Like the *location* field, *direction* is an SFVec3f data type that accepts three floating-point numbers that together specify a 3D coordinate. An imaginary line is drawn from the origin of the coordinate system to this point, the direction of which determines the direction that the sound emitter is aimed. By default, sound emitters are aimed along the positive Z axis.

The *intensity* field controls the volume at which a sound plays. This field accepts a floating-point number in the range of 0.0 to 1.0, where 1.0 represents full volume and 0.0 means that the sound is silent. Sounds are played at full volume unless you specify otherwise.

By default, the Sound node creates spatialized sounds. However, you can set the boolean *spatialize* field to FALSE in cases where you'd like to create ambient sounds, as we've done in Listing 9.18. In this example we've created an ambient sound that plays at a continuous volume regardless of the user's location; by setting the minimum ellipsoid and maximum ellipsoid to the same size we've ensured that the sound won't be attenuated as the user moves about the scene. In addition, these are extremely large ellipsoids that

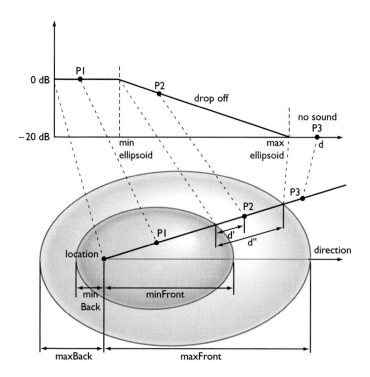

Figure 9-28 Sound is ramped in volume from 0 dB at the minimum ellipsoid to -20 dB at the maximum ellipsoid according to the linear attenuation calculation **attenuation = -20 × (d' / d")**, where **d'** is the distance along the location-to-viewer vector, measured from the transformed minimum ellipsoid boundary to the viewer, and **d"** is the distance along the location-to-viewer vector from the transformed minimum ellipsoid boundary to the transformed maximum ellipsoid boundary.

extend 5000 meters before and after the sound emitter. As a result, this sound can be heard as long as the user stays within 5000 meters of the coordinate-system origin (0 0 0) that this sound emitter is built around by default. Although this sound emitter is positioned at the origin along with the box shape that it is grouped with, the ambient sound seems to emit from everywhere.

Listing 9.19, in contrast, creates a spatialized sound that really seems to come from the center of the box. The sound emitter in this example is also built around the coordinate-system origin (0 0 0) because we didn't bother to set the *location* field. In this case, however, spatialization isn't disabled as it is in Listing 9.18. In addition, we actually created a minimum ellipsoid and maximum ellipsoid of different sizes, meaning that the volume will ramp accordingly as the user moves between these two areas. Finally, this sound emitter is aimed along the positive X axis, overriding the default aim direction supplied by the Sound node.

Listing 9.18   ambientSound.wrl

```
#VRML V2.0 utf8

Group {
  children [

    Sound {
      source AudioClip {
        url "wind.wav"
        loop TRUE
      }
      spatialize FALSE
      minFront 5000
      minBack  5000
      maxFront 5000
      maxBack  5000
    }

    Shape {
      appearance Appearance {
        material Material { }
      }
      geometry Box { }
    }
  ]
}
```

Listing 9.19   spatializedSound.wrl

```
#VRML V2.0 utf8

Group {
  children [

    Sound {
      source AudioClip {
        url "chime.mid"
        loop TRUE
      }
```

```
      minFront 10
      minBack  10
      maxFront 20
      maxBack  20
      direction 1 0 0   # aim along X axis
    }


    Shape {
      appearance Appearance {
        material Material { }
      }
      geometry Box { }
    }
  ]

}
```

Sound Precedence and Performance

The Sound node's *priority* field can be used to prioritize sounds in cases where you place more than one sound emitter in a scene. The *priority* field is a floating-point number that can range in value from 0.0 to 1.0, where 0.0 is the lowest priority and 1.0 is the highest. VRML browsers use this information to determine which sounds to play, when more exist than the underlying hardware can support.

Although sound prioritization is useful, you should avoid the potential for system overload well in advance of deploying your worlds on the Web. First and foremost, you should make judicious use of sound sources, limiting the number that will play at any given time to only one or two if possible. You should also be careful to limit the number and size of MPEG-1 and WAV sounds that you use, as these forms of audio are particularly demanding. MIDI files, in contrast, require less horsepower to play and are also very small (consuming less disk space and bandwidth) and should therefore be used instead of MPEG-1 and WAV sounds whenever possible.

AudioClip Node

The AudioClip node specifies a sound source that can be associated with a Sound node (by setting AudioClip as the Sound node *source*; see above). The VRML97 specification calls for VRML browsers to support both WAV and

MIDI file formats through the AudioClip node, although many browsers also support additional sound formats not required by the specification. Following is the formal definition of the AudioClip node. (The *description* field specifies a text description for an audio source. Browsers can display this information to the user, although they are not required to do so.)

```
AudioClip {
  exposedField    SFString description      " "
  exposedField    SFBool    loop            FALSE
  exposedField    SFFloat   pitch           1.0       # (0,∞)
  exposedField    SFTime    startTime       0         # (−∞,∞)
  exposedField    SFTime    stopTime        0         # (−∞,∞)
  exposedField    MFString url              []
  eventOut        SFTime    duration_changed
  eventOut        SFBool    isActive
}
```

The exposed *url* field is used to specify a sound source file, as shown in Listings 9.18, 9.19 and 9.20. The AudioClip *url* field, like all VRML *url* fields, is an MFString datatype, meaning that you can supply more than one URL to this field. Multiple URL strings are prioritized from high to low in the order you list them. The VRML browser will use the first sound file it can resolve, starting with the first one listed. If a URL can't be resolved, or the file it points to isn't a valid sound source, the browser attempts to load the next one in the list. This process is repeated until a sound file is resolved, or the list is exhausted (no sound is emitted if a sound file can't be resolved). For more details on multiple URLs see the texture discussion in Chapter 8, "Customizing Color and Texture."

Upon loading a sound file, the VRML browser determines its duration. The sound's duration—as measured in seconds—is output to the *duration _changed* eventOut. The value of *duration_changed* is independent of the playback rate specified by the *pitch* field. The exposed *pitch* field is used to control the playback pitch and rate of a sound, which is played at a normal pitch and rate (1.0) by default. *Pitch* values between 0.0 and 1.0 slow the playback rate of the sound, while values higher than 1.0 increase pitch and rate of play. A pitch setting of 2.0, for example, results in a sound that is one octave higher and two times faster than normal. In cases where the sound's duration can't be calculated, *duration_changed* is set to –1.

By default, sounds are not played until their *startTime* is reached, at which point they become active. When a sound becomes active the boolean value TRUE is sent through the *isActive* eventOut and the sound begins playing. The sound will play until its *stopTime* is reached, or until the end of the sound is reached (whichever comes first). Setting the exposed boolean *loop* field to TRUE, however, will repeat the sound indefinitely until its *stopTime* value is reached. In cases where *startTime* is later than *stopTime*, *stopTime* is ignored and the sound will loop forever. When a sound stops playing, the boolean value FALSE is sent through the *isActive* eventOut.

Listing 9.20 uses a TouchSensor to trigger a spatialized sound that loops indefinitely when played. Here a TouchSensor is defined alongside a box shape. When the box is clicked, the sensor's *touchTime* is routed to the AudioClip node's implicit *set_startTime* field (see Chapter 5, "VRML Fundamentals," to learn more about event routing).

Listing 9.21, meanwhile, uses a TimeSensor to play a sound every five seconds. This is achieved by routing the sensor's *cycleTime* eventOut value to the AudioClip node's implicit *set_startTime* field (a TimeSensor node's *cycleTime* time event is generated with each cycle of the sensor, as specified in seconds by the *cycleInterval* field). By setting the node's *loop* field to FALSE, this AudioClip will play only once each time it is trigged by the sensor. We could just as easily have omitted this field altogether for the same effect, because *loop* is set to FALSE by default.

Listing 9.20 TouchSensorSound.wrl

```
#VRML V2.0 utf8

Group {
  children [

    Sound {
      source DEF CHIME AudioClip {
        url "chime.wav"
        loop FALSE
      }
      minFront 10
      minBack  10
      maxFront 20
      maxBack  20
    }

    Shape {
      appearance Appearance {
        material Material { }
      }
      geometry Box { }
    }
    DEF CLICK TouchSensor { }
  ]
```

```
}

ROUTE CLICK.touchTime TO CHIME.set_startTime
```

Listing 9.21   TimeSensorSound.wrl

```
#VRML V2.0 utf8

Group {
  children [

    Sound {
      source DEF CHIME AudioClip {
        url "chime.wav"
        loop FALSE
      }
      minFront 10
      minBack  10
      maxFront 20
      maxBack  20
    }

    Shape {
      appearance Appearance {
        material Material { }
      }
      geometry Box { }
    }

    DEF TIME TimeSensor {
      loop   TRUE
      cycleInterval 5    # REPEAT EVERY 5 SECONDS
    }
  ]
}
ROUTE TIME.cycleTime TO CHIME.set_startTime
```

MovieTexture Node

The MovieTexture node, as you may recall from Chapter 8, "Customizing Color and Texture," is typically used to create animated texture maps from MPEG-1 Systems movies. This node, however, can also act as a sound source, as illustrated in Listing 9.22. This is particularly helpful when you wish to synchronize the movement of a texture map with audio.

A 3D waterfall, for example, might be created by texture mapping an MPEG movie of water to an arched shape. The sound of rushing water contained in the movie file can be associated with the animated shape by simply using the MovieTexture node as the source of a sound emitter. Similarly, a virtual television can easily be created by texture mapping an MPEG movie onto a box shape as shown in Listing 9.22. In this example the movie sound is associated with a sound emitter positioned inside the box. The movie texture starts playing on the surface of the shape when the user clicks on the box, at which point the sound it contains also begins to play.

Following is the VRML97 specification definition for MovieTexture. For details on each field refer to Chapter 8, "Customizing Color and Texture":

```
MovieTexture {
    exposedField SFBool    loop           FALSE
    exposedField SFFloat   speed          1.0      # (-∞,∞)
    exposedField SFTime    startTime      0        # (-∞,∞)
    exposedField SFTime    stopTime       0        # (-∞,∞)
    exposedField MFString  url            []
    field        SFBool    repeatS        TRUE
    field        SFBool    repeatT        TRUE
```

Time-Dependent Nodes

AudioClip, MovieTexture, and TimeSensor are time-dependent nodes that activate and deactivate themselves at specified times. Each of these nodes contains *startTime, stopTime,* and *loop* exposed fields as well as the *isActive* eventOut. The exposedField values are used to determine when the node becomes active or inactive.

Time-dependent nodes can execute for 0 or more cycles. A cycle is defined by field data within the node. If, at the end of a cycle, the value of *loop* is FALSE, execution is terminated. Conversely, if *loop* is TRUE at the end of a cycle, a time-dependent node continues execution into the next cycle. A time-dependent node with *loop*-TRUE at the end of every cycle continues cycling forever if **startTime >= stopTime**, or until **stopTime**, assuming that **startTime < stopTime**. Refer to section 4.6.9 of the VRML97 specification ("Time-dependent nodes") for more details.

```
    eventOut      SFTime    duration_changed
    eventOut      SFBool    isActive
}
```

Listing 9.22   MovieTextureSound.wrl

```
#VRML V2.0 utf8

Group {
  children [
    Shape {
      appearance  Appearance {
        material Material { }
        texture DEF MOVIE MovieTexture {
          url "movie.mpg"
        }
      }
      geometry Box { }
    }

    Sound {
      source USE MOVIE
        minFront 10
        minBack  10
        maxFront 20
        maxBack  20
    }

    DEF CLICK TouchSensor { }
  ]
}

ROUTE CLICK.touchTime TO MOVIE.set_startTime
```

Summary

VRML supports three light nodes in addition to the default headlight provided by VRML browsers. By placing DirectionalLight, PointLight, and SpotLight nodes in your scenes you can create a wide range of lighting effects for your worlds. By default, these nodes generate white light, although you can shine any RGB color through them.

Using the Background node, you can create sky and ground colors for your world, as well as panoramic background images. Conceptually, VRML backgrounds (sky, ground, and panoramic backgrounds) can be thought of as a box sitting inside two spheres. The box, upon each face of which a different image may be placed, represents the panoramic background. Outside the box is the ground sphere, which is a half-sphere that surrounds the bottom of the box. The sky sphere, in turn, encloses both the partial ground sphere and the background box inside it.

The Fog node allows you to add the atmospheric effect of fog, or haze, to a scene. Using the various fields of this node you can specify the color, type, and thickness of fog. As in the real world, objects in the distance are obscured by fog, making them more difficult to see. By setting the visibility range of the Fog node you can control to what extent objects in the distance are affected by this artificial atmosphere.

Sounds are created in VRML by combining a sound emitter with a sound source. The Sound node creates a sound emitter that can be positioned at a specific location in a scene and aimed in a certain direction. Using the AudioClip or MovieTexture nodes you can specify waveform (WAV), Musical Instrument Digital Interface (MIDI), or MPEG-1 Systems sound sources to play through an emitter. WAV and MIDI files are specified with the AudioClip node, while MPEG sound sources are created using the MovieTexture node.

Following is a complete list of URLs referenced in this chapter:

Web3D Gallery VRML Backgrounds   http://www.web3dgallery.com/vrml/background/

Universal Media   http://www.web3d.org/WorkingGroups/media/

Web3D Gallery Textures   http://www.web3dgallery.com/textures/

SkyPaint   http://www.skypaint.com/

Web3D Gallery VRML Tools   http://www.web3dgallery.com/vrml/tools/

Web3D Gallery VRML Fog   http://www.web3dgallery.com/vrml/fog/

Web3D Gallery Sounds   http://www.web3dgallery.com/sounds/

Real Audio and Video   http://www.real.com/

ParallelGraphics Cortona   http://www.parallelgraphics.com/

CREATING NEW VRML WORLDS

Topics in This Chapter

- Creating new VRML worlds using inlined content and prototypes
- Using visual development tools to create custom content

Chapter 10

Although previous chapters have focused on customizing existing VRML worlds that you've either purchased, downloaded from the Web for free, or convinced someone to create for you, in time you'll eventually want to create your own worlds. In this chapter you'll learn how to take advantage of VRML's composition feature, specifically the Inline node, with which you can craft extremely impressive worlds using predefined objects that reside in their own files. In addition, you'll learn about a variety of visual authoring tools that can make the job of assembling your own VRML worlds easier, as well as those that can help you create your own objects from scratch without the headache of sophisticated coding.

Inlining Files

As you may recall from Chapter 2, "Overview of Web3D," one of the major design features of VRML 2.0 (and consequently VRML97) is *composability*, which allows the various objects and scenes that a world is comprised of to be created independently of each other and stored in their own files. A circus scene created in VRML, for instance, might ultimately be made up of a vari-

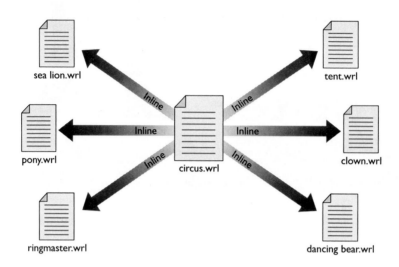

Figure 10-1 VRML's Inline node allows content to be created and stored independently of the worlds in which it appears.

ety of different objects, such as a big-top tent, clowns, fire eaters and sword swallowers, ringmasters, and various performing animals including dancing bears, one-trick ponies, and perhaps even aquatic acts such as beach-ball-balancing sea lions and dolphins. Although these objects could all be defined within a single VRML file, they can, instead, be created and stored independent of each other yet assembled together for the final circus scene, thanks to composability (see Figure 10-1).

To facilitate composability, VRML offers the Inline node whose definition follows:

```
Inline {
  exposedField MFString url        []
  field        SFVec3f  bboxCenter 0 0 0       # (-∞,∞)
  field        SFVec3f  bboxSize   -1 -1 -1    # (0, ∞) or -1,-1,-1
}
```

Using the Inline node, you can weave external VRML files into your own VRML file, a process that is commonly known as *inlining*. Each of the circus objects we've just described, for example, can reside in its own file yet be in-lined directly into your own VRML world with only a few lines of code. Using the Inline *url* field, you merely specify the URL address of an existing

Changing URLs

The Inline node's *url* field is an exposed field, meaning that you can change its value by sending a new URL to the implied *set_url* eventIn, which will result in a corresponding *url_changed* eventOut being generated (see Chapter 5, "VRML Fundamentals," to learn more about events and event routing). The original inlined content will then be replaced by the content pointed to by the new URL (any Script nodes contained in the original inline content will be terminated before the new content is loaded).

VRML file. (That file, in turn, must contain nodes or prototypes that can be treated as children; the Inline node is a grouping node, and the content it pulls into your file is considered a child of the node.) The file pointed to by the *url* field will be fetched by the VRML browser and placed directly into your scene as if you'd actually typed the source code it contains directly into the body of your own file.

In fact, the *url* field is the only one of the three Inline node fields that you must actually supply. If you don't supply a URL to this field, the node will be ignored and nothing will be inlined. (Because the *url* field is an MFString data type, you can supply more than one URL as described in the sidebar "Multiple URLs.") The *bboxCenter* and *bboxSize* fields are not required, however, as they're only used to give the browser hints about the size and position of inlined content, although they're particularly helpful when you want to inline large files that might take a good deal of time to download over the network.

The *bboxSize* field gives the browser an idea of how much 3D space the inlined content will consume, while the *bboxCenter* field tells the browser where the inlined file will appear, once loaded. Specifically, the *bboxSize* and *bboxCenter* fields describe an imaginary bounding box in which the children of the inlined file will fit. The browser can use this information to give the user visual clues about the content being loaded and also to optimize rendering (see "Bounding Boxes").

In the previous chapter you saw a very simplistic use of the Inline node, where a series of sphere shapes was defined in a VRML file called

Multiple URLs

All URL fields in VRML are multivalue, meaning that you can supply more than one absolute or relative Uniform Resource Locator (URL) to these fields. The order in which you supply the URLs determines their priority (the first URL has the highest priority and the last has the lowest priority, while those in between are prioritized accordingly). VRML browsers typically attempt to load URLs in order, starting with the highest-priority one and skipping over those that can't be resolved or that point to unsupported file formats. You may recall that this is the case when it comes to the *url* field of the ImageTexture and MovieTexture nodes, as Chapter 8, "Customizing Color and Texture," explains.

In the case of the Inline node, however, VRML browsers are free to first fetch a lower-priority URL in order to display content to the user immediately while a higher-priority URL continues to load. This assumes, of course, that the highest-priority URL is more time consuming to load than those of lower priority. To continue the circus analogy, the highest-priority URL used in an Inline node might point to a very detailed and richly textured clown, which would take more time to load than a nontextured clown created using only primitive shapes.

Similarly, a browser might first try to load a file URL (file://) that points to a clown stored on the user's hard drive, which could be replaced with a more detailed online version once downloaded. It should be noted, however, that such capabilities are entirely up the browser and aren't defined by the VRML97 specification.

To learn more about supplying multiple URLs to fields such as the Inline node's *url* field, see the texture-mapping discussion in Chapter 8, "Customizing Color and Texture."

sphereColumns.wrl (see Listing 10-3). Because the sphereColumns.wrl file contains valid VRML code, it can be viewed on its own or inlined into other VRML files. To inline this file you can merely add a corresponding Inline node to the top level of your own VRML file, as seen in Listing 10.1.

Alternately, you can place the Inline node inside another grouping node, such as a Transform or Group node, in which case the inlined content becomes a child of that grouping node. In Listing 10.2, for example, we've in-

Bounding Boxes

A number of VRML grouping nodes, including Inline, have *bboxSize* and *bboxCenter* fields that can be used to construct an imaginary bounding box to give the browser hints about the size and location of the children that such nodes contain. The *bboxSize* field defines the size of the bounding box in terms of X, Y, and Z dimensions, while the *bboxCenter* field specifies the center point of the shape in 3D space. Because VRML browsers can compute their own bounding boxes, however, you don't need to supply values for these fields unless they're readily available. (It's tedious and time consuming to manually calculate bounding-box values for complicated worlds; this task is best left to VRML development tools). Consider, however, how a browser might use bounding box information for an Inline node, should you actually set these fields.

Using information supplied by an Inline node's *bboxSize* and *bboxCenter* fields, a browser might draw a simple placeholder 3D box in the location where the inlined content will ultimately appear, giving the user a sense of the world's general structure as the content downloads. This technique is similar in concept to the placeholder rectangle that Web browsers often draw when loading GIF or JPEG images whose width and height is known in advance.

Due to the nature of 3D content it's also possible that one object might be obscured by another (the circus clown might be initially hidden by an elephant, for example, or the clown might even be outside the initial viewpoint when the world is first loaded). In such cases, the *bboxCenter* and *bboxSize* fields can actually provide the browser with valuable placement data, allowing it to defer loading obscured objects until they are actually in view (once the elephant moves, for example, or the user navigates to the part of the world in which the clown resides).

lined the spheres into a top-level Group node, alongside which we also placed a directional light source. Because the inlined spheres are considered children of the Group node, these shapes are illuminated by light cast from the DirectionalLight node (the DirectionalLight node typically illuminates objects that are in its parent node, as these spheres now are; see Chapter 9, "Customizing Light, Background, Fog, and Sound," for details).

Listing 10.1   Inline.wrl

```
#VRML V2.0 utf8

NavigationInfo {
  headlight TRUE
}

Inline {
  url "sphereColumns.wrl"
}
```

Listing 10.2   InlineGroup.wrl

```
#VRML V2.0 utf8

NavigationInfo {
  headlight FALSE
}

Group {
  children [
    DirectionalLight {}

  Inline {
    url "sphereColumns.wrl"
  }
 ]
}
```

Listing 10.3   sphereColumns.wrl

```
#VRML V2.0 utf8

DEF SphereColumn Group {
  children [
    DEF OneSphere Shape {
      appearance Appearance {
        material Material {}
      }
```

```
        geometry Sphere {radius .75}
    }
    Transform { translation 0 6 0 children USE OneSphere }
    Transform { translation 0 4 0 children USE OneSphere }
    Transform { translation 0 2 0 children USE OneSphere }
    Transform { translation 0 -2 0 children USE OneSphere }
    Transform { translation 0 -4 0 children USE OneSphere }
    Transform { translation 0 -6 0 children USE OneSphere }
  ]
}

Transform { translation -6 0 0 children USE SphereColumn }
Transform { translation -4 0 0 children USE SphereColumn }
Transform { translation -2 0 0 children USE SphereColumn }
Transform { translation 2 0 0 children USE SphereColumn }
Transform { translation 4 0 0 children USE SphereColumn }
Transform { translation 4 0 0 children USE SphereColumn }
Transform { translation 6 0 0 children USE SphereColumn }
```

The codings in Listings 10.1, 10.2, and 10.3 are trivial examples of inlining, however, as most of the files that you'll inline will likely contain content that must be translated into the coordinate system of your own VRML file. In other words, the predefined size and orientation of inlined content isn't always appropriate for your own VRML worlds, nor is the default location at which such content is placed (the origin at 0 0 0). The whole idea behind composition is to allow objects to be crafted independently of any particular VRML world, which allows a single VRML file to be inlined into a variety of different scenes. A dancing bear, for instance, could appear just as easily in a circus scene as in a petting zoo. Likewise a clown might appear at a birthday party, the circus, or a Mardi Gras parade, while a dolphin could be found in the ocean or at Sea World.

In each case the inlined objects will need to be sized, oriented, and positioned with respect to the worlds in which they're included, a process that requires the Transform grouping node that you learned about in great detail in Chapter 7, "Customizing Location, Size, and Orientation." Technically speaking, you must perform mathematical translations on the coordinate system of the inlined content relative to the coordinate system in which it is placed. Fortunately, this isn't difficult at all (assuming that you've already read Chapter 7 and as a result are comfortable with the inner workings of the Transform node).

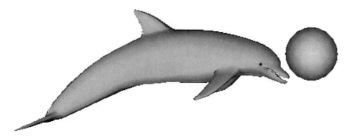

Figure 10-2   This inlined dolphin is treated as a child of the Transform node, through which its location, orientation, and size are altered in order to make it look as if the mammal is playing with the sphere defined in the inlining world.

Listing 10.4 illustrates the use of the Transform node in combination with inlined content, complete with bounding-box settings for good measure (in later examples we'll omit the bounding-box fields altogether, forcing the browser to calculate these fields for itself). As you can see, a VRML file named dolphin.wrl is inlined into a world in which a primitive sphere shape has also been defined. By placing the Inline node inside the Transform node we're now able to move, orient, and change the size of the dolphin in such a way that it appears to be playing with the sphere, as seen in Figure 10-2. However, if we had simply inlined this dolphin into the world without the assistance of a Transform node, as shown in Listing 10.5, the mammal would have appeared too small and in the wrong orientation and location, as seen in Figure 10-3.

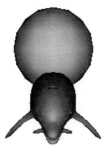

Figure 10-3   Because it has not been inlined in a Transform node in this example, the dolphin is now thrust into the scene at the origin of the world (0 0 0) by default, where it overlaps with the sphere. The dolphin is also too small and not oriented properly.

Listing 10.4   dolphinBall.wrl

```
#VRML V2.0 utf8

Background {
  skyColor 1 1 1
}

NavigationInfo {
  headlight TRUE
}

Shape {
  appearance Appearance {
    material Material {}
  }
  geometry Sphere {}
}

Transform {
  translation -4.5 1.5 0      # move
  rotation 0 1 0 1.571        # reorient
  scale 1.5 1.5 1.5           # grow
  children [
      Inline {
        url "dolphin.wrl"
        bboxSize 6 3 3
        bboxCenter -2.25 .75 0
      }
  ]
}
```

Listing 10.5   dolphinBallNoTranslate.wrl

```
#VRML V2.0 utf8

Background {
  skyColor 1 1 1
}

NavigationInfo {
  headlight TRUE
}
```

```
Shape {
  appearance Appearance {
    material Material {}
  }
  geometry Sphere {}
}

Inline {
  url "dolphin.wrl"
}
```

Nested Inlining

Often, the worlds that you create using inlined content will consist of more than one externally defined object, in which case you'll need to include multiple Tranform nodes (one for each inlined file). However, you'll also find that the worlds that you create in this way are, in fact, worth treating as inlined content themselves. Indeed, VRML files that contain Inline nodes can be inlined by other files, creating a nesting of inlined nodes, as Listing 10.6 illustrates.

In this example the dolphinBall.wrl file created earlier in Listing 10.4 is inlined, meaning that the dolphin and ball are placed into the new world together. To round the scene out we've also inlined an animated clown character (what a strange little circus we now have!), which had to be scaled down a great deal, because this fellow was very large as defined in the clown.wrl file. The result, seen in Figure 10-4, is visually impressive, considering that the only object coded manually was the primitive sphere; thanks to inlined content we've created a compelling scene with very little effort.

Listing 10.6   circus.wrl

```
#VRML V2.0 utf8

Background {
  skyColor 1 1 1
}

Transform {
  translation 1 0 0      # move 1 unit along the +X axis
  scale .75 .75 .75      # scale to 2/3rds normal size
  children [
    Inline {
```

Figure 10-4 Files containing inlined content can themselves be inlined into other worlds. The dolphin and ball in this example were inlined as a single file. The animated clown, meanwhile, is inlined from its own file (http://www.parallelgraphics.com/).

```
        url "dolphinBall.wrl"
      }
  ]
}

Transform {
  translation 4 0 0      # move 4 units along the +X axis
  scale .07 .07 .07      # scale to fraction of normal size
  rotation 0 1 0 -.785   # rotate -45 degrees on Y axis
  children [
    Inline {
      url "clown.wrl"
    }
  ]
}
```

Electronics Showroom

Although the previous examples of inlining are sufficient to give you an understanding of how the Inline node works, you probably aren't in desperate need of a 3D circus for your Web site. In order to convey the full sense of power that inlining can give you in a real-world setting, consider Listing 10.7.

With less than five pages of VRML code we've created a 3D electronics show-room featuring a laptop computer, a digital camcorder, and a palmtop by in-lining these models directly from their home on the Web (see Figure 10-5).

Each model was created by a different vendor, yet we were able to quickly stitch them together into a complete scene using the Inline node in combina-tion with a variety of nodes you've learned about in previous chapters. Of par-ticular note are the camcorder and palmtop models, which are fully interactive product-visualization demos. The camcorder, for example, can be powered on and off, and features a swing-out eyepiece and preview window along with cor-responding zoom controls that users can manipulate using their mouse. The palmtop, meanwhile, features a flip-top screen that can be opened or closed. When opened, a stylus is revealed. Clicking on the stylus triggers an animation that illustrates this product's handwriting-recognition capabilities.

By placing each inlined model in its own Transform node we were able to move, scale, and rotate them to construct the world seen in Figure 10-6. The Text node was used to create a brief description for each product, each of which is the child of a Transform node in order to position descriptions di-rectly below their corresponding model. To facilitate the purchase process, each text description is also wrapped inside an Anchor node. When a text de-scription is clicked, the user is taken directly to the vendor that created the model (in an actual commerce system such a link would take the user to a purchase form or more information about the product).

Warning: Breaking the Law

Before using precreated content in your VRML worlds, you should first ob-tain permission from the company or individual that actually owns it. Unless you've purchased or licensed a piece of content, or the owner has explicitly identified it as being "free for use," it's safe to assume that any piece of precreated content you come across is protected by copyright laws. Not only is it unethical to use content without permission, it's probably illegal in most cases.

To get your hands on freely available VRML content, visit the VRML Repository at http://www.web3d.org/vrml/. Hosted by the Web3D Consor-tium, the VRML Repository contains links to a wealth of freely available ob-jects, textures, sounds, and entire worlds, as well as a bounty of links to free and low-cost VRML development tools.

Figure 10-5 Each of these three models was created by a different vendor, and they reside on different Web servers. Using the Inline node, however, they're easily composed into the same scene.

DirectionalLight nodes are set to shine colored light on the text whenever the mouse is moved over the description, alerting the user that a hyperlink lurks beneath each product description. This is accomplished by defining both a TouchSensor node and DirectionalLight node alongside each Text node, making each product description and its associated sensor and light a child of the same Anchor node.

Rather than duplicate the text-appearance and font-style code for each description, the DEF/USE mechanism is called into action. The first time text-appearance and font-style nodes are specified (in the Laptop text

Figure 10-6 The fully composed electronics showroom scene as seen from the entry viewpoint.

Laptop
366MHz
64MB RAM
4GB HD
Click to Buy!

Camcorder
Digital
Flip lens
Click to Buy!

Palmtop
Ultra thin
Durable
Click to Buy!

description) they are assigned unique names using DEF. The text appearance is defined as TEXT_APPEARANCE, while the text font style is defined as TEXT_STYLE. Later, text appearance and style are reused by referencing these nodes by name. As a result, the source code is more compact (and the world more efficient) than it would be if we had defined a new appearance and style for each text shape.

Using the Viewpoint node we've given the user the ability to quickly and easily examine each product up close. In addition, we've created a default entry viewpoint that displays all three models at a distance of ten meters forward on the Z axis when the world is first loaded (see Figure 10-6). Because each inlined file can contain its own viewpoints, there are actually twelve viewpoints available to the end user (the four we've defined, plus those defined in the inlined models).

Finally, we've used the Background node to set the sky color of this world to solid white, allowing each product and its corresponding text description to be easily seen by the user. In addition, we've added a WorldInfo node that briefly describes the world and gives it a name ("Electronics Showroom").

Listing 10.7   electronicsShowroom.wrl

```
#VRML V2.0 utf8

WorldInfo {
   info   [
       "Copyright (c) 2000, All Rights Reserved",
       "An electronics showroom created using",
       "inlined VRML content. Models courtesy",
       "of MetaCreations, Cybelius, and ParallelGraphics",
   ]
   title "Electronics Showroom"
}

Background {
   skyColor 1 1 1
}

Viewpoint {
   position 0 0 10
   description "Default View"
}
```

```
# LAPTOP MODEL
# Model courtesy of MetaCreations
# Created with MetaCreations Conoma
# http://www.canoma.com/


Transform {
  translation -2 .5 0     # move down X and up Y
  scale .5 .5 .5          # reduce model size by half
  rotation 0 1 0  -.785   # rotate on Y to face viewer

  children [
     Inline {
       url "http://www.canoma.com/vrml/mac/scene.wrl"
     }
   ]
}

# LAPTOP TEXT

Transform {
  translation -4 0 4      # move down X and forward on Z

  children [
     Anchor {
       url "http://www.canoma.com/"
       description "Conoma home page"

       children [
         Shape {
           appearance DEF TEXT_APPEARANCE Appearance {
             material Material {
               diffuseColor .65 .65 .65  # gray
             }
           }
           geometry Text {
             fontStyle DEF TEXT_STYLE FontStyle {
               style "BOLD"
               size .35
             }
             string ["Laptop", "366MHz", "64MB RAM",
                     "4GB HD", "Click to Buy!"]
           }
         }
       }
```

```
        Viewpoint {
          position .9 .75 2
          description "Laptop"
        }

        DEF TS_LAPTOP TouchSensor { }     # sensor

        DEF DL_LAPTOP DirectionalLight { # light
          color 1 0 0   # shine red light when "on"
          on FALSE      # turn "on" only when touched
        }
      ]
    }
  ]
}




# CAMCORDER MODEL
# Model courtesy of Cybelius
# http://www.cybelius.com/

Transform {
  translation 0 .75 3.5  # move up Y and forward on Z
  scale .5 .5 .5         # reduce model size by half
  rotation 0 1 0  -2     # rotate on Y to face viewer

  children [
    Inline {
     url "http://www.cybelius.com/wrlm/Camcorder/Camera_action2406.wrl"
    }
  ]
 }


# CAMCORDER TEXT

Transform {
  translation -1 0 4   # move down X and forward on Z

    children [
      Anchor {
        url "http://www.cybelius.com/"
        description "Cybelius home page"
```

```
      children [
        Shape {
          appearance USE TEXT_APPEARANCE  # reuse
          geometry Text {
            fontStyle USE TEXT_STYLE      # reuse
            string ["Camcorder", "Digital",
                    "Flip lens", "Click to Buy!"]
          }
        }

        Viewpoint {
          position .75 .75 2
          description "Camcorder"
        }

        DEF TS_CAMCORDER TouchSensor { }     # sensor

        DEF DL_CAMCORDER DirectionalLight { # light
          color 0 1 0    # shine green light when "on"
          on FALSE       # turn "on" only when touched
        }
      ]
    }
  ]
}



# PALMTOP MODEL
# Model courtesy of ParallelGraphics
# http://www.parallelgraphics.com/

Transform {
  translation 3 .5 3.5    # move up X and Y, forward on Z
  scale .005 .005 .005    # scale to fraction of normal size

  children [
    Inline {
     url "http://www.parallelgraphics.com/htm/en/demo/concept/clio/clio.wrl"
    }
  ]
}


# PALMTOP TEXT
```

```
Transform {
  translation 2 0 4    # move up X and forward on Z

     children [
       Anchor {
         url "http://www.parallelgraphics.com/"
         description "ParallelGraphics home page"

         children [
           Shape {
              appearance USE TEXT_APPEARANCE  # reuse
              geometry Text {
                fontStyle USE TEXT_STYLE       # reuse
                string ["Palmtop", "Ultra thin",
                        "Durable", "Click to Buy!"]
              }
            }

           Viewpoint {
             position 1.5 .75 2
             description "Palmtop"
           }

            DEF TS_PALMTOP TouchSensor { }     # sensor

            DEF DL_PALMTOP DirectionalLight { # light
              color 0 0 1    # shine blue light when "on"
              on FALSE       # turn "on" only when touched
            }
         ]
       }
     ]
}


# ROUTE TEXT TOUCH SENSORS TO DIRECTIONAL LIGHTS
# IN ORDER TO SHINE COLORED LIGHT ON TEXT WHEN
# USER MOVES MOUSE OVER IT

ROUTE TS_LAPTOP.isOver TO DL_LAPTOP.on
ROUTE TS_CAMCORDER.isOver TO DL_CAMCORDER.on
ROUTE TS_PALMTOP.isOver TO DL_PALMTOP.on
```

Prototypes

In addition to the more than 50 built-in nodes that VRML offers, developers are free to create their own custom nodes as well. Experienced VRML programmers can, in essence, extend the core capabilities of VRML by using the language's powerful PROTO mechanism (short for prototype). Through a corresponding EXTERNPROTO mechanism, which stands for external prototype, PROTO node definitions can reside in a file other than those in which they're actually used, allowing developers to create entire libraries of reusable custom nodes.

Prototypes are often used to construct reusable geometric shapes and models, interface elements (such as progress bars, sliders, buttons, dials, and toggle switches), animated objects, mathematical functions, custom appearances, and special effects (such as exploding objects). Because prototypes can be created using any number of VRML's built-in nodes, including Script nodes that contain programs written in languages such as Java and JavaScript, they can be quite sophisticated. A number of reusable prototype nodes are available on the Web, such as the freely available PROTO Repository (see "PROTO Repository"), which can save content authors a great deal of time and tedium when it comes to implementing advanced features in their VRML worlds.

PROTO

Prototypes are constructed using the PROTO mechanism, which is a special statement in VRML that has the following syntax:

PROTO Repository

The PROTO Repository (http://www.vrml-content.org/) is an online library of reusable, freely available prototypes. At the time of this writing nearly 150 nodes were available free of charge through the growing PROTO Repository. Links to the PROTO Repository and other prototype libraries can be found at the Web3D Gallery (http://www.web3dgallery.com/vrml/proto/).

```
PROTO NodeName [interface] {body}
```

Immediately following the PROTO keyword is the name of the new node being defined. Legal PROTO names begin with a letter and can include a combination of letters, numbers, and symbols. (PROTO names have the same naming restrictions as DEF names; see Appendix B, "VRML Resources," for details.) The node's interface appears within a pair of brackets ("[ ]") and consists of the publicly accessible fields and events that the node supports. It is here that the node's fields, exposed fields, eventIns, and eventOuts are defined. Following the interface is the node's body, where the real meat of the prototype is defined.

Although a comprehensive explanation of how to create PROTO nodes is beyond the scope of this book, you should, at the very least, understand how to take advantage of existing prototypes in your own worlds. Once a PROTO has been defined in a world, instances of that node can then be created in the world as if it were one of VRML's built-in nodes. Listing 10.8, for example, defines a new node type called "Saturn." This particular prototype is not complex by any stretch of the imagination, as it merely combines a primitive sphere and cylinder in order to create a shape that looks like a planet surrounded by a ring. It does, however, illustrate how new nodes are created and used in a scene (later you'll see how EXTERNPROTO allows you to use prototypes in any world, not just the one they are defined in).

Using Prototypes

The first node that appears in the body of a prototype determines where that prototype can be used. If, for example, the first node in a prototype is a Group node, the prototype itself can be used anywhere a Group node is legal. If the first node to appear in the body is a Font, however, the prototype can only be used wherever Font nodes can appear.

Fortunately, most prototypes that you'll find on the Web are typically accompanied by a summary of their capabilities that also describes where they can be used (they often come with at least a VRML sample world that shows the prototype in action as well). As a result you'll only have to peek at the body of prototypes when you're curious about how they're constructed or when (rarely) no documentation or sample code is provided (which means you must determine for yourself where the node may be used).

The Saturn prototype's interface consists of two SFColor fields, *planet-Color* and *ringColor*. The default color of *planetColor* is red, while *ringColor* defaults to yellow. Following the interface definition is the node's body. In this case the body is simply a Group node that contains a primitive sphere shape and a primitive cylinder shape, although real-world prototypes are generally much more complex (the body of a prototype can contain any VRML node, including sensors, routes, and even other PROTO nodes).

Within the Material node of each shape is a reference to IS, which is a special VRML keyword that is used to give the prototype node body access to the interface elements it defines. IS allows connections to be made between the fields found in a prototype body and those in its interface. In this case, the node body uses IS to set the material of each shape to its corresponding interface field. The sphere, which represents the planet, is colored using the prototype's *planetColor* field, while the thin cylinder that represents the ring surrounding the planet is colored with the *ringColor* field.

Once defined, instances of the Saturn node can then be created (in other words, the node can be used only after it is defined). Although PROTO definitions can appear anywhere in a VRML file, they are typically found at the very beginning, as seen in Listing 10.8. In this example a simple Background node follows the node definition, after which two different instances of Saturn are created. The first instance sets the *planetColor* field to green and the *ringColor* field to blue, overriding the prototype's default settings for these colors. The second instance, however, accepts the default colors. To prevent these two Saturn objects from overlapping on screen, the second instance is wrapped inside a Transform node and translated up the X axis and down the Y axis, positioning it below and to the right of the first instance, as seen in Figure 10-7.

Listing 10.8   saturnPROTO.wrl

```
#VRML V2.0 utf8

# Prototypes must first be defined before they can be used.
# Following is the prototype definition for a node named
# "Saturn"

PROTO Saturn [
  field SFColor planetColor   1 0 0   # default is red
  field SFColor ringColor     1 1 0   # default is yellow
] {
  Group {
    children [
```

```
      Shape {
        appearance Appearance {
          material Material {
            diffuseColor IS ringColor
          }
        }
        geometry Cylinder {
          height .5
          radius 3
        }
      }

      Shape {
        appearance Appearance {
          material Material {
            diffuseColor IS planetColor
          }
        }
        geometry Sphere {
          radius 2
        }
      }
    ]
  }
} # End of prototype definition
# The Saturn prototype has been defined above and can
# now be instantiated in this world. The planetColor and
# ringColor fields are public, and so these colors can
# be customized when the node is instanced.
#
# In this first instance below custom colors are set. The
# second instance uses default colors (the second instance
# is also translated to the right and below the first
# instance).

Background {
  skyColor 1 1 1   # white
}


Saturn {
  planetColor  0 1 0   # green planet
  ringColor    0 0 1   # blue rings
}
```

```
Transform {
  translation 4 -3 0
  scale .5 .5 .5

  children [
    Saturn {}   # default colors
  ]
}
```

EXTERNPROTO

Although the PROTO mechanism provides a convenient way for developers to extend the VRML language with custom nodes, it is most powerful when combined with the EXTERNPROTO statement. Whereas PROTO alone restricts access to the new node it defines from within the world in which the node definition appears, as illustrated earlier in Listing 10.8, EXTERNPROTO allows *any* VRML world to tap into a prototype, regardless of where the PROTO definition actually exists. Because it gives VRML files access to externally defined PROTO nodes, EXTERNPROTO is conceptually similar to Java's import statement or the include feature of C and C++.

Figure 10-7 A prototype node called "Saturn" defines the planetlike shapes appearing in this world.

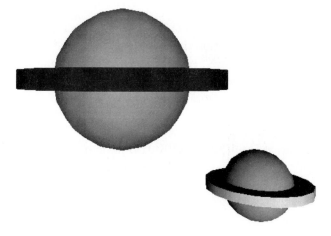

Following is the EXTERNPROTO statement syntax, which is used to create a new node type based on a PROTO definition that resides in a file other than the world you'd like to use it in:

```
EXTERNPROTO NodeName [interface] url [or urls]
```

The name of the new node comes immediately after the EXTERNPROTO, after which the node's interface appears in a pair of square brackets (i.e., the public fields, exposed fields, eventIns, and eventOuts defined in the PROTO interface). In this respect the EXTERNPROTO looks very similar to the PROTO definition, although the name you give an EXTERNPROTO need not be the same as that defined by the PROTO. In addition, you don't actually specify the default values for interface fields, only their class type, data type, and name as seen in Listing 10.9. In cases where a particular interface field isn't needed by your world, it may be omitted from the EXTERNPROTO interface altogether (in which case the omitted field isn't visible to your world; attempting to use a field that isn't listed in the EXTERNPROTO interface is illegal).

The world in Listing 10.9 uses the EXTERNPROTO statement to gain access to the Saturn prototype defined in the file named saturnPROTO.wrl. The Saturn prototype file, whose PROTO definition appears in Listing 10.8, is specified using a relative URL. In this particular case the PROTO definition file and the world in which it is used both reside in the same folder,

---

Naming EXTERNPROTO Nodes

Typically, nodes declared using EXTERNPROTO are given the same name as that of the PROTO node definition they reference. You're free, however, to assign a different name to EXTERNPROTO nodes as long as the name you choose doesn't conflict with VRML's built-in nodes or other prototype nodes defined in your world (the naming restrictions that apply to PROTO also apply to EXTERNPROTO; see "PROTO" for details).

You might, for example, create an EXTERNPROTO node named "Planet" based on the "Saturn" prototype node defined in Listing 10.8. As you'll see in Listing 10.9, however, we've elected to name EXTERNPROTO "Saturn" to maintain consistency with the "Saturn" PROTO node.

although in many cases the two may reside on separate Web servers altogether (in which case an absolute URL would be required).

Although we've supplied only one URL in this example, you can supply more than one, provided they're enclosed in a pair of square brackets. Like the *url* field of the ImageTexture and MovieTexture nodes, multiple EXTERNPROTO URLs are prioritized in the order supplied, from highest to lowest (see Chapter 8, "Customizing Color and Texture"). In such cases, the VRML browser will attempt to resolve the URLs in order, starting with the first one you supply. The browser will use the first URL that can be resolved, skipping over those that it can't resolve or that point to an invalid file.

If the browser is successful in resolving a URL, it then opens the file (if unsuccessful, the EXTERNPROTO is considered incomplete and is ignored as a result). The first PROTO definition listed in the file is associated with the EXTERNPROTO declaration, meaning the EXTERNPROTO implementation is fulfilled by the first PROTO definition that the browser can resolve based on the URL or group of URLs you supply. In cases where two or more PROTO definitions reside in the same file, you can specify the one you wish to use by appending a pound sign (#) and the PROTO name to the URL. To explicitly specify the Saturn prototype, for example, the following URL would be used:

```
saturnPROTO.wrl#Saturn
```

Because the saturnPROTO.wrl file contains only one PROTO definition, however, we didn't bother specifying the Saturn prototype by name in Listing 10.9. If you examine this code carefully, you'll notice that we used the EXTERNPROTO mechanism to construct a world identical to that created earlier in Listing 10.8. The difference, of course, is that the Saturn node is defined external to this world.

Listing 10.9   saturnEXTERNPROTO.wrl

```
#VRML V2.0 utf8

Background {
  skyColor 1 1 1
}


# Because the Saturn prototype resides in a file outside
# of the world, it must be made available to this world
# using the EXTERNPROTO mechanism.
```

```
# Once the prototype has been declared by the EXTERNPROTO
# statement, instances of it may be created.


EXTERNPROTO Saturn [
  field SFColor planetColor
  field SFColor ringColor
] "saturnPROTO.wrl"



Saturn {
  planetColor  0 1 0  # green planet
  ringColor    0 0 1  # blue rings
}


Transform {
  translation 4 -3 0
  scale .5 .5 .5

  children [
    Saturn {}    # default colors
  ]

}
```

Inlining Prototypes

Although PROTO definitions and EXTERNPROTO declarations can't be inlined directly into your worlds, as these structures merely define implementation and usage interfaces for new node types, VRML files that contain instances of prototypes are fair game. You could, for example, inline the VRML files created previously in Listings 10.8 and 10.9, because these files actually contain code that *uses* the Saturn prototype (specifically, two instances of the node are created in both listings as described in the previous sections).

Similarly, the VRML code that is found in Listing 10.10 actually creates an instance of an externally defined PROTO. In this case the PROTO definition is much more sophisticated than the Saturn prototype you've seen so far. Weighing in at 141K when uncompressed, and consuming over 40 pages of VRML code, the animated-dolphin prototype node defined in the file DolphinSrc.wrl is complicated and hefty, to say the least. Because the dolphin PROTO definition is so large, we won't include it here, although you're free to download it from the PROTO Repository (http://www.vrml-content.org/).

Created by Braden McDaniel, the dolphin node is a splendid prototype example. The complex IndexedFaceSet geometry of a dolphin instance is animated over time by routing a TimeSensor event to the node as illustrated in Listing 10.10. The dolphin prototype definition stored in the DolphinSrc.wrl file contains a CoordinateInterpolator node that responds to these events by dynamically altering the coordinates of the shape's IndexedFaceSet geometry, which in turn changes the onscreen appearance of the shape over time, as illustrated in Figure 10.8 (see "Animation" to learn more about VRML animation). By default, the dolphin detects collisions, although you're free to turn this feature off, as we've done in Listing 10.10 (see "Collision Detection").

Animation

VRML97 contains a number of built-in interpolator nodes designed specifically for keyframe animation (an interpolation is a mathematical calculation that estimates an unknown value falling somewhere between two known "key" values). TimeSensor nodes are typically used together with interpolators, allowing the start time, stop time, and speed of animation to be finely controlled (interpolator nodes define linear transformations, meaning that an equal amount of time is taken at each point between any two key values used in an animation).

The PositionInterpolator and OrientationInterpolator nodes, for example, can be used in combination with the TimeSensor node to alter the translation and rotation fields of a Transform node over time. Similarly, ColorInterpolator is used to animate colors, while NormalInterpolator is used to transform surface-normal vectors. ScalarInterpolator, meanwhile, is a general-purpose interpolator that generates floating-point values. To learn more about these nodes, see Appendix B, "VRML Resources."

Although hand-coding sophisticated interpolators isn't impossible, it can be difficult, time consuming, and very tedious. As such, animation is a task best left up to visual authoring tools, as described later in this chapter. If you'd like to learn more about hand-coding animation, however, you can always visit the Web3D Gallery (http://www.web3dgallery.com/vrml/animation/).

Figure 10-8   This dolphin instance is animated by a TimeSensor event that works in combination with a CoordinateInterpolator to alter the coordinates of the node's geometry over time.

Collision Detection

VRML's collision-detection capabilities sense when the viewer's avatar has collided with an object in a scene. Objects in a VRML world are "collidible" by default, meaning you can't walk through them, any more than you might walk through a solid object in the real world. Shapes that are the child of the Collision node, however, can be walked through, as long as that node's *collide* field is set to FALSE.

In addition to being able to disable collision detection for its children, the Collision node can also tell you when the viewer has collided with the shapes it contains (the time the collision occurs is sent to the *collideTime* eventOut in the form of an SFTime value). Collision detection is often used to trigger actions such as sound effects and animation. Colliding with a tree, for example, might cause it to topple over and fall to the ground in a thunderous crash.

See Appendix B, "VRML Resources" to learn more about the Collision node.

Listing 10.10   swimmingDolphin.wrl

```
#VRML V2.0 utf8

# Dolphin PROTO by Braden McDaniel. Freely
# available through the PROTO Repository at
# http://www.vrml-content.org/
```

```
Background {
  skyColor 1 1 1
}


# Cast a blue light on the dolphin
DirectionalLight {
  direction 0 -1 0
  color 0 0 1
}


# Define the external prototype
EXTERNPROTO Dolphin [
  eventIn        SFFloat    set_fraction
  exposedField SFBool     collide
  eventOut       SFTime     collideTime
] "DolphinSrc.wrl"


# Create an instance of the new node
DEF DOLPHIN Dolphin {
  collide FALSE
}

# Specify animation timing, and loop infinitely
DEF TS TimeSensor {
    cycleInterval 1
    loop TRUE
}

ROUTE TS.fraction_changed TO DOLPHIN.set_fraction
```

Although the dolphin PROTO definition itself can't be inlined directly into a world, you can always inline VRML files that contain instances of the prototype. Listing 10.11, for example, inlines the VRML file created in Listing 10.10. The animated dolphin now appears alongside a primitive sphere, courtesy of the Inline node (see Figure 10–9). Of course, we could have achieved the same end result by simply using EXTERNPROTO to bring the dolphin into the world containing the sphere shape. Inlining can be particularly useful, however, when many node instances (prototype or otherwise)

Figure 10-9   The animated dolphin prototype is inlined into a scene containing a primitive sphere.

already exist in an external file. Rather than recompose such complex scenes yourself, you can simply inline the content into your own world.

Listing 10.11   inlineProto.wrl

```
#VRML V2.0 utf8

# This world inlines the swimmingDolphin.wrl file,
# which contains an EXTERNPROTO reference to the
# dolphin PROTO.

Background {
  skyColor 1 1 1
}

NavigationInfo {
  headlight TRUE
}

Shape {
  appearance Appearance {
    material Material {}
  }
  geometry Sphere {}
}

Transform {
  translation -4 0 0
  scale 1.5 1.5 1.5
  children [
    Inline {
```

```
        url "swimmingDolphin.wrl"
      }
  ]
}
```

Inline Loading and Level of Detail (LOD)

VRML browsers often defer loading inlined files until such content actually comes into view of the user. Similarly, inlined files that are the children of LOD nodes may never get loaded. The LOD node is a grouping node used to construct objects with various "Levels of Detail," allowing the browser to load and display different versions of an object based on user proximity.

Typically, highly detailed objects need to be displayed only when the user is close enough to actually see such complexity, while less detailed versions of an object are sufficient when the user is further away. Using the LOD node, VRML developers can make efficient use of bandwidth and computing resources by displaying simpler versions of a model until the time comes when more complicated versions are required.

A car in the far distance, for example, might be adequately represented using a simple combination of primitive box and sphere shapes. When the user moves closer to the car, however, a more realistic version of the model can be loaded and displayed. Finally, a sophisticated and fully interactive model might be loaded when the user is in very close proximity to the car, allowing her to step in and take a spin.

See Appendix B, "VRML Resources" to learn more about the LOD node.

Visual Development Tools

Although the first generation of VRML worlds were entirely hand-coded by programmers, owing to the fact that very few authoring tools existed, much of today's most sophisticated and compelling VRML content is created visually using 3D authoring tools. In recent years VRML97 has become a widely accepted 3D-interchange format. As such, a wide range of traditional 3D authoring tools can import and export VRML files. In addition, a number of VRML-specific authoring tools are now available with which nonprogrammers can construct extremely complex worlds using little more than their mouse and imagination.

Some VRML development tools can be strictly categorized as *geometric modelers* or *behavior modelers*, while *world builders* usually offer modeling tools for both geometry and behaviors, as you'll soon see. In addition, a number of specialty authoring tools can't be neatly classified into one of these three categories. Data visualization tools, terrain generation utilities, avatar creators, and special effects authoring products, for example, are only a few of the types of special-purpose VRML authoring tools available today.

Just as experienced graphics designers become proficient with a number of different drawing and painting programs over the course of their careers, most VRML content developers will assemble a small arsenal of authoring tools in time. It's not uncommon, for instance, for VRML authors to own one or more world builders, geometric modelers, and behavior modelers, in addition to a number of specialty tools. Although various tools may be called into play during the development of very complex worlds, less demanding projects can often be created using little more than a world-building tool.

In the sections that follow you will learn about the different types of development tools that can be used to create VRML content. In addition, these tools can also be used to create VRML models for use with Java 3D, MPEG-4/BIFS, and X3D (see Chapter 2, "Overview of Web3D"). Because VRML97 files work hand-in-glove with these technologies, VRML authoring tools will likely become the backbone for all of your Web3D content development efforts.

Tip: Finding VRML Authoring Tools

In the section that follows I'll introduce you to just a few of the many VRML authoring tools now available. Visit the VRML Tools area of the Web3D Gallery (http://www.web3dgallery.com/vrml/tools/) for links to these and other authoring tools. For even more links you can also visit the Web3D Consortium's VRML Repository (http://www.web3d.org/vrml/), Sandy Ressler's Focus on Web3D site (http://web3d.about.com/), and Bob Crispen's VRMLworks site (http://hiwaay.net/~crispen/vrmlworks/). Between these sites you're certain to find the VRML authoring tools that are right for you.

World Builders

World-builder tools are 3D authoring programs that you can use to create entire VRML scenes from scratch. You can use world builders to assemble preexisting VRML objects into scenes where you can then add hyperlinks, lights, and viewpoints. World builders also allow you to visually customize existing VRML content for your own needs, and many actually offer integrated modeling tools with which you can construct your own objects. Most world builders also let you add behaviors to scenes, meaning that you can animate objects or add support for sophisticated user interactions without having to write the associated VRML code.

World builders typically come with libraries of premade objects, texture maps, background images, and audio files that you can assemble into comprehensive worlds or use as the basis for your own objects. In addition, many world builders come with example scenes that you can use as a starting point for your own worlds. Similar to many of today's HTML authoring tools, world builders often allow you to publish your VRML content directly to the Web after you've created it locally.

Internet Space Builder (see Figure 10-10) from ParallelGraphics (http://www.parallelgraphics.com/), for example, is an inexpensive ($69.95) yet powerful world builder that integrates object geometry modeling with scene assembly. Internet Space Builder, like many world builders, also includes sophisticated texture-mapping and texture-editing tools, giving you great control over the appearance of texture maps used in your scenes. In addition, Internet Space Builder's multimedia capabilities allow you to map texture movies to objects and add MIDI and WAV file sound sources to scenes.

Tip: Free Trial Versions

Free trial versions of most VRML authoring tools can be downloaded directly from the Web. Trial versions typically expire after a specified usage period or a certain number of uses, or they have a limit on the complexity of the scene or object that you can construct. The free trial version of Internet Scene Builder, for example, cannot create scenes containing more then 1400 faces, 7 textures, 2 pictures, 2 movies, and 2 URLs. In addition, the trial version of this product comes with only a small subset of the premade libraries that ship with the full commercial version. For more details visit ParallelGraphics on the Web at http://www.parallelgraphics.com/.

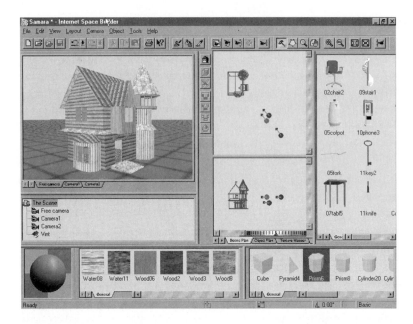

Figure 10-10   Internet Space Builder is an integrated world-building tool that supports geometric modeling, texture editing, and scene creation (http://www.parallelgraphics. com/).

Figure 10-11   Internet Scene Assembler lets you assemble premade objects into interactive, dynamic worlds (http://www.parallelgraphics.com/).

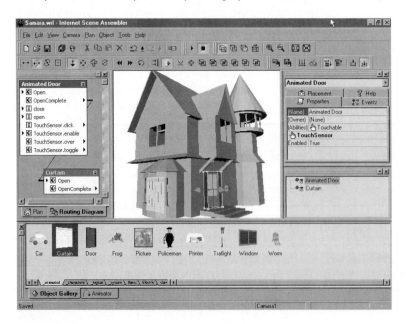

However, because Internet Space Builder doesn't support behavior modeling or event handling, the scenes you create with this world-building tool are static in nature. As a result, you must import the scenes you create with this tool into a behavior-oriented authoring tool such as Internet Scene Assembler in order to add interactively. Also created by ParallelGraphics, Internet Scene Assembler offers no modeling tools whatsoever. Instead, it is focused entirely on adding sophisticated behavior and event handling to *existing* VRML content. As such, Internet Scene Assembler boasts sophisticated event routing and animation capabilities, yet can't construct objects from scratch.

Internet Scene Assembler, however, does come with a number of premade objects. As a result, you can create a wide array of interactive VRML scenes using the library of objects available with this tool, or combine them with other premade content. Figure 10-11, for example, shows how we've used Internet Scene Assembler to add an interactive door and window shade to the otherwise lifeless building created with Internet Space Builder (see Figure 10-11).

The animated door and window shade are just a few of the objects supplied with Internet Scene Assembler; we simply dragged these objects into place, then resized and reoriented them using our mouse. After positioning them into the scene, we used Internet Scene Assembler's event-routing tools to wire together these two objects. When the user clicks on the door, it will swing wide open and trigger the window-shade animation (which, in turn, rolls up so that the user can see outside the building, once inside).

Although the price of Internet Scene Assembler had not been set at the time of this writing, because the product was still under development, it's likely to cost about $175.00. If this is the case, VRML authors can purchase a comprehensive suite of tools for about $250 from the same company that creates the popular Cortona VRML browser (ParallelGraphics Cortona comes with both tools, allowing you to preview your work directly in these authoring environments or a Web browser).

Other solutions exist, of course, such as all-in-one world builders that integrate geometry modeling, behavior modeling, and scene assembly into a single product. Cosmo Worlds, for example, is a popular high-end world-builder tool that was originally created by the Cosmo Software division of Silicon Graphics (SGI). At a cost of nearly $600, Cosmo Worlds isn't an impulse buy. Targeted at professional VRML developers, it is an extremely powerful and capable tool.

Unfortunately, at the time of this writing the future of the entire Cosmo product line, including Cosmo Worlds, was in limbo (see "Cosmo Commotion"). A number of similar high-end, all-in-one VRML authoring tools, however, such as Ligos's V-Realm Builder, are readily available. Although V-Realm Builder is also expensive at $495.00, 50% educational discounts are available to students and educators (see http://www.ligos.com/vrml/ for details).

Not surprisingly, less expensive alternatives to these high-cost tools are available, such as the combination of Internet Space Builder and Internet Scene Assembler described above. In addition, comprehensive low-cost world-building tools such as Spazz3D, are also available. Don't let the name fool you; at $60, Spazz3D is feature-packed. Although billed as a "VRML Animation Editor," Spazz3D is a very capable visual authoring tool (see Figure 10-12). With it you can create interactive objects and entire scenes using only your mouse. Featuring step-by-step wizards, Spazz3D gently leads you through complex tasks such as object animation, text animation, and animated cameras. In addition, Spazz3D is the first VRML authoring tool to support Universal Media, meaning you can craft media-rich worlds that download over the network instantly with this tool (http://www.web3d.org/WorkingGroups/media/for details).

Figure 10-12   Spazz3D is a low-cost, feature-packed world builder with a focus on animation (http://www.spazz3d.com/). It is also the first authoring tool to support Universal Media.

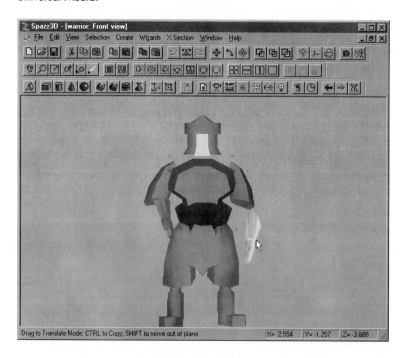

Multiuser (MU) World Builders

VRML does not directly support multiuser (MU) worlds. As a result, the majority of world builders are used to create single-user worlds. Some authoring tools, however, are designed specifically with multiuser environments in mind.

Sony Community Place Conductor, for example, is a multiuser authoring tool used to construct worlds that can be inhabited by more than one person at a time. Because standard VRML plug-ins don't support multiuser environments, users must install the Sony Community Place VRML browser before they can step into such worlds. In addition, these worlds must be delivered by Sony's multiuser Community Place Bureau server (see http://www.community-place.com/ for details).

The blaxxun Contact browser also extends VRML to support multiuser worlds (http://www.blaxxun.com/). Like Sony's Community Place VRML browser, blaxxun Contact communicates with a special multiuser server that keeps track of visitors. The popular multi-user Cybertown site was built around the combination of blaxxun Contact and the blaxxun Community Server (http://www.cybertown.com).

Sony Community Place and blaxxun Contact are fully capable VRML browsers that can also be used to view standard (single-user) VRML content. At the time of this writing, blaxxun had turned the source code for Contact over the Web3D Consortium (see http:/www.web3d.org/fs_pressreleases.htm), from which it will be available under a community source licensing arrangement. It's also likely that Contact will serve as the starting point for a freely available X3D reference browser due from the consortium in the year 2000 (see http://www.web3d.org/TaskGroups/x3d/blaxxun/). The blaxxun Contact browser already supports Universal Media, making it the first VRML browser of its kind.

Cosmo Commotion

At the time this book was written, Computer Associates (http://www
.cai.com) owned the rights to Cosmo Worlds and the entire line of
Cosmo VRML products as a result of its acquisition of Platinum Technologies (http://www.platinum.com/). Originally a division of Silicon
Graphics, Cosmo Software (http://www.cosmosoftware.com/) developed
Cosmo Worlds, Cosmo Player (a VRML browser), Page FX (a VRML
special-effects authoring tool), and other VRML tools.

Silicon Graphics eventually sold Cosmo Software to Platinum Technologies, which also purchased Intervista (makers of the WorldView
VRML browser). After gobbling up a number of leading VRML vendors,
Platinum Technologies itself was acquired by Computer Associates. At
the time of this writing, Computer Associates was in the process of absorbing Platinum Technologies and had not formally stated the direction
it would take with regard to the VRML products it had acquired.

Geometric Modelers

Whereas world builders are typically comprehensive all-in-one products that
allow you to create entire VRML scenes, geometric modelers are specifically
focused on object, or "model," creation. They are typically much more sophisticated in terms of their ability to construct the geometry, or form, of objects
that will eventually be placed in a scene. In addition, geometric modeling tools
usually allow you to apply color and texture maps to objects, meaning that you
can set object appearance and material directly in the modeler.

Although world builders are generally VRML specific, geometric modelers
typically support a wide array of 3D file formats. Nendo, for example, is an integrated modeling and painting program that is capable of exporting objects in
VRML (.wrl), Wavefront (.obj), 3D-Studio (.3ds), and other 3D file formats.
Created by Nichimen Graphics (http://www.nichimen.com/), the same company that produces Mirai (a highly regarded 2D and 3D authoring tool used by
interactive game developers such as Sony, Nintendo, and Electronic Arts),
Nendo's "digital clay" modeling interface is inspired by real-world sculpting.

Considered a breakthrough modeling tool by many 3D artists, the digital
clay metaphor employed by Nendo is quite powerful. By pushing and pulling
polygons' points, edges, or faces, you can create wonderfully complex shapes
by deforming primitives or previously imported objects (see Figure 10-13).
Like other geometric modeling tools, Nendo supports a number of primi-

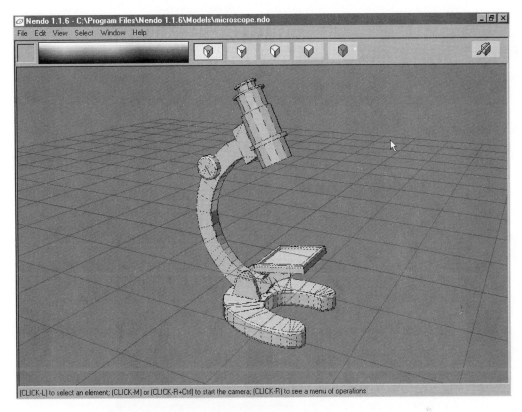

Nendo 1.1.6 - C:\Program Files\Nendo 1.1.6\Models\microscope.ndo

File   Edit   View   Select   Window   Help

(CLICK-L) to select an element; (CLICK-M) or (CLICK-R+Ctrl) to start the camera; (CLICK-R) to see a menu of operations

Figure 10-13   Nendo is an integrated modeling and painting program whose "digital clay" interface is based on traditional sculpting (http://www.nichimen.com/nendo/).

tives that can be used in the construction of more sophisticated objects. In addition to box, cone, cylinder, and sphere shapes, Nendo primitives include:

- **Grid**, a network of uniformly spaced horizontal and perpendicular lines (see Figure 10-14).

- **Torus**, a doughnutlike shape (see Figure 10-14).

- **Dodecahedron**, a twelve-sided polyhedron (a polyhedron is a solid, multifaceted shape created by polygons). A dodecahedron is shaped like a geodesic dome (see Figure 10-14).

- **Icosahedron**, a twenty-sided polyhedron. Like dodecahedrons, icosahedrons resemble geodesic domes (see Figure 10-14).

- **Octahedron**, a eight-sided polyhedron. Octahedrons look like two pyramids attached to each other at the bottom (see Figure 10-14).

- **Tetrahedron**, a four-sided polyhedron. Tetrahedrons look something like pyramids (see Figure 10-14).

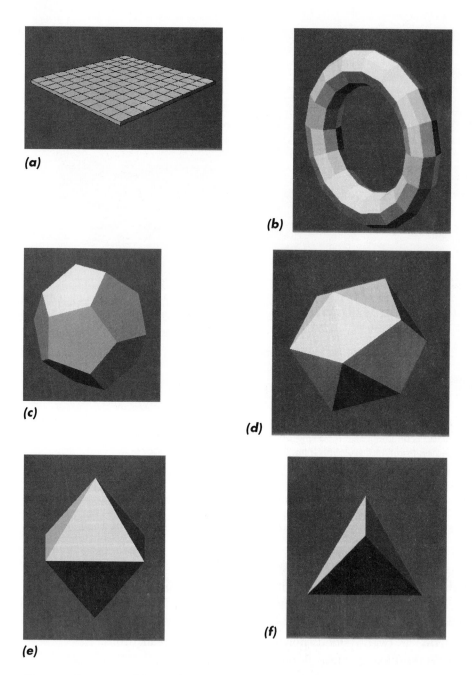

(a)

(b)

(c)

(d)

(e)

(f)

Figure 10-14   In addition to box, cone, cylinder, and sphere primitives, Nendo offers grid (a), torus (b), dodecahedron (c), icosahedron (d), octahedron (e), and tetrahedron (f) primitives.

Like most modelers, Nendo offers a large number of modeling commands that can be applied to objects as they're developed. The Bevel command, for example, can be used to create "rounded" corners on an object. Bridge, meanwhile, is used to automatically create a tunnel (or "bridge") between object faces. Using other modeling commands, entire objects (or selected portions of an object), can be copied, pasted, deleted, mirrored, flipped, inverted, extruded, scaled, smoothed, moved, rotated, and much, much more.

When modeling, you can view objects using wireframe or shaded rendering. These rendering modes are provided to aid in the modeling process. Although you can change the camera angle at any point during the modeling process to look at objects from any viewpoint (similar to changing the viewpoint in a VRML browser), light sources (such as directional, point, and spot lights) are not applied in Nendo. Instead, you must export your models to the VRML format, which can then be inlined into existing VRML scenes or imported into world-building tools as described earlier.

After you construct an object in Nendo, you can you can apply color or texture to it by switching from "Modeling" mode to "Painting" mode (see Figure 10-15). Sporting tools similar to those you'd find in a 2D image-

Figure 10-15   Geometric modeling tools typically allow you to customize the appearance and material of objects. Nendo, for example, offers a large selection of painting tools for such purposes.

editing program such as Adobe Photoshop, Nendo's Painting mode gives you tremendous flexibility and control when it comes to colorizing and texture-mapping objects. Here you can set or change the appearance and material of objects using a variety of visual tools, including pencil, paintbrush, airbrush, stamp, smear, blur, clone, fill, and mask.

Warning: Native VRML Primitives

Some modeling tools, such as Nendo, don't know how to export to the VRML file format using native VRML primitives. Instead, box, cone, cylinder, and sphere shapes are exported as IndexedFaceSet nodes, not the actual VRML Box, Cone, Cylinder, and Sphere nodes that correspond to these shapes.

Such shapes consume much more disk space (and, consequently, more bandwidth) when represented with the IndexedFaceSet node than do their native VRML primitive counterparts. To eliminate this unnecessary baggage you can manually edit the resulting VRML file and replace box, cone, cylinder, and sphere shapes represented by IndexedFaceSet nodes with corresponding hand-coded VRML primitives.

Although Nendo sets the bar for affordable, powerful modelers, it's not the only game in town. Modeling tools capable of exporting to the VRML format abound, all of which strive to provide an intuitive, easy-to-use interface when it comes to constructing 3D objects. Like Nendo, some take a digital clay approach to modeling, others employ entirely different modeling paradigms.

MetaCreations Canoma (http://www.canoma.com/), for example, uses a "push-pin" interface that allows you to create photorealistic models directly from digital images (see Figure 10-16). At nearly $500.00, Canoma is squarely targeted at professional designers and Web developers who have no previous 3D modeling experience. As long as you can point and click, you can construct stunning models with this tool.

To model in Canoma, you simply place various 3D primitives on top of 2D bitmap images (such as a BMP, GIF, JPEG, TIFF, PNG, or other image formats). In other words, you map 3D geometry (such as cubes, pyramids, pyramids, and planes) to similarly shaped portions of a 2D image. Using your mouse, you then align the corners of these 3D primitives to the correspond-

Figure 10-16 Canoma modeling starts with a digital image, such as this scanned photograph of a software box and CD-ROM case that sit atop a wooden table.

ing corners of the image, effectively "pinning" 3D primitive shapes to 2D objects in the image, as seen in Figure 10-17.

When you have finished pinning wireframe primitives onto the image, Canoma will automatically generate a 3D object based on this information. Textures are cut from the image and mapped to the geometry you've constructed, giving the resulting model a photorealistic appearance. Although Canoma can be considered a geometric modeling tool, as its strength lies in creating sophisticated, texture-mapped 3D objects, it also supports animation and scene building.

In addition to the VRML format, Canoma models can be output to a variety of 2D image formats (such as BMP, PNG, and TIFF), animation formats (such as QuickTime, and sequential BMP and PICT images), and 3D formats (such as AutoCAD .DXF, Wavefront .OBJ, and Truespace .SCN). In addition, Canoma models can be output to the 3D MetaStream format jointly developed by MetaCreations and Intel (see "MetaCreations and MetaStream").

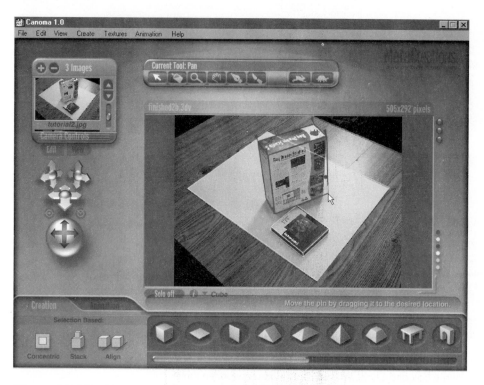

Figure 10-17 Canoma geometry is constructed by "pinning" various 3D wireframe shapes to similarly shaped portions of the digital image. When complete, Canoma will automatically generate a corresponding, photorealistic 3D model (http://www.canoma.com/).

MetaCreations and MetaStream

MetaCreations (http://www.metacreations.com/), a leading vendor of 2D and 3D authoring tools, developed such products as Painter, Kai's Power Tools, Bryce, Ray Dream, Poser, and Infini-D. MetaCreations also offers MetaStream, its own 3D-file format.

Developed with Intel, MetaStream supports progressive download and display of 3D model data. Unlike VRML, which does not support streaming, MetaStream (as the name indicates) is all about streaming 3D. The MetaStream format also compresses 3D geometry and textures to conserve as much bandwidth as possible. Similar to VRML, however, MetaStream requires a special Web browser plug-in. Visit the Meta-Stream home page for details (http://www.metacreations.com/meta-stream/).

Behavior Modelers

Although geometric modeling tools are used to create the form and appearance of objects, they usually can't add behavior to objects. Behaviors bring objects to life, giving them complex capabilities such as animation and interactivity. The interactive camcorder that you earlier inlined into an electronics showroom scene, for example, supported sophisticated behavior that allowed it to act as a functional product visualization (see "Electronics Showroom" for details). Similarly, animated objects such as the circus clown and dolphin prototype are constructed by adding animation behavior to otherwise static, lifeless models.

Comprehensive world-builder tools typically support behavior modeling, although special-purpose behavior modelers are also available that can give your geometric models very specific capabilities. Cybelius TouchMore!, for instance, is designed to create fully interactive product visualizations from existing geometric models (http://www.cybelius.com/). Because TouchMore! is focused entirely on behavior modeling, it doesn't include geometric modeling tools. As a result, this tool is used exclusively to add behavior to otherwise static VRML models.

At a suggested retail price of $995, TouchMore! is among the more expensive commercial VRML authoring products on the market (at the time of this writing the product was available directly from the Cybelius Web site for $499). As a behavior modeler focused specifically on creating functional, interactive product visualizations, however, TouchMore! is commonly used to create sophisticated models for electronic commerce, marketing and sales, new product development, and other fields where such models can result in sales or bottom-line savings that often measure in the hundreds of thousands of dollars.

TouchMore! comes with a library of premade functional components that you can drag and drop onto portions of an existing model (you can also construct your own reusable behavior components in cases where those supplied with TouchMore! don't fit the bill). After assigning behavior components to the model you can visually "wire" together the various input and output fields they contain (see Figure 10-18).

The power-button output of the camcorder shown in Figure 10-19, for example, is connected to the input field of this model's LED display. As Figure 10-19 illustrates, the LED display is initially blank to indicate that the camcorder is off. When the power button is pressed, however, the camera powers up and a sample image appears in the LED display. Additional

Cybelius ShowMore! and Optimizer

In addition to TouchMore!, Cybelius offers a product called ShowMore! Specially targeted at Web developers, ShowMore! allows point-and-click integration of VRML with HTML. At $149, ShowMore! isn't a behavior modeler, however. Instead it is a specialty tool used to create VRML presentations for the Web.

Cybelius Optimizer, on the other hand, is a freely available VRML optimization tool that you can use to reduce the size of any VRML model by 50% or more. For details on the entire Cybelius product line visit http://www.cybelius.com/.

functionality is provided by wiring the camcorder's focus buttons to the LED display, allowing users to zoom in and out of the picture. To complete the experience, behaviors have been assigned to the viewfinder and LED display of the model that allow these parts of the model to be manipulated just as you would expect with a real-world camcorder (see Figure 10-19).

Whereas TouchMore! specializes in interactive behaviors for product visualizations, behavior modelers exist for other purposes as well. ParallelGraphic's Internet Character Animator, for instance, is designed specifically to give life-like movement to VRML characters (http://www.parallelgraphics.com/). Using this tool you can set translation, rotation, and scale values for any part of a character's body at key frames in the animation sequence (see Figure 10-20 and Figure 10-21).

Internet Character Animator can construct a number of animated movements and gestures for characters. Those appearing in an online fashion show or clothing store, for example, might be given the ability to walk, wave, pivot, and bow. Game monsters and virtual sales assistants, on the other hand, would require entirely different movements and gestures unique to them.

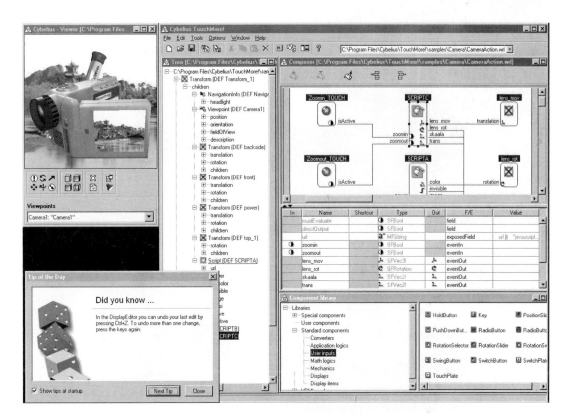

Figure 10-18   TouchMore! is a behavior modeler used to create interactive, functional product models. Functional components are assigned to different parts of an existing VRML model and can then be "wired" together in the FlowEditor window seen in the upper right-hand corner of this screen shot (http://www.cybelius.com/).

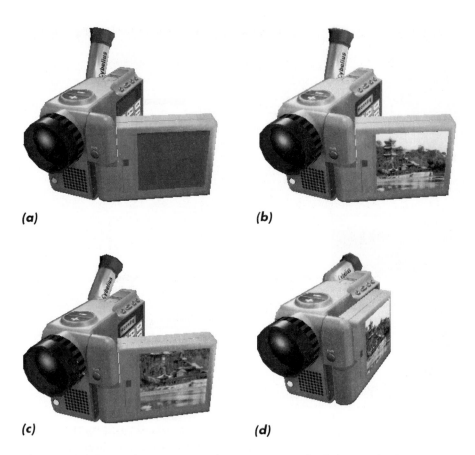

(a) *(b)*

(c) *(d)*

Figure 10-19 TouchMore! was used to construct complex behaviors for this camcorder model. When the camcorder's power is off, the display is blank (a). However, when the power button is selected, an image appears in the LED display (b). Users can zoom in and out of the image by pressing the focus buttons (c), and they can also open and close the display and viewfinder (d).

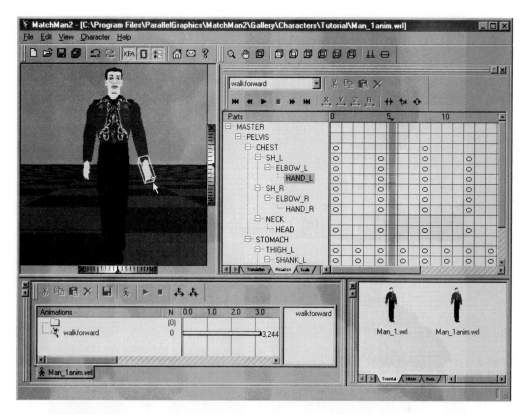

Figure 10-20 Internet Character Animator specializes in adding motion behavior to VRML characters, allowing you to construct sophisticated keyframe animation without writing a line of code (http://www.parallelgraphics.com/).

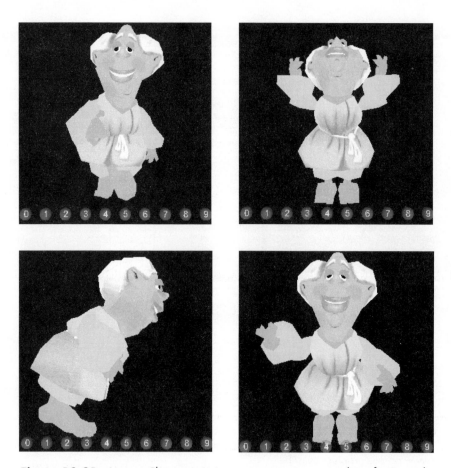

Figure 10-21 Internet Character Animator can construct a number of animated movements and gestures for a single character.

Specialty Tools

Although many VRML authoring tools can be categorized as world builders, geometric modelers, or behavior modelers, a surprising number of specialty tools are also available. A quick trip to the VRML Repository (http://www .web3d.org/vrml/) will reveal a number of authoring tools, utilities, and generators used to create very specific types of objects and scenes. Text animators, titling tools, banner advertisement builders, landscape and terrain generators, avatar constructors, charting and graphing utilities, data visualization tools and many other specialty tools abound.

In most cases, the output generated by such specialty tools is in the form of an object or partial scene that must be integrated into more comprehensive world. As a result, you must either inline this content by hand, or rely on a world builder with which you can visually assemble the results into a complete scene.

Summary

VRML97 was designed with modularity and composability in mind. Using the Inline node, you can compose very sophisticated worlds using premade content that resides in its own file. Inline nodes can be set as the child of a Transform node, allowing you to position, rotate, and scale the inlined content in a manner that is meaningful to your world. Files containing inlined content can themselves be inlined, allowing so-called "nesting" of inlined files.

The PROTO mechanism (short for prototype) gives developers a way to construct custom nodes that extend the base VRML language. Using the corresponding EXTENDPROTO mechanism, you can use externally defined PROTO nodes in your own worlds. In addition, you can inline VRML files that contain instances of prototype nodes. Thanks to inlining and prototypes, modular, reusable libraries of VRML code are possible.

Although you can hand-code impressive VRML worlds by inlining or customizing existing content, at some point you'll want to construct your own content from scratch. Fortunately, a number of visual VRML authoring tools are available that you can use to construct complex objects and entire worlds. All-purpose world builders allow you to assemble scenes and often include basic geometric and behavior-modeling capabilities. Standalone geometric modeling tools and behavior-modeling tools are also available, along with a number of special-purpose authoring tools.

Following is a complete list of URLs referenced in this chapter:

ParallelGraphics   http://www.parallelgraphics.com/

VRML Repository   http://www.web3d.org/vrml/

Canoma   http://www.canoma.com/

Cybelius   http://www.cybelius.com/

Laptop Model   http://www.canoma.com/vrml/mac/scene.wrl

Camcorder Model   http://www.cybelius.com/wrlm/Camcorder/Camera_action2406.wrl

Palmtop Model   http://www.parallelgraphics.com/htm/en/demo/concept/clio/clio.wrl

PROTO Repository   http://www.vrml-content.org/

Web3D Gallery PROTO links   http://www.web3dgallery.com/vrml/proto/

Web3DGallery Animation links   http://www.web3dgallery.com/vrml/animation/

Web3DGallery VRML Tools links   http://www.web3dgallery.com/vrml/tools/

Focus on Web3D   http://web3d.about.com/

VRMLworks   http://hiwaay.net/~crispen/vrmlworks/

Ligos V-Realm   http://www.ligos.com/vrml/

Spazz3D   http://www.spazz3d.com/

Universal Media   http://www.web3d.org/WorkingGroups/media/

Computer Associates   http://www.cai.com/

Platinum Technologies   http://www.platinum.com/

Cosmo Software   http://www.cosmosoftware.com/

Sony Community Place   http://www.community-place.com/

blaxxun   http://www.blaxxun.com/

Cybertown   http://www.cybertown.com/

Web3D Consortium Press Releases   http:/www.web3d.org/fs_pressreleases.htm

X3D and blaxxun   http://www.web3d.org/TaskGroups/x3d/blaxxun/

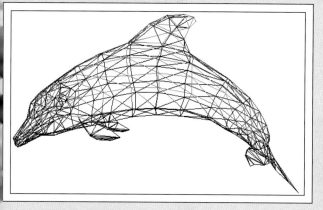

Plate 1a
Wireframe rendering displays the geometry of a shape without taking into account light sources or surface attributes (color, material, and/or texture). As a result, it produces line "skeletons" that are fast and efficient to display at the expense of visual quality.

Plate 1b
Flat rendering paints the surface of a wireframe in a solid (flat) color. Although quite fast and efficient, it does not interpolate color across the surface of a shape and thus produces less-than-realistic results.

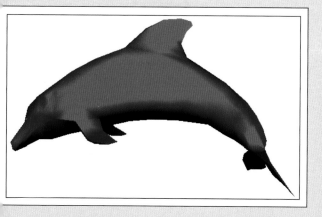

Plate 1c
Smooth rendering takes into account light sources and surface attributes to smoothly interpolate color at each vertex. It is the most realistic of the three types of rendering shown here (and consequently the most demanding in its use of rendering resources).

Plate 2a
Diffuse colors produce relatively flat, dull shapes. Only diffuse colors were used to create this dolphin, giving it a matte appearance.

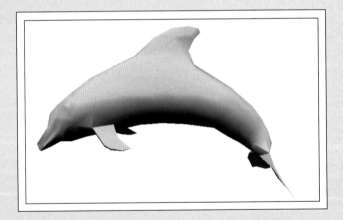

Plate 2b
Specular colors work in combination with "shininess" settings to produce shiny, glossy shapes. They are the source of sparkles, glints, and similar reflective properties. Because this dolphin was created using *only* specular color, however, it lacks the realism of Plate 2c.

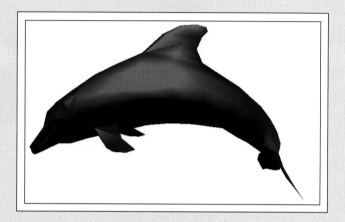

Plate 2c
Visually appealing 3D models are often created using a combination of diffuse and specular colors. Specular colors are combined with shininess settings to produce shiny surfaces; see Plates 2d–2g. This dolphin was created by using both diffuse and specular colors (compare with Plates 2a and 2b).

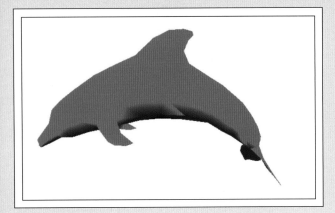

Plates 2d–2g

Shininess works in combination with specular color to produce shiny, glossy shapes. These dolphins are based on the one in Plate 2c. The variety of appearances was created by altering the shininess settings (diffuse and specular color settings remain unchanged).

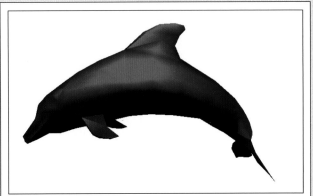

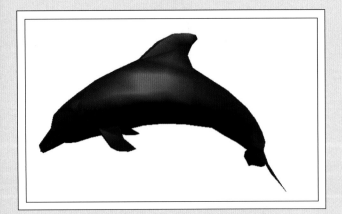

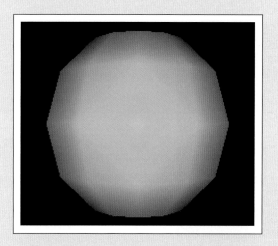

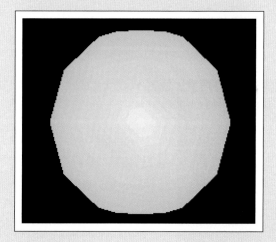

Plates 3a and 3b
Emissive colors create shapes that seem to emit light and glow.
Sphere 3a (top) uses only diffuse color, while 3b (bottom) uses
emissive color.

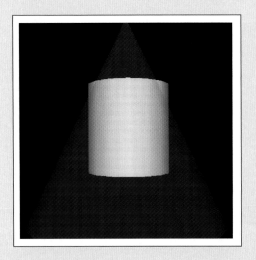

Plate 4a

Screen-door transparency renders transparent shapes using a screening technique, in which a dithered screen mesh (similar in appearance to a screen door or a window screen) is overlaid on a shape. Transparency values control how large or small the "holes" in the screen mesh grid are, thereby dictating the degree to which images behind the screen can be seen. Although screen-door transparency is fast, it's not very realistic looking when compared to blended transparency (Plate 4b, below).

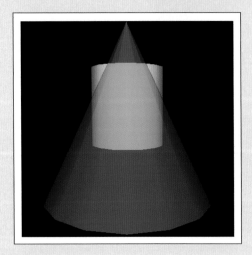

Plate 4b

Blended transparency rendering (also known as "alpha blended transparency") uses mathematical calculations (a "blend equation") to blend the pixels of transparent shapes with underlying pixels, resulting in a very realistic transparency effect. Although blended transparency produces high-quality results, it is computationally expensive compared to screen-door transparency (Plate 4a, above).

Plates 4c and 4d
Our dolphin has been rendered using screen-door transparency (Plate 4c, above) and blended transparency (Plate 4d, below).

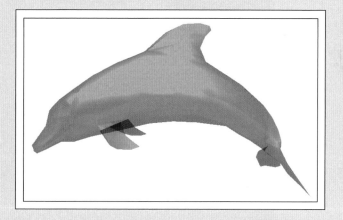

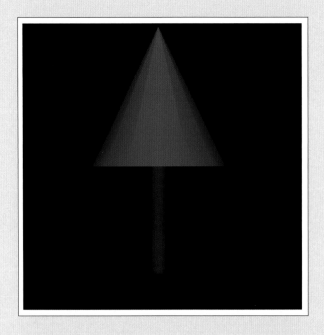

Plates 5a and 5b
Pine tree 5a (top) was created using diffuse colors, while 5b (bottom) was
created using emissive colors. As a result, pine tree 5b appears to glow,
making it easier to see against this black background.

Plates 6a, 6b (top pair) and 7a, 7b (bottom pair)
Textures can bring life to otherwise uninspired geometry. Seaside scene courtesy of Gerardo Quintieri (http://web3dgallery.com/people/gq/), textures courtesy of Universal Media (http://www.web3d.org/WorkingGroups/media/). Dance Party courtesy of Shout Interactive (http://www.shoutinteractive.com/).

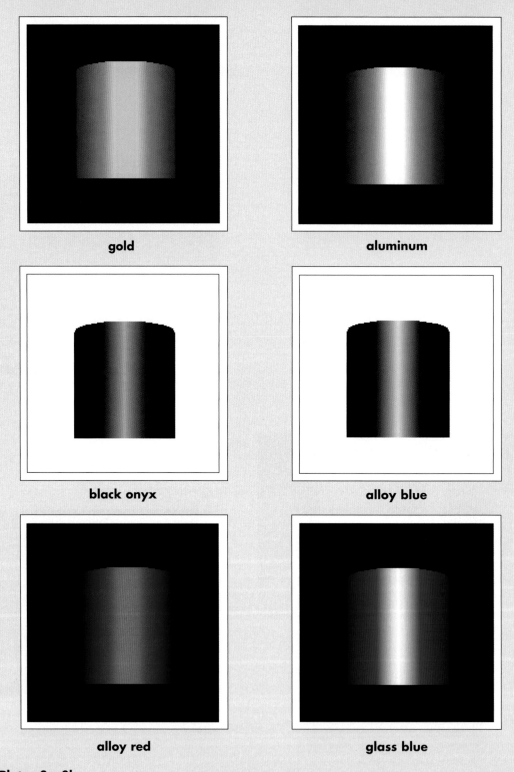

gold

aluminum

black onyx

alloy blue

alloy red

glass blue

Plates 8a–8l

A wide variety of appearances can be created by creatively combining diffuse color, specular color, shininess, and transparency values. The exact formulas for these and many other appearances can be found through the Web3D Gallery at http://www.web3dgallery.com/vrml/color/.

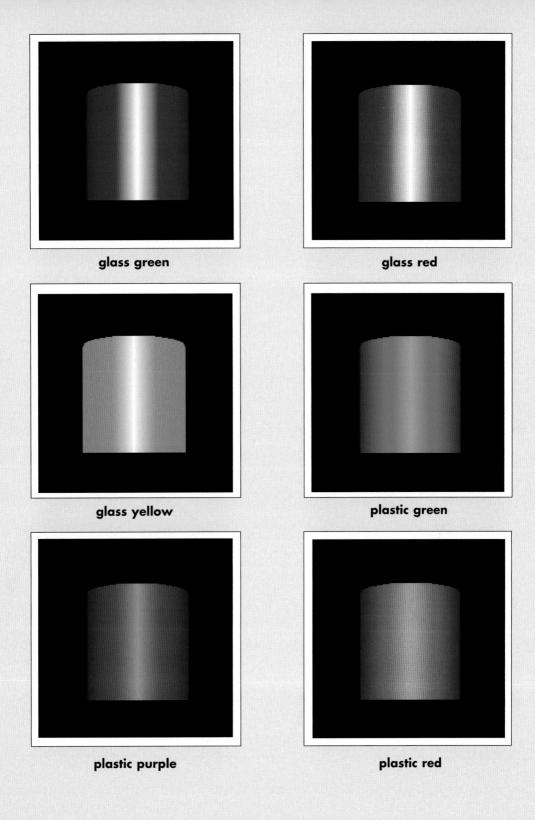

glass green

glass red

glass yellow

plastic green

plastic purple

plastic red

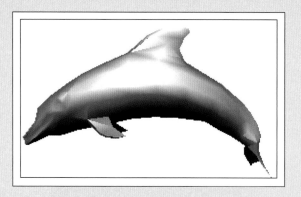

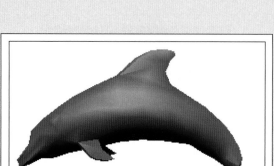

Plates 9a–9e
The appearance of these VRML dolphins varies greatly as a result of their unique Material node settings. Visit the Web3D Gallery (http://www.web3dgallery.com/) to interact with these playful dolphins over the the Internet, and also to find out exactly what Material settings were used to create their colorful appearances.

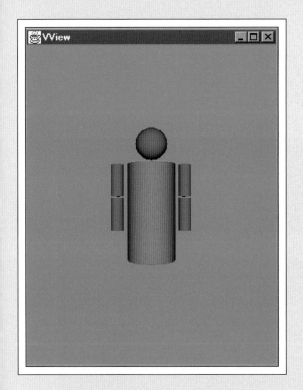

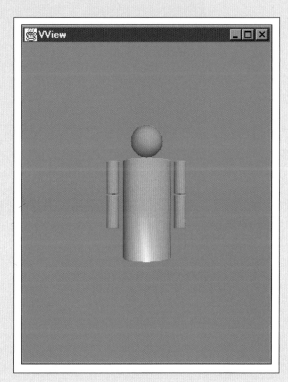

Plates 10a and 10b
Color screenshots from Chapter 15, "Customizing Backgrounds, Fog, Lighting, and Sound." Figure 10a (above left) shows a humanoid VRML avatar integrated with a Java 3D applet courtesy of the VRML loader (Listing 15–1). Figure 10b (above right) shows the same avatar, this time rendered using custom Java 3D light sources (Listing 15–3).

Plates 11a–11g
Altering the textures used in a scene is often a fast and easy way to customize the visual appearance of Web3D content. In this example, Dance Party has been customized (see Plate 7b for the original scene). Every texture in this scene has been altered to create a unique look for the characters and dance floor. Note that the character texture images are actually composites of several textures; hair, clothes, face, and shoe images are contained on a single texture. This technique conserves precious download time, as a single texture is transferred over the wire instead of many (every Internet download requires network connection setup/teardown time, no matter how small the file being transferred). Texture transformations (rotation, scale, etc.) are then used to apply different areas of the texture to the corresponding geometry. Scene courtesy of Shout Interactive (http://www.shoutinteractive.com/).

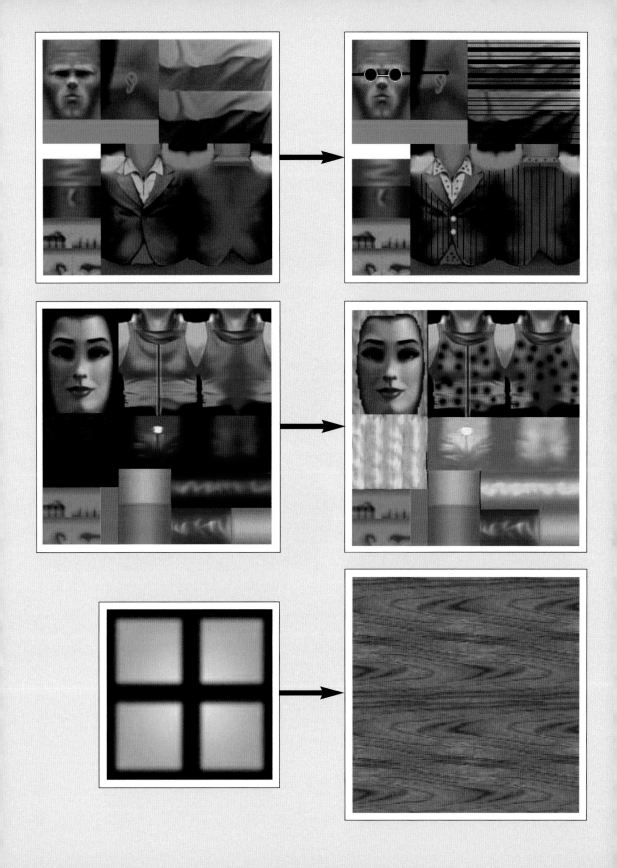

Plate 12
Textures are 2D images that are applied to the surface of a 3D shape. This process, called texture mapping, can create detailed surface appearance with a minimum of effort. These primitive sphere shapes, for example, are texture mapped using freely available, pre-made JPEG images. Images courtesy of Universal Media (http://www.web3d.org/WorkingGroups/media/).

Nendo   http://www.nichimen.com/nendo/

Nichimen Graphics   http://www.nichimen.com/

MetaCreations   http://www.metacreations.com/

MetaStream   http://www.metacreations.com/metastream/

Part 3

JAVA 3D

JAVA 3D OVERVIEW

Topics in This Chapter

- An introduction to the Java 3D API, a member of Sun's Java Media APIs
- Java 3D design goals and version history (1.0, 1.1, and 1.2)
- Key Java 3D features

Chapter 11

Java 3D is a collection of Java classes that define a high-level Application Programming Interface (API) for interactive 3D development. As a standard extension to the base Java technology, Java 3D allows developers to construct comprehensive, platform-independent applets and applications that feature interactive 3D graphics and sound capabilities.

Introduced in mid-1997 by Sun Microsystems, the same company that developed Java itself, the Java 3D API is today licensed by 95 percent of the world's workstation market (according to a 1999 International Data Corporation study), which means that implementations will soon be available for every major operating system and many minor ones as well. At the time of this writing Java 3D was available for Windows 95, Windows 98, Windows NT, and Sun Solaris systems, while SGI IRIX, HP-UX, and Linux implementations were on the horizon.

In this chapter you'll learn how Java 3D relates to Java, and how the two combine to form a powerful 3D-development platform. You'll see that Java 3D is part of the Java Media family of APIs, making it a sibling of many other media-centric Java extensions. In addition, you'll learn essential Java 3D jargon as you explore the fundamental structure common to all Java 3D programs.

Java and Java 3D

Java 3D is an extension to Java, layered on top of Java, as Figure 11-1 illustrates. More specifically, Java 3D is a *standard* extension to the Java 2 platform, which is the most current version of Java now available. Java 2 was unveiled to the public in December of 1998, at the same time that Java 3D was officially released. (Java 2 was originally known as Java 1.2, as "Java 2 vs. Java 1.2" explains, and so you'll often see references to Java 1.2 when reading about Java 3D.) Because of the 3D capabilities that Java 3D delivers as a standard Java extension, Java 3D is actually considered part of a large family of multimedia extensions (see "Java Media APIs," later in this chapter).

Java Programming Required

Although you don't need to be an expert in Java to customize existing Java 3D programs, you should, at the very least, be comfortable with the basics of Java programming. Unlike VRML, which is a relatively simple language to learn, Java 3D is inherently more complicated. Because it is so tightly coupled with Java, Java 3D requires a fundamental knowledge of Java programming from the get-go.

Whereas extremely compelling VRML content can be created using nothing more than your mouse and a visual authoring tool (see Chapter 10, "Creating New VRML Worlds," for details), the same cannot be said for Java 3D. Unfortunately, visual Java 3D authoring tools have yet to hit the market,

Figure 11-1
Java 3D is layered on top of Java, extending Java's core capabilities to include 3D.

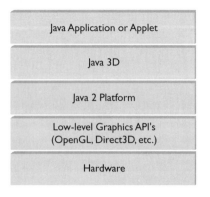

Java Application or Applet

Java 3D

Java 2 Platform

Low-level Graphics API's
(OpenGL, Direct3D, etc.)

Hardware

which means you'll have to deal with Java code if you want to customize existing Java 3D programs or create your own.

If you are not already experienced with Java, you should first familiarize yourself with the language and Sun's Java development tools before continuing with this chapter and those that follow. Sun provides a wealth of Java programming resources free of charge at the official Java home page (http:// java.sun.com/) for just such purposes.

On the Java home page you'll find a link called "Docs and Training." This link will take you to an overwhelming amount of documentation targeted at developers (which you can jump directly to at http://java.sun.com/infodocs/), including the Java Tutorial (available directly at http://java.sun.com/docs/ books/tutorial/). You can learn how to program in Java by working through the Java Tutorial online, or you can download the entire thing to your personal computer for offline reading.

The Java Tutorial's "Your First Cup of Java" lesson should be your first stop, as it starts at the very beginning. Not only does it guide you through the process of creating, compiling, and executing applets and applications, it also includes step-by-step installation instructions for the Java 2 Platform Software Development Toolkit (SDK). Next you should complete all of the other lessons in the "Trails Covering the Basics" portion of the Java Tutorial. You will then have the fundamental experience necessary to learn Java 3D. In particular, you should know:

- Basic Java jargon, including class, class library, object, instance, method, field, bytecode, package, thread, exception, Java Archive (JAR), Java Virtual Machine (JVM), Just-in-Time (JIT) compiler, and so forth.
- The basic code structure of a Java applet and application.
- The basic functionality of the core Java classes, and the packages they are organized into.
- How to compile and run premade Java applets and applications.
- How to stitch an applet into a Web page using the <APPLET> tag.
- How to write a simple Java applet and application from scratch.
- How to import and use premade Java classes, especially those in the core libraries.
- How to create custom classes and bundle them into custom packages.

You'll also find Sun's "Java Platform Documentation" site particularly useful when learning how to program in Java. Located online at http://java.sun.com/docs/, this site provides links to a number of related online resources, including an overview of the Java platform, Frequently Asked Questions (FAQs), technical papers, design guidelines, the Java language specification, coding conventions, and even an overview of the Java standardization process.

Unlike VRML and MPEG, which are established ISO/IEC international standards, neither Java nor Java 3D has been officially standardized (see Chapter 2, "Overview of Web3D"). After a falling out with ISO/IEC, Sun opted to pursue standardization of Java through the ECMA standards organization. At the time of this writing ECMA had *rejected* Java for possible standardization; details can be found through Sun's "Java Platform Documentation" site or directly at http://java.sun.com/aboutJava/standardization/. Although it is unlikely that Java will be endorsed as an ECMA standard in the near future, Java 3D stands on its own.

Although Sun considers Java 3D to be a *standard extension* to Java (also known as an "optional package"), it would not automatically become an international standard for 3D even if Java itself were approved as a standard. Java 3D must undergo a separate, formal review by a standard-setting organization such as ECMA or ISO/IEC. Sun is unlikely to initiate standardization of Java 3D until the outcome of Java standardization is known.

Tip

Although it's possible to plunge headfirst into Java 3D without prior knowledge of Java, programmers are generally well versed in Java before they tackle Java 3D. In the chapters that follow, however, you'll learn how to customize certain aspects of existing Java 3D programs; you don't have to be an expert Java programmer to get your feet wet with Java 3D as discussed in this book.

If you already know how to program in Java, you'll find the chapters that follow to be a gentle introduction to Java 3D. If you're new to Java, you should consider a trip to Sun's Java site (http://java.sun.com/) before continuing with this section of the book. From the Java home page, a "Docs & Training" link will take you to a bounty of free resources that you can use to learn Java, including the online Java Tutorial (http://java.sun.com/docs/books/tutorial/).

Java 2 vs. Java 1.2

Sun Microsystems (http://www.sun.com/) unveiled Java 2 in December of 1998. Prior to its official release, Java 2 was known as Java 1.2, following the previous Java 1.1 (Java 1.1 followed Java 1.0, which was released in 1995). At the last minute Sun decided to recast Java 1.2 as the "Java 2 Platform." Primarily a marketing move to create a "Java 2" brand, the name change emphasized Sun's conviction that the latest version of Java was finally a platform upon which industrial-strength applications could be built.

Unfortunately, many technical publications were caught off guard. As a result, a number of "Java 1.2" books, trade journals, programming magazines, and other publications (including much of Sun's own online Java documentation) were already rolling out the door by the time "Java 2" was officially announced. Sun's most current Java Software Development Toolkit (SDK) is still labeled as SDK 1.2, as it's considered version 1.2 of the Java 2 development platform (although a new SDK 2 may be released in the near future to avoid this unnecessary confusion).

Tip

Because of the amount of Java 1.2 material now on the market, many developers tend to use the terms Java 1.2 and Java 2 interchangeably. To learn more about the lingering and often confusing relationship between Java 2 and Java 1.2, you can read Sun's position paper at http://java.sun.com/products/jdk/1.2/java2.html. To learn more about Java in general you can visit the official Java home page at http://java.sun.com/.

Core Libraries and Extensions

The Java platform is defined by a standard suite of class libraries that are guaranteed to be available on all systems. These "core" Java libraries (also known as the core Java API) constitute the heart and soul of every Java-enabled computing device, allowing developers to take advantage of these features without concern for where their program is ultimately executed (any applet or application can use these core classes, because they're part of the standard Java installation).

As Java has matured over the years, the classes that constitute the core have grown. Java 2 has more classes than its predecessors (Java 1.0 and

Java 1.1) in order to support its added capabilities. Java 2 comes with nearly 4,000 pre-built classes, grouped into almost 200 packages according to their capabilities.

Extensions to the core (AKA "optional packages"), such as Java 3D, add additional classes that aren't considered essential to every Java program. The ability to create a window is considered a core feature available to every Java program, for example, although drawing 3D content in that window is not as critical; consequently, the Java core includes a number of windowing classes but no 3D classes. Java 3D classes, on the other hand, provide very specific

Package Names

Java uses the concept of *packages* to organize and manage classes. Packages are Java-specific namespaces that mimic directory structures, where the top-level (first) name in the package is the most general and subsequent names are more specific. Package name levels are separated by a period. The main Java3D package `javax.media.j3d`, for example, corresponds to the directory path javax/media/j3d, where "javax" is the top-level directory, under which "media" is found. J3d, however, is the most specific portion of the package name, as it appears last. Conceptually, classes in the `javax.media.j3d` package can be thought of as being organized in the following directory structure (in truth, these classes are actually compressed into a single JAR file that is located in the same folder as the JRE):

```
javax
   |------ media
               |------ j3d (classes are in here)
```

Classes that are part of the Java core are assembled into packages that start with "java", such as `java.awt`, `java.io`, `java.lang`, and so forth. Standard extensions to the core, meanwhile, are typically stored in packages that start with "javax" ("x" stands for eXtension). The main Java 3D classes, for example, are packaged under `javax.media.j3d`. Nonstandard extensions, however, are packaged using names chosen by the developer (Sun recommends that such package names start with the reverse domain of the developing company, such as "com.sun", in order to help reduce naming conflicts).

3D graphics and sound capabilities not offered by the core Java class libraries. In this respect, Java 3D classes are analogous to VRML nodes; both are 3D building blocks used in the construction of interactive 3D content.

Because Java 3D is an *extension* to Java, the premade classes that make up the Java 3D implementation are not included in the core Java class libraries. Standard Java runtime environments have no idea how to handle Java 3D programs. You can't, for example, view a Java 3D applet using a typical installation of Netscape Navigator or Internet Explorer, because the runtime environment provided by these systems lacks the Java 3D classes that make up the Java 3D extension. Nor can you run Java 3D applications using Sun's SDK, because it, too, lacks the classes that comprise the Java 3D extension.

Fortunately, Sun provides the Java 3D class libraries free of charge. You can download and install them as explained in a special online Core Web3D chapter located at http://www.CoreWeb3D.com/java3d/install/. (This "Installing Java 3D" chapter is provided online so that you can easily share it with your Web site visitors.) Unfortunately, the Java 3D classes are useful only within the context of a Java 2 runtime environment, which neither Netscape Navigator nor Internet Explorer currently offers. As a result, Java 3D applets must bypass altogether the default runtime provided by these browsers in favor of a full Java 2 runtime equipped with Java 3D classes, a roundabout solution made possible thanks to Sun's Java Plug-in, as described later in this chapter.

Java 3D Specifications and Implementations

As a standard extension to Java, Java 3D is Sun's officially endorsed technology for creating 3D applets and applications in Java. Whereas any developer is free to create a non-standard extension to Java (Java was designed to be extended by developers as needed), only *standard* Java extensions ("optional packages") are endorsed by Sun. As such, Sun itself generally spearheads the development of standard extensions, which are typically collaborative efforts involving a range of industry leaders.

Java 3D, for example, was designed by Sun Microsystems, Silicon Graphics (SGI), Intel, and Apple Computer under the direction of Henry Sowizral, Sun Senior Staff Engineer and chief Java 3D architect. Sowizral, together with fellow Sun engineers and Java 3D coarchitects Kevin Rushforth, Michael Deering, Warren Dale, and Dan Petersen, developed the Java

3D Application Programming Interface (API) specification in cooperation with a number of 3D experts from Sun, SGI, Intel, and Apple. The Java 3D API specification, much like the VRML97 specification discussed in previous chapters, describes precisely the programming units that software developers use to construct Java 3D programs (see Appendix C, "Java 3D Resources").

Unlike the VRML97 specification, however, the Java 3D API specification is expressed entirely in terms of the Java programming language. Using the Java 3D API as a guide, programmers fluent in Java are able to craft 3D applets and applications that can be deployed on any Java 3D-enabled system.

Although the Java 3D specification is a wonderful resource for programmers, it's of little value without a corresponding collection of classes known as a Java 3D implementation. (These are the actual classes described by the Java 3D specification, which must be installed on your computer along with the Java 2 platform.) At the time of this writing Sun had produced Java 3D implementations for Windows 95, Windows 98, Windows NT, and Solaris systems, while ports to SGI IRIX, HP-UX, and Linux were well under way. Nearly all major workstation manufacturers had licensed Java 3D from Sun, so that a variety of Java 3D implementations were likely to emerge in the year 2000 (visit the Java 3D home page at http://java.sun.com/products/java-media/3D/ for details).

Note

Java 3D specifications are developed in advance of corresponding implementations (a specification can be thought of as the blueprint for implementations). The specification detailing Java 3D 1.2 (the most current version of Java 3D at the time this book was written), for example, was written before Sun could produce the first Java 1.2 implementation.

Java 3D Programs

Although the Java 3D API specification gives programmers the information they need in order to write Java 3D applets and applications, it is just a document. Using the Java 3D specification as a guide—for which a corresponding Java 3D implementation must be installed—programmers construct their

Java 3D programs by typing source code written in the Java language (which has a syntax similar to C or C++) into text files.

Java 3D source-code files are run through a Java compiler that generates corresponding bytecode class files based on the instructions they contain. Bytecode is an intermediate, machine-independent format that is more compact and efficient than raw source code. Bytecode class files are ultimately handed to *a Java runtime environment* (JRE) for execution.

Because Java 3D is layered on top of the core Java 2 platform (see Figure 11-1), Java 3D programs cannot run without a Java 2 JRE. Earlier runtimes, such as those based on Java 1.0 or Java 1.1, are simply incapable of handling Java 3D. In order to run Java 3D applications on the desktop, therefore, you must have installed either a Java 2 JRE or a Java 2 development environment (which comes with a JRE) prior to installing a Java 3D implementation. At a minimum, then, Java 3D applications require:

- **A Java 2 platform runtime environment (JRE), or Java 2 software development environment**, both of which are available free of charge from Sun's Java Web site at http://java.sun.com/products/. As explained earlier in this chapter, Java 2 was originally known as Java 1.2. Because Sun has not completely made the transition to the Java 2 name, you'll likely have to look for a Java 1.2 (or greater) runtime at this site. At the time of this writing a new version of Java was nearing release, although it wasn't clear if Sun would call this newest iteration Java 2 or Java 1.3.

- **A Java 3D implementation**, which is a library of Java classes corresponding to those detailed by the Java 3D specification. Sun provides free Java 3D implementations for Windows and Solaris platforms through the Java 3D home page at http://java.sun.com/products/java-media/3D/. Here you'll also find information related to forthcoming Java 3D implementations, such as those for Linux and SGI IRIX.

Because Java 3D requires a Java 2 runtime, however, such applets are unable to run directly in today's commercial Web browsers. When this book went to print, current versions of Internet Explorer or Netscape Navigator shipped with Java 1.1 runtimes. Older browsers, naturally, are built around even older versions of Java (Java 1.0). As a result, end users are unable to experience Java 3D through their stock Web browser.

In order to experience Java 3D applets through a Web browser, users must install a Java 2 runtime environment, followed by a Java 3D implementation. Although these are the same requirements as those for executing Java 3D applications, Java 3D applets also require that Sun's Java Plug-in be installed and activated. As illustrated in Figure 11-2, the Java Plug-in redirects applet execution from the browser's built-in Java runtime environment to a more capable Java 2 runtime. Fortunately, the Java Plug-in is automatically installed when Sun's Java 2 JRE (or Java 2 development environment) is installed; end users need only install the Java 2 JRE in order to obtain the Java Plug-in.

In essence, the Java Plug-in hands applet execution over to a standalone Java 2 JRE, effectively bypassing the browser's own internal JRE. Not all applets are redirected to the Java 2 JRE, however. Any applet woven into a Web page via the <APPLET> tag will execute via the browser's built-in JRE as usual, while those constructed with an appropriately configured <OBJECT> or <EMBED> tag are directed to the Java 2 JRE (see Figure 11-2). As you'll learn in the next chapter (Chapter 12, "Java 3D Fundamentals"), Sun provides a free tool called the **Java Plug-in HTML Converter** that automates the construction of such <OBJECT> and <EMBED> tags.

Figure 11-2 Because Java 3D programs can only execute on a Java 2 JRE, Java 3D applets can't run in today's Web browsers without the help of Sun's Java Plug-in. The Java Plug-in redirects appropriately configured applets away from the browser's internal JRE and onto a more capable Java 2 runtime.

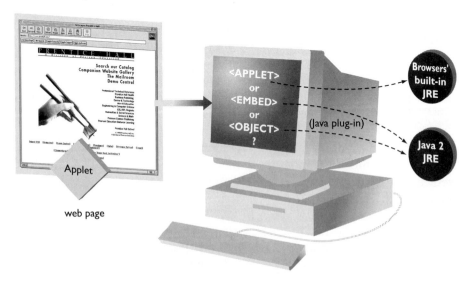

Installing Java 2 and Java 3D

Java 2 is not yet supported by either Netscape Navigator or Internet Explorer; end users must download and install Java 2 and Java 3D manually as detailed in the online Core Web3D "Installing Java 3D" chapter available at http://www.CoreWeb3D.com/java3d/install/. This supplemental Core Web3D chapter also explains how to enable the Java Plug-in, which redirects Java 3D applets to the Java 2 runtime environment.

Although future Web browsers will likely support Java 2 (America Online, for example, is purported to be preparing to carpet-bomb the planet with over 100 million CD-ROMs that contain a Java 2-savvy version of Netscape Navigator), it will be some time before the majority of Web users are properly equipped. To hasten the availability of Java 2 and Java 3D enabled browsers, you're welcome to share the Core Web3D "Installing Java 3D" chapter online with your own users (http://www.CoreWeb3D.com/java3d/install/).

The Java 3D API

As an extension to the core Java technology, the Java 3D API is a standard suite of classes that developers can use to add 3D graphics and sound capabilities to their applets and applications. Java 3D, however, isn't the only option when it comes to extending Java's multimedia capabilities. As a member of the Java Media API family, Java 3D is the 3D component of a compressive multimedia extension system.

Java Media APIs

Although it took the software development industry by storm, the original version of Java was lackluster in terms of its multimedia capabilities. Even today the core Java libraries support only basic sound playback and relatively simplistic line and bitmap graphics, making it difficult, at best, to construct rich multimedia programs. With Java 1.1, however, Sun introduced a framework of multimedia APIs to bolster the Java core with serious multimedia capabilities.

The Java Media APIs (http://java.sun.com/products/java-media/) are a collection of Java extensions that allow developers to create complex multimedia programs, including 3D. As a member of the Java Media family, Java 3D's siblings include:

- **Java 2D,** which offers advanced two-dimensional graphics and imaging. Encompassing line art, text, and images, the Java 2D API supports enhanced lines, colors, image transforms, and composites.

- **Java Advanced Imaging (JAI),** which gives Java programs a wide range of image-processing capabilities, including image scaling, cropping, enhancing, distorting, and warping.

- **Java Media Framework (JMF),** which provides a unified architecture, messaging protocol, and programming interface for media playback, capture, and manipulation. JMF allows developers to synchronize and control audio, video, and other time-based media within their Java applications and applets.

- **Java Shared Data Toolkit (JSDT),** which offers interactive, network-based collaboration capabilities that developers can use to create communication programs such as multiuser whiteboards, chat systems, workflow applications, remote presentations, shared simulations, and networked games.

- **Java Sound,** which extends Java's otherwise limited audio capabilities to provide low-level audio features such as audio mixing, capture, MIDI (Musical Instrument Digital Interface) sequencing, and MIDI synthesis. Whereas Java itself supports only a limited form of AU format audio, Java Sound supports AIFF, AU, and WAV audio formats, as well as MIDI-based song file formats (TYPE 0 MIDI, TYPE 1 MIDI, and RMF).

- **Java Speech,** which gives developers the ability to add support for speech recognition and speech synthesis to their Java programs. Java Speech supports command and control recognizers, dictation systems, and speech synthesizers.

- **Java Telephony**, which integrates telephones with computers. By allowing Java programs to control telephony, Java Telephony can be used to create a wide range of applications including fax systems, voice mail, autodial programs, call logging and tracking, routing, automated attendants, and call center management.

Designed as an interoperable suite of multimedia packages, the Java Media APIs allow developers to integrate audio, video, animation, 2D and

3D graphics, speech, and telephony. Just as Java 3D can be integrated with core Java technologies (such as networking, i/o, database access, and GUI facilities), it can also be integrated with other members of the Java Media family. As a result, media-rich applets and applications can be constructed by combining Java Media APIs with core Java classes.

Java Media Packages and Development Cycles

Although Java Media APIs are interoperable, they're developed and delivered independent of one another. Some Java Media APIs are organized as a subpackage of the main Java Media Framework (JMF) `javax.media` package. Java 3D classes, for example, are found in the `javax.media.j3d` package, while Java Advanced Imaging (JAI) classes are found in the `javax.media.jai` package.

Other Java Media APIs, however, are organized into different packages. Java 2D, for instance, is bundled under the original `java.awt` Abstract Windowing Toolkit package (meaning that Java 2D classes are now considered part of the Java core, as they're delivered under the top-level `java` package instead of as a `javax` "extension" package). Java Sound classes, meanwhile, are found in the `javax.speech` package. Although some Java Media APIs are actually part of the Java core (such as Java 2D), most, like Java 3D, are simply extensions to the core.

Because Java Media APIs are developed and deployed separately, they do not share the same development cycle or version number. Java Media Framework 2.0 was in beta test at the time of this writing, for example, while Java 3D 1.2 and Java Telephony 1.3 were in "early access" release. Visit http://java.sun.com/products/java-media/ to learn more about the various APIs that make up the Java Media family.

Java 3D Packages

Java 3D programs are constructed using classes found in the `javax.media.j3d`, `javax.vecmath`, and `com.sun.j3d` packages (see Table 11-1). The main functionality of Java 3D is provided by the `javax.media.j3d` package, which contains over 100 classes related to 3D graphics. These are often called the *core* Java 3D classes because they are so fundamental to the operation of Java 3D (not to be confused with the core Java classes, which define the base Java platform). Every Java 3D program is constructed using one or more classes from this package.

Table 11.1   Java 3D API Packages

Package Name	Description
javax.media.j3d	The base Java 3D package containing the essential classes that make up the Java 3D standard extension. These classes provide the key functionality of Java 3D and are a required part of any Java 3D implementation.
javax.vecmath	A collection of vector and matrix math classes used internally by the core Java 3D classes and also by many Java 3D programs. Like the classes found in `javax.media.j3d`, these classes are a required part of any Java 3D implementation.
com.sun.j3d	Java 3D "convenience" classes developed by Sun to make life easier on the Java 3D programmer. Inside this top-level package is a subpackage called `com.sun.j3d.util` that contains a collection of "utility" classes. Convenience and utility classes are organized into four general categories (content loaders, scene-graph assembly, geometry, and convenience classes). These classes are optional, not a required part of a Java 3D implementation.

Java 3D programs also use the vector mathematics classes found in the `javax.vecmath` package. Itself a standard extension, the vector math package contains a number of classes related to 3D object representation (points, vectors, and matrices, for instance) and manipulation (such as rotating, scaling, and translation operations). Although `javax.vecmath` isn't a formal part of the Java 3D API, it is vital to Java 3D nonetheless. Many core Java 3D classes rely directly on the `javax.vecmath` package, making the two packages practically inseparable. Vector math classes are also useful outside of the context of Java 3D, however, and so are packaged separately.

In addition to vector math classes, Java 3D programs often use a variety of "convenience" classes defined in the `com.sun.j3d` package. Unlike the core Java 3D and vector math packages, which are both *standard* extensions, the `com.sun.j3d` classes constitute a nonstandard extension to Java that Sun developed to provide developers with a collection of utilities that make writing Java 3D programs a little easier. Inside the main convenience class package is a subpackage called `com.sun.j3d.util` that contains a collection of Java 3D "utility" classes. Convenience and utility classes are organized into four

Note

A convenience class extends a core class in order to make it easier to use. A utility class adds programming capabilities to a core class. Sun's com.sun.j3d *package contains convenience classes, while the* com.sun.j3d.util *subpackage contains utility classes. Both convenience and utility classes are optional; Java 3D does not require them.*

general categories: content loaders, scene graph assembly, geometry, and convenience classes.

Sun's convenience classes provide functionality that is often useful to Java 3D developers, although these classes aren't crucial to the operation of Java 3D in general. In other words, com.sun.j3d classes aren't a required part of a Java 3D implementation and are merely provided as a courtesy to developers. The source code for these classes is available free of charge, allowing utility classes to be used as prebuilt building blocks or as the starting points for a developer's custom-defined classes.

Because they are not a standard extension to Java, Sun's convenience classes aren't bundled into a "javax" package. They are, instead, contained in a package that is named using the reverse domain com.sun, which is Sun's recommended naming practice when it comes to custom packages. Because Sun itself created these classes, they're packaged under the reverse of Sun's own sun.com domain. (If these convenience classes had been created by IBM, for example, they'd be packaged under com.ibm, while the Web3D Consortium would have packaged them under org.web3d.)

Design Goals

The Java 3D specification was developed as a collaborative effort between Sun, SGI, Intel, and Apple. Several major design goals drove its development, including:

- **Integration with Java**, allowing experienced Java developers to take their programming skills into the field of 3D with relatively little effort. By "writing to the Java 3D API," developers can create cross-platform 3D applets and applications using the familiar and popular Java programming language. As a standard extension to Java, the Java

3D API allows developers to create sophisticated 3D programs with a minimal amount of effort. Java 3D programs can access standard Java features (such as windowing, networking, database access, and so forth) and vice versa (standard Java programs can take advantage of 3D through the Java 3D API). In addition, Java 3D programs benefit from key design features common to all Java programs, such as automatic garbage collection (memory management) and multithreading.

- **High performance**, which is particularly important for interactive 3D. Because performance has always been a major concern among Java developers (as well as a pressure point worked devilishly by critics of the technology), Java 3D was designed from the onset with high performance and scalability in mind. Specifically, Java 3D was designed to layer on top of low-level graphics APIs (such as OpenGL and Direct3D). As a layered API, Java 3D supports hardware acceleration when available, a feature that lets Java 3D programs benefit directly from underlying hardware enhancements. In addition, the Java 3D scene graph structure supports high levels of optimization and multiprocessor rendering. (Java 3D takes advantage of Java's threaded architecture, allowing rendering tasks to be shared among more than one processor in cases where the program is run on a multiprocessor system.)

- **Support for runtime "loaders,"** giving Java 3D programs the ability to support a wide range of 3D file formats. Loaders currently exist for VRML, Wavefront (OBJ), AutoCAD Drawing Interchange File (DXF), Caligari trueSpace (COB), Lightwave Scene Format (LSF), Lightwave Object Format (LOF), 3D-Studio (3DS), and many other formats. Developers can create their own loaders in cases where they need to access a file format for which a loader doesn't already exist (allowing Java 3D to accommodate proprietary 3D formats that it otherwise couldn't).

- **Support for a rich suite of critical capabilities,** without succumbing to "feature creep" that might otherwise bloat the core Java 3D API. The main capabilities of Java 3D were intentionally kept tightly focused, while nonessential (or obscure) features that could be layered on top of the Java 3D API were omitted. The convenience and utility classes provided in the `com.sun.j3d` package, for example, were omitted from the Java 3D core because these capabilities are not essential and can be layered on top of the core API.

Note

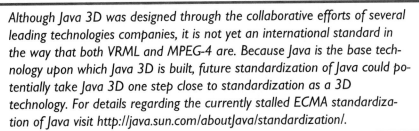

Although Java 3D was designed through the collaborative efforts of several leading technologies companies, it is not yet an international standard in the way that both VRML and MPEG-4 are. Because Java is the base technology upon which Java 3D is built, future standardization of Java could potentially take Java 3D one step close to standardization as a 3D technology. For details regarding the currently stalled ECMA standardization of Java visit http://java.sun.com/aboutJava/standardization/.

Version Overview

Like most software products, Java 3D has matured incrementally since it was first released. Java 3D Version 1.1.2 was the most current implementation at the time of this writing, while Java 3D 1.2 was waiting in the wings. Expected to ship at about the same time this book hits the shelf, Java 3D 1.2 marks the third major version of the API. Following is a brief overview of each:

- **Java 3D 1.0**, the first public release of the Java 3D specification, was unveiled at Sun's JavaOne conference in June 1997. As a high-level 3D API based on Java, the Java 3D 1.0 specification described the classes that developers would use to build 3D applications and applets. Based on a scene graph programming model inspired in part by VRML, the Java 3D 1.0 specification supported interactive 3D scene construction, 3D animation, and basic 3D sound capabilities. Despite its promise, however, an implementation was never delivered for Java 3D 1.0; it remained a specification. The first Java 3D implementation was actually built around an alpha test release of Java 3D 1.1.

- **Java 3D 1.1** was released at the Java Business Exposition in December 1998. Under development for nearly a full year, Java 3D 1.1 was motivated largely by performance issues suffered by the original alpha 1.1 implementation (see Java 3D 1.0 above). Specifically, Java 3D 1.1 addressed rendering and runtime performance problems and also provided a much cleaner interface with the then-emerging Java 1.2 specification (Java 1.2 would eventually be renamed Java 2 upon release, taking the development community by surprise). The result was a dramatic overall performance boost. Although Java 3D 1.1 doesn't quite approach the raw performance typical of native 3D programming libraries, the gap is now marginal. In addition to major performance improvements, Java 3D 1.1 also included a number of convenience and utility classes (packaged under com.sun.j3d) that simplified the development process and made life easier for programmers. File loaders were also introduced, allowing Java 3D to take advantage of a wide variety of 3D formats. Java 3D 1.1 also introduced a common interface to input devices, allowing developers to support devices other than the mouse and keyboard. At the time of this writing Java 3D 1.1.2 is the most current version of the API, representing minor tweaks to the original 1.1 release.

- **Java 3D 1.2,** due to be released in 2000, was under development at the time this book went to press. Considered by some to be the first "mature" Java 3D implementation, version 1.2 is essentially version 1.1 in which the internals have been rewritten for added performance and stability. Although it is basically an industrial-strength implementation of 1.1, Java 3D 1.2 is also expected to include a few new capabilities, including an off-screen rendering mode (permitting rendering to a memory image larger than the screen itself), 3D geometry and texture enhancements, increased appearance functionality, and added sound capabilities. For details, visit the Java 3D 1.2 API page at http://java.sun.com/products/java-media/3D/1_2_api/.

Note

The final release of Java 2 (originally called Java 1.2) caused some problems with Java 3D and the other Java Media APIs. Specifically, combining heavyweight (peer-based) components with lightweight (nonpeer) Swing components caused rendering problems.

Straddling the Middle

A question commonly asked about Java 3D is how it compares existing APIs for doing 3D graphics. On one side of the fence are the established rendering APIs such as OpenGL and Direct3D, while on the other are 3D file formats such as DXF and, to some extent, VRML (VRML isn't merely a 3D file format, although it isn't a full-blown 3D programming API, either).

In short, Java 3D falls somewhere in the middle, with capabilities more like those of rendering APIs than file formats. Although it offers a high-level, scene graph programming model that shields programmers from low-level rendering details (through which many behavioral aspects such as those found in VRML can be produced), it also permits low-level control similar to that of OpenGL and Direct3D. Like VRML, Java 3D allows developers to focus on scene composition rather than rendering (*what* to draw, not *how* to draw), although Java 3D's also offers low-level rendering control that VRML does not provide.

Java 3D vs. Low-level Rendering APIs

Taken at face value, Java 3D is merely a 3D programming API that is similar in nature to OpenGL and Direct3D. Java 3D implementations are, in fact, layered on top of native low-level rendering APIs (OpenGL is the low-level API on top of which UNIX implementations are typically layered, while Windows users have their choice of OpenGL or Direct3D). In this sense, Java 3D can be thought of as a high-level, cross-platform 3D API beneath which a low-level native API such as OpenGL or Direct3D lurks, as illustrated earlier, in Figure 11-1.

Java 3D content is created by writing code; software developers use a source code editor to write Java programs that take advantage of the Java 3D API. Java 3D source code text file(s) are then passed through a Java compiler, which generates corresponding bytecode class files. The compiled class files can then be executed by a Java 2 runtime system (provided a Java 3D implementation is also available). In other words, to create Java 3D content from scratch you must know how to program in Java.

Using Java to write Java 3D programs, therefore, is similar in concept to using C++ to write OpenGL or Direct3D programs. Unlike low-level APIs that are used to create native applications, however, the combination of Java and Java 3D gives developers the ability to construct full-featured applications *and* applets that run across a range of platforms. Java 3D also supports the concept of file loaders, allowing Java 3D programs to take advantage of premade 3D content (such as VRML files). Because a wide variety of 3D files can be loaded into Java 3D programs (where they can be controlled and manipulated by Java code), Java 3D developers can tap into a vast sea of premade content with very little effort.

In addition, Java 3D differs from traditional 3D graphics APIs in its general approach to 3D programming and the facilities it offers. Like low-level APIs, Java 3D allows the programmer to get down to the raw triangles used in rendering, if necessary. While such low-level rendering control can be useful in some cases, most of the time it is an unnecessary burden. 3D developers are typically more concerned with the overall design and implementation of their program. Java 3D is most powerful as a high-level 3D API because it allows the programmer to focus on more general aspects of development, such as user input (mouse, joystick, or keyboard input) and interactive behaviors.

Java 3D also differs from OpenGL and Direct3D in the simplicity with which it integrates with other programming facilities. To display a window of Java 3D content in a typical Java program, for example, you can simply create a frame and add a 3D canvas to it. After registering for mouse and keyboard input, you're ready to rock and roll. With OpenGL, however, the process is much more complicated; you must first determine what screen capabilities are available, select an appropriate one, create your window, separately register for mouse input and sound output, and, finally, render the content to the screen.

Visual Java 3D Authoring Tools

Although visual development tools specifically for Java 3D are on the horizon, they haven't yet emerged to spare us from coding. The best we can do today is to construct geometry with a visual 3D development and export the results to a 3D file format for which a Java 3D loader exists (such as VRML; see Chapter 10, "Creating New VRML Worlds," for details on visual VRML authoring tools). The geometry can then be loaded into a Java 3D scene, although coding is required. For details, see Chapter 13, "Customizing Size, Location, and Orientation."

For links to Java 3D authoring tools, visit the Java 3D tools section of the Web3D Gallery (http://www.web3dgallery.com/java3d/tools/). Check back from time to time if you're interested in visual development tools; when such products eventually become available you'll find links to them here. In the meantime, visit the Web3D Gallery's main Java 3D page (http://www.web3dgallery.com/java3d/) for links to Java 3D applets that you can customize and use on your own Web site.

Java 3D vs. Modeling File Formats

On the other side of the divide are the 3D modeling file formats such as Au-toCAD Drawing Interchange File (DXF), Lightwave Scene Format (LSF), VRML, and, to some extent, MPEG-4/BIFS. Unlike programming APIs that provide full-blown 3D graphics development facilities, 3D modeling file formats typically provide an encapsulated structure for the delivery of 3D content. To be fair, VRML and MPEG-4/BIFS are not merely file formats, as they embody runtime semantics, and a 3D scene description language as well as file format in which this language is stored. Although most 3D file formats simply define 3D scenes, some, such as VRML and MPEG-4/BIFS, also define runtime semantics (such as routes and scripts). Neither VRML nor MPEG-4/BIFS, however, offers as robust an integrated programming language as the combination of Java and Java 3D.

A primary difference between Java 3D and 3D modeling file formats lies in their execution models; 3D files are loaded into a program for display purposes, whereas Java 3D programs are executed directly by a Java runtime system. A VRML file, for example, is of no real value without a VRML browser (in the same way that a text file has no purpose without a text editor or viewer). Standalone Java 3D applications, however, execute like any other software program, whereas Java 3D applets are executed within the context of a Java-enabled Web browser. (As you'll see later, Java 3D programs are often designed to run as dual-purpose standalone applications *and* Web-based applets.)

Using the Java 3D loader mechanism, in fact, Java 3D programs can act as a viewer for a variety of 3D modeling file formats (including VRML). The same cannot be said for 3D models; 3D file formats have no knowledge of Java 3D. You cannot, for example, load Java 3D classes into a VRML world, nor can you integrate Java 3D content directly with an MPEG-4/BIFS scene.

VRML-Java 3D Working Group

The Web3D Consortium's VRML-Java 3D working group is responsible for fostering the relationship between VRML and Java 3D. To this end, Sun has turned development of the Java 3D VRML loader over to this group. In

Note

Java 3D does not have an external file format. Java 3D does, however, offer a file loader mechanism through which a variety of 3D file formats are supported.

addition to the Java 3D loader, the VRML-Java 3D working group has also developed a VRML browser using Java 3D, both of which can be downloaded from the group's site at http://www.web3d.org/WorkingGroups/vrml-java3d/.

Key Java 3D Features

Although Java 3D is fundamentally a programming interface to a comprehensive library of compiled 3D classes, which is quite different from VRML's text-file format and scene description language, the two have a good deal in common. Because VRML inspired the design and development of Java 3D, the two technologies have feature sets that are described in similar terms, as the following sections explain.

Of course, Java 3D and VRML aren't identical twins; they're different in as many ways as they are similar. They are, ultimately, two different approaches to interactive 3D. In the sections that follow you'll learn about the key features of Java 3D, how it resembles VRML, and how it stands on its own as a 3D development API.

Scene Graph Programming Model

Like VRML, Java 3D is based on a high-level scene graph programming model. As you may recall from Chapter 3, "Entering the Third Dimension" and Chapter 5, "VRML Fundamentals," scene graphs are treelike data structures used to store, organize, and render 3D scene information (objects, materials and appearances, lights, and so forth). Similar to VRML (and other scene graph programming models), Java 3D scene graphs are made up of objects called *nodes,* as illustrated in Figure 11-3.

Although Java 3D and VRML both employ a scene graph programming model, Java 3D scene graphs are considerably more difficult to construct,

Note

Like VRML, the elements that populate a Java 3D scene are often called objects. When used in the context of a Java scene, the term object differs from the more general term that is used to describe an instance of a Java class. Although confusing, it's permissible to say that Java 3D scene objects are constructed of Java class objects.

owing to the inherent complexity of full-featured programming languages such as Java. For each Java 3D scene object, transform, or behavior, the programmer must create a new object instance (using corresponding Java 3D classes), set the fields of the instance, and then add it to the scene.

Whereas Java 3D scene graphs are more complicated to construct than their VRML counterparts, the Java 3D approach is much more expressive. All of the code necessary to represent a scene can be placed in a central structure, over which the programmer has direct access. Altering Java 3D node attributes and values is achieved by invoking instance methods and setting fields, which is relatively fast and easy for experienced Java programmers.

Note

The scripting architecture of VRML enforces a highly componentized approach to script-communication, whereas Java 3D allows behaviors to be centralized (or localized) within a shape's geometry or componentized into separate classes. (Unlike modeling languages such as VRML, which are typically restricted to one paradigm, Java's robust programming capabilities allow the developer to use either approach.)

Figure 11-3   Nodes that make up a Java 3D scene graph are rooted to a Locale object, which in turn is rooted to VirtualUniverse object.

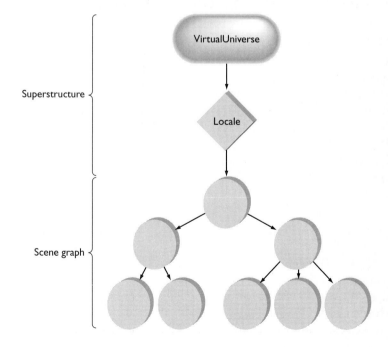

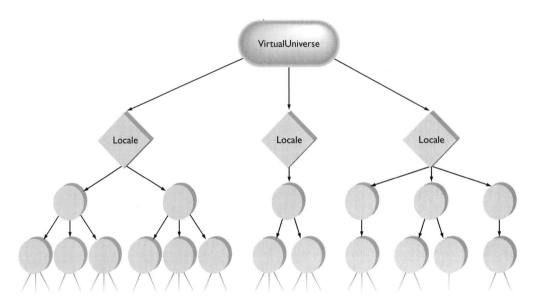

Figure 11-4   A VirtualUniverse object can contain more than one Locale object, meaning that multiple scene graphs can be aggregated under a single virtual universe.

In Java 3D, the term *virtual universe* is used to describe a 3D space populated with 3D objects and is therefore analogous to a VRML world. As Figure 11-3 illustrates, Java 3D scene graphs are rooted to a Locale object, which itself is attached to a VirtualUniverse object. Virtual universes represent the largest possible unit of aggregation in Java 3D, and as such can be thought of as databases. Together, VirtualUniverse and Locale objects comprise what's known as the *scene graph superstructure* (see Figure 11-3).

Virtual universes can be extremely large and can accommodate more than one Locale object. A single VirtualUniverse object, therefore, can act as the database for multiple scene graphs, as depicted in Figure 11-4 (each Locale object is the parent of a unique scene graph). Later in this chapter you'll see that the Locale object specifies a high-resolution coordinate anchor for objects in a scene (objects attached to a Locale are positioned in the scene relative to that Locale's high-resolution coordinates, which are specified using floating-point values).

Rendering Control

The Java 3D renderer is responsible for traversing a Java 3D scene graph and displaying its visible geometry in an on-screen window (e.g., an applet canvas or application frame). In addition to drawing visible geometry, the Java 3D renderer is also responsible for processing user input and performing behaviors. To handle these various tasks the Java 3D renderer runs in an infinite loop that has the following conceptual structure:

```
while(true) {
   Process user input
   If (request to exit == TRUE) break
   Perform Behaviors
   Traverse scene graph and render visible objects
}
Cleanup and exit
```

Unlike modeling languages such as VRML, rendering APIs such as Java 3D typically give the developer complete control over the rendering process (including control over exactly when items are rendered to screen). In graphics parlance, an API's *rendering mode* specifies such control.

The Java 3D API supports three different rendering modes that developers can choose from: **immediate mode**, **retained mode**, and **compiled-retained mode**. These modes correspond to the level of control that the developer has over the rendering process, as well as the amount of liberty that Java 3D has to optimize rendering (each successive rendering mode gives Java 3D more freedom to optimizing program execution). Although most Java 3D developers prefer the convenience and performance enhancements that come with retained and compiled-retained modes provide, some require the fine-grained control offered by immediate mode rendering. Following is an overview of each:

- **Immediate Mode** gives the developer complete control over every aspect of rendering, which in turn gives Java 3D very little opportunity for optimization. For every frame drawn to the screen the developer must provide the raw rendering data (points, lines, or triangles) to a Java 3D draw method. Because Java 3D doesn't bother to retain any of this information between frames, the developer is responsible for managing the rendering data between calls to the draw method. Although intermediate mode rendering can be used in combination with scene graphs, this mode also gives developers the freedom to store and manage scene data in any way they see fit. Immediate mode can be used alone, or it may be combined with retained mode and/or compile-retained mode rendering.

- **Retained Mode** is perhaps the most commonly used rendering mode, as it strikes a balance between the amount of rendering control given to the developer and the amount of optimization control given to Java 3D. Retained mode rendering requires the developer to construct a scene graph and also to specify those parts of the scene graph that may change in the rendering process (see the previous scene graph discussion). The Java runtime system retains this information internally, rendering it as often as necessary without requiring intervention on the developer's part. Scene graphs rendered in retained mode are fully accessible, meaning that the programmer can add nodes, delete existing nodes, or modify nodes at will. Because scene information is always stored in a scene graph structure, however, Java 3D is able to perform a reasonable number of rendering optimizations in an effort to increase performance. In retained mode, parts of a scene graph may be compiled. Compilation of a scene graph has two effects: It allows Java 3D to optimize the scene graph as much as possible, and it makes the "contract" specified by capability bits permanent. The capability bits of a compiled scene graph, therefore, can't be changed (capability bits control access to an object's contents; see Chapter 12, "Java 3D Fundamentals," for details). Because Java 3D is primarily a scene graph API, retained mode is usually the best approach to rendering (making retained mode the most common rendering mode).

- **Compiled-retained Mode** gives Java 3D the most opportunity to optimize rendering performance by limiting the degree to which the developer has access to scene information. Similar to retained mode, compiled-retained mode requires that the developer construct a scene graph and specify those portions of it that may change during rendering. The developer can specify that Java 3D compile some, or all, of the subgraphs that make up a larger scene graph. Although functionally equivalent to their noncompiled counterparts, compiled scene graphs are stored in an internal format that is optimized for rendering purposes. In addition to compiling scene graphs, developers can also compile individual Java 3D objects. Because they have been optimized for performance, compiled objects and scene graphs are, in a sense, "off limits." As a result, programmers have minimal access to the internal structure of compiled objects and scene graphs. Knowing that the majority of components that make up a compiled object or scene will not change, Java 3D can perform any number of optimizations in an effort to boost rendering performance. Geometry compression, geometry grouping, and scene graph flattening are just a few of the many techniques that Java 3D can use to optimize performance.

Java 3D Rendering Model

To avoid multiple APIs and incompatible programs that support indexed and true color, or Z-buffered and non-Z-buffered environments, the Java 3D API assumes a double-buffered, true-color, and Z-buffered rendering model. As minimal requirements for the Java 3D API rendering model, these specifications don't necessarily describe hardware required to run Java 3D programs.

Instead, the Java 3D rendering model simply describes the capabilities of the underlying, low-level API (such as OpenGL) atop which a Java 3D API implementation is layered. Exactly how the underlying low-level API actually implements this functionality is of no concern to programmers working with the high-level Java 3D API.

Because Java 3D is layered on top of lower-level graphics APIs, Java 3D supports hardware acceleration and other performance-enhancing features of the underlying platform. As a high-level, scene graph-based API, however, Java 3D shields the developer from platform-specific details such as hardware acceleration. If hardware acceleration is available, the Java runtime system will take advantage of it transparently without any coding effort on the developer's part.

Scalable Performance

Java 3D was designed to support programs that scale in step with the performance of the systems on which they execute. As computer systems grow in power, for example, Java 3D programs will exhibit increasingly better performance. Developers don't have to rewrite or recompile their Java 3D programs to keep up with advances in hardware; Java 3D applets and applications scale automatically.

Java 3D was designed for scalability in many ways. As a layered API, Java 3D sits atop low-level graphics APIs (such as OpenGL and Direct3D), allowing it to benefit from hardware acceleration when available. The Java 3D scene graph structure was also designed for scalability and incorporates a number of high-level optimization features including view culling, occlusion culling, execution culling, behavior pruning, parallel graph traversal, and parallel rendering.

Because it is based on Java, Java 3D inherently supports multithreading. *Threads*, also known as *lightweight processes* or *execution contexts*, allow large or time-consuming program tasks to be divided into a number of smaller tasks that can be executed independent of one another. When run on systems that have multiple CPUs, commonly known as *multiprocessor systems*, an application's threads can be executed concurrently on different processors. The result is a performance increase, as program execution is effectively spread across CPUs.

Although multiprocessor systems are considered high-end today (primarily reserved for high-capacity servers and scientific workstations), consumer-level computers will eventually benefit from multiple CPUs as well. Because Java 3D supports multithreading by way of Java, a single Java 3D program can scale in performance across a wide variety of computer systems.

When run on a single CPU computer, for example, all threads in a program are executed on a single processor (this can actually result in decreased performance; see "When Multithreading Backfires"). When run on a multiprocessor system, however, the same program can execute across any number of installed CPUs; performance is increased transparently simply because more than one CPU is available for thread execution. The programmer can, therefore, deploy one body of code that scales in performance in step with the underlying hardware.

Although developers are free to construct their own threads, Java 3D implementations typically use multithreading behind the scenes to enhance overall performance, unbeknownst to the developer. Allowing different branches of a scene graph to be traversed concurrently, for example, can greatly increase scene graph traversal speeds. Similarly, processing related to behavior execution and pruning might be handled at the same time as scene graph traversal if more than one CPU is available to handle the load.

Warning: When Multithreading Backfires

Multithreading can actually result in reduced performance on single-processor systems, as the overhead of thread management can be costly on systems that don't have more than one CPU to share the load. This is, unfortunately, the case with Java 3D 1.1. The latest version of Java 3D, however, is expected to eliminate multithreaded performance bottlenecks on single-processor systems.

Java 3D 1.2, due out in 2000, will be largely single threaded when running on single-processor systems. Java 3D 1.2 will also increase the overall runtime performance of Java 3D programs executed on multiprocessor systems. (Java 3D 1.1 performance is increased approximately 15% when executed on a two-processor system, while Java 3D 1.2 is expected to scale even better on multiprocessor systems.)

Behaviors

In order to support various forms of interactivity, Java 3D allows developers to create customized behaviors for the various objects that populate a virtual universe. Behaviors allow program logic to be imbedded into a scene graph and can be thought of as the capacity of an object to change in response to input or a stimulus.

A spinning wheel, for example, would have the behavior of animation associated with it. The input, or stimulus, that the wheel animates in response to might merely be the passage of time (every second the wheel could complete one full rotation, for example). Or, the wheel might be attached to a car and exhibit its animation behavior only when the car itself is put into gear.

Whereas an animated wheel is an example of simple behavior, an interactive sales representative would require more complex behavior capabilities.

Scheduling, Processing, and Pruning

Behavior nodes, or objects, can be added to and removed from a scene graph as needed. Every Behavior object contains a *scheduling region* that defines a spatial volume used to enable the scheduling of the node. (A Behavior node is active, meaning that it can receive stimuli, only when a ViewPlatform's activation volume intersects its scheduling region.) In addition, every Behavior node contains an `initialization()` method that is used to initialize the internal state of the behavior and specify a wakeup condition (or more than one wakeup condition). This method is called when the BranchGroup object containing the behavior is added to the virtual universe.

In addition, all Behavior objects contain a `processStimulation()` method. This method, also known as a *stimulus method*, is responsible for receiving and processing stimulation for a given Behavior node. A behavior's stimulus method is invoked only when the node is active and one of its wakeup criteria is satisfied, allowing Java 3D to "prune" behavior execution and invoke only those that are actually necessary (see Execution Culling). Although not essential in small or trivial Java 3D programs, behavior pruning is particularly useful in cases where every processor cycle counts (i.e., when execution takes place on a low-powered computer system) and for larger virtual universes where hundreds of behaviors must compete for a slice of the CPU pie.

A 3D sales robot could walk visitors through an online purchase, for instance, assuming it had the appropriate behavior associated with it (perhaps some amount of artificial intelligence behavior). A 3D model such as this might also have sophisticated animation behavior that allows it to move about the screen in a natural, human-like way.

A behavior can be associated with the object(s) it interacts with, so that the behavior is active only when the object is in view of (or near) the user. Behaviors can also be associated with the window or keyboard, allowing them to be active at all times. In other words, the Java 3D behavior mechanism is a way of encapsulating program logic into units whose scope can range from local to global.

Behavior nodes give Java 3D programs a wide range of canned and customized behaviors, including animation, keyboard and mouse processing, reaction to movement, and processing pick events. Behavior nodes contain both variables and methods. A Behavior node's methods can interact with other Java objects, modify the state of scene graph nodes, and perform custom calculations specific to that behavior (such as AI processing, in the case of a Behavior node constructed for the previously mentioned sales robot).

Execution Culling

To prune behavior execution, Java 3D builds an internal scheduling-volume tree based on the scheduling regions associated with all Behavior nodes in a virtual universe. In addition, Java 3D constructs an AND-OR tree that contains all Behavior node wakeup criterion. Together these two data structures supply Java 3D with the domain knowledge it needs to skip, or *prune*, unneeded behavior execution.

In order to cull behavior execution, a Java 3D *behavior scheduler* performs the following tests on all behavior objects:

1. Identify all behavior objects with a scheduling region that intersects with the ViewPlatform object's activation volume.

2. Test the WakeupCondition of each behavior object identified in step 1 (Java 3D's WakeupCondition object can specify 14 different criteria used to trigger a behavior's stimulus method, including movement, collision detection, sensor activity, and the elapse of a specific time interval).

3. Schedule the behavior object for execution if its WakupCondition is true (invoke the behavior's stimulus method).

Generic Input Devices

Java 3D supports keyboard and mouse input by way of Java's own input capabilities. In addition, Java 3D offers developers the ability to support a wide range of input devices such as joysticks, position trackers, data gloves, and body suits.

With standard 3D graphics APIs, supporting special-purpose input devices such as these is no trivial matter. For each device that the developer wishes to support, he must write a fair amount of native code, compile it, and then link it into the main application. In addition to being time consuming to develop, support for new input devices can be slow to reach the end user, because a new revision of the entire application must be redistributed with the driver update intact.

Java 3D, in contrast, offers a flexible, generic input-device model that is quite painless by comparison. Handling both polled and continuous input devices, the Java 3D InputDevice interface defines an abstract input device that developers can use to implement specific input-device drivers. Java 3D's built-in *input-device scheduler* can dynamically incorporate special-purpose input-device driver classes into an existing application, meaning that an existing Java 3D program can support new input devices as soon as a new driver class is available. Recompiling and redistribution of the main program is not necessary, only the new input-device driver class is needed.

Note

Java 3D version 1.1 doesn't fully support generic input devices. The forthcoming 1.2 version, however, is expected to do so.

Geometry Compression

Unlike VRML, the Java 3D API allows developers to compress scene geometry. Whereas entire VRML files can be compressed with the standalone GZip utility, Java 3D supports binary compression of specific object geometry through the API itself. Java 3D's geometry-compression capabilities allow an object's geometry, or form, to be represented in an order of magnitude less space than many popular 3D file formats.

With very little loss in object quality, Java 3D's binary compression format is typically used to reduce the overall memory requirement of a scene. Due to the dramatic space savings it affords, this technique is also used to increase the speed at which a virtual universe can download across the network.

Convenience and Utility Classes

The core Java 3D API defines objects only in terms of strips of polygons, or triangles, arranged in various forms. Although a bare 3D object skeleton can be formed using the core API classes, for example, it's up to the programmer to add the required behavior. In many cases, developers construct Java 3D programs by implementing code and structures common to other Java 3D programs. Realizing this, Sun provides a large number of convenience and utility classes designed to save Java 3D developers time, effort, and code.

As you learned earlier, Sun's Java 3D convenience classes are found in the com.sun.j3d package. Here you'll find convenience classes for a range of purposes, from basic scene graph construction, to mouse and keyboard navigation behaviors, to standardized audio-device handling. In addition a number of loaders are included with the convenience classes, allowing Java 3D developers to take advantage of content stored in a variety of popular 3D file formats.

Sun's convenience classes use the Java Sound API (a member of the Java Media family) to produce both 2D and 3D audio output capabilities for Java 3D programs. Although Java 3D uses the Java Sound API to support general sound and MIDI, the Java 3D API also supports fully spatialized audio.

Versatile View Model

Java 3D introduces a unique view model that separates the virtual world (the 3D space in which 3D objects reside) from the physical world that the user resides in. Although the Java 3D view model is more complicated than those found in other 3D graphics APIs, the added complexity allows Java 3D programs to operate seamlessly across a wide range of viewing devices. A single Java 3D applet or application, for example, will work just as well when viewed on a standard desktop monitor as it will when viewed through a pair of stereoscopic virtual reality goggles, in an immersive "cave," or on the walls of a stereo projection system.

The Java 3D view model makes a clean distinction between the virtual world and the user's physical world. In terms of the Java 3D API, the View-Platform object represents the viewpoint in the virtual world, while the physical world is represented by the View object and its associated components, as illustrated in Figure 11–5. Java 3D provides a bridge between the virtual

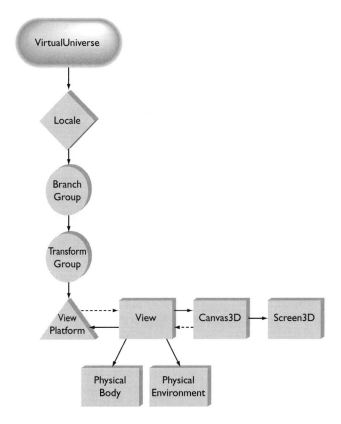

Figure 11-5   In the Java 3D API the ViewPlatform object represents the user's viewpoint in a virtual universe, while the real world is represented by the view object and its associated components.

and physical environment by constructing a one-to-one mapping from one space to another, allowing activity in one space to effect the other.

Conceptually, a Java 3D program manipulates the position, orientation, or scale of its ViewPlatform object. The Java 3D renderer combines this information with information contained in the View object (information about the physical world, such as the user's physical position and orientation in the real world—data that might be provided by a head-tracking system, for example). By combining information about the virtual world with data collected from the physical world, Java 3D is able to render the scene to the user's particular display device.

Camera-based View Model

Traditional camera-based view models, such as the one employed by VRML, emulate a camera placed in a virtual world; programmers continually reposition a virtual camera in 3D space in an attempt to simulate a human being residing in a virtual world. Although camera-based viewing is appropriate in cases where the end user's display device is known (such as a standard computer monitor), it's not flexible enough to handle a wide range of display devices.

The Java 3D view model, on the other hand, was specifically designed to accommodate a variety of end-user configurations. It can handle head-tracking devices seamlessly, without any effort on the programmer's part. In addition, the Java 3D view model can automatically generate stereo views (meaning that various types of VR goggles and stereo viewing devices are supported without extra coding by the programmer).

The Java 3D view model degenerates smoothly to a traditional camera-based model in cases where the display is a single (nonstereo) standard computer monitor, and no head-tracking devices are detected.

Summary

Java 3D is a standard Java 2 platform extension ("optional package") that allows developers to construct comprehensive, platform-independent applets and applications. Featuring interactive 3D graphics, behaviors, and spatialized sound capabilities, Java 3D can be integrated with standard Java programs and vice versa.

As a layered API, the high-level Java 3D API sits atop low-level 3D graphics APIs such as OpenGL and Direct3D. Like VRML, Java 3D is based on a scene graph programming model. Developers use Java 3D classes to construct scene graphs in terms of nodes, which ultimately define a virtual universe (the equivalent of a VRML world). Unlike VRML, however, Java 3D is tied to the object-oriented language of Java. Because Java 3D is based on Java, developers can exert a great deal of programmatic control over the virtual worlds they construct.

Although Java 3D was designed as a collaborative effort by Sun Microsystems, SGI, Intel, and Apple Computer, it is not yet an international standard in the same way that VRML and MPEG-4 are. The base Java technology on which Java 3D builds, however, has recently been rejected by the ECMA standards body. Should ECMA reverse its decision and approve Java as a standard, Java 3D itself will move one step closer to standardization as a 3D graphics API.

Following is a complete list of URLs referenced in this chapter:

Java home page   http://java.sun.com/

Java documentation   http://java.sun.com/infodocs/

Java platform docs   http://java.sun.com/docs/

Java standardization   http://java.sun.com/aboutJava/standardization/

Java tutorial   http://java.sun.com/docs/books/tutorial/

Sun Microsystems   http://www.sun.com/

Java 1.2 vs. Java 2   http://java.sun.com/products/jdk/1.2/java2.html

Java 3D home page   http://java.sun.com/products/java-media/3D/

Java 3D 1.2 API   http://java.sun.com/products/java-media/3D/1_2_api/

Core Java 3D   http://www.CoreJava3D.com/

Installing Java 3D   http://www.CoreWeb3D.com/java3d/install/

Javadoc   http://java.sun.com/products/jdk/javadoc/

Java Media APIs   http://java.sun.com/products/java-media/

Web3D Gallery's Java 3D page   http://www.web3dgallery.com/java3d/

Web3D Gallery's Java 3D tools   http://www.web3dgallery.com/java3d/tools/

VRML-Java 3D working group   http://www.web3d.org/Working-Groups/vrml-java3d/

JAVA 3D
FUNDAMENTALS

Topics in This Chapter

- Introduction to Java 3D scene graphs
- Overview of essential Java 3D packages and classes
- Creating a simple Java 3D virtual universe

Chapter 12

Java 3D is at heart a scene graph API, meaning that Java 3D programs are constructed by assembling nodes into a treelike scene graph data structure. In this chapter you'll learn the fundamentals behind Java 3D's scene graph programming model as you explore several key classes in the API. Once familiar with the basics of scene graph programming you'll create your own Java 3D scene graph by writing a simple Java 3D program that can run as both an application and an applet.

Java 3D Scene Graph and API Basics

Software developers use Java 3D API classes to construct scene graphs that represent virtual universes. In order to customize existing Java 3D programs (or to begin writing your own Java 3D programs, for that matter), you must first become familiar with the basic structure of Java 3D scene graphs and the Java 3D API classes that scene graphs are constructed from.

In the next section we'll explore fundamental properties that are common to all Java 3D scene graphs. Then we'll take a look at the classes in the Java 3D API class hierarchy that correspond to key scene graph elements.

Scene Graph Basics

Java 3D is a high-level scene graph programming model similar to that of VRML. Scene graphs are treelike data structures that are used to store, organize, and render 3D scene information such as objects, materials, appearances, lights, and other aspects of a scene. Together the elements of a Java 3D scene graph define a *virtual universe*, which is analogous to a VRML world. Like VRML (and other scene graph programming models), Java 3D scene graphs are made up of objects called *nodes* (see Chapter 5, "VRML Fundamentals"). Nodes, in turn, contain fields that the programmer manipulates in order to set or change various properties of the node.

Although Java 3D and VRML are similar in that they are both based on a scene graph programming model, Java 3D scene graphs are more difficult to construct. Generally speaking, developers must first be proficient in Java before they can program Java 3D scene graphs (see Chapter 11, "Java 3D Overview"). Assuming that a developer has experience programming in Java, he can then use the Java 3D API to construct Java 3D scene graphs. VRML, by comparison, is a relatively simple language that requires no previous programming skill. As such, the learning curve for VRML isn't nearly as steep as it is for Java 3D (nor is VRML as capable when it comes to creating complex 3D applications).

Using the Java 3D API, developers create object instances for each object, transform, or behavior in a scene (see the tip, "Object Instance vs. Scene Object"). After setting the fields of an instance to give it specific properties, we add it to the scene. The manner in which object instances are added to a scene determines the overall structure of the scene graph. Figure 12-1

Tip: Object Instance vs. Scene Object

Although the term object *is typically used to describe an instance of a Java class, it is also used to describe an item in a Java 3D scene graph (shapes, appearances, behaviors, and so forth). To make matters more confusing, object instances are used to construct scene-graph objects; Java 3D programmers create object instances from Java 3D classes, and then add them to a scene graph (resulting in scene graph objects).*

To avoid potential confusion Java 3D programmers sometimes use the term vi-sual object *to describe a scene-graph object (because the viewer of a Java 3D scene can usually see such objects). In the remainder of this book, however, the term* scene-graph object *describes objects that appear in a Java 3D scene graph, while the term* object instance *(or simply* object*) describes an instance of a class.*

illustrates a relatively simple Java 3D scene graph that consists of two *branch graphs* attached to a *scene graph superstructure*.

As the following sections explain in more detail, the top two levels of every Java 3D scene graph consist of a Locale attached to a VirtualUniverse. Together a Locale and VirtualUniverse comprise what's known as the scene graph superstructure (see the following "Scene Graph Superstructure" discussion). The Locale acts as a coordinate system "anchor" for a scene graph, to which branch graphs may be attached.

A branch graph is a subgraph rooted by a BranchGroup object, which is really where the scene graph begins. Branch graphs contain the various nodes that make up a major segment, or branch, of the treelike scene graph structure. One or more branch graphs can be attached to a Locale, meaning that multiple subgraphs can reside in the same virtual universe. In more simple terms, the BranchGroup object is a grouping node used to hold subgraphs that can be attached ("parented") and detached from the main scene graph.

The scene graph illustrated in Figure 12-1, for example, consists of subgraphs organized under two major branches. The subgraph defined by the

Figure 12-1   Java 3D scene graphs are treelike structures that consist of nodes created from classes found in the Java 3D API.

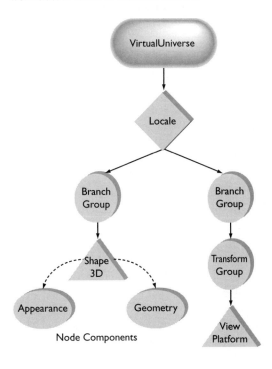

left branch defines the content in this virtual universe (a 3D shape that has an associated appearance and material), while the right branch controls the viewing parameters that apply to this scene graph.

The symbols commonly used to graphically represent Java 3D scene graphs are seen in Figure 12-2. The VirtualUniverse and Locale symbols represent objects created directly from a corresponding VirtualUniverse and Locale Java 3D class. Group, Leaf, and NodeComponent symbols, meanwhile, represent objects derived from one of these three Java 3D classes (BranchGroup, for example, extends the Group class and so is represented with the Group symbol). The plain rectangle symbol represents all other types of objects.

Because a single scene graph symbol often represents more than one type of object, the initials of a specific class of object are usually placed inside the symbol to distinguish it from other objects that share the same symbol. BranchGroup and TransformGroup are both Group nodes, for example. As such, BranchGroup and TransformGroup are both represented by a circle symbol. To distinguish between the two, the scene graph in Figure 12-1 places the initials of each class inside the circular Group symbol. BranchGroup symbols are easily identified as the circle symbols that contain the text "BG," while TransformGroup symbols contain "TG." This approach allows scene graph illustrations to be created without explicit class labels, as seen in Figure 12-3.

Figure 12-2   Symbols commonly used to graphically represent Java 3D scene graphs.

Nodes and NodeComponent (objects)		Arcs (object relationships)	
(VirtualUniverse symbol)	VirtualUniverse	⟶	parent-child link
(Locale symbol)	Locale	- - - ▸	reference
(Group symbol)	Group		
(Leaf symbol)	Leaf		
(NodeComponent symbol)	NodeComponent		
(other objects symbol)	other objects		

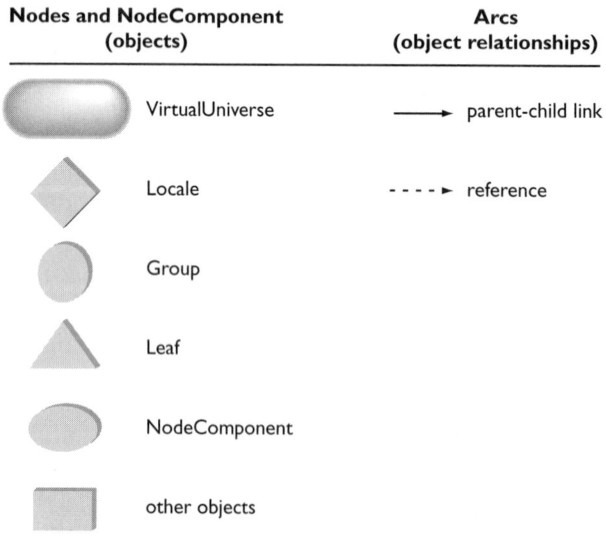

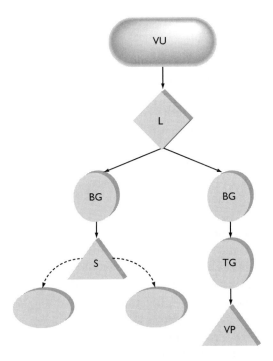

Figure 12-3 This Java 3D scene graph is the same as the one seen in Figure 12-1, with one major exception: Class labels have been omitted.

Like VRML, the nodes in a Java 3D scene graph are organized according to parent-child relationships. A solid arrow represents the directed, parent-child relationship between two objects. A dashed arrow, on the other hand, represents a reference to an object (referenced objects are often shared by different branches of a scene graph). Both solid and dashed arrows can be considered *arcs* that visually convey a relationship between scene graph objects.

Note

Like VRML, the Java 3D scene graph is a directed acyclic graph (DAG). Connections between nodes in a scene graph are represented with lines and arcs that convey a directed, parent-to-child relationship. Because no cycles are allowed between nodes (meaning that a node cannot be its own parent), VRML and Java 3D scene graphs are considered acyclic.

Java 3D API Basics

The bulk of most Java 3D scene graphs are object instances constructed from classes found in the core Java 3D API. These classes are organized into the `javax.media.j3d` package. Java 3D programs can take advantage of classes in other Java APIs, however, such as matrix math classes (`javax.vecmath`), Sun's Java 3D utility classes (`com.sun.j3d`), the core suite of standard Java classes (`java.*`), members of the Java Media Family, and so forth as described in the previous chapter. As a result, Java 3D scene graphs often contain a combination of Java 3D objects and non-Java 3D objects (such objects are represented by the rectangular "other objects" symbol seen earlier in Figure 12-2).

The Java 3D API is a large collection of 3D-specific classes. Approximately 150 classes make up the Java 3D API, a few of which are illustrated in Figure 12-4. Like all Java classes, every class in the Java 3D API ultimately descends from the top-level Object class that is defined in the core Java API (`java.lang.Object`). Java 3D API classes extend the generic Object class to provide developers with a variety of 3D capabilities, many of which are themselves extended by other Java 3D classes to form the Java 3D API class

Figure 12-4
A high-level overview of key classes in the Java 3D API (javax.media.j3d) class hierarchy.

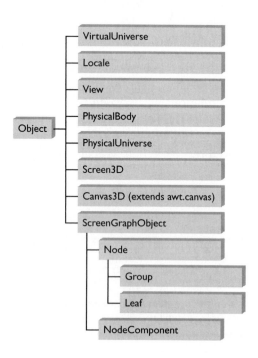

hierarchy (portions of which we'll explore in the following sections). These classes are bundled together in a Java `javax.media.j3d` package, forming a standard extension, or optional package, to the core Java API.

Java 3D Packages

The core Java 3D API classes are bundled into a `javax.media.j3d` subpackage of the main Java Media Framework package (`javax.media`). Java 3D implementations also come with a collection of vector and matrix math classes that are used internally by the core Java 3D classes as well as many Java 3D programs. The "vector math" classes, as they are commonly known, are bundled into the `javax.vecmath` package and define points, vectors, matrices, and similar objects.

In addition to the `javax.media.j3d` and `javax.vecmath` standard extension packages (also known as "optional packages"), Java 3D implementations typically come with Sun's Java 3D "convenience" (or "utility") classes. Bundled into the `com.sun.j3d` package, these classes provide fast and easy access to content loaders, scene graph assembly, geometric primitives, and other capabilities that ease the process of writing full-featured Java 3D programs.

Note: Optional Packages

Beginning with Java 1.3, Sun renamed "standard extension" to "optional packages." For all intents and purposes the terms mean exactly the same thing; they are interchangeable. Classes that are part of the Java core are assembled into packages that start with "java", such as java.awt, java.io, and java.lang. Standard extensions, however, are stored in packages that start with "javax", such as javax.media.j3d and javax.vecmath.

Virtual Universe and Locale Classes

As you learned in the previous section, all Java 3D scene graphs begin with a top-level VirtualUniverse object. The VirtualUniverse object that you saw earlier in Figure 12-1 and Figure 12-3 corresponds to the Java 3D API class of the same name; a VirtualUniverse object is merely an instance of the VirtualUniverse class. Similarly, a Locale object is an instance of a corresponding Locale class.

In other words, the VirtualUniverse and Locale objects depicted in scene graph illustrations are instances of a corresponding class of the same name. The majority of objects that appear in scene graph illustrations, however, are further down in the Java 3D API hierarchy and so don't appear in the high-level overview seen in Figure 12-4. BranchGroup, TransformGroup, and Shape3D nodes, for example, are ultimately descendants of the Scene-GraphObject class (see "Scene Graph Object Classes").

Note: Naming Conventions

By convention, class names begin with an uppercase letter (BranchGroup, Shape3D, SimpleUniverse, and so forth) while method and field (variable) names begin with a lowercase letter (getTransform(), setTransform(), etc.). Fields that are designated as final (meaning that they can't be changed; final fields are the equivalent of constants in other programming languages) typically appear in all uppercase letters (such as ALLOW_TRANSFORM_READ, ALLOW_TRANSFORM_WRITE, PI, BOTTOM, and so on). Nonfinal fields usually begin with a lowercase letter (label, leftSide, radius, etc.).

Scene Graph Object Classes

The SceneGraphObject class is the base class for nearly every object that appears in a Java 3D scene graph. As you'll learn in more detail in the sections that follow, the SceneGraphObject is an abstract class that defines a number of properties common to all *node* and *node component objects*.

Node and Node Component Objects

The Node class is an abstract class that provides a common framework for scene graph objects. Nodes can be categorized as either group nodes or leaf nodes. The primary difference lies in their ability to support children nodes; a group node can contain children, while a leaf node cannot (see "Group and Leaf Nodes" below).

Because scene graph nodes don't always contain all the state information they need, they often reference node component objects that encapsulate such data. The Shape3D leaf node seen in Figures 12-1 and 12-3, for example, references two node component objects: Appearance and Geometry. Appearance data (attributes related to color, material, texture, transparency, and other rendering state data) and geometry data (information that specifies a geometric form, such as a cylinder, sphere, or polygonal mesh) is not included in the Shape3D node.

Instead, this information is stored separately in the Appearance and Geometry node component objects, allowing it to be shared among nodes (multiple Shape3D nodes can share the same appearance and/or geometry, as this data is external to the Shape3D node). It can be said, then, that Appearance and Geometry nodes are a component of the Shape3D node. It can also be helpful to think of node component objects as node "pieces" of information that can be referenced by node objects.

Group and Leaf Nodes

The Node class is the abstract superclass to the Group and Leaf classes, meaning that scene graph nodes can be classified as either group or leaf nodes. The distinction between group and leaf nodes lies in their support for children nodes. Specifically:

- **Group** nodes can contain children, meaning that one or more nodes can be grouped together in a group node. The Group class is the superclass to a number of classes that can specify the location and orientation of scene graph objects. TransformGroup and BranchGroup, for example, are both descendants of the Group class.

- **Leaf** nodes cannot contain children. The Leaf class is the superclass to a number of classes that define the appearance, sound, and behavior of scene graph objects, including Background, Behavior, Fog, Light, Shape3D, and Sound. Although leaf nodes cannot contain children, they can reference node component objects. The Shape3D leaf node, for example, cannot contain children nodes, but it may reference an Appearance node component as well as a Geometry node component, among others, as the previous section explains (see "Node and Node Component Objects").

Scene Graph Viewing Object Classes

The Java 3D API includes five classes that are used in the *viewing* of scene graphs: Canvas3D, Screen3D, View, PhysicalBody, and PhysicalEnvironment. Although these classes are not considered to be a formal part of the Java 3D scene graph, they define important viewing parameters for Java 3D programs and also provide a mechanism for interacting with the physical world.

Fortunately, you don't need to know very much about the scene graph viewing objects to begin customizing existing Java 3D programs. For that matter, you don't need to know a great detail about the Canvas3D, Screen3D, View, PhysicalBody, and PhysicalEnvironment classes even when you begin to write your own Java 3D programs (as you'll do later in this chapter) thanks to Sun's `com.sun.j3d` utility package.

Using the SimpleUniverse utility class (`com.sun.j3d.utils.universe.SimpleUniverse`), developers can create Java 3D programs without dealing directly with Canvas3D, Screen3D, View, PhysicalBody, and Physical-Environment. With the following line of code you can create a Simple-Universe object, which includes a VirtualUniverse, Locale, View, and ViewPlatform with default settings (see "Creating a Simple Virtual Universe," later in this chapter, for more details):

```
SimpleUniverse u = new SimpleUniverse();
```

Digging Deeper into Java 3D

Although Java 3D is similar to VRML in many ways, it's quite a bit more complex (and also more capable). While you may be familiar with VRML from Part II of this book, you've undoubtedly noticed by now that Java 3D introduces a number of new terms and concepts. Once you're comfortable with the basic Java 3D scene graph and API discussions above, you'll need to dig a little deeper into Java 3D fundamentals before you'll feel at ease jumping into source code.

In the sections that follow, we'll explore the Java 3D scene graph and API in more detail, after which you'll write your own simple Java 3D program. If you're particularly anxious to work with Java 3D source code now, you can jump ahead to "Creating A Simple Virtual Universe," although we'd caution against it; that section, like the rest of the Java 3D chapters in this book, assumes a familiarity with the following material.

Scene Graph Superstructure

The term *virtual universe* describes a 3D space populated with Java 3D objects, which is analogous to a VRML world. Virtual universes are the largest unit of aggregate representation in Java 3D and are often thought of as databases, because they can contain a large number of scene graph objects.

Although it's possible for a Java 3D application to contain more than one virtual universe, one is usually adequate for most programs.

Programmers construct a virtual universe by creating an instance of the VirtualUniverse object, to which one or more Locale objects may be attached. A Locale specifies a high-resolution coordinate point of reference, or anchor, for objects in a scene. In other words, a Locale serves as the origin for scene graph objects attached to it (see "Coordinate System," later in this chapter, to learn more about Java 3D's high-resolution coordinates). Together, a VirtualUniverse and Locale object comprise the Java 3D *scene graph superstructure*, as illustrated in Figure 12-5.

SimpleUniverse Utility Class

Because the steps required to construct a scene graph superstructure are the same for many Java 3D programs, Sun has provided utility classes in the `com.sun.java3d` package for such purposes. What would otherwise

Figure 12-5 The VirtualUniverse and Locale object comprise a top-level *scene-graph superstructure* common to all Java 3D scene graphs.

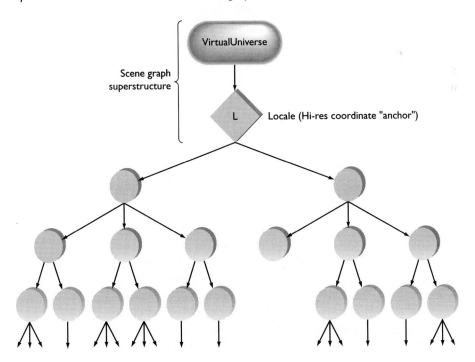

consume a page or more of source code can now be accomplished with just a few lines of utility code. Listing 12.2, for example, contains the complete code of Sun's SimpleUniverse utility class. Developers often use this premade class to implement the basics of a virtual universe, complete with scene graph superstructure and viewing platform, through a single line of code:

```
SimpleUniverse u = new SimpleUniverse();
```

Branch Graphs

The real nuts and bolts of a Java 3D scene graph begin with a BranchGroup node, which is a grouping node that acts as the root for a subgraph known as a *branch graph*. As a grouping node, BranchGroup can contain children nodes (in the same way that VRML's grouping nodes can contain children; see Part II of this book for details). A branch graph contains the various nodes that make up a scene graph, and as such branch graphs can be considered scene graphs in their own right.

In simpler terms, a BranchGroup is merely a collection of elements that can be attached to (and detached from) a scene graph as a single unit. To create a branch graph the programmer first constructs a BranchGroup object, followed by the nodes that it will contain. These nodes are then added to the BranchGroup, which can then be attached to a parent object in the scene graph (typically a Locale). More than one BranchGroup can be attached to a single Locale, although objects other than BranchGroup cannot be attached to a Locale (only BranchGroup objects can be attached to a Locale).

A BranchGroup becomes "live" as soon as it is attached to a scene graph, meaning that the branch graph it describes can be rendered by Java 3D. To prevent rendering of a given branch graph the programmer may "detach" the

Note: Compiling Branch Graphs

Branch graphs can be compiled, allowing Java 3D to optimize them for performance. Typically, compiling a branch graph is the last step before it is attached to a scene graph. Once a branch graph has been attached to a scene graph, it is considered "live." For performance reasons, live portions of a scene graph can only be modified in accordance with capability bit settings (see the "Capability Bits" discussion later in this chapter).

corresponding BranchGroup. By selectively attaching and detaching branch graphs the Java 3D programmer can control when specific portions of a scene are rendered.

Java 3D programs typically contain two BranchGroup objects—one to implement content (such as shapes, appearances, textures, lights, and so forth) and one to implement activity related to viewing the scene (animation and navigation, for example). The scene graph shown in Figure 12-6, for example, contains two BranchGroup objects. The BranchGroup on the left defines content, while that on the right defines the view parameters for this program.

Branch graphs can, and often do, contain subgraphs. The left Branch-Group seen in Figure 12-6, for example, actually consists of two subgraphs. One defines a 3D shape, while the other defines behavior that animates the

Figure 12-6   The left branch of this scene graph contains the contents of this virtual universe, while the right branch handles all aspects related to viewing the scene.

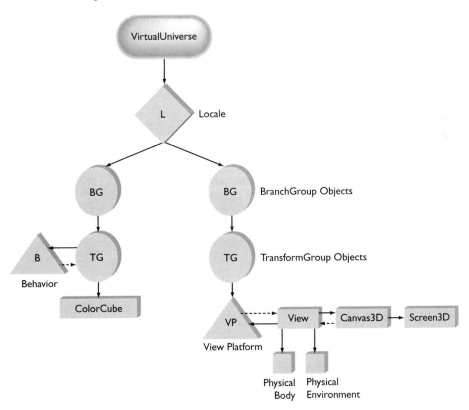

shape. The right BranchGroup, meanwhile, contains only one subgraph—the subgraph that defines the viewing parameters that apply to this virtual universe.

Listings 12.1 and 12.2, later in this chapter, contain the Java 3D source code that corresponds to Figure 12-6. Although the source code may be difficult to comprehend at this stage in your introduction to Java 3D, it should be greatly enhanced by the graphical representation of the scene graph seen in Figure 12-6. Code that defines the left branch is found in Listing 12.1, while Listing 12.2 contains the code that defines the right branch of this scene graph (Listing 12.2 contains the SimpleUniverse utility class provided in the `com.sun.j3d` package, which creates and manages the scene graph viewing branch depicted here).

Scene Graph Objects

As with VRML, the Java 3D scene graph is a treelike structure comprised of nodes that are arranged in directed, parent-to-child relationships. Scene graph nodes can reference other objects in the scene graph, which are commonly referred to as *node component* objects.

As Figure 12-7 illustrates, the abstract SceneGraphObject class (`java.media.j3d.SceneGraphObject`) is the parent class from which all scene graph nodes and components are derived. The SceneGraphObject class has two direct subclasses: Node (`javax.media.j3d.Node`) and NodeComponent (`javax.media.j3d.NodeComponent`). Each has its own descendants, all of which inherit properties from the abstract SceneGraphObject class (see Table 12.1).

To construct a branch graph (a subgraph of a scene graph; see the previous discussion for details), programmers create various instances of these scene graph classes in order to give the subgraph certain properties or capabilities. Specific capabilities of the object instance can be retrieved or altered by invoking an instance's accessor and mutator methods. Accessor methods are often called *get* methods because they begin with the word get (such as `getUserData`) and are used to retrieve information about the instance. Mutator methods, on the other hand, are used to set specific instance properties and so are often called *set* methods. Each *get* method typically has a corresponding *set* method (SceneGraphObject defines both `getUserData()` and `setUserData()`, for example, as seen in Table 12.1).

Scene graph object accessor and mutator methods are not always accessible, however. To facilitate scene graph optimization, Java 3D restricts access to scene graph objects based on *capability bit* settings. Capability bits

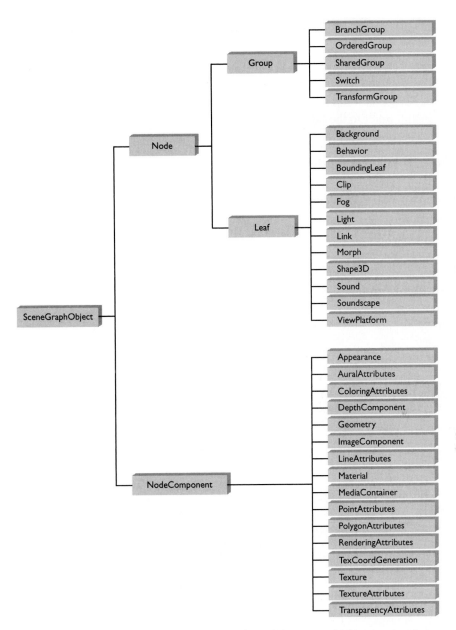

Figure 12-7   SceneGraphObject (java.media.j3d.SceneGraphObject) is the abstract parent class from which all scene graph nodes and components ultimately descend.

Table 12.1	SceneGraphObject Class Summary

Constructor Summary

SceneGraphObject (javax.media.j3d.SceneGraphObject) is the abstract superclass for all scene graph component objects. It's direct subclasses are Node and Node-Component. Refer to the Java 3D Specification for details (http://java.sun.com/products/java-media/3D/).

public SceneGraphObject()
Constructs a SceneGraphObject with the following default parameters:

capability bits: clear (all bits)

isLive: false

isCompiled: false

user data: null

Method Summary

Returns	*Method Name, Parameters, and Description*
void	**clearCapability**(int bit) Clear the specified capability bit.
protected void	**duplicateSceneGraphObject**(SceneGraphObject originalNode) Copies all SceneGraphObject information from originalNode into the current node.
boolean	**getCapability**(int bit) Retrieves the specified capability bit.
java.lang. Object	**getUserData**() Retrieves the userData field from this scene graph object.
boolean	**isCompiled**() Returns a flag indicating whether the node is part of a scene graph that has been compiled.
boolean	**isLive**() Returns a flag indicating whether the node is part of a live scene graph.
void	**setCapability**(int bit) Sets the specified capability bit.
void	**setUserData**(java.lang.Object userData) Sets the userData field associated with this scene graph object.

(often called *cap bits* for short) are scene graph object fields used to establish a strong contract between the Java 3D program and the Java 3D compiler and renderer. By default, capability bits are set to prevent alteration of scene graph objects, which allows Java 3D to optimize objects in a scene as best it can. Programmers must explicitly set capability bits that correspond to the changes they wish to make, effectively warning Java 3D not to optimize these portions of the scene (see the following discussion, "Capability Bits," for more details).

Capability Bits

Once a subgraph has been assembled from node and node component objects it can then be attached to a high-resolution Locale object (before which it can be optionally compiled as described in the previous chapter). This makes the subgraph, and all the objects it contains, *live*. When live, access to scene graph objects is restricted; they cannot be accessed or modified as freely at this stage as they were during the creation stage. In other words, many *get* and *set* methods of a live scene graph object are off limits and can't be invoked by default.

Because access to live scene graph objects is restricted, they can only be accessed or modified in very predictable ways. This predictability allows Java 3D scene graph compiler and renderer to perform scene graph optimizations that would otherwise be impossible. To facilitate predictable access and modification of live scene graph objects Java 3D introduces the notion of *capability bits.*

Capability bits (also known as *cap bits*) are scene graph object fields that are used to establish a contract between the Java 3D application and the Java 3D compiler and runtime. The Java 3D application cannot modify a live scene graph object unless it has set the corresponding capability bits in advance. The Java 3D compiler and runtime, in turn, optimize scene graph objects in accordance with their capability bit settings.

Every scene graph object has a suite of capability bits that apply to it. When a capability bit is set, it enables access to or modification of that specific aspect of the object. When a capability bit is not set, or cleared, access or modification of that aspect of the object is disabled. Capability bits are, in essence, permission flags that tell Java 3D what aspects of a live scene graph object are likely to change.

By default all capability bits of all objects are cleared; programmers must explicitly set these cleared bits in order to access corresponding functionality of live scene graph objects. There is a catch, however: capability bits can only be set *before* a scene graph is compiled or made live (attaching a scene graph to a Locale, for example, makes it "live"). A RestrictedAccessException is thrown when an attempt is made to set the capability bits of an object that is part of a live or compiled scene graph.

Warning: Restricted Access Exception

Capability bits can only be set when a scene graph is not live or compiled. Any attempt to set the capability bits of an object contained in a live or compiled scene graph will result in a RestrictedAccessException exception being thrown.

As Table 12.1 illustrates, three capability bit methods are defined in the abstract SceneGraphObject class: `clearCapability()`, `getCapability()`, and `setCapability()`. These capability bit methods are inherited by all node and node component classes. These classes can also define their own unique capability bit methods, as well as their own capability bit fields.

The TransformGroup class, for example, is a grouping node that performs transform operations on the children it contains (see Chapter 13, "Customizing Size, Location, and Orientation," for details). TransformGroup inherits the `clearCapability()`, `getCapability()`, and `setCapability()` methods from SceneGraphObject. TransformGroup also defines two capability bit fields, ALLOW_TRANSFORM_READ and ALLOW_TRANSFORM_WRITE, as seen in Table 12.2. These capability bit fields correspond to the TransformGroup's `getTransform()` and `setTransform()` methods shown in Table 12.3, meaning that these methods can be invoked on a compiled or live TransformGroup object as long as these capability bits are set in advance (capability bits *must* be set before an object is compiled or becomes live).

The following snippet of source code, for example, is taken from the HelloUniverse program found later in this chapter (see Listing 12.1). In this example the TransformGroup node's ALLOW_TRANSFORM_WRITE capability bit is set before the branch graph that it is part of becomes live. As a result, the corresponding `setTransform()` method can be invoked even while the scene is live, as the following snippet of code illustrates:

```
// Create the transform group. Enable the
// TRANSFORM_WRITE capability so that our
// behavior code can modify it at runtime.
```

```
TransformGroup objTrans = new TransformGroup();
objTrans.setCapability(TransformGroup.ALLOW_TRANSFORM_WRITE);
// a call to objTrans.setTransform() is now legal!
```

Table 12.2 TransformGroup Field Summary

Fields defined by the class javax.media.j3d.TransformGroup. Both of these fields are defined as `public static final int`. These fields are used as capability bits; they allow the corresponding methods listed in Table 12.3 to be invoked when the scene graph is compiled or live. See Chapter 13 to learn more about the TransformGroup class.

ALLOW_TRANSFORM_READ

Specifies that the node will allow read access to its object's transform information.

ALLOW_TRANSFORM_WRITE

Specifies that the node will allow writing of its object's transform information.

Table 12.3 TransformGroup Method Summary

Get and set methods of the class javax.media.j3d.TransformGroup that correspond to the capability bit fields defined by this class (see Table 12-2). See Chapter 13 to learn more about the TransformGroup class.

Returns	Method Name, Parameters, and Description
void	**getTransform**(Transform3D t) Copies the transform component of this TransformGroup into transform *t*.
double	**setTransform**(Transform3D t) Sets the transform component of this TransformGroup to the value of transform *t*.

Node

Java 3D's Node class (`javax.media.j3d.Node`) is a direct descendant of the abstract SceneGraphObject described earlier. Itself an abstract class, Node provides a common framework for constructing Java 3D scene graphs.

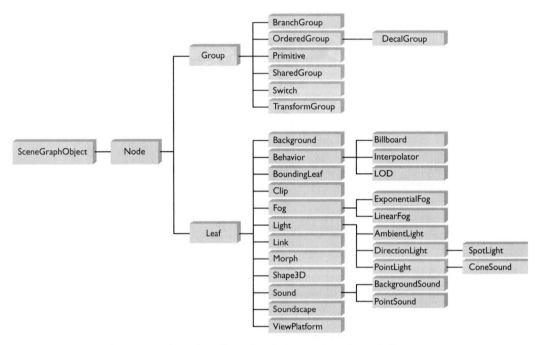

Figure 12-8   Node (java.media.j3d.Node) is the abstract parent class of all scene graph nodes.

Indeed, the subclasses of Node are used to create scene graph nodes. As Figure 12-8 illustrates, there are two immediate subclasses of Node: Group and Leaf.

Group

Java 3D's abstract Group class (`javax.media.j3d.Group`) is a direct descendant of Node and has the distinction of being able to contain children. The primary role of a Group object is to act as the parent of other nodes, specifically other Group nodes and Leaf nodes. As such, all subclasses of Group are considered *grouping* nodes (see Part II of this book to learn more about VRML grouping nodes).

Group serves as the base superclass for a number of classes that position and orient scene graph objects in the virtual universe. Following is an overview of each Group subclass:

- **BranchGroup** is used to create BranchGroup objects, which act as the root for individual scene graph branches (commonly known as branch graphs). BranchGroup objects are the only objects that can be attached directly to a Locale. Contents of BranchGroup objects can be compiled. Attaching or compiling a BranchGroup makes the branch graph it represents "live," allowing Java 3D to optimize it. Access to "live" branch-graph objects is restricted according to their capability bit settings.

- **OrderedGroup** ensures that its children are rendered according to their index order, which guarantees a specific rendering order. Children in an OrderedGroup are rendered in increasing index order (from low to high). Only the OrderedGroup class (and subclasses of OrderedGroup) can render children according to their order in the group. **DecalGroup** is a direct subclass of OrderedGroup that is used to define decal geometry that is rendered on top of other geometry (painted decals and text applied to object surfaces, for example).

- **Primitive** is the base class used by Sun's utilities package to create geometric shapes known as *primitives*. Box, Cone, Cylinder, and Sphere are all descendants of the Primitive class (`com.sun.j3d.utils.geometry.Primitive`). The core Java 3D API does not define primitives directly, although developers can use the Primitive utility class if they wish to create boxes, cones, cylinders, and spheres.

- **SharedGroup** provides the ability to share a subgraph among different portions of a scene graph tree. SharedGroup works in conjunction with the Link leaf node described below (Link leaf nodes are used to store references to SharedGroup nodes).

- **Switch** gives a Java 3D program the ability to dynamically choose which of its children will be rendered. The Switch node assigns a child selection value (a switch value) to each of its children. This value can be used to select a single child for rendering, or a mask value can be used to select multiple children for rendering.

- **TransformGroup** creates a corresponding TransformGroup object that may contain a single spatial transformation used to position, orient, and scale all of the children it contains. TransformGroup is used in combination with the Transform3D object, as described in the next chapter.

Leaf

Like Group, Java 3D's abstract Leaf class (`javax.media.j3d.Leaf`) is a direct descendant of Node. Unlike Group nodes, however, Leaf nodes are not able to contain children. Instead, Leaf nodes specify the shape, sound, and behavior of scene graph objects. Leaf nodes also provide a view platform that is used by the virtual universe to position and orient a view of the scene (see "Scene Graph Viewing Objects," later in this chapter).

Following is a brief description of each top-level Leaf subclass (many of these classes have subclasses of their own):

- **Background** is used to define either a solid background color or an image that fills the window when each new frame is rendered.

- **Behavior** is an abstract class that defines properties common to all behavioral Java 3D components (components that can dynamically modify a scene graph at runtime).

- **BoundingLeaf** defines bounding-region objects that can be referenced by other nodes to define a region of influence for Fog and Light nodes, an activation region for Background, Clip, and Soundscape nodes, or a scheduling region for Sound and Behavior nodes.

- **Clip** defines the back (or "far") clipping distance used to clip objects that appear in the virtual universe.

- **Fog** is an abstract class that defines parameters common to fog environmental effects, as well as the region of influence in which the fog node is active.

- **Light** is an abstract class that defines properties common to all lights.

- **Link** provides a reference to a SharedGroup node, allowing subgroups in a virtual universe to be shared among scene graphs.

- **Morph** allows a Java 3D program to morph between various GeometryArray objects.

- **Shape3D** is used to specify objects that consist of geometric data (the form of an object) and appearance properties (attributes related to color, material, texture, transparency, and so forth).

- **Sound** is an abstract class that defines properties common to all sound sources.

- **Soundscape** defines attributes that characterize the listener's environment as it pertains to sound (the listener's "aural environment"). Soundscape can be used to control reverberation and atmospheric properties that affect rendering (playing) of sound sources.

- **ViewPlatform** controls the location, orientation, and scale of the viewer (the ViewPlatform object is referenced by a View object).

NodeComponent

Java 3D's abstract NodeComponent class (`javax.media.j3d.Node-Component`) is used to specify a variety of node properties, such as geometry, appearance, texture, transparency, and coloring. Node objects don't contain such information directly, as you might expect, but instead reference NodeComponent objects in which this data is encapsulated. This design feature of Java 3D allows NodeComponent objects to be shared by nodes, as you'll see in Chapter 14.

As Figure 12-9 illustrates, a large number of Java 3D classes are derived from NodeComponent. Following is a brief overview of the classes that are immediate descendants of NodeComponent:

- **Appearance** creates objects that are a component of a Shape3D node. Appearance nodes define all rendering-state properties of a Shape3D node, such as color, texture, transparency, and so forth.

- **AuralAttributes** creates objects that are a component object of a Soundscape node. AuralAttributes nodes defines environmental audio parameters that affect sound rendering (playback), such as reverberation, gain scale factor, atmospheric rolloff, distance frequency filtering, and so forth.

Figure 12-9   NodeComponent (javax.media.j3d.NodeComponent) is an abstract parent class used to specify various node properties, including geometry, appearance, color, and texture.

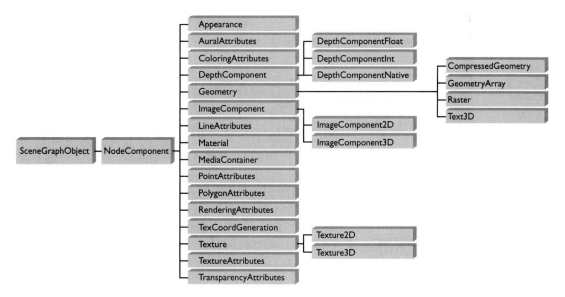

- **ColoringAttributes** defines attributes used in color selection and shading.
- **DepthComponent** creates a 2D array of depth (Z) values.
- **Geometry** creates objects that specify the geometric-form component of a Shape3D node.
- **ImageComponent** is an abstract class used to define 2D or 3D texture images, background images, and raster components of Shape3D nodes.
- **LineAttributes** defines rendering properties that apply to line primitives, such as line width and line pattern.
- **Material** creates objects that are a component of an Appearance object. Material objects define the appearance of an object when it is illuminated (or "lit").
- **MediaContainer** is used to create objects that are components of a Sound node (objects that define audio properties associated with a Sound node).
- **PointAttributes** creates objects that define the rendering properties of point primitives, such as point size and antialiasing (PointAttributes is a component of Shape3D).
- **PolygonAttributes** creates objects that define the rendering properties of polygon primitives, such as face culling and rasterization mode (i.e., POINT, LINE, or FILL). PolygonAttributes is a component of Shape3D.
- **RenderingAttributes** is used to define the per-pixel rendering-state properties common to all primitives.
- **TexCoordGeneration** creates objects that contain parameters related to the generation of texture coordinates (TexCoordGeneration is a component of Appearance).
- **Texture** is an abstract class that defines properties related to texture mapping (Texture is a component of Appearance). Because Texture is an abstract class, all texture objects must be created using the Texture2D or Texture3D classes (both of which are direct subclasses of Texture).
- **TextureAttributes** is used to define texture-mapping attributes, such as texturing mode, blend color, transformation, and perspective correction.
- **TransparencyAttributes** is used to define attributes that affect the transparency of objects.

Scene Graph Viewing Objects

In addition to the previously described classes that are used to construct scene graph objects, Java 3D also includes five classes that are used in the *viewing* of scene graphs: Canvas3D, Screen3D, View, PhysicalBody, and PhysicalEnvironment. Although these classes are not considered to be a formal part of the Java 3D scene graph, they are essential nonetheless. Following is a description of the objects created by these classes:

- **Canvas3D** is an extension of Java's AWT Canvas class that provides a window into which Java 3D content is rendered. Java 3D automatically renders the specified view to all canvases that are attached to an active View object (multiple Canvas3D objects can be attached to a single View object).

- **Screen3D** contains all information related to a specific physical screen, or display device, such as the screen's height and width and physical dimensions.

- **View** contains all parameters necessary to render a scene graph from one viewpoint (all Java 3D viewing parameters are contained directly from within the View object itself or from within the objects referenced by it). A View object contains a list of Canvas3D objects that the view will be rendered into, as well as references to corresponding PhysicalBody and PhysicalEnvironment objects. View objects are attached to a ViewPlatform leaf node, as illustrated in Figure 12-10.

- **PhysicalBody** This object contains a specification of the user's physical characteristics, such as the user's head. Attributes of this object's head parameters are defined in the head coordinate system. The orgin of the head coordinate system is defined to be halfway between the left and right eye in the plane of the face. The X axis extends to the right of the head (looking out from the head). The Y axis extends up. The Z axis extends to the rear of the head (into the skull).

- **PhysicalEnvironment** This object contains a specification of the physical environment in which the view will be generated. It is used to set up input devices (sensors) for head-tracking and other uses, and the audio output device. Sensors are indexed starting at zero.

Thanks to Sun's `com.sun.j3d` utility package, developers can create fully functional Java 3D programs with little or no knowledge of these five viewing classes. The SimpleUniverse utility class (`com.sun.j3d.utils.universe.`

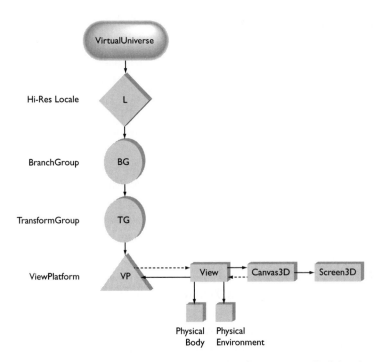

Figure 12-10   Sun's SimpleUniverse utility class creates all of the objects necessary to support scene graph viewing.

SimpleUniverse), shown later in Listing 12.1, for example, implements a basic Java 3D user environment (see Figure 12-10). SimpleUniverse creates all of the objects necessary to support the view portion of a scene graph, allowing developers to get on with the show without getting bogged down with these details. With only one line of code, developers can create a SimpleUniverse object that in turn creates a VirtualUniverse, Locale, View, and ViewPlatform with default settings (see "Creating a Simple Virtual Universe"). For example:

```
SimpleUniverse u = new SimpleUniverse();
```

Coordinate System

Java 3D, like VRML and all other forms of 3D, revolves around the concept of a 3D coordinate system. As with VRML, the Java 3D coordinate system is a right-handed one where X represents the horizontal (left to right) axis, Y the vertical axis (up and down), and Z the depth axis (front to back) when

Behind the Scenes with High-Resolution Coordinates

The HiResCoord class (javax.media.j3d.HiResCoord) implements Java 3D's high-resolution coordinates, which consist of 768 bits of floating-point values in 3-space (X, Y, Z). High-resolution coordinates are made up of three 256-bit fixed-point numbers, one each for the X, Y, and Z axis (together totaling 768 bits). The fixed point of each 256-bit number is located at bit 128, where a value of 1.0 represents 1 meter precisely.

HiResCoord contains methods to add, subtract, negate, and scale high-resolution coordinates. HiResCoord methods are also provided to calculate the difference between two high-resolution coordinates, calculate the distance between specified coordinates, and test for equality between coordinates. Java 3D's high-resolution coordinates operate behind the scenes, allowing developers to express 3D coordinates in a more traditional format (high-resolution coordinates are used by Java 3D to transparently layer traditional floating-point coordinate systems on top of a higher-resolution format). X, Y, Z coordinates specified in a virtual universe, for example, are typically expressed as three floating-point numbers.

viewed straight on. Also like VRML, Java 3D units of measurement are measured in meters, where 1 unit equals 1 meter (see Chapter 7, "Customizing Location, Size, and Orientation," for a more detailed discussion of 3D coordinates and units of measurement).

Unlike VRML, however, Java 3D coordinates are expressed internally in a high-resolution format that is much more precise than the single-precision floating-point values used by VRML. This allows Java 3D scenes to scale in size from the extremely small to the extremely large with great precision. According to the designers of Java 3D, this high-resolution coordinate system is capable of representing a universe that is larger than several billion light-years across as well as objects that are smaller than a proton.

Creating a Simple Virtual Universe

Although you do not have to code Java 3D programs from scratch in order to customize existing Java 3D content (as you'll see in the following chapters), you must understand the basic structure of a Java 3D program nonetheless.

592 Chapter 12 Java 3D Fundamentals

Almost every Java 3D program that you encounter will share fundamental characteristics of the simple program constructed from Listing 12.1 (HelloUniverse.java) and 12.2 (SimpleUniverse.java), and so it is a good exercise to walk through these code examples (appearing later in this chapter) in preparation for customizing more sophisticated Java 3D content later on.

You should note that the source code for HelloUniverse and SimpleUniverse, and many other Java 3D examples, are provided free of charge by Sun Microsystems (see sidebar "Java 3D Demos and Source Code"). If you haven't already installed Java 3D, you should consider doing so now (see Chapter 11, "Java 3D Overview," for details). You will gain a much greater understanding of Java 3D if you take the time to explore and customize the demonstration programs discussed here and in the next few chapters. Not to mention the flat out thrill you'll get upon seeing these programs in action as compared to reading what amounts to static, lifeless source code listings in the pages that follow.

Java 3D Demos and Source Code

Sun provides a number of demonstration programs with its Java 3D implementations (applets and applications, as well as "dual purpose" programs that can run as either an applet *or* an application). Typically these demos are placed inside the "demo" folder of your already installed Java Software Development Toolkit folder (the Java SDK, previously known as the JDK).

If you have installed Java 3D on a Windows machine, for example, the location for the Java 3D demo folder is probably `c:\jdk1.2\demo\java3d\`. Inside this directory you'll find a number of Java 3D demonstration programs, including the HelloUniverse program seen in Listing 12.1.

The SimpleUniverse code found in Listing 12.2, however, is *not* a Java 3D demonstration program; you won't find it in the same demo folder as HelloUniverse. SimpleUniverse, instead, is part of Sun's Java 3D utility package (`com.sun.j3d.utils`). Specifically, SimpleUniverse is found in the `com.sun.j3d.utils.universe` package. Convenience utilities such as SimpleUniverse are usually provided in compiled bytecode form (i.e., SimpleUniverse.class). Fortunately, corresponding source code files such as the one seen in Listing 12.2 (SimpleUniverse.java) are available as a separate download from Sun's Java 3D site at http://java.sun.com/products/java-media/3D/.

Implementing HelloUniverse

The HelloUniverse program found in Listing 12.1 (later in this chapter) is the 3D equivalent of the canonical "Hello World" program used in so many introductory software development texts these days. Instead of displaying a "Hello World" string of characters on the screen, however, HelloUniverse actually creates a simple Java 3D virtual universe in which a spinning 3D cube resides. Unimpressive as it might sound, the HelloUniverse program gives us an excellent introduction to the 7 basic steps required to build any Java 3D program irrespective of complexity. So fundamental are these 7 steps that they're typically called the "recipe" for Java 3D program construction.

A Recipe for Creating Java 3D Programs

The Java 3D Specification describes the 7 fundamental steps, known collectively as a "recipe," that developers typically follow when constructing Java 3D programs:

1. Create a Canvas3D object
2. Create a VirtualUniverse object
3. Create a Locale Object and attach it to the VirtualUniverse object
4. Construct a view branch graph, which consists of the following sub-steps:
   a) Create a View object
   b) Create a ViewPlatform object
   c) Create a PhysicalBody object
   d) Create a PhysicalEnvironment object
   e) Attach ViewPlatform, PhysicalBody, PhysicalEnvironment, and Canvas3D object to the View object
5. Construct one or more content branch graphs
6. Compile view and content branch graphs
7. Insert view and content branch graphs into the Locale

At first blush these steps may seem overkill when all you want to do is display a spinning 3D cube on the screen. And overkill it would certainly be if you actually had to hand-code every step in the recipe yourself, which is thankfully not the case. The SimpleUniverse class shown later in Listing 12.2 takes care of recipe steps 2, 3, and 4 for you entirely, and also facilitates steps 1 and 7. You should note that Listing 12.2 is provided here for reference only; you never even have to deal directly with the SimpleUniverse source code—just use the SimpleUniverse class provided with your Java 3D implementation (`com.sun.j3d.utils.universe.SimpleUniverse`) as explained in the next section.

Steps 1, 2, 3, 4, and 7 (with Help from SimpleUniverse)

Most Java 3D programs have no need for more than one VirtualUniverse object, nor do they require more than one Locale object in most cases. Although more than one of each are possible (and certainly vital to many complex Java 3D programs), the HelloUniverse program and the majority of all other Java 3D programs have no need for more than one of each. As a result, Sun's SimpleUniverse convenience utility automates the construction of a single VirtualUniverse object and the Locale attached to it, sparing you the hassle of doing it yourself.

In addition, many programs don't need multiple views of the virtual universe, and so SimpleUniverse also takes care of constructing a default view branch graph for the programmer. SimpleUniverse completely handles steps 2, 3, and 4 of the Java 3D recipe, freeing programmers from dealing directly with the scene graph superstructure (VirtualUniverse and Locale objects) and the view branch graph. With a single line of code developers can let SimpleUniverse handle these relatively mundane tasks, as illustrated in the HelloUniverse constructor.

Assuming the `com.sun.j3d.utils.universe` package (in which Simple-Universe, ViewingPlatform, and Viewer classes are found) has been imported into your program you can then invoke the SimpleUniverse constructor and hand it a reference to the Canvas3D object created in step 1. In addition, SimpleUniverse can also assist in step 7 via the `addBranchGraph()` method shown below and in Listing 12.1.

Upon constructing a SimpleUniverse object Java 3D programs are automatically supplied with a default scene graph superstructure and view graph. Holding onto a reference of the SimpleUniverse object can be helpful for "fine tuning" the default view you're given by the constructor. In our HelloUniverse program, for example, we use SimpleUniverse to set the nominal viewing distance transform to 2.41 meters. This creates a view distance in which objects that are no more than 2 meters high or wide are generally viewable by the end user (see the "Looking Through the Image Plate" sidebar for details).

Following is the HelloUniverse constructor in which the SimpleUniverse class is put to task in creating a Canvas3D object with a "preferred configuration," along with the essential import statements required by this code. Here the static SimpleUniverse method `getPreferredConfiguration()` is called to get a reference to an ATW GraphicsConfiguration object that contains the best-known graphics configuration information for the system on which the program is run. By looking at SimpleUniverse's `getPreferredConfiguration()` implementation (Listing 12.2) you can see that this method allows Java 3D to determine at runtime if a stereo viewing system must be accommodated, for example.

Although it's convenient and impressive to say that SimpleUniverse constructs your entire view graph in one line of code, in practice most Java 3D programs use SimpleUniverse to aid in the construction of a Canvas3D object in addition to setting the image plate as the following HelloUniverse constructor illustrates:

```java
import com.sun.j3d.utils.universe.*;
import java.awt.GraphicsConfiguration;
import javax.media.j3d.*;

public HelloUniverse() {
  setLayout(new BorderLayout());

  GraphicsConfiguration config =
     SimpleUniverse.getPreferredConfiguration();

  Canvas3D c = new Canvas3D(config);  // STEP 1
  add("Center", c);

    // Create a simple scene & attach to the virtual universe:
    BranchGroup scene = createSceneGraph(); // (STEPS 5, 6; see below)
    SimpleUniverse u = new SimpleUniverse(c); // STEP 2, 3, 4

    // Move the ViewPlatform back so that objects
    // in the scene can be viewed. The default
    // distance is 2.41 meters (see the sidebar
    // "Looking Through the Image Plate"):
    u.getViewingPlatform().setNominalViewingTransform();

    u.addBranchGraph(scene);   // STEP 7 (see SimpleUniverse.java)
}
```

Looking Through the Image Plate

A SimpleUniverse instance constructs a default view branch graph for a virtual universe, which includes a conceptual *image plate.* An image plate can be thought of as a rectangular surface that sits between the end user's eyes and the visible objects in a Java 3D universe, onto which the scene is actually rendered. A Canvas3D object, for example, can be thought of as the image plate for most Java 3D programs; content is rendered onto a Canvas3D object, which in turn appears in a window on the computer monitor. Java 3D content is *projected* onto the image plate, the location of which determines what the end user actually sees.

By default the image plate is centered around the SimpleUniverse origin (0, 0, 0), for which axes orientation is identical to that of VRML: viewer's look down the Z axis. More specifically, the X axis runs horizontally from left to right (negative to positive coordinates), Y is the vertical axis that runs down to up (negative to positive coordinates), and Z is the depth axis that runs back to front (negative to positive coordinates) when the axes are viewed face-on, and normally (in other words, before any orientation in the coordinate system occurs).

Because the image plate is built around the origin it is usually too close to objects initially. The situation is similar, conceptually, to looking at a real-world painting with your nose pushed flat against it. In order to see what's on the canvas you must pull back a few feet, at the very least.

Most Java 3D programs pull the image plate away from the origin at least a few meters in order to give the user a better viewing perspective. To do this the programmer sets a default nominal viewing transform by calling the `setNominalViewingTransform()` method of the ViewingPlatform object, which is retrieved through the SimpleUniverse instance as illustrated in HelloUniverse. This pulls the image plate back 2.41 meters, which is usually enough to allow the end user to drink in Java 3D content from a comfortable distance. At this distance objects that are 2 meters high (or less), and no more than 2 meters wide, are generally within view.

Steps 5 and 6: Construct and Compile a Content Branch Graph

With SimpleUniverse handling all viewing operations, the Java 3D programmer has the luxury of being able to focus a good deal of time and energy on content development. Or, in Java 3D jargon, the programmer can focus on step 5 of the recipe: implementing content branch graphs.

HelloUniverse implements only one content branch graph, which it does through the `createSceneGraph()` method. Although the specifics of this method will be cryptic until you've read the following chapters, the concept that you should walk away with at this time is the notion of separating content branch graphs into methods such as `createSceneGraph()`. You should also note the use of capability bits in this method, as they're an integral part to modifying practically any part of a Java 3D scene. In this particular branch graph construction method a 3D ColorCube shape is created, which has an animation behavior associated with it. When HelloUniverse executes the colored cube appears at the center of the screen, where it spins tirelessly around its Y axis.

The bulk of work here, if you'll pardon the pun, revolves around transforms and rotation vectors that are discussed in detail in Chapter 13, "Customizing Size, Location, and Orientation." Color, on the other hand, is covered in Chapter 14, "Customizing Color and Texture," while the notion of a bounding sphere is discussed in Chapter 15, "Customizing Background, Fog, Lighting, and Sound." You won't, however, find a detailed discussion of the ColorCube class in any of the following chapters. This class creates a simple cube shape whose faces each have a pre-set color. ColorCube is a particularly easy class to use when demonstrating Java 3D concepts as it's entirely self-contained: With one line of code you're up and running with a colorful cube shape. You don't even have to bother creating lights to illuminate the shape, as you must with any other Java 3D geometry class (see "Creating Geometry" for details).

After creating the content branch graph that contains ColorCube and its associated spin behavior the entire structure is compiled for performance purposes, which allows Java 3D to optimize the graph structure before it is rendered. Following is the entire body of code that implements steps 5 and 6 in the HelloUniverse program, along with the most significant import statements required by this method:

```
import com.sun.j3d.utils.geometry.ColorCube;
import javax.media.j3d.*;
import javax.vecmath.*;
```

```java
public BranchGroup createSceneGraph() {

// STEP 5 consumes all but one line of code in this method.
// The one line that is not part of STEP 5 is found at the
// end of this method, and actually comprises STEP 6 of the
// recipe (compiling the graph).

BranchGroup objRoot = new BranchGroup(); // branch graph root

// Create the transform group node and initialize it to the
// identity.  Enable the TRANSFORM_WRITE capability so that
// the behavior code can modify it at runtime.  Add it to the
// root of the subgraph.
TransformGroup objTrans = new TransformGroup();
objTrans.setCapability(TransformGroup.ALLOW_TRANSFORM_WRITE);
objRoot.addChild(objTrans);

// Create a simple shape leaf node, add it to the scene graph.
objTrans.addChild(new ColorCube(0.4));

// Create a new Behavior object that will perform the desired
// operation on the specified transform object and add it into
// the scene graph.
AxisAngle4f axisAngle = new AxisAngle4f(0.0f, 0.0f, 1.0f,
                                        -(float)Math.PI / 2.0f);
Transform3D yAxis = new Transform3D();
Alpha rotationAlpha = new Alpha(-1, Alpha.INCREASING_ENABLE,
                           0, 0,
                           4000, 0, 0,
                           0, 0, 0);

RotationInterpolator rotator =
   new RotationInterpolator(rotationAlpha, objTrans, yAxis,
                       0.0f, (float) Math.PI*2.0f);
BoundingSphere bounds =
   new BoundingSphere(new Point3d(0.0,0.0,0.0), 100.0);
rotator.setSchedulingBounds(bounds);
objTrans.addChild(rotator);

objRoot.compile(); // STEP 6 (the one line not part of STEP 5)

return objRoot;
}
```

Creating Geometry

There are four primary ways to construct geometry for Java 3D programs. The easiest, yet least flexible approach of all is the ColorCube class (`com.sun.j3d.utils.geometry.ColorCube`). This class constructs cube shapes for which the color is pre-set; each face of the cube has a different, predetermined color. The programmer can't specify or change the color of a ColorCube, nor can he change the size a ColorCube after it has been constructed, which limits the practical value of this class. ColorCube, however, is particularly useful when it comes to creating quick scene mock-ups (prototypes) and also for testing purposes because it's easy to use (it is the only Java 3D geometry class that programmers can use without concern for color or lights).

Although the core Java 3D API doesn't come with a suite of primitive shapes, Sun's utility package does. Mirroring VRML's suite of primitives, the `com.sun.j3d.utils.geometry` package contains Box, Cone, Cylinder, and Sphere classes. Unlike ColorCube, programmers can change the appearance of primitive shapes (see Chapter 14 to learn about Java 3D object appearances). In addition, the programmer can dynamically alter their size after initial construction.

The Java 3D loader mechanism is a third option when it comes to bringing geometry into a scene. As you'll learn in Chapter 13, "Customizing Size, Location, and Orientation," high quality VRML files can be loaded into Java 3D programs with very little effort. This technique is particularly important, as it gives Java 3D developers access to a wide range of existing VRML content without breaking a sweat. In addition, Java 3D loaders are available for a number of 3D file formats (see Chapter 11 for details).

Finally, Java 3D programmers have the option of creating geometry by specifying vertex coordinates for points, lines, and polygons. This tedious process would be murder for highly complex, hand-crafted objects that are better created to 3D modeling tools (which can then be brought into Java 3D courtesy of a loader). Algorithmically-generated shapes, however, lend themselves to this approach. Data received by medical probes, for example, would be a good candidate for this technique, as would Geographic Information Systems (GIS) data collected from field instruments.

Listing 12.1 HelloUniverse.java

```
/*
 *  @(#)HelloUniverse.java 1.48 99/05/20 14:07:00
 *
 * Copyright (c) 1996-1998 Sun Microsystems, Inc. All Rights Reserved.
 *
 * Sun grants you ("Licensee") a non-exclusive, royalty free, license to use,
 * modify and redistribute this software in source and binary code form,
 * provided that i) this copyright notice and license appear on all copies
 * the software; and ii) Licensee does not utilize the software in a manner
 * which is disparaging to Sun.
 *
 * This software is provided "AS IS," without a warranty of any kind. ALL
 * EXPRESS OR IMPLIED CONDITIONS, REPRESENTATIONS AND WARRANTIES, INCLUDING AN
 * IMPLIED WARRANTY OF MERCHANTABILITY, FITNESS FOR A PARTICULAR PURPOSE OR
 * NON-INFRINGEMENT, ARE HEREBY EXCLUDED. SUN AND ITS LICENSORS SHALL NOT BE
 * LIABLE FOR ANY DAMAGES SUFFERED BY LICENSEE AS A RESULT OF USING, MODIFYing
 * OR DISTRIBUTING THE SOFTWARE OR ITS DERIVATIVES. IN NO EVENT WILL SUN OR ITS
 * LICENSORS BE LIABLE FOR ANY LOST REVENUE, PROFIT OR DATA, OR FOR DIRECT,
 * INDIRECT, SPECIAL, CONSEQUENTIAL, INCIDENTAL OR PUNITIVE DAMAGES, HOWEVER
 * CAUSED AND REGARDLESS OF THE THEORY OF LIABILITY, ARISING OUT OF THE USE OF
 * OR INABILITY TO USE SOFTWARE, EVEN IF SUN HAS BEEN ADVISED OF THE
 * POSSIBILITY OF SUCH DAMAGES.
 *
 * This software is not designed or intended for use in on-line control of
 * aircraft, air traffic, aircraft navigation or aircraft communications; or in
 * the design, construction, operation or maintenance of any nuclear
 * facility. Licensee represents and warrants that it will not use or
 * redistribute the Software for such purposes.
 */

import java.applet.Applet;
import java.awt.BorderLayout;
import java.awt.event.*;
import java.awt.GraphicsConfiguration;
import com.sun.j3d.utils.applet.MainFrame;  // non-standard utility
import com.sun.j3d.utils.geometry.ColorCube;  // non-standard utility
import com.sun.j3d.utils.universe.*;  // non-standard utility
import javax.media.j3d.*;  // entire Java 3D standard extension package
import javax.vecmath.*;  // entire vector math standard extension package

public class HelloUniverse extends Applet {
  public BranchGroup createSceneGraph() {
    // Create the root of the branch graph
```

```
    BranchGroup objRoot = new BranchGroup();

    // Create the transform group node and initialize it to the
    // identity.  Enable the TRANSFORM_WRITE capability so that
    // our behavior code can modify it at runtime.  Add it to the
    // root of the subgraph.
    TransformGroup objTrans = new TransformGroup();
    objTrans.setCapability(TransformGroup.ALLOW_TRANSFORM_WRITE);
    objRoot.addChild(objTrans);

    // Create a simple shape leaf node, add it to the scene graph.
    objTrans.addChild(new ColorCube(0.4));

    // Create a new Behavior object that will perform the desired
    // operation on the specified transform object and add it into
    // the scene graph.
       AxisAngle4f axisAngle = new AxisAngle4f(0.0f, 0.0f, 1.0f,
                                          -(float)Math.PI / 2.0f);
    Transform3D yAxis = new Transform3D();
    Alpha rotationAlpha = new Alpha(-1, Alpha.INCREASING_ENABLE,
                      0, 0,
                      4000, 0, 0,
                      0, 0, 0);

    RotationInterpolator rotator =
      new RotationInterpolator(rotationAlpha, objTrans, yAxis,
                    0.0f, (float) Math.PI*2.0f);
    BoundingSphere bounds =
        new BoundingSphere(new Point3d(0.0,0.0,0.0), 100.0);
    rotator.setSchedulingBounds(bounds);
    objTrans.addChild(rotator);

       // Have Java 3D perform optimizations on this scene graph.
         objRoot.compile();

    return objRoot;
  }

public HelloUniverse() {
  setLayout(new BorderLayout());
  GraphicsConfiguration config =
     SimpleUniverse.getPreferredConfiguration();

  Canvas3D c = new Canvas3D(config);
  add("Center", c);
```

```
    // Create a simple scene and attach it to the virtual universe
    BranchGroup scene = createSceneGraph();
    SimpleUniverse u = new SimpleUniverse(c);

        // This will move the ViewPlatform back a bit so the
        // objects in the scene can be viewed.
        u.getViewingPlatform().setNominalViewingTransform();

    u.addBranchGraph(scene);
    }


    //
    // The following allows HelloUniverse to be run as an application
    // as well as an applet
    //
    public static void main(String[] args) {
    new MainFrame(new HelloUniverse(), 256, 256);
    }
}
```

Listing 12.2   SimpleUniverse.java

```
/*
 *      @(#)SimpleUniverse.java 1.11 98/11/17 17:27:21
 *
 * Copyright (c) 1996-1998 Sun Microsystems, Inc. All Rights Reserved.
 *
 * Sun grants you ("Licensee") a non-exclusive, royalty free, license to use,
 * modify and redistribute this software in source and binary code form,
 * provided that i) this copyright notice and license appear on all copies of
 * the software; and ii) Licensee does not utilize the software in a manner
 * which is disparaging to Sun.
 *
 * This software is provided "AS IS," without a warranty of any kind. ALL
 * EXPRESS OR IMPLIED CONDITIONS, REPRESENTATIONS AND WARRANTIES, INCLUDING ANY
 * IMPLIED WARRANTY OF MERCHANTABILITY, FITNESS FOR A PARTICULAR PURPOSE OR
 * NON-INFRINGEMENT, ARE HEREBY EXCLUDED. SUN AND ITS LICENSORS SHALL NOT BE
 * LIABLE FOR ANY DAMAGES SUFFERED BY LICENSEE AS A RESULT OF USING, MODIFYING
 * OR DISTRIBUTING THE SOFTWARE OR ITS DERIVATIVES. IN NO EVENT WILL SUN OR ITS
 * LICENSORS BE LIABLE FOR ANY LOST REVENUE, PROFIT OR DATA, OR FOR DIRECT,
 * INDIRECT, SPECIAL, CONSEQUENTIAL, INCIDENTAL OR PUNITIVE DAMAGES, HOWEVER
 * CAUSED AND REGARDLESS OF THE THEORY OF LIABILITY, ARISING OUT OF THE USE OF
 * OR INABILITY TO USE SOFTWARE, EVEN IF SUN HAS BEEN ADVISED OF THE
 * POSSIBILITY OF SUCH DAMAGES.
```

```
 *
 * This software is not designed or intended for use in on-line control of
 * aircraft, air traffic, aircraft navigation or aircraft communications; or in
 * the design, construction, operation or maintenance of any nuclear
 * facility. Licensee represents and warrants that it will not use or
 * redistribute the Software for such purposes.
 */

package com.sun.j3d.utils.universe;

import java.awt.GraphicsEnvironment;
import java.awt.GraphicsConfiguration;
import java.net.URL;

import javax.media.j3d.*;  // entire Java 3D standard extension package
import javax.vecmath.*;  // entire vector math standard extension package

/**
 * This class sets up a minimal user environment to quickly and easily
 * get a Java 3D program up and running.  This utility class creates
 * all the necessary objects on the "view" side of the scene graph.
 * Specifically, this class creates a locale, a single ViewingPlatform,
 * and a Viewer object (both with their default values).
 * Many basic Java 3D applications
 * will find that SimpleUniverse provides all necessary functionality
 * needed by their applications. More sophisticated applications
 * may find that they need more control in order to get extra functionality
 * and will not be able to use this class.
 *
 * @see Viewer
 * @see ViewingPlatform
 */
public class SimpleUniverse extends VirtualUniverse {

    /**
     * Locale reference needed to create the "view" portion
     * of the scene graph.
     */
    protected Locale          locale;

    /**
     * Viewer reference needed to create the "view" portion
     * of the scene graph.
     */
```

```
protected Viewer          viewer;
/**
 * ViewingPlatform reference needed to create the "view" portion
 * of the scene graph.
 */
protected ViewingPlatform viewingPlatform;

/**
 * Creates a locale, a single ViewingPlatform,
 * and a Viewer object (both with their default values).
 *
 * @see Locale
 * @see Viewer
 * @see ViewingPlatform
 */
public SimpleUniverse() {
  // call main constructor with default values.
  this(null, 1, null, null);
}

/**
 * Creates a locale, a single ViewingPlatform (with default values),
 * and a Viewer object.  The Viewer object uses default values for
 * everything but the canvas.
 *
 * @param canvas The canvas to associate with the Viewer object.  Passing
 *   in null will cause this parameter to be ignored and a canvas to be
 *   created by the utility.
 *
 * @see Locale
 * @see Viewer
 * @see ViewingPlatform
 */
public SimpleUniverse(Canvas3D canvas) {
  // call main constructor with default values for everything but
  // the canvas parameter.
  this(null, 1, canvas, null);
}

/**
 * Creates the "view" side of the scene graph.  The passed in parameters
 * override the default values where appropriate.
 *
 * @param origin The origin used to set the origin of the Locale object.
 *   If this object is null, then 0.0 is used.
```

```
 * @param numTransforms The number of transforms to be in the
 *  MultiTransformGroup object.
 * @param canvas The canvas to draw into.  If this is null, it is
 *  ignored and a canvas will be created by the utility.
 * @param userConfig The URL to the user's configuration file, used
 *  by the Viewer object.  Passing in null causes the default values
 *  to be used.
 *
 * @see Locale
 * @see Viewer
 * @see ViewingPlatform
 * @see MultiTransformGroup
 */
public SimpleUniverse(HiResCoord origin, int numTransforms,
  Canvas3D canvas, URL userConfig) {

    // See if the HiResCoord was given
    if (origin == null)
        locale = new Locale(this);
    else
        locale = new Locale(this, origin);

    // Create the ViewingPlatform and Viewer objects, passing
    // down the appropriate parameters.
    viewingPlatform = new ViewingPlatform(numTransforms);
    viewer = new Viewer(canvas, userConfig);

    // Add the ViewingPlatform to the Viewer object.
    viewer.setViewingPlatform(viewingPlatform);

    // Add the ViewingPlatform to the locale - the scene
    // graph is now "live".
    locale.addBranchGraph(viewingPlatform);
}


/**
 * Creates the "view" side of the scene graph.  The passed in parameters
 * override the default values where appropriate.
 *
 * @param viewingPlatform The viewingPlatform to use to create
 *  the "view" side of the scene graph.
 * @param viewer The viewer object to use to create
 *  the "view" side of the scene graph.
 */
```

```java
public SimpleUniverse(ViewingPlatform viewingPlatform, Viewer viewer) {
  locale = new Locale(this);

  // Assign object references.
  this.viewer = viewer;
  this.viewingPlatform = viewingPlatform;

  // Add the ViewingPlatform to the Viewer object.
  this.viewer.setViewingPlatform(this.viewingPlatform);

  // Add the ViewingPlatform to the locale - the scene
  // graph is now "live".
  locale.addBranchGraph(viewingPlatform);
}

/**
 * Returns the Locale object associated with this scene graph.
 *
 * @return The Locale object used in the construction of this scene
 *  graph.
 */
public Locale getLocale() {
  return locale;
}

/**
 * Returns the Viewer object associated with this scene graph.
 * SimpleUniverse creates a single Viewer object for use in the
 * scene graph.
 *
 * @return The Viewer object associated with this scene graph.
 */
public Viewer getViewer() {
  return viewer;
}

/**
 * Returns the ViewingPlatform object associated with this scene graph.
 *
 * @return The ViewingPlatform object of this scene graph.
 */
public ViewingPlatform getViewingPlatform() {
  return viewingPlatform;
}
```

```
/**
 * Returns the Canvas3D object associated with this Java 3D Universe.
 *
 * @return A reference to the Canvas3D object associated with the
 *  Viewer object.  This method is equivalent to calling getCanvas(0).
 *
 * @see Viewer
 */
public Canvas3D getCanvas() {
  return getCanvas(0);
}


/**
 * Returns the Canvas3D object at the specified index associated with
 * this Java 3D Universe.
 *
 * @param canvasNum The index of the Canvas3D object to retrieve.
 *  If there is no Canvas3D object for the given index, null is returned.
 *
 * @return A reference to the Canvas3D object associated with the
 *  Viewer object.  This method is equivalent to calling getCanvas(0).
 */
public Canvas3D getCanvas(int canvasNum) {
  return viewer.getCanvases();
}


/**
 * Used to add Nodes to the geometry side (as opposed to the view side)
 * of the scene graph.  This is a short cut to getting the Locale object
 * and calling that object's addBranchGraph() method.
 *
 * @param BranchGroup The BranchGroup to attach to this Universe's Locale.
 */
public void addBranchGraph(BranchGroup bg) {
  locale.addBranchGraph(bg);
}


/**
 * Finds the preferred GraphicsConfiguration object
 * for the system.  This object can then be used to create the
 * Canvas3D object for this system.
 *
 * @return The best GraphicsConfiguration object for
 *  the system.
 */
```

```
public static GraphicsConfiguration getPreferredConfiguration() {
  GraphicsConfigTemplate3D template = new GraphicsConfigTemplate3D();
  String stereo;

  // Check if the user has set the Java 3D stereo option.
  // Getting the system properties causes appletviewer to fail with a
  //  security exception without a try/catch.
  stereo = (String) java.security.AccessController.doPrivileged(
      new java.security.PrivilegedAction() {
      public Object run() {
          return System.getProperties().getProperty("j3d.stereo");
      }
  });

  // update template based on properties.
  if (stereo != null) {
      if (stereo.equals("REQUIRED"))
          template.setStereo(template.REQUIRED);
      else if (stereo.equals("PREFERRED"))
          template.setStereo(template.PREFERRED);
  }

  // Return the GraphicsConfiguration that best fits our needs.
  return GraphicsEnvironment.getLocalGraphicsEnvironment().
          getDefaultScreenDevice().getBestConfiguration(template);
}

}
```

Running HelloUniverse

The HelloUniverse program can be run as both an application *and* an applet, as can most Java 3D programs. This dual-purpose capability is possible thanks to the presence of a public HelloUniverse constructor described earlier, which the applet version utilizes, as well as a main() method required by all Java applications. Once compiled, for example, HelloUniverse can be executed as an application by issuing the following command line (where > is the command line prompt):

> java HelloUniverse

When executed in this fashion, the Java loader will invoke HelloUniverse's `main()` method, which contains a single line of code that accomplishes two important tasks. First, a top-level frame is constructed inside of which the program can render its ColorCube content. Second, the HelloUniverse constructor is called, which is the real entry point for this program. To make life a little easier on the programmer Sun has included a MainFrame class with the Java 3D utility package. By importing this line of code the HelloUniverse main() method can do its magic:

```java
import com.sun.j3d.utils.applet.MainFrame;

public static void main(String[] args) {
    new MainFrame(new HelloUniverse(), 256, 256);
}
```

To run HelloUniverse as an applet, however, an appropriate <APPLET> tag must be woven into an HTML file. As illustrated in Listing 12.3, the <APPLET> tag for HelloUniverse is quite simple as this program isn't capable of handling parameters (hence the glaring lack of PARAM attributes). The best we can do to bulk up this <APPLET> tag is to provide a line or two of alternate HTML code that is displayed by browsers that can't run Java applets.

For testing purposes you can load this page with the appletviewer tool that comes with Sun's Java Software Development Toolkit (SDK):

```
> appletviewer HelloUniverseTest.html
```

Listing 12.3   HelloUniverseTest.html

```html
<HTML>
<HEAD>
<TITLE>Hello Universe Applet</TITLE>
</HEAD>
<CODE>

<APPLET CODE="HelloUniverse.class" WIDTH=256 HEIGHT=256>
Sorry! You need a Java2-capable browser to view this applet.
</APPLET>

</BODY>
</HTML>
```

When you want to deploy this applet on the Web, however, you'll have to jump through one more hoop (fortunately it's an easy one to clear, and not on fire as so many hoops seem to be these days). Because none of today's commercial Web browsers support Java 2, this applet must be redirected to run on Sun's Java 2 runtime rather than the browser's own Java runtime. To do this the HTML code we just wrote must be modified to work in concert with Sun's Java Plug-in, which facilities the Java runtime handoff as explained in the previous chapter.

By default, Sun's Java 2 implementations come with the Java Plug-in. As a result, all you have to do is configure your HTML page to work with the Java Plug-in (you can safely assume that anyone equipped with Sun's Java 2 implementation also has the Java Plug-in needed to run Java 3D applets in a Web browser). This involves creating an <EMBED> tag that Netscape Navigator can handle, as well as an <OBJECT> tag that Internet Explorer will respect (see Chapter 6, "Weaving VRML into Web Pages," to learn more about these tags). Luckily, you don't have to hand-code either.

Sun's freely available Java Plug-in HTML Converter automates the task for you. Itself a Java application, the HTML Converter takes as input one or more HTML pages that contain <APPLET> tags. The tool then converts every <APPLET> tag it finds into a pair of corresponding <EMBED> and <OBJECT> tags that Navigator and Internet Explorer require. Listing 12-4 shows the resulting Web page generated by the HTML Converter when handed Listing 12.3 as input.

Note: Java Plug-in and HTML Converter

To learn more about the Java Plug-in and get your free copy of the Java Plug-in HTML Converter visit Sun's Java Plug-in home at http://java.sun.com/products/plugin/.

Tip: Shout3D and Blaxxun3D

Java 3D's end user requirements are high, to say the least. In addition to a complete installation of the Java 2 platform users must also have a Java 3D implementation installed (see Chapter 11 for details). Because of the extremely large download sizes for these implementations, it will be several years before the average computer user has a "Java 3D ready" system without substantial effort on their part. This will likely come as the result of a future version of Navigator or Internet Explorer shipping with support for Java 2, together with a transparent network installation of Java 3D, two major events that would make Java 3D readily accessible to the masses.

In the meantime, there are lightweight alternatives to Java 3D. Shout3D
(http://www.shout3d.com/) and blaxxun3D (http://www.blaxxun.com/) are
two stunning examples of Java-based Web3D technology that run seamlessly within today's Web browsers and without a stitch of effort on the end
users part. Although not as comprehensive as Java 3D, Shout3D and
blaxxun3D are blazing a trail for plug-in-less Web 3D. Both Shout3D and
blaxxun3D surfaced as core proposals for X3D, as Part 5 of this book explains, and have continued to evolve outside of the X3D development
process. Response to Shout3D and blaxxun3D has been tremendous, and
as of this writing these powerful applets seem to be blossoming all over the
Web like tulips following an April shower.

| Listing 12.4 PluginTest.html |

```html
<HTML>
<HEAD>
<TITLE>Hello Universe Applet</TITLE>
</HEAD>
<BODY>
<!--"CONVERTED_APPLET"-->
<!-- CONVERTER VERSION 1.0 -->
<OBJECT classid="clsid:8AD9C840-044E-11D1-B3E9-00805F499D93"
WIDTH = 256 HEIGHT = 256
codebase="http://java.sun.com/products/plugin/1.2/jinstall-12-
win32.cab#Version=1,2,0,0">
<PARAM NAME = CODE VALUE = "HelloUniverse.class" >

<PARAM NAME="type" VALUE="application/x-java-applet;version=1.2">
<COMMENT>
<EMBED type="application/x-java-applet;version=1.2"
java_CODE = "HelloUniverse.class" WIDTH = 256 HEIGHT = 256
pluginspage="http://java.sun.com/products/plugin/1.2/plugin-
install.html"><NOEMBED></COMMENT>
Sorry! You need a Java2-capable browser to view this applet.
</NOEMBED></EMBED>
</OBJECT>


<!--
<APPLET  CODE = "HelloUniverse.class" WIDTH = 256 HEIGHT = 256 >
Sorry! You need a Java2-capable browser to view this applet.

</APPLET>
```

```
-->
<!--"END_CONVERTED_APPLET"-->

</BODY>
</HTML>
```

Summary

Java 3D uses a scene graph programming model similar to that of VRML. Like VRML, Java 3D scene graphs are treelike data structures that contain node objects arranged into directed, parent-to-child relationships. Nodes, in turn, contain fields that the programmer can manipulate in order to alter their properties.

Java 3D scene graphs are assembled primarily from object instances created using Java 3D API classes, although references to other Java objects are also legal. Most of the nodes found in a typical scene graph are descendants of the abstract SceneGraphObject class, which is the parent of Java 3D's Node and NodeComponent classes. Nodes can be categorized as either Group nodes or Leaf nodes; a Group node, can contain children, while a Leaf node cannot. Node components can be thought of as bundles of information that are referenced by nodes. A Shape3D node, for example, can reference Appearance and Geometry node components. Because node components encapsulate data used by a node, they are external to the node (and can therefore be shared by nodes if needed).

The BranchGroup node is a grouping node that is used to construct and manage major branches of a Java 3D scene graph. BranchGroup acts as the root of a branch graph and can be selectively attached and detached from the scene graph. BranchGroups are typically attached to a Locale, which acts as a coordinate-system anchor for objects in a scene branch graph (only BranchGroup objects can be attached to a Locale). A Locale, in turn, is attached to a VirtualUniverse object, which is the top-level object in every Java 3D scene graph. The VirtualUniverse is the largest single unit of aggregate measurement in Java 3D and can be thought of as a database in which a large number of scene graphs can be stored.

Once a BranchGroup is attached, or compiled, it becomes "live." Access to objects in a live branch graph is limited according to capability bit settings, which form a strong contract between the Java 3D program and the Java 3D compiler and renderer (allowing Java 3D to optimize the subgraph contents).

In order to modify a live scene graph object the capability bits that correspond to the modification must be set in advance.

Following is a complete list of URLs referenced in this chapter:

Java 3D Web site   http://java.sun.com/products/java-media/3D/

Java Plug-in and HTML Converter   http://java.sun.com/products/plugin/

Shout3D   http://www.shout3d.com/

blaxxun3D   http://www.blaxxun.com/

CUSTOMIZING SIZE, LOCATION, AND ORIENTATION

Topics in This Chapter

- Changing the scale, location, and orientation of objects
- Creating object hierarchies
- Loading and transforming VRML worlds

Chapter 13

In this chapter you'll learn how to change the location, orientation and scale of three-dimensional objects in the virtual world. Because VRML and Java 3D have a lot in common when it comes to transforming objects in this way, you may find Chapter 7, "Customizing Location, Size, and Orientation," to be a good general introduction to the various concepts found here (although it's not necessary to read Chapter 7 in advance, you might find it a valuable primer to this chapter). You'll also learn how those objects can be arranged into hierarchies, and how VRML worlds can be loaded into a Java 3D universe.

Introduction

By default, every virtual object in a Java 3D scene is initially stationary and unchanging. Every light source, view platform, sound source, and shape remains at its starting location unless you write code that specifies otherwise. In this chapter you'll learn how to move and rotate these objects, as well as how to change the size of a three-dimensional object. These three basic operations are known as "translation," "rotation," and "scaling."

Note

Like VRML, Java 3D is based on a right-handed coordinate system. To determine the direction of rotation, for example, the "right hand rule" may be applied. For details, see Chapter 7, "Customizing Location, Size, and Orientation."

Translation

Translation simply means moving an object from one location in space to another. It's accomplished by adding an offset to each of the X, Y and Z components of the object's location. For example, if an object is located at (7, 15, 2) (that is, seven meters along the X axis, 15 meters up the Y axis, and 2 meters forward along the Z axis) and you add a translation of (2, 0, 5), the object will end up at (9, 15, 7). In Java 3D, as with VRML, all translations are expressed in terms of meters (one meter is about 39.37 inches, or just a little over three feet).

Rotation

Rotation is more complex. An object can be rotated around any combination of the X, Y, and Z axes simultaneously, which can result in every point on the object's surface getting moved to a different location. To understand this more clearly, imagine a simple box that's oriented along the X, Y, and Z axes as shown in Figure 13-1. If you rotate the box around the vertical (Y) axis, all four corners of the box end up in a different location than they were before the rotation, as shown in Figure 13-2. Now imagine taking that rotated box and rotating it yet again, this time around the X axis—once again, all the points have changed location, as shown in Figure 13-3. Like VRML, Java 3D rotation angles are always expressed in units called radians (one radian is about 57.296 degrees; see "Angles vs. Radians").

Scaling

Scaling an object means changing its size. Because of the way Java 3D handles scaling internally, it's important to distinguish between two different types of scaling operation: uniform and nonuniform. A uniform scale simply changes the size of an object, making it larger in all directions. A cube that gets uniformly scaled by some amount will still be a cube, and a sphere will

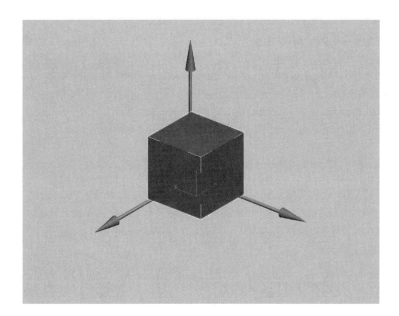

Figure 13-1   This box is oriented along the X, Y, and Z axes of the Java 3D coordinate system.

Figure 13-2   The box has been rotated around the Y axis.

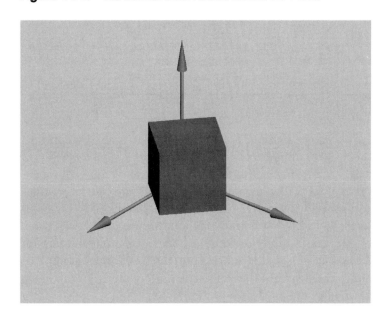

Radians vs. Degrees

Java 3D, like VRML, deals with rotation angles in terms of radians. Although degrees are generally easier for people to deal with than radians, computers prefer radians when calculating with angles. Fortunately, the formula for converting from degrees to radians isn't terribly difficult:

$$radians = degrees/180 \times 3.142$$

To convert 45 degrees into radians, for example, divide 45 by 180 and then multiply the result by 3.142. The answer, .785, is the number of radians in 45 degrees. To convert radians to degrees, the formula is applied in reverse:

$$degrees = radians/3.142 \times 180$$

Following are a few of the more common angles you'll use in Java 3D, expressed in both degrees and radians:

DEGREES	*RADIANS*
0	0.000
10	0.175
45	0.785
90	1.571
180	3.142
270	4.712
360	6.283

remain a sphere, as shown in Figure 13-4. A nonuniform scale, by contrast, actually changes the relative dimensions of an object by scaling it by different amounts in each axis.

Uniform scaling involves taking a single value (a floating-point or double-precision value) and multiplying the X, Y, and Z components of every point on the surface of an object by that amount. Nonuniform scaling uses three different values, one for the X direction, one for the Y direction, and one for the Z direction. A box that gets scaled more along the X axis than along Y or Z will become oblong, and a sphere that gets scaled more along Y than along X or Z will become an ellipsoid, as shown in Figure 13-5.

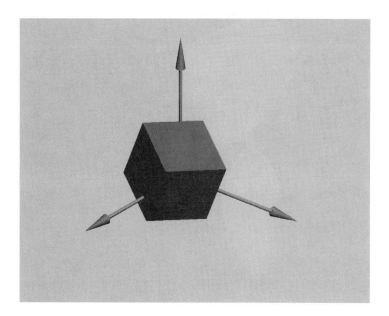

Figure 13-3   The box has been rotated around the X axis.

Figure 13-4   Uniform scaling changes the size of an object in all directions.

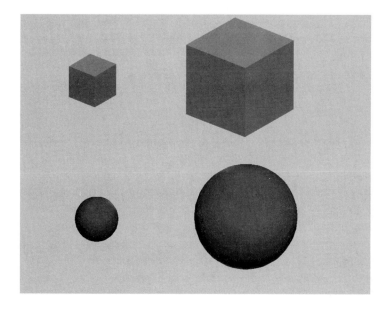

Figure 13-5   Whereas uniform scaling merely changes the shape of an object, nonuniform scaling is used to resize an object along a specific axis (or any combination of axes).

In general, you should use uniform scaling whenever possible. Java 3D was originally designed to support only uniform scaling, and support for nonuniform scaling was added later. The API still reflects this, and many of the functions that affect scale will take only a single floating-point or double-precision value as a scale factor rather than three values.

Note

Java 3D initially avoided nonuniform scaling because it is much more mathematically complex than uniform scaling, particularly when taking the inverse of a matrix (which many Java 3D implementations will do internally every time they render the scene). Nonuniform scaling operations greatly increase the complexity of these inverse operations and therefore have an adverse effect on rendering speed and frame rate.

Scale factors: In Java 3D, scaling is expressed as a multiplier. A value of 1.5 means that the object is one and a half times its original size.

Transforms (javax.media.j3d.Transform3D)

Collectively, these three operations (translation, rotation, and scaling) are known as "transformations" or simply "transforms." In Java 3D, they are represented by a class of objects known as a Transform3D (`javax.media.j3d.Transform3D`). A single Transform3D object can represent a translation, a rotation, a scaling, or any combination of the three.

In order to understand the various methods of the Transform3D object, it's necessary to understand how a transform is represented mathematically. Each transform consists of an array of 16 numbers, arranged in a four-by-four array:

```
m00 m01 m02 m03
m10 m11 m12 m13
m20 m21 m22 m23
m30 m31 m32 m33
```

This array of numbers, called a "matrix," is a compact way of representing all the numeric values that are required for any combination of translation, rotation, and scaling. The top three values in the rightmost column (m03 m13 m23) are used to store the X, Y, and Z translation values, respectively. The remaining 3×3 submatrix is used to store both rotation and scaling. In practice, the last row (m30 m31 m32 m33) is usually (0, 0, 0, 1). The situations where this is not the case are beyond the scope of this book, but details can be found in most 3D computer graphics books (see http://www.web3dgallery.com/3d/ for a list of valuable 3D resources).

When a Transform3D is applied to a three-dimensional shape, each point in that shape is transformed by the matrix. In other words, the coordinates for the point are multiplied by the matrix in the Transform3D object, producing a new set of X, Y, and Z values for that point.

Another way of looking at this is that the matrix represents the following set of equations:

```
x' = m00 * x + m01 * y + m02 * z + m03
y' = m10 * x + m11 * y + m12 * z + m13
z' = m20 * x + m21 * y + m22 * z + m23
```

Upon close examination it becomes clear that the new value of the point (x', y', z') is merely the old value of the point (x, y, z) multiplied by the values in the matrix.

When dealing with transformations, a particularly useful concept is that of an "identity matrix":

```
1 0 0 0
0 1 0 0
0 0 1 0
0 0 0 1
```

If you examine the equations above, and plug in the "m" values from the identity matrix, you find it just boils down to:

```
x' = x
y' = y
z' = z
```

That means the identity matrix doesn't change the coordinates at all. If you take a matrix that starts off as the identity matrix, and set the m03, m13, and m23 values to be the translation values, you get:

```
x' = x + m03
y' = y + m13
z' = z + m23
```

This is exactly what you would expect—adding an offset to the original values to get the new ones.

Now what happens if you want to scale the point, instead of translate it? Well, you would start off with the identity matrix and multiply all its values by the appropriate amount. For example, to uniformly scale an object to seven times its original size, you would use the following matrix:

```
7 0 0 0
0 7 0 0
0 0 7 0
0 0 0 1
```

Notice that the bottom right element didn't change—it didn't need to, so it's still 1. If you plug those matrix values into the equations above, you find the following to be true:

```
x' = 7 * x
y' = 7 * y
z' = 7 * z
```

This produces a uniform scaling, as expected. Of course, the scaling can be nonuniform. To scale a sphere into a horizontal ellipsoid, you might use the following:

```
7 0 0 0
0 3 0 0
0 0 3 0
0 0 0 1
```

This would multiply Y and Z by 3, but X by 7, which would stretch the sphere more along the horizontal axis than along the up-down or front-back axes.

Rotations are more complex and are based on the sine and cosine values for the angle of rotation. The details are beyond the scope of this chapter but can be found in any good graphics textbook. The only thing you need to know at this point is that a rotation will produce a particular set of values in the top left three-by-three submatrix of a Transform3D object.

This introduces an interesting problem—since the same part of the matrix is used to store both the scaling and the rotation, how do you separate them? The short answer is that you generally don't need to. Once the Transform3D is built, it simply gets used to transform points. However, if you want to modify just the rotation or just the scale, you need to be able to access them separately. For the most part, Java 3D handles this for you. When you call a method on a Transform3D object that changes the rotation, for example, Java 3D will internally factor out the scale (a process known as Singular Value Decomposition, or SVD), then apply the rotation, and then reapply the scale. Something similar happens when you change the scale—the original scale is factored out, and the new scale is applied in its place while keeping the rotation the same.

The TransformGroup Class (javax.media.j3d.TransformGroup)

Although a Transform3D object is a handy way to represent a transformation matrix, it can't alter objects in a scene by itself. In order for a Transform3D to actually translate, rotate, and scale objects it needs to be copied into a Java 3D TransformGroup object (`javax.media.j3d.TransformGroup`).

The TransformGroup class subclasses the Group class, giving Transform-Group the ability to store and retrieve its children. It also offers the standard methods related to cloning and duplicating nodes. Aside from that, the only methods that TransformGroup provides are those that allow you to set and get the Transform3D object for the TransformGroup.

A TransformGroup node contains a Transform3D, as well as some number of "children." Each of the children is itself a node, which may be a leaf node (such as a shape or sound) or a grouping node that contains children of its own. When the scene is rendered and the renderer encounters a TransformGroup, that node's Transform3D is used to transform the coordinates of all the objects that are children of the TransformGroup. If some of those children are grouping objects, their children are transformed as well, and so on (VRML's Transform node is equivalent to the Java 3D TransformGroup; see Chapter 7, "Customizing Location, Size, and Orientation," for details). All of this fits naturally into the basic scene structure discussed in the previous chapter. Specifically, a VirtualUniverse contains one or more Locale objects. Each Locale contains one or more BranchGroup objects. Each BranchGroup object can contain any arbitrary nodes, some of which may be TransformGroup objects. Those TransformGroup objects can contain any kind of node as children, including additional TransformGroup objects. This entire collection of nested nodes is typically called a "scene graph." Figure 13-6 shows the full structure of a Java 3D scene graph.

Note that a TransformGroup starts out with an identity matrix in its Transform3D. This means that the translation is (0, 0, 0), the scale is (1, 1, 1) and all the rotation angles are set to zero. Tables 13.1 through 13.3 provide a summary of the TransformGroup constructors, fields, and methods.

Table 13.1   TransformGroup Constructor Summary

Constructors for the class javax.media.j3d.TransformGroup. Vector, matrix, and quaternion parameters used by many of these constructors are defined in the javax.vecmath package. See the Java 3D API Specification (http://java.sun.com/products/java-media/3D/) for details.

`public` **`TransformGroup`**`()`
    Default (no argument) constructor initializes a TransformGroup using an identity matrix.

`public` **`TransformGroup`**`(Transform3D t)`
    Constructs and initializes a TransformGroup from the transform *t*.

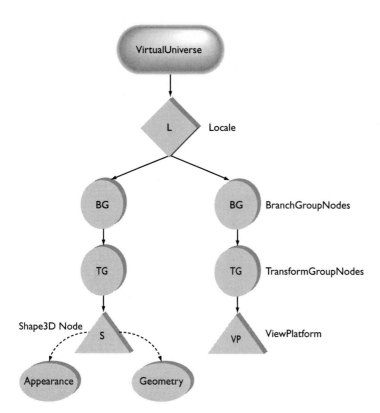

Figure 13-6 A Java 3D scene graph is a collection of nested nodes, of which the TransformGroup node can contain children to which translations may be applied (a TransformGroup can also contain any type of node, including other TransformGroup objects).

Table 13.2   TransformGroup Field Summary

Only two fields are defined by the class javax.media.j3d.TransformGroup (both are defined as `public static final int`). See the Java 3D API Specification (http://java.sun.com/products/java-media/3D/) for details.

`ALLOW_TRANSFORM_READ`
Specifies that the node will allow read access to its object's transform information.

`ALLOW_TRANSFORM_WRITE`
Specifies that the node will allow writing of its object's transform information.

Table 13.3	TransformGroup Method Summary

Public methods of the class javax.media.j3d.TransformGroup. See the Java 3D API Specification (http://java.sun.com/products/java-media/3D/) for details.

Returns	Method Name, Parameters, and Description
node	**cloneNode**(boolean forceDuplicate) Creates a new instance of the node (javax.media.j3d.Node)
void	**getTransform**(Transform3D t) Copies the transform component of this TransformGroup into transform *t*.
double	**setTransform**(Transform3D t) Sets the transform component of this TransformGroup to the value of transform *t*.

Hierarchies

When a TransformGroup contains another TransformGroup, the effects of their Transform3D objects are combined so that all the children of the "inner" TransformGroup are affected by both sets of transforms. For example, if a TransformGroup specifies a translation of (2, 17.5, 18) and also contains a TransformGroup that specifies a translation of (3, 4.2, 27), their combined effect would be a translation of (5, 21.7, 45). Another way of looking at this is to say that the innermost TransformGroup is used to transform the coordinates of any nodes that it contains. The resulting coordinates are then transformed by the next outer TransformGroup, and so on. Each TransformGroup defines a translation, rotation, and scaling relative to the next TransformGroup up in the hierarchy.

Imagine, for example, that you're writing a Java 3D application that will display and animate a human being. Each body part in the human will be attached to the one above it...the shin bone is connected to the thigh bone, the thigh bone connected to the hip bone, and so on. In Java 3D the concept of being "attached to" another object is expressed by being a child of the corresponding grouping object. In other words, the hip joint would be a TransformGroup object, and its children would be a Shape3D node (for the geometry of the thigh) and another TransformGroup for the knee joint. The knee joint would also have two children—a Shape3D object for the calf, and another TransformGroup object for the ankle joint. If you change the rotation of the hip joint by modifying the rotation value of the Transform3D node and then writing it back into the TransformGroup for the hip joint, all the children of that TransformGroup will be rotated around that joint. This will not only change the orientation of the Shape3D object for the thigh, it will also move the knee, the calf, the ankle, the foot, the toes, and so on. The same principles are applied to other hierarchical structures. When you rotate your shoulder, for instance, you find that your upper arm, lower arm, hands, and fingers all "come along for the ride."

Tip

When you change the value of a Transform3D node, the effect is not instantaneous. You need to set that Transform3D node into the Transform-Group again in order for it to affect the scene. The reason is that the TransformGroup stores a copy of the Transform3D rather than a reference to it, so updating the original Transform3D has no direct effect.

This means that you can create a Transform3D object and use it over and over again to set values in a number of different TransformGroup objects. This ability to reuse a Transform3D can help reduce the need for garbage collection, which is significant, since every time Java's garbage collection runs it takes CPU cycles away from rendering.

Another example would be a solar system. There would be a Transform-Group for the sun, which would allow you to position and orient the entire solar system relative to the galaxy it's contained within (although you're likely to use a Locale in such a case). The sun's TransformGroup would have a child for each planet, and each of those children would itself be a Transform-Group. The sun TransformGroup would also store the geometry for the sun in a Shape3D node, as well as a PointLight node to generate sunlight. Each subsiding planetary TransformGroup node would contain a Shape3D node for the planet's geometry, as well as a child TransformGroup for each moon of the planet. Each of those TransformGroups would contain the geometry for that moon.

Note

While we're talking about nested TransformGroup nodes, it's worth noting that a Locale is very much like a TransformGroup. The main difference is that a Locale does not contain any rotations or scaling factors—just a translation value. The translation value in a Locale is expressed in very high-resolution coordinates, much higher than those used in a Transform Group. Despite these differences, a Locale does offer another level of transformation hierarchy.

Representing Rotations

Translation and scaling are easy to represent, since they're just three simple floating-point or double-precision numbers. Rotation, however, is more complex. There are several ways of expressing a rotation, and Java 3D supports all of them.

If your application is able to generate a rotation matrix directly, you can have Java 3D set that matrix directly into a Transform3D object. That works, but it puts the burden of computing the matrix onto your application software. Alternatively, you can create a separate rotation matrix for the X rotation, the Y rotation, and the Z rotation, and then tell Java 3D to combine them into a single matrix.

If you prefer, you can create a rotation matrix from a set of three rotation angles, often referred to as "Euler angles." You simply store the roll, pitch, and yaw values into the three elements of a vector and set it as the Euler angles for the Transform3D.

Another approach is to use an axis/angle representation, which provides an axis around which to rotate the object and an angle through which to rotate it. This will be familiar to you if you've read Chapter 7, since this is the rotation system that VRML uses.

Yet another approach is to use quaternions, which are mathematical entities that store rotations in a form that's easy to interpolate. It's easy to move back and forth between quaternions and axis/angle. Quaternions are very useful for animation, but they can be difficult to visualize.

The Transform3D Class

The Transform3D class provides a large number of methods for getting and setting the various components of its transform matrix (see Table 13.6). Its constructors also accept a variety of different parameters for creating a Transform3D object. A Transform3D can be built from a 4×4 matrix, or from a 3×3 matrix plus a vector and a scale factor (see Tables 13.4 and 13.5).

You can set the rotations from a vector of Euler angles, a matrix, a quaternion, or an AxisAngle object. A uniform scale can be set as a floating-point or double-precision value, and a nonuniform scale can be set from a vector of three such values. You can set both the rotation and scale at the same time from a matrix. You can invert a Transform3D, multiply it by another Transform3D (thereby accumulating the two transforms), or normalize the matrix. You can reset a matrix to all zeroes or to an identity matrix.

The matrix stored in a Transform3D object can be any of several different types. You can get the type of the matrix, in order to determine whether it's an identity matrix, a zero matrix, a pure scale matrix, a pure translation matrix, an orthogonal matrix (rotation only), a rigid matrix (rotation and translation only, no scale), congruent (translation, rotation and uniform scale), or affine (translate, rotate, and nonuniform scale).

The fact that Java 3D provides so many different methods for creating and updating a transform matrix should tell you that these operations are a very important part of most Java 3D applications. Once a developer has built a scene, most of his or her time may very well be spent animating it, and this is invariably done by changing the transforms that control the location, orientation, and scale of objects in a Java 3D universe.

Table 13.4　Transform3D Constructor Summary

Constructors for the class javax.media.j3d.Transform3D. Vector, matrix, and quaternion parameters used by many of these constructors are defined in the javax.vecmath package. See the Java 3D API Specification (http://java.sun.com/products/java-media/3D/) for details.

`public` **`Transform3D()`**
Default (no argument) constructor initializes a transform to the identity matrix.

`public` **`Transform3D_`**`(double[] m)`
Constructs and initializes a transform from the double-precision array of length 16 matrix (m). The top row of the matrix is initialized to the first four elements of the array, and so forth.

`public` **`Transform3D`**`(float[] m)`
Constructs and initializes a transform from the float array of length 16 matrix (m). The top row of the matrix is initialized to the first four elements of the array, and so forth.

`public` **`Transform3D`**`(GMatrix m)`
Constructs and initializes a transform from the upper 4×4 of matrix (m).

`public` **`Transform3D`**`(javax.vecmath.Matrix3d m,`
`javax.vecmath.Vector3d t, double s)`
Constructs and initializes a transform from rotation matrix (m), translation vector (t), and scale (s) values.

`public` **`Transform3D`**`(Matrix3f m, Vector3d t, double s)`
Constructs and initializes a transform from rotation matrix (m), translation vector (t), and scale (s) values.

```
public Transform3D(Matrix3f m, Vector3f t, float s)
```
Constructs and initializes a transform from rotation matrix (m), translation vector (t), and scale (s) values.

```
public Transform3D(Matrix4d m)
```
Constructs and initializes a transform from a 4×4 matrix (m).

```
public Transform3D(Matrix4f m)
```
Constructs and initializes a transform from a 4×4 matrix (m).

```
public Transform3D(Quat4d q, Vector3d t, double s)
```
Constructs and initializes a transform from quaternion (q), translation vector (t), and scale (s) values.

```
public Transform3D(Quat4f q, Vector3d t, double s)
```
Constructs and initializes a transform from quaternion (q), translation vector (t), and scale (s) values.

```
public Transform3D(Quat4f q, Vector3f t, float s)
```
Constructs and initializes a transform from quaternion (q), translation vector (t), and scale (s) values.

```
public Transform3D(Transform3D t)
```
Constructs and initializes a transform from a Transform3D object.

Table 13.5   Transform3D Field Summary

Fields defined by the class javax.media.j3d.Transform3D. All fields are defined as `public static final int`. See the Java 3D API Specification (http://java.sun.com/products/java-media/3D/) for details.

AFFINE

An affine matrix can translate, rotate, reflect, scale anisotropically, and shear.

CONGRUENT

This is an angle- and length-preserving matrix, meaning that it can translate, rotate, and reflect about an axis, and scale by an amount which is uniform in all directions.

IDENTITY

An identity matrix.

NEGATIVE_DETERMINANT

This matrix has a negative determinant; an orthogonal matrix with a positive determinant is a rotation matrix; an orthogonal matrix with a negative determinant is a reflection and rotation matrix.

ORTHOGONAL

The four row vectors that make up an orthogonal matrix form a basis, meaning that they are mutually orthogonal; an orthogonal matrix with positive determinant is a pure rotation matrix; a negative determinant indicates a rotation and a reflection.

RIGID

This matrix is a rotation and a translation with unity scale; the upper 3×3 of the matrix is orthogonal, and there is a translation component.

SCALE

A uniform scale matrix with no translation or other off-diagonal components.

TRANSLATION

A translation-only matrix with ones on the diagonal.

ZERO

A zero matrix.

Table 13.6   Transform3D Method Subset Summary

The javax.media.j3d.Transform3D class contains a large number of methods related to transform representation and manipulation. This table summarizes a **small subset** of the many public methods defined in the Transform3D class. Most of the methods listed below are overloaded, meaning that many variations on the same methods exist. (A method is typically overloaded to accommodate vector, matrix, and quaternion parameters in the javax.vecmath package.) Many of the "set" mutator methods listed below have a corresponding "get" accessor method. See the Java 3D API Specification (http://java.sun.com/products/java-media/3D/) for details.

Returns	*Method Name, Parameters, and Description*
void	**add**(Transform3D t) Adds this transform to transform *t* and places the result into this (i.e., this = this + 1).
boolean	**equals**(Object obj) Returns true if the Object *obj* is of type Transform3D and all of the data members of *obj* are equal to the corresponding data members in this Transform3D.
void	**invert**() Inverts this transform in place.

void	**lookAt**(Point3d eye, Point3d center, Vector3d up) Helping function that specifies the position and orientation of a view matrix.
void	**mul**(double scalar) Multiplies each element of this transform by a scalar.
void	**mulInverse**(Transform3D t) Multiplies this transform by the inverse of transform *t*.
void	**mulTransposeBoth**(Transform3D t1, Transform3D t2) Multiplies the transpose of transform *t1* by the transpose of transform *t2* and places the result into this transform (i.e., this = transpose(t1) ° transpose(t2)).
void	**normalize**() Normalizes the rotational components (upper 3 × 3) of this matrix in place using a Singular Value Decomposition (SVD).
void	**ortho**(double left, double right, double bottom, double top, double near, double far) Creates an orthographic projection transform that mimics a standard, camera-based view-model.
void	**perspective**(double fovx, double aspect, double zNear, double zFar) Creates a perspective projection transform that mimics a standard, camera-based view-model.
void	**rotX**(double angle) Sets the value of this transform to a counterclockwise rotation about the x axis.
void	**rotY**(double angle) Sets the value of this transform to a counterclockwise rotation about the y axis.
void	**rotZ**(double angle) Sets the value of this transform to a counterclockwise rotation about the z axis.
void	**set**(Vector3d t) Sets the translational value of this matrix to the vector *t*, and sets the other components of the matrix as if this transform were an identity matrix. *Note: a variety of set() methods are defined in this class (see Java 3D API for details).*

void	**setEuler**(Vector3d e)
	Sets the rotational component (upper 3 × 3) of this transform to the rotation matrix converted from the Euler angles *e*; the other nonrotational elements are set as if this were an identity matrix.
void	**setIdentity**()
	Sets this transform to the identity matrix.
void	**setRotation**(AxisAngle4f a)
	Sets the rotational component (upper 3 × 3) of this transform to the matrix equivalent values of the axis-angle *a*; the other elements of this transform are unchanged; any preexisting scale in the transform is preserved.
void	**setScale**(double s)
	Sets the scale component of the current transform to the scale *s*; any existing scale is first factored out of the existing transform before the new scale is applied.
void	**setTranslation**(Vector3f t)
	Replaces the translational components of this transform to the values in the vector *t*; the other values of this transform are not modified.
void	**setZero**()
	Sets this transform to all zeros.
void	**sub**(Transform3D t)
	Subtracts transform *t* from this transform and places the result into this (i.e., this = this − t).
void	**transform**(Vector3f n)
	Transforms the normal *n* by this transform and places the value back into normal.

Examples

By now, your head must be spinning. And possibly translating as well, and perhaps undergoing a horrible nonuniform scale. Well, a few examples should help you find your identity again.

Let's start with a little code fragment to position an imaginary pencil object in space:

```
// Assume there's already a Shape3D node called
// pencil_geometry

// Create a new TransformGroup, to allow us
// to position the pencil

TransformGroup pencil = new TransformGroup();
pencil.addChild(pencil_geometry);

// Create a new Transform3D

Transform3D transform = new Transform3D();
transform.setTranslation(new Vector3f(2, 15,
8.9));

// Position the pencil

pencil.setTransform(transform);
```

Now, let's get a little fancier. Let's rotate the pencil, so it lies on its side.

```
transform.setRotation(new Vector3d(1.57, 0, 0));
pencil.setTransform(transform);
```

This creates a 1.57-radian (90-degree) roll value in a vector and sets the rotation part of the transform to that value. The translation part is unaffected. The second line sets the transform back into the TransformGroup of the pencil. If we don't do this, the pencil will continue to have its old transform.

Now let's try our hand at building our first object hierarchy. We're going to put the pencil on a table.

```
// Assume there's already a Shape3D node called
// table_geometry

TransformGroup table = new TransformGroup();
table.addChild(table_geometry);

// Now put the pencil on the table

table.addChild(pencil);

// Now move the pencil
```

```
transform.setIdentity();   // back to original state
transform.setTranslation(5, 0.75, 5);
pencil.setTransform(transform);

// Now move the table

transform.setIdentity(); // we're reusing this Transform3D
transform.rotY(Math.PI/4);   // rotate 45 degrees
transform.setTranslation(new Vector(2, 0, 0);   // move table
```

This will put the pencil on the table (assuming the table's origin is at ground level, and the table is 0.75 meters tall). It will then rotate the table 45 degrees around the vertical axis, and move the table 2 meters in the X direction. The pencil will move as well and will maintain its position relative to the table. Congratulations! You've just constructed your first object hierarchy. Tables 13.4 through 13.6 provide a summary of the Transform3D constructors, fields, and method subsets used in these sample snippets of code.

Loading and Transforming VRML Worlds

In Part 2 of this book you learned how to create simple VRML worlds and also how to customize the appearance of premade VRML content for your own needs. Chapter 10, "Creating New VRML Worlds," even showed you how to assemble more sophisticated worlds by inlining existing VRML files, and how to get started creating complex VRML worlds from scratch using a visual authoring tool.

Unfortunately, visual Java 3D authoring tools do not yet exist. However, as a result of Java 3D's close relationship with VRML (see Chapter 11, "Java 3D Overview") you can use a great deal of existing VRML content in your Java 3D programs.

VRML and Java 3D actually have a shared history. For a while, engineers from Sun Microsystems (where Java was developed) and Silicon Graphics (which had supported VRML since its inception) were collaborating with each other in order to ensure that these two 3D technologies were compatible with each other. In fact, much of Java 3D ended up being based on VRML, right down to individual nodes. However, the VRML and Java 3D efforts began to diverge, partly due to differing goals. VRML is a file format for describing both three-dimensional scenes and their runtime behavior. Java 3D, on the other hand, is a scene graph API that provides a means for applications to control a 3D scene. Which one you would choose depends on the application, but quite often a combination of the two is effective. Using the Java 3D loader mechanism, object geometry (form) can be created in VRML and then loaded into Java 3D for control by a Java application (even non-programmers can create VRML content using a visual development tool as described in Chapter 10, "Creating New VRML Worlds").

The Concept of a "Loader"

Java 3D supports a special class of objects called "loaders," which are able to load data from various file formats and construct a Java 3D scene graph from them. For example, one might have a loader for Lightwave files, another for 3D Studio Max files, another for files from Softimage, and so on. What's more, a single application can have multiple loaders and can therefore integrate files created in a variety of authoring tools with no need for file format conversion. This effectively makes Java 3D independent of the underlying graphics file formats that are used by the content creators.

Note

The latest VRML97 loader is available through the Web3D Consortium's VRML-Java3D working group at http://www.vrml.org/WorkingGroups/ vrml-java3d/.

A loader is a utility class that implements the `com.sun.j3d.loaders` interface (see Tables 13.7 and 13.8). A loader can be told to load a world from a filename on your local system, from a URL, or from a Reader object. Loaders can also be instructed to load only certain elements of the scene, such as the geometry, the lights, the viewpoints, and so on. This is done by setting corresponding flags for the loader (see Table 13.8).

Table 13.7	Loader Methods

The following methods are defined in the com.sun.j3d.loaders interface. As a result, all loaders (such as the VRML97 loader) support these methods. See the Java 3D API Specification (http://java.sun.com/products/java-media/3D/) for details.

Returns	*Method Name, Parameters, and Description*
String	**getBasePath**() Returns the current base path setting in the form of a string (java.lang.String).
URL	**getBaseUrl**() Returns the current base URL setting (`java.net.URL`).
int	**getFlags**() Returns the current loader flags (see Table 13.8).
Scene	**load**(Reader r) Loads the Reader (`java.io.Reader`) and returns the Scene containing the scene.
Scene	**load**(String fileName) Loads the file specified by the string (`java.lang.String`) and returns the Scene containing the scene.
Scene	**load**(URL u) Loads the file specified by the URL (`java.net.URL`) and returns the Scene containing the scene.
void	**setBasePath**(String pathName) Sets the base path name for data files associated with the file passed into the `load(String)` method.
void	**setBaseUrl**(URL url) Sets the base URL (`java.net.URL`) name for data files associated with the file passed into the `load(URL)` method.
void	**setFlags**(int flags) Sets the load flags for the file (see Table 13.8).

Table 13.8   Loader Field Summary

The following fields are defined in the com.sun.j3d.loaders interface. As a result, all loaders (such as the VRML97 loader) support these fields. These fields are defined as `public static final int`. See the Java 3D API Specification (http://java.sun .com/products/java-media/3D/) for details.

LOAD_ALL
  Enables loading of all objects into the scene.

LOAD_BACKGROUND_NODES
  Enables loading of background objects into the scene.

LOAD_BEHAVIOR_NODES
  Enables loading of behaviors into the scene.

LOAD_FOG_NODES
  Enables loading of fog objects into the scene.

LOAD_LIGHT_NODES
  Enables loading of light objects into the scene.

LOAD_SOUND_NODES
  Enables loading of sound objects into the scene.

LOAD_VIEW_GROUPS
  Enables loading of view (camera) objects into the scene.

Making a Scene

The object returned by a loader is called a Scene. It stores several important pieces of information, the most significant being a BranchGroup containing the nodes created by the loader. It also contains an array of all the lights in the scene, an array of viewpoints, and so on.

Note that loading a VRML world does not automatically make it part of the scene graph in your Java 3D application. The Scene object returned by the loader contains a BranchGroup for the scene, but you need to explicitly add that BranchGroup to a Locale in order to make it "live." If you're going to access any of the nodes in the loaded VRML world, you need to set the ca- pabilities bits on those nodes before making the VRML BranchGroup live. All of this will be made clear in the example code presented later in this section.

Tip

When you are loading VRML worlds it is often convenient to place the named nodes they contain in a Hashtable (Java's java.util.Hashtable class maps keys to values). When placed into a Hashtable, every node in a VRML world that has a DEF name associated with it can be easily accessed by name (the "key").

Following is a snippet of code that places the objects contained in a scene into a Hashtable structure, then outputs each to standard output (the complete program in which this snippet is found appears later in this chapter). This is made possible by the getNamedObjects() method defined in the Scene class, which returns a Hashtable containing the scene's objects:

```
Hashtable ht =               // load the Hashtable with
  scene.getNamedObjects();      scene objects
Enumeration en = ht.keys();  // build an Enumeration
                                from its keys
while (en.hasMoreElements()) // iterate over in the
                                Enumeration
  System.out.println         // output each Enumeration
  ("\t" + en.nextElement());
```

The VView Application

In order to show how a VRML loader works, we're going to create a Java 3D program from scratch that will load and display a VRML world. And to show how easy it is to combine Java 3D and VRML, our entire application is going to be less than two pages of code!

Let's begin at the very beginning (a very good place to start). We need to import a number of packages that will handle the nitty-gritty part of the job for us. First there are the standard Java packages you use when writing graphical applications:

```
import java.awt.*;
import java.applet.Applet;
import java.util.*;
```

Next come the Java 3D packages:

```
import javax.media.j3d.*;
import javax.vecmath.*;
```

All of this should be familiar territory from previous chapters. In order to keep our example short, we're going to use a couple of utility packages:

```
import com.sun.j3d.utils.applet.MainFrame;
import com.sun.j3d.utils.universe.*;
```

Note that these are `com.sun.j3d` packages, which means that they aren't officially a Java 3D "standard extension" but are useful packages provided by Sun to make your job as a developer easier. Mainframe is a class that handles all the grunt work of creating a frame into which you can place your 3D graphics application, and the universe package contains a SimpleUniverse class which will save us a huge amount of work when it comes to actually building a scene. Finally, we get to the loader itself:

```
import com.sun.j3d.loaders.vrml97.VrmlLoader;
import com.sun.j3d.loaders.Scene;
```

The first line simply imports the VRML97 loader. The second imports the Scene class, which we talked about earlier.

So much for importing packages. Our next step is to define the VView (or "VRML Viewer") class itself:

```
public class VView extends Applet {
    SimpleUniverse universe;
    Scene scene = null;
```

The class contains two variables. The first stores a reference to the universe we create, and the other stores the scene that gets loaded from the VRML file. We may need to access information about either of these objects from a variety of methods within the class, so we declare them here for convenience.

Since we want our VView class to be able to function as either an applet or an application, we need to define a main method which will invoke the applet. It's very simple:

```
public static void main(String[] args) {
    new MainFrame(new VView(args[0]), 320, 400);
}
```

This creates a new instance of the VView class, passing it the single command-line argument, which is the name of the VRML file with no extension. It then hands that class to MainFrame, along with the dimensions of the frame it should create (in this case, 320 pixels wide by 400 pixels high).

Most of the work in our application will be done in the constructor of the VView class. We start out by setting the layout of the frame we're running in and creating a 3D canvas for Java 3D to render into. We'll use a simple BorderLayout and place the canvas in the center. Since we won't be putting anything in the north, south, east, or west parts of the layout, the center canvas will fill the whole screen.

```
VView(String avatar) {
  setLayout(new BorderLayout());
  Canvas3D canvas = new Canvas3D(null);
  add("Center",canvas);
```

Notice that the Canvas3D object is a component and can therefore be added using the standard add method.

Now it's time to actually create our universe. Here we see how much time and effort is saved by using the SimpleUniverse class:

```
universe = new SimpleUniverse(canvas);
ViewingPlatform viewingPlatform =
    universe.getViewingPlatform();
TransformGroup vpTransGroup =
    viewingPlatform.getViewPlatformTransform();
View view = (universe.getViewer()).getView();
```

Complicated? Only at first glance. The SimpleUniverse class really saves us a lot of effort. It not only creates the universe, it also creates a Locale for us to add BranchGroups to. Since the vast majority of Java 3D applications don't need more than one Locale, it's nice not to have to worry about it. SimpleUniverse also creates a ViewingPlatform for us, as well as a View. All we have to do is read them, which we do in lines 2 and 4 above. We also get the TransformGroup for the ViewingPlatform, since we'll need to move the viewpoint, which we'll do in a moment.

In the Beginning . . .

We're making good progress—just a few lines into our application, and we've already created a whole universe. However, it's still empty and without form. We need to fill it with VRML. Just a few more lines of code will do it:

```
VrmlLoader loader = new VrmlLoader();
try { scene = loader.load(avatar + ".wrl"); }
catch (Exception e) {
```

```
            System.out.println("Exception loading file!");
            System.exit(1);
    }
```

The first line creates a VrmlLoader object. We won't bother setting any flags on it, since our simple example will be loading the whole file kit 'n kaboodle. The second line takes the avatar name (the fact that we're calling it an "avatar" may give you a hint of things to come...) and tacks on a ".wrl" extension. VRML files all have .wrl extensions unless they are GZip compressed as described in Part 2 of this book. We then tell the loader to load the file and store the result in the scene variable. If an exception is thrown by the loader, we print an error message and exit.

At this point, assuming there were no exceptions, we've got our VRML world loaded and ready to go. Well, almost. We still need to add it to the universe we created earlier. But just before we do, we'll set a few capability bits:

```
    // get the scene group from the loaded VRML scene
    BranchGroup sceneGroup = scene.getSceneGroup();
    sceneGroup.setCapability(BranchGroup.ALLOW_DETACH);
    sceneGroup.setCapability(BranchGroup.ALLOW_BOUNDS_READ);
```

The first line simply asks the scene for a reference to the BranchGroup containing all the nodes that were loaded from the VRML file. The second line gives us the ability to detach this group later, and the third lets us read the bounding volume information from the BranchGroup (which we'll be using later on to figure out where to put the viewpoint).

And now, at last, we're ready to actually add the VRML scene to the world:

```
            universe.addBranchGraph(sceneGroup);
```

A long way to go, but well worth the trip. Our VRML scene is now loaded.

Finding a Good Vantagepoint

However, there may still be a problem. What if the scene was modeled in such a way that it's too far away to be seen from the default viewpoint? Or what if it's behind us, or off to one side? What we would like to do is position the viewpoint to give us a nice overall view of the scene. To do this, let's start by figuring out where in the world the scene is, and how big it is.

```
BoundingSphere sceneBounds =
    (BoundingSphere)sceneGroup.getBounds();
double radius = sceneBounds.getRadius();
Point3d center = new Point3d();
sceneBounds.getCenter(center);
```

Okay, so now we know the center and radius of a bounding sphere that just encloses the scene. Where do we put our viewpoint? Well, let's move it along the +Z axis, away from the center of the scene, far enough so that everything fits into our field of view. We do this using some clever math, borrowed from the SimpleVrml97Viewer class that comes with the VRML97 package (available at http://www.web3d.org/WorkingGroups/VRML-java3d/).

```
Vector3d temp = new Vector3d(center);
temp.z += 1.4 * radius
            / Math.tan(view.getFieldOfView() / 2.0);
```

What does this do? The first line just creates a vector and copies the location of the bounding sphere's center into it. The second line is more interesting. The field of view is the viewing angle through which we see the scene, and we obtain it from our current View object. We divide this angle by two to get the angle called alpha (see Figure 13-7). From the diagram, we can see that the radius of the bounding sphere, divided by the distance from the viewpoint to the center of the bounding sphere, is tan(alpha). Solving for the

Figure 13-7 The alpha angle is obtained by dividing the viewing angle by two (view.getFieldOfView() / 2.0).

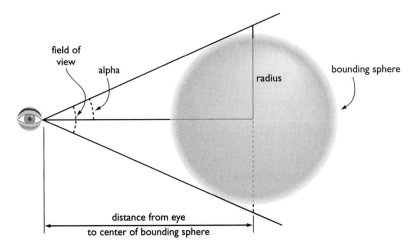

distance, we find it's just the radius divided by tan(alpha). We multiply by 1.4 to move us a little further back and make sure we have some space around the scene we're viewing, and add this distance to the Z location of the center of the bounding sphere. We leave X and Y unchanged, since we want the bounding sphere centered on our screen.

Now that we have this new viewpoint location, we set it into the viewing platform's TransformGroup.

```
Transform3D viewTransform = new Transform3D();
viewTransform.set(temp);
vpTransGroup.setTransform(viewTransform);
```

And now we're done. We can compile our new application (make sure that the VRML97.jar loader file is in the CLASSPATH) and run it to view a VRML world.

Listing 13.1 contains the complete listing of the VRML Viewer (available online at http://www.CoreWeb3D.com/):

Listing 13.1   VView.java (Example 1)

```
// Very simple VRML world viewer
// Written by Bernie Roehl, October 1999
//
// CONVERTING TO AN APPLET:
// To convert this application into an applet you must construct
// a standard init() method that contains the code now in the VView
// constructor. From within the init() method you will invoke the VRML
// loader's load(URL) method, as the load(String) method currently used
// by this application can't be used in an applet (a security exception
// is thrown by the applet when loading a VRML world from a String).
//
// To convert to an applet, simply rename the following method:
//              public VView(String avatar)
// to:
//              public void init()
//
// Next, use the applet's getParameter() method to retrieve the
// name of the VRML file to load and place the resulting string into the
// "avatar" variable. The following code assumes that a PARAM named
// "world" is in the corresponding HTML Web page for this applet:
//    String  avatar = getParameter("world");
//
```

```
// Finally, change the VRML loader's load(String) method so that it
// is passed an absolute URL. For example:
//   scene = loader.load(new java.net.URL(getCodeBase(), avatar + ".wrl"));
//
// Visit the Core Web3D web site at http://www.CoreWeb3D.com/ to
// obtain code listings from this book, including an applet version of this
// VView program.

import java.awt.*;
import java.applet.Applet;
import java.util.*;
import javax.media.j3d.*;
import javax.vecmath.*;
import com.sun.j3d.utils.applet.MainFrame;
import com.sun.j3d.utils.universe.*;
import com.sun.j3d.loaders.vrml97.VrmlLoader;
import com.sun.j3d.loaders.Scene;

public class VView extends Applet {

    SimpleUniverse universe; // the universe
    Scene scene = null;      // the VRML scene that we load

    public VView(String avatar) {
        setLayout(new BorderLayout());
        Canvas3D canvas = new Canvas3D(null);
        add("Center",canvas);

        universe = new SimpleUniverse(canvas);
        ViewingPlatform viewingPlatform =
                universe.getViewingPlatform();
        TransformGroup vpTransGroup =
                viewingPlatform.getViewPlatformTransform();
        View view = (universe.getViewer()).getView();

        VrmlLoader loader = new VrmlLoader();
        try { scene = loader.load(avatar + ".wrl"); }
        catch (Exception e) {
                System.out.println(
                "Exception loading file! from path:" + avatar + ".wrl");
                System.exit(1);
        }

        // get the scene group from the loaded VRML scene
        BranchGroup sceneGroup = scene.getSceneGroup();
```

```
        sceneGroup.setCapability(BranchGroup.ALLOW_DETACH);
        sceneGroup.setCapability(BranchGroup.ALLOW_BOUNDS_READ);

    // make the VRML scene live
    universe.addBranchGraph(sceneGroup);

    // find the radius and center of the scene's
    // bounding sphere
    BoundingSphere sceneBounds =
        (BoundingSphere)sceneGroup.getBounds();
    double radius = sceneBounds.getRadius();
    Point3d center = new Point3d();
    sceneBounds.getCenter(center);

    // now move the viewpoint back so we
    // can see the whole scene
    Vector3d temp = new Vector3d(center);
    temp.z += 1.4 * radius
            / Math.tan(view.getFieldOfView() / 2.0);

    // and finally, set that viewpoint into the
    // viewing transform
    Transform3D viewTransform = new Transform3D();
    viewTransform.set(temp);
    vpTransGroup.setTransform(viewTransform);
  }

  public static void main(String[] args) {
      new MainFrame(new VView(args[0]), 320, 400);
  }
}
```

There you have it—a complete VRML Viewer application in less than two pages of code, including comments and lots of whitespace.

Now it's time to try it on an actual VRML file. At http://www.CoreWeb3d. com/ you will find a file called "Human.wrl". It's a simple humanoid figure, made up of cylinders and spheres (see Listing 13.2).

Listing 13.2   Human.wrl

```
#VRML V2.0 utf8

DirectionalLight { direction 0 0 -1 }

DEF Human_body Transform {
  children [
      Transform {
        translation 0 1.5 0
        children [
          Shape {
            appearance Appearance {
              material Material {
                diffuseColor 0.8824 0.3451 0.7804
              }
            }
            geometry Cylinder { radius 0.75 height 3 }
          }
    ] }
    DEF Human_r_shoulder Transform {
     translation -1.067 2.987 -0.01011
      children [
          Transform {
            translation 0 -0.5 0
            children [
              Shape {
                appearance Appearance {
                  material Material {
                    diffuseColor 0.549 0.3451 0.8824
                  }
                }
                geometry Cylinder { radius 0.2 height 1 }
              }
        ] }
        DEF Human_r_elbow Transform {
          translation 0 -1.054 0
          children [
              Transform {
                translation 0 -0.5 0
                children [
                          Shape {
                            appearance Appearance {
                              material Material {
```

```
                        diffuseColor 0.549 0.3451 0.8824
                      }
                    }
                    geometry Cylinder { radius 0.2 height 1 }
                  }
              ] }
            ]
          }
        ]
      },
      DEF Human_l_shoulder Transform {
        translation 1.046 2.987 -0.01011
        children [
            Transform {
              translation 0 -0.5 0
              children [
                Shape {
                  appearance Appearance {
                    material Material {
                      diffuseColor 0.549 0.3451 0.8824
                    }
                  }
                  geometry Cylinder { radius 0.2 height 1 }
                }
          ] }
          DEF Human_l_elbow Transform {
            translation 0 -1.054 0
            children [
                Transform {
                  translation 0 -0.5 0
                  children [
                    Shape {
                      appearance Appearance {
                        material Material {
                          diffuseColor 0.549 0.3451 0.8824
                        }
                      }
                      geometry Cylinder { radius 0.2 height 1 }
                    }
              ] }
            ]
          }
        ]
      }
      DEF Human_skullbase Transform {
```

```
    translation 0 3.632 0
    rotation -1 0 0 -1.571
    children [
      Shape {
        appearance Appearance {
          material Material {
            diffuseColor 0.549 0.3451 0.8824
          }
        }
        geometry Sphere { radius 0.5 }
      }
    ]
  }
 ]
}
```

At long last, we can load this file into our VRML Viewer by simply giving the command:

```
    java VView Human
```

Figure 13-8 shows the Human.wrl file being displayed using this viewer.

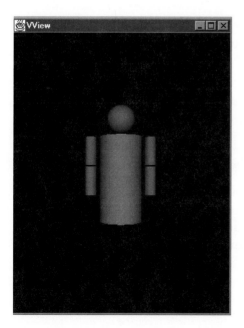

Figure 13-8   The Java 3D loader mechanism makes it possible to store the geometry of this Java 3D program in VRML format (Human.wrl).

Making It Move

Now that we can load a VRML file, what's the next step? How about changing its posture? To do this, we're going to modify our VRML Viewer application and take advantage of the Scene class to obtain references to individual nodes.

Recall that a VRML world is made up of nodes, and that these nodes correspond roughly to Java 3D objects. For example, the VRML Transform node corresponds to a Java 3D TransformGroup object. Also recall that the transformation hierarchies we've discussed in this chapter also apply to VRML, which uses nested Transform nodes to create articulated figures, as described in Chapter 7, "Customzing Location, Size, and Orientation."

When we load a VRML file into Java 3D using the VRML loader, a complete transformation hierarchy is automatically built for us. The nested Transform nodes in the VRML file produce a set of hierarchically structured Java 3D TransformGroup objects. All we need to do in order to pose our figure is get references to the appropriate nodes and set the transforms on them.

Getting the node references is easy, assuming that the Transform nodes we're after were given DEF names in the VRML file. The Scene class lets us get a Hashtable object through which we can look up node references, using their DEF names.

As a check, let's modify our program to print out the names of the nodes in the file it loads. Right after we set the capabilities on the BranchGroup for our scene, we add the following lines of code:

```
// list all the nodes found in the file
System.out.println("Named nodes in file:");
Hashtable ht = scene.getNamedObjects();
Enumeration en = ht.keys();
while (en.hasMoreElements())
        System.out.println("\t" + en.nextElement());
```

The getNamedObjects() method returns a Hashtable containing all the DEF names in the scene and the nodes they correspond to. From that Hashtable, we create an Enumeration and iterate through it, printing out the DEF names. When we run this program on our Human.wrl example, we get the following output:

```
Named nodes in file:
    Human_r_elbow
```

The H-Anim Standard

How do we know what the nodes are named? After all, the person who built the VRML file could have called the shoulder joint "shoulder_left", "shoulder_joint_2," or even "left_upper_arm". We would have to look at every file we want to load, and then modify our program to read that particular file. Tedious? You bet!

Fortunately, there's a solution. The Web3D Consortium's Humanoid Animation Working Group (http://www.h-anim.org/) has developed a standard called H-Anim that defines what each joint in a humanoid is named. It also defines a neutral pose, so you know what position the figure is in when you first load it. That makes it a lot easier to set a new posture.

For example, let's say we want to pose the avatar as if it's waving. This involves bending the shoulder and elbow joints of the left arm. From the H-Anim specification, we see that the names for those two joints are "l_shoulder" and "l_elbow" respectively. We insert the name of the avatar in front of these, just in case there's more than one avatar in the file (and therefore more than one "l_shoulder" joint) and in our case we get "Human_l_shoulder" and "Human_l_elbow". These are the actual DEF names of the TransformGroups we want.

```
Human_l_shoulder
Human_r_shoulder
Human_body
Human_skullbase
Human_l_elbow
```

As we can see, the nodes have the names we expect. However, before we can make them move, we need to make sure they remain accessible even after the scene graph goes live. To do this, we access the node and set its capabilities:

```
// make sure left shoulder is accessible
TransformGroup l_shoulder =
(TransformGroup) ht.get(avatar + "_l_shoulder");
```

```
l_shoulder.setCapability(TransformGroup.ALLOW_TRANSFORM_READ);
l_shoulder.setCapability(TransformGroup.ALLOW_TRANSFORM_WRITE);
// make sure right shoulder is accessible
TransformGroup l_elbow =
(TransformGroup) ht.get(avatar + "_l_elbow");
l_elbow.setCapability(TransformGroup.ALLOW_TRANSFORM_READ);
l_elbow.setCapability(TransformGroup.ALLOW_TRANSFORM_WRITE);
```

We use ht.get() to look up the avatar's left shoulder in the Hashtable. We then set the ALLOW_TRANSFORM_READ and ALLOW_TRANS-FORM_WRITE capabilities. This will allow us to read and write the transform in the TransformGroup even after the scene is live. We repeat this for the left elbow, since we'll be bending it as well.

To actually move the joints of our articulated figure, we need to read and write the transforms. This can be done at any time, even after the scene goes live. To change the joint angles, we just do the following:

```
// now rotate the shoulder
Transform3D trans = new Transform3D();
l_shoulder.getTransform(trans);
trans.setRotation(new AxisAngle4f(0, 0, 1, 2.7057f));
l_shoulder.setTransform(trans);
// and the elbow
l_elbow.getTransform(trans);
trans.setRotation(new AxisAngle4f(0, 0, 1, 0.7057f));
l_elbow.setTransform(trans);
```

We start by creating a new Transform3D object. Even though we'll be rotating two joints, we only need one transform. This is because the contents of the Transform3D gets copied into the TransformGroup, leaving the Transform3D available for reuse.

Next we get the shoulder's current transform. This will consist of a rotation and a translation. We replace the rotation part, giving it an axis-angle representation of (0, 0, 1, 2.7057). The (0, 0, 1) part says that we're rotating around the positive Z axis, and the 2.7057 is the angle in radians. Notice that setting the rotation does not affect the translation part at all. Once we've up-

Capability Bits and Optimization

Java 3D tries to do everything it can to improve the performance of the scenes it renders. It can perform many optimizations, some of them quite drastic, which is why the capabilities settings are needed. The capabilities bits serve as "hints" to Java 3D about what parts of the scene graph the application will need to change at runtime and what parts won't be changed. Things that don't change at runtime can be more heavily optimized than things that do.

By default, Java 3D will optimize the transform hierarchy in such a way that it may no longer be possible to read or write individual transforms. If you need to be able to access those transforms, you need to set the appropriate capabilities flags.

Not all implementations of Java 3D will actually use the capabilities bits, and the degree of optimization will vary from one implementation to another. Keep in mind that there's a price to pay for this. By turning on those bits, you prevent Java 3D from performing certain types of optimizations. This in turn will result in decreased performance.

This is why, in our example, we have chosen to turn on those capability flags only on the two nodes we'll be moving, instead of just iterating through the Hashtable and setting them on all the nodes.

dated the transform, we copy it back into the TransformGroup using set-Transform().

We repeat the process for the elbow. Notice that the getTransform() call replaces all the values in the transform, both rotation and translation, with the values from the elbow. We then update the rotation, and write it back to the TransformGroup.

Keep in mind everything that we talked about earlier in this chapter: When you rotate the left shoulder, it affects the upper arm and the lower arm. The upper arm moves, and the lower arm "comes along for the ride." Moving the lower arm, however, has no effect on the upper arm. Listing 13.3 shows our modified program in its entirety.

Listing 13.3   VView.java (Example 2)

```
// Very simple VRML world viewer
// Written by Bernie Roehl, October 1999
//
// CONVERTING TO AN APPLET:
// To convert this application into an applet you must construct
// a standard init() method that contains the code now in the VView
// constructor. From within the init() method you will invoke the VRML
// loader's load(URL) method, as the load(String) method currently used
// by this application can't be used in an applet (a security exception
// is thrown by the applet when loading a VRML world from a String).
//
// To convert to an applet, simply rename the following method:
//              public VView(String avatar)
// to:
//              public void init()
//
// Next, use the applet's getParameter() method to retrieve the
// name of the VRML file to load and place the resulting string into the
// "avatar" variable. The following code assumes that a PARAM named
// "world" is in the corresponding HTML Web page for this applet:
//    String  avatar = getParameter("world");
//
// Finally, change the VRML loader's load(String) method so that it
// is passed an absolute URL. For example:
//   scene = loader.load(new java.net.URL(getCodeBase(), avatar + ".wrl"));
//
// Visit the Core Web3D web site at http://www.CoreWeb3D.com/ to
// obtain code listings from this book, including an applet version of this
// VView program.

import java.awt.*;
import java.applet.Applet;
import java.util.*;
import javax.media.j3d.*;
import javax.vecmath.*;
import com.sun.j3d.utils.applet.MainFrame;
import com.sun.j3d.utils.universe.*;
import com.sun.j3d.loaders.vrml197.VrmlLoader;
import com.sun.j3d.loaders.Scene;
import com.sun.j3d.utils.image.TextureLoader;

public class VView extends Applet {
```

```
SimpleUniverse universe; // the universe
Scene scene = null;      // the VRML scene that we load

VView(String avatar) {
      setLayout(new BorderLayout());
      Canvas3D canvas = new Canvas3D(null);
      add("Center",canvas);

      universe = new SimpleUniverse(canvas);
      ViewingPlatform viewingPlatform =
            universe.getViewingPlatform();
      TransformGroup vpTransGroup =
            viewingPlatform.getViewPlatformTransform();
      View view = (universe.getViewer()).getView();

      VrmlLoader loader = new VrmlLoader();
      try { scene = loader.load(avatar + ".wrl"); }
      catch (Exception e) {
            System.out.println(
                "Exception loading file from path:"
                    + avatar + ".wrl");
            System.exit(1);
      }

      // get the scene group from the loaded VRML scene
      BranchGroup sceneGroup = scene.getSceneGroup();
      sceneGroup.setCapability(
            BranchGroup.ALLOW_DETACH);
      sceneGroup.setCapability(
            BranchGroup.ALLOW_BOUNDS_READ);

      // list all the nodes found in the file
      System.out.println("Named nodes in file:");
      Hashtable ht = scene.getNamedObjects();
      Enumeration en = ht.keys();
      while (en.hasMoreElements())
            System.out.println("\t" + en.nextElement());

      // make sure left shoulder is accessible
      TransformGroup l_shoulder =
            TransformGroup) ht.get(avatar +
                                   "_l_shoulder");
      l_shoulder.setCapability(
            TransformGroup.ALLOW_TRANSFORM_READ);
      l_shoulder.setCapability(
```

```
                TransformGroup.ALLOW_TRANSFORM_WRITE);

// make sure right shoulder is accessible
TransformGroup l_elbow =
        (TransformGroup) ht.get(avatar +
                                "_l_elbow");
l_elbow.setCapability(
        TransformGroup.ALLOW_TRANSFORM_READ);
l_elbow.setCapability(
        TransformGroup.ALLOW_TRANSFORM_WRITE);

// make the VRML scene live
universe.addBranchGraph(sceneGroup);

// find the radius and center of
// the scene's bounding sphere
BoundingSphere sceneBounds =
        (BoundingSphere)sceneGroup.getBounds();
double radius = sceneBounds.getRadius();
Point3d center = new Point3d();
sceneBounds.getCenter(center);

// now move the viewpoint back so we can
// see the whole scene
Vector3d temp = new Vector3d(center);
temp.z += 1.4 * radius /
        Math.tan(view.getFieldOfView() / 2.0);

// and finally, set that viewpoint into
// the viewing transform
Transform3D viewTransform = new Transform3D();
viewTransform.set(temp);
vpTransGroup.setTransform(viewTransform);

// now rotate the shoulder
Transform3D trans = new Transform3D();
l_shoulder.getTransform(trans);
trans.setRotation(
        new AxisAngle4f(0, 0, 1, 2.7057f));
l_shoulder.setTransform(trans);

// and the elbow
l_elbow.getTransform(trans);
trans.setRotation(
```

```
                new AxisAngle4f(0, 0, 1, 0.7057f));
            l_elbow.setTransform(trans);
    }

    public static void main(String[] args) {
        new MainFrame(new VView(args[0]), 320, 400);
    }

}
```

And in Figure 13-9, we see our happy avatar waving back at us!

Figure 13-9   By transforming our Human VRML model we have made it "wave" at the user.

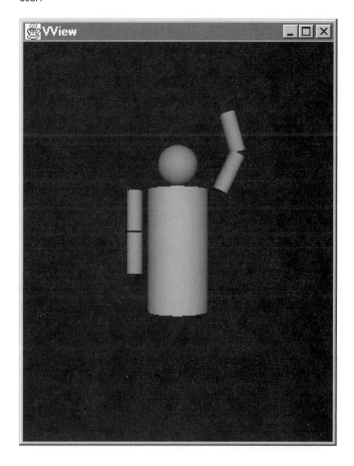

Warning: Dislocated Joints

The "Human.wrl" file uses the naming convention and neutral pose defined by the H-Anim standard. However, it does not use the PRO-TOs from that specification. This is because of some limitations in the VRML97 class library, which cause the joint centers to be in the wrong location. Future versions of the class library may correct this problem, but for the time being you should not assume that the VRML97 support in Java 3D is capable of handling arbitrary H-Anim compliant files.

Note

The software in this chapter will also be used in Chapter 15, "Customizing Background, Fog, Lighting, and Sound," to illustrate the use of lighting, backgrounds, and fog.

Summary

In this chapter you've learned how to move objects in virtual space, as well as rotate them, stretch them, and scale them. You've also learned how to assemble objects into hierarchies. To do this, you've learned about two important classes of object in Java 3D—the Transform3D class, which stores translation/rotation/scale information, and the TransformGroup, which uses a Transform3D to affect objects in the scene graph. You've also learned how to read VRML files into your Java 3D applications, and how to access individual nodes and change their values.

Following is a complete list of URLs referenced in this chapter:

Web3D Gallery 3D Resources   http://www.web3dgallery.com/3d/

Java 3D API Specification   http://java.sun.com/products/java-media/3D/

VRML-Java3D Working Group   http://www.Web3d.org/WorkingGroups/vrml-java3d/

VRML97 Loader   http://www.web3d.org/WorkingGroups/vrml-java3d/

Humanoid Animation (H-Anim) Working Group http://www.h-anim.org/

CUSTOMIZING COLOR AND TEXTURE

Topics in This Chapter·

- Customizing the color of shapes using the Appearance and Material nodes
- Creating dull, shiny, glowing, and transparent surfaces
- Wrapping images around shapes ("texture mapping")
- Using the TextureTransform node to control texture mapping

Chapter 14

In the previous chapter you learned how to customize Java 3D scenes by moving objects around and changing their physical attributes. As you have seen with VRML in Part 2 of this book, however, you can customize more than just the position, orientation, and scale of objects in a 3D scene. In this chapter you learn how to customize the color and texture of Java 3D objects, just as you learned how to customize these properties of VRML objects in Chapter 8, "Customizing Color and Texture."

In comparison to the techniques discussed in the previous chapter, customizing color and textures will seem somewhat awkward at first. Modifying the position, orientation, and scale of objects as you did in Chapter 13 revolved around modifying portions of the scene graph that corresponded to externally loaded files. By simply wrapping an extra TransformGroup node around each piece of the scene graph delivered by the loader you were able to customize the position, orientation, and scale of objects in the scene.

In comparison, customizing the color and texture of Java 3D content is a entirely different story. Both of these attributes are relative to the *individual* object. In a complex model, you can easily have hundreds of surfaces, each of which might have its own unique color and texture (we say *might*, because colors and textures can be shared by objects, as you'll learn later in this chapter). All of this is hidden from view by the convenience of the loader mechanism, meaning that you won't have easy access to color and texture information of externally loaded objects.

For the purposes of this chapter, therefore, we'll assume that you will be customizing the contents of a Java 3D program whose objects are created directly in Java 3D code. In other words, you can view, edit, and recompile the Java 3D code that corresponds to the objects that you wish to customize (i.e., any object that is not brought into the program through a loader). If you don't already have a suitable program to customize, you can get your feet wet by customizing one of the demonstration programs provided with your Java 3D implementation. Sun's Java 3D implementation, for example, comes with a sample program called AppearanceTest that is an ideal companion to this chapter. Alternately, you can use the source-code examples provided in the text that follows (visit the Core Web3D Web site at http://www.CoreWeb3D .com/ to download code samples used in this book).

Note: Java 3D and VRML

Java 3D's color, shading, and lighting models are very similar to those used by VRML; once you know how to customize object appearances in VRML you'll find that it is relatively simple to do the same in Java 3D. With this in mind (and in an effort to reduce redundancy), many of the basic concepts introduced in Chapter 8, "Customizing Color and Texture," do not appear in this chapter.

The concept of mixing RGB colors, for example, is covered in detail in Chapter 8, and so it's assumed that you already know the basic principles behind RGB colors as you read the material that follows. Likewise, a detailed overview of light reflections (specular reflections and shininess, for example) and texture mapping (applying an image to the surface of shape) is not provided here, as these and other general color and texture topics are covered in detail in Chapter 8. This chapter instead focuses on fundamental, Java 3D-specific concepts that you must know to customize the color and texture of Java 3D objects.

Appearance and Material

Visible Java 3D objects are typically created using the Shape3D node, which is analogous to VRML's Shape node. Like the Shape node, Shape3D allows developers to specify the form, or geometry, of a shape independent from

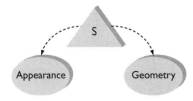

Figure 14-1 *Geometry and appearance components are stored independently of shapes. Shapes, therefore, are said to reference geometry and appearance components rather than contain them (as indicated by the dashed-arrow reference).*

its appearance. Appearance and Geometry are actually separate shape components that are referenced by the Shape3D node (see Figure 14-1). Because the geometric form of a shape is independent of its appearance, you can easily alter the *look* of a shape without concerning yourself with code that defines its shape. To customize the color or texture of a Java 3D shape you simply modify its Appearance component—or, more accurately, the shape's appearance "bundle."

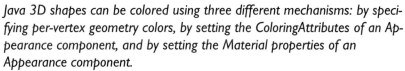

Note: Color Me Beautiful

Java 3D shapes can be colored using three different mechanisms: by specifying per-vertex geometry colors, by setting the ColoringAttributes of an Appearance component, and by setting the Material properties of an Appearance component.

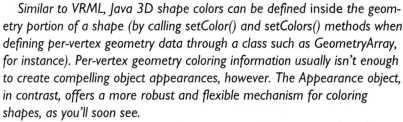

Similar to VRML, Java 3D shape colors can be defined inside the geometry portion of a shape (by calling setColor() and setColors() methods when defining per-vertex geometry data through a class such as GeometryArray, for instance). Per-vertex geometry coloring information usually isn't enough to create compelling object appearances, however. The Appearance object, in contrast, offers a more robust and flexible mechanism for coloring shapes, as you'll soon see.

Appearance Bundles

Java 3D's Appearance class is a node component that defines Shape3D rendering properties, such as color, transparency, material, and texture (Appearance is a subclass of NodeComponent, which is in turn a subclass of SceneGraphObject; see Figure 14-2). Tables 14.1, 14.2, and 14.3 summarize the Appearance class constructors, capability bit fields, and mutator ("setter") methods.

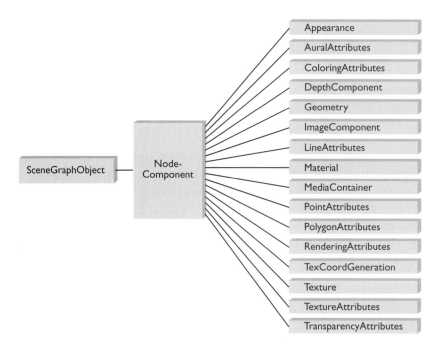

Figure 14-2   Appearance is ultimately a node component that defines Shape3D rendering properties (such as color, transparency, material, and texture) by referencing other NodeComponent objects (see Figure 14-3 on page 668).

Contrary to what you might assume, Appearance objects don't actually *contain* rendering information. Instead, they reference one or more *appearance attribute* objects that encapsulate this information, as illustrated in Figure 14-3 (page 668). This highly modular design lends to the notion of an "appearance bundle," which is really nothing more than a collection of appearance attributes referenced by an Appearance object that together determine the on-screen appearance of a shape.

The following snippet of code, for example, creates a simple appearance bundle consisting of default coloring attributes:

```
Appearance app = new Appearance();
ColoringAttributes ca = new ColoringAttributes();
app.setColoringAttributes(ca);
```

In the above code the Appearance object is created first, followed by a ColoringAttributes object. In both cases the default constructor is called, resulting in default values being assigned to each object instance (you'll learn

Table 14.1 Appearance Constructor Summary

```
public Appearance()
```

Constructs a default Appearance component object. All component object references (attribute references) are initialized to null and assigned the following default values:

color: white (1, 1, 1)

texture environment mode: TEXENV_REPLACE

texture environment color: white (1, 1, 1, 1)

depth test enable: true

shade model: SHADE_GOURAUD

polygon mode: POLYGON_FILL

transparency enable: false

transparency mode: FASTEST

cull face: CULL_BACK

point size: 1.0

line width: 1.0

line pattern: PATTERN_SOLID

point antialiasing enable: false

line antialiasing enable: false

---

more about default values later in this chapter). A reference to the ColoringAttributes object is then passed to Appearance by calling Appearance's corresponding `setColoringAttributes()` method (see Table 14.3).

The resulting appearance bundle can now be referenced by a Shape3D object as follows:

```
Shape3D myShape = new  Shape3D();   // create a shape
myShape.setAppearance(app); // give it our appearance bundle
```

Java 3D will now render this shape according to the attributes referenced in the associated appearance bundle. Exactly what these appearance attributes are and how you use them, however, is the $64,000 question. Before you can create useful appearance bundles you must first have a solid understanding of the various attributes available to you, and so we turn our attention to appearance attributes.

Table 14.2   Appearance Capability Bits

Capability bit fields are defined by the class javax.media.j3d.Appearance. When set by a call to the `setCapability()` method, these capability bit flags allow corresponding methods to be invoked on live or compiled objects. Each of these fields is defined as `public static final int`. See the Java 3D API Specification for details (http://java.sun.com/products/java-media/3D/).

`ALLOW_COLORING_ATTRIBUTES_READ, ALLOW_COLORING_ATTRIBUTES_WRITE`
Allows reading/writing of coloringAttributes component information.

`ALLOW_LINE_ATTRIBUTES_READ, ALLOW_LINE_ATTRIBUTES_WRITE`
Allows reading/writing of line component information.

`ALLOW_MATERIAL_READ, ALLOW_MATERIAL_WRITE`
Allows reading/writing of material component information.

`ALLOW_POINT_ATTRIBUTES_READ, ALLOW_POINT_ATTRIBUTES_WRITE`
Allows reading/writing of point component information.

`ALLOW_POLYGON_ATTRIBUTES_READ, ALLOW_POLYGON_ATTRIBUTES_WRITE`
Allows reading/writing of polygon component information.

`ALLOW_RENDERING_ATTRIBUTES_READ,`
`ALLOW_RENDERING_ATTRIBUTES_WRITE`
Allows reading/writing of rendering/rasterization component information.

`ALLOW_TEXGEN_READ, ALLOW_TEXGEN_WRITE`
Allows reading/writing of texture coordinate-generation component information.

`ALLOW_TEXTURE_ATTRIBUTES_READ, ALLOW_TEXTURE_ATTRIBUTES_WRITE`
Allows reading/writing of textureAttributes component information.

`ALLOW_TEXTURE_READ, ALLOW_TEXTURE_WRITE`
Allows reading/writing of texture component information.

`ALLOW_TRANSPARENCY_ATTRIBUTES_READ, ALLOW_TRANSPARENCY`
`_ATTRIBUTES_WRITE`
Allows reading/writing of transparency component information.

Appearance Attributes

Appearance objects can reference a number of node components known as *appearance attributes*, which encapsulate rendering properties related to a shape's color, transparency, texture, lines, points, polygons, and material. Each of these attributes is a descendant of the NodeComponent class, just as

Table 14.3	Appearance Mutator Method Summary

This table contains a summary of mutator ("setter") methods defined in the class javax.media.j3d. Appearance. Accessor ("getter") methods are not included in an effort to reduce the length of this table. (Most mutators have a corresponding accessor. The setMaterial() mutator method, for example, has a corresponding getMaterial() accessor method.) See the Java 3D API Specification (http://java.sun.com/products/java-media/3D/) for a complete listing of all methods.

Returns	*Method Name, Parameters, and Description*
void	**setColoringAttributes**(ColoringAttributes coloringAttributes) Sets the coloringAttributes object to the specified object.
void	**setLineAttributes**(LineAttributes lineAttributes) Sets the lineAttributes object to the specified object.
void	**setMaterial**(Material material) Set the material object to the specified object.
void	**setPointAttributes**(PointAttributes pointAttributes) Sets the pointAttributes object to the specified object.
void	**setPolygonAttributes**(PolygonAttributes polygonAttributes) Sets the polygonAttributes object to the specified object.
void	**setRenderingAttributes**(RenderingAttributes renderingAttributes) Sets the renderingAttributes object to the specified object.
void	**setTexCoordGeneration**(TexCoordGeneration texCoordGeneration) Sets the texCoordGeneration object to the specified object.
void	**setTexture**(Texture texture) Sets the texture object to the specified object.
void	**setTextureAttributes**(TextureAttributes textureAttributes) Sets the textureAttributes object to the specified object.
void	**setTransparencyAttributes**(TransparencyAttributes transparencyAttributes) Sets the transparencyAttributes object to the specified object.

the Appearance node is (see Figure 14-2). The sections that follow give an overview of each appearance attribute class covering some in more detail than others.

Specifically, appearance attributes related to the color and texture of shapes are covered in detail, as these topics are the focus of this chapter,

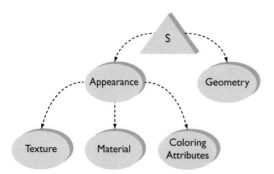

Figure 14-3   Appearance components are sometimes called "appearance bundles" because they can reference various NodeComponent subclasses, including ColoringAttributes, TransparencyAttributes, Material, and Texture (see Figure 14-2).

while other attributes are given less attention. Although we'll focus primarily on the ColoringAttributes, TextureAttributes, and TransparencyAttributes classes in the following section, you can always turn to Sun's Java 3D API specification (http://java.sun.com/products/java-media/3D/) for details related to other appearance attributes.

Color Classes (javax.vecmath)

Before we dive into appearance attribute classes, you should be aware that you'll often find yourself working with Color3f and Color4f classes (found in the vector math package `javax.vecmath`) when customizing the color and texture attributes of an object. These classes are used to specify three- and four-component colors in terms of single-precision floating-point numbers (Color3b and Color4b classes are also available in cases where you need to specify colors using byte values).

As you may recall from Chapter 8, three-component colors are colors expressed in terms of red, green, and blue (r, g, b) color components, while four-component colors use an additional component value to specify the alpha (transparency) of a color (r, g, b, a). The term RGB is commonly used to describe three-component colors (red, green, blue), while four-component colors are often referred to as RGBA colors (red, green, blue, alpha).

Like VRML, Java 3D color components are represented using a floating-point value in the range of zero (0.0f) to one (1.0f), where (0.0f) specifies that no amount of light for a given color component should be used and (1.0f) specifies that all (100%) of that color component should be used. Values between (0.0f) and (1.0f) are used to specify varying degrees of color-component intensity.

Table 14.4 provides a summary of each Color3f and Color4f constructor, although the methods available for use with these classes are not listed here. Color3f and Color4f classes do not have methods of their own, and instead inherit critical methods from the specific Tuple class that they extend (tuple objects, also found in the `javax.vecmath` package, are used to create and manipulate values comprised of two, three, or four elements, such as points, coordinates, and colors). A variety of tuple methods are available for use with color objects, including mutator (setter) methods that allow you to change the value of an existing color object by passing another color object or raw (r, g, b) values to a `set()` method, as the following snippet of code illustrates:

```
// Start by constructing a few basic colors:
Color3f black  = new Color3f(0.0f, 0.0f, 0.0f);
Color3f white  = new Color3f(1.0f, 1.0f, 1.0f);
Color3f red    = new Color3f(1.0f, 0.0f, 0.0f);
Color3f green  = new Color3f(0.0f, 1.0f, 0.0f);
Color3f blue   = new Color3f(0.0f, 0.0f, 1.0f);
Color3f yellow = new Color3f(0.8f, 0.8f, 0.0f);

// Now create a color that we'll modify a few times:
Color3f myColor = new Color3f(black); // start as black

// Change by passing a new color object to the set() method:
myColor.set(white); // set to white
myColor.set(red);   // set to red
myColor.set(green); // set to green
myColor.set(blue);  // set to blue
myColor.set(yellow);  // set to yellow

// Change by passing raw (r,g,b) values to the set() method:
myColor.set(1.0f, 1.0f, 1.0f); // set to white
myColor.set(1.0f, 0.0f, 0.0f); // set to red
myColor.set(0.0f, 1.0f, 0.0f); // set to green
myColor.set(0.0f, 0.0f, 1.0f); // set to blue
myColor.set(0.8f, 0.8f, 0.0f); // set to yellow
```

ColoringAttributes (javax.media.j3d.ColoringAttributes)

The ColoringAttributes object is used to specify color values for "unlit" shapes. Shapes whose appearance bundle has a `null` or unspecified Material object are not lighted and so are considered to be unlit. In other words,

Table 14.4   Color Classes

The vector math package (javax.vecmath) contains four color classes:

Color3b (three-byte color vector)

Color3f (three single-precision floating-point color vector)

Color4b (four-byte vector primarily used for colors with alpha)

Color4b (four single-precision floating-point vector primarily used for colors with alpha).

Following is a summary of Color3f and Color4f, as these two classes are commonly used to customize object color and texture. All color classes extend a corresponding Tuple class, representing two-, three-, and four-element values (Color3f extends Tuple3f, for example, while Color4f extends Tuple4f). See the Java 3D API Specification (http://java.sun.com/products/java-media/3D/) for details.

Color3f

A three-element vector that is represented by single-precision floating-point x, y, z coordinates that correspond to red, green, and blue (r,g,b) color components. Color components should be in the range of zero (0.0f) to one (1.0f).

Constructors

public Color3f()
  Constructs and initializes a Color3f to black (0,0,0).

public Color3f(Color3f v1)
  Constructs and initializes a Color3f from the specified Color3f.

public Color3f(float[] v)
  Constructs and initializes a Color3f from a 3 element array.

public Color3f(float x, float y, float z)
  Constructs and initializes a Color3f from the specified coordinates.

public Color3f(Tuple3d t1)
  Constructs and initializes a Color3f from the specified Tuple3d.

public Color3f(Tuple3f t1)
  Constructs and initializes a Color3f from the specified Tuple3f.

Color4f

A four-element color represented by single-precision floating-point x, y, z, w coordinates that correspond to red, green, blue, and alpha (r, g, b, a) color components. Color and alpha components should be in the range of zero (0.0f) to one (1.0f).

Constructors

public Color4f()
  Constructs and initializes a Color4f to white (0,0,0,0).

public Color4f(Color4f c1)
  Constructs and initializes a Color4f from the specified Color4f.

public Color4f(float[] c)
 Constructs and initializes a Color4f from a 4-element array.

public Color4f(float x, float y, float z, float w)
 Constructs and initializes a Color4f from the specified x, y, z, w
   coordinates.

public Color4f(Tuple4d t1)
 Constructs and initializes a Color4f from the specified Tuple4d.

public Color4f(Tuple4f t1)
 Constructs and initializes a Color4f from the specified Tuple4f.

if a shape references an appearance bundle that has a null or unspecified
Material object, that shape will be rendered without the benefit of 3D lighting and shading.

When a shape is unlit, it is colored using either ColoringAttributes object
color settings or per-vertex colors specified in the shape's Geometry node
(i.e., colors directly assigned to the geometry of a shape as described earlier
in this chapter; see "Color Me Beautiful"). If neither ColoringAttributes nor
Geometry colors exist, the shape is rendered as solid white.

Lit shapes, on the other hand, are colored using Material object color settings (for details see "Lighting and Shading" and the discussion on the Material object and lighting later in this chapter). You should note, however, that
per-vertex Geometry colors always override colors defined by ColoringAttributes and Material objects, regardless of whether or not the object is lit
(per-vertex colors take precedence over ColoringAttributes colors and diffuse and ambient colors specified by Material).

Simply put, colors specified in a ColoringAttributes object are never used
in shading. Interestingly, however, the ColoringAttributes object is used to
specify the shade model that is applied to lit shapes (see "Lighting and Shading"). This apparent contradiction in purpose can sometimes be confusing,
since you wouldn't normally expect to set the shade model for a shape using
an object whose color settings aren't actually used in shading!

The ColoringAttributes object can contain a single color that is used to
render the surface of a shape when no material is specified, or when no lighting exists. This color can be set when the ColoringAttributes object is constructed (Table 14.5), or by calling the setColor() method (Table 14.7).

Table 14.5   ColoringAttributes Constructor Summary (javax.media. j3d.ColoringAttributes)

`public ColoringAttributes()`

Constructs a ColoringAttributes node with the following default parameters:

color: white (1,1,1)

shade model: SHADE_GOURAUD

`public ColoringAttributes(Color3f color, int shadeModel)`

Construct ColoringAttributes object with specified color and shade model (see Table 14.6).

`public ColoringAttributes(float red, float green, float blue, int shadeModel)`

Construct ColoringAttributes object with specified color and shade model (see Table 14.6).

Table 14.6   ColoringAttributes Field Summary

Fields defined by the class javax.media.j3d.ColoringAttributes. Each of these fields is defined as `public static final int`. See the Java 3D API Specification for details (http://java.sun.com/products/java-media/3D/).

`ALLOW_COLOR_READ, ALLOW_COLOR_WRITE`

Capability bits that allow reading/writing of color component information.

`ALLOW_SHADE_MODEL_READ, ALLOW_SHADE_MODEL_WRITE`

Capability bits that allow reading/writing of shade-model component information.

`FASTEST`

Fastest available shade model (usually SHADE_FLAT).

`NICEST`

Nicest available shade model (usually SHADE_GOURAUD).

`SHADE_FLAT`

Flat shade model (do not interpolate color across the primitive).

`SHADE_GOURAUD`

Gouraud shade model (smoothly interpolate color at each vertex across the primitive).

Lighting and Shading

The Material object enables lighting for a shape. A shape whose appearance bundle references a non-null Material object, and whose geometry is under the influence of a light source (such as a point, directional, or spot light; see Chapter 15 for details), is said to be "lit." Unlit objects, on the other hand, either fall outside the influence of a light source (no light can reach them) or they have a `null` or unspecified Material object. Shapes that fall outside the influence of light are rendered as black.

Lit shapes are shaded for 3D effect using the shade model specified by their associated ColoringAttributes object, while unlit objects are not shaded at all. The shade model determines how Java 3D renders colors in the presence of a light source. Java 3D supports "flat" and "Gouraud" shading, as well as "fastest" and "nicest" shading (keep in mind that "fastest" almost always corresponds to "flat" for most systems, while "nicest" almost always corresponds to "Gouraud"). ColoringAttributes fields and methods related to shading are listed in Tables 14.6 and 14.7.

The following snippet of code illustrates the first (constructor-based) technique; a full source-code listing can be found in Listing 14.1:

```
// First, create an Appearance object:
Appearance app = new Appearance();

// Next, create a ColoringAttributes object:
ColoringAttributes ca = new ColoringAttributes(1.0f, 0.0f,
  0.0f, ColoringAttributes.SHADE_FLAT);

// Set Appearance object to reference ColoringAttributes:
app.setColoringAttributes(ca);

// Finally, let a shape use our new appearance bundle:
Sphere shape = new Sphere(0.5f, app);
```

In this example the shade model was set to flat because Gouraud shading would have no effect on this particular scene. As you can see from the full listing (Listing 14.1), this scene lacks a light source and a Material node. As a result, the Gouraud shade model isn't necessary because light and material settings aren't available to help create the illusion of smooth, 3D shading (see

Table 14.7	ColoringAttributes Mutator and Accessor Method Summary

This table contains a summary of the javax.media.j3d.ColoringAttributes mutator and accessor methods. See the Java 3D API Specification (http://java.sun.com/products/java-media/3D/) for a complete listing of all methods.

Returns	*Method Name, Parameters, and Description*
void	**getColor**(Color3f color) Gets the intrinsic color of this ColoringAttributes component object.
int	**getShadeModel**() Gets the shade mode for this ColoringAttributes component object.
void	**setColor**(Color3f color) Sets the intrinsic color of this ColoringAttributes component object.
void	**setColor**(float r, float g, float b) Sets the intrinsic color of this ColoringAttributes component object.
void	**setShadeModel**(int shadeModel) Sets the shade mode for this ColoringAttributes component object.

"Shade Models"). Figure 14-4 contains a screen shot that shows the results of the appearances created with Listing 14.1, in addition to a variety of lighting and shading combinations possible with Java 3D and the ColoringAttributes object.

Listing 14.1	ColoringAttributes Demonstration

```
/*
 *  SimpleSphere.java
 *  A simple primitive sphere colored using ColoringAttributes.
 */

// import core Java packages used by this program
import java.applet.*;
import java.awt.*;

// import core Java 3D package (standard extension,
// aka "optional package")
import javax.media.j3d.*;
```

```
// import Sun's convenience utilities (nonstandard extensions)
import com.sun.j3d.utils.applet.MainFrame;
import com.sun.j3d.utils.universe.*;
import com.sun.j3d.utils.geometry.Sphere;

public class SimpleSphere extends Applet {

 // main() method allows this program
 // to run as an application or an applet
 public static void main(String[] args) {
   new MainFrame(new SimpleSphere(), 500, 500);
 }

  // Default constructor
 public SimpleSphere() {
  setLayout(new BorderLayout());
  GraphicsConfiguration config =
      SimpleUniverse.getPreferredConfiguration();

  Canvas3D c = new Canvas3D(config);
  add("Center", c);
```

Figure 14-4   This figure shows the sphere shape created in Listing 14.1, as well as several variations on the same theme created by combining coloring attributes with lighting and material.

Shade Models

As seen in Table 14.6, the ColoringAttributes object can be set to one of four possible shade models:

```
SHADE_GOURAUD

SHADE_FLAT

NICEST

FASTEST
```

Gouraud shading uses trilinear interpolation to shade pixels across the surface of a shape (based on the color of each vertex of the enclosing polygon), which produces a smooth, 3D effect when combined with a light source and material settings. Flat shading, by comparison, sets all pixels in a given polygon to the same color (based on one vertex color of the enclosing polygon).

While SHADE_GOURAUD and SHADE_FLAT allow the developer to specify a specific shade model (Gouraud or flat, respectively), a setting of NICEST and FASTEST allows Java 3D to determine the appropriate shading mode at runtime. In most cases "nicest" shading uses the Gouraud shade model, while "fastest" uses flat shading, but not always. (Rendering performance varies greatly from system to system depending on the underlying graphics hardware. On some systems Gouraud shading is actually faster than flat shading; on others the difference in performance between Gouraud and flat shading can be dramatic, which can make the end-user experience quite unpleasant if Gouraud shading is specified instead of flat or fastest.)

```java
// Create a simple scene and attach it to the virtual universe
BranchGroup scene = createSceneGraph();
SimpleUniverse u = new SimpleUniverse(c);

// Move the ViewPlatform back so the
// objects in the scene can be viewed.
u.getViewingPlatform().setNominalViewingTransform();

u.addBranchGraph(scene); // add it
}
```

```java
private BranchGroup createSceneGraph() {
  // Create the root of the branch graph
  BranchGroup objRoot = new BranchGroup();

  // Create shape with appearances next...
  // First, create an Appearance object:
  Appearance app = new Appearance();

  // Next, create a ColoringAttributes object:
  ColoringAttributes ca = new ColoringAttributes(1.0f, 0.0f, 0.0f,
                            ColoringAttributes.SHADE_FLAT);

  // Set Appearance object to reference ColoringAttributes:
  app.setColoringAttributes(ca); // set coloring attributes

  // Finally, let a shape use our new appearance bundle:
  Sphere shape = new Sphere(0.5f, app);

  objRoot.addChild(shape);  // add shape to the scene graph
  objRoot.compile(); // allow optimizations on scene graph

  return objRoot;
}
}
```

TransparencyAttributes
(javax.media.j3d.TransparencyAttributes)

Java 3D's TransparencyAttributes node component object is used to define the opacity and transparency properties of rendered shapes. Unlike VRML, whose transparency properties are specified by a field in the Material node (the Material node's *transparency* field), Java 3D encapsulates these attributes into a separate object. Specifically, a TransparencyAttributes object contains the following two attributes:

- **transparency value**, which is a single-precision floating-point number used to specify the overall transparency or opacity of a shape. Transparency values can range from 0.0f to 1.0f, where 0.0f represents full opacity (solid; not transparent at all) and 1.0f represent complete transparency (an invisible shape).

Table 14.8   TransparencyAttributes Constructor Summary (javax. media.j3d.TransparencyAttributes)

public TransparencyAttributes()
Constructs a TransparencyAttributes object with the following default parameters.
transparency mode: NONE
transparency value: 0.0

public TransparencyAttributes(int tMode, float tVal)
Construct TransparencyAttributes object with specified transparency mode and transparency value.

- **transparency mode**, which is an integer value that specifies the rasterization technique to be used (if any) when rendering the transparency of a shape. Transparency modes correspond to the TransparencyAttributes fields BLENDED, FASTEST, NICEST, NONE, or SCREEN_DOOR (see Table 14.9), giving Java 3D developers the ability to control transparency rendering modes in a way that VRML developers cannot (VRML developers can specify only the transparency value of shapes, not their mode).

The transparency value and mode of an object can be created through a TransparencyAttributes constructor (see Table 14.8) or set using one of two related mutator methods (see Table 14.10). The appearance of transparent shapes can further be controlled using the more advanced RenderingAttributes object described later in this chapter (see "Line, Point, Polygon, and Rendering Attributes"), although TransparencyAttributes alone will probably provide all of the control you will require in most cases.

The following snippet of code illustrates how to use the TransparencyAttributes setTransparency() and setTransparencyMode() mutator methods to specify the transparency value and transparency mode for a simple sphere shape rendered in SCREEN_DOOR mode (this code is a slight variation on the transparency appearance created in Listing 14.2 later in this chapter; see Material for details). The resulting sphere can be seen in Figure 14-5, which also shows a sphere rendered using the BLENDED transparency mode:

```
// Set up the transparency properties
TransparencyAttributes ta = new TransparencyAttributes();
```

Table 14.9   TransparencyAttributes Field Summary

Fields defined by the class javax.media.j3d.TransparencyAttributes. Each of these fields is defined as `public static final int`. See the Java 3D API Specification for details (http://java.sun.com/products/java-media/3D/).

ALLOW_MODE_READ, ALLOW_MODE_WRITE
Capability bits that allow reading/writing of transparency mode component information.

ALLOW_VALUE_READ, ALLOW_VALUE_WRITE
Capability bits that allow transparency value reading/writing.

BLENDED
Alpha blended transparency. This color-blending technique creates realistic-looking transparency when compared to the `SCREEN_DOOR` technique, although it is usually more time consuming. When enabled, this mode blends pixel colors based on both source and destination pixels values (overlapping pixels) using a blend equation of `(alpha*src + (1-alpha)*dst)`, where alpha equals `(1 - transparency value)`.

FASTEST
Fastest available method for transparency (usually `SCREEN_DOOR`).

NICEST
Nicest available method for transparency (usually `BLENDED`).

NONE
No transparency; renders an opaque object.

SCREEN_DOOR
Screen-door transparency. This technique is faster but less realistic than `BLENDED`. Screen-door transparency uses a stipple (on/off) pattern to render the shape in which the percentage of percentage of transparent pixels is approximately the same as the transparency value.

```
ta.setTransparencyMode(TransparencyAttributes.SCREEN_DOOR);
ta.setTransparency(0.5f);
app.setTransparencyAttributes(ta);

// Set up the material properties
Color3f black = new Color3f(0.0f, 0.0f, 0.0f);
Color3f white = new Color3f(1.0f, 1.0f, 1.0f);
Color3f objColor = new Color3f(1.0f, 0.0f, 0.0f);
```

Table 14.10	TransparencyAttributes Mutator and Accessor Method Summary

This table contains a summary of the javax.media.j3d.TransparencyAttributes mutator and accessor methods. See the Java 3D API Specification (http://java.sun.com/products/java-media/3D/) for a complete listing of all methods.

Returns	*Method Name, Parameters, and Description*
float	**getTransparency**() Retrieves this appearance component's transparency (see Table 14.9).
int	**getTransparencyMode**() Gets the transparency mode for this appearance component object (see Table 14.9).
void	**setTransparency**(float transparency) Sets this appearance component's transparency (see Table 14.9).
void	**setTransparencyMode**(int transparencyMode) Sets the transparency mode for this appearance component object (see Table 14.9).

Figure 14-5   Sphere A is rendered using the alpha-blending technique specified by BLENDED, which typically corresponds to NICEST mode. Sphere B was rendered using the faster but less realistic looking screen-door technique specified by SCREEN_DOOR (which typically corresponds to FASTEST mode).

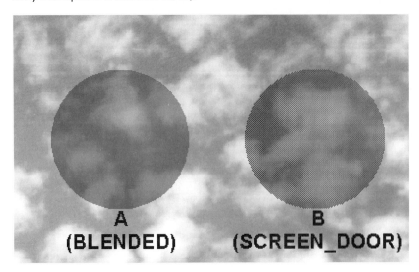

A (BLENDED)   B (SCREEN_DOOR)

```
app.setMaterial(new Material(objColor, black, objColor,
                white, 80.0f));

// Finally, let a shape use our new appearance bundle:
Sphere shape = new Sphere(0.5f, app);
```

TextureAttributes (javax.media.j3d. TextureAttributes)

The TextureAttributes object is used to specify attributes that apply to the process of texture mapping, a process in which texture pixels, or *texels* (short for texture element), are used to color a 3D shape. (See the "Textures" section later in this chapter for details.) If you're already familiar with the details of VRML texture mapping discussed earlier in Chapter 8, you'll soon notice that Java 3D's texture-mapping controls are much more sophisticated than VRML's. Like VRML, Java 3D allows you to specify a bitmap image for texturing purposes, as well as a transformation matrix that can stretch, rotate, and shift the texture on the surface. TextureAttributes store this information, in addition to several other attributes used in the texture-mapping process (see Table 14.11).

Specifically, a TextureAttributes object encapsulates four key attributes related to texture mapping:

- **texture mode**, which specifies how the texture should be applied to a shape (VRML doesn't give you this option). TextureAttributes

---

Table 14.11   TextureAttributes Constructor Summary (javax.media. j3d.TextureAttributes)

`public TextureAttributes()`
    Constructs a TextureAttributes object with the following default parameters:

texture mode: REPLACE

blend color: black (0, 0, 0, 0)

transform: null

perspective correction mode: NICEST

`public TextureAttributes(int textureMode, Transform3D transform, Color4f textureBlendColor, int perspCorrectionMode)`
    Construct a TextureAttributes object with specified values.

supports four texture modes: REPLACE, DECAL, BLEND, or MODULATE (see Table 14.12). Following is a brief description of each: REPLACE mode pastes the texture directly onto the object, with no regard for the object's underlying material properties. Texture color and transparency values override all other colors (except specular color in the case of lit shapes) and transparency settings. The default texture mode is REPLACE.

Table 14.12   TextureAttributes Field Summary

Fields defined by the class javax.media.j3d.TextureAttributes. Each of these fields is defined as `public static final int`. See the Java 3D API Specification for details (http://java.sun.com/products/java-media/3D/).

ALLOW_BLEND_COLOR_READ, ALLOW_BLEND_COLOR_WRITE
Capability bits that allow reading/writing of blend color component information.

ALLOW_MODE_READ, ALLOW_MODE_WRITE
Capability bits that allow reading/writing of texture mode component information and perspective correction mode.

ALLOW_TRANSFORM_READ, ALLOW_TRANSFORM_WRITE
Specifies that this TextureAttributes object allows reading its texture transform component information.

BLEND
Blend the texture blend color with the object color.

DECAL
Apply the texture color to the object as a decal.

FASTEST
Use the fastest available method for perspective correction.

MODULATE
Modulate the object color with the texture color.

NICEST
Use the nicest (highest-quality) available method for texture-mapping perspective correction.

REPLACE
Replace the object color with the texture color.

DECAL applies the texture to the object, yet allows the texture's own transparency values to dictate how much of the underlying material will show through. This technique is similar in nature to applying a decal to a model airplane in real life (opaque decals replace underlying colors entirely, while those with transparency allow underlying colors through). Textures used in this mode must be in the RGB or RGBA format.

BLEND combines the color of the texture with the color of the shape to which it is mapped. Transparency in this mode is a combination of the transparency values in the texture and those defined in material settings. An optional "blend color" can also be specified (see ***texture blend color*** below).

MODULATE mixes the material color with the texture so that both material and texture have an effect on the final color of the surface. Transparency in this mode is a combination of the transparency values defined in the texture and those defined in material settings.

- **texture blend color** is an RGBA color used in combination with the BLEND texture mode (see above). When BLEND mode is enabled, this color is combined with each texel color, resulting in the pixel colors of the rendered shape. This technique can be used to create a variety of texture maps from the same texture image. The default texture blend color is black (0, 0, 0) with an alpha value of 0, or (0, 0, 0, 0).

- **texture map transform**, which is a Transform3D object used to dynamically alter the texture map at runtime. Texture map transforms are used to translate, rotate, and scale textures before they are mapped to the surface of a shape. By default no texture map transform is provided; developers must create their own Transform3D object if they wish to transform textures, as explained later in this chapter (see Chapter 13, "Customizing Size, Location, and Orientation," to learn more about Transform3D objects).

- **perspective correction mode**, which describes the technique Java 3D uses to correct the perspective of textures mapped to shapes. Because a texture is mapped to an image in terms of the image's space, texture planes often appear distorted when viewed from an angle. To remedy the situation Java 3D automatically applies perspective correction when mapping textures. By default, the perspective correction mode is FASTEST. You can, however, change this mode to NICEST at the expense of processing power (FASTEST and NICEST are the only two options available for perspective correction).

Tip

Texture mapping is often a computationally intensive process, particularly when using software-only rendering and no 3D acceleration. One of the most expensive aspects of rendering a texture-mapped polygon involves per-spective correction, so Java 3D allows you to specify NICEST *or* FASTEST *correction with a call to* setPerspectiveCorrectionMode() *(see Tables 14.12 and 14.13). The fastest mode avoids an expensive per-pixel division operation and is well suited for textures that will be seen face-on. For textures that will mostly be seen at an angle to the viewer, this no-division approach will produce severe distortion, so using the nicest perspective correction is preferred.*

As you'll learn later in this chapter, an image used for texture mapping must first be loading into memory using the TextureLoader class. An appearance bundle can then reference the loaded image with a call to the *setTexture()* method (defined in the Appearance class; see Table 14.3). Along with a Texture object reference, an appearance bundle can also contain a reference to a corresponding TextureAttributes object, as the following snippet of code illustrates:

```
// Load a texture map:
TextureLoader tex =
    new TextureLoader("images/checkers.jpg", this);
app.setTexture(tex.getTexture());

// Specify texture attributes (see Table 14-13):
TextureAttributes texAttr = new TextureAttributes();
texAttr.setTextureMode(TextureAttributes.MODULATE);
app.setTextureAttributes(texAttr);

// Specify material properties:
app.setMaterial(new Material(white, black, white,
                 black, 1.0f));

// Associate a shape with our new appearance bundle.
// Note that shapes must have texture coordinates in order
// to be texture mapped (see Textures later in this chapter).
// Fortunately, primitive Sphere constructors can generate
// texture coordinates for us automatically:
Sphere shape = new Sphere(1.0f, Sphere.GENERATE_TEXTURE_COORDS +
                 Sphere.GENERATE_NORMALS, app);
```

Table 14.13	TextureAttributes Mutator and Accessor Method Summary

This table contains a summary of the javax.media.j3d.TextureAttributes mutator and accessor methods. See the Java 3D API Specification (http://java.sun.com/products/java-media/3D/) for a complete listing of all methods.

Returns	*Method Name, Parameters, and Description*
int	**getPerspectiveCorrectionMode**() Gets perspective correction mode value.
void	**getTextureBlendColor**(Color4f textureBlendColor) Gets the texture blend color for this appearance component object.
int	**getTextureMode**() Gets the texture mode parameter for this texture attributes object.
void	**getTextureTransform**(Transform3D transform) Retrieves a copy of the texture transform object.
void	**setPerspectiveCorrectionMode**(int mode) Sets perspective correction mode to be used for color and/or texture coordinate interpolation.
void	**setTextureBlendColor**(Color4f textureBlendColor) Sets the texture blend color for this texture attributes object.
void	**setTextureBlendColor**(float r, float g, float b, float a) Sets the texture blend color for this appearance component object.
void	**setTextureMode**(int textureMode) Sets the texture mode parameter for this appearance component object.
void	**setTextureTransform**(Transform3D transform) Sets the texture transform object used to transform texture coordinates.

In this code example a black-and-white checkerboard image is mapped to a primitive sphere shape, the results of which are seen in Figure 14-6.

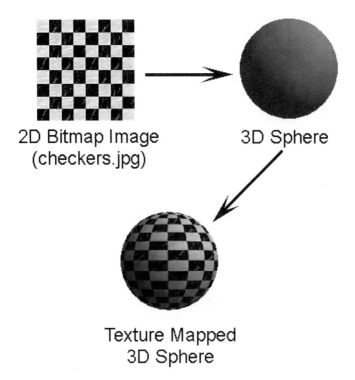

Figure 14-6   The pixels of a 2D "checkerboard" bitmap image are mapped to the surface of a primitive 3D sphere shape.

Note: Free Textures

The Web3D Consortium's Universal Media system comes with a variety of high-quality, freely available textures that you can use to customize your Java 3D worlds. Universal Media textures can be downloaded free of charge at http://www.web3d.org/WorkingGroup/media/.

Line, Point, Polygon, and Rendering Attributes

In addition to the three attribute classes described above (ColoringAttributes, TransparencyAttributes, and TextureAttributes), Java 3D also offers NodeComponent subclasses that encapsulate attributes for lines, points, and polygons (the three basic forms of geometry in Java 3D) and general rendering. Although these attributes aren't discussed in detail here, as they aren't essential to our discussion of color and texture, a brief description of each follows to give you a basic understanding of their purposes. For a detailed overview of the constructors, fields, and methods offered by these classes refer to the Java 3D API Specification available online at http://java.sun.com/products/java-media/3D/.

PolygonAttributes (javax.media.j3d.PolygonAttributes)

The PolygonAttributes class is used to specify how Java 3D polygons should be rendered (see Table 14.14). Using the culling methods of this class, you can instruct Java 3D to render both sides of polygon, or only one. PolygonAttributes also gives you the option of rendering polygons as lines, points, or a normal filled area (by default, polygons are filled). Listing 14.2 illustrates how to use the PolygonAttributes class to render a primitive sphere in wireframe (line) and point form; see `case 1` and `case 2` of the `switch` statement defined in the `createAppearance()` method for details.

Table 14.14   PolygonAttributes Class Summary

For details see the Java 3D API Specification http://java.sun.com/products/java-media/3D/.

PolygonAttributes Constructors

```
public PolygonAttributes()

public PolygonAttributes(int polygonMode, int cullFace,
        float polygonOffset)

public PolygonAttributes(int polygonMode, int cullFace,
        float polygonOffset, boolean backFaceNormalFlip)

public PolygonAttributes(int polygonMode, int cullFace,
        float polygonOffset, boolean backFaceNormalFlip,
        float polygonOffsetFactor)
```

Fields

static int	**ALLOW_CULL_FACE_READ, ALLOW_CULL_FACE_WRITE** Capability bits that allow reading/writing of cull face information.
static int	**ALLOW_MODE_READ, ALLOW_MODE_WRITE** Capability bits that allow reading/writing of polygon mode information.
static int	**ALLOW_NORMAL_FLIP_READ, ALLOW_NORMAL_FLIP_WRITE** Capability bits that allow reading/writing of back face normal flip flag.
static int	**ALLOW_OFFSET_READ, ALLOW_OFFSET_WRITE** Capability bits that allow reading/writing of polygon offset information.

static int	**CULL_BACK**
	Cull all back-facing polygons.

static int	**CULL_FRONT**
	Cull all front-facing polygons.

static int	**CULL_NONE**
	Don't perform any face culling.

static int	**POLYGON_FILL**
	Render polygonal primitives by filling the interior of the polygon.

static int	**POLYGON_LINE**
	Render polygonal primitives as lines drawn between consecutive vertices of the polygon.

static int	**POLYGON_POINT**
	Render polygonal primitives as points drawn at the vertices of the polygon.

Mutators

void	**setBackFaceNormalFlip**(boolean backFaceNormalFlip)
	Sets the back face normal flip flag to the specified value.

void	**setCullFace**(int cullFace)
	Sets the face culling for this appearance component object.

void	**setPolygonMode**(int polygonMode)
	Sets the polygon rasterization mode for this appearance component object.

void	**setPolygonOffset**(float polygonOffset)
	Sets the constant polygon offset to the specified value.

void	**setPolygonOffsetFactor**(float polygonOffsetFactor)
	Sets the polygon offset factor to the specified value.

LineAttributes (javax.media.j3d.LineAttributes)

Assuming that you have specified line mode rendering in the PolygonAttributes object (see above), you can further refine how those line primitives appear using a LineAttributes object. Through LineAttributes you can specify the thickness, pattern (dashes or dots), and antialiasing properties of lines (see Table 14.15). By default, line primitives are one pixel thick, have a solid pattern (no dashes or dots), and do not utilize antialiasing.

Table 14.15 LineAttributes Class Summary

For details see the Java 3D API Specification http://java.sun.com/products/ java-media/3D/.

LineAttributes Constructors

```
public LineAttributes()
public LineAttributes(float lineWidth, int linePattern,
        boolean lineAntialiasing)
```

Fields

static int   **ALLOW_ANTIALIASING_READ, ALLOW_ANTIALIASING_WRITE**
Specifies that this LineAttributes object allows reading its line antialiasing flag.

static int   **ALLOW_PATTERN_READ, ALLOW_PATTERN_WRITE**
Specifies that this LineAttributes object allows reading its line pattern information.

static int   **ALLOW_WIDTH_READ, ALLOW_WIDTH_WRITE**
Specifies that this LineAttributes object allows reading its line width information.

static int   **PATTERN_DASH**
Draw dashed lines.

static int   **PATTERN_DASH_DOT**
Draw dashed-dotted lines.

static int   **PATTERN_DOT**
Draw dotted lines.

static int   **PATTERN_SOLID**
Draw solid lines with no pattern.

static int   **PATTERN_USER_DEFINED**
Draw lines with a user-defined line pattern.

Mutators

void   **setLineAntialiasingEnable**(boolean state)
Enables or disables line antialiasing for this LineAttributes component object.

void   **setLinePattern**(int linePattern)
Sets the line pattern for this LineAttributes component object.

void	**setLineWidth**(float lineWidth)
	Sets the line width for this LineAttributes component object.
void	**setPatternMask**(int mask)
	Sets the line pattern mask to the specified value.
void	**setPatternScaleFactor**(int scaleFactor)
	Sets the line pattern scale factor to the specified value.

PointAttributes (javax.media.j3d.PointAttributes)

PointAttributes is similar in nature to the LineAttributes object, although it is (not surprisingly) used to specify attributes related to points instead of lines. If you have specified point mode rendering in the PolygonAttributes object (see above), for example, you can further refine how these point primitives are rendered using a PointAttributes object. Through PointAttributes you can define the thickness and antialiasing properties of points (see Table 14.16). By default, point primitives are one pixel in size and do not utilize antialiasing (note that points rendered without antialiasing resemble squares; enabling antialiasing will color point corners in such a way that they appear rounded).

Material

The Material node component is used to describe the appearance of illuminated objects. A shape whose appearance bundle references a valid, non-null Material object is said to be "lit," provided the geometry of the shape intersects the influence of a light source (such as a point light, directional light, or spot light; see Chapter 15, "Customizing Background, Fog, Lighting, and Sound," for details). In other words, shapes with material settings are rendered using light and 3D shading, provided light can actually reach them; otherwise, they are considered unlit and rendered without the benefit of light or shading.

Shapes positioned outside of the influence of a light source are rendered solid black, while those without an associated Material node are colored according to ColoringAttributes or per-vertex geometry colors (see "Coloring Chain of Command"). In cases where color isn't specified, a shape is rendered pure white.

Table 14.16   PointAttributes Class Summary

For details see the Java 3D API Specification http://java.sun.com/products/
java-media/3D/.

PointAttributes Constructors

```
public PointAttributes()
public PointAttributes(float pointSize, boolean pointAntialiasing)
```

Fields

static int	**ALLOW_ANTIALIASING_READ, ALLOW_ANTIALIASING_WRITE** Specifies that this PointAttributes object allows reading its point an- tialiasing flag.
static int	**ALLOW_SIZE_READ, ALLOW_SIZE_WRITE** Specifies that this PointAttributes object allows reading its point size information.

Mutators

void	**setPointAntialiasingEnable**(boolean state) Enables or disables point antialiasing for this appearance component object.
void	**setPointSize**(float pointSize) Sets the point size for this appearance component object.

Like VRML's Material node, the Material node used by Java 3D encapsulates a variety of color settings, including:

- **ambient color**, which specifies how much ambient light is reflected
  from the surface of the shape associated with this Material object.
  Ambient light is the scattered, randomly reflected light bounced
  around a scene as the result of direct lighting (see **diffuse color**
  below). The amount of ambient light in a scene is calculated based
  on the number of direct light sources and is a rough approximation of
  how light is reflected off objects in the real world. Ambient lights are
  often used to eliminate the "harshness" of lighting effects in an attempt to simulate the manner in which light fills a room in the real
  world. The default ambient color is (0.2f, 0.2f, 0.2f).

Coloring Chain of Command

Material colors are used when rendering lit objects, while Coloring-Attributes colors are used to render unlit objects. As a result, colors defined by a Material node override those specified by ColoringAttributes colors when rendering in the presence of light (in the absence of light, however, the Java 3D renderer uses colors defined by Coloring-Attributes even if Material colors are available, because Material colors are only used to render lit objects).

Both Material and ColoringAttributes colors, however, are overridden by per-vertex geometry colors (assuming per-vertex geometry colors are defined) regardless of lighting conditions. Specifically, per-vertex colors override diffuse and ambient colors defined in the Material object.

- **emissive color** produces glowing colors that seem to emanate from within the shape itself. Whereas a diffuse color might be used to color a light bulb that has not been lit up, an emissive color can be used to render a light that is turned on; light appears to be emitted from within the bulb, making it glow. Although emissive colors seem to create shapes that emit light, you should note that they do not actually illuminate objects around them (emissive colors don't act as light sources). The default emissive color is (0.0f, 0.0f, 0.0f).

- **diffuse color** describes flat, matte colors that are based on *diffuse reflection*, which is a term used to describe light that bounces off objects in random directions. Because light rays that strike a diffuse reflection surface are reflected in random directions, objects colored only with the diffuse color have a soft, consistent overall look; there are no bright or shiny spots (compare with **specular color**). Diffuse colors can also be combined with other Material node properties to create shiny, glossy colors. The default diffuse color is white (1.0f, 1.0f, 1.0f).

- **specular color** describes colors created based on *specular reflection*, which bounces light off objects in a mathematically predictable manner to create shiny reflective spots on objects (such as the sparkle of a diamond ring or the twinkling of sun off a car hood on a summer day). Specular color is combined with shininess settings (see **shini-**

ness below) to create reflective color spots on the surface of shapes, while diffuse colors are flat or dull by comparison. Often, however, these fields are used together; the diffuse color field sets the base color for an object, while specular color and shininess settings specify the color and size of reflective spots. The default specular color is white (1.0f, 1.0f, 1.0f).

- **shininess** controls the size of reflective spots created using specular colors. Shininess values must be in the range of 1.0 to 128.0, where 1.0 creates a surface that is not shiny and 128.0 creates an extremely shiny surface (values outside this range are clamped). The default shininess value is 64.

Table 14.17 lists the constructors for the Material class, while Table 14.18 lists the two capability bit fields supported by this class. Table 14.19, meanwhile, lists the various mutator methods supported by Material objects. Here you'll find the methods used to set ambient, emissive, diffuse, and specular

---

Table 14.17   Material Constructor Summary (javax.media. j3d.Material

```
public Material()
```
Constructs and initializes a Material object using the following default parameters:

lighting enable: true

ambient color: (0.2, 0.2, 0.2)

emissive color: (0.0, 0.0, 0.0)

diffuse color: (1.0, 1.0, 1.0)

specular color: (1.0, 1.0, 1.0)

shininess: 64

```
public Material(Color3f ambientColor, Color3f emissiveColor,
                Color3f diffuseColor, Color3f specularColor,
                float shininess)
```
Constructs and initializes a new material object using the specified parameters. Note that `shininess` values must be in the range (1.0f, 128.0f), where 1.0 is not shiny and 128.0 is very shiny (values outside this range are clamped).

Table 14.18   Material Field Summary

Fields defined by the class javax.media.j3d.Material. Each of these fields is defined as `public static final int`. See the Java 3D API Specification for details (http://java.sun.com/products/java-media/3D/).

ALLOW_COMPONENT_READ, ALLOW_COMPONENT_WRITE
  Capability bits that allow reading/writing of individual component field information.

---

colors, as well as methods to set the shininess value that is used in combination with specular colors. Several of these methods are used in Listing 14.2, which renders a primitive sphere shape using a variety of appearance and material settings.

Listing 14.2   Appearance and Material Demonstration

```
/*
 * Appearances.java
 *
 * Based on Sun's AppearanceTest.java demonstration program.
 * In the interest of simplicity this variation on
 * AppearanceTest.java creates primitive, nonanimated
 * Sphere shapes for the sole purpose
 * of demonstrating various appearance settings.
 */

// import core Java packages used by this program
import java.applet.*;
import java.awt.*;

// import core Java 3D and matrix math packages
// (standard extensions, aka "optional packages")
import javax.media.j3d.*;
import javax.vecmath.*;

// import Sun's convenience utilities (nonstandard extensions)
import com.sun.j3d.utils.applet.MainFrame;
```

Table 14.19	Material Mutator Method Summary

This table contains a summary of the javax.media.j3d.Material mutator methods. Accessor methods are not included in order to create a table of manageable length. See the Java 3D API Specification (http://java.sun.com/products/java-media/3D/) for a complete listing of all methods.

Returns	*Method Name, Parameters, and Description*
void	**setAmbientColor**(Color3f color) Sets this material's ambient color based on the supplied Color3f object.
void	**setAmbientColor**(float r, float g, float b) Sets this material's ambient color based on the supplied floating-point r, g, b values.
void	**setDiffuseColor**(Color3f color) Sets this material's diffuse color based on the supplied Color3f object.
void	**setDiffuseColor**(float r, float g, float b) Sets this material's diffuse color based on the supplied floating-point r, g, b values.
void	**setDiffuseColor**(float r, float g, float b, float a) Sets this material's diffuse color based on the supplied floating-point r, g, b and alpha values.
void	**setEmissiveColor**(Color3f color) Sets this material's emissive color based on the supplied Color3f object.
void	**setEmissiveColor**(float r, float g, float b) Sets this material's emissive color based on the supplied floating-point r, g, b values.
void	**setLightingEnable**(boolean state) Enables or disables lighting for this appearance object (true = enabled, false = disabled).
void	**setShininess**(float shininess) Sets this material's shininess based on the supplied parameter. Note that shininess values must be in the range [1.0, 128.0], where 1.0 is not shiny and 128.0 is very shiny (values outside this range are clamped).
void	**setSpecularColor**(Color3f color) Sets this material's specular color based on the supplied Color3f object.
void	**setSpecularColor**(float r, float g, float b) Sets this material's specular color based on the supplied floating-point r, g, b values.

```java
import com.sun.j3d.utils.universe.*;
import com.sun.j3d.utils.image.TextureLoader;
import com.sun.j3d.utils.geometry.Sphere;

public class Appearances extends Applet {

  // main() method allows this program
  // to run as an application or an applet
  public static void main(String[] args) {
     new MainFrame(new Appearances(), 700, 700);
  }

   // Default constructor
  public Appearances() {
    setLayout(new BorderLayout());
    GraphicsConfiguration config =
        SimpleUniverse.getPreferredConfiguration();

    Canvas3D c = new Canvas3D(config);
    add("Center", c);

    // Create a simple scene and attach it to the virtual universe
    BranchGroup scene = createSceneGraph();
    SimpleUniverse u = new SimpleUniverse(c);

    // Move the ViewPlatform back so the
    // objects in the scene can be viewed.
    u.getViewingPlatform()
.setNominalViewingTransform();

    u.addBranchGraph(scene);
  }

  private BranchGroup createSceneGraph() {
    // Create the root of the branch graph
    BranchGroup objRoot = new BranchGroup();

    // Create light settings. See Chapter 15 for details
    // on how to create Java 3D lights.

    // First, create a bounding sphere for lights
    BoundingSphere bounds =
        new BoundingSphere(new Point3d(0.0,0.0,0.0), 100.0);

    // Next create global lights
    Color3f lColor1 = new Color3f(0.7f, 0.7f, 0.7f);
```

```
Vector3f lDir1  = new Vector3f(-1.0f, -1.0f, -1.0f);
Color3f alColor = new Color3f(0.2f, 0.2f, 0.2f);

AmbientLight aLgt = new AmbientLight(alColor);
aLgt.setInfluencingBounds(bounds);
DirectionalLight lgt1 = new DirectionalLight(lColor1, lDir1);
lgt1.setInfluencingBounds(bounds);
objRoot.addChild(aLgt);
objRoot.addChild(lgt1);

// Set up the background texture. See Chapter 15 for details.
TextureLoader bgTexture =
                new TextureLoader("images/clouds.jpg", this);
Background bg = new Background(bgTexture.getImage());
bg.setApplicationBounds(bounds);
objRoot.addChild(bg);

// Create shapes and appearances next...
// Create 9 shapes, each with a unique appearance,
// and add them to the scene graph. Each shape is
// associated with a unique "index" value (row * 3 + col)
// that determines its position and appearance settings.
//
// Shapes are positioned starting at the lower left
// hand corner of the canvas (index = 0) and run
// from left to right, bottom to top, ending with the
// last shape in the upper right hand corner (index = 8).
int row, col;
Appearance[][] app = new Appearance[3][3];

for (row = 0; row < 3; row++)
  for (col = 0; col < 3; col++)
   app[row][col] = createAppearance(row * 3 + col);

for (int i = 0; i < 3; i++) {
 double ypos = (double)(i - 1) * 0.5;
   for (int j = 0; j < 3; j++) {
    double xpos = (double)(j - 1) * 0.5;
    objRoot.addChild(createObject(app[i][j], 0.12,  xpos, ypos));
   }
}
objRoot.compile(); // allow optimizations on scene graph

 return objRoot;
}
```

```
private Appearance createAppearance(int index) {
    Appearance app = new Appearance();

  // Globally used colors
  Color3f black = new Color3f(0.0f, 0.0f, 0.0f);
  Color3f white = new Color3f(1.0f, 1.0f, 1.0f);

  // Create unique appearance based on shape's index
  // value. Positions start at the lower left
  // hand corner of the canvas (index = 0) and run
  // from left to right, bottom to top, ending with the
  // last shape in the upper right hand corner (index = 8).

  switch (index) {

    case 0:  // Null (no appearance or material)
      { break; }

    case 1:  // Unlit wire frame
        {
        // Set up the coloring properties
        Color3f objColor = new Color3f(0.5f, 0.0f, 0.2f);
        ColoringAttributes ca = new ColoringAttributes();
        ca.setColor(objColor);
        app.setColoringAttributes(ca);

        // Set up the polygon attributes
        PolygonAttributes pa = new PolygonAttributes();
        pa.setPolygonMode(pa.POLYGON_LINE);
        pa.setCullFace(pa.CULL_NONE);
        app.setPolygonAttributes(pa);
      break;
        }


    case 2:  // Unlit points
        {
        // Set up the coloring properties
        Color3f objColor = new Color3f(0.2f, 0.2f, 1.0f);
        ColoringAttributes ca = new ColoringAttributes();
        ca.setColor(objColor);
        app.setColoringAttributes(ca);

        // Set up the polygon attributes
        PolygonAttributes pa = new PolygonAttributes();
```

```
    pa.setPolygonMode(pa.POLYGON_POINT);
    pa.setCullFace(pa.CULL_NONE);
    app.setPolygonAttributes(pa);

    // Set up point attributes
    PointAttributes pta = new PointAttributes();
    pta.setPointSize(5.0f);
    app.setPointAttributes(pta);
  break;
  }


case 3:   // Lit solid
    {
    // Set up the material properties
    Color3f objColor = new Color3f(0.8f, 0.0f, 0.0f);
    app.setMaterial(new Material(objColor, black, objColor,
                    black, 80.0f));
    break;
    }


case 4:   // Texture mapped, lit solid
    {
    // Set up the texture map
    TextureLoader tex =
      new TextureLoader("images/checkers.jpg", this);
    app.setTexture(tex.getTexture());

    TextureAttributes texAttr = new TextureAttributes();
    texAttr.setTextureMode(TextureAttributes.MODULATE);
    app.setTextureAttributes(texAttr);

    // Set up the material properties
      app.setMaterial(new Material(white, black, white,
                    black, 1.0f));
    break;
    }


case 5: // Transparent, lit solid
    {
    // Set up the transparency properties
    TransparencyAttributes ta = new TransparencyAttributes();
    ta.setTransparencyMode(TransparencyAttributes.BLENDED);
```

```
            ta.setTransparency(0.5f);
            app.setTransparencyAttributes(ta);

            // Set up the material properties
            Color3f objColor = new Color3f(1.0f, 0.0f, 0.0f);
            app.setMaterial(new Material(objColor, black, objColor,
                            white, 80.0f));
        break;
        }


    case 6: // Lit solid with white specular reflection
        {
         // Set up the material properties
         Color3f objColor = new Color3f(0.0f, 1.0f, 0.0f);
          app.setMaterial(new Material(objColor, black, objColor,
                          white, 80.0f));
        break;
         }


    case 7: // Lit solid with no specular reflection
        {
         // Set up the material properties
         Color3f objColor = new Color3f(0.0f, 1.0f, 0.0f);
          app.setMaterial(new Material(objColor, black, objColor,
                          black, 80.0f));
        break;
         }

    case 8: // Glowing solid (glows yellow)
        {
         // Set up the material properties
         Material mat = new Material();
         mat.setEmissiveColor(0.8f, 0.8f, 0.0f);
         app.setMaterial(mat);
        break;
         }

    default: // null settings (no appearance or material)
        {System.out.println("not a valid index!");}
    }

    return app;
}
```

```
private Group createObject(Appearance app, double scale,
                          double xpos, double ypos) {

  // Create a transform group node to scale and position the object
  Transform3D t = new Transform3D();
  t.set(scale, new Vector3d(xpos, ypos, 0.0));
  TransformGroup objTrans = new TransformGroup(t);

  // Create a simple primitive shape and set its appearance.
  // Note that in Sun's original AppearanceTest.java program
  // a Shape3D node is set to a custom Tetrahedron
  // shape (coded in Tetrahedron.java) like so:
  //     Shape3D shape = new Tetrahedron();
  // We simply use a primitive Sphere defined in Sun's
  // utility package (com.sun.j3d.utils.geometry.Sphere).
  // In order to texture map and light the Sphere we must
  // generate texture coordinates and normals:
  Sphere shape = new Sphere(1.5f, Sphere.GENERATE_TEXTURE_COORDS +
                                  Sphere.GENERATE_NORMALS, app);

  objTrans.addChild(shape);   // add it to the scene graph

  return objTrans;
  }
}
```

Textures

Although color can go a long way when it comes to sprucing up Java 3D content, it's not the only way to customize the visual appeal of objects in a scene. As with VRML, Java 3D supports texture mapping of shapes. Conceptually, a texture map can be thought of as a sheet of rubber on which an image appears. This sheet is wrapped around an object, where it is stretched or pinched as needed in a process called texture mapping.

More specifically, the pixels in a texture image are mapped to the pixels of a 3D form. In other words, a geometric shape gets its colors from the pixels in an image when texture mapping is applied. Because images can be applied to shapes, texture mapping offers a wonderfully simply way to increase the visual appeal of objects in a scene without the need for added geometry. In many cases, texture maps are the only option when it comes to producing a specific visual appearance. Finely detailed grain in a piece of wood, for example, or bark on the trunk of a tree are quite easy to represent with a texture image, yet would be extremely time consuming (not to mention tedious or even downright painful) to create using only geometry (see Figure 14-7).

The texture mapping options available to Java 3D programmers are similar to those for VRML. For this reason, you should read the Textures section found in Chapter 8, "Customizing Color and Texture," before proceeding with the following material. You'll find, however, that while VRML and Java 3D share a common set of texture mapping capabilities, Java 3D offers several advanced features not available to VRML developers. For example, 3D texture maps (also known as volume textures) are not directly supported by

Figure 14-7   Texture mapping is commonly used to add the appearance of great detail to otherwise uninspired geometry. In this example various texture maps have been applied to primitive sphere shapes, which radically changes their appearance. The full color version of this image can be seen in the color insert of this book.

VRML, although Java 3D offers this powerful capability. Similarly, VRML doesn't support multiple levels of textures (a technique known as "MIP mapping"), while Java 3D does.

Note: TextureAttributes

The TextureAttributes object, described earlier in this chapter, defines attributes that apply to texture mapping. For details refer to the previous TextureAttributes section and Tables 14.11, 14.12, and 14.13.

Texture Coordinates

Like VRML, the height and width dimensions of a Java 3D texture are expressed in terms of S and T coordinates that each range from 0 to 1. The S coordinate describes the horizontal direction of a texture, while T describes the texture's vertical direction as explained in Chapter 8, "Customizing Color and Texture."

As with VRML texture coordinates, the origin of Java 3D texture coordinates is located at the lower left hand corner of the texture. The S coordinate ranges from 0.0 at the origin and extends to 1.0 at the far right corner of the texture image (the S coordinate runs from left to right along the bottom of the texture). Similarly, the T coordinate ranges from 0.0 at the origin and extends up to the top of the texture image at 1.0 (the T coordinate runs from bottom to top along the left edge of the texture).

Text 2D and Line Textures

Sun's Text2D convenience utility (com.sun.j3d.utils.geometry.Text2D) is used to create textures from text, which can then be applied to a 3D shape (in other words, Text2D allows text to act as the source for a texture map). The ability to create textures from text isn't possible within VRML, nor is the ability to texture map lines (Java 3D also supports texture mapping of lines). Sun's Text2D utility class shouldn't be confused with the core Java 3D Text3D class (javax.media.j3d.Text3D) which is used to create 3D geometry from a text string.

In keeping with VRML, Java 3D's texture coordinates are in no way related to the physical size of the texture image itself; S and T coordinates *always* range from 0.0 to 1.0 no matter how large or small the texture is. This allows developers to specify a location on a texture in terms of (S, T) only, irrespective of the texture's actual size. The developer only has to know that S and T range from 0.0 to 1.0, and the basic concepts behind (S, T) coordinates; they don't have to know how large a texture actually is in each dimension. A texture coordinate specified as (0.5f, 0.5f), for instance, always pinpoints the exact center of the texture, regardless of the texture image's size. A texture coordinate of (1.0f, 1.0f), meanwhile, will always specify the upper right hand corner of the texture. If this concept is unfamiliar, you should turn to Chapter 8 to learn more about the S and T coordinate system used by both VRML and Java 3D.

Texture coordinates are used to specify the application of a texture to geometry on a per-vertex basis. In other words, developers specify a specific point on a texture image via a texture coordinate (S,T). This point on the texture is mapped to the geometry of an image, the precise location of which is specified as a vertex value (x, y, z). Technically, a point on a texture is known as a *texel* (short for texture element, as explained earlier). Texels are mapped to the geometry vertex points, or pixels, during the texture mapping process (which involves trilinear interpolation of the vertices' texture coordinates to determine how texels are applied to pixels).

Generating Primitive Coordinates

Because the process of aligning texture coordinates to geometry, vertices is tedious, time consuming, and prone to error, most developers don't do it by hand. Instead of hand-coding the assignment of texture coordinates to geometry many developers will let Java 3D automatically generate coordinates for them. Primitive objects, for example, can be instructed at construction time (via constructor parameters) to automatically generate coordinates, as seen earlier in Listing 14.2. Following is the snippet of code from that listing, which illustrates this technique:

```
// Create a simple primitive Sphere defined in Sun's
// utility package (com.sun.j3d.utils.geometry.Sphere).
// In order to texture map and light the Sphere we must
// generate texture coordinates and normals:
Sphere shape = new Sphere(1.5f, Sphere.GENERATE_TEXTURE_COORDS +
                Sphere.GENERATE_NORMALS, app);
```

In this example, the Sphere is instructed to generate both texture coordinates and surface normals. Whereas texture coordinates are used to map a point on an image to a point on an object's geometry, normals are used to light the sphere. In both cases, a static field is available in the primitive Sphere class in order to specify these settings during object construction. These fields aren't defined directly in the Sphere class but are instead defined in the Primitive class (`com.sun.j3d.utils.geometry.Primitive`) that all primitive shapes extend. Thus, the fields seen in Table 14.20 are available to all primitives, not just Sphere. Box, Cone, Cylinder, and Sphere are all capable of generating texture coordinates and normals thanks to the Primitive superclass they are each derived from (refer to the Java 3D specification for details about the constructor, fields, and methods defined by Box, Cone, Cylinder, and Sphere).

Warning: Normal and Texture Coordinates Requirements

A normal is a vector that defines the orientation of a shape's surface (Java 3D normals are associated with geometry coordinate points). If lighting is enabled in a Java 3D scene, the objects in that scene must have surface normals specified in order to reflect the light source(s). When texture mapping is enabled, however, texture coordinates are needed. When both texture mapping and lighting are enabled (as seen in Listing 14-2) both normals texture coordinates are required.

Tip: Primitive Appearances

Primitives are part of Sun's convenience utility packages; they aren't included in the core Java 3D API. Although primitive shapes are not derived from Shape3D, you can still set their appearance by calling setAppearance() methods just as you might with any other geometric shape. You can also specify the appearance of a primitive at construction time by passing an appearance object to the primitive's constructor, as illustrated in Listing 14-2. To learn more about Java 3D primitives, turn to the Java 3D specification at http://java.sun.com/products/java-media/3D/.

Table 14.20	Primitive Field Summary

Fields defined by the class com.sun.j3d.utils.geometry.Primitive, which are inherited by Box, Cone, Cylinder, and Sphere. Each of these fields is defined as public static final int. See the Java 3D API Specification for details (http://java.sun.com/products/java-media/3D/).

static int	**ENABLE_APPEARANCE_MODIFY** Specifies that the ALLOW_APPEARANCE_READ and ALLOW_APPEARANCE_WRITE bits are to be set on the generated geometry's Shape3D nodes.
static int	**ENABLE_GEOMETRY_PICKING** Specifies that the ALLOW_INTERSECT capability bit should be set on the generated geometry.
static int	**GENERATE_NORMALS** Specifies that normals are generated along with the positions.
static int	**GENERATE_NORMALS_INWARD** Specifies that normals are to be flipped along the surface.
static int	**GENERATE_TEXTURE_COORDS** Specifies that texture coordinates are generated along with the positions.
static int	**GEOMETRY_NOT_SHARED** Specifies that the geometry being created will not be shared by another scene graph node.

TexCoordGeneration (javax.media.j3d.TexCoordGeneration)

Generating texture coordinates in the constructor of primitive shapes is a cinch, as Listing 14.2 illustrates. In cases where geometry is represented without primitives, however, an alternate means of texture coordinate generation is necessary. You can't, for example, specify automatic coordinate generation during the construction of Shape3D objects. Nor can you specify texture coordinate generation in the constructor of a GeometryArray object. (GeometryArray objects contains arrays of positional coordinates, colors, normals, and texture coordinates that describe point, line, or polygon geometry; descendants of this class are used to create lines, triangle strips, and other geometric forms.)

In these cases, you can instead use the TexCoordGeneration class found in the core Java 3D API (`javax.media.j3d.TexCoordGeneration`). Tex-CoordGeneration, which is short for *texture coordinate generation*, contains all the parameters necessary for texture coordinate generation (a TexCoord-Generation object can be part of an Appearance component object). Developers can create a TexCoordGeneration object with a variety of texture coordinate parameters, and then add it to the Appearance bundle of a Java 3D geometric shape as the following code illustrates:

```
TexCoordGeneration textureCoordinates = new
  TexCoordGeneration(TexCoordGeneration.OBJECT_LINEAR,
  TexCoordGeneration.TEXTURE_COORDINATE_2);

Appearance app = new Appearance();
app.setTexCoordGeneration(textureCoordinates);
```

TexCoordGeneration constructors are found in Table 14.19, fields are listed in Table 14.22, and mutator methods are presented in Table 14.23. Following is a brief overview of each TexCoordGeneration parameter:

- **enable flag**: Enables or disables texture coordinate generation for this appearance component object. This flag can be set to *true* or *false*. The default setting is *true*.

- **texture generation mode**: Specifies whether linear projection (OBJECT_LINEAR) or spherical mapping (SPHERE_MAP) is used in the generation of texture coordinates. The default texture generation mode is OBJECT_LINEAR.

  Linear projection generated coordinates are specified with planes. With two dimensional textures (S, T), for example, two corresponding planes are used: planeS and planeT. In cases where three-dimensional Texture3D texture images are created for mapping purposes, three planes are used (planeS, planeT, and planeR). In either case, the distance from a vertex to one plane represents the texture coordinate in the corresponding dimension. With linear projection, two texture coordinate methods exist: object linear and eye linear. With object linear projection, the texture coordinates do not change when the shape moves; the image appears to be glued to the surface of the shape. Eye linear projection, however, creates texture coordinates that change dynamically in response to the movements of the object (relative to the eye coordinates of the viewer). Such texture maps appear to move, or glide, over the surface of the shape to which they are applied whenever the shape moves.

Spherical mapping, however, generates texture coordinates based on surface normals and viewing direction. This process is used to create special texture maps that reflect shapes around them. Keep in mind, however, that Java 3D doesn't actually support real time reflection maps. Spherical mapping is typically used in combination with special texture images (usually created with a camera and fisheye lens) to create the illusion of reflections.

- **format**: Specifies whether the texture coordinates should be generated for a 2D or 3D texture map. Format can be set to TEXTURE_COORDINATE_2 to generate 2D coordinates (S, T), or TEXTURE_COORDINATE_3 to generate 3D coordinates (S, T, R). The default format setting is TEXTURE_COORDINATE_2.

Table 14.21   TexCoordGeneration Constructor Summary (javax.media.j3d. TexCoordGeneration)

Constructor Summary

`public TexCoordGeneration()`
Constructs and initializes a TexCoordGeneration object with the following default parameters:

enable flag: true

texture generation mode: OBJECT_LINEAR
format: TEXTURE_COORDINATE_2
plane S: (1,0,0,0)
plane T: (0,1,0,0)
plane R: (0,0,0,0)

`public TexCoordGeneration (int genMode, int format)`
Constructs a TexCoordGeneration object with the specified genMode and format.

`public TexCoordGeneration (int genMode, int format, Vector4f planeS)`
Constructs a TexCoordGeneration object with the specified genMode, format, and the S coordinate plane equation.

`public TexCoordGeneration (int genMode, int format, Vector4f planeS, Vector4f planeT)`
Constructs a TexCoordGeneration object with the specified genMode, format, and the S and T coordinate plane equations.

`public TexCoordGeneration (int genMode, int format, Vector4f planeS, Vector4f planeT, Vector4f planeR)`
Constructs a TexCoordGeneration object with the specified genMode, format, and the S, T, and R coordinate plane equations.

- **plane S**: The plane setting corresponding to the S texture coordinate. The default plane S setting is (1,0,0,0).

- **plane T**: The plane setting corresponding to the T texture coordinate. The default plane T setting is (0,1,0,0).

- **plane R**: The plane setting corresponding to the R texture coordinate (for use with Texture3D, not Texture2D). The default plane R setting is (0,0,0,0).

Table 14.22	TexCoordGeneration Field Summary

Fields defined by javax.media.j3d.TexCoordGeneration. Each of these fields is defined as public static final int. See the Java 3D API Specification for details (*http://java.sun.com/products/java-media/3D/*).

static int	**ALLOW_ENABLE_READ, ALLOW_ENABLE_WRITE** Specifies that this TexCoordGeneration object allows reading/writing of its enable flag.
static int	**ALLOW_FORMAT_READ** Specifies that this TexCoordGeneration object allows reading its format information.
static int	**ALLOW_MODE_READ** Specifies that this TexCoordGeneration object allows reading its mode information.
static int	**ALLOW_PLANE_READ** Specifies that this TexCoordGeneration object allows reading its planeS, planeR, and planeT component information.
static int	**EYE_LINEAR** Generates texture coordinates as a linear function in eye coordinates.
static int	**OBJECT_LINEAR** Generates texture coordinates as a linear function in object coordinates.
static int	**SPHERE_MAP** Generates texture coordinates using a spherical reflection mapping in eye coordinates.
static int	**TEXTURE_COORDINATE_2** Generates 2D texture coordinates (S and T).
static int	**TEXTURE_COORDINATE_3** Generates 3D texture coordinates (S, T, and R).

Table 14.23   TexCoordGeneration Mutator Method Summary

This table contains a summary of the javax.media.j3d.TexCoordGeneration mutator methods. Accessor methods are not included in order to create a table of manageable length. Almost every mutator method listed here has a corresponding accessor method. See the Java 3D API Specification (http://java.sun.com/products/java-media/3D/) for a complete listing of all methods.

Returns	*Method Name, Parameters, and Description*
void	**setEnable**(boolean state) Enables or disables texture coordinate generation for this appearance component object.
void	**setFormat**(int format) Sets the TexCoordGeneration format to the specified value.
void	**setGenMode**(int genMode) Sets the TexCoordGeneration generation mode to the specified value.
void	**setPlaneR**(Vector4f planeR) Sets the R coordinate plane equation.
void	**setPlaneS**(Vector4f planeS) Sets the S coordinate plane equation.
void	**setPlaneT**(Vector4f planeT) Sets the T coordinate plane equation.

TextureLoader
(com.sun.j3d.utils.image.TextureLoader)

Sun's TextureLoader utility class gives Java 3D developers a convenient mechanism for loading images into a format suitable for texture mapping purposes. This process, known as texture loading, is quite simple thanks to TextureLoader, and it requires only a few lines of code (without Texture-Loader this process would require considerably more code).

As you can see from Table 14.25, a variety of TextureLoader constructors exist that allow the Java 3D developer to load textures from Java's standard AWT Image and BufferedImage objects, or even String and URL objects (pointers that lead to images stored on disk or somewhere on the network). By default TextureLoader expects images to be in RGBA format, although it can also accommodate images stored in other formats, including RGB,

INTENSITY, LUMINANCE, ALPHA, and LUMINANCE_ALPHA. To load an image in a specific format you can supply any one of these types as the *format* argument in a corresponding TextureLoader constructor (see Table 14.25, as well as Table 14.27).

In cases where a TextureLoader constructor is supplied with an Image, String, or URL, a reference to an *image observer* object is also required. This is consistent with the image loading methods found in the core Java API, as there may be latency associated with loading such images (an image that resides on the network will take considerably longer to load as compared to an image already buffered in memory, for example). An image observer is merely any AWT component that that can watch, or observe, the loading process. Image observers may be queried, so that the progress of the image being loaded can be monitored if desired, but in most cases developers are content to supply a reference to the observer as a formality and simply wait for the image load.

Because any AWT component can act as an image observer, Java 3D developers typically pass a reference to the applet itself for such purposes (all Java applets ultimately descend from the Component class and so can act in the capacity of an image observer when the need arises). To do this, the developer supplies the Java keyword "this" as the TextureLoader image observer (see Listing 14.3), which is a reference to the applet itself. Consider, for example, the following code:

```
// First, load the image:
TextureLoader t = new TextureLoader("treebark.gif", this);
ImageComponent2D image = t.getImage();

// Next, set it as the base level (level 0) mipmap
// of a Texture2D object:
Texture2D t2D = new Texture2D(Texture.BASE_LEVEL,
                Texture.RGBA,
                image.getWidth(),
                image.getHeight());

t2D.setImage(0, image); // the base level mipmap = 0

// Finally, set the texture into an appearance bundle,
// which can then can be associated with a shape:
Appearance app = new Appearance();
app.setTexture(t2D);
Sphere shape = new Sphere(1.5f,
        Sphere.GENERATE_TEXTURE_COORDS, app);
```

In this case, the image named "treebark.gif" is loaded using the Texture-Loader constructor that accepts a String object argument, for which the applet is set as the image observer. Once loaded, the loader's `getImage()` method is invoked to extract the image into an ImageComponent2D object. The Image-Component2D is then set into a Texture2D object, where it is specified as being the base level (level = 0) mipmap. As you'll learn later in this chapter, Java 3D's mipmap texture capability allows developers to specify multiple levels of textures. Because we're only creating one texture map level in this example, we set the mipmap level for this image to zero, which is the base level.

Finally, the resulting Texture2D object is used to create an appearance bundle for a primitive sphere shape. Now when the sphere is rendered, it will be texture mapped with the treebark.gif image that was originally handed to our TextureLoader in the first line of code.

The TextureLoader class can also be used to load a background image for the virtual universe, as the following lines of code taken from Listing 14.2 illustrate (see Chapter 15 for details on background images):

```
TextureLoader bgTexture =
new TextureLoader("images/clouds.jpg", this);
Background bg = new Background(bgTexture.getImage());
```

Table 14.26 summarizes the four methods defined by the TextureLoader class, all but one of which return references to a `javax.media.j3d.Image-Component2D` object. TextureLoader's `getTexture()` method instead returns a Texture object reference, which can also be used in texture mapping, as you can see from Listing 14.3 and the excerpts of code from this listing provided below (keep in mind that Texture is actually an abstract class, from which concrete Texture2D and Texture3D classes are derived as explained in the following sections). The one and only field defined by TextureLoader is related to MIP mapping, as seen in Table 14.24, which is an advanced Java 3D texture mapping capability described later in this chapter.

Note

Java 3D's ImageComponent2D class defines a two-dimensional image component (a 2D array of pixels) that is used for texture images, background images and raster components of Shape3D nodes, while javax.media.j3d. ImageComponent3D defines a corresponding three-dimensional image component (a 3D array of pixels) used for texture images (see Texture3D below). Both ImageComponent2D and ImageComponent3D are node component objects (both descend from javax.media.j3d.ImageComponent, which itself descends from javax.media.j3d.NodeComponent).

Below are key excerpts from the TextureImage.java program that relate directly to the issue of loading an image for texture mapping purposes. The complete program, found in Listing 14.3, texture maps a user-specified image file onto a spinning 3D box. The user specifies the texture map image on the command line when the program is run thusly (where > is the command line prompt):

```
> java TextureImage woodpanel.jpg
```

The image name specified on the command line is passed to the program as the first element of the String array defined by the `main()` method. In the case of this program, the String array is named `args` (short for "arguments"). The `main()` method passes the `args` array to the TextureImage constructor, which ultimately passes it to the `createSceneGraph()` method where a TextureLoader object loads the image it specifies. After the image is loaded, it is set as the TextureAttributes component of the box's Appearance bundle, which assigns it as the texture map for this box. Following are the most significant lines of code related to this process (see Listing 14.3 for the complete program):

```
// Use Sun's TextureLoader utility class to load a
// texture map from an image file whose name is passed
// to this program on the command line.
//
// The image file name is stored in the first element
// of the command line argument array, which is
// specified in code as args[0]
//
// After the texture is loaded use the TextureLoader
// object's getTexture() method to return the
// associated Texture object:

import com.sun.j3d.utils.image.TextureLoader;

Appearance app = new Appearance(); // holds texture info

Texture tex =
 new TextureLoader(args[0], this).getTexture();

app.setTexture(tex);   // set into Appearance bundle

// Use a TextureAttributes component of an
// Appearance bundle to specify that this
// texture map be applied in MODULATE
// mode (see the earlier discussion about
```

```
// TextureAttributes for details):
TextureAttributes texAttr = new TextureAttributes();
texAttr.setTextureMode(TextureAttributes.MODULATE);
app.setTextureAttributes(texAttr);

// Finally, use this texture map by associating the
// Appearance bundle with a shape (a Box primitive):
Box textureCube = new Box(0.4f, 0.4f, 0.4f,
            Box.GENERATE_TEXTURE_COORDS, app);
```

Warning

Java 3D requires that texture images be a mathematical power of two (1, 2, 4, 8, 16, 32, 64, 128, 256, and so forth) in each dimension. If you supply images that are not a mathematical power of two in each dimension, the Java runtime will throw a java.lang.IllegalArgumentException exception (this exception is also thrown when in invalid image format or mipmapMode is supplied to a Texture2D or Texture3D constructor).

Table 14.24   TextureLoader Field Summary

The com.sun.j3d.utils.image.TextureLoader class defines only one field. This field is defined as public static final int. See the Java 3D API Specification for details (http://java.sun.com/products/java-media/3D/).

static int   **GENERATE_MIPMAP**
                Optional flag - specifies that mipmaps are generated for all levels

Table 14.25   TextureLoader Constructor Summary (com.sun.j3d.utils.image.TextureLoader)

public TextureLoader(java.awt.image.BufferedImage bImage)
Constructs a TextureLoader object using the specified BufferedImage and default format RGBA.

public TextureLoader(java.awt.image.BufferedImage bImage, int flags)
Constructs a TextureLoader object using the specified BufferedImage, option flags and default format RGBA

public TextureLoader(java.awt.image.BufferedImage bImage, java.lang.String format)
Constructs a TextureLoader object using the specified BufferedImage and format

public TextureLoader(java.awt.image.BufferedImage bImage, java.lang.String format, int flags)

Constructs a TextureLoader object using the specified BufferedImage, format, and option flags.

```
public TextureLoader(java.awt.Image image, java.awt.Compo-
nent observer)
```
Constructs a TextureLoader object using the specified Image and default format RGBA

```
public TextureLoader(java.awt.Image image, int flags, java
.awt.Component observer)
```
Constructs a TextureLoader object using the specified Image flags and default format RGBA

```
public TextureLoader(java.awt.Image image, java.lang
.String format, java.awt.Component observer)
```
Constructs a TextureLoader object using the specified Image and format

```
public TextureLoader(java.awt.Image image, java.lang
.String format, int flags, java.awt.Component observer)
```
Constructs a TextureLoader object using the specified Image format and option flags

```
public TextureLoader(java.lang.String fname, java.awt.Com-
ponent observer)
```
Constructs a TextureLoader object using the specified file and default format RGBA

```
public TextureLoader(java.lang.String fname, int flags,
java.awt.Component observer)
```
Constructs a TextureLoader object using the specified file, option flags and default format RGBA

```
public TextureLoader(java.lang.String fname,
java.lang.String format, java.awt.Component observer)
```
Constructs a TextureLoader object using the specified file, and format

```
public TextureLoader(java.lang.String fname, java.lang
.String format, int flags, java.awt.Component observer)
```
Constructs a TextureLoader object using the specified file, format and option flags

```
public TextureLoader(java.net.URL url, java.awt.Component
observer)
```
Constructs a TextureLoader object using the specified URL and default format RGBA

```
public TextureLoader(java.net.URL url, int flags,
java.awt.Component observer)
```
Constructs a TextureLoader object using the specified URL, option flags and default format RGBA

```
public TextureLoader(java.net.URL url, java.lang.String
format, java.awt.Component observer)
```
Constructs a TextureLoader object using the specified URL and format

```
public TextureLoader(java.net.URL url, java.lang.String
format, int flags, java.awt.Component observer)
```
Constructs a TextureLoader object using the specified URL, format, and options flags

Table 14.26 TextureLoader Method Summary	

This table contains a summary of the com.sun.j3d.utils.image.TextureLoader methods. See the Java 3D API Specification for details (http://java.sun.com/products/java-media/3D/).

Returns	*Method Name, Parameters, and Description*
`ImageComponent2D`	`getImage()` Returns the associated ImageComponent2D object
`ImageComponent2D`	`GetScaledImage`(float xScale, float yScale) Returns the scaled ImageComponent2D object
`ImageComponent2D`	`GetScaledImage`(int width, int height) Returns the scaled ImageComponent2D object
`Texture`	`getTexture()` Returns the associated Texture object

Texture (javax.media.j3d.Texture)

Java 3D's Texture class is the abstract superclass of Texture2D and Texture3D. Because Texture is an abstract class, objects can not be created directly from it; only Texture2D and Texture3D objects can be instantiated for texture mapping purposes. Texture does, however, define the basic framework common to both Texture2D and Texture3D. As a result, the concrete Texture2D and Texture3D classes inherit Texture's basic constructor capabilities (Table 14.27) as well as a great detail of Texture's fields and methods (see Tables 14.26 and 14.27).

Texture is a direct descendant of the NodeComponent class (`javax.media.j3d.NodeComponent`), which indirectly makes Texture2D and Texture3D node components as well. As node components, Texture2D and Texture3D objects can be used to specify texture properties of an appearance bundle. Once set into an appearance bundle, texture mapping is then enabled for any shape that references that bundle (in other words, a 3D shape will be mapped with the texture referenced by its appearance bundle).

Texture, and consequently Texture2D and Texture3D, supports a number of texture mapping settings that you can customize when working with these classes. Following is a summary of several of these settings:

- **Texture Format** is used to provide details about the format of the texture image, specifically the number of component values used to represent each texel and how these values are applied during the mapping process. The texture format can be either INTENSITY, LUMINANCE, ALPHA, LUMINANCE_ALPHA, RGB, or RGBA (see Table 14-28 for a description of each). RGB is the default texture format.

- **Boundary Mode** specifies whether to CLAM or WRAP texture coordinates when a given texture coordinate is beyond the 0 to 1 range allowed by the S and T directions of texture coordinate space. When Boundary Mode is set to WRAP (the default), the image is repeated as necessary. When Boundary Mode is set to CLAMP, however, the image's edge color is used to map texture coordinates that fall outside of the legal 0 to 1 range (see Boundary Color below).

- **Boundary Color** augments the boundary mode setting by allowing the developer to specify a boundary color to use in cases where texture mode is CLAMP and textures coordinates fall outside of the legal 0 to 1 range. Keep in mind that only one boundary color can be specified (one color is used for both texture dimensions in situations where both S and T are set to CLAMP).

- **MIP Map Mode and Level** specify the type of mipmap mode used in texture mapping, as well as the level of mipmap for which an image is set into a Texture object. Mipmap mode may be either BASE_LEVEL or MULTI_LEVEL_MIPMAP. By default, the BASE_LEVEL mipmap mode is used, which means that multiple levels of texture maps are not utilized. The base mipmap level is level 0, which can be explicitly specified through the `setImage()` method (see MIP Mapping later in this chapter for details).

- **Filter Functions** specify the type of filter to apply during the texture mapping process when texels don't map precisely to pixels. Generally speaking, it's not uncommon for there to be a size mismatch between the texels on a texture map and the pixels that they are being applied to on a 3D shape: a precise 1-to-1 mapping is rare. In cases where the pixel being rendered maps to an area that is less than (or equal to) one texel, a *magnification filter* can be applied to produce better looking results (the texture's pixels are magnified as they are applied to the pixels of the geometric form). The magnification filter can be set to perform point sampling (BASE_LEVEL_POINT), where the color of the nearest texel is used, or biliner interpolation on the four closest texels in the level 0 texture map (BASE_LEVEL_LINEAR). The former is usually fastest, while the latter is more computationally expensive, though it produces better quality results (BASE_LEVEL_LINEAR magnification helps reduce the possibility of "texelization", a condition where the individual textures are obvious after texture mapping).

In the opposite case, where the pixel being rendered maps to an area that is larger than one texel, a *minification filter* can be applied. Here the texels are squeezed (minified) to fit onto the pixels. As with the magnification filter, a minification filter can be set to use point sampling (BASE_LEVEL_POINT) so that the color of the nearest texel is used. Alternately, the minification filter can be set to perform bilinear interpolation on the four closest texels in the level 0 texture map (BASE_LEVEL_LINEAR). The minification filter also supports multi-level settings of MULTI_LEVEL_POINT and MULTI_LEVEL_LINEAR for situations where multiple levels of textures have been specified (see MIP Mapping later in this chapter). By default, both magnification and magnification filters use BASE_LEVEL_POINT settings. In cases where the programmer does not explicitly specify a filter to apply during the mapping process, the Java 3D runtime typically chooses the most appropriate one for the task at hand.

Table 14.27   Texture Constructor Summary (javax.media.j3d.Texture)

`public Texture()`

Constructs and initializes a Texture object using the following default parameters:

enable flag: true
width: 0
height: 0
mipmap mode: BASE_LEVEL
format: RGB
boundary mode S: WRAP
boundary mode T: WRAP
min filter: BASE_LEVEL_POINT
mag filter: BASE_LEVEL_POINT
boundary color: black (0,0,0,0)
image: null

Note that this constructor creates a texture object having a width and height of 0, which isn't useful in most cases.

public **Texture**(int mipMapMode, int format, int width, int height)

Constructs an empty Texture object with specified mipMapMode format, width and height. Image at level 0 must be set by a call to setImage(). In cases where mipmapMode is set to MULTI_LEVEL_MIPMAP images for ALL levels must also be set. Notice that width and height must be a power of 2 (i.e., 2, 4, 8, 16, 32, 64, 128, 256, etc.) otherwise java.lang.IllegalArgumentException will be thrown (this exception is also thrown when an invalid image format or mipmapMode is specified).

Following is a description of parameters accepted by this constructor:

mipmapMode: BASE_LEVEL or MULTI_LEVEL_MIPMAP
format: INTENSITY, LUMINANCE, ALPHA, LUMINANCE_ALPHA, RGB, or RGBA
width: width of image at level 0 (must be power of 2)
height: height of image at level 0 (must be power of 2)

Table 14.28   Texture Field Summary

Fields defined by the class javax.media.j3d.Texture. Each of these fields is defined as public static final int. See the Java 3D API Specification for details (http://java.sun.com/products/java-media/3D/).

static int	**ALLOW_BOUNDARY_COLOR_READ** Specifies that this Texture object allows reading its boundary color information.
static int	**ALLOW_BOUNDARY_MODE_READ** Specifies that this Texture object allows reading its boundary mode information.
static int	**ALLOW_ENABLE_READ, ALLOW_ENABLE_WRITE** Specifies that this Texture object allows reading/writing of its enable flag.
static int	**ALLOW_FILTER_READ** Specifies that this Texture object allows reading its filter information.
static int	**ALLOW_FORMAT_READ** Specifies that this Texture object allows reading its format information.
static int	**ALLOW_IMAGE_READ, ALLOW_IMAGE_WRITE** Specifies that this Texture object allows reading/writing of its image component information.
static int	**ALLOW_MIPMAP_MODE_READ** Specifies that this Texture object allows reading its mipmap mode information.

static int   **ALLOW_SIZE_READ**
Specifies that this Texture object allows reading its size information (e.g., width, height, number of mipmap levels).

static int   **ALPHA**
Specifies Texture contains only Alpha values.

static int   **BASE_LEVEL**
Indicates that Texture object only has one level.

static int   **BASE_LEVEL_LINEAR**
Performs bilinear interpolation on the four nearest texels in level 0 texture map.

static int   **BASE_LEVEL_POINT**
Select the nearest texel in level 0 texture map.

static int   **CLAMP**
Clamps texture coordinates to be in the range [0, 1].

static int   **FASTEST**
Uses the fastest available method for processing geometry.

static int   **INTENSITY**
Specifies Texture contains only Intensity values.

static int   **LUMINANCE**
Specifies Texture contains only luminance values.

static int   **LUMINANCE_ALPHA**
Specifies Texture contains Luminance and Alpha values.

static int   **MULTI_LEVEL_LINEAR**
Performs tri-linear interpolation of texels between four texels each from two nearest mipmap levels.

static int   **MULTI_LEVEL_MIPMAP**
Indicates that this Texture object has multiple images, one for each mipmap level.

static int   **MULTI_LEVEL_POINT**
Selects the nearest texel in the nearest mipmap.

static int   **NICEST**
Uses the nicest available method for processing geometry.

static int   **RGB**
Specifies Texture contains Red, Green and Blue color values.

static int   **RGBA**
Specifies Texture contains Red, Green, Blue color values and Alpha value.

static int   **WRAP**
Repeats the texture by wrapping texture coordinates that are outside the range [0,1].

Table 14.29	Texture Mutator Method Summary

This table contains a summary of the javax.media.j3d.Texture mutator methods. Accessor methods are not included in order to create a table of manageable length. Almost every mutator method listed here has a corresponding accessor method. See the Java 3D API Specification (http://java.sun.com/products/java-media/3D/) for a complete listing of all methods.

Returns	*Method Name, Parameters, and Description*
void	**setBoundaryColor**(Color4f boundaryColor) Sets the texture boundary color for this texture object.
void	**setBoundaryColor**(float r, float g, float b, float a) Sets the texture boundary color for this texture object.
void	**setBoundaryModeS**(int boundaryModeS) Sets the boundary mode for the S coordinate in this texture object.
void	**setBoundaryModeT**(int boundaryModeT) Sets the boundary mode for the T coordinate in this texture object.
void	**setEnable**(boolean state) Enables or disables texture mapping for this appearance component object.
void	**setImage**(int level, ImageComponent image) Sets the image for a specified mipmap level.
void	**setImages**(ImageComponent[] images) Sets the array of images for all mipmap levels.
void	**setMagFilter**(int magFilter) Sets the magnification filter function.
void	**setMinFilter**(int minFilter) Sets the minification filter function.
void	**setMipMapMode**(int mipMapMode) Sets mipmap mode for texture mapping for this texture object.

Texture2D (javax.media.j3d.Texture2D)

Texture2D is a concrete subclass of the abstract Texture class described in the previous section. As such, Texture2D inherits most of its fields and methods from Texture. Texture2D enhances Texture by merely adding the Texture2D-specific constructors seen in Table 14.30.

Table 14.30   Texture2D Constructor Summary (javax.media.j3d.Texture2D)

`public Texture2D()`

Constructs a texture object using default values.

`public Texture2D(int mipmapMode, int format, int width, int height)`

Constructs an empty Texture2D object with specified mipmapMode format, width and height.

The TextureImage.java program shown in Listing 14.3 illustrates how to use a TextureLoader object to create a texture map from an image file. In this example, anobject reference of type Texture is retrieved through the TextureLoader object with a call to the `getTexture()` method defined by the Texture class (see Table 14.26). You'll notice that Texture is an abstract class, which means that you can not create instances of it. You can, however, retrieve an object reference that is of the Texture data type as shown in Listing 14.3. Once you have a reference to a Texture data type, you can then use it to construct an appearance bundle for texture mapping purposes, just as this program does.

The TextureTest.java program found in Listing 14.4, meanwhile, creates an actual Texture2D instance from raw pixel data. The pixel data for the texture map used in this program is generated procedurally; it's not loaded from an image file, as is the case with TextureImage.java. Instead, TextureTest. java creates an array of bytes to store individual pixel colors, which are assigned programmatically in a `for` loop. This raw buffered image data is then used in the construction of an ImageComponent2D object, which is ultimately set into a Texture2D object for texture mapping purposes.

Note: Texture2D Fields and Methods

Texture2D is a concrete class derived from the abstract Texture class described in the previous section. As such, Texture2D inherits all of its fields and methods directly from Texture; Texture2D does not define its own fields and methods.

Although very different in approach, both programs illustrate common Java 3D texture mapping techniques. TextureImage.java and TextureTest. java are supplied as demonstration programs along with Sun's Java 3D implementation for Windows environments. You can run them yourself without typing in a line of code, assuming you've installed Java 3D, as described earlier in this chapter.

Listing 14.3　TextureImage.java

```
/*
 *      @(#)TextureImage.java 1.16 99/05/19 14:29:48
 *
 * Copyright (c) 1996-1998 Sun Microsystems, Inc. All Rights Reserved.
 *
 * Sun grants you ("Licensee") a non-exclusive, royalty free, license to use,
 * modify and redistribute this software in source and binary code form,
 * provided that i) this copyright notice and license appear on all copies of
 * the software; and ii) Licensee does not utilize the software in a manner
 * which is disparaging to Sun.
 *
 * This software is provided "AS IS," without a warranty of any kind. ALL
 * EXPRESS OR IMPLIED CONDITIONS, REPRESENTATIONS AND WARRANTIES, INCLUDING ANY
 * IMPLIED WARRANTY OF MERCHANTABILITY, FITNESS FOR A PARTICULAR PURPOSE OR
 * NON-INFRINGEMENT, ARE HEREBY EXCLUDED. SUN AND ITS LICENSORS SHALL NOT BE
 * LIABLE FOR ANY DAMAGES SUFFERED BY LICENSEE AS A RESULT OF USING, MODIFYING
 * OR DISTRIBUTING THE SOFTWARE OR ITS DERIVATIVES. IN NO EVENT WILL SUN OR ITS
 * LICENSORS BE LIABLE FOR ANY LOST REVENUE, PROFIT OR DATA, OR FOR DIRECT,
 * INDIRECT, SPECIAL, CONSEQUENTIAL, INCIDENTAL OR PUNITIVE DAMAGES, HOWEVER
 * CAUSED AND REGARDLESS OF THE THEORY OF LIABILITY, ARISING OUT OF THE USE OF
 * OR INABILITY TO USE SOFTWARE, EVEN IF SUN HAS BEEN ADVISED OF THE
 * POSSIBILITY OF SUCH DAMAGES.
 *
 * This software is not designed or intended for use in on-line control of
 * aircraft, air traffic, aircraft navigation or aircraft communications; or in
 * the design, construction, operation or maintenance of any nuclear
 * facility. Licensee represents and warrants that it will not use or
 * redistribute the Software for such purposes.
 */

import java.applet.Applet;
import java.awt.*;
import java.awt.event.*;
import com.sun.j3d.utils.applet.MainFrame;
```

```
import com.sun.j3d.utils.universe.*;
import com.sun.j3d.utils.image.TextureLoader;
import com.sun.j3d.utils.geometry.Box;
import javax.media.j3d.*;
import javax.vecmath.*;

public class TextureImage extends Applet {

 public BranchGroup createSceneGraph(String[] args) {
   // Create the root of the branch graph
   BranchGroup objRoot = new BranchGroup();

   // Create the transform group node and initialize it to the
   // identity.  Enable the TRANSFORM_WRITE capability so that
   // our behavior code can modify it at runtime.  Add it to the
   // root of the subgraph.
   TransformGroup objTrans = new TransformGroup();
   objTrans.setCapability(TransformGroup.ALLOW_TRANSFORM_WRITE);
   objRoot.addChild(objTrans);

   // Create appearance object for textured cube
   Appearance app = new Appearance();

   if (args.length > 0) {
     Texture tex = new TextureLoader(args[0], this).getTexture();
     app.setTexture(tex);
     TextureAttributes texAttr = new TextureAttributes();
     texAttr.setTextureMode(TextureAttributes.MODULATE);
     app.setTextureAttributes(texAttr);

     if (tex == null)
       System.out.println("Warning: Texture is disabled");

   } else {
     System.out.println("Warning: Texture is disabled");
     System.out.println("Usage: java TextureImage " +
       "<image file name> [-f ImageComponent format]");
   }

   // Create textured cube and add it to the scene graph.
   Box textureCube = new Box(0.4f, 0.4f, 0.4f,
                 Box.GENERATE_TEXTURE_COORDS, app);

   objTrans.addChild(textureCube);
```

```
      // Create a new Behavior object that will perform the desired
      // operation on the specified transform object and add it into
      // the scene graph. See Chapter 13 for details.
      Transform3D yAxis = new Transform3D();
      Alpha rotationAlpha = new Alpha(-1, Alpha.INCREASING_ENABLE,
                             0, 0,
                             4000, 0, 0,
                             0, 0, 0);
      RotationInterpolator rotator =
       new RotationInterpolator(rotationAlpha, objTrans, yAxis,
                    0.0f, (float) Math.PI*2.0f);
      BoundingSphere bounds =
       new BoundingSphere(new Point3d(0.0,0.0,0.0), 100.0);

      rotator.setSchedulingBounds(bounds);
      objTrans.addChild(rotator);

      // Have Java 3D perform optimizations on this scene graph.
      objRoot.compile();

      return objRoot;
    }

    public TextureImage(String[] args) {
     setLayout(new BorderLayout());
     GraphicsConfiguration config =
      SimpleUniverse.getPreferredConfiguration();

     Canvas3D c = new Canvas3D(config);
     add("Center", c);

      // Create a simple scene and attach it to the virtual universe
      BranchGroup scene = createSceneGraph(args);
      SimpleUniverse u = new SimpleUniverse(c);

      // This will move the ViewPlatform back a bit so the
      // objects in the scene can be viewed.
      u.getViewingPlatform().setNominalViewingTransform();

      u.addBranchGraph(scene); // add scene to universe
    }


    // The following allows TextureImage to be run as an
    // application as well as an applet:
```

```
   public static void main(String[] args) {
     new MainFrame(new TextureImage(args), 256, 256);
   }
}
```

Listing 14.4   TextureTest.java

```
/*
 *   @(#)TextureTest.java 1.35 99/05/19 14:29:45
 *
 * Copyright (c) 1996-1998 Sun Microsystems, Inc.
 * All Rights Reserved.
 *
 * SEE COPYRIGHT NOTICE IN LISTING 14-3.
 */

import java.applet.Applet;
import java.awt.*;
import java.awt.event.*;
import com.sun.j3d.utils.applet.MainFrame;
import com.sun.j3d.utils.universe.*;
import com.sun.j3d.utils.geometry.Box;
import javax.media.j3d.*;
import javax.vecmath.*;
import java.awt.image.*;
import java.awt.color.ColorSpace;


public class TextureTest extends Applet {

  public BranchGroup createSceneGraph() {
    Color3f aColor  = new Color3f(0.2f, 0.2f, 0.2f);
    Color3f eColor  = new Color3f(0.0f, 0.0f, 0.0f);
    Color3f dColor  = new Color3f(0.2f, 1.0f, 0.6f);
    Color3f sColor  = new Color3f(1.0f, 1.0f, 1.0f);
    Color3f lColor1 = new Color3f(0.7f, 0.7f, 0.7f);
    Color3f lColor2 = new Color3f(0.7f, 0.7f, 0.35f);
    Vector3f lDir1  = new Vector3f(-1.0f, -1.0f, -1.0f);
    Vector3f lDir2  = new Vector3f(0.0f, 0.0f, 1.0f);
    Color3f alColor = new Color3f(1.0f, 1.0f, 1.0f);

    // Create the root of the branch graph
    BranchGroup objRoot = new BranchGroup();
```

```
// Create the transform group node and initialize it to
// the identity. Enable the TRANSFORM_WRITE capability
// so that our behavior code can modify it at runtime.
// Add it to the root of the subgraph.
TransformGroup objTrans = new TransformGroup();
objTrans.setCapability(TransformGroup.ALLOW_TRANSFORM_WRITE);
objRoot.addChild(objTrans);

// Create some simple geometry (without an appearance node).
// Create a new shape leaf node using the specified geometry
// and add it into the scene graph.
int width = 16;
int height = 16;

ColorSpace cs = ColorSpace.getInstance(ColorSpace.CS_sRGB);
int[] nBits = {8, 8, 8};

ComponentColorModel colorModel =
 new ComponentColorModel(cs, nBits,
         false, false,
         Transparency.OPAQUE, 0);

WritableRaster raster =
 colorModel.createCompatibleWritableRaster(width, height);

BufferedImage bImage =
 new BufferedImage(colorModel, raster, false, null);

byte[] byteData =
 ((DataBufferByte)raster.getDataBuffer()).getData();

int i, j, k, cc;
 for (i=0;i < height;i++){
   for (j=0;j < width;j++){
   if  (((( i & 0x2) == 0)^((j & 0x02)) == 0)) cc =255;
   else cc = 0;
   k = (i*15 + j) *3;
   byteData[k] = (byte)cc;
   byteData[k+1] = (byte)cc;
   byteData[k+2] = (byte)cc;
   }
 }

ImageComponent2D pArray =
 new ImageComponent2D(ImageComponent.FORMAT_RGB,
         width, height);
```

```
pArray.set(bImage);

Texture2D tex = new Texture2D(Texture.BASE_LEVEL,
                Texture.RGB, width, height);
tex.setImage(0, pArray);
tex.setEnable(true);

// Create a simple shape leaf node
Appearance a = new Appearance();
a.setTexture(tex);

TextureAttributes texAttr = new TextureAttributes();
texAttr.setTextureMode(TextureAttributes.MODULATE);
a.setTextureAttributes(texAttr);

Box textureCube = new Box(0.4f, 0.4f, 0.4f,
            Box.GENERATE_TEXTURE_COORDS, a);

objTrans.addChild(textureCube);

// Set up some lights (see Chapter 15 for details)
BoundingSphere bounds =
 new BoundingSphere(new Point3d(0.0,0.0,0.0), 100.0);

AmbientLight aLgt = new AmbientLight(alColor);
aLgt.setInfluencingBounds(bounds);
DirectionalLight lgt1 = new DirectionalLight(lColor1, lDir1);
lgt1.setInfluencingBounds(bounds);
DirectionalLight lgt2 = new DirectionalLight(lColor2, lDir2);
lgt2.setInfluencingBounds(bounds);
objRoot.addChild(aLgt);
objRoot.addChild(lgt1);
objTrans.addChild(lgt2);

// Create a new Behavior object that will perform the desired
// operation on the specified transform object and add it
// into the scene graph. See Chapter 13 for details.
Transform3D yAxis = new Transform3D();
Alpha rotorAlpha = new Alpha(-1, Alpha.INCREASING_ENABLE,
                0, 0,
                4000, 0, 0,
                0, 0, 0);

RotationInterpolator rotator =
 new RotationInterpolator(rotorAlpha,
```

```java
                    objTrans,
                    yAxis,
                    0.0f,
                    (float) Math.PI*2.0f);

    rotator.setSchedulingBounds(bounds);
    objTrans.addChild(rotator);

    // Have Java 3D perform optimizations on this scene graph.
    objRoot.compile();

    return objRoot;
  }

  public TextureTest() {
   setLayout(new BorderLayout());
    GraphicsConfiguration config =
    SimpleUniverse.getPreferredConfiguration();

    Canvas3D c = new Canvas3D(config);
    add("Center", c);

    // Create a simple scene and attach it to the virtual universe
    BranchGroup scene = createSceneGraph();
    SimpleUniverse u = new SimpleUniverse(c);

    // This will move the ViewPlatform back a bit so the
    // objects in the scene can be viewed.
    u.getViewingPlatform().setNominalViewingTransform();

    u.addBranchGraph(scene); // add scene to universe
  }

  // The following allows TextureTest to be run as an
  // application as well as an applet
  public static void main(String[] args) {
   new MainFrame(new TextureTest(), 256, 256);
  }
}
```

Texture3D (javax.media.j3d.Texture3D)

Like Texture2D, Texture3D is a concrete subclass of the abstract Texture class. Texture3D extends Texture by adding a third coordinate, R, which allows developers to create three dimensional texture images that have depth. Texture3D is typically used to create volume textures, such as those often used in scientific or medical imaging (MRI scans, for example, might produce 3D volume textures that can be used to texture map the *inside* of a human body as well as the body surface). Texture3D extends Texture by adding new constructors (Table 14.31) and methods (Table 14.32) related the extra R depth dimension supported by these unique textures.

Because Texture3D extends Texture, it supports all of the features describe in the previous Texture and Texture2D sections. Texture3D's dimension of depth is the only feature that Texture2D does not support, although in in-depth discussion of this capability is beyond the scope of this book.

Tip

Volume texture is an advanced topic that is beyond the scope of this book. For links to various volume texture resources, including Java 3D sites, visit the Web3D Gallery at http://www.web3dgallery.com/.

Note: Texture3D Fields and Methods

Like Texture2D, the Texture3D class is a concrete class derived from the abstract Texture class described earlier. Unlike Texture2D, which does not define its own fields and methods, the Texture3D actually defines a number of its own methods in addition to using those defined by the abstract Texture class. Of particular interest are the two getBoundaryModeR() methods shown in Table 14.32, which are unique to Texture3D.

Table 14.31	Texture3D Constructor Summary (javax.media.j3d.Texture3D)

```
public Texture3D()
```
Constructs a Texture3D object with default parameters.

```
public Texture3D(int mipmapMode, int format, int width,
int height, int depth)
```
Constructs an empty Texture3D object with specified mipmapMode format, width, height, and depth.

Table 14.32	Texture3D Method Summary

This table contains a summary of accessor and mutator methods defined in the class javax.media.j3d.Texture3D. See the Java 3D API Specification (http://java.sun.com/products/java-media/3D/) for a complete listing of all methods supported by this class.

Returns	*Method Name, Parameters, and Description*
int	**getBoundaryModeR**() Retrieves the boundary mode for the R coordinate.
int	**getDepth**() Retrieves the depth of this Texture3D object.
void	**setBoundaryModeR**(int boundaryModeR) Sets the boundary mode for the R coordinate in this texture object.

MIP Mapping

Unlike VRML, Java 3D supports multiple levels of textures, a technique commonly known as *MIP mapping*. MIP is an acronym for the Latin saying *multum in parvo* ("many things in a small space"), while the 3D computer graphics term "MIP map" (and its simplified contraction "mipmap") refer to the practice of using a series of images to texture map a single object. In other words, mipmap refers to multilevel texturing where an image is supplied for texture mapping a single geometric form.

MIP mapping is the texture-mapping equivalent of geometric Level of Detail (LOD), a popular optimization technique that allows the quality of the geometric shape to change depending on the user's proximity to it (Java 3D supports LOD through the javax.media.j3d.DistanceLOD class). A car created with LOD might actually be comprised of three or four different models, for example, which range in quality and polygon count from very high (best quality, slowest to render) to very low (worst quality, fastest to render). The level of detail can change dynamically depending on how close the user is to the vehicle; the highest quality model is used when the car is closest to the user, while progressively lower quality models can be displayed as the car moves further and further away.

Similarly, a MIP mapped car might be mapped with an extremely high quality texture image when the model is very close to the viewer and progressively lower quality images for progressively further distances. Because the high quality image is only necessary when the car is closest to the user, there is no need to waste precious CPU cycles in the mapping process when the car is further away. Instead, lower quality images created at smaller dimensions can be used, taking a significant burden off the rendering engine (why map a large, full color image to the car when it is too far away to be appreciated?).

Java 3D's texture mapping classes inherently support MIP mapping, as you can see from the various Texture, Texture2D, and Texture3D tables that appear earlier in this chapter. Using this technique, you can supply a unique texture image for each "level" of quality, as specified by the *level* field of Texture's `setImage()` method (see Table 14.29). The base level is equal to 0, which is why we've supplied 0 as the *level* parameter in all previous examples. MIP mapping wasn't used in these examples, and so a single texture map image was loaded at the base level of 0.

To actually utilize mipmap textures in Java 3D, the developer must alert the Texture2D or Texture3D objects accordingly. This involves setting the *mipMapMode* MULTI_LEVEL_MIPMAP flag (see Table 14.28) when invoking the texture constructor as illustrated in the following code sample:

```
Texture2D t = new Texture2D(Texture.MULTI_LEVEL_MIPMAP,
        Texture.RGB, imageWidth, imageHeight);

// ..assume that we're loading this image into
// mipmap level 5 now, after having loaded all previous
// levels already:
t.setImage(5, image);
```

Typically, the size of each mipmap texture dimension is _ the size of the previous image, continuing in such a fashion until a height or width of 1 pixel is reached. For instance, if the highest quality texture image is 256x64, the succeeding texture dimensions would be 128x32, 64x16, 32x8, 16x4, 8x2, 4x1, 2x1, and finally 1x1. Such textures can be created programmatically in Java 3D (a new image can be created at each size by scaling the original, full-sized image), or using an image editing tool such as Adobe Photoshop. When rendering an on-screen object that has been outfitted with mipmap textures, Java 3D uses the texture image that is closest in size the size of the object.

Transforming Textures

When customizing the appearance of Java 3D objects with textures, you will often find that the texture doesn't map onto the object exactly as you'd like. At other times, you might prefer to have the texture tile across the surface of the object, rather than stretch to cover it. In such cases, you must transform the texture during the mapping processes.

Using the `setBoundaryMode()` methods, you can control how a texture is rendered across the surface of an object. There are separate methods for the both the S and T directions (corresponding to the width and height of the surface, respectively), providing us with a great deal of precision over how the object is rendered. For example, you could stretch the texture for the height and tile it across the width with the following bit of code:

```
texture.setBoundaryModeS(Texture.WRAP);
texture.setBoundaryModeT(Texture.CLAMP);
```

As you may recall from the previous discussion on WRAP and CLAP, the CLAMP mode tells Java 3D to pin the edge of the texture to the edge of the object. As the object changes in size, that direction of the texture is stretched to fit. By using WRAP, the texture stays the same size, as it is tiled across the object as many times as necessary to cover the entire surface.

Regardless of whether you tile or stretch textures, you'll often find that they do not map onto the surface to your satisfaction. Perhaps, for example, the center of the image and the center of the surface don't quite match up as you expected they would. Similarly, you might feel the urge to rotate the texture just a bit to make it more attractive when applied to a particular shape. In such situations, you will use the `setTextureTransform()` method defined by the TextureAttributes class described earlier in this chapter.

The `setTextureTransform()` method takes a Transform3D instance (created from the same Transform3D class discussed in Chapter 13, "Customizing Size, Location, and Orientation") and uses the values it contains to modify the appearance of the texture. Using the Transform3D to move textures as described here is not much different than using it to move whole objects as described in Chapter 13. In both cases, the methods that you use are the same (just be sure to keep the values that you supply between 0 and 1 for translations in order to stay within the legal range for texture coordinates).

When translating an image, a value of 1 refers to the width of the image. Therefore, if you translate the image by a value of 1, you will move it along the object's surface by the full width of the image. A value of 2 will move it two widths, and so on. This transform is independent of the size of the image. Usually there is no good reason to supply a translation value of 1, as the texture will move off the end of the object as a result. Instead, it makes better sense to use a small value between 0 and 1 to tweak the final position.

Note

To dynamically change the texture transformation, you must first set the ALLOW_TRANSFORM_WRITE capability bit. You should also note that changing the Transform3D values alone does not automatically update the texture; you must set the transform again by calling the setTexture-Transform() method every time that you make a change, as explained in Chapter 13, "Customizing Size, Location, and Orientation."

Summary

Java 3D's color, lighting, and shading models are very similar to those used by VRML. As a result, having a familiarity with VRML coloring and texturing (as discussed in Chapter 8) makes it relatively easy to learn how to customize the color and texture of Java 3D objects.

Like VRML, Java 3D appearances are encapsulated into an Appearance node. A subclass of NodeComponent, Appearance objects are node components that can be referenced by Shape3D objects (as well as primitive shapes defined by Sun's convenience utility package). Appearance objects can reference one or more node component objects (such as ColoringAttributes, TransparencyAttributes, TextureAttributes, Material, and Texture objects), leading to the notion of an *appearance bundle*.

Adding a Material component to an appearance bundle enables lighting for a shape, in which case the colors defined by Material are used. Shapes that are not lit are colored with ColoringAttributes colors (ColoringAttributes is also used to specify the shade model used to render a shape). Shapes that specify per-vertex geometry colors are rendered using per-vertex colors even if ColoringAttributes or Material colors are specified; per-vertex colors have precedence over ColoringAttributes and Material colors.

Adding a TransparencyAttributes object to a shape's appearance bundle allows you to customize transparency, although these transparency values may be overridden if a Texture object is also added. The Texture object is used to map a texture image to the surface of a shape (the rendering properties of which can be customized using a corresponding TextureAttributes object).

Java 3D appearances and materials can be shared by objects (referenced by more than one shape), just as VRML supports sharing of appearances (via

the DEF/USE mechanism). Sharing appearances can conserve valuable memory and processing cycles, resulting in faster and more efficient programs.
    Following is a complete list of URLs referenced in this chapter:

Core Web3D Web   http://www.CoreWeb3D.com/

Java 3D API Specification http://java.sun.com/products/java-media/3D/

Universal Media   http://www.web3d.org/WorkingGroup/media/

CUSTOMIZING BACKGROUND, FOG, LIGHTING, AND SOUND

Topics in This Chapter

- Understanding bounding regions
- Creating background colors and images
- Creating linear and exponential fog effects
- Lighting scenes with directional, point, and spot light sources
- Adding point and background sound sources to scenes

Chapter 15

By now you know the basics of creating virtual worlds. You can create an empty universe, fill it with objects, adjust the colors and materials of those objects, build object hierarchies, and even load complete VRML worlds. However, there's still more to learn about Java 3D. In this chapter we'll see how to enhance our worlds by adding backdrops, lights, sound sources, and fog. We'll be building on our VRML Viewer example from Chapter 13, "Customizing Size, Location, and Orientation," and enhancing it using these new techniques.

In this chapter you'll learn how to enhance your Java 3D universes with backgrounds, fog, lighting, and sound. You'll also discover the importance of bounding regions, which are used to limit the effects of these features.

Note

Although a number of vital Java 3D concepts are covered in this section of Core Web3D, *we've only scratched at the surface of Java 3D. If you'd like to learn about programming Java 3D in greater detail, visit the* Core Java 3D *web site at http://www.CoreJava3D.com/. As a companion title to* Core Web3D, Core Java 3D *is dedicated entirely to Java 3D programming. Because you've already purchased* Core Web3D, *you'll be given access to several online* Core Java 3D *chapters that are not available to the general public.*

Note: Core Web3D Code

Source code listings for this (and all other) Core Web3D *chapters are available online at http://www.CoreWeb3D.com/.*

Bounding Regions

Before we start using these new features, though, you must understand a concept that's common to all of them—bounding regions. A bounding region is a volume of space that contains objects that are affected by a particular background, light, sound, or fog. By associating each of these "environmental" nodes with a bounding region, we can easily limit the range of their effect on the scene.

To see why this is important, consider the following hypothetical example. You've built a small virtual house, three stories high with a number of rooms. Your living room is well lit, with a number of floor lamps and an overhead light. The basement, immediately below it, is quiet and dark, lit by a single candle. The television is on in the living room, while upstairs a small portable radio is playing. The kitchen is full of smoke from a roast that's burning in the oven.

Sounds great, but it won't work! Without bounding regions, the lights from the living room would illuminate the basement as well, the transistor radio overhead would be louder than the television across the room from you, and the smoke from the kitchen would fill the house. This is because light, sound, and fog nodes normally have no limits to their effect aside from plain old distance, and the result is a virtual world that's not very much like our real one.

The way to get around these problems is to use bounding regions. You would set up regions such that your television could be heard only within the living room, and the radio could be heard only upstairs. The bounds around the kitchen would contain the fog for the smoke, and the lights from the living room wouldn't affect the basement.

There are three basic types of bounding volume in Java 3D: BoundingBox, BoundingSphere, and BoundingPolytope (see Tables 15.1 and 15.2). A *bounding box* is a rectangular box aligned with the X, Y, and Z axes. A *bounding sphere* is simply a sphere with a particular center point and radius. A *bounding polytope* is a set of mathematical planes that enclose a convex region of space, which is ideal for enclosing an arbitrary volume.

Which shape to use depends on your application. If you're creating the interior of a house, as we did in our little "thought experiment" above, then it makes sense to use bounding boxes that correspond to the rectangular rooms. If you're dealing with something like the sphere of influence of a light source or sound source, a bounding sphere might make more sense. And if you're dealing with a really peculiar shape, a bounding polytope might be the best way to go.

Every light, sound, background, and fog node must have a bounding region associated with it. By default, the bounding regions are null and the nodes have no effect, leading to one of the most common problems encountered by programmers new to Java 3D. For example, they will create a fog bank and then wonder why it has no effect on their scene. To remedy the situation a bounding region must be set, as the following code examples illustrate.

Tip

By default bounding regions are null, and the nodes have no effect. In order to use bounding regions you must actually set them, as shown in the following code examples.

Table 15.1   Bounding-Region Constructors

BoundingBox, BoundingSphere, and BoundingPolytope classes are used to create bounding-region objects. These classes extend the abstract class javax.media.j3d.Bounds. (See the Java 3D API Specification (http://java.sun.com/products/java-media/3D/) for details.)

BoundingBox

BoundingBox defines an axis-aligned bounding box for use as a bounding region.

`public BoundingBox()`

Constructs and initializes a default bounding box (a 2X unity cube built around the origin 0 0 0, such that $-1 <= x,y,z <= 1$).

`public BoundingBox(Bounds boundsObject)`

Constructs a bounding box from a bounding object.

`public BoundingBox(Bounds[] bounds)`

Constructs a bounding box from an array of bounding objects.

```
public BoundingBox(Point3d lower, Point3d upper)
```

Constructs and initializes a bounding box from the given minimum and maximum in x,y,z.

BoundingSphere

BoundingSphere defines a spherical bounding region that is defined by a center point and a radius.

```
public BoundingSphere()
```

Constructs and initializes a default bounding sphere (built around the origin 0 0 0, with radius = 1).

```
public BoundingSphere(Bounds boundsObject)
```

Constructs and initializes a bounding sphere from a bounding object.

```
public BoundingSphere(Bounds[] boundsObjects)
```

Constructs and initializes a bounding sphere from an array of bounding objects.

```
public BoundingSphere(Point3d center, double radius)
```

Constructs and initializes a bounding sphere from a center and radius.

BoundingPolytope

BoundingPolytope defines a polyhedral bounding region from the intersection of three or more half-spaces. The region defined by a BoundingPolytope is always convex and must be closed.

```
public BoundingPolytope()
```

Constructs and initializes a default bounding polytope as a set of 6 planes that defines a cube (such that -1 <= x,y,z <= 1).

```
public BoundingPolytope(Bounds boundsObject)
```

Constructs a BoundingPolytope from the specified bounds object.

```
public BoundingPolytope(Bounds[] boundsObjects)
```

Constructs a BoundingPolytope from the specified array of bounds objects.

```
public BoundingPolytope(Vector4d[] planes)
```

Constructs a BoundingPolytope using the specified planes.

Table 15.2	Common Bounding Region Methods

As bounding regions, the BoundingBox, BoundingSphere, and BoundingPolytope classes have a large number of methods in common. Each class also has methods that are unique to it, such as "get" and "set" methods, which are not listed here. BoundingSphere objects, for example, support a **setRadius**(double r) method that is used to set spherical bounding region to a radius based on a double-precision value. See the Java 3D API Specification (http://java.sun.com/products/java-media/3D/) for details.

Common Methods

Returns	*Method Name, Parameters, and Description*
Object	**clone**()
	Creates a copy of this bounding region.
Bounds	**closestIntersection**(Bounds[] boundsObjects)
	Finds closest bounding object that intersects this bounding region.
void	**combine**(Bounds boundsObject)
	Combines this bounding region with a bounding object.
void	**combine**(Bounds[] bounds)
	Combines this bounding region with an array of bounding objects.
void	**combine**(Point3d point)
	Combines this bounding region with a point.
void	**combine**(Point3d[] points)
	Combines this bounding region with an array of points.
boolean	**equals**(java.lang.Object bounds)
	Indicates whether the specified bounds object.
int	**hashCode**()
	Returns a hash-code value for this bounding-region object.
boolean	**intersect**(Bounds boundsObject)
	Tests for intersection with another bounds object.
boolean	**intersect**(Bounds[] boundsObjects)
	Tests for intersection with an array of bounds objects.
boolean	**intersect**(Point3d point)
	Tests for intersection with a point.
boolean	**intersect**(Point3d origin, Vector3d direction)
	Tests for intersection with a ray.

Common Methods

Returns	Method Name, Parameters, and Description
boolean	**isEmpty**() Tests whether the bounding region is empty.
void	**set**(Bounds boundsObject) Sets the value of this bounding region.
String	**toString**() Returns a string representation of this class.
void	**transform**(Bounds boundsObject, Transform3D matrix) Modifies the bounding region so that it encloses the volume generated by transforming the given bounding object.
void	**transform**(Transform3D matrix) Transforms this bounding region by the given matrix.

Backgrounds

If you're already familiar with the Background node in VRML...then forget everything you know! Java 3D has a much simpler (and unfortunately, less flexible) background capability than VRML. As you may recall from Chapter 9, "Customizing Light, Background, Fog, and Sound," VRML can surround the user with six different texture-mapped images and a sky/ground background beyond that. In contrast, Java 3D offers a Background class that gives you only a choice of a solid color or a single, static background image (see Tables 15.3 through 15.5). The background image does not move as you change your point of view—it's like a backdrop that gets drawn first, before the scene is rendered in front of it.

This can be fairly limiting, but for many applications it works just fine. If you need something more sophisticated, you can always implement it yourself by creating a texture-mapped sphere around your world. This sphere (or box, or any other shape) can be made part of the "background geometry" of the scene, so that it's always rendered first before anything else.

In order to illustrate how backgrounds work, we're going to use our VView application from a previous chapter (see Chapter 13, "Customizing Size, Location, and Orientation"). We'll start by creating a bounding region, which will be a slightly scaled-up version of the bounding sphere we computed in order to position our viewpoint (see Listing 15.1).

```
sceneBounds.setRadius(temp.z * 2.0);
```

This doubles the size of the bounding sphere, which should be plenty even if we move around a bit. Next, we'll create a new BranchGroup that will contain the background, fog, and light nodes we'll be creating in this chapter.

```
BranchGroup environment = new BranchGroup();
```

Now we're ready to actually create the background. We'll start with a simple greenish-blue sky:

```
Background bg = new Background(0.0f, 0.75f, 0.25f);
```

The three floating-point numbers that are passed to the constructor are the RGB values (see Chapter 14, "Customizing Color and Texture," for details). The red component is 0.0, the green component is 0.75, and the blue component is 0.25. Note that simply creating this Background isn't enough—we need to set its bounding region like so:

```
bg.setApplicationBounds(sceneBounds);
```

This tells the Background that it should be active whenever the user is within the specified bounds, which in our case is a sphere centered on the world, with a radius twice that of the world's bounding sphere.

Our next step is to add the Background node to the environment Branch-Group:

```
environment.addChild(bg);
```

Even though the Background is part of a different BranchGraph than the rest of the world, it will still affect everything within its ApplicationBounds.

Our final step is to add the environment BranchGroup to the universe. Note that we do this last, since it has the effect of making this BranchGroup "live" and therefore unchangeable:

```
universe.addBranchGraph(environment);
```

Notice that again we are taking advantage of the handy methods that the SimpleUniverse class provides to relieve us of the burden of dealing with Locales.

Listing 15.1 provides a completed background example.

Listing 15.1   VView.java (Example 3)

```
// Show how the Background node works
// Written by Bernie Roehl, October 1999
// CONVERTING TO AN APPLET:
// To convert this application into an applet you must construct
// a standard init() method that contains the code now in the VView
// constructor. From within the init() method you will invoke the VRML
// loader's load(URL) method, as the load(String) method currently used
// by this application can't be used in an applet (a security exception
// is thrown by the applet when loading a VRML world from a String).
//
// To convert to an applet, simply rename the following method:
//               public VView(String avatar)
// to:
//               public void init()
//
// Next, use the applet's getParameter() method to retrieve the
// name of the VRML file to load and place the resulting string into the
// "avatar" variable. The following code assumes that a PARAM named
// "world" is in the corresponding HTML Web page for this applet:
//    String  avatar = getParameter("world");
//
// Finally, change the VRML loader's load(String) method so that it
// is passed an absolute URL. For example:
//   scene = loader.load(new java.net.URL(getCodeBase(), avatar +
//   ".wrl"));
//
// Visit the Core Web3D web site at http://www.CoreWeb3D.com/ to
// obtain code listings from this book, including an applet version of this
// VView program.

import java.awt.*;
import java.applet.Applet;
import java.util.*;import javax.media.j3d.*;
import javax.vecmath.*;
import com.sun.j3d.utils.applet.MainFrame;
import com.sun.j3d.utils.universe.*;
import com.sun.j3d.loaders.vrml97.VrmlLoader;
import com.sun.j3d.loaders.Scene;

public class VView extends Applet {

    SimpleUniverse universe;    // the universe
    Scene scene = null;         // the VRML scene
```

```
public VView(String avatar) {
      setLayout(new BorderLayout());
      Canvas3D canvas = new Canvas3D(null);
      add("Center",canvas);

      universe = new SimpleUniverse(canvas);
      ViewingPlatform viewingPlatform =
            universe.getViewingPlatform();
      TransformGroup vpTransGroup =
            viewingPlatform.getViewPlatformTransform();
      View view = (universe.getViewer()).getView();

      VrmlLoader loader = new VrmlLoader();
      try { scene = loader.load(avatar + ".wrl"); }
      catch (Exception e) {
            System.out.println(
                  "Exception loading file from path:"
                  + avatar + ".wrl");
            System.exit(1);
      }

      // get the scene group from the loaded VRML scene
      BranchGroup sceneGroup = scene.getSceneGroup();
      sceneGroup.setCapability(
            BranchGroup.ALLOW_DETACH);
      sceneGroup.setCapability(
            BranchGroup.ALLOW_BOUNDS_READ);

      // make the VRML scene live
      universe.addBranchGraph(sceneGroup);

      // find the radius and center of
      // the scene's bounding sphere

      BoundingSphere sceneBounds =
            (BoundingSphere)sceneGroup.getBounds();
      double radius = sceneBounds.getRadius();
      Point3d center = new Point3d();
      sceneBounds.getCenter(center);

      // now move the viewpoint back
      Vector3d temp = new Vector3d(center);
      temp.z += 1.4 * radius
            / Math.tan(view.getFieldOfView() / 2.0);

      // set that viewpoint into the viewing transform
```

```
    Transform3D viewTransform = new Transform3D();
    viewTransform.set(temp);
    vpTransGroup.setTransform(viewTransform);

    // increase the size of the sceneBounds,
    // for later use
    sceneBounds.setRadius(temp.z * 2.0);

    // create a new branchgroup for holding the
    // lights, sounds, background and fog
    BranchGroup environment = new BranchGroup();

    // add a background to the scene
    Background bg = new Background(
            0.0f, 0.75f, 0.25f);
    bg.setApplicationBounds(sceneBounds);
    environment.addChild(bg);

    universe.addBranchGraph(environment);
  }

  public static void main(String[] args) {
    new MainFrame(new VView(args[0]), 320, 400);
  }
}
```

We'll run it again, using the simple "Human.wrl" file:

```
java VView Human
```

The result is shown in Figure 15-1.

Now we'll enhance our example by adding a texture map. To do this, we have to import the TextureLoader class from the Java 3D image utilities:

```
import com.sun.j3d.utils.image.TextureLoader;
```

Next we'll load a sky texture and set it as the image for the Background node. Following is the revised code for setting up the background.

```
// add a background to the scene
Background bg = new Background(0.0f, 0.75f, 0.25f);
bg.setApplicationBounds(sceneBounds);
TextureLoader sky = new TextureLoader("sky.jpg", this);
bg.setImage(sky.getImage());
environment.addChild(bg);
```

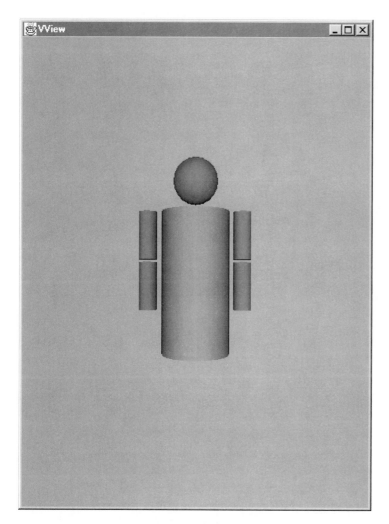

Figure 15-1   Our simple humanoid, against a solid background color.

Notice that we still create the Background node with a color. If we set a texture, the color value is ignored—the image takes priority over the color. The texture gets tiled if necessary, so be sure to choose a "tileable" image. Figure 15-2 shows the Human.wrl file with a cloudy sky behind it.

When we say that a texture gets "tiled," we mean that it gets repeated many times and laid side-to-side and end-to-end, like the tiles on a floor. In order for the tiles to fit together properly, you need to make sure that the

Figure 15-2   Using an image as a backdrop, rather than a solid color.

left and right edges of the image match up and the top and bottom edges match up.

The easiest way to do this is to bring the image into a paint program, copy it, and lay it side-to-side left-to-right, but with the right half mirror-imaged so that you have the right edge lined up against a copy of itself on the left.

Then smooth out the differences between the two. Repeat with the top and bottom edges, then pick some subimage (with the same dimensions as the original image) and save it out as the tile.

If you're not up to creating your own textures, you can always use the freely available Universal Media textures. Available through the Web3D Consortium at http://www.web3d.org/WorkingGroups/media/, Universal Media contains thousands of professional-level textures, sounds, and 3D objects that you can use free of charge in your own worlds.

Table 15.3   Background Constructor Summary

The Background class extends javax.media.j3d.Leaf. Background defines either a solid background color or a background image that fills the window at the beginning of each new frame. It optionally allows background geometry to be referenced (pretessellated onto a unit sphere, drawn at infinity). The Background class specifies an application region in which this background is active. See the Java 3D API Specification (http://java.sun.com/products/java-media/3D/) for details.

`public Background()`

Constructs a Background node with default parameters of color = black (0, 0, 0) while image, geometry, application bounds, and application bounding leaf are all set to null.

`public Background(BranchGroup branch)`

Constructs a Background node with the specified geometry.

`public Background(Color3f color)`

Constructs a Background node with the specified color.

`public Background(float r, float g, float b)`

Constructs a Background node with the specified color.

`public Background(ImageComponent2D image)`

Constructs a Background node with the specified image.

Table 15.4   Background Field Summary

Fields defined by the class javax.media.j3d.Background. All fields are defined as `public static final int`. See the Java 3D API Specification (http://java.sun.com/products/java-media/3D/) for details.

`ALLOW_APPLICATION_BOUNDS_READ`

Specifies that the Background allows read access to its application bounds and bounding leaf at runtime.

ALLOW_APPLICATION_BOUNDS_WRITE

Specifies that the Background allows write access to its application bounds and bounding leaf at runtime.

ALLOW_COLOR_READ

Specifies that the Background allows read access to its color at runtime.

ALLOW_COLOR_WRITE

Specifies that the Background allows write access to its color at runtime.

ALLOW_GEOMETRY_READ

Specifies that the Background allows read access to its background geometry at runtime.

ALLOW_GEOMETRY_WRITE

Specifies that the Background allows write access to its background geometry at runtime.

ALLOW_IMAGE_READ

Specifies that the Background allows read access to its image at runtime.

ALLOW_IMAGE_WRITE

Specifies that the Background allows write access to its image at runtime.

Table 15.5   Background Method Summary

Public methods defined in the class javax.media.j3d.Background. See the Java 3D API Specification (http://java.sun.com/products/java-media/3D/) for details.

Returns	*Method Name, Parameters, and Description*
Node	**cloneNode**(boolean forceDuplicate)
	Creates a new instance of the node.
void	**duplicateNode**(Node originalNode, boolean forceDuplicate)
	Copies all node information from originalNode into the current node.
BoundingLeaf	**getApplicationBoundingLeaf**()
	Retrieves the Background node's application bounding leaf.
Bounds	**getApplicationBounds**()
	Retrieves the Background node's application bounds.
void	**getColor**(Color3f color)
	Retrieves the background color.
BranchGroup	**getGeometry**()
	Retrieves the background geometry.

Returns	Method Name, Parameters, and Description
ImageComponent2D	**getImage**()
	Retrieves the background image.
void	**setApplicationBoundingLeaf**(BoundingLeaf region)
	Sets the Background's application region to the specified bounding leaf.
void	**setApplicationBounds**(Bounds region)
	Sets the Background's application region to the specified bounds.
void	**setColor**(Color3f color)
	Sets the background color to the specified color.
void	**setColor**(float r, float g, float b)
	Sets the background color to the specified color.
void	**setGeometry**(BranchGroup branch)
	Sets the background geometry to the specified Branch-Group node.
void	**setImage**(ImageComponent2D image)
	Sets the background image to the specified image.
void	**updateNodeReferences**(NodeReferenceTable referenceTable)
	Callback used to allow a node to check if any scene-graph objects referenced by that node have been duplicated via a call to cloneTree.

Fog

Fog is a surprisingly useful feature that can increase the realism of your scenes and improve their performance by allowing you to reduce the amount of detail required in the distance. In the real world, distant objects seem to fade slightly because the light reflected from them has to travel farther through the earth's atmosphere (see Chapter 3, "Entering the Third Dimension" for details). Depending on the atmospheric conditions, this fading effect can be quite extreme. This fog effect is sometimes called "depth cueing" (since it gives the brain a visual cue as to the depth of an object in the scene) and it is implemented in Java 3D by simply blending the fog color with the objects in the scene based on distance from the viewer. The farther away a particular pixel on the screen is from the viewpoint (in terms of Z-depth), the more it gets blended with the fog color.

Like VRML, Java 3D supports two basic types of fog. Linear fog has a constant density, so that an object that's twice as far away appears to be twice as "fogged" (see Tables 15.6 through 15.8). Exponential fog has a density value that can be set by your application (see Tables 15.9 through Table 15.11). In general, linear fog is useful for depth cueing, while exponential fog is better for simulating atmospheric effects (see Chapter 9, "Customizing Light, Background, Fog, and Sound," to learn more about linear and exponential fog types used by VRML).

Linear fog has a pair of distance values that define the "fog bank." Anything closer than the front distance is not fogged at all, anything beyond the back distance is completely obscured by the fog, and anything in between the two distances is fogged depending on the distance.

Tip

Set your far fog distance to correspond with the back distance in a Clip object, so that anything which would be completely obscured by fog will be clipped out and not even rendered.

Exponential fog does not use distances but instead provides a "density" value that is, essentially, an exponent of the fogging based on distance. Therefore a nearby object will hardly be fogged at all, but a distant object will be exponentially more heavily fogged.

Adding fog to a scene is easy. First we get rid of the background image, since it doesn't get fogged and therefore spoils the effect. Next, we add the following lines of code to our example program:

```
LinearFog fog = new LinearFog(0.25f, 0.75f, 0.0f);
fog.setInfluencingBounds(sceneBounds);
fog.setBackDistance(temp.z * 2.0f);
environment.addChild(fog);
```

This creates a linear fog that's greenish-red in hue (red is set to 0.25, green to 0.75, and blue to 0.0). The same bounds that we computed earlier are now set as the influencing bounds for the fog bank. Although the front distance remains at its default value of 0.1 meter, the back distance has been pushed back from 1.0 to twice the depth value (so that the fog doesn't obscure anything completely). Finally, the fog is added to the environment. Figure 15-3 shows the effect of this linear fog.

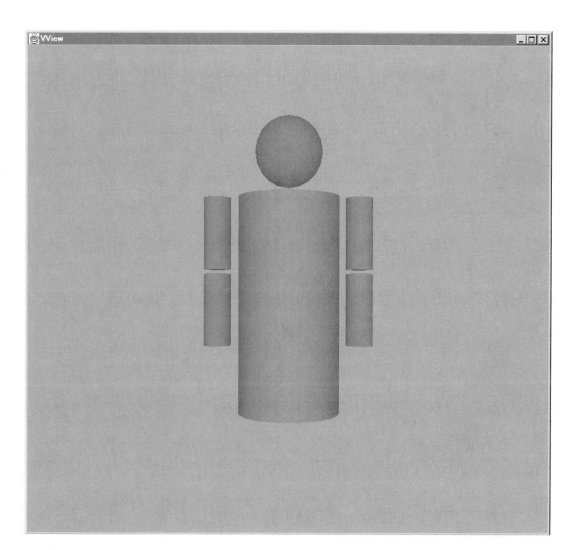

Figure 15-3 A foggy day in the virtual world. This linear fog effect was created using the LinearFog class.

Using Java 3D's exponential fog class is not much different. Instead of setting the back distance, we set an exponent value (or density), as the following snippet of code illustrates:

```
ExponentialFog fog = new ExponentialFog(
    0.25f, 0.75f, 0.0f);
fog.setInfluencingBounds(sceneBounds);
```

```
fog.setDensity(5.0f);
environment.addChild(fog);
```

A high density value, such as 5.0 used in this example, produces a heavy fog. In this example the effect is much like pea soup, as seen in Figure 15-4.

Tip

For maximum effect, the fog color and the background color should be the same. Then objects that are far away and heavily fogged appear to blend into the background color and disappear.

Note that LinearFog and ExponentialFog are both subclasses of the abstract Fog class. This means that (in theory) other types of fog could be defined and added later on. Also notice that there are strong similarities between the fog nodes in Java 3D and those in VRML, which can again be attributed to their common history.

Figure 15-4   This heavy fog effect was created using the ExponentialFog class.

Table 15.6   LinearFog Constructor Summary

Constructors for the class javax.media.j3d.LinearFog, which is a leaf node that defines fog distance parameters for linear fog. LinearFog is a subclass of the abstract javax.media.j3d.Fog class. See the Java 3D API Specification (http://java.sun.com/products/java-media/3D/) for details.

public LinearFog()

Constructs a LinearFog node with default parameters.

public LinearFog(Color3f color)

Constructs a LinearFog node with the specified fog color.

public LinearFog(Color3f color, double frontDistance, double backDistance)

Constructs a LinearFog node with the specified fog color and distances.

public LinearFog(float r, float g, float b)

Constructs a LinearFog node with the specified fog color.

public LinearFog(float r, float g, float b, double frontDistance, double backDistance)

Constructs a LinearFog node with the specified fog color and distances.

Table 15.7   LinearFog Field Summary

Fields defined by the class javax.media.j3d.LinearFog. These fields are defined as `public static final int`. LinearFog also inherits a number of fields from the abstract Fog class (see Table 15.12). See the Java 3D API Specification (http://java.sun.com/products/java-media/3D/) for details.

ALLOW_DISTANCE_READ

Specifies that this LinearFog node allows read access to its distance information.

ALLOW_DISTANCE_WRITE

Specifies that this LinearFog node allows write access to its distance information.

Table 15.8   LinearFog Method Summary

Public methods defined in the class javax.media.j3d.LinearFog. LinearFog also inherits a number of methods from the abstract Fog class (see Table 15.13). See the Java 3D API Specification (http://java.sun.com/products/java-media/3D/) for details.

Returns	*Method Name, Parameters, and Description*
Node	**cloneNode**(boolean forceDuplicate)
	Used to create a new instance of the node.
double	**getBackDistance**()
	Gets back distance for fog.
double	**getFrontDistance**()
	Gets front distance for fog.
void	**setBackDistance**(double backDistance)
	Sets back distance for fog.
void	**setFrontDistance**(double frontDistance)
	Sets front distance for fog.

Table 15.9   ExponentialFog Constructor Summary

Constructors for the class javax.media.j3d.ExponentialFog, which is a leaf node used to set fog density parameters for exponential fog. Like LinearFog, ExponentialFog is a subclass of the abstract javax.media.j3d.Fog class. See the Java 3D API Specification (http://java.sun.com/products/java-media/3D/) for details.

public ExponentialFog()

Constructs an ExponentialFog node with default parameters.

public ExponentialFog(Color3f color)

Constructs an ExponentialFog node with the specified fog color.

public ExponentialFog(Color3f color, float density)

Constructs an ExponentialFog node with the specified fog color and density.

public ExponentialFog(float r, float g, float b)

Constructs an ExponentialFog node with the specified fog color.

public ExponentialFog(float r, float g, float b, float density)

Constructs an ExponentialFog node with the specified fog color and density.

Table 15.10   ExponentialFog Field Summary

Fields defined by the class javax.media.j3d.ExponentialFog. These fields are defined as public static final int. ExponentialFog also inherits a number of fields from the abstract Fog class (see Table 15.12). See the Java 3D API Specification (http://java.sun.com/products/java-media/3D/) for details.

ALLOW_DENSITY_READ

Specifies that this ExponentialFog node allows read access to its density information.

ALLOW_DENSITY_WRITE

Specifies that this ExponentialFog node allows write access to its density information.

Table 15.11   ExponentialFog Method Summary

Public methods defined in the class javax.media.j3d.ExponentialFog. Exponential-Fog also inherits a number of methods from the abstract Fog class (see Table 15.13). See the Java 3D API Specification (http://java.sun.com/products/java-media/3D/) for details.

Returns	Method Name, Parameters, and Description
Node	**cloneNode**(boolean forceDuplicate)
	Used to create a new instance of the node.
void	**duplicateNode**(Node originalNode, boolean forceDuplicate)
	Copies all node information from originalNode into the current node.
float	**getDensity**()
	Gets fog density.
void	**setDensity**(float density)
	Sets fog density.

Table 15.12   Fog Field Summary

Fields defined by the abstract class javax.media.j3d.Fog inherited by LinearFog and ExponentialFog subclasses (these fields are defined as public static final int). The Fog class is a leaf node (derived from javax.media.j3d.Leaf) that defines parameters common to all types of fog. Fog also specifies a region of influence in which this fog node is active. See the Java 3D API Specification (http://java.sun.com/products/java-media/3D/) for details.

ALLOW_COLOR_READ

Specifies that this Fog node allows read access to its color information.

ALLOW_COLOR_WRITE

Specifies that this Fog node allows write access to its color information.

ALLOW_INFLUENCING_BOUNDS_READ

Specifies that this Fog node allows read access to its influencing bounds and bounds leaf information.

ALLOW_INFLUENCING_BOUNDS_WRITE

Specifies that this Fog node allows write access to its influencing bounds and bounds leaf information.

ALLOW_SCOPE_READ

Specifies that this Fog node allows read access to its scope information at runtime.

ALLOW_SCOPE_WRITE

Specifies that this Fog node allows write access to its scope information at runtime.

Table 15.13   Fog Method Summary

Public methods defined in the abstract class javax.media.j3d.Fog that are inherited by LinearFog and ExponentialFog subclasses. The Fog class is a leaf node (derived from javax.media.j3d.Leaf) that defines capabilities and settings common to all types of fog. Fog also specifies a region of influence in which this fog node is active. See the Java 3D API Specification (http://java.sun.com/products/java-media/3D/) for details.

Returns	*Method Name, Parameters, and Description*
void	**addScope**(Group scope)
	Appends the specified Group node to this Fog node's list of scopes.
Enumeration	**getAllScopes**()
	Returns an enumeration of this Fog node's list of scopes.
void	**getColor**(Color3f color)
	Retrieves the fog color.
BoundingLeaf	**getInfluencingBoundingLeaf**()
	Retrieves the Fog node's influencing bounding leaf.
Bounds	**getInfluencingBounds**()
	Retrieves the Fog node's influencing bounds.
Group	**getScope**(int index)
	Retrieves the Group node at the specified index from this Fog node's list of scopes.
void	**insertScope**(Group scope,int index)
	Inserts the specified Group node into this Fog node's list of scopes at the specified index.
int	**numScopes**()
	Returns the number of nodes in this Fog node's list of scopes.

Returns	Method Name, Parameters, and Description
void	**removeScope**(int index)
	Removes the node at the specified index from this Fog node's list of scopes.
void	**setColor**(Color3f color)
	Sets the fog color to the specified color.
void	**setColor**(float r, float g, float b)
	Sets the fog color to the specified color.
void	**setInfluencingBoundingLeaf**(BoundingLeaf region)
	Sets the Fog's influencing region to the specified bounding leaf.
void	**setInfluencingBounds**(Bounds region)
	Sets the Fog's influencing region to the specified bounds.
void	**setScope**(Group scope, int index)
	Replaces the node at the specified index in this Fog node's list of scopes with the specified Group node.
void	**updateNodeReferences**(NodeReferenceTable referenceTable)
	Callback used to allow a node to check if any nodes referenced by that node have been duplicated via a call to `cloneTree`.

Lighting

There are four basic types of lighting in Java 3D. If you've already read the chapter on lighting in VRML (Chapter 9, "Customizing Light, Background, Fog, and Sound"), Java 3D's directional lights, point lights, and spot lights will seem quite familiar. There's also an ambient light, which has no explicit equivalent in VRML. In VRML, ambient light is a result of the ambient contribution from each of the light sources in the scene, whereas in Java 3D it's actually created explicitly.

All Java 3D lighting nodes are derived from an abstract Light base class. As a result, all Java 3D lights have an influencing bounds region, an on/off flag, and a color. Naturally, each type of light has unique features as well.

For the lighting examples that follow we'll be using the simple white sphere created in Listing 15.2. The VRML sphere created in Listing 15.2 offers enough detail that we can easily see the effects produced by each Java 3D light source discussed in the sections that follow. See Listing 15.3, later in this chapter, for the complete lighting example source code listing (snippets of Listing 15.3 are used in following sections to explain the various light classes offered by Java 3D).

Listing 15.2   VRMLSphere.wrl

```
#VRML V2.0 utf8

Shape {
    geometry Sphere { }
    appearance Appearance {
      material Material {
      diffuseColor 1 1 1
      }
    }
}
```

Note

Turn to the color plate section of this book to see various color screen shots of the Java 3D topics discussed in this chapter.

Table 15.14   Light Field Summary

Fields defined by the abstract class javax.media.j3d.Light. These fields are defined as public static final int and are inherited by subclasses AmbientLight, DirectionalLight, and PointLight (described in the following sections). The Light class is a leaf node (derived from javax.media.j3d.Leaf) that defines parameters common to all types of light. See the Java 3D API Specification (http://java.sun.com/products/java-media/3D/) for details.

ALLOW_COLOR_READ

Specifies that this Light allows read access to its color information at runtime.

ALLOW_COLOR_WRITE

Specifies that this Light allows write access to its color information at runtime.

ALLOW_INFLUENCING_BOUNDS_READ

Specifies that this Light allows read access to its influencing bounds and bounds leaf information.

ALLOW_INFLUENCING_BOUNDS_WRITE

Specifies that this Light allows write access to its influencing bounds and bounds leaf information.

ALLOW_SCOPE_READ

Specifies that this Light allows read access to its scope information at runtime.

ALLOW_SCOPE_WRITE

Specifies that this Light allows write access to its scope information at runtime.

ALLOW_STATE_READ

Specifies that this Light allows read access to its current state information at runtime.

ALLOW_STATE_WRITE

Specifies that this Light allows write access to its current state information at runtime.

Table 15.15   Light Method

Public methods defined in the abstract class javax.media.j3d.Light inherited by subclasses AmbientLight, DirectionalLight, and PointLight. The Light class is a leaf node (derived from javax.media.j3d.Leaf) that defines capabilities and settings common to all types of light. See the Java 3D API Specification (http://java.sun.com/products/java-media/3D/) for details.

Returns	*Method Name, Parameters, and Description*
void	**addScope**(Group scope) Appends the specified Group node to this Light node's list of scopes.
Enumeration	**getAllScopes**() Returns an enumeration of this Light node's list of scopes.
void	**getColor**(Color3f color) Gets this Light's current color and places it in the parameter specified.
boolean	**getEnable**() Retrieves this Light's current state (on/off).
BoundingLeaf	**getInfluencingBoundingLeaf**() Retrieves the Light node's influencing bounding leaf.
Bounds	**getInfluencingBounds**() Retrieves the Light node's influencing bounds.
Group	**getScope**(int index) Retrieves the Group node at the specified index from this Light node's list of scopes.

Returns	*Method Name, Parameters, and Description*
void	**insertScope**(Group scope, int index)
	Inserts the specified Group node into this Light node's list of scopes at the specified index.
int	**numScopes**()
	Returns the number of nodes in this Light node's list of scopes.
void	removeScope(int index)
	Removes the node at the specified index from this Light node's list of scopes.
void	**setColor**(Color3f color)
	Sets the Light's current color.
void	**setEnable**(boolean state)
	Turns the light on or off.
void	**setInfluencingBoundingLeaf**(BoundingLeaf region)
	Sets the Light's influencing region to the specified bounding leaf.
void	**setInfluencingBounds**(Bounds region)
	Sets the Light's influencing region to the specified bounds.
void	**setScope**(Group scope, int index)
	Replaces the node at the specified index in this Light node's list of scopes with the specified Group node.
void	**updateNodeReferences**(NodeReferenceTable referenceTable)
	Callback used to allow a node to check if any scene-graph objects referenced by that node have been duplicated via a call to `cloneTree`.

Directional Lights

A directional light source acts very much like the sun, in that all of its rays are parallel to one another and strike surfaces from a particular direction but with no particular source. In other words, the location of a DirectionalLight is irrelevant—it has the same effect no matter where it's located. The only properties you can set with a directional light source are the direction it's pointing in and the color of the light (see Tables 15.16, 15.17, and 15.18). (Learn more about directional light sources in Chapter 9, "Customizing Light, Background, Fog, and Sound.")

Creating a directional light source in Java 3D is easy. First we create a vector that gives the direction the light should point in:

```
Vector3f direction = new Vector3f(-1f, -1f, -1f);
```

Next, specify the color of light you want:

```
Color3f lightColor = new Color3f(1f, 0f, 0f);
```

After that, create the light itself and set its influencing bounds:

```
DirectionalLight dirLight = new DirectionalLight(
                        lightColor, direction);
dirLight.setInfluencingBounds(sceneBounds);
```

And finally, add the light to the environment:

```
environment.addChild(dirLight);
```

That's all there is to it. The scene is now illuminated by a sunlike directional light source, pointing down, to the left, and away from us as shown in Figure 15-5.

Figure 15-5   A directional light source, courtesy of the Java 3D DirectionalLight class, now illuminates our sphere.

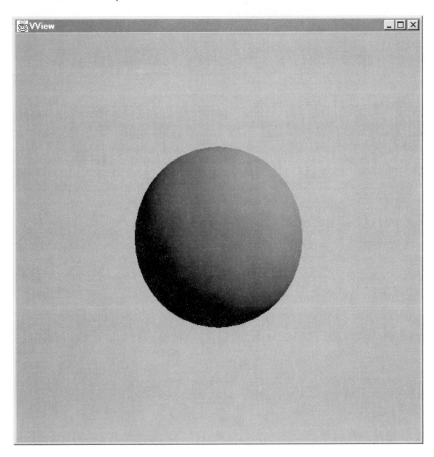

Table 15.16   DirectionalLight Constructor Summary

Constructors for the class javax.media.j3d.DirectionalLight, which implements directional light sources. See the Java 3D API Specification (http://java.sun.com/products/java-media/3D/) for details.

```
public DirectionalLight()
```

Constructs a default directional light node where direction = (0,0,-1).

```
public DirectionalLight(boolean lightOn, Color3f color,
                        Vector3f direction)
```

Constructs and initializes a directional light node with the specified color and direction. When *lightOn* is true, the light is turned on, otherwise the light is turned off.

```
public DirectionalLight(Color3f color, Vector3f direction)
```

Constructs and initializes a directional light node with the specified color and direction.

Table 15.17   DirectionalLight Field Summary

Fields defined by the class javax.media.j3d.DirectionalLight. These fields are defined as `public static final int`. DirectionalLight also inherits a number of fields from the abstract class javax.media.j3d.Light (Table 15.14). See the Java 3D API Specification (http://java.sun.com/products/java-media/3D/) for details.

`ALLOW_DIRECTION_READ`

Specifies that the Node allows access to its object's direction information.

`ALLOW_DIRECTION_WRITE`

Specifies that the Node allows writing to its object's direction information.

Table 15.18   DirectionalLight Method Summary

Public methods defined in the class javax.media.j3d.DirectionalLight. DirectionalLight also inherits a number of methods from the abstract javax.media.j3d.Light class (Table 15.15). See the Java 3D API Specification (http://java.sun.com/products/java-media/3D/) for details.

Returns	Method Name, Parameters, and Description
Node	**cloneNode**(boolean forceDuplicate)
	Creates a new instance of this directional light node.
void	**getDirection**(Vector3f direction)
	Gets the direction of this light and places it in the parameter specified.
void	**setDirection**(float x, float y, float z)
	Sets the direction of this directional light.
void	**setDirection**(Vector3f direction)
	Sets the direction of this directional light.

Point Lights

If a directional light is like the sun, a point light source is like a firefly. A point light emits light in all directions, and it has a specific point of origin. In Java 3D, a point light can have a color, a position, and some attenuation factors (see Tables 15.19, 15.20, and 15.21).

Attenuation is just a fancy word for "weakening" or "petering out." In the real world, all light is attenuated by a variety of factors. Simple distance causes the light from a source to be spread out over a larger area as you get farther away, in an inverse-square relationship. In other words, if you move twice as far from the light source, it'll seem only one-fourth as bright (see Chapter 9, "Customizing Light, Background, Fog, and Sound," to learn more about point light sources).

Java 3D supports a full inverse quadratic for attenuation based on the following formula:

```
brightness = intensity / (const + ln * d + quad * d²)
```

where `quad` is the quadratic coefficient, `ln` is the linear coefficient, and `const` is the constant term. The variable `d` is the distance from the light source to the object being illuminated. The three factors (constant, linear, quadratic) are stored in a `Point3f`, as is the position of the light source. The X component of the `Point3f` stores the constant factor, the Y component the linear factor, and the Z component the quadratic factor.

To add a point light source to the scene, we start by defining its location and attenuation factors:

```
Point3f position = new Point3f(-2f, 0f, 0f);
Point3f attenuation = new Point3f(0.5f, 0f, 0f);
```

This will put the light source two meters to the left of our sphere, with a constant attenuation of 0.5 and no linear or quadratic attenuation at all.

Next we'll define the color of our light source. We'll make this light blue, so that it stands out against the red directional light:

```
lightColor = new Color3f(0f, 0f, 1f);
```

Note that we're reusing the `lightColor` variable. Our next step is to create the point light source itself and set its influencing bounds:

```
PointLight pointLight = new PointLight(
    lightcolor, position, attenuation);
PointLight.setInfluencingBounds(sceneBounds);
```

And, of course, we need to add it to our environment:

```
environment.addChild(pointLight);
```

The resulting scene, with both a red directional light and a blue point light off to the left, is shown in Figure 15-6.

Table 15.19   PointLight Constructor Summary

Constructors for the class javax.media.j3d.PointLight, which implements point light sources (an attenuated light that radiates light equally in all directions from a fixed point in space). See the Java 3D API Specification (http://java.sun.com/products/java-media/3D/) for details.

public PointLight()

Constructs a default point light node where position = (0, 0, 0) and attenuation = (1, 0, 0).

public PointLight(boolean lightOn, Color3f color,
                   Point3f position, Point3f attenuation)

Constructs and initializes a point light node with the specified color, position, and attenuation (constant, linear, quadratic). When *lightOn* is true, the light is turned on, otherwise the light is turned off.

public PointLight(Color3f color, Point3f position,
                   Point3f attenuation)

Constructs and initializes a point light node with the specified color, position, and attenuation (constant, linear, quadratic).

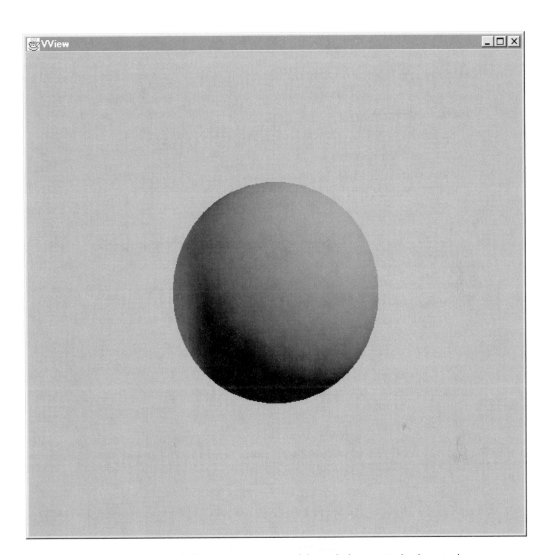

Figure 15-6 Java 3D point light sources are created through the PointLight class. In this example a blue point light is positioned two meters to the left of our sphere.

Table 15.20   PointLight Field Summary

Fields defined by the class javax.media.j3d.PointLight. These fields are defined as public static final int. PointLight also inherits a number of fields from the abstract class javax.media.j3d.Light (Table 15.14). See the Java 3D API Specification (http://java.sun.com/products/java-media/3D/) for details.

ALLOW_ATTENUATION_READ

Specifies that this PointLight node allows reading its attenuation information.

ALLOW_ATTENUATION_WRITE

Specifies that this PointLight node allows writing its attenuation information.

ALLOW_POSITION_READ

Specifies that this PointLight node allows reading its position information.

ALLOW_POSITION_WRITE

Specifies that this PointLight node allows writing its position information.

Table 15.21   PointLight Method Summary

Public methods defined in the class javax.media.j3d.PointLight. PointLight also inherits a number of methods from the abstract class javax.media.j3d.Light (Table 15.15). See the Java 3D API Specification (http://java.sun.com/products/java-media/3D/) for details.

Returns	*Method Name, Parameters, and Description*
Node	**cloneNode**(boolean forceDuplicate)
	Creates a new instance of this point light node.
void	**getAttenuation**(Point3f attenuation)
	Gets this point light's attenuation values and places them in the parameter specified.
void	**getPosition**(Point3f position)
	Gets this point light's position and places it in the parameter specified.
void	**setAttenuation**(float constant, float linear, float quadratic)
	Sets this point light's current attenuation values.
void	**setAttenuation**(Point3f attenuation)
	Sets this point light's attenuation values.
void	**setPosition**(float x, float y, float z)
	Sets this point light's position.
void	**setPosition**(Point3f position)
	Sets this point light's position.

Spot Lights

In Java 3D, a spot light is a point light that has a direction (similar to that for the DirectionalLight), a spread angle, and a concentration factor (the SpotLight class that defines spot light sources is actually a subclass of the PointLight class). The spread angle controls how wide the spotlight beam is, and the concentration controls how sharp the edges are. In Java 3D, the concentration ranges from 0 to 128 (see Tables 15.22, 15.23, and 15.24 for Java 3D Spotlight node details; see Chapter 9, "Customizing Light, Background, Fog, and Sound," to learn more about spot light sources.)

To create our spotlight, we're going to reuse the position, direction, color, and attenuation variables. Let's start by setting the color to yellow, which is a mixture of red and green light components:

```
lightColor = new Color3f(1f, 1f, 0f);
```

Next we'll position the light source 2 meters toward us, along the +Z axis, and point it backward in the –Z direction (back at the sphere).

```
position = new Point3f(0f, 0f, 2f);
direction = new Vector3f(0f, 0f, -1f);
```

We'll set up quadratic attenuation, just for a change:

```
attenuation = new Point3f(0f, 0f, 0.5f);
```

Finally, we'll create our `SpotLight`:

```
SpotLight spotlight = new SpotLight(
lightColor, position, attenuation, direction, 0.47f, 50f);
```

The value 0.47 is the angle in radians, equivalent to about 27 degrees (see Chapter 13 to learn about radians and angles). The value 50 is the concentration factor, which is fairly moderate.

Finally, we set the influencing bounds and add the spotlight to our world (the resulting scene, with three lights, is shown in Figure 15-7):

```
spotLight.setInfluencingBounds(sceneBounds);
```

Table 15.22   SpotLight Constructor Summary

```
environment.addChild(spotLight);
```

Constructors for the class javax.media.j3d.SpotLight, which implements spot light sources. A spot light is an attenuated light source that radiates light in a specified direction from a fixed point in space (a spread angle limits the effect of the light, while a concentration exponent attenuates the light based on angular deviation from the

Figure 15-7 Java 3D spot light sources are created using the SpotLight node. In this example a yellow spot light shines down the Z axis (this spot light is combined with two other light sources: a directional light and a point light).

light's direction). SpotLight is a subclass of the PointLight class summarized in Tables 15.19, 15.20, and 15.21. See the Java 3D API Specification (http://java.sun.com/products/java-media/3D/) for details.

public SpotLight()

Constructs a default spot light node where direction = (0, 0, −1), spread angle = PI, and concentration = 0.0.

public SpotLight(boolean lightOn, Color3f color, Point3f position,
              Point3f attenuation, Vector3f direction,
              float spreadAngle, float concentration)

Constructs and initializes a spot light node based on the following parameters: *lightOn* (whether the light is on or off), *color* (color of the light source), *position* (location of the light in 3D-space), *attenuation* (attenuation—constant, linear, quadratic—of the light), *direction* (direction of the light), *spreadAngle* (spread angle of the light), and *concentration* (concentration of the light).

```
public SpotLight(Color3f color, Point3f position,
                 Point3f attenuation, Vector3f direction,
                 float spreadAngle, float concentration)
```

Constructs and initializes a spot light node based on the same parameters as the above constructor, with the exception of *lightOn* (which is not passed to this constructor).

Table 15.23   SpotLight Field Summary

Fields defined by the class javax.media.j3d.SpotLight. These fields are defined as `public static final int`. SpotLight also inherits a number of fields from the abstract class javax.media.j3d.Light (Table 15.14) and the javax.media.j3d.PointLight class it extends (Table 15.20). See the Java 3D API Specification (http://java.sun.com/products/java-media/3D/) for details.

ALLOW_CONCENTRATION_READ
Specifies that the Node allows reading to its spot lights concentration information.

ALLOW_CONCENTRATION_WRITE
Specifies that the Node allows writing to its spot lights concentration information.

ALLOW_DIRECTION_READ
Specifies that the Node allows reading to its spot lights direction information.

ALLOW_DIRECTION_WRITE
Specifies that the Node allows writing to its spot lights direction information.

ALLOW_SPREAD_ANGLE_READ
Specifies that the Node allows reading to its spot lights spread-angle information.

ALLOW_SPREAD_ANGLE_WRITE
Specifies that the Node allows writing to its spot lights spread-angle information.

Table 15.24   SpotLight Method Summary

Public methods defined in the class javax.media.j3d.SpotLight. SpotLight also inherits a number of methods from the abstract class javax.media.j3d.Light (Table 15.15) and the javax.media.j3d.PointLight class it extends (Table 15.21). See the Java 3D API Specification (http://java.sun.com/products/java-media/3D/) for details.

Returns	*Method Name, Parameters, and Description*
Node	**cloneNode**(boolean forceDuplicate)
	Used to create a new instance of the node.
float	**getConcentration**()
	Gets spot light concentration.
void	**getDirection**(Vector3f direction)
	Gets this Light's current direction and places it in the parameter specified.
float	**getSpreadAngle**()
	Gets spot light spread angle.
void	**setConcentration**(float concentration)
	Sets spot light concentration.
void	**setDirection**(float x, float y, float z)
	Sets light direction.
void	**setDirection**(Vector3f direction)
	Sets this Light's current direction and places it in the parameter specified.
void	**setSpreadAngle**(float spreadAngle)
	Sets spot light spread angle.

Ambient Light

Ambient light is completely sourceless and nondirectional. It doesn't emanate from any specific location, and it doesn't point in any particular direction. In the real world, ambient light is actually the result of light reflecting off objects, then being reflected off other objects, and so on until it completely fills a space. (Read Chapter 8, "Customizing Color and Texture," to learn more about ambient light and reflection.)

In Java 3D, an ambient light does the same thing. It provides a source of light that fills the room, shining equally on all objects from all directions. Ambient light sources are often used to "soften" the look of a Java 3D scene, removing some of the harsh elements of light sources (see Tables 15.25, 15.26, and 15.27).

For our example, we'll create a kind of amber ambient light that's bright enough to be noticeable over the effects of the directional, point, and spot lights that we've already created. We'll start by setting the color:

```
lightColor = new Color3f(0f, 1f, 1f);
```

Notice that by using a color component intensity of 1, we've increased the brightness of this light considerably. Next, we create the ambient light, set its influencing bounds, and add it to our environment:

```
AmbientLight ambLight = new AmbientLight(lightColor);
ambLight.setInfluencingBounds(sceneBounds);
environment.addChild(ambLight);
```

That's all there is to it. Figure 15–8 shows the results of adding this ambient light.

Figure 15-8   Java 3D ambient light sources are created with the AmbientLight node. In this example a relatively high level of yellow-colored Ambient light is added to our scene, complementing the directional, spot, and point lights created previously.

Table 15.25   AmbientLight Constructor Summary

Constructors for the class javax.media.j3d.AmbientLight, which implements ambient light sources. See the Java 3D API Specification (http://java.sun.com/products/java-media/3D/) for details.

public AmbientLight()

　Constructs and initializes an ambient light using default parameters.

public AmbientLight(boolean lightOn, Color3f color)

　Constructs and initializes an ambient light using the specified parameters.

public AmbientLight(Color3f color)

　Constructs and initializes an ambient light using the specified parameters.

Table 15.26   AmbientLight Field Summary

No fields are defined directly by javax.media.j3d.AmbientLight; all fields are inherited from its superclass javax.media.j3d.Light (Table 15.14). See the Java 3D API Specification (http://java.sun.com/products/java-media/3D/) for details.

Table 15.27   PointLight Method Summary

Public methods defined in the class javax.media.j3d.AmbientLight. AmbientLight also inherits a number of methods from the abstract class javax.media.j3d.Light (Table 15.15). See the Java 3D API Specification (http://java.sun.com/products/java-media/3D/) for details.

Returns	*Method Name, Parameters, and Description*
Node	**cloneNode**(boolean forceDuplicate)
	Used to create a new instance of the node.
void	**duplicateNode**(Node originalNode, boolean forceDuplicate)
	Copies all node information from originalNode into the current node.

The Complete Lighting Example

Listing 15.3 contains the complete source listing for our lighting examples, allowing you to see how the various snippets of code we've added fit into the context of a complete Java 3D program.

Listing 15.3   VView.java (Example 4)

```java
// Our complete lighting example
// Written by Bernie Roehl, October 1999
//
// CONVERTING TO AN APPLET:
// To convert this application into an applet you must construct
// a standard init() method that contains the code now in the VView
// constructor. From within the init() method you will invoke the VRML
// loader's load(URL) method, as the load(String) method currently used
// by this application can't be used in an applet (a security exception
// is thrown by the applet when loading a VRML world from a String).
//
// To convert to an applet, simply rename the following method:
//                public VView(String avatar)
// to:
//                public void init()
//
// Next, use the applet's getParameter() method to retrieve the
// name of the VRML file to load and place the resulting string into the
// "avatar" variable. The following code assumes that a PARAM named
// "world" is in the corresponding HTML Web page for this applet:
//     String  avatar = getParameter("world");
//
// Finally, change the VRML loader's load(String) method so that it
// is passed an absolute URL. For example:
//  scene = loader.load(new java.net.URL(getCodeBase(), avatar + ".wrl"));
//
// Visit the Core Web3D web site at http://www.CoreWeb3D.com/ to
// obtain code listings from this book, including an applet version of this
// VView program.

import java.awt.*;
import java.applet.Applet;
import java.util.*;
import javax.media.j3d.*;
import javax.vecmath.*;
import com.sun.j3d.utils.applet.MainFrame;
import com.sun.j3d.utils.universe.*;
import com.sun.j3d.loaders.vrml97.VrmlLoader;
import com.sun.j3d.loaders.Scene;

public class VView extends Applet {

    SimpleUniverse universe;    // the universe
    Scene scene = null;         // the VRML scene
```

```
VView(String avatar) {
      setLayout(new BorderLayout());
      Canvas3D canvas = new Canvas3D(null);
      add("Center",canvas);

      universe = new SimpleUniverse(canvas);
      ViewingPlatform viewingPlatform =
            universe.getViewingPlatform();
      TransformGroup vpTransGroup =
            viewingPlatform.getViewPlatformTransform();
      View view = (universe.getViewer()).getView();

      VrmlLoader loader = new VrmlLoader();
      try { scene = loader.load(avatar + ".wrl"); }
      catch (Exception e) {
            System.out.println(
                  "Exception loading file from path:"
                  + avatar + ".wrl");
            System.exit(1);
      }

      // get the scene group from the loaded VRML scene
      BranchGroup sceneGroup = scene.getSceneGroup();
      sceneGroup.setCapability(
            BranchGroup.ALLOW_DETACH);
      sceneGroup.setCapability(
            BranchGroup.ALLOW_BOUNDS_READ);

      // make the VRML scene live
      universe.addBranchGraph(sceneGroup);

      // find the radius and center of the
      // scene's bounding sphere
      BoundingSphere sceneBounds =
            (BoundingSphere)sceneGroup.getBounds();
      double radius = sceneBounds.getRadius();
      Point3d center = new Point3d();
      sceneBounds.getCenter(center);

      // now move the viewpoint back
      // so we can see the whole scene
      Vector3d temp = new Vector3d(center);
      temp.z += 1.4 * radius
                  / Math.tan(view.getFieldOfView() / 2.0);
```

```
// set that viewpoint into the viewing transform
Transform3D viewTransform = new Transform3D();
viewTransform.set(temp);
vpTransGroup.setTransform(viewTransform);

// increase the size of the sceneBounds,
// for later use
sceneBounds.setRadius(temp.z * 2.0);

// create a new BranchGroup to hold the
// lights, sounds, background, and fog
BranchGroup environment = new BranchGroup();

// add a background to the scene
Background bg = new Background(
     0.0f, 0.75f, 0.25f);
bg.setApplicationBounds(sceneBounds);
environment.addChild(bg);

// create a new DirectionalLight
// and add it to the scene
Vector3f direction = new Vector3f(-1f, -1f, -1f);
Color3f lightColor = new Color3f(1f, 0f, 0f);
DirectionalLight dirLight =
  new DirectionalLight(lightColor, direction);
dirLight.setInfluencingBounds(sceneBounds);
environment.addChild(dirLight);

// create a new PointLight
// and add it to the scene
lightColor = new Color3f(0f, 0f, 1f);
Point3f position = new Point3f(-2f, 0f, 0f);
Point3f attenuation = new Point3f(0.5f, 0f, 0f);
PointLight pointLight =
     new PointLight(lightColor, position,
          attenuation);
pointLight.setInfluencingBounds(sceneBounds);
environment.addChild(pointLight);

// create a new SpotLight
// and add it to the scene
lightColor = new Color3f(1f, 1f, 0f);
position = new Point3f(0f, 0f, 2f);
direction = new Vector3f(0f, 0f, -1f);
```

```
    attenuation = new Point3f(0f, 0f, 0.5f);
    SpotLight spotLight =
        new SpotLight(lightColor, position,
            attenuation, direction, 0.47f, 50f);
    spotLight.setInfluencingBounds(sceneBounds);
    environment.addChild(spotLight);

    // create a new AmbientLight
    // and add it to the scene
    lightColor = new Color3f(0f, 1f, 1f);
    AmbientLight ambLight =
        new AmbientLight(lightColor);
    ambLight.setInfluencingBounds(sceneBounds);
    environment.addChild(ambLight);

    universe.addBranchGraph(environment);
    }

    public static void main(String[] args) {
        new MainFrame(new VView(args[0]), 320, 400);
    }

}
```

Our little example has certainly grown, but it now serves as a good jumping-off point for creating some interesting applications.

Sound

Java 3D provides extensive support for the use of 3D sound. Sounds are represented by audio data files, typically stored in Sun's ".au" file format or in ".wav" format. Most sound editing programs (such as Goldwave or CoolEdit) are able to read and write sounds in a variety of formats, including ".wav" and ".au".

If you're familiar with the way VRML handles sound, then you already know the basics of sound in Java 3D. (To learn about VRML sound refer to Chapter 9, "Customizing Light, Background, Fog, and Sound.") VRML defines an AudioClip node that contains the actual audio data, whereas Java 3D defines a MediaContainer that does the same thing. Despite its generic name, a MediaContainer can currently store only audio data—not general multimedia data such as AVI or MPEG files.

VRML defines a single Sound node that is used to define a sound source position, orientation, and other sound parameters (see Tables 15.28 and 15.29). Java

3D has an abstract Sound class, which is subclassed by the BackgroundSound class in order to define an "ambient" sound having no particular source location, and by the PointSound class to define a sound source that has a position in the virtual world. The PointSound class is in turn subclassed by the ConeSound class, which adds the notion of sound that has a direction associated with it.

Java 3D provides some sense of spatialization to the sound as it's played back. As a sound source moves around the virtual world (relative to the listener), Java 3D's sound subsystem will modify the volume, left/right balance, and interaural delay of the audio emission in order to create the illusion that the sound is coming from a different direction. As the sound moves closer to the listener, it gets louder. As it moves off to the left, it is panned over to the left speaker. As it moves around the listener, a delay is added between the left and the right channel. At the moment, Java 3D's sound subsystem does not support 3D sound hardware, but even using these few simple techniques it does manage to create a very effective illusion of spatialized audio.

In this section, we're going to create a simple application that allows the user to move a sound source around and hear it coming from different directions. We'll be starting with our familiar VRML Viewer, but we'll make some important changes in order to support audio. We'll also be adding some mouse-based object-manipulation controls, which will provide the user with some interactivity.

Table 15.28   Sound Field Summary

Fields defined by the abstract class javax.media.j3d.Sound. These fields are defined as `public static final int` and are inherited by subclasses BackgroundSound, ConeSound, and PointSound (described in the following sections). The Sound class is a leaf node (derived from javax.media.j3d.Leaf) that defines capabilities and settings common to all types of sound. A scene graph can contain multiple sounds, each having an associated reference to: Sound data ("Sound Data"), an amplitude scale factor ("Initial Gain"), a flag denoting that the sound will play to the end when disabled ("Release Flag"), a flag indicating the number of times sound is to be repeated ("Loop"), the sound's state ("State"), a scheduling region ("Scheduling Bounds"), and a flag denoting whether the sound is to continue playing "silently" even while it is inactive ("Continuous Flag"), priority, and duration. See the Java 3D API Specification (http://java.sun.com/products/java-media/3D/) for details.

`ALLOW_CHANNELS_USED_READ`
Specifies that this node allows access to its number of channels used by this sound.

`ALLOW_CONT_PLAY_READ`
Specifies that this node allows access to its object's continuous-play information.

`ALLOW_CONT_PLAY_WRITE`
Specifies that this node allows writing to its object's continuous-play information.

ALLOW_DURATION_READ
Specifies that this node allows access to its object's sound-duration information.

ALLOW_ENABLE_READ
Specifies that this node allows access to its object's sound-on information.

ALLOW_ENABLE_WRITE
Specifies that this node allows writing to its object's sound-on information.

ALLOW_INITIAL_GAIN_READ
Specifies that this node allows access to its object's initial-gain information.

ALLOW_INITIAL_GAIN_WRITE
Specifies that this node allows writing to its object's initial-gain information.

ALLOW_IS_PLAYING_READ
Specifies that this node allows access to its object's sound audibly-playing or playing-silently status.

ALLOW_IS_READY_READ
Specifies that this node allows access to its object's sound status denoting if it is ready to be played "immediately."

ALLOW_LOOP_READ
Specifies that this node allows access to its object's loop information.

ALLOW_LOOP_WRITE
Specifies that this node allows writing to its object's loop information.

ALLOW_PRIORITY_READ
Specifies that this node allows read access to its priority-order value.

ALLOW_PRIORITY_WRITE
Specifies that this node allows write access to its priority-order value.

ALLOW_RELEASE_READ
Specifies that this node allows access to its object's release-flag information.

ALLOW_RELEASE_WRITE
Specifies that this node allows writing to its object's release-flag information.

ALLOW_SCHEDULING_BOUNDS_READ
Specifies that this node allows read access to its scheduling-bounds information.

ALLOW_SCHEDULING_BOUNDS_WRITE
Specifies that this node allows write access to its scheduling-bounds information.

ALLOW_SOUND_DATA_READ
Specifies that this node allows access to its object's sound-data information.

ALLOW_SOUND_DATA_WRITE
Specifies that this node allows writing to its object's sound-data information.

DURATION_UNKNOWN
Denotes that the sound's duration could not be calculated.

INFINITE_LOOPS
When used as a loop count, sound will loop an infinite number of times until explicitly stopped (setEnabled(false)).

NO_FILTER
Denotes that there is no filter value associated with its object's distance or angular
attenuation array.

Table 15.29   Sound Method

Sound methods are public methods defined in the abstract class
javax.media.j3d.Sound that are inherited by subclasses BackgroundSound, Cone-
Sound, and PointSound. The Sound class is a leaf node (derived from
javax.media.j3d.Leaf) that defines capabilities and settings common to all types of
sounds. See the Java 3D API Specification (http://java.sun.com/products/java-
media/3D/) for details.

Returns	*Method Name, Parameters, and Description*
boolean	**getContinuousEnable**() Retrieves sound's continuous-play flag.
long	**getDuration**() Get the Sound's duration.
boolean	**getEnable**() Retrieves sound's enabled flag.
float	**getInitialGain**() Get the overall gain applied to the sound data associated with source.
int	**getLoop**() Retrieves loop count for this sound.
int	**getNumberOfChannelsUsed**() Retrieves number of channels (on executing audio device) that are being used by this sound.
float	**getPriority**() Retrieves sound's priority value.
boolean	**getReleaseEnable**() Retrieves release flag for sound associated with sound.
BoundingLeaf	**getSchedulingBoundingLeaf**() Retrieves the Sound node's scheduling bounding leaf.
Bounds	**getSchedulingBounds**() Retrieves the Sound node's scheduling bounds.
MediaContainer	**getSoundData**() Retrieves description/data associated with this sound source.
boolean	**isPlaying**() Retrieves sound's play status.

Returns	*Method Name, Parameters, and Description*
boolean	**isPlayingSilently**() Retrieves sound's silent status.
boolean	**isReady**() Retrieves sound's "ready" status, denoting that the sound is fully prepared for playing (audibly or silently) to begin.
void	**setContinuousEnable**(boolean state) Enables or disables continuous-play flag.
void	**setEnable**(boolean state) Enables or disables sound.
void	**setInitialGain**(float amplitude) Sets the overall gain scale factor applied to data associated with this source to increase or decrease its overall amplitude.
void	**setLoop**(int loopCount) Sets a sound's loop count.
void	**setPriority**(float priority) Sets sound's priority value.
void	**setReleaseEnable**(boolean state) Enables or disables the release flag for the sound associated with this sound.
void	**setSchedulingBoundingLeaf**(BoundingLeaf region) Sets the Sound's scheduling region to the specified bounding leaf.
void	**setSchedulingBounds**(Bounds region) Sets the Sound's scheduling region to the specified bounds.
void	**setSoundData**(MediaContainer soundData) Sets fields that define the sound source data of this node.
void	**updateNodeReferences**(NodeReferenceTable referenceTable) Callback used to allow a node to check if any scene-graph objects referenced by that node have been duplicated via a call to cloneTree.

Common Elements

A number of things are common to BackgroundSound, PointSound, and ConeSound sources, and a few are common to all applications that use audio. For starters, the audio device must be explicitly created, based on the Viewer object for the universe. The sound sources must be assigned a bounding region that defines when they're audible (or, more accurately, when they can be "scheduled"). The sound sources all need to have a MediaContainer object associated with them, and they all need to be enabled and told how often to loop. In addition, a sound source can be made the child of some other object in the scene, so that it moves right along with that object. For example, you might create a transistor radio object and attach a sound source to it, so that when the radio gets moved the sound travels with it.

We're going to start by modifying our VRML Viewer example. We'll assume that the VRML file we load is a humanoid, and that there's a light source already in the VRML file so we don't need to create one in Java 3D. Everything from our Viewer example will remain the same, up to the point where we have the VRML file loaded and the sceneGroup's capabilities set. Before we add the sceneGroup to the universe, we have some additional work to do.

Since we'll be attaching a sound source to the head of our avatar, we need access to the appropriate node from the VRML file. And since we'll be letting the user move the humanoid around, we need access to the root node of the humanoid as well. As we saw in Chapter 13, "Customizing Size, Location, and Orientation," the loaded VRML scene contains a Hashtable that gives us access to all the VRML nodes that have DEF names associated with them. From the H-Anim specification (http://www.h-anim.org/) we know that the node we want to attach the sound to is called "skullbase," and the name of the root node is "HumanoidRoot." We take our avatar name (which is the name passed on the command line of our application) and use it as a prefix to these names, as the following snippet of code illustrates:

```
// find the list of DEF names
Hashtable defnames = scene.getNamedObjects();

// find the body
TransformGroup body = (TransformGroup) defnames.get(
                      avatar + "_HumanoidRoot");

// find the head
TransformGroup head = (TransformGroup) defnames.get(
                      avatar + "_skullbase");
```

Since we'll be manipulating the body with the mouse, and this will be done after the scene graph has gone live, we need to set the appropriate capability flags on the body:

```
body.setCapability(TransformGroup.ALLOW_TRANSFORM_READ);
body.setCapability(TransformGroup.ALLOW_TRANSFORM_WRITE);
```

Now, since we'll be using audio in our examples, we need to create an audio device and associate it with the Viewer object. Since we're basing our universe on SimpleUniverse, we can use the `getViewer()` method to find the Viewer. The Viewer itself has a method for creating an audio device and initializing it:

```
// create an audio device
(universe.getViewer()).createAudioDevice();
```

At this point, we will be adding the sound objects and setting them up. We'll come back to that later, when we discuss the sound nodes themselves. Once they've been added, we can add the scene graph to the universe and compute the bounding sphere as before. We can also set up our viewpoint, as we have in our previous examples.

```
// make the VRML scene live by adding it to the universe
universe.addBranchGraph(sceneGroup);

// find the radius and center of the scene's bounding sphere
BoundingSphere sceneBounds = (BoundingSphere)
                              sceneGroup.getBounds();
double radius = sceneBounds.getRadius();
Point3d center = new Point3d();
sceneBounds.getCenter(center);

// now move the viewpoint back so we can see the whole scene
Vector3d temp = new Vector3d(center);
temp.z += 1.4 * radius / Math.tan(view.getFieldOfView()
                / 2.0);

// and set that viewpoint into the viewing transform
Transform3D viewTransform = new Transform3D();
viewTransform.set(temp);
vpTransGroup.setTransform(viewTransform);
```

Manipulators

Now we're going to add some manipulators to our scene that will allow the user to move the humanoid around in space and rotate it, using the mouse. These manipulator objects are very handy, since they do a lot of very difficult and complicated math for us. By holding down the first button and dragging the mouse around, the user will be able to rotate the humanoid. Holding down the second button and dragging the mouse will move the humanoid up/down and left/right. The third button will be used to move the humanoid forward and backward as the mouse is dragged up and down on the screen. On machines that have only a two-button mouse, or a mouse driver that supports only two buttons, the ALT key should be held down along with the first mouse button to achieve the effect of a third button.

These manipulators are part of the behavior utilities of Java 3D. To use them, we must import the appropriate classes:

```
import com.sun.j3d.utils.behaviors.mouse.MouseRotate;
import com.sun.j3d.utils.behaviors.mouse.MouseZoom;
import com.sun.j3d.utils.behaviors.mouse.MouseTranslate;
```

These manipulators also have to be part of the scene graph, so we'll create a new BranchGroup to contain them:

```
BranchGroup manipulatorGroup = new BranchGroup();
```

We'll start with rotation. We create a new MouseRotate object, called mr. We tell that object what TransformGroup it will be manipulating:

```
MouseRotate mr = new MouseRotate();
mr.setTransformGroup(body);
```

The `setTransformGroup()` method tells the MouseRotate object which TransformGroup it will be updating. MouseRotate needs to be able to read the transform from that TransformGroup, modify it based on the mouse movement, and write it back again. That's why we set the appropriate capability bits on the body object.

Our next step is to set the scheduling bounds for this manipulator to be the sceneBounds we computed earlier.

```
mr.setSchedulingBounds(sceneBounds);
```

Now that the MouseRotate object is set up, we add it to the manipulator-Group:

```
manipulatorGroup.addChild(mr);
```

We repeat this whole procedure for the MouseTranslate manipulator:

```
MouseTranslate mt = new MouseTranslate();
mt.setTransformGroup(body);
mt.setSchedulingBounds(sceneBounds);
manipulatorGroup.addChild(mt);
```

And finally, we do the same for the MouseZoom manipulator (which actually doesn't perform a "zoom" operation, but instead moves the object in the Z direction):

```
MouseZoom mz = new MouseZoom();
mz.setTransformGroup(body);
mz.setSchedulingBounds(sceneBounds);
manipulatorGroup.addChild(mz);
```

Now that all the manipulators have been created and added to the manipulatorGroup, we can add the manipulatorGroup itself to the universe:

```
universe.addBranchGraph(manipulatorGroup);
```

At this point, we're ready to roll. And tilt, and pan, and zoom. . . .

PointSound

We've done everything we need to do, except set up the sound source itself. We'll start with the simplest type of sound source—the PointSound node. It radiates sound uniformly in all directions, very much as a PointLight radiates light.

We begin by creating the PointSound itself:

```
// create a new point sound
PointSound sound = new PointSound();
```

A sound source has a bounding region just like all the other nodes we've looked at in this chapter. Instead of reusing the bounding sphere we computed earlier, though, we're going to create a new one that's as large as the entire universe. We do this to illustrate how easy it is to create and use such a default bounding sphere.

```
BoundingSphere soundBounds = new BoundingSphere(
                new Point3d(), Double.MAX_VALUE);
sound.setSchedulingBounds(soundBounds);
```

The `Point3d()` constructor creates a new point for the center of the sphere. Since we didn't pass any arguments to the constructor, the point is created at the origin (0, 0, 0). We set the radius of the bounding sphere to be the largest possible double-precision value, `Double.MAX_VALUE`. We know we'll never move outside of a sphere with that radius! Once we have the bounding sphere, we set it as the scheduling bounds for the sound source we just created.

Next, we have to load the actual sound data itself. Sound data gets stored in a MediaContainer object, which can be initialized with a String containing the URL of the sound. In this case, we'll assume the existence of a file called "testing.au" in the "j3d" subdirectory of our current drive:

```
sound.setSoundData(
new MediaContainer("file:/j3d/testing.au"));
```

This loads the data into a MediaContainer and sets that MediaContainer as the sound data of the sound source we created earlier. In this particular case we want our sound to start off enabled, in which case we need to pass the Boolean value true to the sound's `setEnable( )` method as follows:

```
sound.setEnable(true);
```

Java 3D allows us to play sounds once, or loop them a specific number of times. If we want the sound to loop indefinitely without stopping, we give it a loop count of –1 as follows:

```
sound.setLoop(-1);
```

And finally, we want to attach this sound source to the head of our avatar:

```
head.addChild(sound);
```

From this point on, the sound should be playing and moving around with the avatar's head. That's all there is to it. Listing 15.4 contains complete source code for our PointSoundViewer example. To run our application, we simply enter the following at the command line:

```
java PointSoundViewer Human
```

The result looks just like it did before, but we now hear the sound playing. We can use our mouse to drag the humanoid around, even off-screen, and the sound moves right along with it. You may want to drag the PointSound-Viewer window to the middle of your screen, so that you can move the humanoid off-screen to the left. The same thing applies with ConeSound, but with angular attenuation features that are beyond the scope of this chapter. (Visit the Core Java 3D web site at http://www.CoreJava3D.com/ to learn how to use the ConeSound node.)

Listing 15.4   PointSoundViewer.java (Example 5)

```
// Very simple point sound "viewer"
// Written by Bernie Roehl, October 1999
// CONVERTING TO AN APPLET:
// To convert this application into an applet you must construct
```

```
// a standard init() method that contains the code now in the VView
// constructor. From within the init() method you will invoke the VRML
// loader's load(URL) method, as the load(String) method currently used
// by this application can't be used in an applet (a security exception
// is thrown by the applet when loading a VRML world from a String).
//
// To convert to an applet, simply rename the following method:
//                public VView(String avatar)
// to:
//                public void init()
//
// Next, use the applet's getParameter() method to retrieve the
// name of the VRML file to load and place the resulting string into the
// "avatar" variable. The following code assumes that a PARAM named
// "world" is in the corresponding HTML Web page for this applet:
//    String  avatar = getParameter("world");
//
// Finally, change the VRML loader's load(String) method so that it
// is passed an absolute URL. For example:
//   scene = loader.load(new java.net.URL(getCodeBase(), avatar + ".wrl"));
//
// Visit the Core Web3D web site at http://www.CoreWeb3D.com/ to
// obtain code listings from this book, including an applet version of this
// VView program.

import java.awt.*;
import java.applet.Applet;
import java.util.*;

import javax.media.j3d.*;
import javax.vecmath.*;
import com.sun.j3d.utils.applet.MainFrame;
import com.sun.j3d.utils.universe.*;
import com.sun.j3d.loaders.vrml97.VrmlLoader;
import com.sun.j3d.loaders.Scene;
import com.sun.j3d.utils.behaviors.mouse.MouseRotate;
import com.sun.j3d.utils.behaviors.mouse.MouseZoom;
import com.sun.j3d.utils.behaviors.mouse.MouseTranslate;

public class PointSoundViewer extends Applet {

    SimpleUniverse universe;    // the universe
    Scene scene = null;         // the VRML scene

    PointSoundViewer(String avatar) {
        setLayout(new BorderLayout());
```

```
Canvas3D canvas = new Canvas3D(null);
add("Center", canvas);

universe = new SimpleUniverse(canvas);
ViewingPlatform viewingPlatform =
      universe.getViewingPlatform();
TransformGroup vpTransGroup =
      viewingPlatform.getViewPlatformTransform();
View view = (universe.getViewer()).getView();

VrmlLoader loader = new VrmlLoader();
try { scene = loader.load(avatar + ".wrl"); }
catch (Exception e) {
      System.out.println(
            "Exception loading file from path:"
                  + avatar + ".wrl");
      System.exit(1);
}

// get the scene group from the loaded VRML scene
BranchGroup sceneGroup = scene.getSceneGroup();
sceneGroup.setCapability(
      BranchGroup.ALLOW_DETACH);
sceneGroup.setCapability(
      BranchGroup.ALLOW_BOUNDS_READ);

// find the list of DEF names
Hashtable defnames = scene.getNamedObjects();

// find the body itself
// and allow it to be manipulated
TransformGroup body = (TransformGroup)
         defnames.get(avatar + "_HumanoidRoot");
body.setCapability(
      TransformGroup.ALLOW_TRANSFORM_READ);
body.setCapability(
      TransformGroup.ALLOW_TRANSFORM_WRITE);

// find the head, and allow it to have
// children added later
TransformGroup head = (TransformGroup)
         defnames.get(avatar + "_skullbase");

// create an audio device
(universe.getViewer()).createAudioDevice();
```

```
// create a new point sound
PointSound sound = new PointSound();
BoundingSphere soundBounds =
    new BoundingSphere(new Point3d(),
        Double.MAX_VALUE);
sound.setSoundData(
    new MediaContainer("file:/j3d/testing.au"));
sound.setSchedulingBounds(soundBounds);
sound.setLoop(-1);
sound.setEnable(true);

// attach the sound to the head
head.addChild(sound);

// make the VRML scene live by
// adding it to the universe

universe.addBranchGraph(sceneGroup);

// find the radius and center of the
// scene's bounding sphere
BoundingSphere sceneBounds =
        (BoundingSphere) sceneGroup.getBounds();
double radius = sceneBounds.getRadius();
Point3d center = new Point3d();
sceneBounds.getCenter(center);

// now move the viewpoint back so we can
// see the whole scene
Vector3d temp = new Vector3d(center);
temp.z += 1.4 * radius
        / Math.tan(view.getFieldOfView() / 2.0);

// and set that viewpoint into the
// viewing transform
Transform3D viewTransform = new Transform3D();
viewTransform.set(temp);
vpTransGroup.setTransform(viewTransform);

// add some manipulators to let us
// move the object around

BranchGroup manipulatorGroup = new BranchGroup();

MouseRotate mr = new MouseRotate();
```

```
        mr.setTransformGroup(body);
        mr.setSchedulingBounds(sceneBounds);
        manipulatorGroup.addChild(mr);

        MouseTranslate mt = new MouseTranslate();
        mt.setTransformGroup(body);
        mt.setSchedulingBounds(sceneBounds);
        manipulatorGroup.addChild(mt);

        MouseZoom mz = new MouseZoom();
        mz.setTransformGroup(body);
        mz.setSchedulingBounds(sceneBounds);
        manipulatorGroup.addChild(mz);

        universe.addBranchGraph(manipulatorGroup);

    }

    public static void main(String[] args) {
        new MainFrame(
            new PointSoundViewer(args[0]), 320, 400);
    }

}
```

Table 15.30 PointSound Constructor Summary

Constructors for the class javax.media.j3d.PointSound, which defines a spatially located sound source whose waves radiate uniformly in all directions from a given location in 3D-space. As a subclass of javax.media.j3d.Sound (Table 15.28 and Table 15.29), PointSound has the same attributes as a Sound object with the addition of a location and the specification of distance-based gain attenuation for listener positions between an array of distances. See the Java 3D API Specification (http://java.sun.com/products/java-media/3D/) for details.

public PointSound()

Constructs and initializes a new PointSound node using default parameters.

public PointSound(MediaContainer soundData, float initialGain,
                float posX, float posY, float posZ)

Constructs a PointSound node object using only the provided parameter values for sound data, sample gain, and position.

```
public PointSound(MediaContainer soundData, float initialGain,
                  int loopCount, boolean release, boolean con-
                  tinuous, boolean enable, Bounds region, float
                  priority, float posX, float posY, float posZ,
                  float[] attenuationDistance, float[] attenua-
                  tionGain)
```

Constructs a PointSound object accepting individual float parameters for the elements of the position points, and accepting separate arrays for the distance and gain scale factors components of distance attenuation.

```
public PointSound(MediaContainer soundData, float initialGain,
                  int loopCount, boolean release, boolean con-
                  tinuous, boolean enable, Bounds region, float
                  priority, float posX, float posY, float posZ,
                  Point2f[] distanceGain)
```

Constructs a PointSound object accepting individual float parameters for the elements of the position point, and accepting an array of Point2f for the distance attenuation values, where each pair in the array contains a distance and a gain scale factor.

```
public PointSound(MediaContainer soundData, float initialGain,
                  int loopCount, boolean release, boolean con-
                  tinuous, boolean enable, Bounds region, float
                  priority, Point3f position, float[] attenua-
                  tionDistance, float[] attenuationGain)
```

Constructs a PointSound object accepting points as input for the position.

```
public PointSound(MediaContainer soundData, float initialGain,
                  int loopCount, boolean release, boolean con-
                  tinuous, boolean enable, Bounds region, float
                  priority, Point3f position, Point2f[] dis-
                  tanceGain)
```

Constructs a PointSound object accepting Point3f as input for the position and accepting an array of Point2f for the distance attenuation values, where each pair in the array contains a distance and a gain scale factor.

```
public PointSound(MediaContainer soundData, float initialGain,
                  Point3f position)
```

Constructs a PointSound node object using only the provided parameter values for sound data, sample gain, and position.

Table 15.31	PointSound Field Summary

Fields defined by the class javax.media.j3d.PointSound. These fields are defined as `public static final int`. PointSound also inherits a number of fields from the abstract class javax.media.j3d.Sound (Table 15.28). See the Java 3D API Specification (http://java.sun.com/products/java-media/3D/) for details.

ALLOW_DISTANCE_GAIN_READ
Specifies that this node allows access to its object's distance gain attenuation information.

ALLOW_DISTANCE_GAIN_WRITE
Specifies that this node allows writing to its object's distance gain attenuation information.

ALLOW_POSITION_READ
Specifies that this node allows access to its object's position information.

ALLOW_POSITION_WRITE
Specifies that this node allows writing to its object's position information.

Table 15.32	PointSound Method Summary

Public methods defined in the class javax.media.j3d.PointSound. PointSound also inherits a number of methods from the abstract class javax.media.j3d.Sound (Table 15.29). See the Java 3D API Specification (http://java.sun.com/products/java-media/3D/) for details.

Returns	*Method Name, Parameters, and Description*
Node	**cloneNode**(boolean forceDuplicate) Creates a new instance of the node.
void	**duplicateNode**(Node originalNode, boolean forceDuplicate) Copies all node information from originalNode into the current node.
void	**getDistanceGain**(float[] distance, float[] gain) Gets this sound's distance gain attenuation values in separate arrays.
void	**getDistanceGain**(Point2f[] attenuation) Gets this sound's distance attenuation.
int	**getDistanceGainLength**() Get the length of this node's distance gain attenuation arrays.
void	**getPosition**(Point3f position) Retrieves this sound's direction and places it in the vector provided.

Returns	Method Name, Parameters, and Description
void	**setDistanceGain**(float[] distance, float[] gain)
	Sets this sound's distance gain attenuation as an array of Point2fs.
void	**setDistanceGain**(Point2f[] attenuation)
	Sets this sound's distance gain attenuation—where gain scale factor is applied to sound based on distance listener is from sound source.
void	**setPosition**(float x, float y, float z)
	Sets this sound's position from the three values provided.
void	**setPosition**(Point3f position)
	Sets this sound's location from the vector provided.

ConeSound

The ConeSound node extends PointSound to create a sound source that can be directed along a 3D vector. Although the ConeSound node's complicated angular attenuation features are beyond the scope of this book, you're welcome to visit the Core Java 3D web site at http://www.CoreJava3D.com/. As a reader of *Core Web3D* you're given online access to *Core Java 3D* chapters that aren't available to the general public, including a chapter that describes in detail how to construct and use sophisticated cone sound sources.

BackgroundSound

The BackgroundSound node (Tables 15.33, 15.34, and 15.35) is similar to the PointSound node but does not have a location in space. The following code snippet illustrates how to use BackgroundSound to create ambient background music:

```
BackgroundSound bgsound = new BackgroundSound();
bgsound.setSoundData(
    new MediaContainer("file:/j3d/bgsound.au"));
bgsound.setSchedulingBounds(soundBounds);
bgsound.setLoop(-1);
bgsound.setEnable(true);
bgsound.setInitialGain(0.25f);
body.addChild(bgsound);
```

This is very similar to the initialization of the PointSound, but notice that we set the initial gain to 0.25f. This is to make the background sound quieter than the "foreground" sound. If we didn't do this, it would be hard to make out either sound clearly. Also notice that we attach the background sound to the body, instead of the head. In fact, it doesn't matter where we attach it, since it has no point of origin and will be heard throughout the scene. However, it must be attached somewhere, or it won't be heard at all.

Table 15.33   BackgroundSound Constructor Summary

Constructors for the class javax.media.j3d.BackgroundSound, which defines a sound source that has no specific location in 3D-space (sometimes called "ambient" sound). As a subclass of javax.media.j3d.Sound (Tables 15.28 and 15.29), BackgroundSound has the same attributes as a Sound object. See the Java 3D API Specification (http://java.sun.com/products/java-media/3D/) for details.

`public BackgroundSound()`

Constructs a new BackgroundSound node using the default parameters for Sound nodes.

`public BackgroundSound(MediaContainer soundData, float initial-Gain)`

Constructs a BackgroundSound node object using only the provided parameter values for sound data and sample gain.

`public BackgroundSound(MediaContainer soundData, float initial-`
`        Gain, int loopCount, boolean release, boolean continuous,`
`        boolean enable, Bounds region, float priority)`

Constructs a BackgroundSound object accepting all the parameters associated with a Sound node.

Table 15.34   BackgroundSound Field Summary

No fields are defined directly by javax.media.j3d.BackgroundSound; all fields are inherited from its superclass javax.media.j3d.Sound (Table 15.28). See the Java 3D API Specification (http://java.sun.com/products/java-media/3D/) for details.

Table 15.35 BackgroundSound Method Summary

Public methods defined in the class javax.media.j3d.BackgroundSound. BackgroundSound also inherits a number of methods from the abstract class javax.media.j3d.Sound (Table 15.29). See the Java 3D API Specification (http://java.sun.com/products/java-media/3D/) for details.

Returns	*Method Name, Parameters, and Description*
Node	**cloneNode**(boolean forceDuplicate) Creates a new instance of the node.
void	**duplicateNode**(Node originalNode, boolean forceDuplicate) Copies all node information from originalNode into the current node.

Summary

In this chapter we've discussed the various "environmental" nodes in Java 3D. We've discussed the idea of bounding regions and shown examples of Backgrounds, Fog, AmbientLight, PointLight, DirectionalLight, and SpotLight objects. We've also introduced the notion of spatialized audio and looked at how 3D sound programs are created.

Following is a complete list of URLs referenced in this chapter:

Core Web3D   http://www.CoreWeb3D.com/

Core Java 3D   http://www.CoreJava3D.com/

Universal Media   http://www.web3d.org/WorkingGroups/media/

H-Anim   http://www.h-anim.org/

Part 4

MPEG-4/BIFS

MPEG-4 OVERVIEW

Topics in This Chapter

- An Introduction to MPEG

- Fundamental MPEG concepts

- An overview of the MPEG-4 standard

Chapter 16

In Part 2, "Virtual Reality Modeling Language (VRML)," you learned the fundamentals of this language and how the scene-graph data structure is used by VRML programmers to represent a 3D world. Here, you'll learn about a new standard adopted by ISO (International Standard Organization) called MPEG-4.

It is assumed that you are familiar now with VRML concepts developed in the previous part—in particular the scene-graph structure of a VRML scene as well as the event-routing mechanism. This part overviews MPEG standards and focuses on the last one to be released: MPEG-4. Next the binary scene composition will be discussed, and finally, you will learn how to create more dynamic content with MPEG-J, a Java interface extending the concepts of EAI.

This chapter begins with a brief introduction to fundamental concepts and to some terms that are used throughout the MPEG specifications and in this part of the book, then gives a general overview of MPEG standards with focus on MPEG-4 standard. You will learn the necessary jargon to understand MPEG standard as well as the fundamental concepts underlying this technology.

What Is MPEG?

MPEG-4 was developed through an open, collaborative effort among the member countries of the Geneva-based International Standardization Organization ISO/IEC JTC1/SC29/WG11, better known as the Moving Pictures Expert Group, or MPEG. This organization explores every possibility of the digital environment. MPEG-4 is the third standard it has released, following MPEG-1 and MPEG-2 (and MPEG-7 has just started).

Note

The official MPEG web site is located at http://www.cselt.it/mpeg/. Information related to each MPEG standard is available at this site, as well as links to other MPEG resources.

MPEG demonstrations, sites, and material discussed in this book can be found at the Web3D Gallery. Visit http://www.web3dgallery.com/mpeg/ for details.

An MPEG standard defines precise requirements and the technologies needed to achieve the requirements. It defines a common model as a platform to assess the relative merits and integrate the different technologies. This common model is implemented in software and validated through core experiments and bitstreams exchange in an effort to identify and remove bugs and to verify the performance of the standard. While MPEG-1 and MPEG-2 standards have informative softwares that need not be followed, MPEG-4 has a normative one, considering that many MPEG-4 products will be software based. Consequently, products claiming MPEG-4 compliance must decode bitstreams as MPEG-4 reference software.

Fundamental Concepts

MPEG-4 is the first standard that views multimedia content as a set of audio-visual objects that are presented, manipulated, and transported individually. It shares fundamental concepts with previous MPEG standards that we will review.

Audio or video entities that participate as individual elements in a scene are termed *audiovisual objects*. Such objects can be either natural or synthetic. Natural objects are time-variant data and are conveyed separately in different *channels* or *streams*. Throughout this and subsequent chapters the term *media stream* is used to describe any type of elementary audiovisual stream in the MPEG-4 system.

As is the general paradigm in MPEG, all information is conveyed in a streaming manner (even if MPEG-1 is intended to be a storage protocol). The term *elementary stream* refers to data that fully or partially contains the encoded representation of a single audio or visual object, scene description information, or control information.

The process of combining multiple elementary streams into a single stream is called *multiplexing*. It consists of mixing packets of audiovisual elementary streams in an efficient manner based on constraints such as network considerations or error resilience.

The smallest entity in an audiovisual stream is called an *access unit* (AU). Each elementary stream is partitioned in a sequence of such AUs. The content of an AU depends on individual media encoders. In general, this content is not relevant for the system. However, as it is the smallest entity to which timing information can be associated, AU is essential to the system for synchronization purpose.

In general, the timing information consists of *timestamps* needed to synchronize many streams that may be quasi-concurrently generated and consumed. Timestamps are associated with all streamed data and may signal the time at which the data has to be decoded (the *decoding timestamp,* or DTS) or the time at which decoded data should be presented to the user (the *composition timestamp,* or CTS).

Timestamps help in reducing loading delays and ambiguities in execution times. They are useful when the order of arrival of AU is not exactly the same as the order of sending, which is often the case in the Internet environment. Timestamps are also useful to detect if an AU has not been received, in which case the terminal may need to ask the server to resend it. They can also be used for sending AUs ahead of time to the terminal for efficiency (in this case AUs are already present at the terminal; it is not necessary to retransmit them).

Timestamps refer to a *timebase*, which provides a source of time much like a crystal oscillator. A timebase provides only a representation of the current time. On the other hand, a *clock* defines a transformation on the time that its timebase keeps, typically marking time for a particular media stream.

In delivering data in a streaming manner, one cannot guarantee that the sender and receiver are locked to the same clock. Samples of the sender time base can be communicated to the receiver by means of *object clock reference* (OCR) timestamps. The receiver can then estimate, and therefore reconstruct, the speed of the sender clock by observing the arrival times of such OCRs. A number of well-known techniques, such as phase-locked loops (PLLs), are detailed in related publications (see Appendix D, "MPEG-4 Resources," for links). In our networked world, even distributed sources may all be locked to a single timebase such as the Network Time Protocol (NTP) or the Global Positioning System (GPS). In such cases, OCRs might still be used to indicate an arbitrary phase offset in the encoding of time stamps, although a timebase recovery is no longer necessary.

Note

Conceptually, MPEG standards can be thought of as toolkits, where tools are specific functions required to achieve certain functionalities. MPEG defines profiles as groups of tools to satisfy major application domains and maximize interoperability between domains.

Other concepts will be introduced later in this chapter when the topic of MPEG-4 is covered in detail. Following is a review of MPEG standards, from MPEG-1 to MPEG-7.

MPEG-1: Coding of Moving Pictures and Associated Audio or Digital Storage Media at up to About 1.5 Mbit/s

The MPEG-1 project started in May 1988 and became an official international standard (ISO/IEC 11172) in November 1992. MPEG-1 is widely used for storage of interactive movies on CDs at a rate of 1.4 megabits per seconds (1.4 Mbps), which produces video equivalent in quality to VHS's and CD-quality stereo audio. It was the first audiovisual standard defining the receiver (the client) instead of the transmitter (the server). MPEG-1 is also unique in that it operates independently of a particular video format (NTSC, PAL, SECAM, and so forth).

The MPEG-1 standard consists of three parts: systems, video, and audio. One or more audio and video streams with timing information are combined together to form a single stream (Figure 16-1). A number of techniques are used to achieve a high compression ratio on audio and video streams. In terms of MPEG standards, *Systems* describes the heart of the decoder and controls synchronization and composition of all media such as audio and video.

In video, the algorithm uses motion compensation for causal prediction of the current picture from a previous picture, for noncausal prediction of the current picture from a future picture, or for interpolative prediction from past and future pictures. The difference signal, the prediction error, is further compressed using the discrete cosine transform (DCT) to remove spatial correlation and is then quantized. Finally, the motion vectors are combined with the DCT information and coded, using variable-length codes.

In audio, a coded representation is used to compress both mono and stereo audio sequences. Audio samples are filtered and subsampled, and a psychoacoustic model creates a set of data to control the encoding. Refer to Appendix D, "MPEG-4 Resources," if you're interested in learning more about the algorithms used in MPEG-1. Here you'll find links to the MPEG-1 standard (ISO/IEC 11172) as well as a number of related resources. ISO/IEC 11172 part 2 (video) describes the MPEG-1 video encoding algorithms, while part 3 (audio) details MPEG-1 audio encoding.

Note

MPEG-1 is the standard of choice when it comes to representing audio and video on today's PC. Microsoft Windows 95, 98, 2000, and NT come with a built-in MPEG-1 decoder, meaning that over 90% of computers produced today are able to play MPEG-1 content out of the box.

In addition, MPEG-1 Audio layer 3 (more commonly known as MP3) has become an extremely popular format for web-based music, further extending the reach of this international standard.

Europe and Canada have adopted MPEG-1 by way of Digital Audio Broadcasting (DAB), which utilizes MPEG-1 audio. Today you can even find lightweight MPEG-1 video cameras for sale at many electronics stores.

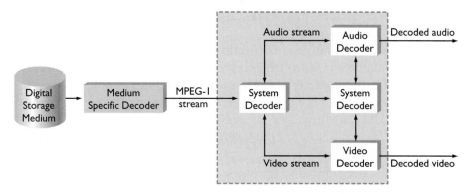

Figure 16-1   MPEG-1 systems.

MPEG-2: Generic Coding of Moving Pictures and Audio

Development of the second MPEG project, MPEG-2, started in July 1990 and was standardized by ISO/IEC in November 1994 (MPEG-2 is ISO/IEC international standard 13818). The main goal was to migrate television from analog to digital with composite quality at 6 Mbps, component quality at 9 Mbps, multichannel audio coding, and multiprogram transport.

The MPEG-2 standard addresses the combining of one or more elementary streams of video and audio, as well as other data, into single or multiple streams which are suitable for storage or transmission. These capabilities are specified in two forms: the Program Stream and the Transport Stream.

The Program Stream is similar to MPEG-1 systems multiplex. It results from combining one or more Packetized Elementary Streams, which have a common time base, into a single stream. The Program Stream is designed for use in relatively error-free environments and is suitable for applications that may involve software processing. Program stream packets may be of variable and relatively great lengths.

The Transport Stream combines one or more Packetized Elementary Streams with one or more independent time bases into a single stream. Elementary streams sharing a common timebase form a *program*. The Transport Stream is designed for use in environments where errors are likely, such as storage or transmission in lossy or noisy media. Transport Streams have a fixed packet size of 188 bytes.

The MPEG-2 standard is widely used in satellite and cable television and is a fundamental technology utilized by tens of millions of set top boxes. Digital television uses MPEG-2 for UHF/VHF broadcasting, and over 2 million DVD players have already been sold as of this writing.

Note

To implement MPEG-2 Video MP@ML—the complete profile, ISO reports that more than 40 patents are licensed.

MPEG-4: Coding of Audiovisual Objects

MPEG-4, the third MPEG project, started in July 1993. The first version became an international standard in March 1999 (ISO/IEC 14496), while the second version was scheduled for standardization in December 1999.

The MPEG-4 standard addresses the coded representation of both natural and synthetic (i.e., computer-generated) audio and visual objects. MPEG-4 was developed to provide the necessary facilities for specifying how such objects can be composed together in a terminal to form complete scenes, how a user can interact with the content, as well as how the streams should be multiplexed for transmission or storage. The MPEG-4 term *terminal* is used in a generic sense and includes computer programs hosted on general-purpose computers.

Possibly the greatest advance made by MPEG-4 is that viewers and listeners need no longer be passive. Most state-of-the-art audiovisual systems today allow users to stop or start a video at will. MPEG-4, however, is quite different: it allows the user to interact with the objects within the scene, whether they derive form real sources, such as natural video, or from synthetic sources, such as computer-generated cartoons. Content creators can give the user the power to modify scenes by deleting, adding, or replacing objects or to alter the behavior of the objects. In essence, the overall MPEG-4 architecture was designed to solve the *global media* problem, namely how to deliver, communicate, consult, synchronize, resource, and network rich-media services, on any platform and any network.

The extraordinary strength of MPEG-4 comes from its radical object-oriented paradigm, allowing audio and video to be easily manipulated. Unlike previous standards, MPEG-4 is composed of objects. They can exist independently, or multiple ones can be grouped together to form higher-level audiovisual entities. The grouping of audiovisual objects for presentation purposes is called *composition* and the result is an MPEG-4 scene.

In addition to the Internet, the standard is also designed for low-bitrate communications devices, which are usually wireless (such as mobile phones). Nevertheless, depending on the type of connection and traffic, all devices have the potential to suffer from low access speed or narrow bandwidth. In response, MPEG-4 supports *scalable content*. Scalable content allows content be encoded once and automatically played out at different rates with acceptable quality for the communication environment at hand.

Visual objects in a scene are described mathematically and given a position in a two- or three-dimensional space. Similarly, audio objects are placed in a sound space. When placed in 3D space, the video and audio objects need only be defined once. The viewer can change his position, and the calculations to update the scene and sound are done accordingly at the user's terminal. This is an extremely important feature if the response needs to be fast and the available bitrate is limited, or when no return channel is available, as in broadcast situations.

MPEG-4/BIFS

MPEG-4's language for describing and dynamically changing the scene is called the *Binary Format for Scenes* (BIFS). BIFS commands are available not only to add or remove objects from the scene but also to change visual or acoustic properties of an object without changing the object itself. BIFS can also animate objects just by sending commands or by using the BIFS-Anim streaming protocol (both protocols are discussed in the following chapters). It can be used to define behaviors of objects in response to user input at the decoder. Because of the way it is designed, BIFS might even be used to treat an application screen (such as a Web browser) like a texture, allowing it to be composed into a scene (see Figure 16-2).

BIFS borrows many concepts from the Virtual Reality Modeling Language (VRML), which is the method used most widely on the Internet to describe 3D objects and users' interaction with them (see Part 1 of this book). In VRML, 3D scenes are described using plain text commands. BIFS,

Figure 16-2 A complex scene showing different types of multimedia that can be transmitted by MPEG-4. Here, web browser screens are texture mapped onto the walls of a 3D scene.

however, is a binary format and thus produces more compact scenes (typically on the order of 10 to 15 times smaller). Unlike VRML, which does not support streaming, MPEG-4 uses BIFS for real-time data streaming. BIFS, therefore, allows MPEG-4 scenes to be incrementally displayed as they come across the wire.

BIFS defines 2D objects such as circles, lines, and rectangles, which are currently found in VRML (VRML is strictly a 3D scene language and at present integrates poorly with 2D content). It also defines facial and body animation objects compatible with the Web3D Consortium's H-Anim Working Group definitions, as well as optimized compression for heavy mesh objects (these new nodes are discussued in more detail in the following chapters).

Note

The Web3D Consortium's H-Anim Working Group is responsible for developing humanoid animation extensions to VRML. For details visit http://www.web3d.org/WorkingGroups/.

For audio, BIFS has entered a new terrain with its provision for *structured audio*, a very efficient method for creating sounds at extremely low bitrates. The concept comes from the MIT Media Laboratory's work on the NetSound library, which uses the popular synthesis language Csound. Rather than a method of synthesis, structured audio is a format for describing methods of synthesis (Figure 16-3).

In structured audio, descriptors for many signal-processing elements for sound synthesis, such as oscillators and digital filters, are specified, and small networks of elements are chosen to create the specific sounds. Each network is termed an *instrument,* whether, for example, it is a piano or a siren. These instruments can be downloaded and then played through commands in the bitstream.

The spirit of the method is musical-score-driven synthesis. The scoring uses two languages: the structured audio orchestra language (SAOL) and the structured audio score language (SASL). Instruments can be defined and downloaded with the first and controlled with the second. Virtually any kind of sound can be generated with these two languages from real-sounding instruments to crackling fire.

As it is a description framework, the output is guaranteed to sound the same from terminal to terminal. Other audio options are already familiar to

MPEG-4 Resources

The MPEG-4 Systems web site is located at http://garuda.imag.fr/MPEG4/. The MPEG-4 Synthetic Audio web site (structured audio coding) is located at http://sound.media.mit.edu/mpeg4/, while the synthetic visual coding site is located at http://www.es.com/mpeg4-snhc/ (natural video encoding information is available at http://bs.hhi.de/mpeg-video/).

Links to these and other MPEG-4 sites are available through the Web3D Gallery MPEG area (http://www.web3dgallery.com/mpeg/) and Appendix D, "MPEG-4 Resources."

MAIN CONVERSION STEP	ENCODING	BIT-RATE

Conventional sampling

Analog-to-digital converter

```
0100111111111
0001111111111
1100001111111
1100001111111
```

High

Digital device interface

Digital saxophone

Performance parameters:
• air pressure
• key open/key closed

Low

Structured audio

DEFINE vibrato as pitch

DEFINE source as buzzer

DEFINE resonance as bandpass filter

OUTPUT source/ 2 + resonance

Low

Structured audio workstation

Figure 16-3   Comparison of sound synthesis methods. Image courtesy of Eric Scheirer, Massachussets Institute of Technology.

users of mass-market synthesizers such as the popular Musical Instrument Digital Interface (MIDI), which can be used to control the MPEG-4 audio if no fine control is needed, or the wavetable bank synthesis, already found on many PC sound cards.

Recently, digital copying of audio on the internet has become a popular practice. In response, MPEG-4 provides features for protection of intellectual property rights. The Intellectual Property Management and Protection (IPMP) interface defines a set of methods a content provider can use to secure the delivery and presentation of data to the user. For example, set top box makers may use this interface as an access to smart cards. A terminal may choose not to use IPMP systems, thereby offering no management and protection features.

To allow more interactivity, MPEG-4 defines in version 2 of the standard a set of Java interfaces called MPEG-J to access elements in the scene, network resources, terminal resources, and input devices. MPEG-J is to MPEG-4 what the External Authoring Inteface (EAI) is to VRML and is similar in concept to EAI. With these interfaces, a terminal can intelligently scale down the content and thus will allow the content creators not only to create highly interactive multimedia content but also to make optimal use of terminal and network resources. An author can programmatically define complex interaction with the scene that would be difficult or even impossible to achieve with the current specification. For example, suppose you want to display a dialog box for a user login and password. It would be much easier to program it in Java than in BIFS. In this scenario, the BIFS *backchannel* may be used to transmit the encrypted information back to the server.

Anatomy of an MPEG-4 Terminal

Unlike MPEG-2, MPEG-4 does not define a transport-layer facility but provides a very flexible multiplexing structure. MPEG-4 was developed to accommodate both client-server (including broadcast) as well as mass-storage based playback scenarios (on hard disk, CD, DVD, and so forth). The sender transmits multiplexed streams containing compressed audiovisual objects and the associated scene and object description. At the receiver these streams are demultiplexed and the resulting objects are decompressed, composed according to the scene description, and presented to the end user. The end user may be allowed to interact with the presentation. Interaction information can be processed locally or transmitted to the sender.

Before being composed, objects traverse the following three layers (as illustrated in Figure 16-4):

- The *delivery layer* consists of the transport multiplex (TransMux) and the MPEG-4 multiplex (FlexMux). MPEG-4 does not define any specific transport layer but provides an interface to access existing ones, which is network independent. This interface is termed *DAI*

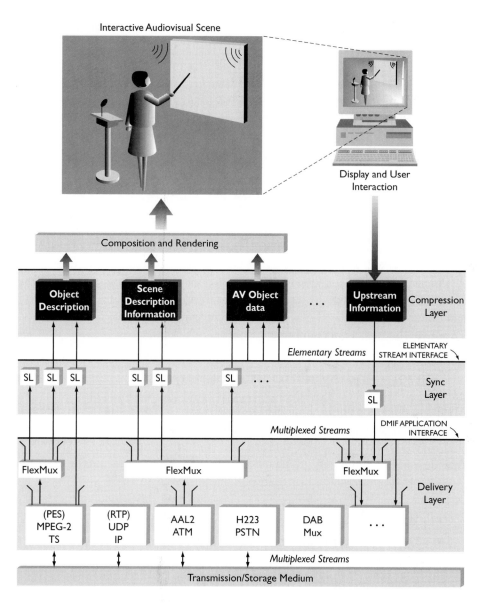

Figure 16-4 Layers of an MPEG-4 client terminal. From the delivery to the composition and rendering, MPEG-4 Systems define how the elementary streams are composed and synchronized.

for *Delivery Multimedia Interchange Format Application Interface*. This layer is media unaware and delivery aware.

- The *sync layer* adapts elementary stream data for communication across the *Elementary Stream Interface*, providing timing and synchronization information, as well as fragmentation and random-access information. This layer is media unaware and delivery unaware.

- The *compression layer* recovers data from its encoded format (elementary stream) through the elementary stream interface and performs the necessary operations to reconstruct the original information. It incorporates the media object decoders. This layer is media aware but delivery unaware.

Between each layer, *Intellectual Property Rights* (IPR) may apply and are handled by IPMP modules.

Finally, at the Presentation layer, the decoded information is used by the terminal's composition, presentation, and rendering subsystems. The user can now interact with the scene and even send information back to the server via the upstream channel.

Delivery and Synchronization Layers

MPEG-4 does not define how data are transported, hence the term *delivery layer* is used as a generic abstraction of any existing transport protocol stack that may be used to transmit and/or store content complying with MPEG-4. A wide variety of delivery mechanisms serve for transmission as well as for storage of streaming data. For example, one might use:

- MPEG-2 Transport Stream (TS) for digital television and DVD
- Digital Audio Broadcasting (DAB)
- UDP protocol over TCP/IP for internet applications
- AAL2 protocol on ATM networks
- Or any other transmission or storage format

In addition, an MPEG-4 application can use any combination of these protocols to access streams on many servers. For applications where the desired transport facility does not fully address these requirements, MPEG-4 defines a simple multiplexing tool called FlexMux with low delay and low overhead.

To facilitate content management, an MPEG-4 file format has been designed based on Apple's Quicktime file format. It is not intended for transmission of MPEG-4 streams but rather for authoring, exchanging, and composition (to combine and extract elementary streams). This format supports use of multiple files and is multiprotocol.

MPEG-4 does not define the functionality of the delivery layer, more commonly known as Delivery Multimedia Interchange Format *(DMIF)*. It only defines the interface to access the streams, called *DMIF Application Interface (DAI)*. The DAI defines an interface not only for the delivering of streaming data but also for signaling information required for session and channel setup as well as teardown.

The DAI allows opening channels to retrieve streams. There is one channel of communication per stream. The streams are termed *elementary streams* (ES) as they represent basic abstractions for any streaming data source. Along with these streams, synchronization and timing information is conveyed using the Synchronization Layer packets. The Sync Layer (SL) extracts this timing information to enable synchronized decoding and, subsequently, composition of the elementary stream data.

There are six different types of elementary streams, as described below.

Object Description Framework (OD)

Object Descriptors (ODs) identify and describe elementary streams and associate them appropriately with an audiovisual scene description. An OD is similar in structure to a URL, containing pointers to elementary streams.

For example, consider an AudioSource node. In VRML, to access the content you specify the source of the audio stream by supplying a URL in the node's *url* field. In MPEG-4, you use a number called an OD id to refer to the Object Descriptor structure and an ES id to refer to the stream itself. If the audio stream is located inside the multiplexed stream, the OD can be used to retrieve it, as depicted in Figure 16-5. If it is located on another server, the OD will contain the URL to the stream instead of the ES id.

Each object descriptor is assigned a unique identifier (OD id) in a defined name scope. This identifier is used to associate audiovisual objects in the scene description with a particular object descriptor and thus the elementary streams related to that object. An OD contains one or more elementary stream descriptors that contain the source of the stream data. It also contains information about the encoding format, configuration information for the decoding process and the sync layer packetization, quality of service requirements for the transmission of the stream, and intellectual property identification, as shown in Figure 16-6.

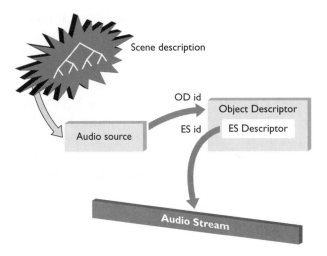

Figure 16-5   An audio node uses an Object Descriptor identifier (OD id) to refer to a unique OD in the name scope. The OD contains one elementary stream descriptor to uniquely identify the audio stream.

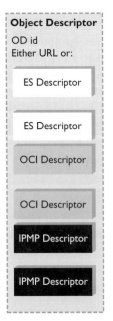

Figure 16-6   Anatomy of an Object Descriptor. An OD is composed of an identifier (OD id), a URL or a list of Elementary Stream Descriptors, and other descriptors such as OCI and IPMP.

A scene defines a unique *name scope.* A subscene is opened by an Inline node and defines its own. In a name scope, the scene description stream serves to compose all the audiovisual streams. The object descriptors are the links between nodes using streamed data and the elementary streams themselves. Figure 16–7 shows an example of such a composition.

Dependency between streams can also be signaled in the elementary stream descriptors. This functionality may be used to describe alternative representations for the same content (e.g. the same speech content in various language), as shown in Figure 16-7, or, for scalable audio or visual streams, it can be used to indicate logical dependency of a stream containing enhancement information to a stream containing the base information. One can use this for lip synchronization between an animated face model and an audio stream or simply to synchronize independent audio and video streams, as in Figure 16-8.

Object descriptors decouple the scene description and the streams. This fundamental concept makes it possible for a content creator to create many versions of the same streams and to store them once, and to play them anywhere, without touching them.

Figure 16-7   An audio node uses an object descriptor which points to two audio streams in the English and French languages.

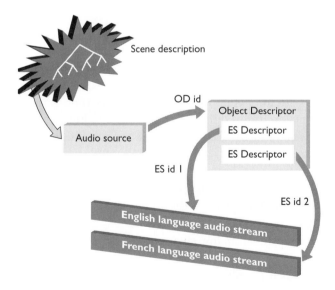

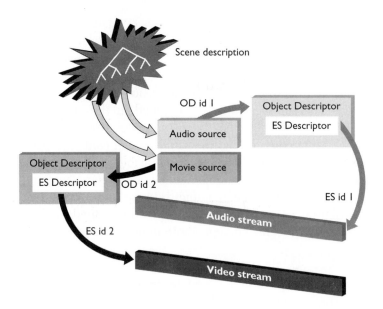

Figure 16-8   Audio and Video nodes, their object descriptors pointing to the respective streams.

Intellectual Property Management and Protection (IPMP)

The IPMP framework consists of a normative interface that permits an MPEG-4 terminal to host one or more IPMP systems. The IPMP interface consists of IPMP descriptors and IPMP streams. The IPMP descriptors are part of the object descriptors stream, while IPMP streams carry time-variant information that can be associated to multiple object descriptors. Figure 16-9 gives an overview of one conceptual MPEG-4 terminal and all the possible control points for IPMP systems.

IPMP systems themselves are nonnormative components. They use the information conveyed in the IPMP streams to protect MPEG-4 content. A terminal may choose not to use IPMP systems, thereby offering no management and protection features.

The IPMP framework can protect many stages in the presentation of MPEG-4 content: at the Sync Layer before decoding a stream, after decoding, and before composition. As it is unlikely that a single IPMP system will be used for MPEG-4 content, this framework allows coexistence of multiple

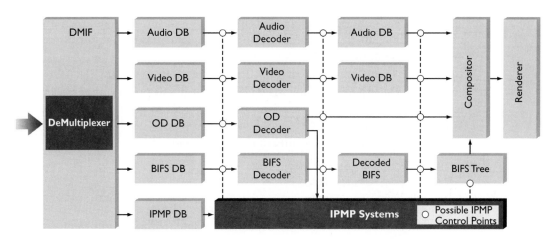

Figure 16-9 MPEG-4 terminal and IPMP systems. Control points may translate, for example, to decrypting or enabling data flows or to reporting about this data flow.

IPMP systems that govern conditional access to specific content streams or entire presentations.

IPMP descriptors convey proprietary information that may help decrypt elementary streams or that contain authorization or entitlement information evaluated by an IPMP subsystem (also proprietary) in the receiving terminal. IPMP descriptors have id's that may be assigned to individual vendors of IPMP systems by a registration authority, so that descriptors for different systems may be attached to content without conflict. Examples of such descriptors include ISBN (International Standard Book Number), ISMN (International Standard Music Number), and DOI (Digital Object Identifier).

IPMP descriptors may be changed over time, but IPMP information that needs frequent updates in a streaming fashion should be conveyed in IPMP streams. Such streams allow keeping IPMP information separate from the original MPEG-4 information. Consequently, an author can create a content, and a vendor might add its own proprietary controls.

Object Content Information (OCI)

Object Content Information descriptors convey descriptive information about audiovisual objects. OCI descriptors can be included in the related object descriptor or elementary stream descriptor, or, if they are time variant, they can be conveyed in separate elementary streams. OCI streams can be associated with multiple object descriptors. OCI descriptors can contain content classification descriptors, keyword descriptors, rating descriptors, language descriptors, textual descriptors, and content-creation descriptors. Finally, it should be noted that OCI is a first step toward MPEG-7, in the sense that the expectation for MPEG-7 is that it will provide much more extensive semantic information about media content in a standardized format. It is therefore likely that OCI will be only a temporary solution to be superseded or extended by the results of this new standard.

Quality of Service (QoS)

The Quality of Service (QoS) descriptor is an optional descriptor that may occur in elementary stream descriptors. It qualifies the requirements a specific elementary stream might impose on the QoS of the transport channel for this stream. At the elementary stream level, an obvious use in interactive scenarios is when the terminal has to select between individual elementary streams based on their traffic and their QoS requirements, as well as the associated communication cost. Unfortunately, it is difficult to agree on a universal set of QoS parameters that is valid for a variety of transport networks. Therefore, a generic set of QoS ␣ Qualifiers has been adopted that needs to be refined in the scope of specific applications.

Audiovisual Streams

The coding of video and audio streams is described in parts 2 and 3 of the MPEG-4 standard. Once decoded, such data are made available to the composition process for potential use during scene rendering.

Upchannel Streams

This stream may be used to allow a better interactivity between client and server. Downstream channels (coming from server to the receiving terminal) may require upchannel information to be transmitted from the receiving terminal to the sending terminal.

Scene Description Streams—BIFS

Scene description streams information addresses the organization of audiovisual objects in a scene, in terms of both spatial and temporal attributes. This information allows the composition and rendering of audiovisual objects after the respective decoders have reconstructed the streaming data for them. Note that video composition is implementation dependent, since MPEG-4 does not mandate particular composition algorithms. For audio data, the composition process has been specified in a normative manner. The scene description is represented using a parametric approach. The description consists of an encoded hierarchy (tree) of nodes with attributes and other information such as event routing. Leaf nodes in this tree may be simple values or elementary audiovisual data, whereas intermediate nodes group this material to form audiovisual objects and perform grouping, transformation, and other such operations on audiovisual objects. The scene description can also evolve by using scene description updates called BIFS commands. As with VRML, BIFS provides support for user and object interactions in the form of linked event sources and targets (via the ROUTE mechanism) as well as sensors (special nodes that can trigger events based on specific conditions). However, MPEG-4, like VRML, does not specify any specific user interface or mechanism that maps user actions (keyboard, mouse, etc.) to such events. With such an interactive environment, it is not necessary to have an upstream channel, but MPEG-4 provides one to enable client-server interactive sessions. This upstream channel may be useful for telelearning applications or for interactive communication with a sales person. In fact, you can think of BIFS commands as acting on an encoded VRML scene. These commands allow insertion, deletion, and modification of nodes, fields, and routes in a scene. A special command is used to replace the whole scene.

BIFS-Anim

This is another protocol used for streamed animation. BIFS-Anim allows modifications of field values over time and can be thought of as a video stream acting on the scene description. In the next chapter you will learn more about these two protocols.

We now have a collection of elementary streams containing compressed data. They are presented to the corresponding decoders. If the terminal does not provide a necessary decoder, then the stream is discarded. The layer where all the decoders reside is called the compression layer.

Compression Layer

The compression layer receives elementary streams in compressed form in the decoders' decoding buffers. The compressed data are decoded by the corresponding decoders and stored in composition memory. The decoded

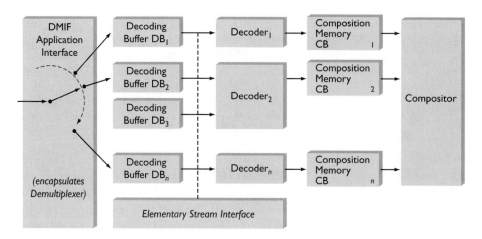

Figure 16-10   MPEG-4 Decoder model.

data is then composed and rendered. In this model (Figure 16-10), the decoding buffer size is given by elementary stream descriptors in associated object descriptors. This buffer size may be fixed by an authoring tool or, for some decoders, known a priori. The composition memory size is variable and depends on each decoder and/or each content.

A decoder decodes one or many access units to produce a composition unit. To each unit is attached a timestamp in order to specify when an access unit should be decoded and when a composition unit should be ready for composition, respectively.

Composition and Rendering

The composition is done according to the scene description. Audiovisual streams decoded in the compression layer can now be composed with other objects and presented to the end user. Figure 16-11 shows an example of scene composition with audio and video streams. This virtual environment is an example of a virtual meeting room in 2D. An audiovisual stream is attached to each person participating in the meeting. The background is a 2D scene with elements each user can grab, such as notebooks, a task list, or a projector to make a presentation to everyone. Alternatively each user can set up a private channel to communicate to another user and exchange data.

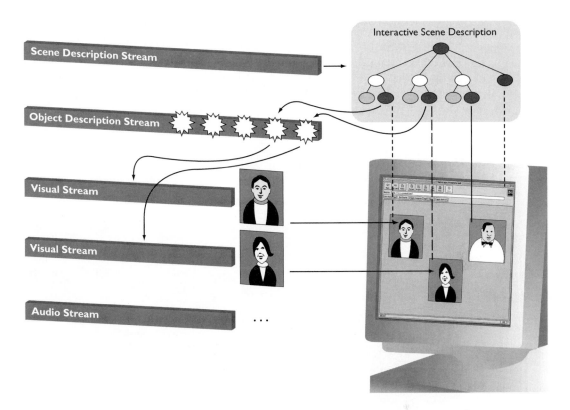

Figure 16-11 Example of scene description and associated streams. Picture courtesy of Olivier Avaro, Deutsche Telekom-Berkom.

In composition, as with VRML, nodes and fields can be viewed as data structures with no special meaning. But in rendering, these nodes need to be interpreted. A cone must be rendered as a cone, while a sensor defines a functionality but could not be rendered graphically.

Rendering is used as a generic term for semantic interpretation of nodes as well as user interaction. User interaction can come from specific devices (keyboard, mouse, etc.) as well as programmatically from scripts that can be written in ECMAScript or Java through the MPEG-J interface. This interface not only can manipulate the scene, as with EAI in the VRML world, but also enables graceful degradation as well as access to the network and to the decoders. In other words, MPEG-J enables controlling all the resources of the terminal.

In version 1 of the standard, facial animation, audio mixing capabilities, and animation of 2D meshes (Figure 16-12) have been introduced.

In version 2, advanced BIFS features allow view-dependent coding of synthetic textures, body animation of virtual humans, 3D model compression, progressive decoding of 3D meshes (Figure 16-13), and structured audio.

Figure 16-12   Some new features introduced by BIFS as compared to VRML. Pictures courtesy of Peter van Beek, Sharp Laboratories of America (a, b) and Touradj Ebrahimi, EPFL (c).

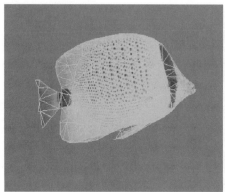 

a. 2D mesh and texture mapped of a fish   b. 2D mesh of a speaker

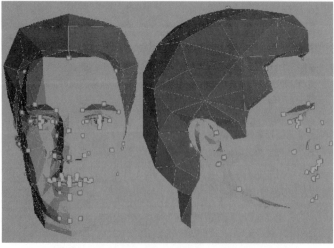

c. 3D face and possible animation control points

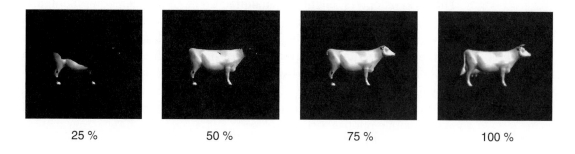

25 %   50 %   75 %   100 %

Figure 16-13   Example of progressive downloading, with each percentage of bitstream received illustrated. Pictures courtesy of Touradj Ebrahimi, EPFL.

MPEG-7: Multimedia Content Description Interface

Development of MPEG-7, the last project of the MPEG series, started in July 1997. MPEG-7 is expected to become international standard ISO/IEC 15938 in September 2001. It's overarching goal is to provide a standardized mechanism to semantically search audio and video databases (MPEG-7 will standardize descriptors and description definition languages for such purposes). For details, visit http://www.cselt.it/mpeg.

The Future of MPEG-4

Given its great potential, the question, of course, is "When will MPEG-4 be available?" The first commercial MPEG-4 systems are expected to be used for internet delivery of multimedia content in early 2000. One MPEG-4 server and a software decoder were previewed by Philips Digital Video Systems at the September 1998 International Broadcasting Convention in Amsterdam. The video decoder in Microsoft's Windows Media Player, in fact, now operates according to the text of the final MPEG-4 standard. Recently, Sharp introduced a digital camera capable of storing MPEG-4 video.

The next adopters might be manufacturers of mobile equipment and providers of mobile services. For such devices, implementing the entire standard would be too much. Instead, a number of profiles, which define a subset of the standard, have been included for their designers to choose from. In fact, MPEG-4 has been found usable for streaming wireless video transmission by using GSM (Global System for Mobile communications) at 10 Kbps, which is the currently used data rate for voice communications. We might soon see mobile phones with video!

Some audio broadcasters have already expressed interest in MPEG-4, whose quality has been judged by the European Narrowband Digital Audio Broadcasting Group to be better than that of analog AM broadcasting for the same bandwidth. The Advanced Audio Coding (AAC) algorithm of the MPEG-2 standard is used for audio of the highest quality, and it provides not only multichannel surround sound support but also considerably lower bitrates than the MP3 audio format widely used on the Internet today.

Some reactions have been hostile to MPEG-4, in the belief that the standard is intended to supersede MPEG-2. But MPEG-4 is not intended to do so; instead, it enables new applications and new types of content, as well as more types of connections. In addition, the Moving Picture Experts Group is now designing ways for MPEG-4 and MPEG-2 to work together. As MPEG-4 does not define a transport layer, MPEG-2 Transport stream could be used. MPEG-2 conveys audio, video, and data. The data part may be used to convey MPEG-4 streams, thus enabling MPEG-4 features on set top boxes (and DVD) already using MPEG-2. Subsequent chapters will discuss the Binary Format for Scenes (BIFS), presenting the new functionalities and the new nodes as compared to VRML. The binary encoding of BIFS will be revealed as well as the two protocols: BIFS-Commands and BIFS-Anim.

Summary

The Moving Picture Experts Group (MPEG) is a working group of the ISO/IEC international standards community charged with the development of international standards for compression, decompression, processing, and coded representation of moving pictures (video), audio, and the combination of both audio and video. To date, MPEG has produced three international standards: MPEG-1 (ISO/IEC 11172), MPEG-2 (ISO/IEC 13818), and MPEG-4 (ISO/IEC 14496). The fourth MPEG project, MPEG-7, is expected to be standardized as ISO/IEC 15938 in September 2001.

Whereas the MPEG-1 and MPEG-2 standards are designed for fixed media and high-bandwidth applications (such as CD-ROM, DVD, and digital television), MPEG-4 is a toolkit of technologies created specifically to enable multimedia over slow and variable-bitrate networks (such as wireless communications devices and the Internet). MPEG-4 version 1 was standardized by ISO/IEC in October 1998, while version 2 received international standardization in December 1999.

MPEG-4 supports coded representation of natural and synthetic (computer-generated) audio and visual objects. MPEG-4 provides the necessary facilities for specifying how such objects can be composed together in a terminal to form complete scenes, how a user can interact with the content, as well as how the streams should be multiplexed for transmission or storage. Binary Format for Scenes (BIFS) is the MPEG-4 language for describing and dynamically changing scenes. Although it is based on VRML, BIFS is a highly compressed binary format that supports streaming (VRML is a text-based format that does not support streaming) and additional capabilities not found in VRML.

Following is a complete list of URLs referenced in this chapter:

MPEG Home Page   http://www.cselt.it/mpeg/

Web3D Gallery MPEG Area   http://www.web3dgallery.com/mpeg/

Web3D Consortium Working Groups   http://www.web3d.org/Working-Groups/

MPEG-4 Systems   http://garuda.imag.fr/MPEG4/

MPEG-4 Synthetic Audio   http://sound.media.mit.edu/mpeg4/

Synthetic visual encoding   http://www.es.com/mpeg4-snhc/

Natural video encoding   http://bs.hhi.de/mpeg-video/

MPEG-4 Industry Forum   http://www.mphil.org

MPEG-4 BINARY FORMAT FOR SCENES (BIFS)

Topics in This Chapter

- An overview of BIFS

- Fundamental differences between BIFS and VRML97

- A crash course on quantization

- BIFS-Commands protocol

- BIFS-Anim protocol

Chapter 17

The preceding chapter introduced MPEG standards and revealed the fundamental concepts of MPEG-4. This chapter presents the MPEG-4 scene description mechanism known as the Binary Format for Scenes (BIFS). While very similar in syntax and functionalities to VRML97, from which it is derived, BIFS is also quite unique in many ways, as you'll soon see.

Binary Format for Scenes (BIFS)

MPEG-4 Systems handles the composition of objects as well as how a user may interact with such objects. The audio, video, and SNHC (synthetic natural hybrid coding) objects provide their own encoding algorithms. In order to combine these media objects into complete presentations, a scene description capability is needed. Binary Format for Scenes is a standard mechanism that provides input data to the presentation layer of the MPEG-4 terminal. Based on VRML97, BIFS includes all the functionalities of this standard (see Part 2 of this book to learn more about VRML). As a text-based 3D scene description language, it describes VRML objects and their actions in plain text format. BIFS code is binary, however, and as such it is capable of representing the same scene in much less space. BIFS content is typically 10 to 15 times smaller in size than when represented in VRML text format. (VRML files can be compressed with GZip, as explained in Chapter 6, "Weaving VRML into Web Pages," although GZip does not compress files as much as BIFS.)

To build interactive applications, BIFS defines commands that can modify, delete, or replace objects in the scene. It is possible to change visual or acoustic properties of an object without changing the object itself; thus, the color alone of a 3D object might be varied. Sending only BIFS-Commands can produce animations, and it is even possible to define the behavior of animated objects in response to user input at the receiver. For streamed animations, BIFS-Anim offers better compression and the ability to synchronize with other media in the scene. A typical example is lip synchronization.

A review of the major differences between VRML97 and BIFS will clarify the fundamental concepts introduced by BIFS, after which you will learn how to use the new 2D and 3D nodes. Then, we'll look at the compression used in the BIFS-Command and BIFS-Anim protocols.

Fundamental Differences with VRML97

In the second version of the MPEG-4 standard, BIFS supports all VRML97 nodes. BIFS also extends VRML97 nodes and capabilities with:

- **2D composition.** 2D primitives can be composed in a 2D hierarchical scene graph. The same operations available for 3D nodes are possible for 2D ones: translation, scaling, and rotations. In addition, MPEG-4 provides specific scrolling and automatic layout capabilities for 2D primitives, similar to a 2D window graphic environment such as Microsoft Windows or X-Motif.

- **2D objects.** To ease integration of 2D graphics primitives with 3D, the design of 2D primitives follows the design of the 3D ones. For instance, the 2D Circle primitive corresponds to the 3D Sphere primitive, while a 2D Rectangle shape corresponds to the 3D Box.

- **2D/3D scene composition.** In addition to the 2D nodes, MPEG-4 defines how to mix 2D and 3D primitives. This is a major difference with VRML97 as well as other 3D graphic formats. Usually, 2D/3D composition is done by restricting 3D primitives to 2D environments or by interfacing a 3D engine with a 2D engine. Both of these approaches are inefficient in terms of rendering and often complex. MEPG-4 defines three ways to solve this issue:

- 2D primitives can be directly included in the 3D space by drawing them in a local x,y plane.
- Transparent regions can be composed on top of the others as layers. MPEG-4 defines Layer2D and Layer3D nodes to render 2D or 3D scenes, respectively. Each layer can be viewed as a rendering of a subscene with its own viewpoint. This allows MPEG-4 to show different views of the same scene, add a 3D logo on a 2D video, or use a 2D interface to a 3D scene as a menu.
- Scenes can be rendered as textures and mapped on any objects with CompositeTexture2D and CompositeTexture3D nodes. The first renders 2D scenes as textures, the second as 3D scenes.

- **Facial and body animation nodes.** Animating a face is a complex task that involves nonrigid deformations. This requires special libraries to render the displacements of vertices on the mesh. MPEG-4 defines facial nodes with a default face model (though the mesh itself is not standardized) or one that can be customized by a content creator. State-of-the-art virtual worlds nowadays use a limited set of predefined models; customization allows developers to use their own models. The body nodes define displacements of joints in a skeleton. In VRML, the Web3D Consortium's Humanoid Animation (H-Anim) Working Group has already defined these specific nodes and scripts to bound and to control the displacements of a humanoid (see http://www.web3d.org/WorkingGroups). These nodes are included in MPEG-4, so that animation scripts do not have to be included with the scene as they are with VRML (making humanoid animation more efficient in MPEG-4).

- **Extended sound composition.** In VRML, the sound model supports attaching sounds to object geometry and the user's point of view. MPEG-4 enhances this model by attaching physical properties to material in the scene, by defining some environmental sound rendering parameters, and by composing sound based on physical and perceptual modeling. MPEG-4 defines an audio scene graph, where sound composition is accomplished by applying signal-processing transformations to the input audio streams (which in turn produces the audio output stream). This approach allows simple, yet flexible mixing control of sound sources. Advanced features allow defining of "instruments" (real instruments, such as horns or drums, as well as conceptual instruments, such as rushing water or blowing wind), defining synthetic music, or producing special effects on natural audio streams.

- **Scalability and scene control.** When dealing with rich multimedia content, a challenging issue is to be sure that the content will be shown as the author intended shown on every client platform. The diversity of client platforms makes it difficult to predict how the content will behave. MPEG-4 defines mechanisms (sometimes called "graceful degradation" mechanisms) that allow content to be scaled down at the client terminal in order to adapt it according to specific environment parameters:

  - The TermCap node contains a list of system capabilities such as frame rate, memory, or CPU load. At any time during scene-graph traversal, the current capabilities of the system can be estimated and the scene graph adapted accordingly. A typical example is to use different sets of models according to the frame rate.
  - Enhancing the EAI interface of VRML97, MPEG-4 defines a Java layer called MPEG-J. An MPEG-J application can access the system resources and act on network, decoders, and composition interfaces.

The BIFS-Command protocol allows dynamic modifications of scenes in time. The BIFS-Anim protocol allows modifications of fields in a streaming manner. The BIFS-Command protocol can be used in two ways:

- The server sends a complete scene and at some point in time issues commands to modify this scene.
- The server sends a small scene and issues many commands to progressively build the scene.

When a VRML scene is downloaded, for example, you must wait until the entire scene has come across the wire. With BIFS, however, the content may be sent in parts. As a result, the user will wait less, see the content progressively on the screen, and start interacting with it immediately. Also, sending parts of the content improves *error resilience*. You may have experienced downloading huge documents on the Web. After a while, the stream is broken and you have to retry until you have a better connection. Sending parts in such noisy environments will reduce this.

In VRML, when you want to produce an animation, you use interpolators with lengthy fields. Consequently, VRML files tend to be much bigger, and the whole file has to be downloaded before it can be rendered. The BIFS-Anim protocol is used for continuous animation of the scene and comes as a separate stream. It allows modification of any values in the scene.

New Scene Features and New Nodes

BIFS includes 2D nodes in its scene graph. This allows 2D scenes and mixing of 2D and 3D primitives in a 3D engine, or layering 2D and 3D scenes, or mapping 2D/3D scenes as composite textures on primitives.

BIFS proposes facial and body nodes to be placed in a 3D space and allows interacting with the models. Advanced features enable defining custom faces and their animation.

2D Nodes

The BIFS 2D nodes are usually 3D nodes with one dimension removed. Their functionalities are identical. There are basic 2D primitives such as *Circle*, *Curve2D*, *IndexedFaceSet2D*, *IndexedLineSet2D*, *PointSet2D*, and *Rectangle*. Other nodes are *Background2D*, *CoordinateInterpolator2D*, *Material2D*, *PlaneSensor2D*, *PositionInterpolator2D*, *ProximitySensor2D*, *Sound2D*, and *Transform2D*. Removing "2D" leads to the corresponding 3D node. Consequently, using 2D nodes is as simple as using 3D nodes in VRML.

Layout and *Form* control the disposition of 2D graphic elements in the display window in the same manner as a windowing system such as Microsoft

Note

BIFS introduces a variety of nodes and capabilities beyond those offered by VRML. New audio capabilities, graceful degradation, and upstream channel management, however, are beyond the scope of this book. Refer to Appendix D, "MPEG-4 Resources," for links to BIFS sites that cover these and other MPEG-4 topics in great detail. Alternately you can visit the MPEG area of Web3D Gallery at http://www.web3dgallery.com/mpeg/ to access these and other online resources.

Windows or X-window. *Layout* specifies the placement of its children in various alignment modes as specified. *Form* specifies the placement of its children according to relative alignment and distribution constraints. Distribution spreads objects regularly, with an equal spacing between them.

2D/3D Nodes

2D/3D nodes mix 2D and 3D functionality. In this category, BIFS offers:

- **Layer2D and Layer3D.** These nodes enable piling different scenes (or layers) on top of one another. Using VRML's DEF/USE mechanism (see Chapter 5, "VRML Fundamentals"), layers can share objects. An example is given in Figure 17-1, where one scene is viewed from different viewpoints, defining a view system as in CAD/CAM applications with top, left, face, and perspective views. If an object is moved in a layer, it is also moved in other layers with respect to the corresponding viewpoints. The second example is to have a 3D layer with a 3D scene inside and a 2D layer with a navigation menu bar.

- **CompositeTexture2D and CompositeTexture3D.** These nodes allow developers to define a scene and map a picture of it as a texture

Figure 17-1   Mixing layers.

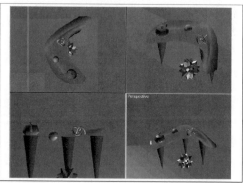

France Télécom Boutique Bleue.
The 3D scene in the background is in a Layer3D, while the 2D buttons in the menu bar are in a Layer2D. By clicking on the buttons, the user is taken to a demonstration stand of pagers, mobile phones, and special offers for the individual and the professional.
The current Java-based player plays BIFS-command contents only.

Different views of the same scene as in a modeler. Each view is Layer3D. Moving an object in a view makes it move in the other views.

on any geometry node. CompositeTexture2D maps 2D scenes while CompositeTexture3D maps 3D ones.

- **OrderedGroup** controls the visual layering order of its children. Each child is rendered on top of another by default or in a specified order. With 3D nodes, this order is along the z-axis of the viewpoint. With 2D nodes, nodes are rendered on top of others, as a painter would do.

Facial and Body Animation Nodes

Face and Body nodes control the rendering and animation of a face and a body. When used as 2D or 3D nodes, with no other parameters, an MPEG-4 terminal should use a default synthetic face and body. These default models are not standardized and consequently vary from renderer to renderer. BIFS defines other parameters in order to create and to animate custom proprietary faces and bodies.

There exist 66 facial animation parameters (Figure 17-2) and 260 body animation parameters. To animate these objects, MPEG-4 defines control points or facial animation parameters (FAPs, shown in Figure 17-3) and body animation parameters (BAPs, shown in Figure 17-4). FAPs can be viewed as muscle anchor points, while BAPs are human body joints.

Body animation relies on forward kinematics (i.e., rotation of each joint has to be specified to produce an animation), while face animation translates feature points on a face mesh. The rendering of these parameters is not standardized. Depending on the complexity of the deformation library, rendering of face models may vary from synthetic appearance to realistic. Dedicated low-bitrate animation bitstreams have been developed to animate these

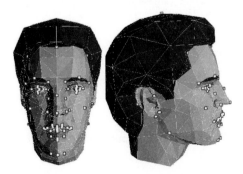

Figure 17-2   The 66 facial feature points or animation parameters (FAPs). (Image courtesy of Touradj Ebrahimi, EPFL.)

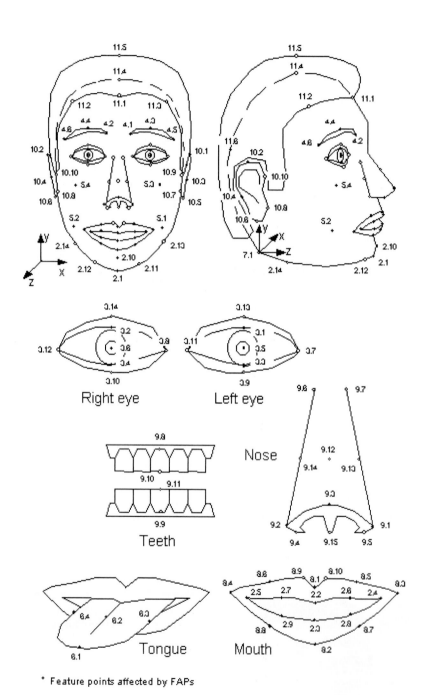

* Feature points affected by FAPs

Figure 17-3   Facial animation parameters. (Image courtesy of Touradj Ebrahimi, EPFL.)

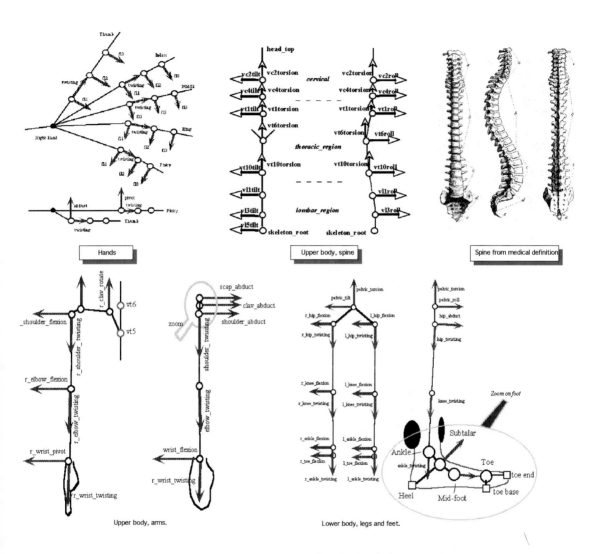

Figure 17-4   Body animation parameters. (Image courtesy of Touradj Ebrahimi, EPFL.)

objects and require specific decoders. (Details of the bitstreams are beyond the scope of this book, although you'll find the resources in Appendix D, "MPEG-4 Resources," invaluable should you wish to learn about bitstreams online.)

To define a custom face, one may send his proprietary face, then define how the FAPs should be applied to this face model. The Face node has the following prototype:

```
Face {
  exposedField      SFNode      fit             NULL
  exposedField      SFNode      fdp             NULL
  exposedField      SFNode      fap             NULL
  exposedField      SFNode      ttsSource       NULL
  exposedField      MFNode      renderedFace    NULL
}
```

A Face node with non-NULL fdp and fit fields defines a custom face.

- **fdp** stands for *facial deformation parameters*. It may contain an FDP node. It defines the particular look of a face by means of downloading the position of face definition points or an entire model.

- **fit** stands for *facial interpolation tables*. It may contain an FIT node. It allows a set of FAPs to be defined in terms of another set of FAPs.

- **ttsSource** determines if the facial animation parameters are to be received from an audio text-to-speech (TTS) source. In this case, ttsSource should contain an AudioSource node, and the face is animated using the phonemes and bookmarks received from the TTS.

- **renderedFace** contains the scene graph of the face after it is rendered (i.e., after all FAPs are applied).

Note

To learn more about TTS, FDP, FIT, and facial animation nodes such as FaceDefMesh, FaceDefTransform, FaceDefTables, Expression, and Viseme, see Appendix D, "MPEG-4 Resources," or visit the MPEG area of the Web3D Gallery at http://www.web3dgallery.com/mpeg/.

Body is defined in similar manner, and custom behavior may be specified as for Face. If you are interested in learning about body animation nodes, refer to the MPEG-4 standard part 1 and to part 2 for a detailed discussion of corresponding animation bitstreams.

This section has given you some highlights on the new graphic functionalities BIFS provides. However, BIFS does not take into account the functionality provided by each node. BIFS is a compressed binary representation of the scene graph. Once decoded, it is interpreted and rendered by the renderer. The remainder of this chapter provides details of BIFS encoding, showing you how to send commands acting on the scene graph and how to send an animation bitstream. BIFS is a low-level process that simply parses a binary scene description, comparable to a VRML browser parsing the textual description of a scene graph.

Let's Shrink the Scene...

VRML uses an ASCII representation that has the advantage of being human readable. However, for transport and storage, a binary format enables optimal data compression as well as faster parsing at the terminal. MPEG-4 defines a binary format for all VRML97 nodes and BIFS additional nodes. Typically, you can expect a compression rate of 10 to 15. If you use advanced features of BIFS, such as mesh compression, it can go up to 30 times! As a comparison, compression tools such as GZip reduce VRML files about 8 times. To achieve these impressive results and preserve the field values, BIFS uses a context-dependent way of encoding, as you will see in the next section.

If you want to compress even more and to allow some loss of data in field values, you can use quantization. For example, if values of an SFInt32 field are in range 0 to 63, they can be coded in 7 bits instead of 32. This is a compression rate of 4.6! You will learn more on quantization in the next section and, in general, be reminded that quantization is a lossy process.

A Crash Course on Quantization

This section describes uniform linear scalar quantization, as it is the type used in BIFS. Other types of quantization that may be used in MPEG-4 streams won't be reviewed. For detailed information, refer to the literature referenced in Appendix D, "MPEG-4 Resources."

In many lossy compression applications, each source output x is represented using one of a small number of code words y (Figure 17-5). The number of possible distinct source output values is generally much greater than the number of codewords available to represent them. The process of representing a large—possibly infinite—set of values with a much smaller set is called *quantization*.

Consider a source that generates numbers between –10 and 10. Suppose we represent each output of the source with the integer value nearest to it. If the source output is equally close to two integers, we will randomly pick one of them. For example, if the source output is 2.47, we represent it as 2, and if the source output is 3.1415927, we represent it as 3.

There are an infinite number of values between –10 and 10. In this example, we are representing this infinite set with a set that contains only 21 values ($\{-10, \ldots, 0, \ldots, 10\}$). These 21 values can be represented on $\log_2(21) \cong$ 5 bits. However, given the representation or reconstruction value, we can never recover the source output. If we are told the reconstruction value is 3, we cannot tell whether the source output was 2.56, 2.95, 3.16, or any other of an infinite set of values between 2.5 and 3.5. In other words, we have lost some information. This loss of information is the reason for the use of the word "lossy" in many compression schemes. The reconstruction error or simply the error is defined as the difference between the source output and the reconstructed value. In the literature, it is called the *difference distortion measure*. Two popular measures of distortion are

- The squared-error measure:

$$d(x, y)=(x-y)^2$$

- The absolute-difference measure:

$$d(x,y)=|x-y|$$

In some applications the distortion is not perceptible as long as it is below some threshold. In these situations, we might be interested in the maximum value of the error magnitude,

$$d_\infty=max_n|x_n-y_n|$$

Figure 17-5 A quantizer maps an input value *x* to a code value *y*. The mapping is a step function. In BIFS, the code is always in the range [0, 2^N-1], where *N* is the number of bits used to store the code in the bitstream.

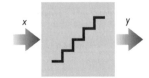

In general, a number of average measures are used to summarize the information in the difference sequence, as it is often difficult to examine the difference on a term-by-term basis. The most often used average measure is the average of the squared-error measure, called the *mean squared error (mse)* and represented as σ^2 or σ_d^2:

$$\sigma^2 = \frac{1}{N} \sum_{n=1}^{N} (x_n - y_n)^2$$

Often you may be interested in the size of the error relative to the signal, called the *signal-to-noise ratio (SNR)*, which represents the ratio of the average squared value of the source output and the *mse*:

$$SNR = \frac{\sigma_x^2}{\sigma^2}$$

Sometimes we are more interested in the size of the error relative to the peak value of the signal, x_{peak}, than in the size of the error relative to the average squared value of the signal. This ratio is called *the peak-signal-to-noise ratio (PSNR) and is measured in decibels (dB)*:

$$PSNR_{dB} = 10 \log_{10} \frac{x_{peak}^2}{\sigma_d^2}$$

The set of inputs and outputs of the quantizer can be scalar or vectors. If they are scalars, we call the quantizers *scalar quantizers*. If they are vectors, we call the quantizers *vector quantizers*.

BIFS has identified 13 different quantizers (see Table 17.1), one for each type of field value in possible nodes of the scene. Therefore, BIFS uses 13 scalar quantizers defined the same way. As it does not use vector quantizers, vector data are considered as a set of independent values using the same quantizer. In other words, quantizer 1 will be used for each of the 3 components of a 3D position.

A quantizer acts on a description of the scene and is used to store this scene on fewer bits. While optional in BIFS-Command, usage of quantizers is mandatory in BIFS-Anim in order to reduce the amount of data

Table 17.1   The 13 BIFS Quantizers. Notation [a, b] means values are between a and b inclusive, while]a, b] means between a exclusive and b inclusive.

Quantizer	Type of value	Dimension of values	Example
0	None		
1	3D positions	3 floats	(0.5, 5, –2.8)
2	2D positions	2 floats	(5.6, –7.8)
3	Drawing order	1 integer	2
4	RGB colors	3 floats in [0, 1]	(0.56, 0.78, 1)
5	Texture coordinate	2 floats in [–1, 1]	(–0.5, 0.89)
6	Angle	1 float in [0, 2π[	0.3456
7	Scale	1 to 3 floats in [0, +∞[	
8	Interpolator keys	1 float in [0, 1]	0.678
9	Unitary normals	3 floats in [–1, 1]	(0.56, –0.76, 0.329)
10	Rotations	1 normal and 1 angle	(0.56, –0.76, 0.329,–0.345)
11	Object size 3D	3 floats in [0, +∞[	
12	Object size 2D	2 floats in [0, +∞[	
13	Linear scalar quantization		

transmitted between two frames. This description is similar to VRML files, and if we look at a particular type of field, say a 3D position, we know what are the minimal v_{min} and maximal v_{max} values for this type of data. Thus, we know the bounds of this type of field. The distortion we will introduce in the data will come from the number of bits we will use to represent data inside these bounds. Let's call N the number of bits used. Consequently, we have 2^N reconstruction values, and quantizing a value v is defined as:

$$v_q = \left[\frac{v - v_{min}}{v_{max} - v_{min}} (2^N - 1) \right]$$

Equation 1 —Quantizing a value in BIFS. This is the method $v_q = quantize(v_{min}, v_{max}, N, v)$.

where [.] returns the integer part of the value. The reconstructed value is:

$$v_r = v_{\min} + v_q \frac{v_{\max} - v_{\min}}{2^N - 1}$$

Equation 2—Reconstructing (or dequantizing) a value from its quantized version. This is the method $v_r = inverse(v_{min}, v_{max}, N, v_q)$.

As the number of reconstruction values is always even in BIFS, this type of quantizer is often called in the literature a *uniform midrise quantizer* (Figure 17-6).

Regarding the definition of the quantized value, the quantizer need not be symmetric, but each step is constant and has the value:

$$\Delta = \frac{v_{max} - v_{min}}{2^N}$$

Figure 17-6 A uniform midrise quantizer as used in BIFS.

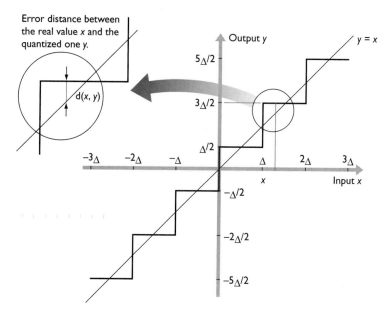

One can show that the mean squared error is $mse = \Delta^2/12$ and the $SNR_{dB} = 6.02N$ dB. This last result says that for every additional bit in the quantizer, we get an increase in the signal-to-noise ratio of 6.02 dB. This means that if the quantizer uses more bits, the SNR will be higher, and intuitively the error on each value will be lower. This well-known result is often used to get an indication of the maximum gain available if we increase the rate (N). However, remember that these results are valid for these particular types of quantizers used in BIFS. If we used different assumptions and quantizer design, the results may not hold. In the next chapter we will reuse these results to see how rate-distortion theory can be used to find the best optimal set of quantizers for a minimal distortion, leading to a minimal bitrate.

Later, the two protocols defined by BIFS will be reviewed. They both use the quantizers presented earlier. For BIFS-Command protocol, usage of the quantizers is not necessary, but for BIFS-Anim it is mandatory.

How Quantization Is Used in BIFS

For each type of field, quantization may be used. When traversing a scene, if a QuantizationParameter node is encountered, the BIFS decoder uses it to decode values of subsequent fields. Quantization parameters may act locally or globally. When used locally, only the node following the QuantizationParameter will use the quantization parameters (if the node has children, its children use them also). If used globally, all subsequent nodes will use the quantization parameters. In the definition of the node below, each color represents a set of quantization parameters (whether it is used or not, bounds, and number of bits) for a quantizer:

Quantizer ID QuantizationParameter {

	field	SFBool	isLocal	FALSE
1	field	SFBool	position3DQuant	FALSE
	field	SFVec3f	position3DMin	$-\infty, -\infty, -\infty$
	field	SFVec3f	position3DMax	$+\infty, +\infty, +\infty$
	field	SFInt32	position3DNbBits	16
2	field	SFBool	position2DQuant	FALSE
	field	SFVec2f	position2DMin	$-\infty, -\infty$
	field	SFVec2f	position2DMax	$+\infty, +\infty$
	field	SFInt32	position2DNbBits	16

3	field	SFBool	drawOrderQuant	TRUE
	field	SFVec3f	drawOrderMin	$-\infty$
	field	SFVec3f	drawOrderMax	$+\infty$
	field	SFInt32	drawOrderNbBits	8
4	field	SFBool	colorQuant	TRUE
	field	SFFloat	colorMin	0.0
	field	SFFloat	colorMax	1.0
	field	SFInt32	colorNbBits	8
5	field	SFBool	textureCoordinateQuant	TRUE
	field	SFFloat	textureCoordinateMin	0.0
	field	SFFloat	textureCoordinateMax	1.0
	field	SFInt32	textureCoordinateNbBits	16
6	field	SFBool	angleQuant	TRUE
	field	SFFloat	angleMin	0
	field	SFFloat	angleMax	$2.\pi$
	field	SFInt32	angleNbBits	16
7	field	SFBool	scaleQuant	FALSE
	field	SFFloat	scaleMin	0.0
	field	SFFloat	scaleMax	$+\infty$
	field	SFInt32	scaleNbBits	8
8	field	SFBool	keyQuant	TRUE
	field	SFFloat	keyMin	0.0
	field	SFFloat	keyMax	1.0
	field	SFInt32	keyNbBits	8
9, 10	field	SFBool	normalQuant	TRUE
	field	SFInt32	normalNbBits	8
11, 12	field	SFBool	sizeQuant	FALSE
	field	SFFloat	sizeMin	0.0
	field	SFFloat	sizeMax	$+\infty$
	field	SFInt32	sizeNbBits	8
	field	SFBool	useEfficientCoding	FALSE
	}			

In this node are defined the quantization parameters for 10 quantizers: `position3D`, `position2D`, `drawOrder`, `color`, `textureCoordinate`, `angle`, `scale`, `interpolator key`, `normal`, `size`. The three remaining quantizers are built using a combination of these quantizers:

- *Object size 3D* (quantizer 11) and *2D* (quantizer 12) use `size` quantizer for each component.

- *Linear scalar quantization* (quantizer 13) uses a number of bits and minimum bounds specified in the fields. These values are known by the BIFS codec and cannot be changed. The quantized value is an integer shifted to fit the interval $[0, 2^N - 1]$:

$$v_q = v - v_{min}$$

Equation 3—Quantizing with the linear scalar quantizer 13.

The reconstructed value is:

$$v_r = v_{min} + v_q$$

Equation 4—Reconstructing a value using linear scalar quantization.

- *Rotation* (quantizer 10) and *normal* (quantizer 9) use the `normal` quantizer. Quantizing normals and rotations is special. The method described here is different from the traditional sampling of Euler angles. Sampling Euler angles leads to a nonuniform sampling on a sphere, while this method provides a uniform one. At the poles, Euler angle sampling will provide fine approximation, while at the equator it will lead to a crude one. As normals and rotations are vectors lying on a unit sphere (in 3D for normals and in 4D for rotations using quaternions, as we will see later), a uniform sampling is desirable.

Normals are unitary; that is, their norm is equal to 1. If a normal has components $\vec{n} = (n_x, n_y, n_z)$, then its norm is defined as:

$$\left\| \vec{n} \right\|^2 = n_x^2 + n_y^2 + n_z^2 = 1$$

A unit vector is defined on a 3D unit sphere. SFRotations (n_x, n_y, n_z, α) can be represented as 4-dimensional unit vectors called unit quaternions:

$$q_0 = \cos\frac{\alpha}{2}, \quad q_1 = \frac{n_x}{\|\vec{n}\|}\sin\frac{\alpha}{2}, \quad q_2 = \frac{n_y}{\|\vec{n}\|}\sin\frac{\alpha}{2}, \quad q3 = \frac{n_z}{\|\vec{n}\|}\sin\frac{\alpha}{2}$$

Equation 5—Converting an SFRotation to a quaternion.

That is, if a rotation has quaternion components $\vec{q} = (q_0, q_x, q_y, q_z)$, then $\|\vec{q}\|^2 = q_0^2 + q_x^2 + q_y^2 + q_z^2 = 1$. As it is a 4D unit vector, a quaternion is defined in a 4D unit sphere. For both, the encoding process is the same and takes advantage of the fact that they lie on unit spheres. To explain how the process works, we give the description for normals. Let us define a normal as

$$\vec{n} = \{n_i\}_{i=1,\ldots,3}$$

The coordinate largest in absolute value n_k determines the *orientation* k of the normal and its sign, its *direction*. The orientation is between 0 and C, which, at most, is 2 for normals and 3 for rotations; thus, this index is encoded on 2 bits and the direction on 1 bit (+1 is 0, –1 is 1). For rotations, *direction* is not written because of the property: Two quaternions lying in opposite directions on the unit sphere actually represent the same rotation.

If we divide all coordinates n_i by n_k, we obtain a reduced normal $n_r = \{n_i/n_k\}$, with the largest coordinate of value 1, which won't need to be encoded. Thus, a normal is encoded using 2 components or a rotation 3. The reduced normal lies inside a unit box, and the angle between the reduced normal and each plane of normal other than k is determined and quantized.

Obviously, $0 < \left|\dfrac{n_i}{n_k}\right| < 1$, so each angle is in range $[-\pi/4, \pi/4]$ and has the value

$$\alpha_1 = \frac{4}{\pi} tan^{-1} \frac{n_{(i+k+1)\bmod C}}{n_k}, \quad i = 0, \ldots, C-1$$

where C is the number of components, 3 for a normal, 4 for a rotation. With this process, $\alpha_i \in [0, 1]$. It will be quantized on $N-1$ bits and a shift of 2^{N-1} is added so as to have a positive value stored in the bitstream on N bits. The encoded value is

$$n_q[i] = 2^{N-1} + quantize(0, 1, N-1, \alpha_i), \quad i = 0, \ldots, C-1$$

Equation 6—Quantizing the reduced components.

where quantize() is given by Equation 1; 0, 1 are the bounds for the angle; and N is the number of bits used in the bitstream.

Reconstruction is given by

$$\hat{n}_q[i] = inverse(0, 1, N-1, n_q[i]) - 2^{N-1}, \quad i = 0, ..., C-1$$

$$\hat{n}_k = direction \frac{1}{\sqrt{1 + \sum_{i=0}^{i=C-1} \tan^2 \frac{\pi \hat{m}_q[i]}{4}}}$$

$$\hat{n}_{(i+k+1) \bmod C} = \tan \frac{\pi \hat{m}_q[i]}{4}, \quad i = 0, ..., C-1$$

Equation 7—Reconstructing normals and rotation components.

If the object is a rotation, the quaternion $\vec{q} = (\hat{n}_0, \hat{n}_1, \hat{n}_2, \hat{n}_3)$ can be converted to a rotation (n_x, n_y, n_z, α):

$$\alpha = 2\cos^{-1}\hat{n}_0, \quad n_x = \frac{\hat{n}_1}{\sin\alpha/2}, \quad n_y = \frac{\hat{n}_2}{\sin\alpha/2}, \quad n_y = \frac{\hat{n}_3}{\sin\alpha/2}$$

Equation 8—Converting a quarternion to an SFRotation.

When the scope of a local QuantizationParameter ends, the previous QuantizationParameter is used, if any. One might view this mechanism as stacking local QuantizationParameter nodes as the scene is traversed. When the scope of such a node ends, it is popped out of the stack. This stack is maintained inside the BIFS decoder.

But, how does the BIFS decoder know which field should use one quantizer or another? In fact, the decoder knows all the nodes it can decode. It also knows all their fields, their default values, and which quantizer should be used for each field, if any. In the appendix we give the prototypes of all BIFS version 1 nodes. The field %q at the end of each field indicates which quantizer should be used.

BIFS-Command Protocol

BIFS-Command protocol is used to send commands acting on a scene from a server to a client terminal in which the scene resides. A *scene* is a set of objects or nodes with specific behavior and an optional list of routes to propagate events between objects. A scene is represented by a scene graph in which leaves are nodes (this graph is the same as the one defined by VRML). Nevertheless, BIFS imposes some constraints on the scene graph:

- It must start with only one top node. If you look at a VRML file, you will realize that you can have many top-level nodes such as Group or Transform.

- All the routes must be at the end of the scene description. In VRML, they can be placed anywhere in the textual description of the scene.

- As BIFS is a binary format, DEF names used in VRML for nodes are replaced by integers on a fixed number of bits. This means that references of such a node (in commands such as USE name and ROUTE name.field) are replaced by numeric identifiers.

- ROUTEs can be DEF'd as nodes, which is not possible in VRML. This is used to reference routes when using commands.

The two first constraints are a result of the BIFS compression scheme's being context dependent. Consider, for example, the following scene (refer to Part 1 of this book if you're unfamiliar with this code):

```
Transform {
  children [
    Shape {
      appearance Appearance {
        material Material { diffuseColor .5 .7 1 }
      }
      geometry Box {}
    }
  ]
}
```

For the *appearance* field, only the Appearance node can be used. For the *material* field, only a Material node is valid. For *geometry*, a set of 3D nodes may be used, such as Sphere, Cone, IndexedFaceSet, or ElevationGrid.

BIFS-Command Examples

La Boutique Bleue, created by France Télécom in 1998, was the first example of BIFS-Command content for the Internet. Available online at http://www.lorraine.region.francetelecom.fr, this virtual shop allows you to interact with 3D models of France Télécom pagers and phones.

For links to this and other BIFS-Command examples, visit the MPEG-4 area of the Web3D Gallery at http://www.web3dgallery.com/mpeg/.

Thus, each field may use a subset of all possible nodes. Such a subset is called a *context*. A node may be part of one or many contexts. For example, a Group node may be used as a top-level node (i.e., a root of the scene graph), but it may also be used as a simple 3D node as a child of another Group or Transform node.

In BIFS version 1, 32 contexts are defined (Table 17.2).

Table 17.2   The 32 contexts defined in BIFS version 1.

Context	*BIFS nodes in this context*	
SF2DNode	Anchor	PlaneSensor2D
32 nodes	AnimationStream	PositionInterpolator2D
	Background2D	ProximitySensor2D
	ColorInterpolator	QuantizationParameter
	Conditional	ScalarInterpolator
	CoordinateInterpolator2D	Script
	DiscSensor	Shape
	Face	Sound2D
	Form	Switch
	Group	TermCap
	Inline	TimeSensor
	LOD	TouchSensor
	Layer2D	Transform2D
	Layer3D	Valuator
	Layout	WorldInfo
	OrderedGroup	

Context   *BIFS nodes in this context*

SF3DNode   Anchor   OrientationInterpolator
52 nodes   AnimationStream   PlaneSensor
                            Background   PlaneSensor2D
                            Background2D   PointLight
                            Billboard   PositionInterpolator
                            Collision   PositionInterpolator2D
                            ColorInterpolator   ProximitySensor2D
                            Conditional   ProximitySensor
                            CoordinateInterpolator   QuantizationParameter
                            CoordinateInterpolator2D ScalarInterpolator
                            CylinderSensor   Script
                            DirectionalLight   Shape
                            DiscSensor   Sound
                            Face   Sound2D
                            Fog   SphereSensor
                            Form   SpotLight
                            Group   Switch
                            Inline   TermCap
                            LOD   TimeSensor
                            Layer2D   TouchSensor
                            Layer3D   Transform
                            Layout   Transform2D
                            ListeningPoint   Valuator
                            NavigationInfo   Viewpoint
                            NormalInterpolator   VisibilitySensor
                            OrderedGroup   WorldInfo

SFAppearanceNode   Appearance

SFAudioNode   AudioBuffer   AudioMix
7 nodes   AudioClip   AudioSource
                            AudioDelay   AudioSwitch
                            AudioFX

SFBackground2DNode   Background2D

SFBackground3DNode   Background

SFColorNode   Color

SFCoordinate2DNode   Coordinate2D

SFCoordinateNode   Coordinate

SFExpressionNode   Expression

SFFAPNode   FAP

SFFDPNode   FDP

Context	*BIFS nodes in this context*	
SFFITNode	FIT	
SFFaceDefMeshNode	FaceDefMesh	
SFFaceDefTablesNode	FaceDefTables	
SFFaceDefTransform-Node	FaceDefTransform	
SFFogNode	Fog	
SFFontStyleNode	FontStyle	
SFGeometryNode	Bitmap	IndexedFaceSet2D
17 nodes	Box	IndexedLineSet
	Circle	IndexedLineSet2D
	Cone	PointSet
	Curve2D	PointSet2D
	Cylinder	Rectangle
	ElevationGrid	Sphere
	Extrusion	Text
	IndexedFaceSet	
SFLinePropertiesNode	LineProperties	
SFMaterialNode	Material	Material2D
SFNavigationInfoNode	NavigationInfo	
SFNormalNode	Normal	
SFStreamingNode	AnimationStream	Inline
5 nodes	AudioClip	MovieTexture
	AudioSource	
SFTextureCoordinate-Node	TextureCoordinate	
SFTextureNode	CompositeTexture2D	MovieTexture
5 nodes	CompositeTexture3D	PixelTexture
	ImageTexture	
SFTextureTransform-Node	TextureTransform	
SFTopNode	Group	Layer3D
4 nodes	Layer2D	OrderedGroup
SFViewpointNode	Viewpoint	
SFVisemeNode	Viseme	
SFWorldNode	Anchor	IndexedLineSet2D
All the 100 nodes	AnimationStream	Inline
	Appearance	LOD

Context

BIFS nodes in this context

AudioBuffer	Layer2D
AudioClip	Layer3D
AudioDelay	Layout LineProperties
AudioFX	ListeningPoint
AudioMix	Material
AudioSource	Material2D
AudioSwitch	MovieTexture
Background	NavigationInfo
Background2D	Normal
Billboard	NormalInterpolator
Bitmap	OrderedGroup
Box	OrientationInterpolator
Circle	PixelTexture
Collision	PlaneSensor
Color	PlaneSensor2D
ColorInterpolator	PointLight
CompositeTexture2D	PointSet
CompositeTexture3D	PointSet2D
Conditional	PositionInterpolator
Cone	PositionInterpolator2D
Coordinate	ProximitySensor2D
Coordinate2D	ProximitySensor
CoordinateInterpolator	QuantizationParameter
CoordinateInterpolator2D	Rectangle
Curve2D	ScalarInterpolator
Cylinder	Script
CylinderSensor	Shape
DirectionalLight	Sound
DiscSensor	Sound2D
ElevationGrid	Sphere
Expression	SphereSensor
Extrusion	SpotLight
Face	Switch
FaceDefMesh	TermCap
FaceDefTables	Text
FaceDefTransform	TextureCoordinate
FAP	TextureTransform
FDP	TimeSensor
FIT	TouchSensor
Fog	Transform
FontStyle	Transform2D

Context	*BIFS nodes in this context*	
	Form	Valuator
	Group	Viewpoint
	ImageTexture	VisibilitySensor
	IndexedFaceSet	Viseme
	IndexedFaceSet2D	WorldInfo
	IndexedLineSet	

The first node in a scene is always an SFTopNode, and each field opens a new context. For example, the definition of a Group node in VRML and BIFS is:

```
          VRML definition                         BIFS definition

Group {                              Group {
  eventIn      MFNode addChildren      eventIn      MF3DNode addChildren
  eventIn      MFNode removeChildren   eventIn      MF3DNode removeChildren
  exposedField MFNode Children         exposedField MF3DNode Children
}                                    }
```

And for Shape:

```
          VRML definition                         BIFS definition

Shape {                              Shape {
  exposedField SFNode  appearance      exposedField SFAppearanceNode appearance
  exposedField SFNode  geometry        exposedField SFGeometryNode   geometry
}                                    }
```

In both cases, each field is an SFNode or an MFNode, but BIFS defines the context of the node we should use for each field. In the case of Group, only 3D nodes can be used as children. For Shape, only appearance nodes and geometry nodes should be used. By looking at the previous tables, we have a choice among 52 nodes for the *geometry* field, 1 node for the *appearance* field, and 17 nodes for the *geometry* field. This contextual information gives us a hint on how many bits should be used to encode a node in a context: Knowing how many nodes are in a context leads to the number of bits necessary and sufficient to encode an index of a node in a context.

For example, suppose we want to use a Sphere as geometry node for the *geometry* field of Shape. We have 17 geometry nodes to choose from. Consequently, $\log_2 17 \approx 5$ bits are necessary to encode the index of Sphere, which is the sixteenth in this context. We will code 16 on 5 bits.

When a context has only one node (like SFAppearanceNode), using 1 bit with value 0 would be useless and save only one bit. To avoid this, no context index is encoded.

To go a step further, you might have noticed that `eventIn` and `eventOut` fields are never used when describing a scene graph. As a result, BIFS-Command encodes only the indices of `field` and `exposedField` field types. The indices of the event fields are used only to encode routes. This separation between fields describes four categories in BIFS, as shown Table 17.3. DEF, IN, OUT, and DYN are used to encode VRML field types (field, exposedField, eventIn, eventOut). When encoding a node, only DEF fields are used. When encoding a ROUTE, only IN and OUT fields are used. DYN fields are used for BIFS-Anim protocols and have no corresponding fields in VRML.

As stated earlier, only nodes' DEF field indexes are used when encoding a static description of a scene graph. OUT and IN fields indices are used when encoding a ROUTE from an OUT field to an IN field respectively. For instance, the field-coding table of a Transform node will be:

```
Transform {                                      DEF    IN     OUT    DYN
  eventIn       MF3DNode     addChildren                 000
  eventIn       MF3DNode     removeChildren              001
  exposedField  SFVec3f      center             000      010    000    000
  exposedField  MF3DNode     children           001      011    001
  exposedField  SFRotation   rotation           010      100    010    001
  exposedField  SFVec3f      scale              011      101    011    010
  exposedField  SFRotation   scaleOrientation   100      010    100    011
  exposedField  SFVec3f      translation        101      111    101    100
}
```

Table 17.3	BIFS field types.			

	DEF	*IN*	*OUT*	*DYN*
eventIn		√		
eventOut			√	
field	√			(√)
exposedField	√	√	√	(√)

Here the notation of the index is in binary: 101 signifies the value 7 will be encoded on 3 bits of value 1, 0, and 1. These values are determined by the type of the fields and in order. For example, there are 6 DEF fields, so $\log_2 6 = 3$ bits are necessary. The first DEF field has number 0 on 3 bits, thus 000 is stored in the bitstream. Similarly, there are 8 IN fields (eventIn and exposedField) and 6 OUT fields (eventOut and exposedField). Again, as $\log_2 8 = 3$, 3 bits are used for IN fields. As for context with only one node, if there is only one field of a certain type, its index is not coded. This is the case for the Group node, which has only one DEF field (children).

So far we have detailed the background concepts in encoding a scene graph in BIFS. In the next section you will see the complete encoding of nodes, fields, and their values. These three parts are the building blocks of BIFS. BIFS does not take into account the functionality of each node. For BIFS, there exist only commands, scene, routes, nodes, fields and their values. In an MPEG-4 terminal, the renderer does the interpretation of each node. This component will render each node according to its name and its field values. At this stage, you may look at BIFS as a specialized text encoder dedicated to VRML scene graphs.

To describe the encoding process of a scene, we will use the Syntactic Description Language, or SDL, which extends C-like syntax into a well-defined object-oriented framework in which bitstream units consist of classes. SDL extends the C++ or Java programming language by providing facilities for defining bitstream-level quantities and how they should be parsed. We review some rules of this language that we will use to describe BIFS encoding.

Syntactic Description Language (SDL)

Rule 1: Classes

```
class class_name [( type param1, type param2, … )] {
  // class body
  …
}
```

A class must have a name and an optional list of default parameters. It may extend another class.

```
class B extends A {
  // class body
  …
  // class parameters
```

```
unsigned int(5) param; // instantiate param
...
 // class code
 if(param == SOME_VALUE {

   ...
 }
}
```

Rule 2: Parameters

```
type[(length)] element_name [=value]; // C++-style comment
```

A type can be any of the following: **int** for integers, **unsigned int** for
unsigned integers, **long** for long integers, **float** for floating-point value,
double for double-precision floating-point value, or **bit** for raw binary data.
The *length* attribute indicates the length of the element in bits, as it is
stored in the bitstream. Note that it is between squared brackets, so *length*
is optional. If *length* is not specified, the type default length should be used:
32 bits for **int**, **unsigned int,** and **float**, 64 bits for **long** and **double**. The
value attribute should be present only when the value is fixed, and it may
also indicate a range of values ('0x01..0xAF'). In many cases the length is
not fixed by a number but rather stored in another value; this can be represented as:

```
int(nbBits) length; // length is stored on nbBits bits
```

Type may also be a class, and the variable is instantiated as in C++ or Java
with as many parameters as in its default constructor.

```
class variable_name
class variable_name (class_parameter1, class_parameter2, ...);
```

Method calls are the same as in C, C++, or Java:

```
[return_value=] a_method ( [param1, param2, ...] )
```

and flow control also:

```
if(condition) {
  ...
} [else if (condition) {
  ...
}] [else {
  ...
}]

for (expression1; condition; expression2) {
```

```
 ...
}

switch (condition) {
[case label1: ...]
[default: ...]
}

do {
 ...
} while (condition);

while (condition) {
 ...
}
```

The SDL language will be used to describe how bits in the BIFS bit-stream are interpreted to decode a complete scene and commands. Compared to the decoding process, the encoding one is straightforward but may require additional configuration parameters, which we will discuss in the next chapter.

Decoding Scene Graph Elements

In a scene we have three types of elements: nodes, fields, and ROUTEs. Figure 17-7 presents a model of the classes in a scene using the Uniform Modeling Language (UML). This is just an object-oriented model; it may not reflect a real implementation, which might require optimizations, real-time constraints, or anything else.

This model shows that BIFS does not take into account the functionality of a node or even what this node is: There is no mention of Transform, Group, Shape, Material, or other nodes. The concept is that a node has a name and is simply a collection of named fields. With this powerful concept in mind, we can now continue our description of decoding a scene.

A BIFS decoder needs some configuration parameters to decode a scene:

```
class BIFSConfig {
nodeIDbits          Number of bits to decode node
                    identifiers
routeIDbits         Number of bits to decode route
                    identifiers
...
```

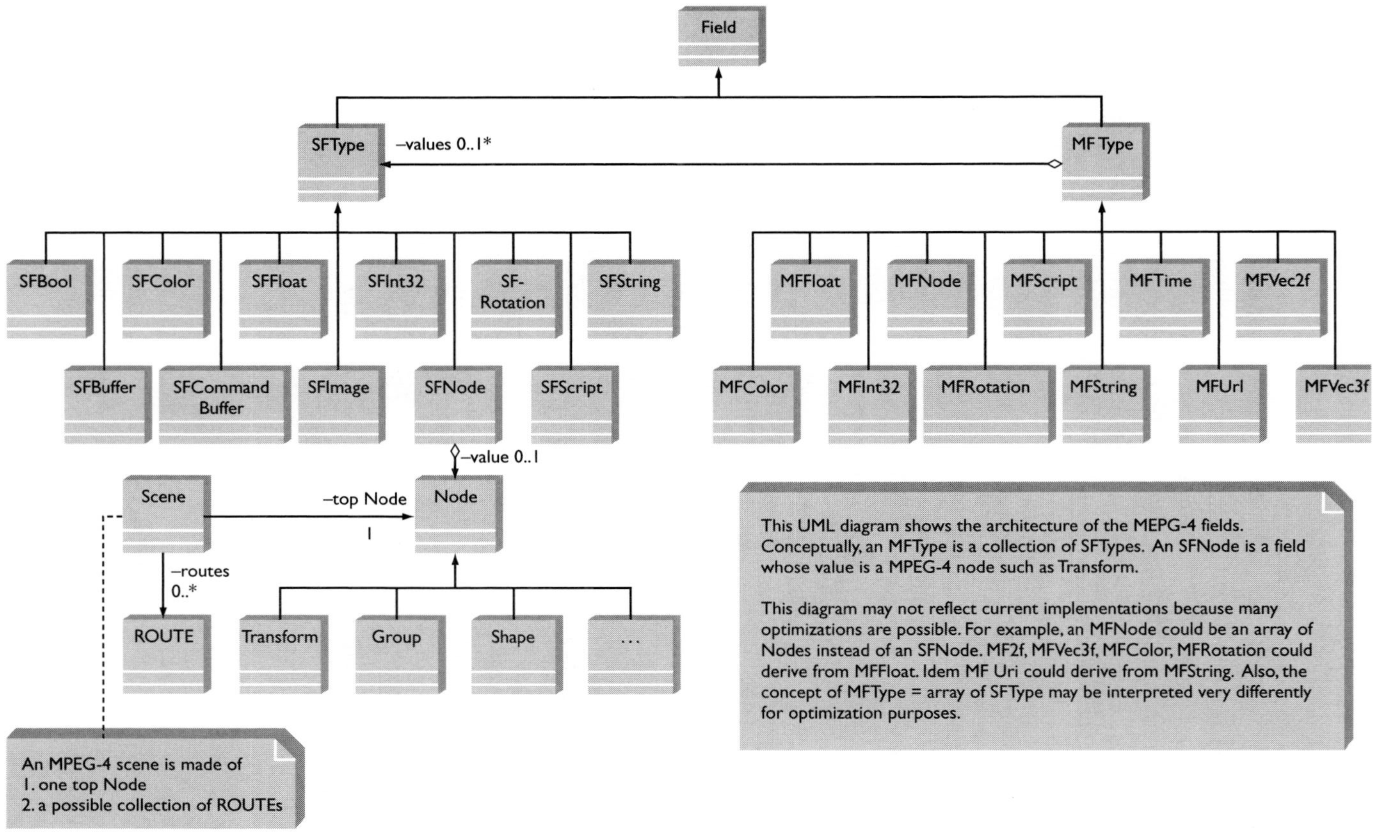

Field
SFType
–values 0..1*
MF Type
SFBool
SFColor
SFFloat
SFInt32
SF-
Rotation
SFString
SFBuffer
SFCommand
Buffer
SFImage
SFNode
SFScript
MFFloat
MFNode
MFScript
MFTime
MFVec2f
MFColor
MFInt32
MFRotation
MFString
MFUrl
MFVec3f
–value 0..1
Scene
–top Node
1
Node
–routes
0..*
ROUTE
Transform
Group
Shape
...
This UML diagram shows the architecture of the MEPG-4 fields. Conceptually, an MFType is a collection of SFTypes. An SFNode is a field whose value is a MPEG-4 node such as Transform.
This diagram may not reflect current implementations because many optimizations are possible. For example, an MFNode could be an array of Nodes instead of an SFNode. MF2f, MFVec3f, MFColor, MFRotation could derive from MFFloat. Idem MF Uri could derive from MFString. Also, the concept of MFType = array of SFType may be interpreted very differently for optimization purposes.
An MPEG-4 scene is made of
1. one top Node
2. a possible collection of ROUTEs

Figure 17-7 A UML model of a scene.

```
bit(1) randomAccess;        These parameters are used
AnimMask animMask();        by BIFS-Anim decoder.
}
```

and knowledge of nodes in each context. These configuration parameters are part of the BIFSConfig descriptor; see the introduction on object descriptors in the preceding chapter. Describing object descriptors is beyond the scope of this book, and so, even if the BIFSConfig descriptor contains other config-uration parameters, we won't detail all of them with regard to decoding a scene. In the BIFS-Anim chapter, which follows, we will use the AnimMask.

To create a node from a context, our BIFS decoder will have the following methods:

```
class BIFSDecoder {
  getContextBits(context)     Returns the number of bits used
                              to encode a node index in this
                              context.
  createNode(context, index)  Returns a node at index position
                              in a context.
  getNodeFromID(nodeID)       Returns a node from a node iden-
                              tifier or NULL if none.
  QuantizationParameter qp;   The current QuantizationParame-
                              ter node if any.
}
```

Each type of node (Transform, Group, Shape, ...) must have the following methods for decoding:

```
class NodeData {
  int nodeType;               The type of the node: Trans-
                              form, Shape, Face, ...
  int getNumDefFields()       Returns the number of DEF
                              fields
  int getNumInFields()        Returns the number of IN
                              fields
  int getNumOutFields()       Returns the number of OUT
                              fields
  int getNumDynFields()       Returns the number of DYN
                              fields
  int getNumDefBits()         Returns the number of bits to
                              encode a DEF field, this is
                              log₂(getNumDefFields())
  int getNumInBits()          Returns the number of bits to
                              encode an IN field, this is
                              log₂(getNumInFields())
```

```
int getNumOutBits()               Returns the number of bits to
                                  encode an OUT field, this is
                                  log₂(getNumOutFields())
FieldData getDefField(index)      Returns the DEF FieldData at
                                  index in the node or NULL if
                                  none.
FieldData getInField(index)       Returns the IN FieldData at
                                  index in the node or NULL if
                                  none.
FieldData getOutField(index)      Returns the OUT FieldData at
                                  index in the node or NULL if
                                  none.
FieldData getDynField(index)      Returns the DYN FieldData at
                                  index in the node or NULL if
                                  none.
}
```

And FieldData class holds quantization information about a field in a node while decoding:

```
class FieldData {
  boolean isQuantized;            TRUE if the BIFS decoder has
                                  a QuantizationParameter node
                                  acting on this type of field.
  boolean useEfficientCoding;     TRUE if this field uses effi-
                                  cient float coding. This is
                                  the case if the decoder has a
                                  QuantizationParameter node
                                  with useEfficientCoding set
                                  to TRUE.
  int quantType;                  The quantizer index from 1 to
                                  13 used by this field.
  int nbBits;                     Number of bits used to quan-
                                  tize this field.
  int nbComp;                     Number of components for nu-
                                  meric fields. SFFloat and
                                  SFInt32 have 1 component,
                                  SFVec2f has 2, SFColor and
                                  SFVec3f have 3, and SFRota-
                                  tion has 4 components.
  AnimFieldQP qp                  Animation quantizer of this
                                  field. This is the same as
                                  QuantizationParameter.
}
```

At the beginning of this section, we discussed the concept of BIFS contexts. To encode an SFNode, we need to know in which context it is and what is the index of the node in it. The first node of the scene is always in SFTopNode context, and each SFNode or MFNode field will open a new context for its values.

class	*number of bits*

```
class Scene {
  bit(8) reserved;                    8
  SFNode node(SFTopNode);
  bit(1) hasROUTEs;                   1
  if(hasROUTEs) {
    ROUTEs routes;
  }
}
```

A Scene object (recall that in object-oriented languages an *object* is an instantiation of a *class*) first reads 8 reserved bits that will be used in future versions of BIFS. In MPEG-4 version 1 we simply discard their value. Then an SFNode object node is read with SFTopNode context. The boolean (i.e., a 1-bit value) hasROUTEs indicates, if nonzero, that we have ROUTEs to read.

As in VRML, an SFNode might be reused via the DEF/USE mechanism. BIFS does not use names but numeric identifiers, unique to each DEF.

VRML	*BIFS*

```
DEF MyBox Shape {              DEF 5 Shape {
  appearance Appearance {        appearance Appearance {
    material Material {            material Material {
      diffuseColor 1 .5 .1          diffuseColor 1 .5 .1
    }                             }
  }                             }
  geometry Box { size 2 3 1 }   geometry Box { size 2 3 1 }
}                              }


Transform {                    Transform {
  children [                     children [
    USE MyBox                      USE 5
  ]                              ]
}                              }
```

The node identifier or nodeID is also used by the commands to update the scene graph.

class	*number of bits*

```
class SFNode (int context) {
  bit(1) isReused;                              1
  if(isReused) {
    bit(BIFSConfig.nodeIDbits) nodeID;    BIFSConfig.nodeIDbits
  }
  else {
    bit(getContextBits(context)) nodeIndex;   getContextBits
                                                (context)

    node = createNode(context, nodeIndex);
    bit(1) isUpdatable;                         1
    if(isUpdatable) {
      bit(BIFSConfig.nodeIDbits) nodeID;  BIFSConfig.nodeIDbits
    }
    bit(1) maskDescription;                     1
    if(maskDescription) {
      MaskNodeDescription mnode(node);
    }
    else {
      ListNodeDescription lnode(node);
    }
  }
}
```

If the node uses another one (isReused=1), we decode the nodeID of the used node, otherwise we decode the nodeIndex of the node in this context and instantiate the node. If the node isUpdatable, we decode the nodeID. As the node has been created, the number of fields it has is known, and the decoding process has to decode their values. BIFS defines two ways of encoding fields: mask and list descriptions. Depending on the number of DEF fields, one description will save some bits compared to the other. One can show that if equation 9 holds:

$$k\,(D+1) \le 1 + nD$$

Equation 9—Choose Rash Node Description if this equation holds.

where k is the number of DEF fields with default values, n the total number of DEF fields, and D the number of DEF bits, which is $[1 + \log_2 n]$, where $[.]$ rounds a number down, toward zero. Note also that a node with only one DEF field used 0 DEF bits.

class	*number of bits*

```
class MaskNodeDescription(NodeData node) {
 for(i=0; i<node.getNumDefFields(); i++) {
  bit(1) mask;                                        1
  if(mask)
   Field value(node.getDefField(i));                  V
 }
}
```

In the `MaskNodeListDescription`, the encoder encodes a field if its value is different from its default value. For each field, it writes a Boolean `mask` to indicate whether the field has default value (`false`) or not (`true`), and if `true`, writes its `value` in the bitstream.

class	*number of bits*

```
class ListNodeDescription(NodeData node) {
 bit(1) endFlag;                                      1
 while(!endFlag) {
  int(node.getDefBits()) fieldIndex;            node.getDef
                                                   Bits()
  Field value(node.getDefField(fieldIndex));         V
  bit(1) endFlag;                                     1
 }
}
```

In the `ListNodeDescription`, if the field has a value different from its default one, the encoder writes its `fieldIndex` and `value` in the bitstream.

When the node was instantiated, the fields were created with default values. In the two descriptions, the field to be decoded is retrieved from the node description and its value is decoded.

class	*number of bits*

```
class Field(FieldData field) {
 if(isSF(field))
```

```
  SFField svalue(field);
 else
  MFField mvalue(field);
}
```

The method isSF(field) returns true if the field is a single-valued field and false if the field has multiple values. In an object-oriented framework this class is not necessary, since each object inherits from Field and has its own parsing method. This class is used here for clarity.

class   *number of bits*

```
class MFField(FieldData field) {
 bit(1) reserved;                                          1
 if(!reserved) {
  bit(1) isListDescription;                                1
  if(isListDescription)
   MFListDescription lfield(field);
  else
   MFVectorDescription vfield(field);
 }
}
```

The choice between MFListDescription and MFVectorDescription is made by the encoder; if

$$n \leq \lceil 5 + \log_2 n \rceil$$

Equation 10—The list description should be preferred
for MFFields with less than 10 fields.

where n is the number of fields, the MFListDescription should be preferred.

class   *number of bits*

```
class MFListDescription (FieldData fd) {
 bit(1) endFlag;                                           1
 while(!endFlag) {
  Field field(fd);                                         F
  bit(1) endFlag;                                          1
 }
}
```

This representation leads to $1 + n(F + 1)$ bits in the bitstream.

class	*number of bits*

```
class MFVectorDescription (FieldData fd) {
  int(5) nbBits;                            5
  int(nbBits) numFields;                   nbBits
  Field field[numFields](fd);          NumFields*F
}
```

This representation leads to $6 + \log_2 n + nF$ bits in the bitstream.

As Field is the base class of all fields, the decoding process will use the correct Field type (SFBool, SFFloat, MFInt32, ...). BIFS defines an efficient way to encode a floating-point value if quantization is used. If not, the traditional IEEE 754 floating-point representation is used (which is the one used in most computer hardware).

class	*number of bits*

```
class GenericFloat {
  if(BIFSDecoder.qp.useEfficientcoding)
    EfficientFloat value;                  4 to 29
  else
    float value;                              32
}
```

```
class EfficientFloat {
  unsigned int(4) mantissaLength;             4
  if(mantissaLength) {
    int(3) exponentLength;                    3
    int(1) mantissaSign;                      1
    int(mantissaLength-1) mantissa;     mantissaLength-1
    if(exponentLength) {
      int(1) exponentSign;                    1
      int(exponentLength-1) exponent;   exponentLength-1
    }
  }
}
```

Using `EfficientFloat` representation, zero is stored on 4 bits only (`mantissaLength=0`) compared with 32 bits. This representation encodes floats in a variable length from 4 to 29 bits. The reconstructed float is:

$$value = (1 - 2 \cdot mantissaSign) \cdot (2^{mantisaLength-1} + mantisa)$$
$$\cdot 2^{(1-2 \cdot exponentSign) \cdot (2exponentLength-1+exponent)}$$

class	*number of bits*

```
class SFBool (FieldData field) extends Field {
 bit(1) value;                                              1
}
```

```
class SFInt32 (FieldData field) extends Field {
 if(field.isQuantized)
  QuantizedField qvalue(field);
 else
 int value;                                                32
}
```

```
class SFFloat (FieldData field) extends Field {
 if(field.isQuantized)
  QuantizedField qvalue(field);
 else
  GenericFloat value;                                   4 to 32
}
```

```
class SFTime (FieldData field) extends Field {
 double value;                                             64
}
```

```
class SFVec2f (FieldData field) extends Field {
 if(field.isQuantized)
  QuantizedField qvalue(field);
 else {
  GenericFloat x;                                      4 to 32
  GenericFloat y;                                      4 to 32
 }
}
```

```
class SFVec3f (FieldData field) extends Field {
 if(field.isQuantized)
  QuantizedField qvalue(field);
 else {
  GenericFloat x;                                      4 to 32
  GenericFloat y;                                      4 to 32
```

```
  GenericFloat z;                                          4 to 32
 }
}

class SFColor (FieldData field) extends Field {
 if(field.isQuantized)
  QuantizedField qvalue(field);
 else {
  GenericFloat red;                                        4 to 32
  GenericFloat green;                                      4 to 32
  GenericFloat blue;                                       4 to 32
 }
}

class SFRotation (FieldData field) extends Field {
 if(field.isQuantized)
  QuantizedField qvalue(field);
 else {
  GenericFloat nx;                                         4 to 32
  GenericFloat ny;                                         4 to 32
  GenericFloat nz;                                         4 to 32
  GenericFloat angle;                                      4 to 32
 }
}
class SFString (FieldData field) extends Field {
 unsigned int(5) nbBits;                                      5
 unsigned int(nbBits) length;                              NbBits
 char(8) value[length];                                   8.length
}
```

SFString value is encoded using UTF-8 character encoding. The encoding of SFUrl is as follows:

class	*number of bits*

```
class SFUrl (FieldData field) extends Field {
  bit(1) isOD;                                               1
  if(isOD)
    bit(10) ODid;                                           10
  else
    SFString url;
 }
```

SFUrl extends the VRML definition, since an object descriptor (OD) may be used to access a stream in the MPEG-4 bitstream. This stream is uniquely referenced by an OD identifier ODid. When url is used, it specifies the location where a stream has to be fetched, as in VRML.

class	*number of bits*

```
class SFImage (FieldData field) extends Field {
  unsigned int(12) width;                              12
  unsigned int(12) height;                             12
  bit(2) numComponents;                                2
  bit(8) pixels[(numComponents+1)*width*height]        8*(numComponents
                                                       +1)*width*height
}
```

An SFImage is a new type of field and can store a raw image defined as an array of characters (8-bit). numComponents defines the number of color components:

0	Greyscale image
1	Greyscale + alpha channel
2	RGB image
3	RGB + alpha channel

class	*number of bits*

```
class SFBuffer (FieldData field) extends Field {
  unsigned int(5) nbBits;                              5
  unsigned int(nbBits) length;                         nbBits
  bit(8) value[length];                                8*length
}
```

SFBuffer does not exist in VRML and enables storing an array of raw data.

```
class SFCommandBuffer (FieldData field) extends Field {
  CommandFrame();
}
```

The SFCommandBuffer type is specific to BIFS and is used to handle BIFS commands. We will review commands later in this section. At the time of this writing, the SFScript field encoding is poorly defined in the MPEG-4 framework, so it won't be presented here.

If the field is quantized, i.e., if the BIFS decoder contains a Quantization-Parameter node, which acts on this class of field, then a quantized value is decoded:

```
class QuantizedField (FieldData field) {
 switch(field.quantType) {
 case 9:
 int(1) direction; 1
 case 10:
 int(2) orientation;      2
 default:
 break;
 }
 for(i=0; i < field.nbComp; i++)
 int(field.nbBits) vq[i];
}
```

Cases 9 and 10 are for normals and rotations, respectively. From vq[i] and the field's quantizer bounds, the reconstructed values vr[i] are determined using equation 7 for normals and rotations, equation 4 for linear scalar quantization, and equation 2 for other values.

Finally, scene encoding isn't complete without ROUTEs. Their encoding is similar to that for MFFields.

class	*number of bits*

```
class ROUTEs {
 bit(1) isListDescription;               1
 if(isListDescription)
  ListROUTEs lroutes;
 else
  VectorROUTEs vroutes;
}
```

class	*number of bits*

```
class ListROUTEs {
 do {
  ROUTE route;                            R
  bit(1) moreRoutes;                      1
 } while(moreRoutes);
}
```

class   *number of bits*

```
class VectorROUTEs {
   int(5) nbBits;                              5
   int(nbBits) length;                       nbBits
   ROUTE route[length];                     length*R
}
```

As for MFField, the choice of list representation may be made by solving the equation:

$$n \leq \lceil 6 + \log_2 n \rceil$$

Equation 11 — The list description should be preferred for less than 11 ROUTEs.

where n is the number of routes in the scene. The encoding of a route defined as:

ROUTE nodeOut.fieldOut TO nodeIn.fieldIn

where fieldOut is an OUT field and fieldIn is an IN one, it is:

class   *number of bits*

```
class ROUTE {
bit(1) isUpdatable;                              1
if(isUpdatable)
bit(BIFSConfig.routeIDbits) routeID;          routeIDbits

bit(BIFSConfig.nodeIDbits) outNodeID;          nodeIDbits
NodeData nodeOut = getNodeFromID(outNodeID);
int(nodeOut.getOutBits()) outFieldRef;      nodeOut.getOutBits()

bit(BIFSConfig.nodeIDbits) inNodeID;           nodeIDbits
NodeData nodeIn = getNodeFromID(inNodeID);
int(nodeIn.getInBits()) inFieldRef;          nodeIn.getInBits()
}
```

So far, we have presented the encoding and decoding of a scene and detailed the quantization process of each field. Before concluding with the

BIFS commands, we will review some real examples to understand how this process works.

Example: Encoding a Simple Scene Step-by-Step

Suppose we have the following simple scene composed of a blue box centered at the origin and a red unit sphere moving from corner to corner:

```
Group {
 children [
  DEF TS TimeSensor {}
  Shape {
   appearance Appearance {
    material Material { diffuseColor 0 0 1 }
   }
   geometry Box { size 2 1 3 }
  }

  DEF PI PositionInterpolator {
   key [ 0 0.125 0.25 0.375 0.5 0.625 0.75 0.875 ]
   keyValue [ -1 0.5 1.5, 1 0.5 1.5, 1 0.5 -1.5, -1 0.5 -1.5,
   -1 -0.5 -1.5, -1 -0.5 1.5, 1 -0.5 1.5, 1 -.5 -1.5 ]
  }

  DEF XF Transform {
   children [
    Shape {
     appearance Appearance {
      material DEF SMAT Material { diffuseColor 1 0 0 }
     }
     geometry Sphere {}
    }
   ]
  }
 ]
}

ROUTE DEF R1 TS.fraction_changed TO PI.set_fraction
ROUTE DEF R2 PI.value_changed TO XF.translation
```

   This simple scene will be encoded as follows (without quantization, though): We choose that each time we encounter a DEF name, we convert the name to an integer we increment, starting from 0. Note also how the node encoding is affected by the context when the encoder enters an SFNode or MFNode. In BIFS, ROUTEs may have a routeID, in order to update them with commands.

In all our examples, we suppose the number of bits used to encode a nodeID or a routeID to be 10 bits:

```
BIFSDecoder.nodeIDbits = BIFSDecoder.routeIDbits = 10.
```

Scene	Encoding	Comments
	bit (8) reserved = 0	BIFSScene
Group {	bit (1) isReused = 0	SFNode(SFTopNode)
	bit (3) nodeIndex = 1	
	bit (1) isUpdatable = 0	
	bit (1) maskDescription = 0	We use ListNodeDescription
children [	bit (1) endFlag = 0	children is the first DEF
	bit (0) fieldIndex = 0	field of Group
	bit (1) reserved = 0	
	bit (1) isListDescription = 1	
	bit (1) endFlag = 0	
DEF TS TimeSensor {}	bit (1) isReused = 0	SFNode(SF3DNode)
	bit (6) nodeIndex = 45	
	bit (1) isUpdatable = 1	First DEF name in the scene
	bit (10) nodeID = 0	has ID 0 in this encoding.
	bit (1) maskDescription = 0	We use ListNodeDescription
	bit (1) endFlag = 1	
	bit (1) endFlag = 0	
Shape {	bit (1) isReused = 0	SFNode(SF3DNode)
	bit (6) nodeIndex = 38	
	bit (1) isUpdatable = 0	
	bit (1) maskDescription = 0	
appearance	bit (1) endFlag = 0	appearance is the first DEF
	bit (1) fieldIndex = 0	field of Shape.
Appearance {	bit (1) isReused = 0	SFNode(SFAppearanceNode)
	bit (1) nodeIndex = 1	
	bit (1) isUpdatable = 0	
	bit (1) maskDescription = 0	
material	bit (1) endFlag = 0	material is the first DEF
	bit (2) fieldIndex = 0	field of Appearance.
Material {	bit (1) isReused = 0	SFNode(SFMaterialNode)
	bit (2) nodeIndex = 1	
	bit (1) isUpdatable = 0	
	bit (1) maskDescription = 0	
	bit (1) endFlag = 0	diffuseColor is the second
diffuseColor 0 0 1	bit (3) fieldIndex = 1	field of Material.

Scene	*Encoding*	*Comments*
	float r = 0.000000	As no QuantizationParameter
	float g = 0.000000	is used, floats are stored
	float b = 1.000000	as 32 bits IEEE 754.
}	bit (1) endFlag = 1	
}	bit (1) endFlag = 1	
geometry	bit (1) endFlag = 0	geometry is the second field
	bit (1) fieldIndex = 1	of Shape.
Box {	bit (1) isReused = 0	SFNode(SFGeometryNode)
	bit (5) nodeIndex = 2	
	bit (1) isUpdatable = 0	
	bit (1) maskDescription = 0	Using ListNodeDescription,
size 2 1 3	bit (1) endFlag = 0	size is the first field of
	bit (0) fieldIndex = 0	Box.
	float x = 2.000000	Again, encoded as IEEE 754
	float y = 1.000000	on 32 bits.
	float z = 3.000000	
}	bit (1) endFlag = 1	
}	bit (1) endFlag = 1	
	bit (1) endFlag = 0	
DEF PI		
PositionInterpolator {	bit (1) isReused = 0	SFNode(SF3DNode)
	bit (6) nodeIndex = 31	
	bit (1) isUpdatable = 1	PI is the second DEF name in
	bit (10) nodeID = 1	this scene.
	bit (1) maskDescription = 0	Using ListNodeDescription.
key [0 0.125 0.25		
0.375 0.5 0.625 0.75		
0.875]	bit (1) endFlag = 0	
	bit (1) fieldIndex = 0	
	bit (1) reserved = 0	This MFInt32 is encoded using
	bit (1) isListDescription = 1	MFListDescription, since we
	bit (1) endFlag = 0	have 8 values.
	float value = 0.000000	
	bit (1) endFlag = 0	
	float value = 0.125000	
	bit (1) endFlag = 0	
	float value = 0.250000	
	bit (1) endFlag = 0	
	float value = 0.375000	
	bit (1) endFlag = 0	
	float value = 0.500000	
	bit (1) endFlag = 0	
	float value = 0.625000	
	bit (1) endFlag = 0	
	float value = 0.750000	
	bit (1) endFlag = 0	
	float value = 0.875000	
	bit (1) endFlag = 1	

Scene	Encoding	Comments
keyValue [-1 0.5 1.5, 1 0.5 1.5, 1 0.5 -1.5, -1 0.5 -1.5, -1 -0.5 -1.5, -1 -0.5 1.5, 1 -0.5 1.5, 1 -.5 -1.5]		
	bit (1) endFlag = 0	
	bit (1) fieldIndex = 1	
	bit (1) reserved = 0	This MFVec3f is encoded using
	bit (1) isListDescription = 1	MFListDescription, as for key.
	bit (1) endFlag = 0	
	float x = -1.000000	Each SFVec3f is separated by
	float y = 0.500000	an endFlag in this de-
		scription
	float z = 1.500000	
	bit (1) endFlag = 0	
	float x = 1.000000	
	float y = 0.500000	
	float z = 1.500000	
	bit (1) endFlag = 0	
	float x = 1.000000	
	float y = 0.500000	
	float z = -1.500000	
	bit (1) endFlag = 0	
	float x = -1.000000	
	float y = 0.500000	
	float z = -1.500000	
	bit (1) endFlag = 0	
	float x = -1.000000	
	float y = -0.500000	
	float z = -1.500000	
	bit (1) endFlag = 0	
	float x = -1.000000	
	float y = -0.500000	
	float z = 1.500000	
	bit (1) endFlag = 0	
	float x = 1.000000	
	float y = -0.500000	
	float z = 1.500000	
	bit (1) endFlag = 0	
	float x = 1.000000	
	float y = -0.500000	
	float z = -1.500000	
	bit (1) endFlag = 1	
}	bit (1) endFlag = 1	
	bit (1) endFlag = 0	
DEF XF Transform {	bit (1) isReused = 0	SFNode(SF3DNode)
	bit (6) nodeIndex = 47	
	bit (1) isUpdatable = 1	XF is the third DEF name in

Scene	*Encoding*	*Comments*
	bit (10) nodeID = 2	this scene.
	bit (1) maskDescription = 0	
children [	bit (1) endFlag = 0	children is the second DEF
	bit (3) fieldIndex = 1	field of Transform.
	bit (1) reserved = 0	
	bit (1) isListDescription = 1	
	bit (1) endFlag = 0	
Shape {	bit (1) isReused = 0	SFNode(SF3DNode)
	bit (6) nodeIndex = 38	
	bit (1) isUpdatable = 0	
	bit (1) maskDescription = 0	
	bit (1) endFlag = 0	
appearance	bit (1) fieldIndex = 0	
Appearance {	bit (1) isReused = 0	SFNode(SFAppearanceNode)
	bit (1) nodeIndex = 1	
	bit (1) isUpdatable = 0	
	bit (1) maskDescription = 0	
material	bit (1) endFlag = 0	
	bit (2) fieldIndex = 0	
DEF SMAT Material {	bit (1) isReused = 0	SFNode(SFMaterialNode)
	bit (2) nodeIndex = 1	
	bit (1) isUpdatable = 1	SMAT is the fourth node in
	bit(10) nodeID = 3	the scene.
	bit (1) maskDescription = 0	
	bit (1) endFlag = 0	
diffuseColor 1 0 0	bit (3) fieldIndex = 1	
	float r = 1.000000	
	float g = 0.000000	
	float b = 0.000000	
}	bit (1) endFlag = 1	
}	bit (1) endFlag = 1	
	bit (1) endFlag = 0	
geometry	bit (1) fieldIndex = 1	
Sphere {}	bit (1) isReused = 0	SFNode(SFGeometryNode)
	bit (5) nodeIndex = 16	
	bit (1) isUpdatable = 0	
	bit (1) maskDescription = 0	
	bit (1) endFlag = 1	
}	bit (1) endFlag = 1	
]	bit (1) endFlag = 1	
}	bit (1) endFlag = 1	
]	bit (1) endFlag = 1	
}	bit (1) endFlag = 1	
	bit (1) hasRoutes = 1	
ROUTE DEF R1		
TS.fraction_changed		
TO PI.set_fraction	bit (1) listDescription = 1	We use ListROUTEs description
	bit (1) isUpdatable = 1	The first DEF'd route has
	bit (10) RouteID = 0	a routeID of 0.
	bit (10) NodeID = 0	ID of TS

Scene	Encoding	Comments
	bit (4) outFieldRef = 6	
	bit (10) NodeID = 1	ID of PI
	bit (2) inFieldRef = 0	
	bit (1) moreRoutes = 1	One more ROUTE to encode
ROUTE DEF R2		
PI.value_changed		
TO XF.translation	bit (1) isUpdatable = 1	The second DEF'd route has
	bit (10) RouteID = 0	a routeID of 1.
	bit (10) NodeID = 1	ID of PI
	bit (2) outFieldRef = 2	
	bit (10) NodeID = 2	ID of XF
	bit (3) inFieldRef = 7	
	bit (1) moreRoutes = 0	No more ROUTEs, BIFSScene encoding is finished.

Example 2: Using QuantizationParameter Node

Taking the previous example, a QuantizationParameter node will be used to quantize the *diffuseColor* of the Box locally, while the Sphere one will use the efficient float encoding. To do that, two QuantizationParameter nodes are needed: one local for the box, and a global one for other values. The textual scene description becomes:

```
Group {
 children [
  DEF TS TimeSensor {}

  QuantizationParameter {
   isLocal TRUE
   colorNbBits 1
  }

  Shape {
   appearance Appearance {
    material Material { diffuseColor 0 0 1 }
   }
   geometry Box { size 2 1 3 }
  }

QuantizationParameter {
 colorQuant FALSE
 useEfficientCoding TRUE
}
```

```
DEF PI PositionInterpolator {
 key [ 0 0.125 0.25 0.375 0.5 0.625 0.75 0.875 1 ]
   keyValue [ -1 0.5 1.5, 1 0.5 1.5, 1 0.5 -1.5, -1 0.5 -1.5,
-1 -0.5 -1.5, -1 -0.5 1.5, 1 -0.5 1.5, 1 -.5 -1.5 ]
   }

  DEF XF Transform {
   children [
    Shape {
     appearance Appearance {
      material DEF SMAT Material { diffuseColor 1 0 0 }
      }
     geometry Sphere {}
     }
    ]
   }
  ]
}

ROUTE DEF R1 TS.fraction_changed TO PI.set_fraction
ROUTE DEF R2 PI.value_changed TO XF.translation
```

The first QuantizationParameter is local, so it applies to the node following its definition (i.e., the Shape node and its children). It uses default values
such as colorMin = 0 and colorMax = 1. colorNbBits is set to 1 instead of 8
by default because the color is made of 0 and 1.

The second QuantizationParameter is global and applies to all nodes following its definition—i.e., to the PositionInterpolator and to the Transform
and its children.

Note also that for color quantizer it is not necessary to set colorQuant to
TRUE, since it is already by default.

The encoding of the scene remains identical at the beginning. After Time-
Sensor, the fisrt QuantizationParameter is encoded as:

```
bit (1) isReused = 0
bit (6) nodeIndex = 35
bit (1) isUpdatable = 0
bit (1) maskDescription = 0
bit (1) endFlag = 0
bit (6) fieldIndex = 0
bit (1) value = 1
bit (1) endFlag = 0
bit (6) fieldIndex = 16
bit (5) value = 1
```

Then, the encoding of the Shape remains until the encoding of the material node, which becomes:

```
bit (1) isReused = 0
bit (2) nodeIndex = 1
bit (1) isUpdatable = 0
bit (1) maskDescription = 0
bit (1) endFlag = 0
bit (3) fieldIndex = 1
bit (1) quantized value R = 0
bit (1) quantized value G = 0
bit (1) quantized value B = 1
bit (1) endFlag = 1
```

As expected, the color values are encoded using 1 bit 0 or 1. The Box size is not affected, since no size quantizer is used. The encoding remains the same until the end of the Shape. The second QuantizationParameter is encoded as follows:

```
bit (1) isReused = 0
bit (6) nodeIndex = 35
bit (1) isUpdatable = 0
bit (1) maskDescription = 0
bit (1) endFlag = 0
bit (6) fieldIndex = 13 // for colorQuant
bit (1) value = 0
bit (1) endFlag = 0
bit (6) fieldIndex = 39 // for useEfficientCoding
bit (1) value = 1
bit (1) endFlag = 1
```

The encoding of the PositionInterpolator is affected only when the key and keyValues are encoded. There, efficient float encoding is used.

```
0          bit (4) mantissaLength = 0
           bit (1) endFlag = 0              Next value follows

0.125      bit (4) mantissaLength = 1
           bit (3) exponentLength = 2
           bit (1) mantissaSign = 0
           bit (1) mantissa = 0
           bit (1) exponentSign = 1
           bit (2) exponent = 1
           bit (1) endFlag = 0              Next value follows

0.25       bit (4) mantissaLength = 1
```

```
        bit (3) exponentLength = 2
        bit (1) mantissaSign = 0
        bit (1) mantissa = 0
        bit (1) exponentSign = 1
        bit (2) exponent = 0
        bit (1) endFlag = 0                Next values follows


Etc... for the other key values
```

In addition, for the keyValues, each float is encoded using the efficient float coding:

```
-1      bit (4) mantissaLength = 1
        bit (3) exponentLength = 0
        bit (1) mantissaSign = 1
        bit (1) mantissa = 0
0.5     bit (4) mantissaLength = 1
        bit (3) exponentLength = 1
        bit (1) mantissaSign = 0
        bit (1) mantissa = 0
        bit (1) exponentSign = 1
        bit (1) exponent = 0
1.5     bit (4) mantissaLength = 1
        bit (3) exponentLength = 0
        bit (1) mantissaSign = 0
        bit (1) mantissa = 1
        bit (1) endFlag = 0             Next 3-float
                                        value follows

1       bit (4) mantissaLength = 1
        bit (3) exponentLength = 0
        bit (1) mantissaSign = 0
        bit (1) mantissa = 0
0.5     bit (4) mantissaLength = 1
        bit (3) exponentLength = 1
        bit (1) mantissaSign = 0
        bit (1) mantissa = 0
        bit (1) exponentSign = 1
        bit (1) exponent = 0
1.5     bit (4) mantissaLength = 1
        bit (3) exponentLength = 0
        bit (1) mantissaSign = 0
        bit (1) mantissa = 1
        bit (1) endFlag = 0             Next 3-float
                                        value follows
Etc... for remaining keyValue values.
```

After the encoding of the keyValues, the bitstream is unchanged until the encoding of the SMAT Material node, where the diffuseColor's values are encoded using the efficient float representation:

```
1    bit (4) mantissaLength = 1
     bit (3) exponentLength = 0
     bit (1) mantissaSign = 0
     bit (1) mantissa = 0
0    bit (4) mantissaLength = 0
0    bit (4) mantissaLength = 0
```

The rest of the bitstream is unchanged. With the efficient float representation, SMAT's diffuseColor used 17 bits compared to 3 if using QP1 parameters. Compared to normal float encoding, $3 \times 32 = 96$ bits would be used. Using QuantizationParameter node, we saved many bits in the bitstream and, with these judicious parameters, the values were not even affected by the quantizers.

So far we have described BIFS contextual encoding of a scene graph. This encoding is part of the BIFS-Command protocol framework, which can modify the scene at any time. These commands are explained in the next section.

BIFS Commands

The sender can insert, delete, or replace nodes, field values, and routes in the scene (Figure 17-8). He can also send a complete scene via the ReplaceScene command, which is the first command sent in to a terminal to create the very first scene. These commands are sent randomly in the sense that a terminal cannot predict when it will receive a command. On the other hand, BIFS-Anim protocol defines field replacement commands in a stream that may happen at a known frame rate.

The four possible commands are:

- Insert
  - A node can be inserted in an MFNode field.
  - A field value can be inserted in a multiple-value (MF) field.
  - A route can be added to the scene.
- Delete
  - A node can be deleted from an SFNode or MFNode field.
  - A field value can be deleted from a multiple-value (MF) field.
  - A route can be deleted from the list of routes in a scene.

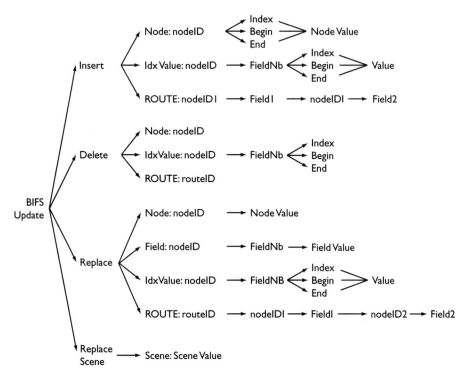

Figure 17-8   All possible BIFS commands.

- Replace
  - A node can be replaced by another one of the same kind. We will explain later what we mean by "kind."
  - A field value can be replaced by another one.
  - A route can be replaced by a new one.
- SceneReplace: A new scene replaces the previous one. It erases all objects and routes that were previously created. This is the first command sent.

At any time, a list of commands can be sent. The encoding of commands is as follow:

class   *number of bits*

```
class CommandFrame {
 do {
```

```
  Command command();
  bit(1) continue;                          1
} while(continue);
}
```

Each individual commands is encoded as follows: For each command, a 2-bit `code` determines which command is used.

class   *number of bits*

```
class Command {
 bit(2) code;                                                                 2
 switch(code) {
 case 0:
  InsertCommand insert();
  break;
 case 1:
  DeleteCommand delete();
  break;
 case 2:
  ReplaceCommand replace();
  break;
 case 3:
  SceneReplaceCommand sceneReplace();
  break;
 }
}
```

Insert Commands

The `type` of insert command is stored on 2 bits:

class   *number of bits*

```
class InsertCommand {
 bit(2) type;                                                                 2
 switch(type) {
 case 0:
  NodeInsertCommand nodeInsert();
  break;
 case 2:
  FieldInsertCommand fieldInsert();
  break;
```

```
case 3:
 ROUTEInsertCommand routeInsert();
 break;
 }
}
```

NodeInsertCommand inserts a node in an SFNode's children field. The node ID of the SFNode is first decoded, then the children field is retrieved. Using this command with nodes other than grouping nodes (i.e., without a children field) will produce an error here. Then, the node is decoded and inserted at the specified position:

class   *number of bits*

```
class NodeInsertCommand {
 bit(BIFSConfig.nodeIDbits) nodeID;          nodeIDbits
 NodeData sfnode = getNodeFromID(nodeID);
 int context=sfnode.getContext();

 bit(2) position;                            2
 switch(position) {
 case 0: // at a specified index
  bit(8) index;                              8
  break;
 case 2: // at the beginning
  break;
 case 3: // at the end
  break;
 }
 SFNode node(context);

 sfnode.getChildrenField().insert(position,
node);
}
```

The FieldInsertCommand is the same as NodeInsertCommand, except that it inserts a field value in an MFField. First the node ID is decoded, then the index of the IN field in which a value will be inserted. An SFField corresponding to the type of field in the MFField is decoded using the FieldData information of the MFField. Finally, this field is inserted at the desired position:

class	*number of bits*
`class FieldInsertCommand {`	
`bit(BIFSConfig.nodeIDbits) nodeID;`	nodeIDbits
`Nodedata sfnode = getNodeFromID(nodeID);`	
`int(node.getInBits()) inID;`	node.inBits
`MFField mffield= node.getInField(inID);`	
`bit(2) position;`	2
`switch(position) {`	
`case 0: // at a specified index`	
`  bit(16) index;`	16
`  break;`	
`case 2: // at the beginning`	
`  break;`	
`case 3: // at the end`	
`  break;`	
`}`	
`SFField value(mffield);`	
`mffield.insert(position, index, value);`	
`}`	

The RouteInsertCommand works even more simply: A ROUTE is simply decoded and inserted in the scene:

class	*number of bits*
`class ROUTEInsertCommand {`	
`bit(1) isUpdatable;`	1
`if(isUpdatable)`	
`  bit(BIFSConfig.routeIDbits) routeID;`	routeIDbits
`bit(BIFSConfig.nodeIDbits) departureNodeID;`	nodeIDbits
`NodeData nodeOut=getNodeFromID`	
`(departureNodeID);`	
`int(nodeOut.getOutBits()) departureID;`	nodeOut.outBits
`bit(BIFSConfig.nodeIDbits) arrivalNodeID;`	nodeIDbits
`NodeData nodeIn=getNodeFromID(arrivalNodeID);`	
`int(nodeIn.getInBits()) arrivalID;`	nodeIn.inBits
`}`	

Delete Commands

In order to determine the `type` of delete command, 2 bits are read from the stream:

class   *number of bits*

```
class DeleteCommand {
 bit(2) type;                                                2
 switch(type) {
 case 0:
  NodeDeleteCommand nodeDelete ();
  break;
 case 2:
  FieldDeleteCommand fieldDelete();
  break;
 case 3:
  ROUTEDeleteCommand routeDelete();
  break;
 }
}
```

NodeDeleteCommand simply reads the nodeID of the node to be deleted from the scene:

class   *number of bits*

```
class NodeDeleteCommand {
 int(BIFSConfig.nodeIDbits) nodeID;            nodeIDbits
}
```

FieldDeleteCommand needs to know in which MFField of SFNode and at which position a value should be removed. It should be noted that if the inID does not lead to a MFField, this will generate an error:

class   *number of bits*

```
class FieldDeleteCommand {
 int(BIFSConfig.nodeIDbits) nodeID;              nodeIDbits
 NodeData node=getNodeFromID(nodeID);
 int(node.getInBits()) inID;                     node.inBits

 bit(2) position;                                      2
```

```
switch(position) {
case 0: // at a specified index
 bit(16) index;                                  16
 break;
case 2: // at the beginning
 break;
case 3: // at the end
 break;
 }

 node.getInField(inID).delete(position, index);
}
```

ROUTEDeleteCommand is as simple as for NodeDeleteCommand: Only the routeID is needed.

```
class ROUTEDeleteCommand {
int(BIFSDecoder.routeIDbits) routeID;        routeIDbits
}
```

Replace Commands

There are four types of Replace commands. The type is stored on 2 bits:

class   *number of bits*

```
class ReplaceCommand {
 bit(2) type;                                     2
 switch(type) {
 case 0:
  NodeReplaceCommand nodeReplace ();
  break;
 case 1:
  SFFieldReplaceCommand sffieldReplace();
  break;
 case 2:
  MFFieldReplaceCommand mffieldReplace();
  break;
 case 3:
  ROUTEReplaceCommand routeReplace();
  break;
 }
}
```

Compared to previous commands, case 1 has been introduced because one might need to replace values of an SFField and not only of an MFField.

The NodeReplaceCommand retrieves the node to be replaced from its nodeID and reads a new node in the SFWorldNode contex:

class   *number of bits*

```
class NodeReplaceCommand {
 bit(BIFSConfig.nodeIDbits) nodeID;              nodeIDbits
 SFNode node(SFWorldNode);
}
```

The SFFieldReplaceCommand needs to know which IN field in which node has to be replaced by a new value:

class   *number of bits*

```
class SFFieldReplaceCommand {
 bit(BIFSConfig.nodeIDbits) nodeID;               nodeIDbits
 NodeData node=getNodeFromID(nodeID);
 int(node.getInBits()) inID;               node.getInBits()
 Field value(node.getInField(inID));
}
```

The MFFieldReplaceCommand works as the SFFieldReplaceCommand and needs to know at which position in the MFField the value will be replaced:

class   *number of bits*

```
class MFFieldReplaceCommand {
 bit(BIFSDecoder.nodeIDbits) nodeID;               nodeIDbits
 NodeData node=getNodeFromID(nodeID);
 int(node.getInBits()) inID;               node.getInBits()

 bit(2) position;                                        2
 switch(position) {
 case 0: // at a specified index
  bit(16) index;                                        16
  break;
 case 2: // at the beginning
  break;
```

```
case 3: // at the end
 break;
}

Field value(node.getInField(inID));
node.getInField(inID).replace(position, index, value);
}
```

The ROUTEReplaceCommand needs to know the routeID of the ROUTE to be replaced, then the new parameters of the ROUTE:

class	*number of bits*

```
class ROUTEReplaceCommand {
 bit(BIFSConfig.routeIDbits) routeID;                     routeIDbits
 bit(BIFSConfig.nodeIDbits) departureNodeID;              nodeIDbits
 NodeData nodeOut=getNodeFromID(departureNodeID);
 int(nodeOut.getOutBits()) departureID;              nodeOut.outBits

 bit(BIFSConfig.nodeIDbits) arrivalNodeID;                nodeIDbits
 NodeData nodeIn=getNodeFromID(arrivalNodeID);
 int(nodeIn.getInBits()) arrivalID;                   NodeIN.inBits
}
```

SceneReplaceCommand

The SceneReplaceCommand needs only to decode a BIFSScene.

class	*number of bits*

```
class SceneReplaceCommand {
 BIFSScene scene();
}
```

Example: Encoding a Simple Scene

Let's take the simple scene in the previous section, made of a blue box and a red sphere moving from corner to corner. We want this scene to replace any existing scene. We will send a SceneReplaceCommand with this scene inside:

```
Command                              Encoding

CommandFrame {
  SceneReplaceCommand {              bit(2)  code = 3
    BIFSScene scene()                The previous bitstream encoding
  }
}                                    bit(1)  continue=0
```

As we have only one command here, the continue flag has value 0 (FALSE).

Example: Applying Commands to the Scene

Now let's change the color of our sphere from red to green. We need the FieldReplaceCommand:

```
Command                              Encoding

CommandFrame {
  ReplaceCommand {                   bit(2)  code = 2
    FieldReplaceCommand {            bit(2)  type = 1
      SMAT.diffuseColor BY 0 1 0     bit(10) nodeID = 3
                                     bit(3)  fieldID = 1
                                     float r= 0.000
                                     float g= 1.000
                                     float b= 0.000

    }
  }
}                                    bit(1)  continue=0
```

We'll delete the XF Transform and at the same time the two ROUTEs R1 and R2. We need a NodeDeleteCommand and two ROUTEDelete Commands.

```
Command                              Encoding

CommandFrame {
  DeleteCommand {                    bit(2)  code = 1
    NodeDeleteCommand {              bit(2)  type = 0
      XF                             bit (10) nodeID = 2
    }
  }
                                     bit(1)  continue=1
```

```
DeleteCommand {                    bit(2) code = 1
  ROUTEDeleteCommand {             bit(2) type = 3
    R1                             bit (10) routeID = 0
  }
}
                                   bit(1) continue=1
DeleteCommand {                    bit(2) code = 1
  ROUTEDeleteCommand {             bit(2) type = 3
    R2                             bit (10) routeID = 1
  }
  }
}                                  bit(1) continue=0
```

Summary

MPEG-4 scenes are encoded according to the Binary Format for Scenes (BIFS). An extension of VRML, BIFS supports all VRML97 nodes in the second version of the MPEG-4 standard. In addition, BIFS introduces a number of new nodes and capabilities not found in VRML, including support for 2D shapes, 2D/3D composition, streaming, and facial and body animation. As a binary format that utilizes quantization compression, BIFS content is encoded in an extremely compact and efficient manner (BIFS files are typically 10 to 15 times smaller than corresponding VRML files).

To build interactive applications, BIFS defines commands that can modify, delete, or replace objects in the scene. The BIFS-Command protocol is used to send commands acting on a scene from a server to a client terminal in which the scene resides. Although the BIFS-Command protocol can be used to produce scene animation, the BIFS-Anim protocol (discussed in detail in the next chapter) offers better compression and synchronization capabilities for such purposes.

Following is a complete list of URLs referenced in this chapter:

Web3D Gallery MPEG-4 Area   http://www.web3dgallery.com/mpeg/

La Boutique Bleue   http://www.lorraine.region.francetelecom.fr/

ANIMATING SCENES WITH BIFS-ANIM

Topics in This Chapter

- Introducing BIFS-Anim
- Animating Scenes with BIFS-Anim

Chapter 18

In this chapter we'll explore BIFS-Anim, the MPEG-4 protocol designed specifically to allow animation of scenes. This material—like the discussion of MPEG-4 quantization and the BIFS-Command in the previous chapter—is quite technical in nature. In time MPEG-4 authoring tools will emerge that spare content authors from such details. Until such tools arrive, however, an intimate understanding of the BIFS-Anim protocol is necessary to control MPEG-4 scene animation.

The BIFS-Anim Protocol

BIFS-Anim is a streaming protocol. It behaves like a video or audio streaming protocol: a header (the *anim mask*) is first sent to configure the BIFS-Anim decoder, then *frames* are sent at a specified frame rate. Frames contain values for fields that have been declared animated in the mask and that are animated in these frames.

While BIFS-Anim and BIFS-Command seem to be two different protocols, they both use the same BIFS decoder: the mask is stored in the BIFS-Command decoder. It will serve to configure a BIFS-Anim decoder to which the animation stream will be attached (Figure 18-1). One can view the

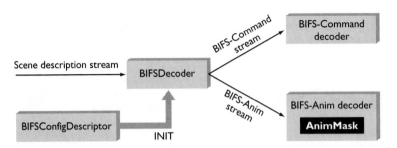

Figure 18-1 Instantiating the BIFS-Anim decoder.

BIFS-Anim process as a special case of FieldReplacement command, replacing values of any kind of field except SF/MFNode, SF/MFUrl, SF/MFString, SF/MFScript, SFCommandBuffer, SFImage, and SFBuffer.

The mask contains initial quantization information for fields of nodes that may be animated. The quantizers are the same as for BIFS-Command and may be modified in frames.

A frame consists of a *header* part and a *data* part. The *header* contains information on the frame itself: whether it is Intra or Predictive, whether it has a frame rate or a time code, and whether a number of frames should be skipped. The header specifies also which nodes are animated in this frame. The *data* part contains the field values of animated nodes for this frame.

A field value may be encoded in Intra or Predictive mode. In *Intra* mode, the value is quantized and stored in the bitstream. In *Predictive* mode, the difference between the previous value and the current value is quantized. As the value is determined from a previous value, this is called a prediction, thus the name of this mode.

BIFS-Anim uses an adaptive arithmetic encoder to store the quantized values in the bitstream. In general, values of a field follow a smooth curve, and the difference between two successive quantized values will be the same from frame to frame. An arithmetic encoder takes advantage of this situation. It adapts its statistics to the value to be encoded, so that it will produce more bits for uncommon values and fewer bits for common ones (see "Arithmetic Coding Resources" in Appendix D, "MPEG-4 Resources"). At the Web3D Gallery (http://www.web3d.gallery.com/mpeg/), the code of the arithmetic encoder is given. The same encoder is used in other standards such as H.26x.

While quantization is not necessary in the BIFS-Command protocol, it is mandatory in BIFS-Anim. BIFS-Anim uses the same quantizers, as shown in Table 18.1.

Note

The following three publications are recommended reading if you're interested in learning more about about arithmetic coding:

G. G. Langdon, Jr., "An Introduction to Arithmetic Coding," IBM Journal of Research and Development, 28:135–149, March 1984.

J. J. Rissanen and G. G. Langdon, "Arithmetic Coding," IBM Journal of Research and Development, 23(2):149–162, March 1979.

I. H. Witten, R. Neal, and J. G. Cleary. "Arithmetic Coding for Data Compression," Communications of the ACM, 30:520–540, June 1997.

Quantizers 3 and 5 do not exist in BIFS-Anim; they are reserved for future use. Quantizers 7 and 8 are used to quantize floats bounded in a range [min, max], in fact in the same way a 1D scale is. Quantizer 8 may use predefined bounds, while bounds must be specified for quantizer 7. For all other quantizers, usages are the same. As each DEF field might be animated, an

Table 18.1   BIFS-Command and BIFS-Anim Quantizers

BIFS-Command quantizer	BIFS-Anim quantizer	Type of value
0	0	None
1	1	3D positions
2	2	2D positions
3		Drawing order
4	4	RGB colors
5		Texture coordinate
6	6	Angle
7	7	Scale / Float
8	8	Interpolator keys / BoundFloat
9	9	Unitary normals
10	10	Rotations
11	11	Object size 3D
12	12	Object size 2D
13	13	Linear Scalar Quantization / Integer

AnimFieldQP—an animation quantizer—is part of the FieldData and is defined as follows:

```
class AnimFieldQP {
  boolean useDefault;          If TRUE, default values are used.
  int getNbBounds();           Returns the number of bounds or com-
                               ponents of the field.
  float Imin[], Imax[];        Bounds [min, max] in Intra mode.
  int IminInt;                 Lower bound for quantizer 13.
  int InbBits, PnbBits;        Number of bits in Intra and Predic-
                               tive mode.
  float PMin[];                Lower bound in Predictive mode.
  boolean isTotal;             For MFFields, if TRUE, all fields
                               values are given at each frame.
  int indexList[];             If isTotal = FALSE, a list of in-
                               dices of animated fields is speci-
                               fied.

}
```

Decoding the BIFS-Anim Mask

The animation mask has the following structure:

class   *number of bits*

```
class AnimationMask {
 int numNodes=0;
 do {
  ElementaryMask elemMask();
  numNodes++;
  bit(1) moreMasks;                                              1
 } while(moreMasks);
}
```

AnimationMask handles a list of elementary masks and maintains a number of animated nodes numNodes.

class   *number of bits*

```
class ElementaryMask {
 bit(BIFSDecoder.nodeIDbits) nodeID;            nodeIDbits
 NodeData node=getNodeFromID(nodeID);
 switch(node.nodeType) {
```

```
  case FaceType:
  case BodyType:
  case IndexedFaceSet2D:
   Break;
  default:
   InitialFieldsMask initMask(node);
 }
}
```

An ElementaryMask retrieves the animated node in the scene and, depending on its type, decodes the initial masks for the animated fields. Face, Body, and IndexedFaceSet2D are handled by specific animation decoders. BIFS-Anim simply conveys their bitstreams.

class	*number of bits*

```
class InitialFieldsMask(NodeData node) {
 for(i=0; i<node.getNumDynFields(); i++)
  bit(1) isAnimField[i];                              1

 for(i=0; i<node.getNumDynFields(); i++) {
  if(isAnimField[i]) {
   FieldData field=node.getDynField(i);
   AnimFieldQP aqp = field.aqp;
   if(!isSF(field)) {
    bit(1) aqp.isTotal;                               1
    if(!aqp.isTotal) {
     unsigned int(5) nbBits;                          5
     do {
       int(nbBits) aqp.indexList[aqp.numElements++];nbBits
       bit(1) moreIndices;                            1
     } while(moreIndices);
    }
   }
   InitialAnimQP QP[i](field.aqp);
  }
 }
}
```

An array of Boolean is first decoded to indicate whether a DYN field is animated (`true`) or not (`false`). Then, for each animated DYN field, if the field is an MFField, we read an array of index that will be modified if it is not the whole array (`isTotal=true`). Finally, the initial animation quantization parameters (QP) are read.

class	*number of bits*

```
class InitialAnimQP(AnimFieldQP aqp) {
 aqp.useDefault=FALSE;
 switch(aqp.animType) {
  case 4:  // color
  case 8:  // bound float
   bit(1) aqp.useDefault;                                      1
  case 1:  // position 3D
  case 2:  // position 2D
  case 7:  // floats
  case 11: // size 3D
  case 12: // size 2D
    if(!aqp.useDefault) {
     for(i=0; i<aqp.getNbBounds(); i++) {
      bit(1) useEfficientCoding;                               1
      GenericFloat aqp.Imin[i](useEfficientcoding);       4 to 32
     }
     for(i=0; i<aqp.getNbBounds(); i++) {
      bit(1) useEfficientCoding;                               1
      GenericFloat aqp.Imax[i](useEfficientcoding);       4 to 32
     }
    }
    break;
   case 13:  // integers
    int(32) aqp.IminInt[0];                                   32
    break;
  }
 unsigned int(5) aqp.INbBits;                                  5
 for(i=0; i<aqp.getNbBounds(); i++) {
  int(INbBits+1) vq;                                    INbBits+1
  aqp.Pmin[i] = vq - 2^aqp.InbBits;
 }
 unsigned int(4) aqp.PNbBits;                                  4
}
```

The bounds of the quantizer are first read if different from default ones. For each field, the %b=[min, max] tag specifies the default bounds of the field value (see the Web3D Gallery at http://www.web3dgallery.com/mpeg). If min = −∞ or max = +∞, there is no bound, and the encoder must provide them. Then the number of bits in which values in Intra mode are encoded and the offset v_q are decoded. Finally, the number of bits used in Predictive mode is decoded. In this mode, the difference between two successive quantized values is stored.

Consequently, P_{min} may have values in the range $-2^{INbBits}$ to $2^{INbBits}-1$. The value is coded as an integer using *INbBits+1* bits and has the value $P_{min}-2^{INbBits}$.

The quantization process is used in Intra frames only, and the prediction process in Predictive ones.

The BIFS decoder is now configured with nodes and their fields that may be animated in the scene as well as the quantization and prediction parameters for each possibly animated field. The decoding of each frame will be done by the Anim decoder.

Decoding the BIFS-Anim Frames

The frames consist of a header and a data part. The header contains timing information and the type of the frame data (Intra mode or Predictive mode), and the data part field values. In the data part it is also possible to change the initial quantization parameters. Frames use the animMask of the BIFSDecoder as well as the randomAccess flag, as shown later. Decoding of the values uses an adaptive arithmetic decoder, which is available online at the Web3D Gallery (http://www.web3dgallery.com/mpeg).

```
class AnimationFrame {
 AnimationFrameHeader header(BIFSConfig.animMask);
 AnimationFrameData data(BIFSConfig.animMask);
}
```

The AnimationFrameHeader keeps timing information of the frame as well as its type—Intra or Predictive. It has the following structure:

class	*number of bits*

```
class      AnimationFrameHeader(AnimationMask
mask) {
 bit(23)* next;                          Check 23 bits, not read
 if(next == 0)
  bit(32) animationStartCode;                  32

 bit(1) mask.isIntra;                           1
 bit(1) mask.isActive[mask.numNodes];    mask.numNodes

 if(isIntra) {
  bit(1) isFrameRate;                           1
```

```
if(isFrameRate)
  FrameRate rate;                                    13
bit(1) isTimeCode;                                    1
if(isTimeCode)
  unsigned int(18) timeCode;                         18
}
bit(1) hasSkipFrame;                                  1
if(hasSkipFrame)
  SkipFrames skip;
}
```

next is used to determine if we have a start code or not. The first 23 bits are checked, but the pointer in the bitstream is not moved. If these bits are all zeros, a 32-bit start code is read. This start code is very important in a streaming environment. In a broadcast environment such as television, once a television is switched on, it receives images as part of a program. On the other hand, on the Internet, you connect to a server and receive images from the beginning of the program. In both cases, resynchronization is needed. The start code enables a decoder to scan the bitstream as received until a start code is found and the frame is Intra.

Then a mask of Booleans is read to determine which of the declared animable nodes in the animMask are animated in this frame. There are as many bits to read as nodes declared in AnimationMask.

FrameRate and SkipFrames are read as follows:

class	*number of bits*

```
class FrameRate {
  unsigned int(8) frameRate;                          8
  unsigned int(4) seconds;                            4
  bit(1) frequencyOffset;                             1
}
```

The real frame rate is computed as

$$frame\ rate = frame\_rate\ +\ seconds/16$$

frequency_offset, when set to 1, indicates that the frame rate uses the NTSC frequency offset of $1000/1001 - frame\ rate *= 1000/1001$. This is typically the case when $frame\_rate = 24$, 30 or 60.

class	*number of bits*

```
class SkipFrames {
  int nFrame=0;
```

```
do {
 bit(4) numFramesToSkip;                                    4
 nFrame += numFramesToSkip;
} while (numFramesToSkip == 15);
}
```

SkipFrame indicates the number of frames to skip. When num-FramesToSkip = 15, 4 bits are read again and added to nFrame, the total number of frames to skip.

AnimFrameData uses the AnimationMask and the array of Booleans of active nodes decoded in the header to decode their field values.

class   *number of bits*

```
class AnimFrameData (AnimationMask mask) {
 decoder_reset();

 for(int i=0; i<mask.numNodes; i++) {
  if(mask.isActive[i]) {
   NodeData node = mask.animNode[i];
   switch (node.nodeType) {
   case Face:
    FaceFrameData fdata;
    break;
   case Body:
    BodyFrameData bdata;
    break;
   case IndexedFaceSet2D:
    Mesh2DFrameData mdata;
    break;
   default:
    for(int j=0; j<node.getNumDynFields(); j++)
     if(node.isAnimField[j])
      AnimationField afield(node.getDynField(j),mask.isIntra);
   }
  }
 }
}
```

At the beginning of the AnimFrameData, the arithmetic decoder is reset using decoder_reset() (see http://www.web3dgallery.com/mpeg). This method reads 16 bits in the bitstream to initialize the decoder.

If the node is active but is of type Face, Body, or IndexedFaceSet, dedicated decoders are called and the rest of the bitstream is passed to them. The details of these decoders are beyond the scope of this book, and details can be found in MPEG-4 standard, part 2. For these nodes, extra care should be taken, using the arithmetic decoder provided at the Web3D Gallery. Implemented as such, the arithmetic decoder holds some extra bits in its buffer; thus, the pointer in the bitstream is ahead of its normal position. When the bitstream pointer is passed to these dedicated decoders, the pointer in the bitstream must be rewound as many extra bits as in the arithmetic decoder. Note that each of these decoders uses an arithmetic decoder. When they finish decoding their values, they also have to rewind the bitstream pointer.

For other nodes, each declared animated field in the mask uses the field's quantization parameters. These parameters may be updated if necessary.

If `randomAccess` = `TRUE`, the InitialAnimQP of the field should be used and is valid until the next Intra frame. It is possible to perform random access to a particular predictive frame in the stream until the next Intra frame. The field's predictive arithmetic models should be reset to uniform models by using `model_reset(PnbBits)`.

If `randomAccess` = `FALSE`, the AnimFieldQP that was valid at the previous frame is used; no random access is possible. The field's predictive models are reset to uniform models only if a new AnimFieldQP is read:

class   *number of bits*

```
class AnimationField (FieldData field, boolean isIntra) {
 AnimFieldQP aqp = field.aqp;
 if(randomAccess)
  model_reset(PnbBits);

 if(isIntra) {
  bit(1) hasQP;                                                        1
  if(hasQP) {
   AnimQP qp(aqp);
   model_reset(PnbBits);
  }
 }

 if(isTotal || isSF(field))
  AnimIValue ivalue(field);
 else // for MFField
  for(int i=0; i<aqp.numElements; i++)
   AnimIValue ivalue(field.getValue(aqp.indexList[i]));
 }
```

```
  else {
   if(isTotal || isSF(field))
    AnimPValue pvalue(field);
   else // for MFField
    for(int i=0; i<aqp.numElements; i++)
     AnimPValue pvalue(field.getValue(aqp.indexList[i]));
  }
 }
```

If the field is an SFField or if it is an MFField and isTotal=TRUE, then the field is read entirely. If the field is an MFField and only some of its fields are animated (isIntra=FALSE), then only these indices are read. The indices are in indexList, and there are numElements (obviously numElements is less than the number of fields of the MFField).

If the field's quantization parameters have changed, they are read in a similar manner as InitialAnimQP:

class	*number of bits*

```
class AnimQP (AnimFieldQP aqp) {
 bit(1) IMinMax;                                          1
 if(IMinMax) {
  aqp.useDefault = FALSE;
  switch(aqp.animType) {
   case 4:  // color
   case 8:  // BoundFloats
    bit(1) aqp.useDefaults;                               1
   case 1:  // position 3D
   case 2:  // position 2D
   case 7:  // floats
   case 11: // size 3D
   case 12: // size 2D
    if(!aqp.isDefault) {
     for(int i=0; i< aqp.getNbBounds(); i++) {
      bit(1) useEfficientCoding;                          1
      GenericFloat aqp.Imin[i](useEfficientCoding);    4 to 32
     }
     for(int i=0; i< aqp.getNbBounds(); i++) {
      bit(1) useEfficientCoding;                          1
      GenericFloat aqp.Imax[i](useEfficientCoding);    4 to 32
     }
    }
    break;
```

```
    case 13:
    int(32) aqp.IminInt[0];                                        32
    break;
  }
bit(1) hasInbBits;                                                  1
if(hasInbBits)
 unsigned int(5) aqp.InbBits;                                       5

bit(1) hasPminMax;                                                  1
if(hasPminMax) {
 for(int I=0; I< aqp.getNbBounds(); I++) {
  int(INbBits+1) vq;                                         INbBits+1
  aqp.Pmin[I] = vq - 2^aq.InbBits;
 }
}
bit(1) hasPnbBits;                                                  1
if(hasPnbBits)
 unsigned int(4) aqp.PnbBits;                                       4
}
```

For each value, bounds in Intra mode may be read. The number of bits used in Intra mode is then determined. In Predictive mode, the minimal bound is in the range $[-2^{InbBits}, 2^{Inbbits}-1]$ around a central value vq. The number of bits used in Predicitive mode is finally read.

The value in Intra mode uses quantization in the same manner as in BIFS-Command protocol. In Predictive mode, vqDelta is read from the bitstream using an adaptive arithmetic decoder (AAD); see the Web3D Gallery.

class	*number of bits*

```
class AnimIValue (FieldData field) {
 switch(field.animType) {
  case 9:  // normal
   int(1) direction;                                               1
  case 10: // rotation
   int(2) orientation;                                             2
   break;
  default:
   break;
 }
 for(int j=0; j< field.getNbComponents(); j++)
  int(field.nbBits) vq[j];                              field.nbBits
}
```

Using bounds and number of bits in the AnimQP, values are decoded using quantization equations 2 and 4 for quantizer 13, and equation 1 for normals and rotations (see the quantization discussion in Chapter 17, "MPEG-4 Binary Format for Scenes (BIFS)," for details). As explained previously, the direction of rotations is not needed because of a property of quaternions.

```
class AnimPValue (FieldData field) {
 switch(field.animType) {
  case 9:   // normal
   int(1) inverse;
   break;
  default:
   break;
 }
 for(int j=0; j< field.getNbComponents(); j++)
   int(aaNbBits) vqDelta[j];
}
```

The predictive values are decoded using a prediction process, illustrated in Figure 18-2.

At frame t, the prediction process adds the arithmetic decoded value vqDelta(t) to PMin bound and to the previous reconstructed value vq(t-1). This value is then unquantized using IMin and IMax bounds, and PnbBits for the number of bits. To summarize the process:

$$v'(t) = v_{aac}(t) + \text{PMin}$$
$$vq(t) = vq(t - 1) + v'(t)$$
$$v(t) = inverse\ (\text{IMin, IMax, InbBits, } vq(t))$$

The '+' sign in the second equation is conceptual addition. For each value an addition is performed component-by-component, except for normals and rotations, which require special treatment.

For positions 2D and 3D, each component has its own bounds PMin[i], but uses the same number of bits. For all other types of fields, PMin is simply a scalar.

Figure 18-2 Prediction process in decoding values in BIFS-Anim's Predictive mode. Z^{-1} means a delay of one frame is introduced.

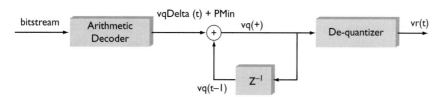

For rotations and normals, the prediction process requires special treatment. However, for normals, if `inverse=0`, then let $inv = 1$ and if inverse=1, $inv = -1$. For rotations, $inv=1$. Recall that if N is the number of components, we are dealing with $N_r = N - 1$ reduced components: 2 for normals and 3 for rotations. The process starts by adding $PMin$ to each component decoded by the arithmetic decoder. Then $vq(t - 1)$ is added to $v'(t)$, as previously, but stored in a temporary array:

$$vq_{temp}[i] = vq[i](t - 1) + v'[i]$$

Let $scale = 2^{max(0, nbBits-1)} - 1$; three cases have to be considered:

1. $vq_{temp}[i] \leq scale$, then
$$\begin{cases} vq[i](t) & = & vq_{temp}[i] \\ orientation(t) & = & orientation(t - 1) \\ direction(t) & = & direction(t - 1) \circ inverse \end{cases}$$

2. If there exists only one index k such that $|vq_{temp}[k]| > scale$, then let $inv = 1$ if $vq_{temp}[k] \geq 0$ and $inv = -1$ else. Let $k' = k + 1$; then the components of vq are:

$$\begin{cases} 0 \leq i \leq N_r - k', & vq[i] = inv \cdot vq_{temp} [(i + k') \bmod N_r] \\ i = N_r - k', & vq[i] = inv \cdot 2 \cdot scale - vq_{temp} [k' - 1] \\ N_r - k' < i < N_r, & vq[i] = inv \cdot vq_{temp} [(i + k' - 1) \bmod N_r] \end{cases}$$

$$orientation(t) = (orientation(t - 1) + k') \bmod N$$

$$direction(t) = direction(t - 1) \cdot inverse.inv$$

3. If there exist many indices k such as $|vq_{temp}[k]| > scale$, then results are undefined. In practice, interpolating rotations between frames is usually smooth, and this case should never happen.

Having `orientation(t)`, `direction(t)` and `vq(t)`, reconstruction of rotations and normals at time t is done using quantization equations 7 and 8 in Chapter 17, "MPEG-4 Binary Format for Scenes."

The procedure used by BIFS-Anim requires some care. The PnbBits are used to instantiate the arithmetic model for a field. In theory, there are at max $2^{InbBits+1}$ values. Using PMin and PnbBits enables us to use a subset of these values. However, in an interactive process, a "live" encoder would have to monitor these two parameters to avoid an overflow of the arithmetic encoder. This overflow will happen when the difference between two consecutive values is out of bounds, i.e., out of $[PMin - 2^{PnbBits-1}, PMin + 2^{PnbBits-1}]$. In this case, an Intra frame should be sent with new Imin, Imax, InbBits, vq, and PnbBits (recall that $PMin = vq - 2^{InbBits}$). You might think that if PnbBits

= InbBits + 1 and PMin = 0, you should be safe. However, in general, this would result in using too many unnecessary values in the arithmetic model: twice the number possible in Intra! For each field, this might waste a lot of memory as well as CPU efficiency and use more bits in the bitstream.

As the BIFS-Anim protocol involves coding of field values and not nodes themselves, it is possible to write a BIFS-Anim encoder without any knowledge of the scene itself. However, the decoder needs to know the scene itself, and at the time the animation mask is decoded, the scene has to be there. This is an important restriction in practice, because if the scene is not present when the animation mask is received, the BIFS-Anim decoder cannot retrieve the node from the scene and thus is unable to determine which type of field has to be animated.

At the time of writing, proposals to solve this problem had been made at MPEG [French NB comments on 14496-1 & 14496-1/FPDAM1, Proposal m5100, Melbourne meeting, October 1999] and were included in the standard at the same time as BIFS version 2 in December 1999.

Summary

BIFS-Anim is a streaming protocol used to control MPEG-4/BIFS scene animation. It can be thought of as a mechanism for dynamically altering node field values over a network connection. BIFS-Anim behaves like a video or audio streaming protocol, in that a header (the *anim mask*) is first sent to configure the BIFS-Anim decoder, after which frames are sent at a specified frame rate (frames contain values for fields that have been declared animated in the mask and that are animated in these frames).

Although they appear to be separate protocols, both BIFS-Anim and BIFS-Command utilize the same BIFS decoder (the anim mask is stored in the BIFS-Command decoder). While quantization is not necessary in the BIFS-Command protocol, it is mandatory in BIFS-Anim (BIFS-Anim uses an adaptive arithmetic encoder to store the quantized values in the bitstream).

In the next chapter you will learn how to encode existing VRML content in BIFS format. Because MPEG-4 is so new, however, commercial visual authoring tools for this technology are not yet available. Visit the MPEG area of the Web3D Gallery (http://www.web3dgallery.com/mpeg/) to learn about MPEG-4 authoring tools now under development and to find commercial tools as they become available.

Following is a complete list of URLs referenced in this chapter:

Web3D Gallery MPEG Area   http://www.web3dgallery.com/mpeg/

CUSTOMIZING VRML FOR BIFS

Topics in This Chapter

- How to convert VRML contents to BIFS
- Enhancing the content
- What's next?

19

In the previous chapters you were introduced to MPEG-4 Binary Format for Scenes (BIFS) and its two protocols: BIFS-Commands and BIFS-Anim. The binary formats were described and some techniques for using these protocols were discussed. In this chapter you will learn how to use existing VRML content with MPEG-4, by converting it to BIFS. VRML content can be converted to BIFS protocols to take advantage of the compression schemes. However, higher compression rates can be achieved at the cost of introducing a small, unnoticeable error in the original values. This powerful concept is the whole idea behind using quantization. Here you will learn how to optimize the encoding presented in previous chapters. Algorithms will be presented to automate usage of quantization from a few user-provided parameters. The last part of the chapter gives examples of customization of VRML contents with BIFS functionalities.

Converting VRML Contents to BIFS

In earlier chapters you learned about BIFS-Commands and BIFS-Anim protocols. BIFS-Commands adds some constraints in the VRML scene:

- Scenes must start with a top-level node. In the case of VRML contents it can only be a Group node. All nodes must be children of this top-level node. Adding a Group on top of each VRML content does not change the functionalities of the scene.

- All ROUTEs must be put at the end of the scene description.

- DEF names must be converted to unique integer identifiers. The easiest way to do this is to create and maintain a hash table with keys as DEF names and values as identifiers. Each time a new DEF name is encountered, the identifier number is incremented. When a VRML command using DEF names such as USE or ROUTE is parsed, the identifier corresponding to the DEF name is already in the hash table.

Converting textual content description to binary format leads to a compact representation of the data. Constraints may govern the process, such as efficiency versus size of the BIFS stream. As we will see later, in order to obtain a better compression ratio, the encoding may require iterative techniques to estimate the set of quantization parameters that best match requirements a user may provide, such as size of bitstream and the error made on values. These types of techniques are rooted in rate-distortion theory (Jain 1989, Sayood 1996), as we will see later. As they are iterative over the scene description, real-time encoding is not possible. On the other hand, if compression ratio is not important, encoding without quantization parameter nodes or with a set of predefined ones should be sufficient in most cases. The conversion technique is illustrated graphically in Figure 19-1.

Considering these parameters, a complete VRML scene can be encoded in BIFS-Commands protocol. BIFS-Anim deals with values changing over

Figure 19-1   Encoding a VRML scene in BIFS-Commands (BIC) protocol.

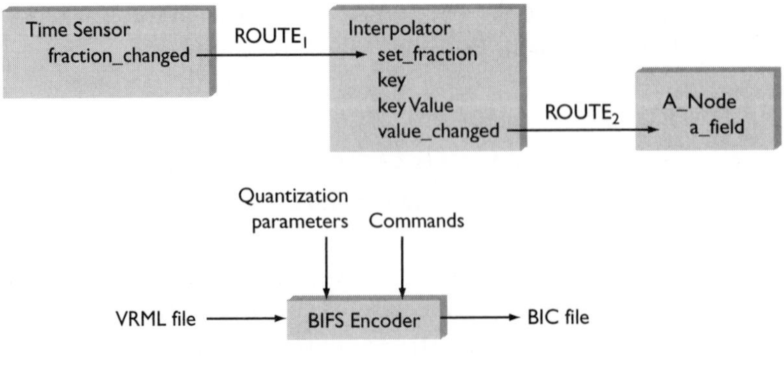

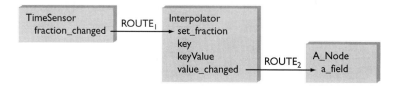

Figure 19-2 Typical use of value changing over time in VRML. As the fraction of time changes in the TimeSensor, it is routed to an interpolator which interpolates a value between two key values. The changed value is then routed to a field in a node.

time. In VRML content, these values are contained in interpolator nodes such as PositionInterpolator and ColorInterpolator. To make them change over time, a TimeSensor is routed to an interpolator and the interpolator is routed to a node field (Figure 19-2).

To create a BIFS-Anim stream, it is sufficient to extract the interpolator values, timing information (for example, when it starts, how long the stream lasts, speed of the clock), and where the values are routed from the interpolator. Removing TimeSensors, interpolators, and associated ROUTEs from the scene and adding quantization parameters enables the creation of the BIFS-Anim stream and a smaller BIFS-Command bitstream.

Figure 19-3 shows the complete conversion process we will discuss in this chapter. There are four parts to the process:

1. extracting information from the VRML file (TimeSensors, interpolators, ROUTEs)
2. converting the file to BIFS-Command protocol, subject to possible placement of a QuantizationParameters node
3. converting extracted interpolators to BIFS-Anim protocol, subject to judicious animation quantization parameters
4. customizing BIFS-Command (BIC) file by adding commands and the BIFS-Anim (BIA) file

Converting from VRML to BIFS

Converting from VRML to BIFS is a straightforward process, since BIFS includes all VRML nodes. BIFS-Command imposes some of the constraints mentioned in the description above: only one top node (Group for example),

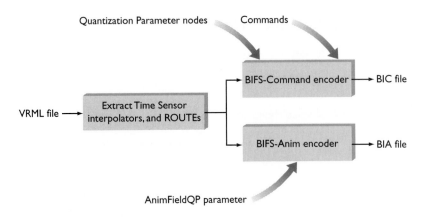

Figure 19-3   Complete block diagram of converting a VRML scene description to BIFS-Commands (BIC) and BIFS-Anim protocols (BIA).

DEF names have to be converted to unique identifiers, and ROUTEs have to be grouped together.

The BIC file will be significantly (6 to 9 times) smaller than the VRML file. The compression can be improved using QuantizationParameter nodes placed as we saw in Chapter 17, "MPEG-4 Binary Format for Scenes (BIFS)." In fact, many values in a VRML file can be truncated without visually modifying the behavior an author created. This is typically the case with floats. If no quantization is used, each float uses 32 bits. By simply using the efficient float representation, each float will use 4 to 29 bits.

BIC files are typically sent in a streaming manner. The smaller they are, the faster they will reach the client. If the file is too big, the underlying communication protocol will transmit it in smaller chunks that may not arrive sequentially. It will take more time to reassemble the whole file, and some chunks may be lost. That is one reason the download of large files over the Internet may take quite a long time before ultimately failing. Using judiciously placed QuantizationParameter nodes will reduce the size of the bitstream, but careful authoring may achieve this as well. For example, try to avoid unnecessary polygons in meshes. Visually, it is often better to have a good texture mapped on a simple mesh rather than an expressively detailed mesh. On flat parts of meshes, try to use very few polygons, while on near edges and corners try to have smaller polygons.

In the remainder of this section we will discuss the use of quantization parameters for BIFS-Command and BIFS-Anim.

Encoding in BIFS-Commands

To better compress a BIFS-Command (BIC) file, use of Quantization-Parameter nodes in the scene graph is typically necessary. This leads to a lossy compression scheme. The simplest use of a QuantizationParameter node may be to use only `useEfficientFloat = TRUE` placed as the first node of the scene. All floats in the scene will be compressed, using from 4 to 29 bits instead of 32 bits, and for most of the scenes there will be no loss.

In Chapter 17 we saw that QuantizationParameter has 13 quantizers, one for each kind of quantizable field, as shown in Table 19.1.

There are two ways of setting quantizer bounds (for example, position3DMin and position3DMax) and setting the number of bits (for example, position3DnbBits): either manually or automatically. Manually, these values are set after estimating what error would result on the values where the quantizers will act. Automatically, the encoder will determine these values with respect with constraints imposed, such as the error on the values (the distortion) and/or the number of bits for each value or for the whole file (the rate).

Table 19.1   Type of field for each of the 13 BIFS-Command quantizers

Quantizer	Type of value	Type of field
1	Positions 3D	SFVec3f
2	Positions 2D	SFVec2f
3	Drawing order	SFInt32
4	Color	SFFloat/SFColor
5	Texture coordinates	SFVec2f
6	Angle	SFFloat
7	Scale	SFFloat/SFVec2f/SFVec3f
8	Interpolator keys	SFFloat
9	Normals	SFVec3f
10	Rotations	SFRotation
11	Size 3D	SFFloat/SFVec2f/SFVec3f
12	Size 2D	SFFloat/SFVec2f/SFVec3f
13	Integers	SFInt32

Rate distortion theory is concerned with the trade-offs between distortion D and rate R in lossy compression schemes. Rate is defined as the average number of bits used to represent each sample value. Distortion is defined as the distance between the original value v and the reconstructed value $\hat{v}$:

$$D = d(v,\hat{v}) = \|v - \hat{v}\|$$

The distance $d(.,.)$ may be defined as the absolute value of the difference, the squared value of the difference, or in general as:

$$D = \sum_{i=0}^{M-1} \sum_{j=0}^{M'-1} d(v_i, \hat{v}_j) P(\hat{v}_j \mid v_i)$$

where $P(v_i)$ is the probability of occurrence of value v_i and $P(\hat{v}_j \mid v_i)$ is the conditional probability (i.e., the probability of occurrence of $\hat{v}_j$ if v_i is known).

One way of representing the trade-offs is via *a rate distortion function $R(D)$*. This function specifies the lowest rate at which the output of a source can be encoded while keeping the distortion less than or equal to D. Given a distortion constraint D^*, we could look at all encoders with distortion less than D^* and pick one with the lowest output entropy. This entropy would be the rate corresponding to the distortion D^*.

The *entropy* is defined as a measure of the average number of binary symbols needed to code the output of a source. Shannon (Shannon 1948; see Appendix D, "MPEG-4 Resources") showed that the best a compression scheme can do is to encode the output of a source with an average of bits equal to the entropy. The entropy for an independent, identically distributed (iid) random variable that takes values from the source alphabet $\chi = \{x_0, x_1, \ldots, x_{M-1}\}$ is defined as:

$$H(X) = -\sum_{i=0}^{M-1} P(x_i) \log_2 P(x_i)$$

where $P(x_i)$ is probability of occurrence of symbol x_i.

For our present concern, the source alphabet is the output of a quantizer. If a quantizer has 2^N steps, the source alphabet has $M = 2^N$ values. We will use a distortion defined as the difference between the original value and the reconstructed one: $D = \|v - \hat{v}\|$. We have two options:

1. Given a maximal distortion not to be exceeded, we will try to find a set of quantizers and a placement for them in the scene graph so as to have a minimal rate.

2. Given a maximal rate not to be exceeded, we will try to find the quantization parameters leading to a minimal distortion.

Let's define a rate distortion function $C(R, D, Q)$, where R is the rate, D is the distortion, and Q is the cost of adding QuantizationParameter nodes (with its fields and values) in the scene. The goal here is to minimize this cost function. In practice, this problem is very difficult due to the nature of the scene. The algorithms presented below are in general suboptimal, because we try to minimize the cost function locally and not globally.

Some local constraints may be added, such as rate and distortion for a node and its children, resulting in a local QuantizationParameter to be placed before this node.

Algorithm 1: For a Simple Scene

Before describing the complete algorithm, let's take a simple case. Suppose we have a grouping node with some child nodes. The quantization parameters of each quantizer are first determined for each node. Let's define

- D^* as the maximal distortion allowed by the user.
- $v_{\min q,k}$ and $v_{\max q,k}$ as the bounds of node k for quantizer q. They are determined by parsing each field to which the quantizer q applies.
- $$N_{0,k} = \log_2\left(1 + \frac{v_{\max q,k} - v_{\min q,k}}{2D^*}\right)$$ as the minimal number of

   bits to achieve the distortion specified by the user, for node k.

For all nodes, the global bounds are

$$v_{\min q} = \min_k v_{\min q,k}$$

$$v_{\max q} = \min_k v_{\max q,k}$$

and the minimal number of bits to achieve the user's maximal distortion is

$$N_0 = \log_2\left(1 + \frac{v_{\max\ q} - v_{\min\ q}}{2D^*}\right)$$

Consequently, if $N_0 \geq N_{0.k}$ for all nodes k, we can achieve the user's distortion D^* for all nodes, and move these parameters in a global Quantization-Parameter node as first child of the grouping node. However, if there exists a node k such that $N_0 < N_{0.k}$, we cannot use these global parameters and we must insert a local QuantizationParameter before node k.

In some cases the distortion specified by the user cannot be achieved, so we need to limit $N_0 \leq 32$ bits, which is the maximal size of an integer we can store in the bitstream. In other cases it might cost less to use efficient float coding instead of quantization. In this case, we will deactivate the quantizer and use only `useEfficientFloats = TRUE` in the global quantizer.

The cost Q of inserting a QuantizationParameter node is:

Cost of adding an SFNode	9
Cost of describing F fields	
If ListNodeDescription	$1 + 7F + C_F$
If MaskNodeDescription	$40 + C_F$
endFlag, if grouping node's `children` field uses ListNodeDescription	1

where C_F is the cost of the used fields themselves. Thus, if we use more than 5 fields among the 40 fields of a QuantizationParameter node, we should use the MaskNodeDescription.

However, if we could reuse an already defined QuantizationParameter, the cost would be $1 + nodeIDbits\ (+\ 1)$, where $nodeIDbits$ is the number of bits used to represent the nodeID of a DEF'd node (and depends on the number of DEF'd nodes in the scene), and $(+1)$ if ListNodeDescription is used for the grouping the node's children field.

Finally, what do we gain by using QuantizationParameters? Every non-quantized field costs 32 bits per component (an SFFloat and SFInt32 have 1 component, SFVec2f 2 components, SFVec3f and SFColor 3 components, and SFRotation 4 components). Using the quantizer q, we use only N_{0q} bits per component for a field. If we use efficient float representation instead, this number may vary per component from 4 to 29 bits. Note also that quantization of normals and rotations uses one less component (i.e., 2 for normals and 3 for rotations). Depending on the number of fields to which quantization is applied, using the QuantizationParameter node will reduce the bitstream.

Algorithm 2: For a Complete Scene

We can now extend this simple algorithm to a complete scene made of a top grouping node, which may contain other grouping nodes. The scene can be represented as a tree where each branching node is a grouping node and each leaf a node (and possibly a grouping node with no children). See Figure 19-4.

Remember that a QuantizationParameter node applies to all sibling nodes and their children. Thus, if we insert a QuantizationParameter in a grouping node, it will apply to the nodes following it inside the grouping node, and if it is local, to the following node only.

We use the same definitions as the previous algorithm. Then algorithm 2 is as follows:

1. We start at the highest level in the tree, i.e., $l = L - 2$.

2. We apply algorithm 1 at level l.

   Algorithm 1 ends by inserting a global QuantizationParameter before the first node and possibly local QuantizationParameters before some nodes at level $l + 1$. We move the bounds and number of bits of each quantizer to the grouping node at level l. Adding a global QuantizationParameter at level $l + 1$ as first node of a grouping node at level l is equivalent to adding a local QuantizationParameter before the grouping node at level l.

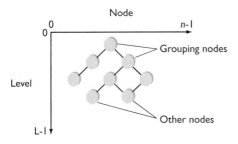

Level

0
0

Node

n-1

Grouping nodes

Other nodes

L-1

Figure 19-4   A scene represented as a tree. The top grouping node is at level 0. A grouping node at level l has children at level $l + 1$. Child nodes at a level are numbered from left (the first node) to right (the last node).

3. We repeat step 2 for level $l = l - 1$ until we reach the root of the tree, i.e., level $l = 0$.

However, at level 0, we cannot add a local QuantizationParameter before the grouping node. Thus, we will leave the global QuantizationParameter at level 1.

At the end of the algorithm, we may add the following refinement:

4. From level 0 to level $L - 1$, if there exist QuantizationParameters with the same field's values, i.e., same quantizers at level $l' > l$, then replace the QuantizationParameter at level l' by USE Quantiza-tionParameter at level 1.

Algorithm 2 ends in general with a suboptimal scene, because we minimized the cost function locally and not globally. Minimizing the cost function globally is difficult because the position and the parameters of the QuantizationParameters may change all the time. Moreover, for another distortion, even close to D^*, QuantizationParameters may be placed in a very different manner, may be grouped, or we may have more local QuantizationParameters. It may happen that even for a higher distortion, the algorithm ends with a higher rate. A refinement may be to try different values of D^* and pick the one leading to the smallest rate.

Encoding in BIFS-Anim

BIFS-Anim optimization is much simpler than for BIFS-Commands, thanks to the nature of the encoding scheme. In the preceding chapter we showed the decoding of the animation decoder. Figure 19-5 shows the encoder process.

At frame t, a value of a field $v(t)$ is quantized using the field's animation quantizer Q_I, where I denotes that parameters of the Intra frame are used to quantize value $v(t)$ to a value $vq(t)$. The sent value is $\varepsilon(t) = vq(t) - vq(t-1)$. In an Intra frame, the sent value is simply $vq(t)$ as there exists no previous value $vq(t-1)$. Finally, an arithmetic encoder performs a variable-length coding of $\varepsilon(t)$.

Let us summarize the parameters involved in this encoding process:

- I_{min}, I_{max}, N_I: parameters of the quantizer Q_I: respectively minimal and maximal bounds of value $v(t)$ over all frames, and number of bits

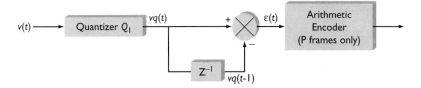

Figure 19-5 Encoding a field's values in BIFS-Anim. Z^{-1} means a delay of one frame is used.

used to quantize the value (which implies 2^{N_I} steps for the quantizer).

- $P_{min} = K - 2^{N_I}$, N_P: the lower bound in Predictive mode, which depends only on a constant K, and the number of bits in Predictive mode. N_P is used only to initialize the arithmetic model for this field (see the appendix) with 2^{N_P} values.

As for the BIFS-Command, our goal is to find these parameters so as to have a smaller bitstream with a small distortion. As we will see later, we must also determine when to insert Intra frames in the bitstream among the Predictive ones.

We will suppose we know all the values in advance (for example, the animation has been done with some authoring tool, as opposed to being created in real time). We will refer to the first case as the broadcast scenario and to the second as the interactive scenario.

If we know all the values of a field, we are able to determine its bounds. We also know that the quantizer introduces a maximal distortion D of

$$D \le \frac{\Delta}{2}, \quad \Delta = \frac{I_{max} - I_{min}}{2^{N_I} - 1}$$

So, given a distortion D^* not to cross, the minimal number of bits N^*_I is

$$N^* = \log_2 \left(1 + \frac{I_{max} - I_{min}}{2D^*} \right)$$

If we use $N_I \ge N_I^*$, this leads to a distortion $D \le D^*$, which is exactly what we want.

In Predictive mode, the difference between two consecutive values is sent in the bitstream:

$$
\begin{aligned}
0 &\leq v_q(t) & &< 2^{N_I} \\
-2^{N_I} &< v_q(t) - v_q(t-1) & &< 2^{N_I} \\
0 &< v_q(t) - v_q(t-1) + 2^{N_I} & &< 2^{N_I+1}
\end{aligned}
$$

This equation shows that in the worst case, we might have a difference of 2^{N_I+1}. This means that the predictive arithmetic model for the field might need 2^{N_I+1} values, i.e., $N_p^* = N_I + 1$, which can be a lot of memory wasted! Fortunately, values of a field over time are often correlated and the difference is bounded to a subset of these values:

$$
K \leq v_q(t) - v_q(t-1) + 2^{N_I} \leq L
$$

and

$$
\begin{aligned}
L - K + 1 &= 2^{N_p} \\
N_p &= \log_2 (L - K + 1)
\end{aligned}
$$

Consequently, if on a set of frames we know K and L, then we know how many bits N_p we should use to initialize the arithmetic model of this field. On the other hand, if we fix a number of bits not to cross in Predictive mode, we will have to find a set of frames such that $L - K + 1 \leq 2^{N_p}$. Before and after this set of frames, we will have to insert Intra frames.

Even if both approaches are possible, we will focus on the first one and determine N_p from a set of frames, keeping in mind that we want it small.

Previously, we said $N_p^* = N_I + 1$ was the worst case. In some cases, however this will not use so much memory, and it is interesting to use these parameters because the whole bitstream will consist of:

$$
\text{I P P } \dots \text{ P} \qquad \textit{ideal case}
$$

where I stands for Intra frames and P for Predictive ones.

In general, this is not possible, and the bitstream will consist of frames in this order:

$$
\text{I P P } \dots \text{ P I P } \dots \text{ P I P } \dots \text{ P} \qquad \textit{general case}
$$

However, as we introduced I frames, we also changed the quantization parameters for the set of values between two I frames, lowering the distortion of the whole stream. We gain in distortion, but as an I frame costs more than a P frame, the general case has a higher rate than the ideal one.

The worst case will happen when the previous value is $v(t-1) = I_{min}$ and the current one is $v(t-1) \geq I_{max}$, or vice versa. If this happens, it would be wise to insert an Intra frame before sending the current value and to find other quantization parameters for the following values.

On the other hand, it is important to save memory, since it is generally not possible to know the capabilities of a receiving terminal. If it is a set-top box or a mobile phone, or any low-memory device, the user won't be able to play the stream.

We now have everything we need in order to propose a general conversion technique.

Algorithm

Let us define

- $v(f)$ as the value of a field at frame f
- D^* as the distortion not to be exceeded, specified by the user
- N_I^u and N_P^u as the number of bits not to be exceeded, specified by the user in Intra and Predictive mode, respectively.

The general technique proposed is as follows:

1. Determine quantization parameters for the Intra frame at time t_0 that we will call frame f_0.
   a. Parse all values for frames $f \geq f_0$.
      Update I_{min}, I_{max}, and N^* such that

$$I_{min} = \min_{f = 0, \ldots, M-1} v(f)$$

$$I_{max} = \max_{f = 0, \ldots, M-1} v(f)$$

$$N^* = \log_2\left(1 + \frac{I_{max} - I_{min}}{2D^*}\right)$$

b. Stop if $N^° > N^u_I$

At this stage, we have parsed M values (and possibly all values).

2. Determine quantization parameters for Predictive frames.

a. For frames $1 \le f \le M - 1$, determine

$$K = 2^{N_I} + \min_{f = 1, ..., M - 1} v_q(f) - v_q(f - 1)$$

$$L = 2^{N_I} + \max_{f = 1, ..., M - 1} v_q(f) - v_q(f - 1)$$

b.   Stop if L > 2Nup - 1 + K

If we meet this criterion at frame $M' < M$, we can no longer use predictive frames because we overflow the arithmetic model. We have to resend an Intra frame. Go to step 1.

3. Go to step 1 until all values of all frames are processed.

At the end of this process we have a complete sequence of Intra and Predictive frames meeting the criteria imposed by the user: not to exceed a distortion D^* and a specified number of bits.

This algorithm is suboptimal in the sense that it leads to a local minimum of the complex function $R(D^*)$—rate versus distortion.

Algorithm 2

To find the global minimum, we can restart the Algorithm 1 with other values of D^* using a bisection algorithm. In this way, the previous algorithm can be viewed as a subroutine of Algorithm 2. As the rate distortion curve is convex, this algorithm is guaranteed to find an optimum value. From rate distortion theory, we know there exists an optimal distortion D^* such that

$$D_{\min} \le D^* \le D_{\max}$$

minimizes the rate, i.e., the total number of bits used to send the values. We can simply use our algorithm in a bisection algorithm:

- Use the first algorithm with some low value $D_{min} = D_1$. This leads to rate R_1.
- Use the first algorithm for some high value $D_{max} = D_2$. This leads to rate R_2.
- If $R_1 < R_2$, then let $D_{min} = D_1$ and $D_{max} = (D_2 - D_1)/2$. Restart the first algorithm for D_{max}. The optimal distortion we are looking for is now between D_{min} and D_{max}.
- If $R_2 < R_1$, then let $D_{min} = (D_2 - D_1)/2$ and $D_{max} = D_2$. Restart the first algorithm for D_{min}.
- Stop this procedure if $R_1 \approx R_2$.

At the end of the second algorithm, we find the lowest distortion leading to the best minimal rate.

We assume that the user gives N_I^u and N_P^u. As stated earlier, these parameters are mainly to avoid waste of memory. Moreover, for efficiency, it would be better to keep N_P^u constant for all predictive frames in the first algorithm. This would avoid reallocating new arrays for the arithmetic model at each Intra frame. If N_P^u is kept constant, we just have to reset it.

Algorithm 3: For Piecewise Linear Interpolated Values

When converting VRML contents to BIFS-Anim (Figures 19-3 and 19-5), encoded values typically come from interpolators. In interpolators, values are linearly interpolated between two keys. In BIFS-Anim, values will also be interpolated linearly between two key frames, which are typically Intra frames. Key frames correspond to interpolator's keys. The slope of a linear segment between two keys is constant. However, $\varepsilon(t) = v_v(t) - v_v(t - 1) = v(t) - v(t - 1) + q(t) - q(t - 1)$ does not remain constant unless quantization noise $q(t)$ and $q(t - 1)$ are identical, which is rarely the case in practice.

VRML interpolators last for a period of T seconds given by a TimeSensor node. In BIFS-Anim, a frame rate f is specified in frames per second. The interpolators' keyValues will be sampled at this fixed frame rate. Each frame will have duration of $1/f$ seconds, and Tf frames will be generated. The following simple algorithm assumes that keys coincide with BIFS-Anim frames, i.e., $= k_j/f$, where k_j is an integer. In general, this may not be true.

1. Between two interpolator keys key_i and key_{i+1},

   a. Determine the slope:

$$s = \frac{keyValue_{i+1} - keyValue_i}{\Delta t_i} = f\,\frac{keyValue_{i+1} - keyValue_i}{k_{i+1} - k_i}$$

   where $\Delta t_j = (k_{j+1} - k_j)/f$ is the elapsed time between the two keys.

   b. Determine Intra quantization parameters:

$$I_{min} = min(keyValue_j, keyValue_{I+1})$$
$$I_{max} = max(keyValue_j, keyValue_{I+1})$$

$$N_I^\circ = \log_2\left(1 + \frac{I_{max} - I_{min}}{2D^*}\right)$$

   c. Determine Predictive quantization parameters.

$$K = \lfloor \Delta q_{min} + s/f + 2^{N_I^\circ} \rfloor$$
$$N_P^\circ = 1$$

   Empirically, one can show that $\Delta q_{min} \approx 4.825 \times 2^{N_I^\circ - 9}$ is a good estimate for this type of quantizer and data.

2. Go to step 1, until end of keys.

At this point, we have proposed 3 algorithms for offline or broadcast scenarios where the content is created with an authoring tool and all values are known over time.

Extension to Interactive Scenario

In the interactive scenario, knowledge of all the values of a field over time is impossible; we cannot predict the future! Given values of v_{min}, v_{max}, N_I, and K for each field's quantizer, a monitoring of the values is needed to avoid:

- A value may be out of the range $[v_{min}, v_{max}]$.

- A quantized value $e(t) = v_q(t) - v_q(t - 1)$ may be out of range $[0, 2^{N_p} - 1]$.

If one of these criteria is met, we need to send an Intra frame with new quantization parameters. By doing so, arithmetic models are re-allocated, decreasing the performance. Nevertheless, you may wonder what the new quantization parameters are, since we have no knowledge of the future. A hint may be given by the previous values: we know how fast the values are varying. We can assume that they will vary in the same way. Note that this is just a hint and this assumption may not be true in general, leading to more distortion in the reconstructed values.

Customizing VRML Contents

The preceding sections used a lot of mathematics. In this section we will focus on customizing existing VRML contents with new nodes provided by BIFS. One of the applications could be to add 2D objects in a 3D VRML world. A possible application is to add a 2D menu with text and graphics on top of a 3D world. Another is to add a 2D contextual menu. Other applications might use the synchronization model provided by MPEG-4 to make rich multimedia content with audio, video, and scene objects synchronized. Alternatively, a VRML world may be refined with new 3D objects such as face and body animation nodes. The possibilities are endless!

In the sections that follow, we describe a few applications. They all assume that we have a VRML file we want to customize.

Displaying Multiple Views of a Scene at Once

Suppose you have a scene and you would like to display it from different points of view in the same manner as a modeler: left view, top view, front view, and a custom view. In addition, you would like to see changes made to the scene in a window reflected in other windows. We need to use different layers having their own viewpoints and sharing the same scene.

Let's assume the VRML scene is inside a Group with DEF id 1. The textual BIFS description of the scene is as follows:

```
Layer2D {
 children [
  Transform {
   translation -0.5 0.5
    children [
     Layer3D { # left view
      size 1 1
      children [
       Viewpoint { … } # positioned at left of the scene
       DEF 1 Group {
          # put your VRML scene here, without ROUTEs
       }
      ]
     }
    ]
  }

  Transform {
   translation 0.5 0.5
    children [
     Layer3D { # face view
      size 1 1
      children [
       Viewpoint { … } # positioned in front of the scene
       USE 1
      ]
     }
    ]
  }

  Transform {
   translation -0.5 -0.5
    children [
     Layer3D { # top view
      size 1 1
      children [
       Viewpoint { … } # positioned on top of the scene
       USE 1
      ]
     }
    ]
  }

  Transform {
```

```
  translation 0.5 -0.5
  children [
   Layer3D { # custom view
    size 1 1
    children [
     Viewpoint { … } # positioned anywhere in the scene
      USE 1
     ]
    }
  ]
 }

 ]
}
```

```
# put all the ROUTEs of your VRML scene here
```

Adding a 2D Menu Bar

Suppose you have a 3D scene and you want to add a 2D menu bar on top of it. In this menu bar, you would like to have icons so that when the user clicks on them, some actions are performed on the 3D scene. For example, this could be used for a navigation system. Each icon may represent a special position in a 3D environment so as to help the user.

This application is another example of Layer usage. We will use two layers: one Layer3D for the 3D scene, and one Layer2D for the menu bar, as shown in Figure 19-6.

To place the user at a specific position, we need to use a Viewpoint corresponding to this position. In VRML, Viewpoints are bindable nodes. This means we can define multiple viewpoints in the VRML scene and only one will be active at a time. Clicking on an icon will result in activating a specific Viewpoint.

For each icon, we will use a TouchSensor that is activated when the user clicks on it. We route this isActive eventOut to a Viewpoint's set_bind field. The example will use three viewpoints and thus three icons.

The code for this application is as follows:

```
Layer3D {
 children [
  Layer3D {
```

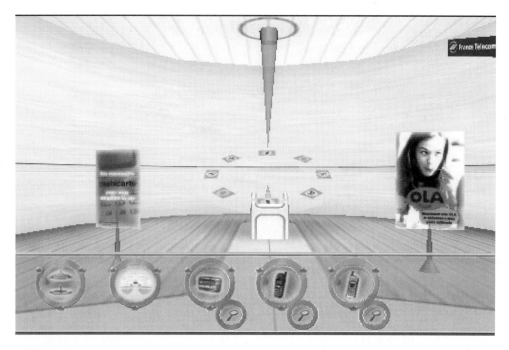

Figure 19-6 Example of 2D menu bar over a 3D scene. Image courtesy of France Télécom (France Telecom 1998).

```
    children [
      DEF 10 Viewpoint { … }
      DEF 11 Viewpoint { … }
      DEF 12 Viewpoint { … }

      # add your 3D scene here without ROUTEs
      ]

Layer2D {
  children [
    Transform { # position first icon
      children [
        DEF 20 TouchSensor {}
        # define the icon here
      ]
    }
```

```
Transform { # position second icon
 children [
  DEF 21 TouchSensor {}
  # define the icon here
 ]
}

Transform { # position third icon
 children [
  DEF 22 TouchSensor {}
  # define the icon here
 ]
}

]
}

# define the ROUTEs from TouchSensors to Viewpoints
ROUTE 20.isActive TO 10.set_bind
ROUTE 21.isActive TO 11.set_bind
ROUTE 22.isActive TO 12.set_bind

# add the ROUTEs in your scene
```

What's Next?

The previous examples outlined some of the possibilities provided by BIFS. At the time of this writing, BIFS version 2 is under development and will provide more functionalities:

- **Perceptual audio coding.** In BIFS version 1, physical modeling of sound has been standardized. In version 2, perceptual modeling opens a new way of synthetically representing audio.
- **Hierarchical 3D mesh.** Instead of sending the whole mesh at once, we send it progressively. This enables us to have smaller access units, avoiding loss of packets during transmission of big models and rendering the model faster from a coarse shape to a finer one.

- **PROTO node** as defined in VRML.

- **ApplicationWindow node** allows us to place an application's window inside a BIFS scene. You can imagine your favorite Internet browser embedded in a virtual world.

- **Progressive encoding of big MFFields.** In a BIFS scene, meshes and interpolators use a lot of values. As there is a clear correlation between each value, efficient compression schemes will be standardized.

- **New sensors** such as sliders or dialog-like boxes to enter some text.

- **Specification of usage of the backchannel** to send informations about the terminal status back to the server so to improve interaction between server and client.

- **MPEG-J,** a Java API extending VRML's EAI (External Authoring Interface). Through this interface one can access the scene and the terminal resources. It is then possible to scale them down in a graceful manner and to design more interactive scenes.

MPEG-4 is the first standard that enables a truly rich multimedia experience with high-quality audio, video, 2D and 3D objects, dynamic interactive modifications of the scene, and all in a streaming manner. The new possibilities are endless. Moreover, as MPEG-4 introduces the concept of versions, we may in the near future have new versions of BIFS providing new nodes and functionalities (it won't take long for MPEG-4 products to appear in the market).

Summary

This chapter presented the process of converting existing VRML files to BIFS. We saw how to customize VRML files by adding commands to create BIFS-Command files. We also saw how to extract animation data to generate BIFS-Anim files.

Along the way we gave some algorithms to optimize the binary encoding, resulting in small bit-streams along with small distortions in the values. The algorithms lead to optimal representation of data. Depending on the evaluation criterion (the measure) smaller bit-streams may be achieved for the same distortion.

Tip

To learn more about MPEG-4 and BIFS (including BIFS v2, which was published at the time this book went to print), and for all source code listings in this book visit the Core Web3D Web site at http://www.CoreWeb3D.com.

Following is a complete list of URLs referenced in this chapter:

Core Web3D Web site   http://www.CoreWeb3D.com/

Part 5

X3D

WHY X3D?

Topics in This Chapter

- The motivation behind Extensible 3D (X3D)
- Barriers to VRML ubiquity
- A hint of things to come with X3D

Chapter 20

As you learned in Parts 1 and 2 of this book, VRML97 defined an international standard for 3D on the Web. Thanks to VRML, 3D worlds of astonishing quality and impact have invaded the Internet over the years (see Chapter 2, "Overview of Web3D," to see just a few of the many ways in which VRML is used today). As a pioneer Web3D technology, VRML was the seed from which a multitude of nonstandard 3D technologies sprung forth. Today, VRML is at the core of the most popular 3D virtual communities on the net. The MPEG-4 group adopted VRML as their way to define 3D geometry, while the Java 3D API not only emulates many VRML nodes and concepts but can utilize VRML files directly through a loader mechanism (see Part 3 of this book for details).

With all of this positive activity surrounding VRML, why would anyone want to cast it aside in favor of a radical new idea like Extensible 3D (X3D)? X3D, after all, is a modern-day replacement for VRML, isn't it? No—not exactly.

Today it's clear that X3D is merely an evolutionary step in the life of VRML. Designed to allow the best capabilities of VRML to be expressed in terms of the red-hot Extensible Markup Language (XML), X3D is being crafted with the benefit of 20/20 hindsight. X3D is, for all intents and purposes, the next generation of VRML.

> # X3D vs. VRML-NG
>
> Extensible 3D (X3D) began life as VRML Next Generation (VRML-NG). In time the name VRML-NG was changed to X3D to reflect its close ties to the Extensible Markup Language (XML) developed by the World Wide Web Consortium (http://www.w3.org/XML/). X3D allows 3D to be expressed in terms of XML tags. For details see Chapter 22, "Weaving X3D into Web Pages."
>
> X3D is being developed through the Web3D Consortium (the same organization that developed VRML). As an open process, development of X3D is open to all potential contributors. For details visit the Web3D Consortium's X3D Task Group at http://www.web3d.org/x3d.html.

If you've invested time or money in VRML, or are just starting a VRML project, you can rest assured that your investment is safe. So far as anyone is able to predict, X3D isn't a wholesale replacement for VRML; it's an incremental step forward based on the past success and failures of VRML.

Although VRML is considered by many to be the premier 3D technology for the Web, it's certainly not the only game in town. This book, in fact, describes two major technologies that up the ante for Web-based 3D technologies (Java 3D and MPEG-4/BIFS), while other forms of Internet 3D are nipping at its heels from every side (see Appendix F, "Other 3D Technologies for the Web," for details). While some people have been able to make a very decent living building VRML content, it isn't exactly a road to riches. Nor has VRML become the ubiquitous form of Web 3D that early hype promised it would be (see Chapter 1, "Why Bother?", for details). So what happened? A lot of things, as you'll soon see.

Size Matters

Netscape Navigator at one time included a VRML browser in their standard distribution. Internet Explorer also came standard with a built-in VRML browser at one time. Today, VRML browsers are relegated to full installations (no longer part of standard installations) for one simple reason: VRML browsers are too big, most weighing in at over 3 MB in size.

VRML browsers became so large and complex because the VRML97 specification is so large and complex. The VRML97 specification defines a dazzling array of 3D capabilities and requirements that browser vendors must implement in order to be considered "spec compliant." Those requirements ultimately translate into lines of code (which in turn contribute to a browser's size) and CPU cycles (which means speed, or lack thereof). All the will and skill in the world can't reduce those lines of code and those CPU cycles below a certain number.

To complicate matters, installing a VRML browser in the early years was far from the relatively painless process we enjoy today. For a significant period of time after the release of the VRML97 specification, frustrated users actually found installing a VRML browser to be harder than installing a DOS game (a notoriously difficult, if not impossible task for the average user).

Typically the user had to modify `autoexec.bat` and, often, manually install a Java Virtual Machine, DirectX, and a host of other accessories. Heaven help the user who wanted to install more than one VRML browser, which was often an exercise in futility for all but the most experienced computer users.

VRML browsers were inevitably too big as a result of VRML97 specification compliance requirements, an obstacle that was made more formidable by cumbersome installation schemes. As a result, many end users opted to pass when it came to viewing VRML content, and VRML browsers failed to find a home on every desktop.

Cortona Components Battle Browser Bloat

Most commercial VRML browsers are larger than 3 MB, making them impractical to bundle with standard, or "typical," Web browser distributions. To combat browser bloat, ParallelGraphics has broken its popular Cortona VRML browser into pieces. Cortona's component-based design revolves around a core VRML 3D engine that can be distributed independently of other nonessential components (such as sound and External Authoring Interface components). Weighing in at a svelte 500 KB, the core Cortona component can be downloaded transparently over the Internet without requiring user intervention. For details visit ParallelGraphics on the Web at http://www.parallelgraphics.com/.

VRML Lite

After it became obvious that the VRML97 specification engendered browsers that were too big and overly complicated, VRML architects Rikk Carey and Gavin Bell proposed a subset of VRML that eventually became known as "VRML Lite." VRML Lite excluded a number of VRML97 nodes, among them the predefined primitive shapes and the PROTO mechanism that allowed developers to extend VRML.

The VRML community, however, decided that VRML Lite wasn't worth pursuing, and the idea withered on the vine for lack of support. Surprisingly, the basic concept of VRML Lite has reappeared in many of today's X3D proposals. As you'll learn in the next chapter, X3D is shaping up to be a functional subset of VRML that is capable of being expressed in terms of XML.

The Corporate Soap Opera

Silicon Graphics, Inc. (SGI) was a driving force behind the design and development of VRML. A leader in high-performance computing, SGI has consistently produced world-class graphics technologies since it was formed in 1982. SGI workstations are the workhorses behind many of today's most complex simulation and 3D visualization projects, and they largely fueled the explosion of special effects we now take for granted in movies and television.

SGI was an early and vigorous supporter of VRML. The VRML 1.0 specification was essentially a subset of SGI's Inventor file format, and many of the key people behind VRML97 were SGI employees (see Chapter 4, "VRML Overview"). As a testimony to its commitment to VRML, SGI formed a subsidiary company called Cosmo Software (http://www.cosmosoftware.com/) at about the same time the VRML97 specification was released. Consisting of SGI employees, Cosmo Software produced commercial VRML authoring tools and a VRML browser called Cosmo Player.

Cosmo Software was the result of SGI's heavy investment in 3D technology in general and VRML in particular, boasting many of the most experienced VRML developers on the planet. It came as no surprise when Cosmo Player quickly dominated the budding VRML97 browser market. In early 1998, Cosmo Software employee David Frerichs claimed that approximately 38 million downloads of Cosmo Player had been logged.

Intervista WorldView, meanwhile, was widely recognized as the second most popular VRML browser in existence. Although WorldView wasn't used by as many people as Cosmo Player, Intervista had developed close ties with Microsoft that would eventually lead to WorldView's forming the basis of Microsoft's VRML 2.0 Viewer. Bundled with Internet Explorer, Microsoft's VRML 2.0 Viewer brought the dream of "VRML browser ubiquity" one step closer to reality.

If early 1998 was brimming with the promise and potential of VRML, late 1998 was a brush with disaster.

Under pressure from increasingly aggressive competition, the once-dominant SGI eventually saw its market share erode and its stock price tumble. By late 1998, the company announced that it would sell Cosmo Software in an effort to focus on its core business. After failing to close a deal with a potential buyer, Cosmo Software closed its doors to the stunned VRML community it helped build.

In September of 1998, however, PLATINUM Technology, Inc., came to the rescue and acquired the defunct Cosmo Software company. PLATINUM had acquired Intervista earlier that year and now planned to consolidate Cosmo Player and WorldView into a single VRML browser. In addition to Cosmo Software and Intervista, PLATINUM had also acquired VREAM (developers of a popular VRML modeler and browser). Clearly the enterprise business-solutions company had big plans for Web3D, specifically Internet-based 3D data visualization.

But PLATINUM ran into some setbacks itself. As a publicly held company, PLATINUM (like SGI) was under continual pressure to perform to Wall Street expectations. Following a particularly bad quarter the company downsized, laying off over 1,000 employees in a cost-cutting measure that included 3D developers. Cosmo Software was once again on the ropes, and with it Intervista and VREAM. Many of the most significant people driving commercial VRML development found themselves without an employer.

Shortly thereafter PLATINUM was acquired by Computer Associates International (CAI), which now owns the rights to Cosmo Software, Intervista, and VREAM products. CAI also acquired 3D content development houses Viewpoint Datalabs and 3Name3D, indicating that CAI, like PLATINUM before it, sees a big future in 3D technology married to enterprise business solutions. Although it's a good bet that CAI will use VRML for Internet-based data visualization, the company had not publicly announced its plans at the time this book went to press. As a result, a number of commercial VRML products have been stagnant for over a year.

Although these events haven't brought VRML to a screeching halt, they've certainly slowed it down. The overall quality of VRML content, like that of most Web media, is directly related to the authoring tools available to content developers. With several commercial VRML authoring tools (and leading VRML browsers) in limbo, VRML content development suffered a serious slowdown, and industry insiders began to question the future of VRML. Fortunately, a new generation of powerful authoring tools and browsers has recently emerged to fill the void (see "The Beat Goes On").

The Beat Goes On

Although a series of unfortunate corporate circumstances have beset Cosmo Software and Intervista, the beat goes on. This particular line of VRML browsers and authoring tools has been dealt a serious setback, unquestionably, but others have emerged. Today a new generation of VRML browsers and authoring tools are making their way to users and content developers (see the discussion in Chapter 10 for details).

In the Right Place at the Wrong Time

A significant number of the early VRML specification designers, as well as VRML browser and modeler makers, had SGI workstations on their desktops. Consequently, their vision of what was possible with computerized 3D was in large part driven by the ample processing power at their fingertips. Not surprisingly, many of these high-powered notions of 3D went straight into the VRML specification.

Until recently, however, the average home PC lacked the CPU horsepower and 3D graphics acceleration necessary to bring rich VRML worlds to life (Chapter 1, "Why Bother?"). In many respects, VRML's graphics capabilities were simply too good for the computer in the average home at the end of 1997. Understanding this fundamental gap between VRML's capabilities and those of the average home computer, VRML architect Rikk Carey posted what we see in Table 20.1 to the www-vrml email list some time ago.

VRML's color and lighting model, collision-detection capabilities, atmospheric effects, texturing, animation, and a virtually unlimited number of

Table 20.1 Frame Rate vs. Effect	
Frames per second	*Effect*
20–60	Perfect illusion, full 3D experience, dreamlike clarity
12–20	Reasonable illusion of 3D, good enough
8–12	Operable 3D interface, subconscious frustration, boatlike navigation, ok for design/expert tool
1–8	Unusable 3D interface, poor navigation, conscious frustration, in need of different UI techniques (e.g., *Myst*)

objects and polygons all add up to CPU cycles. Although high-end graphics workstations at the time were up to the task, home computers were not. VRML browsers running on ordinary PCs couldn't make it into the "good enough" frame rate. Many content developers had to struggle just to make some of their worlds fast enough to be considered "unusable."

As we enter the year 2000, the situation has vastly improved. Inexpensive 3D graphics cards now approach, and often exceed, the capabilities of SGI workstations that were state-of-the-art when the VRML97 specification was released. At the time of this writing 400-MHz CPUs and 64 MB of RAM seem to be the minimum for new PCs, with 3D hardware acceleration a commonplace enhancement. Consumer-level CPUs now have special hardware for doing matrix operations on floating-point numbers—one of the biggest CPU hogs for any form of 3D, not just VRML.

Finding a Use for Real-Time 3D

Today's consumer-level desktop computers are up to the challenge of processing 3D in real time. The challenge for content authors, however, lies in finding appropriate uses for real-time 3D (RT3D). There are plenty of compelling, effective, useful applications of real-time 3D. If you want your application to be one of them, you need to be ruthless in weeding out the bad ideas before you start. To learn about the minimum criteria of RT3D authoring, read Bob Crispen's paper, "Finding a Use For Real Time 3D," at http://www.web3dgallery.com/go/rt3d/.

Although hardware advances are great news for VRML developers and users today, early VRML adopters weren't so fortunate. Unfortunately, a good deal of VRML97 content was too ambitious for the hardware of its time. As a result, many people who didn't have cutting-edge equipment were turned off by the VRML worlds they encountered.

Ten Pounds in a Five-Pound Bag

The VRML file format is based on plain text. The best thing about that is that anybody can code a VRML world. The worst thing about it is that *anybody* can code a VRML world. And many of them did. Designing good VRML worlds takes time and experience, particularly 3D experience, something many early VRML content developers didn't have. As a result, a tremendous amount of poorly designed (and often downright ugly) VRML content is floating around on the Web today. The harsh but true reality is that only a very small percentage of the worlds on the Web today are really impressive; the rest usually aren't worth the download time.

Today's VRML authoring tools are a major advance over those available just a few years ago, and many content developers are beginning to embrace them (see Chapter 10, "Creating New VRML Worlds," to learn about visual authoring tools). A good deal of VRML content produced in the past, however, was actually exported from traditional 3D tools such as CAD programs. Unfortunately, many traditional 3D programs export to the VRML format without consideration of file sizes required for efficient Web distribution.

Most CAD modelers and animation modelers were designed for an environment where the models stayed on or near the computer they were designed on. As a result, they produced huge files with many more polygons than were strictly necessary. And the mesh decimators (software programs that reduce the number of points and polygons on surfaces) that might have reduced these models to a sensible size were either expensive or unavailable.

Bob Crispen (*CoreWeb 3D* co-author, and the main author of this chapter), for example, is the proud owner of a 20-MB VRML model of a Space Station airlock that he converted from CAD drawings being used to build the real-world Space Station. Although Bob's VRML model is gigantic, it's considerably reduced from the original CAD format. The original Space Station CAD drawings were packed with detail (the threads on each individual bolt looked realistic, for instance). Still, the model he was left with is almost good enough that you could build a Space Station airlock from it.

Despite the temptation, Bob hasn't uploaded his 20-MB VRML Space Station to the Web, and for good reason: It's too big to be viewed by anyone connected to the Internet with a dial-up modem. If only others had the same self-restraint! A surprising number of VRML worlds now on the Web consume several megabytes (or more) of disc space, putting them out of the reach of the average user. Courteous VRML authors sometimes provide low-bandwidth versions of large models, although not often enough.

The fact that so many people built huge worlds gave the completely false impression that VRML itself is too big. In fact, the opposite is true. A properly designed animated banner advertisement constructed in VRML is often smaller than the compressed JPEG image that it takes to adequately represent *one frame* of the same ad. The IrishSpace project on which Bob worked has to be delivered on a CD-ROM because it's far too big to transmit over the Internet. Yet 95% of the size of IrishSpace is from the audio and image files (http://www.ovrt.nist.gov/voyage/). The VRML geometry, which arguably gives the greatest impact, comprises only 5%. VRML is a tremendously efficient way to represent geometry, and of the media that come over the Internet, VRML can deliver one of the biggest bangs per byte.

At the VRML 98 Symposium, David Frerichs presented a summary of the bandwidth required for various forms of VRML. According to David's calculations, immersive VRML worlds are practical only when delivered over high-speed data connections (or on fixed media). If you're trying to build an immersive VRML world (which, after all, was a significant part of the reason VRML was created in the first place), a significant portion of the Web population won't be able to able to participate today (see Table 20.2).

These aren't limitations on VRML alone; they're limitations on *anything* delivered over the Internet. If you GZip-compress VRML files, you can get

Note

The Web3D Consortium's Universal Media Working Group has developed a cross-platform solution designed to eliminate media download bottlenecks. Libraries of freely available, standardized media elements (textures, sounds, and 3D objects) are stored locally on the end user's computer. By referencing Universal Media, media-rich 3D worlds can be constructed without regard for download times (only the world geometry is downloaded because the media is stored locally). For details visit the Universal Media site at http://www.web3d.org/WorkingGroups/media/.

Table 20.2 Connection Requirements		
Download Speed	*Type*	*Maximum Size*
28.8 Kbps	Nano-VRML	12 KB
56 Kbps, ISDN	Vignette	200 KB
CD-ROM, T1	Immersive	1 MB+

quite a bit of distance out of 12 KB. Still, making small worlds that look good is as much an art as it is a science. Until recently, very few tools have supported the art and science of VRML.

Conformance Concerns

In 1997 the VRML Consortium asked Mary Brady of the National Institute of Standards and Technology (NIST) to develop a series of conformance tests for VRML browsers. You can see them at http://www.itl.nist.gov/div897/ctg/vrml/vrml.htm. In addition, because our goal was to make VRML worlds look the same everywhere, Eric Haines developed a Java applet called Pellucid (http://www.acm.org/tog/resources/applets/vrml/pellucid.html) which was a "perfect" implementation of the VRML color and lighting model. Browser makers can compare their renderings with Pellucid's to see how well their color and lighting matches the standard.

Unfortunately, no one ever put a process in place that would issue a certification for conformance to the VRML97 specification, so testing was strictly voluntary. While a number of people in the major browser companies used Mary's and Eric's tests, browser makers who claimed conformance often did so based on less-than-perfect performance on the tests.

Why does that matter? Because it gave a huge advantage to proprietary Web3D applications. In VRML, if you build a VRML world that misbehaves or gives results you don't expect, you're never quite sure whether it's your fault or whether you're chasing a browser bug. Tools such as Trapezium's Vorlon (http://www.trapezium.com/) weed out overt syntax errors, but once you fixed those errors and sent legal VRML to your browser, it was difficult to nail down just what that legal VRML code was supposed to do.

It also placed companies developing VRML at a financial disadvantage. As Bob discovered working on the Monterey world his team built for the VRML

98 Symposium Website (http://ece.uwaterloo.ca/vrml98/vrml/monterey.wrl), you can spend as much time working around browser bugs and accounting for browser peculiarities as you do building the original world. Some early content-development houses had one price if their client wanted a VRML world to work in a single VRML browser and a considerably higher price if they wanted it to work in multiple browsers. That's why you see so many VRML content sites that recommend a specific VRML browser.

Although over 90% of VRML worlds work the same and pretty much look the same in every browser, the other 10% or so cause a real problem. It's human nature for content creators to push the boundaries of their tools and browser. It's equally human nature for engineers at browser companies not to test (or even know) all the boundaries as strictly as they test the normal cases. That combination adds up to potential problems.

Makers of proprietary Internet 3D applications just sat back and grinned. If you've got a proprietary 3D application, only one browser, and often only one file format and development toolset are needed. There isn't a single doubt about what a given file is supposed to do; by definition, whatever it does is what it's supposed to do.

Working with the Web

As you may recall, you can have VRML worlds as Web pages by themselves. That is, they take up all your Web browser's viewing area. Or you can put a VRML world in a frame on a Web page. Or you can embed a VRML world in a Web page, so that the VRML world and other Web-page elements like text and graphics and Java can reside on the same page. Using the External Authoring Interface (EAI) you can even have Java controls that talk to your VRML world.

But your VRML world is still inevitably inside a box, whether the box is the Web page, a frame, or a box in the Web page.

Wouldn't it be something if VRML could break out of its box? Wouldn't it be lovely to have 3D objects interact fluidly with the other elements on your Web page? Wouldn't it be nice to use a 3D element on your Web page as easily as you use a 2D graphics image?

That was the promise of Microsoft's Chromeffects (originally called Chrome) in 1998. And in fact, Chromeffects did deliver on that promise at least well enough to produce some spectacular demos at SIGGRAPH 98.

The fact that Chromeffects died shortly after it was born probably says more about the internal politics of the various product groups at Microsoft than it does about the technology itself. Mind you, there was no way to get as immersive in Chromeffects as you can in VRML, but that wasn't the point. Chromeffects for the first time showed that you could have 3D components as an integral part of the Web page. Furthermore, you could place 2D Web pages inside a 3D container (an extremely exciting prospect for 3D folks). While it's technically possible to make a decent *simulation* of 2D Web pages in a 3D VRML world, it's not easy; the process is extremely tedious, and unless you compute the proper viewpoint and force the user to stand in *exactly* that place, it will look terrible.

The main thing that people thinking about 3D on the Web took away from working on or seeing the Chromeffects demos was that integration between 3D and 2D on the Web could be much better than it was with VRML. Chromeffects gave us a look at what it meant to take 3D out of its box, allowing it to play freely with the entire Web page. Although Chromeffects is no longer alive, the concept of 3D integrated with the Web lives on in X3D.

I Want It NOW!

In 1998 a company called MetaCreations came out with an exciting 3D technology for the Web called MetaStream (http://www.metastream.com/). Developed in cooperation with Intel, MetaStream is based on a technology called *progressive rendering*. When you create a file for progressive rendering, you put certain data right at the front of it. As soon as the application gets that data, it can render a first approximation of the object. Then, as more data comes down the slow pipe that connects you to the Internet, your plug-in can render a slightly better looking object, then an object that looks pretty good, and finally the whole 3D object in all its glory.

That's the best of all possible outcomes. Unless you figure out how to instantaneously transmit 3D objects by telepathy or sneak into everyone's home in the dead of night and plant 3D objects on their computers, as Universal Media does, you're always going to want to show something that takes longer to download than your average visitor's attention span. By showing progressively better images, you can keep your visitors interested while the file downloads. Shockwave has this capability as well, and there are streaming MPEG players, streaming RealAudio and streaming RealVideo players.

(The seed from which this idea grew was planted in the GIF-89a standard for progressive GIF images, which was followed by the progressive JPEG image format.)

Sadly, VRML is high and dry as far as this technology goes. While a few early beta browsers tried to render things as they got them, they were faced with the inescapable problem illustrated in the following VRML file snippet:

```
#VRML V2.0 utf8
Transform {
    children [
        <100,000 lines of VRML code go here>
    ]
    rotation 0 1 0 1.57
}
```

Although this is a perfectly legal VRML file, it's deadly as far as progressive rendering is concerned. The next-to-last line of this file rotates the whole works 90 degrees around the Y axis, making any attempt to progressively render the 100,000 lines of code practically impossible; why draw something to the screen in one position if it's supposed to be rotated after it arrives? In this case, all of the children in the transform node have to come across the wire before they can be rendered.

Worse still, the VRML standard does not support streaming media. The VRML specification doesn't require or even recommend that browsers support streaming media. Consequently, browser vendors haven't bothered to support streaming formats until recently (see "Cortona Streams"). Without support for progressive rendering or streaming media, very large and media-rich VRML worlds are simply impractical as far as the average dial-up Internet user is concerned, unless technologies such as Universal Media are employed.

Cortona Streams

Cortona 2.0 supports RealAudio and RealVideo, meaning that VRML content created for this browser can tap into streaming media. Because other browsers don't support these media formats, however, such content cannot be viewed without Cortona. For details visit ParallelGraphics at http://www.parallelgraphics.com/.

I Hear You Calling

As you may recall from Chapter 9, "Customizing Light, Background, Fog and Sound," VRML's sound model provides support for MIDI and WAV files. Unfortunately, most VRML browsers' support of MIDI isn't what you might hope for. Many of the browsers that implement MIDI tend to slow navigation down to a crawl when the sound is playing, and MIDI rarely synchronizes properly to other events in the world unless you have a very high-end computer and an undemanding VRML world.

Synchronization is a serious problem. Often you don't want to start a sound track until all the geometry has downloaded that goes along with it. At other times you'd like to have your sounds play in sync with events taking place in the world (when a blacksmith strikes his anvil, for example, the "clang" sound should play when the hammer strikes, not before or after). It turns out that doing either of these things is a very difficult problem in VRML.

Despite these synchronization problems, MIDI is often the only reasonable VRML sound to use because of its small file sizes (WAV files are considerably larger than MIDI files). Nobody wants to wait five minutes for a bird chirp to download, making MIDI the sound format of choice in most cases despite the difficulty that many VRML browsers have with MIDI files.

Indeed, VRML's integration with multimedia as a whole is less than stellar. MovieTextures, for example, are normally unsatisfying when you consider the bytes that must be downloaded in order to achieve a desired effect (a problem that would be a nonissue if VRML supported streaming media). Even ImageTextures can cause quality problems, as many VRML browsers render them grainier and more pixelated than they should be (see Chapter 8, "Customizing Color and Texture" to learn about VRML textures).

Worlds that are constructed using only 3D VRML geometry are usually quite small, because they don't include any media. When properly designed, such worlds can load very quickly without sacrificing visual appeal (a combination that gives an excellent impression to visitors). Add media, however, and you'll often bloat the size of your world while introducing potential quality problems (the world will require more CPU cycles at the very least).

Note: Universal Media

Universal Media is a recent solution for creating media-rich VRML worlds without the overhead of extra downloads. Visit http://www.web3d.org/ WorkingGroups/media/ for details.

The Real World

Bob Crispen once had an interesting real-world experience after collaborating on a virtual world of Monterey, CA, for the VRML98 Symposium held there. J. Eric Mason had built a morphing duck, and Bob animated a viewpoint behind the duck so that it flew through the Monterey Bay area. At the end of the tour, the duck dropped the user off in the water by a sandcastle created by Margaret Pomeroy. Once there, the visitor could click on various parts of the scene and go directly to registration or view other information about the Symposium.

Paul Jensen put together the virtual terrain for this world from real-world Digital Elevation Model (DEM) data of Monterey. Norman Maher collected some bathymetry data so that visitors could see the fascinating underwater terrain of Monterey Bay. And Robert Stacey put the cherry on top by providing some Landsat images of the actual terrain that were mapped to the DEM. Virtual Monterey was a terrific little world, thanks to the efforts of everyone involved. And it had an interesting side effect in the real world that Bob remembers fondly:

> I got to my hotel in Monterey a day early, planning to help set some things up, but the net was down so I sat on the balcony of my hotel room and looked out the window at the bay, and suddenly it struck me—I've been here. After all the hours I'd spent in that VRML world, I had a familiarity with the terrain of the Monterey Bay area that was better than my familiarity with the town I live in. Oh, I was too lazy to put in all the feature data that should have gone along with the 3D map so that you could click and find out where the stores are and what that big building across the bay was. But I still came away with a conviction: This is the way maps are going to be created in the 21st century.

To this end, Martin Reddy and members of the Web3D Consortium's GeoVRML working group are developing innovative ways to use georeferenced data in VRML (http://www.web3d.org/WorkingGroups/).

There are, however, two major problems. First, all coordinates in VRML are represented using single-precision floating-point numbers. Although this isn't a problem in most virtual worlds, single-precision floating-point numbers are not precise enough when using real-world geo data. Eventually, there'll be a map of the Earth, and you'll click on it and zoom in to a 3D map of anywhere. But VRML hasn't got the precision to make that happen.

The second problem is that no matter how much memory and disk space you've got on your computer, you can't cope with all the geo data you'll want to see in even an average visit to this 3D map of the world. The GeoVRML folks have got that licked, too. They have a technology that lets you get progressively more detail as you zoom in, and even loads terrains in front of you and unloads it when behind you. The only catch is, you can't tell a VRML browser to unload data. There's no way to do it. You can't even control when the browser loads in data without some difficulty—that's normally left up to the browser. While it might be reasonable to leave it up to the browser in most worlds, in worlds of the *real world,* or any time you need to manage huge data sets, that's almost certain to be unsatisfactory.

VRML, as it stands, is inadequate when it comes to creating virtual maps of the real world without the GeoVRML solution. Amazingly, it's inadequate for these purposes mostly because of what seem to be insignificant shortcomings that could be easily rectified in a new iteration of the technology.

Science Marches On

The plan after the VRML97 specification was released in December 1997 was to have 18 months of stability to let the content grow and let opinions clarify about what was needed next. Those 18 months have passed, and at the time of this writing the Web3D Consortium is hard at work on X3D, the successor to VRML. In the next chapter we'll be looking under the hood of some current proposals for X3D.

It's important to note here, however, that VRML was never intended to be the final answer to 3D on the Web. No matter how much you aim your specification at future capabilities, technology will still surprise you. Many capabilities omitted from the VRML97 specification are today considered important (if not essential) to any future-ready Web3D technology such as X3D.

For example, when VRML97 was designed it was widely believed that Non-Uniform Rational B-Splines (NURBS) could not be rendered in real time on consumer-level computers (NURBS is an extremely compact way of describing geometry; see Chapter 3, "Entering the Third Dimension"). The engineers at blaxxun, however, punched a gaping whole in that theory when they added NURBS support to their Contact browser (see Appendix A, "VRML Browsers"). Thanks to blaxxun, a NURBS proposal is now on the table for X3D.

Superscape (http://www.superscape.com/), on the other hand, has demonstrated that VRML's Gouraud-like shading model isn't the last word in shading for Internet 3D technologies. As you may recall from Chapter 8, "Customizing Color and Texture," VRML's specular highlights (sparkles and glints, such as the type of reflections that you get off a fender of a car) are specified as a single prespecified color. Superscape's Viscape browser, however, now has true specular reflections (if the car is parked next to a yellow building, the yellow shows up in the reflection from the fender). Can real mirrors be far behind? Viscape also supports shadows, another thing missing from the VRML standard because we all believed they'd take too long to render back then. Wrong again.

These and other previously unthinkable capabilities are now possible thanks to the amazing pace at which computer technology in general, and 3D hardware in particular, has developed. Today's 3D accelerator boards can handle a dazzling array of advanced rendering features that can't even be specified in VRML. As a result, X3D proposals now exist for bump mapping, multitexture rendering, and particle systems. Because X3D is the next generation of VRML, these and other important 3D capabilities that weren't part of VRML97 are likely to make it into the new standard.

3D Everywhere

If VRML failed to take over the Web, 3D in general failed to take over our lives. A handful of years ago it was thought that 3D would revolutionize, if not dominate, our daily computing experience. This didn't happen for a number of reasons, including those described above.

Today, X3D is being designed as the next generation of VRML. X3D, naturally, benefits from our being able to see where VRML97 succeeded and where it failed. As you'll see in the next chapter, the core of X3D will ultimately be less complicated than VRML97. It will, however, accommodate a component-based extension mechanism that will allow it to grow as needed. Today the primary target of X3D is the World Wide Web, although it's not a Web-only technology. Like Java 3D and MPEG-4, X3D has every possibility of appearing across a wide range of devices, including television set-top boxes, game consoles, and information appliances.

Summary

Extensible 3D, better known as X3D, is the next generation of VRML. As such, it is motivated by both the successes and failures of VRML97. As the first international standard for 3D on the Internet, VRML succeeded in becoming today's dominant Web3D technology. It didn't reach the ubiquity that everybody had hoped for, however. It failed to do so in large part because the specification was ahead of its time. As a result, browsers were overly large and complicated, comprehensive authoring tools were difficult to produce, and end-user systems at the time weren't powerful enough to handle rich VRML worlds.

Currently under development by the Web3D Consortium (the same organization that developed VRML), X3D is being designed to solve these problems while introducing new features and capabilities. Originally known as VRML Next Generation (VRML-NG), the name Extensible 3D reflects the close relationship this forthcoming technology has with the Extensible Markup Language (XML).

Following is a complete list of URLs referenced in this chapter:

Extensible Markup Language (XML)   http://www.w3.org/XML/

X3D Task Group   http://www.web3d.org/x3d.html

ParallelGraphics   http://www.parallelgraphics.com/

Cosmo Software   http://www.cosmosoftware.com/

Finding a Use for Real-Time 3D
   http://www.web3dgallery.com/go/rt3d/

IrishSpace   http://www.ovrt.nist.gov/voyage/

Universal Media   http://www.web3d.org/WorkingGroups/media/

NIST VRML Conformance Tests
   http://www.itl.nist.gov/div897/ctg/vrml/vrml.htm

Pellucid ("perfect" color & lighting)   http://www.acm.org/tog/
   resources/applets/vrml/pellucid.html

Trapezium Vorlon   http://www.trapezium.com/

VRML98 Symposium Web Site
  http://ece.uwaterloo.ca/vrml98/vrml/monterey.wrl

MetaStream   http://www.metastream.com/

Web3D Working Groups   http://www.Web3d.org.com/Working-
  Groups/

Superscape   http://www.superscape.com/

X3D OVERVIEW

Topics in This Chapter

- How X3D began as VRML Next Generation (VRML-NG)
- Requirements driving the development of X3D
- Core X3D specification proposals
- Proposed X3D specification contributions
- Proposed X3D extensions

Chapter 21

At the time of this writing, Extensible 3D (X3D) was under active development, to such a degree that much about this next generation of VRML was still up in the air. Although it's nice to be able to construct conceptual X3D examples without having to run them through a (presently nonexistent) syntax checker, it's practically impossible to predict the future.

Fortunately, we don't have to. The ultimate outcome of the X3D development process will be found through the Web3D Consortium's X3D Task Group Web site (see http://www.web3d.org/x3d.html). As this book goes to press, the site is chock full of materials related to development of the X3D specification, including proposals from various companies.

It contains a huge pile of documents—some new, some old, and few consistent with one another. These materials make it clear that contributors to the X3D development effort are all looking out the same window. The largest objectives are well in view, and some of the smaller details have begun to emerge as well. This chapter presents a summary of the most essential of these materials, giving you an overview of X3D as it currently stands as this book goes to press.

There's another good reason to review these materials. Looking back at the VRML97 development process, it is now obvious that key elements of technology described in various VRML proposals eventually surfaced in other Internet 3D technologies, even though they didn't make it into

VRML97. Many ideas from the Sun Microsystem's VRML proposal, for example, later appeared in Java 3D, while concepts described in Microsoft's ActiveVRML proposal turned up in ActiveX and Chromeffects (interestingly, the now defunct Chromeffects effort was an early influence on X3D; see Chapter 20, "Why X3D?"). There's every reason to suspect that the same will happen with regard to the X3D proposals described below. In other words, concepts rejected by X3D may well surface in future Web3D technologies.

Finally, learning some of the concepts currently proposed for X3D will help you understand not only what X3D is about, but how to speak a common language that's starting to emerge among Web3D developers.

Note: X3D Task Group

X3D is being developed by the Web3D Consortium (http://www.web3d. org/), the same organization that developed VRML (see Chapter 2, "Overview of Web3D," and Chapter 4, "VRML Overview," for details). As the successor to VRML, X3D allows 3D content to be expressed through the Extensible Markup Language (XML) as described in Chapter 22, "Weaving X3D into Web Pages."

X3D is the newest of all Web3D technologies discussed in this book. Because it was under active development at press time, the X3D material discussed in these chapters is designed to give you a conceptual understanding of the technology rather than a concrete one. If you're interested in using X3D, you should visit the X3D Task Group site to get your hands on the most current X3D specification and tools available (http://www. web3d.org/x3d.html).

You can also visit the X3D area of the Web3D Gallery (http://www. web3dgallery.com/x3d/) for easy access to a variety of X3D resources and example content.

Early Beginnings

As the previous chapter explains, X3D was a planned change. VRML97 was always intended to have an 18-month period of stability, after which it would be replaced by next-generation technology. We also saw in the last chapter how unanticipated events interrupted these plans and stretched that time period.

SIGGRAPH

The Association for Computing Machinery's Special Interest Group (SIG) on Graphics (SIGGRAPH) holds a conference each year. That conference often has over 30,000 people attending, and while it's more correct to say "The annual SIGGRAPH Conference," just about everyone simply calls it SIGGRAPH. There are two significant dates on every VRML person's calendar: the annual Web3D/VRML Symposium (informally called VRML 95, VRML 96, VRML 2000, etc., for the year in which it's held), usually around the start of the year, and SIGGRAPH in the summer. These dates are significant because they give us a good excuse to meet one another face to face and get some work done at the same time. They're also convenient deadlines for delivering Working Group materials and for announcing new products related to Web3D.

But the Web3D Consortium kept on track. The SIGGRAPH 98 conference fell right between Cosmo Software's collapse and its subsequent acquisition by PLATINUM, unquestionably some of VRML's darkest days. During that conference, the Web3D Consortium, undaunted, began work on requirements for what was then called VRML Next Generation (VRML-NG).

At SIGGRAPH 98, Rick Rafey and Rob Glidden started a 3D Integrated Media Working Group (3dim) whose charter was "to facilitate 3D-based media integration—the creation, delivery, rendering and interaction of synchronized 3D, 2D, video, text, and audio media types."

At the same time, the Consortium organized an Intellectual Property Rights (IPR) Task Group, one of whose jobs was—in light of the collapse of Cosmo Software and various other events, including the community source release of Java 3D—to investigate the possibilities and pitfalls of Open Source for VRML.

Tip

Links to active Web3D Consortium Working Groups and Task Groups can be found at http://www.web3d.org/WorkingGroups/.

Shortly before SIGGRAPH, Dan Ancona of Intervista wrote a white paper on 3DXML (http://www.web3d.org/WorkingGroups/dbwork/ancona/home.html), an integration of 3D and XML, and even worked toward a demonstration.

Before August was over, the www-vrml list had started to discuss the successor to VRML, and by September the discussion was in full swing, with Jeff Close issuing a call for requirements. The threads that will form the final tapestry began to spin.

X3D (VRML-NG) Requirements

In addition to the list of requirements that Jeff Close had collected and published before the VRML 99 Symposium, a number of other requirements for the next generation of VRML were starting to form. In particular, David Frerichs surveyed the Consortium membership on their needs, Cindy Ballreich conducted a survey of the content developer community, and Tony Parisi wrote a paper on X3D market requirements (all of these documents can be found on the X3D Task Group site at http://www.web3d.org/x3d.html).

Don Brutzman, Web3D Consortium Vice-President of Technology and current X3D Task Group chair, extracted the base X3D requirements from these surveys and various related documents. Based on this information, which is available at http://www.web3d.org/TaskGroups/x3d/requirements.html, the following summary sections were constructed.

Primary Target Applications

The design and development of X3D is driven in large part by a growing demand from the community for a 3D technology that can be used to build a wide range of Internet-based applications. To this end, X3D is being created with a number of target applications in mind, including:

- **E-commerce Product and Technology Demonstration**
- **Visual Simulation**
- **Database Visualization** and large-scale data visualization, regardless of how the data is stored
- **Advertising and Web Page Animation**
- **Augmented News and Documentaries**
- **Training** (includes education and other uses of 3D on the Web to explain and teach)

- **MultiUser** (includes virtual communities, virtual meetings, and collaboration facilitated by 3D)

Market Requirements

A technology without a market is like a ship without an ocean: No matter how well it was designed, it won't reach the far corners of the world. For X3D to be a success, the Internet 3D market must embrace it when it arrives; and for this to happen, it is believed that X3D must satisfy the following market requirements:

- **Address the Shortcomings of VRML97** (see the previous chapter).
- **Interoperation with Other Relevant Standards**, including XML, XHTML, and MPEG-4
- **Tighter Media Integration** (see the previous chapter)
- **Improved Visual Quality** (see the previous chapter)
- **Component-Based Approach** (see the sidebar "Components, Levels of Functionality, and Profiles," at the end of the next section)
- **VRML97 Compatibility** through converters or through profiling. When many VRML97 browsers find a VRML 1.0 file, they convert it either with a built-in converter or by launching a converter process. Apart from a second or two of extra time, users don't even notice it. Profiling would define a "VRML97 Profile" for X3D that would include the full capabilities of VRML97.
- **File Format Issues**, including streaming, a binary file format for fast download, and a text-based format for authoring and interchange
- **Time to Market** (sooner is better, particularly when proprietary 3D applications are proliferating)

Technical Requirements

According to a number of developers, VRML is in many ways a successful technology in search of a successful application. Although it can be argued that this was inevitable, not only for VRML but for any real-time 3D technology on the Web today, as explained in the previous chapter, it's an overarching issue that does not rest well the X3D team. To truly be considered a success, the X3D effort must define a form of Web 3D that is widely *used*.

To achieve widespread use, X3D must satisfy a number of technical requirements. A summary of these substantive requirements follows.

Note

The X3D technical requirements document contains functional require-ments that describe what X3D must be able to do, as well as process re-quirements that describe what the X3D team must do in order to create X3D; consequently, it can be rather difficult to digest. In the section that follows, therefore, all process requirements are marked with an asterisk (*) and not commented upon further (since they are of more interest to the browser and tool designer than to the general reader).

GENERAL

- **Aggressive Schedule***
- **Iterative Development***
- **Components/Levels/Profiles**—see the "Components, Levels of Functionality, and Profiles" sidebar at the end of this section
- **Integrate with existing Web and Media Standards and Technologies**—including:
    - XML—unified representation of all tree-based document structures for the web
    - DOM—unified document object model for tree-based documents
    - GIF, JPEG, PNG—common image file formats
    - WAV, MP3—common audio file formats
    - MPEG2, QuickTime—common movie file formats
    - MPEG4—streaming media and synchronization protocol, 2D nodes, compression
    - Metacreations—progressive rendering
    - HTML+TIME, SMIL—synchronized time for html pages
- **RealPlayer**—streaming media
- **Platform Independence**—"X3D shall be designed so that it relies only on functionality reasonably expected to exist on any target platform"

CORE

- **Unified Typing System**—VRML97 has strongly typed fields, but weakly typed nodes. By using strong typing for nodes, the base type of the node can help the browser determine which types can be used in which contexts, and it can provide the basis for a mechanism of extensibility.

- **Namespaces**—Upper-level objects in VRML97 can't refer to objects in inlined files, nor can inlined files refer to one another, because each file has a separate namespace. Adding namespaces would resolve this and would give much more flexibility to world builders, while giving browser makers fewer problems related to namespaces to worry about.

- **High-Precision Numerical Representation**—required for data visualization and geographic data navigation (see the preceding chapter).

- **Deterministic Design**—Writing a specification is one thing. Building a browser or a modeler that conforms to that specification is quite another. All of the companies that built VRML browsers discovered areas in the VRML specification that were unclear. One way to avoid this ambiguity in the future is through:
  - Verifiability*
  - Determinism*
  - Formalism*
  - Programmability (APIs)

- **Powerful Capabilities**—VRML97 has a very small, nonextensible set of Application Programming Interfaces (APIs). X3D needs to have:
  - Extensive scene-graph traversal/modification/creation abilities
  - Full access and discovery of dynamically created objects
  - Advanced picking and intersection (ray, cone, box)
  - Collision detection/behavior
  - Navigation control
  - Input-device feedback
  - Rendering methods
  - Persistence of state
  - Embedded runtime environment interfaces
  - Runtime context to determine platform capabilities/available browser components, and adjust the experience appropriately

- Notification for completion of asynchronous operations
- Debugging support (console output, breakpoint API)

- **Consistent and Understandable**—Each API should be consistent with the others. The most significant change resulting from this requirement and the following one is that the specification will no longer describe the VRML node syntax, the External Authoring Interface syntax, the Java Scripting Application Interface syntax, or the syntaxes of other APIs that come along as though each of them described separate things. X3D will be defined in a language-neutral fashion, using IDL. IDL is Interface Definition Language, first developed by Sun Microsystems and very commonly used, especially by the Object Management Group (OMG), to permit the same interfaces to be reused from multiple programming languages.

- **Extensible and Object Oriented**—Prototypes (PROTOs) are used in VRML97 to provide both the collection of existing nodes (one very simple example is that you can define a RedSphere PROTO in VRML97) and to add additional capability (the NURBS nodes some browsers are now supporting are declared as PROTOs). This requirement provides a much stronger way of adding capabilities to the runtime by using the object-oriented mechanisms of polymorphism and inheritance.

- **Write-once/Run-anywhere**—This applies to the design, not the code, and doesn't preclude high-performance platform-specific applications.

- **Interoperate with Standard API Models**—In particular, *Document Object Model* (DOM).

- **Synchronization**—between the X3D object model and the enclosing environment (e.g., Web browser).

- **Content Development (File Format)**

- **Fast Content Delivery**—Minimize the time between the start of download and the initial user experience.

- **Authoring/Publishing File Format Encodings**—at least two encodings: one that is readable and writeable by hand, and another that uses lossless binary compression.

- **Author Control over Tradeoffs**—Some performance/fidelity/bandwidth constraints are legitimately the province of the browser, as they are in VRML97, but others need to be within the domain of the author. For example, it's very important for geography applications to be able to control when Inline nodes load and unload, since no machine can reasonably be expected to hold, much less render, all the data that is available from geographic databases.

- **Declaration of Profile**—The name of the profile will be declared in the file, most likely within the first few bytes.

- **Compatibility with VRML97**—One of the profiles must be a VRML97 compatibility profile to preserve the value of existing VRML97 content.

- **Prototype Nodes**—Although the VRML97 prototype that adds functionality to the runtime is now handled by inheritance and polymorphism, there is still a need for the simpler use of prototypes that aggregate nodes.

- **Metadata**—Some metadata (data about data) might be the identification of the world and its author. Other metadata might show its relationship to other 2D, 3D, and text objects. Still other metadata might provide information that's generated and used by modelers but isn't used in the scene graph. During the discussion on this item, the Dublin Core was mentioned as being very desirable.

- **Scene Graph Optimization Hints**—An example in the previous chapter showed why VRML browsers can't prerender files while they're downloading them (recall the example of 100,000 lines of VRML followed by a rotation that turns the whole thing 90 degrees). Yet most worlds aren't like that. In fact, if an author (or an authoring tool) is able to help the browser by providing nodes and fields in an order that will help the browser, it should be able to tell the browser what it's doing so that the browser can take advantage of it.

END-USER EXPERIENCE (RUNTIME)

- **Small Extensible Runtime Core**—The longer it takes to download and install a 3D plug-in, the less likely it is to be used and the less likely it is to be included by default in Web browsers. The requirements define "small" as "in the range between Flash and RealPlayer." How do you extend the runtime core? That isn't covered in the requirements, but it will be an important decision—perhaps *the* important decision—on how well X3D is accepted by end users.

- **Integration of 2D/3D/Multimedia into the User Experience**— Both 2D content within the 3D scene (e.g., Web pages with working links) and 3D content anywhere on the 2D Web page.

- **Reliable and Tractable**—It took many months to develop the first VRML browser that came close to passing conformance tests. This is directly attributable to the complexity required by the specification. That, in turn, restricted browser and modeler development to companies with ample resources. This must not happen with X3D.

- **Minimal, Reasonable Core Functionality**—The details of this requirement will no doubt be the hardest for the designers to meet. Following are these requirements quoted in full:

The Runtime Core profile shall be designed to incorporate the features of VRML97 that require system services in order to be implemented (fundamental features), as well as commonly used features that provide a high level of optimization (core composable features). Any features of VRML97 that can be composed from other core features without a significant loss of optimization, or are rarely used, shall not be included in the Runtime Core profile. The Runtime Core profile of X3D shall not be significantly less functional than VRML97. In addition to a Runtime Core profile, at least one File Format profile shall be specified for the interchange of 3D data among applications.

You'll notice that this requirement requires the designers of X3D to make the core profile smaller and simpler, though not *too* small or *too* simple.

- **Behavior Culling**—VRML has several mechanisms for behavior culling (i.e., skipping over behavior execution, such as animation, when it's not necessary for the current scene). For example, the world builder can (and should) use VisibilitySensor nodes to turn off the animation of nodes that aren't visible. The specification does not provide culling for Scripts however. As a result, inactive Scripts remain in the scene graph long after the guest in the virtual world can see anything the Script controlled. X3D is expected to offer a more thorough behavior culling mechanism

- **Error Reporting/Handling**—Every VRML97 browser handles runtime differently. Some simply fail quietly, or fail to render part of the scene but continue to render the rest of the scene without notifying the guest in the virtual world. Other browsers report every single error and specification nonconformance they come across. If you tested your world only on a forgiving browser, you'd very often get angry email from people who used more persnickety browsers. Worse, people would get the impression that VRML worlds really aren't interoperable across browsers.

- **High Performance**—In some applications, such as training simulations, quality is secondary to speed. If you're coming in for a landing on a flight simulator, for example, and the visual system introduces a lag between the time you bank the plane and the time you see that happen, the simulator will be teaching you the wrong thing. The design of X3D must not preclude it from being used in such high performance applications.

- **High Fidelity**—In other applications, such as animation for the movies, speed is secondary to quality. In a recent animated feature film, some frames took over a hundred hours to render. The design of X3D must not preclude it from being used in those applications.

In summary, X3D will consist of a reasonably sized core (between the sizes of Flash and RealPlayer), plus some extensions. One of those extensions *has* to be VRML97. Don Brutzman has gone so far as to publicly announce that a VRML97 compatibility profile is a "nonnegotiable constraint" of the X3D development process. The precise mechanism by which the additional components may be added has yet to be determined. Ideally, your X3D plug-in would read the profile identifier at the start of a X3D file, determine which components it needed, and get them automatically and quickly, perhaps without your even noticing. How practical that is remains to be seen, but it's considered by many as critical to the success of X3D.

There will be new capabilities in some profiles: support for high-quality rendering (rendering styles were even mentioned, such as rendering the scene as a pen-and-ink drawing), support for high-performance rendering, and support for large data sets like aerodynamic data and geographic information. Browser makers will be able to use familiar object-oriented mechanisms like inheritance and polymorphism to extend the capabilities of the browsers, and it may be that world builders will also have some of this capability. Finally, and perhaps most importantly, X3D won't be put in a box. There will be 2D in 3D worlds and 3D in 2D Web pages.

Components, Levels of Functionality, and Profiles

A **component** is a replaceable unit of functionality. For example, a VRML browser built with a component architecture, yet doesn't support the AudioClip node might have a method like this:

```
int doAudioClip(...) {
       return NOT_IMPLEMENTED_YET;
}
```

That is, it would do nothing and report that it did nothing. If a component architecture were allowed for VRML97, the browser could then either go to a site where a working AudioClip component was available and automatically download it, or it could pop up a message asking the visitor to buy a component, or it could simply fail silently.

In the X3D requirements, several **levels of functionality** are defined. Many VRML browsers already have this feature built in: the user can choose between high-quality and high-speed rendering. Some VRML browsers also let you choose the rendering library and tell the browser whether your graphics card has hardware acceleration. X3D rendering levels might include no highlights, VRML style specular highlights, specular reflections, reflection mapping, or fully reflective mirror surfaces.

The X3D design requirements also provide for **profiles.** A profile represents a product, a useful grouping of component levels, and perhaps a salable group of component levels. For example, you might have a GeoVRML profile that let you display special geographical nodes and use extended-precision numbers for some coordinates, or a raytracing profile that groups together all the highest-quality levels of the rendering components.

The most important profile is the **core profile,** the functionality that must exist in *all* X3D browsers.

What X3D Isn't

After reading the previous chapter and the earlier part of this one, you probably have a good understanding of what X3D is supposed to be. However, it's also important to understand what X3D is not in order to properly set your sights on this coming technology. Following is a summary that describes what X3D is not:

- **X3D isn't a language.** VRML is a language, but X3D isn't. X3D is a defined set of objects, methods, and interfaces, collected together in an Application Programming Interface (API). There will be X3D bindings to various languages. There will be an XML binding, almost certainly a Java binding, probably a compressed binary file format, and perhaps a human-readable file format that looks something like VRML (a consensus is building to meet the "human-readable" requirement with the XML binding).

- **X3D isn't a stripped-down version of VRML for ad banners.** There will be a Core X3D Profile, but that's just one product in a long product line. Another *required* profile will be fully compatible with VRML, and other profiles will add capabilities that VRML never had and even some that VRML *couldn't* have.

- **X3D isn't a product.** It's a product *line.* You'll see a whole range of products (some free, some for sale) that implement X3D and its various profiles.

- **X3D isn't one *kind* of product.** VRML exists primarily on the Web and is accessed by Web browser plug-ins. You may see X3D on PCs, set-top boxes, game systems, and other platforms.

Meet the Candidates

There are, at the time of this writing, five full X3D specification proposals on the table:

- **Core X3D Specification** by Paul Isaacs, Jim Stewartson, and David Westwood of Shout Interactive

- **Core X3D Specification** by Holger Grahn and Kristof Nast-Kolb of blaxxun
- **Core X3D Specification** by Paul Diefenbach, Bryan Housel, Prakash Mahesh, and Jeffry Nimeroff of Computing Associates, Inc., and Open Worlds.
- **Core X3D Specification and G3D Components API** by Clay Graham and Kamal Shah of newObjectivity (for small values of "full")
- **Blendo: An Extensible Media Modeling Architecture** by Peter Broadwell, Jim Kent, Chris Marrin, and Rob Myers of Sony

In addition, there are two contributions to an X3D specification:

- **Jamal: Components Framework and Extensibility** by Mark Rudolph of Lucid Actual
- **Uniform Resource Names (URNs)** by Aaron E. Walsh and the Universal Media Working Group

Finally, there are three proposed X3D extensions:

- **X3D Multitexture Approach** by Rob Glidden of Quadramix
- **X3D ParticleSet Proposal** by Rob Glidden of Quadramix
- **NURBS Proposal and Overview** by Holger Grahn of blaxxun

This isn't a beauty contest. With VRML97 we had a number of competing proposals, from which the VRML community selected one winner (see Chapter 4, "VRML Overview"). Most of the supporters of losing VRML proposals eventually supported the winning one, some to a greater extent than others. This time it's different. The X3D contributors will reach a consensus, and the participating companies (and perhaps individuals) will create separate implementations of a common standard.

Let's look at each of these proposals and try to identify some common elements.

Shout Core X3D Proposal

Shout Interactive (http://www.shoutinteractive.com/) is best known in the Web3D community for its award-winning MOD characters that, using nothing but standard VRML and Java, were able to perform significantly better animation and on-the-fly scene-graph culling than most people had seen before. Besides Shout's reputation as a content house, it does significant work in systems integration, mostly involving 3D.

We'll begin each of these sections with a table of what's in and what has been retained from VRML97 in each of the Core X3D Profile proposals. Shout's specifics are listed in Table 21.1. More attention will be given to the Shout proposal in general because it introduces a number of key concepts that are acknowledged or referenced by other proposals. This allows us to say "they like that, and do it too" and save paper.

Warning

Keep in mind that Core X3D proposals (such as Shout's) describe a Core *X3D Profile, which is the absolute minimum set to which other components will be added for other profiles. Many* `www-vrml` *list members have misunderstood this and interpreted the Core X3D Profile as defining* all *the functionality that X3D will have (a major misconception that can lead to panic and shortness of breath). This is not so; the Core X3D Profile merely defines a base functionality to which a variety of extensions can be made (think of it as a kernel).*

Geometry

In Shout's proposal all geometry primitives (Box, Cone, Cylinder, and Sphere) have been removed, as have ElevationGrid and Extrusion. Does this mean you won't be able to put these shapes in a scene? Not at all. All those nodes can be mimicked by the IndexedFaceSet, and most modeling programs do just that. The only remaining geometry nodes are PointSet, IndexedLineSet, and IndexedFaceSet. While Shout's Core Profile is probably not very easily editable by hand, other profiles would be, and the three geometry nodes in the Core Profile happen to be nodes that modelers can generate very easily. IndexedLineSet now includes lineWidth, and PointSet now includes a pointSize field.

Color, Lighting, and Rendering

All lights but DirectionalLights were removed. Additionally, the color and lighting model was changed to remove the effects of ambient color,

Table 21.1   Shout Core X3D Profile

Kept*	Removed	New	Moved to fields
Anchor	AudioClip	RenderInfo	Color
Appearance	Billboard	*(gets the headlight*	Coordinate
Background	Box	*and visibilityLimit*	TextureCoordinate
CoordinateInterpolator	Collision	*from the former*	
DirectionalLight	ColorInterpolator	*NavigationInfo node)*	
Group	Cone		
ImageTexture	Cylinder		
IndexedFaceSet	CylinderSensor		
IndexedLineSet	ElevationGrid		
Material	Extrusion		
OrientationInterpolator	Fog		
PointSet	FontStyle		
PositionInterpolator	Inline		
ScalarInterpolator	LOD		
Shape	MovieTexture		
TimeSensor	Normal		
Transform	NormalInterpolator		
Viewpoint	PixelTexture		
	PlaneSensor		
	PointLight		
	ProximitySensor		
	Script		
	Sound		
	Sphere		
	SphereSensor		
	SpotLight		
	Switch		
	Text		
	TextureTransform		
	TouchSensor		
	VisibilitySensor		
	WorldInfo		

*Nearly all the nodes that have been kept in this proposal are changed.

shininess, and specular color of materials, as well as ambient intensity of lights. Two additions were made to the color and lighting model: transparency now modulates textures, and diffuse color now modulates diffuse color in the lighting model.

In addition to sparing the DirectionalLight node, Shout's proposal allows it to name the nodes which it affects. Careful light designers in VRML97 would often have dozens of lights, each of which affected only a few nodes.

In Shout's proposal fog is missing, which is understandable since relatively few content creators actually use fog atmospheric effects in their worlds.

Events, Interaction, and Animation

There are two sensors: the Anchor and the TimeSensor. The Anchor node has the badly needed activateTime parameter, so event observers outside the scene know when the user clicked the anchor's geometry. Additionally, Anchor, Group, and Transform have a Boolean "hidden" field which can be used to easily turn part of a scene on and off.

Interpolator semantics have been changed considerably. Here's an example, converted to VRML syntax:

```
PositionInterpolator {
        key               [ 0.0 0.5 1.0]
        keyValue          [ 0 0 0, 1 0 0, 2 0 0]
        timeSensor        TimeSensor { … }
        toNode            [ThisNode, ThatNode, TheOtherNode]
}
```

The key and keyValue fields are exactly the same as in VRML. The time-Sensor field *contains* the TimeSensor that drives the interpolator, and the toNode field *contains* the nodes that are affected.

The result is much cleaner, but some effects that are fairly easy to achieve in VRML, like rotating an object around multiple axes and simultaneous translation and rotation changes, seem to be more difficult.

There is no requirement for navigation capability or for gravity or collision detection. Shout also removes the distinction between field, eventIn, eventOut, and exposedField. All fields are exposed, and there are both field types and field usages.

Field types describe the size and shape of the elements and how they can be used. For example, a FloatField is 32 bits long, and an application should perform arithmetic on it according to the IEEE standard for floating-point numbers. A FloatArrayField is an array of FloatFields (of any length). A BooleanField's length is machine dependent and has a value of FALSE or TRUE. Field usages constrain the value of what's in a field. For example, a FIELD_OF_VIEW usage is permitted to have values between 0 and π. A COORD3 usage means that the FloatArrayField making up the array has exactly 3 elements, and the permissible range for each of the 3 numbers is $-\infty..+\infty$ (i.e., there is no constraint on their permissible values, except that they must be numeric).

There's no reason why a system designer *has* to separate size/shape/use and value constraints into types and usages. In the Ada programming language, for example, you can declare `type MyInteger is new Integer range 0..10;`. It's a design choice.

Programming API and Extensibility

All the nodes are classes, as are all fields. The classes all derive from a base Node class, and it is possible to derive new node classes from Bindable, Geometry, Interpolator, Light, and Texture abstract node classes. The Shout specification has only an ImageTexture node, but another browser implementing, for example, a MovieTexture or HTMLTexture or BumpMapTexture node could extend the capabilities of the core by implementing these new node classes as derived from the Texture abstract class. Once it did that, its new node could go anywhere that any other node derived from Texture is allowed.

The API includes the abstract DeviceInput class (from which MouseInput, KeyboardInput, and WindowInput classes are derived). It also includes interfaces called FieldObserver (which watches the status of a field and reports through its onMethodChange method), Searcher (hunts inside a scene of one or all instances of a node), Picker (implements some of the traditional mouse technology by intersecting rays with the geometry of the scene), ResourceListener and ResourceObserver (obtain access to system resources such as files), and DeviceListener and DeviceObserver (for access to devices such as joysticks and 3D trackballs).

Language Bindings

Shout has provided a Java implementation demo of their proposal called Shout3D (http://www.shout3d.com/). Shout3D loads the whole core browser and runs a 3D animated demo in about the same amount of time as it takes to load a medium-sized 2D image. So it's clear that at least a part of this proposed specification has already been given Java bindings.

It's important to repeat that X3D is language independent. Some people have seen the demo and mistakenly thought that this was Shout's product. Not so. Java happens to be very convenient to demonstrate on the Web. But the specification defines the behavior of a *family* of products, which just as easily could be a Web browser plug-in, a stand-alone X Windows application, or a CAD program.

Shout has also provided an XML tagset. Since this is the first time we've talked about XML and 3D, let's look at an example. Following is Shout's IDL description of a familiar VRML node:

```
class Material {
  FloatArrayField diffuseColor = 0.8 0.8 0.8; // RGB COLOR
  FloatArrayField emissiveColor = 0 0 0;// RGB COLOR
  FloatField      transparency  = 0; // NORMALIZED_FLOAT
  }
```

and here's the equivalent in XML. First, the declaration:

```
<!ELEMENT Material (diffuseColor?, emissiveColor?)>
    <!ATTLIST Material transparency CDATA "0">
    <!ELEMENT diffuseColor  EMPTY>
    <!ELEMENT emissiveColor EMPTY>
    <!ATTLIST diffuseColor  r CDATA "0"
                            g CDATA "0"
                            b CDATA "0">
    <!ATTLIST emissiveColor r CDATA "0"
                            g CDATA "0"
                            b CDATA "0">
```

"ATTLIST" can be thought of XML's user-friendly way of specifying default values (see Chapter 22, "Weaving X3D into Web Pages," for details). Here's an example of Shout's XML tagsets being used to create a Material with transparency and diffuseColor explicitly defined, while the default emmisiveColor setting is accepted:

```
            <Material transparency="0.3">
             <diffuseColor r=".33" g=".33" b="0" />
            </Material>
```

It's important to recall the requirement that X3D be defined in a language-independent way. That means that the syntax of the Java bindings, the ECMAScript bindings, and the XML bindings should mirror one another and that the semantics should remain the same (within the parameters of the individual language).

blaxxun Core X3D Proposal

blaxxun, Inc. (http://www.blaxxun.com/) has in some ways assumed the mantle of leadership of VRML as a result of its hugely successful virtual community Cybertown (formerly Colony City, http://www.cybertown.com/) and its accompanying Contact browser. When American companies in the Web3D Consortium were saying "call it anything but VRML, that's the kiss of death," Franz Buchenberger and his colleagues at blaxxun were quick to remind us that the perceived death of VRML was purely an American phenomenon and that the four letters have considerable value to the rest of the world.

It's not too surprising then that blaxxun's proposal looks very familiar to VRML developers (see Table 21.2).

Table 21.2   blaxxun Core X3D Profile

Kept	*Removed*	*New*	*Changed Function*
Anchor	Box		AudioClip
Appearance	Collision		Background
Billboard	Color		ImageTexture
ColorInterpolator	Cone		IndexedFaceSet
Coordinate	Cylinder		Material
CoordinateInterpolator	CylinderSensor		NavigationInfo
DirectionalLight	ElevationGrid		Sound
Group	Extrusion		TouchSensor
IndexedLineSet	Fog		
Inline	FontStyle		
LOD	MovieTexture		
OrientationInterpolator	Normal		
PointSet	NormalInterpolator		

Kept	*Removed*	*New*	*Changed Function*
PositionInterpolator	PixelTexture		
ProximitySensor	PlaneSensor		
ROUTE	PointLight		
ScalarInterpolator	Script		
Switch	Sphere		
TextureCoordinate	SpereSensor		
TimeSensor	SpotLight		
Transform	Text		
Viewpoint	TextureTransform		
VisibilitySensor			
WorldInfo			

Geometry

Under the blaxxun proposal, geometry primitives, Extrusion, and Elevation-Grid have been removed, while PointSet, IndexedLineSet, and Indexed-FaceSet remain. The IndexedFaceSet is very heavily reduced in functionality, with explicit color-per-face, color-per-vertex, and all normal information removed. The creaseAngle, which controls the rounding and smoothing of the object, is limited to 0 (flat shaded) and π (smooth shaded).

Color, Lighting, and Rendering

blaxxun's lighting model is very similar to Shout's. In addition, all Indexed-FaceSets are assumed to be convex, and two-sided lighting is not provided for nonsolid meshes.

Events, Interaction, and Animation

blaxxun's proposal removes the requirement for navigation, gravity, and collision detection from the browser. Its model includes standard event ROUT-ING, but not Scripting. As with the other proposals, most of the things world builders will do to make their worlds animated and interactive will be accomplished through the API.

Programming API and Extensibility

blaxxun's proposal does not support PROTOs or Scripts but instead puts that functionality into the API. Its API is based in large part on the VRML External Authoring Interface (EAI) Working Group's proposal located online at http://www.web3d.org/WorkingGroups/vrml-eai/.

Language Bindings

The grammar in the blaxxun proposal is largely VRML-style but also includes an EAI and XML interface. Here's an example of the blaxxun XML definition (by Jeff Sonnstein) for a Material node:

```
<!ELEMENT Material   (diffuseColor? )>
    <!ATTLIST Material   transparency NMTOKEN  '0.0'
                         DEF          ID       #IMPLIED
                         USE          IDREF    #IMPLIED >
    <!ELEMENT diffuseColor EMPTY>
    <!ATTLIST diffuseColor   r   NMTOKEN  '0.0'
                             g   NMTOKEN  '0.0'
                             b   NMTOKEN  '0.0'
                             DEF ID       #IMPLIED
                             USE IDREF    #IMPLIED >
```

DRaW Computing Core X3D Proposal

DRaW Computing Associates, Inc. (http://www.drawcomp.com/) is best known as a content house and system integrator with a strong background in visual scenes and objects for the modeling and simulation industry. Their proposal acknowledges and borrows from the Shout and blaxxun proposals and attempts to integrate those ideas with their OpenWorlds product (http://www.openworlds.com/).

They have also contributed a proposal for an X3D Full Profile. To keep the tables similar, if a node was removed in the X3D Core Profile, it's placed in the "Removed" column. If it's present in the X3D Full Profile, it's marked with an asterisk (*). The nodes in the "New" column marked "**" are present in the X3D Full Profile only (see Table 21.3).

Table 21.3   DRaW Computing Core X3D Profile

Kept	Removed	New	Changed Function
Appearance	Anchor°	Pyramid°°	AudioClip
DirectionalLight Group	Billboard°	Torus°°	Background
ImageTexture	Box°	VectorInterpolator	
IndexedFaceSet	Collision°		
IndexedLineSet	Color		
LOD	ColorInterpolator		
Material	Cone°		
PointSet	Coordinate		
ScalarInterpolator	CoordinateInterpolator		
Shape	Cylinder°		
TextureTransform	CylinderSensor		
Timer	ElevationGrid°		
TouchSensor	Extrusion°		
Transform	Fog°		
VectorInterpolator	FontStyle		
Viewpoint	Inline°		
WorldInfo	MovieTexture°		
	NavigationInfo°		
	Normal		
	NormalInterpolator		
	OrientationInterpolator		
	PixelTexture°		
	PlaneSensor		
	PointLight°		
	PositionInterpolator		
	ProximitySensor°		
	Script°		
	Sound°		
	Sphere°		
	SphereSensor		

Kept	*Removed*	*New*	*Changed Function*
	SpotLight		
	Switch°		
	Text°		
	TextureCoordinate		
	VisibilitySensor		

Geometry

The geometry proposed by the DRaW proposal is similar to that of other proposals. In the Full Profile, they put back all the primitives, ElevationGrid, and Extrusion, and even add a couple of primitives. In this respect and in many others, as we'll see, this proposal calls for a much more fully featured specification. There are different definitions of "lightweight," of course. This is not a bad thing. What everybody really wants is a full-featured VRML browser that's 50K in size, that loads a world faster than a Web browser loads a JPEG image, and that executes with raytraced quality at 60 frames a second. Since we must inevitably compromise many of our wishes, it's natural that there's a range of opinion on what's small enough, but not too small.

This proposal retains, as others do not, normals, backface rendering of nonsolid objects, and full crease angle.

Color, Lighting, and Rendering

This is the first proposal that removes the TextureCoordinate node and keeps TextureTransform. The other proposals have done the opposite. Although many developers have found VRML's TextureCoordinate node to be quite useful, others (including the developers at DRaW) have found that it isn't an absolute necessity. The DRaW proposal also keeps specular color, ambient intensity, and the PointLight node (though it removes SpotLight), and the Full Profile even retains Fog.

Events, Interaction, and Animation

The DRaW proposal retains PROTOs, EXTERNPROTOs, and ROUTEs.

Programming API and Extensibility

DRaW has a very thoroughly specified API that's different from others we've seen so far. The DRaW API is divided into a Browser Interface, a Database API, a Simulation Manager API, a Graphics Interface (GFX) API, a Node Interface, and a Field Interface. The Browser, Node, and Field interfaces are defined in DRaW's IDL specification. It isn't clear whether the other interfaces are intended to be public, in the sense that content developers are enabled and encouraged to use them; but considering the methods defined in those interfaces, it seems more likely that they'd be of use to browser and tool makers.

It's worth noting, though, that this is the first specification that seeks to nail down the under-the-hood interfaces of X3D browsers and tools.

Language Bindings

As with the other proposals, DRaW has IDL and XML bindings. It also shows Java bindings.

Following is an example of DRaW's XML definitions, after which an example usage created by Len Bullard and Tim Bray appears:

```
<!ELEMENT Material (diffuseColor?)>
    <!ELEMENT diffuseColor  EMPTY>
    <!ATTLIST diffuseColor  r CDATA "0"
                            g CDATA "0"
                            b CDATA "0">

<Material>
    <diffuseColor r=".33" g=".33" b="0" />
</Material>
```

newObjectivity Core X3D Proposal

newObjectivity (http://www.newobjectivity.com/) is a startup company whose mission is to bring distributed 3D visualization to the enterprise. Its founder, Clay Graham, is well known and highly respected in the VRML and 3D graphics community. The newObjectivity proposal is very terse and lacks any reference to VRML, preferring to define the objects, methods, interfaces, and properties of the objects on a blank sheet of paper. But so that it will fit into the format of the previous discussions, it seems to keep and remove the VRML 97 nodes listed in Table 21.4.

Table 21.4   newObjectivity Core X3D Profile

Kept	Removed	Unknown
Appearance	AudioClip	OrientationInterpolator
Background	Billboard	PositionInterpolator
DirectionalLight	Box	ScalarInterpolator
Group	Collision	CoordinateInterpolator
ImageTexture	ColorInterpolator	TimeSensor
IndexedFaceSet	Cone	TouchSensor
IndexedLineSet	Cylinder	
Material	CylinderSensor	
PointSet	ElevationGrid	
Shape	Extrusion	
Transform	Fog	
Viewpoint	FontStyle	
	Inline	
	LOD	
	MovieTexture	
	Normal	
	NormalInterpolator	
	PixelTexture	
	PlaneSensor	
	PointLight	
	ProximitySensor	
	Script	
	Sound	
	Sphere	
	SphereSensor	
	SpotLight	
	Switch	
	Text	
	TextureTransform	
	VisibilitySensor	
	WorldInfo	

Geometry

The newObjectivity proposal has the same nodes present and absent as Shout, although it keeps all the fields offered by VRML97.

Color, Lighting, and Rendering

This proposal eliminates the PointLight and SpotLight but keeps specular color and ambient intensity and renames Material to Color. It seems to allow backface rendering of nonsolid meshes and the same variability of creaseAngle and specification of normals as VRML97.

Events, Interaction, and Animation

All animation seems to be through the API. There are get...() and set...() methods for the usual VRML97 fields, and there are mouse events and picking; however, there seem to be no time sensor or interpolators defined.

Programming API and Extensibility

newObjectivity has defined both IDL and XML binding. Following is the XML definition (unfortunately there are no examples of XML used in this proposal):

```
<!ELEMENT IX3dColor EMPTY >
<!ATTLIST IX3dColor
    ID                      ID              #IMPLIED
    ambientIntensity        CDATA           #IMPLIED
    emissiveColor           CDATA           #IMPLIED
    shininess               CDATA           #IMPLIED
    specularColor           CDATA           #IMPLIED
    diffuseColor            CDATA           #IMPLIED
    transparency            CDATA           #IMPLIED
>
```

Sony Blendo Proposal

Sony has been involved in VRML from the very earliest days. Their Cyber Passage browser (later named Community Place) was one of the first VRML97 browsers. Cyber Passage (Community Place) was also the first

VRML browser to offer multi-user technology that was reliable enough to build successful virtual communities.

Sony has always had a slightly different slant on things. For example, their browser supported Java, but not ECMAScript. Their mechanism for sharing virtual words required each participant to download the world onto his or her own machine, unzip it, and then use the net connection solely for communicating with other people sharing that world. When you consider that your favorite VRML browser does exactly the same thing, except that you're sitting there staring at the screen while it's doing it, you can appreciate Sony's strategy.

That unique point of view shows up in Blendo with a vengeance.

Blendo began life as Extensible Media Modelling Architecture (EMMA), a technology conceived by VRML architect Chris Marrin. When Chris came to Sony, he teamed up with a group in the Distributed Systems Lab who were working on "Steerable Media" ("giving users control of a rich, declaratively authored, multimedia experience"). The result of that collaboration was Blendo.

One thing Emma did, and Blendo does after it, is eliminate routes in a particularly elegant fashion. For an example:

```
DEF T Transform { ... }
DEF SENSOR IntervalSensor { ... }
DEF PI PositionInterpolator {
    key ...
    keyValue ...
    fraction FROM SENSOR.fraction
    value TO T.translation
}
```

By declaring the "comes from" and "goes to" right in the interpolator's fields, Emma, and Blendo after it, eliminate the ROUTE mechanism that many developers believe is the ugliest thing about VRML. Nevertheless, Blendo retains ROUTES for those cases where they might be needed and in some cases replaces IS mapping with ROUTEs.

Incidentally, the above example has been made somewhat clearer by declaring the Transform node before the interpolator, but in Sony's actual example the Transform appears after the interpolator. Blendo evidently keeps a pile of unresolved references around as it passes through the file, and it only complains if the pile isn't empty by the time it gets to the bottom.

Blendo also has strong 2D integration with its SurfaceNode class. Surfaces can be used to display 2D text or imagery, streaming movies, composite textures, or other 3D geometry.

Blendo's timing model is derived from a TimeBase node and claims to be able to support synchronization of animation and media.

Like the Shout proposal, Blendo has event listeners and adds the capability to notify listeners in the order in which they were added, as well as standard EventsProcessed() notification. Also, like the Shout proposal both nodes and fields are typed in Blendo, and the distinction between field, eventIn, eventOut, and exposedField vanishes.

Blendo lets PROTOs execute scripting directly with less authoring overhead than is currently possible in VRML. Following, for example, is a piece of Blendo code that adds one to the Y value of a coordinate as it goes from an interpolator to a Transform:

```
DEF PI PositionInterpolator {
    key ...
    keyValue ...
    value TO S.in
}
DEF S PROTO [
    field SFVec3f out
    field SFVec3f in {
        out = new Vec3f(in.x, in.y+1, in.z);
    }
] { }
DEF T Transform {
    translation FROM S.out
}
```

There is a well defined list of objects and methods in the API, but Blendo also has a native scripting language, a subset of ECMAScript, and the interpreter for this native scripting is built into the browser. The purpose of this scripting is to let world builders who want to do simple things avoid the difficulties of an API (there are many people for whom the phrase "and then you compile it" means the same thing as "this technology is not for me.")

Geometry

Blendo's geometry and node set are essentially the same as Shout's except that Blendo retains separate Coordinate, Normal, TextureCoordinate and VertexColor nodes.

Color, Lighting, and Rendering

Blendo doesn't subset VRML's color and lighting capabilities, but Chris Marrin has expressed a willingness to do so.

Events, Interaction, and Animation

Blendo doesn't support Anchor, leaving that to the API. Blendo has event listeners like the Shout proposal, but also supports routing within the file. Blendo's timing is derived from a TimeBase object, and all event notification comes through an EventManager object.

Programming API and Extensibility

Blendo doesn't have field usage. Instead, they have a larger set of types that specifies both the size and shape and the constraints on permissible values.

X3D Specification Contribution Proposals

In addition to the several core X3D proposals described above, several X3D specification contribution proposals were also submitted to the Web3D Consortium for consideration. These proposals describe possible enhancements or additions to the forthcoming Core X3D specification regardless of the Core X3D proposal (or combination of proposals) that the X3D specification is ultimately based on.

The Jamal Components Framework

Mark Rudolph of Lucid Actual (http://www.biorococo.com/) has made a significant contribution not to the substance of what each X3D class and field should look like, but to the potential architecture of X3D.

Mark's Jamal claims to permit easy integration and extension of components with an X3D core—something that has to happen or X3D won't work. It functions similarly to JavaBeans components in this regard (Jamal is based in part on IBM's Bean Markup Language). Jamal also raises the level of granularity from individual components to component frameworks. To learn more about Jamal, visit http://www.web3d.org/TaskGroups/x3d/lucidActual/jamal/Jamal.html.

Uniform Resource Names (URNs)

As a Web developer, you're undoubtedly familiar with Uniform Resource Locators (URLs). URLs are used by many VRML nodes to reference resources (such as textures, see Chapter 8, "Customizing Color and Texture," for details). Annex F of the VRML97 specification, however, also describes how developers can use Uniform Resource Names (URNs) as a means to extend the capabilities of a VRML browser. The URN proposal for X3D is an enhancement to Annex F of the VRML97 specification that builds on the cross-platform URN bindings system developed by the Web3D Consortium's Universal Media Working Group (http://www.web3d.org/WorkingGroups/media/). This proposal describes a standard, cross-platform solution for storing and retrieving URN resolution information, such as that used by browsers to support Universal Media.

URNs describe a resource by *name*, not an explicit path as URLs do. This approach allows URNs to act as persistant resource identifiers, meaning they aren't as brittle and likely "break" as URLs are. When a resource pointed to by a URL is moved, for example, it can no longer be located. URNs, however, point to resources by name and can be resolved regardless of where that resource actually resides.

A slightly modified example from Annex F illustrates how URNs might be used in the VRML ImageTexture node:

```
ImageTexture {
url [
   "urn:inet:foo.com:textures:wood001.gif",
   "http://www.foo.com/textures/woodblock_floor.gif"
]
}
```

If a VRML browser supports URNs, it will approach the foo.com server and ask for image named "textures:wood001.gif". The server, in turn, is responsible for hunting down the appropriate image and returning it to the browser. In other words, it's up to the foo.com server to figure out how to respond to the URN request. The server might fetch it from a file, create it dynamically from a webcam stream, or refer the request to another server. If the server doesn't know where to get the file, it simply fails the request. In this case the VRML browser skips over the URN entry in the node and attempts to load to the next link (which is a standard URL).

Why is this approach significant? Suppose that you maintain a site of sailing ship images and have organized your fleet by color (red ships, green ships, blue ships, and so forth). In time you might realize that this particular organization method isn't very effective, yet you'd be loth to reorganize them in another manner for fear of breaking URLs that refers to these images. A system based on URNs, however, gives you the freedom to move the images about at will, since each is referenced by name instead of a hard-coded URL path. Your server will always be able to return the proper image, regardless of their location or name (even renaming resources won't break the system as long as your server understands how to resolve URN requests). You could even move the entire library of images to another server without fear of breaking references to them.

But URNs can be even more powerful than that. Here's an example of a Universal Media URN:

```
urn:web3d:media:textures/materials/oak.gif
```

In this URN, "web3d" is the *namespace,* like "inet" was the namespace for the URN in the previous example. The namespace simply instructs the browser how to start looking. In this case, the browser should start looking among the names assigned by the Web3D Consortium (everything to the right of "web3d" belongs to the Web3D Consortium).

The second field, "media," is called the assigner. The Web3D Consortium has given the Universal Media Working Group (http://www.web3d.org/ WorkingGroups/media/) the right to assign names. Everything to the right of "media" belongs to the Universal Media Working Group, whereas everything to the right of "h-anim" assigner might belong to the Humanoid Animation Working Group, and so on.

The X3D proposal for URNs would require browsers that encounter URN strings beginning "urn:web3d:" check a specific, standardized platform-dependent location on their machines to see if a given library (e.g., the Universal Media Library) had been installed. If so, the browser would get the image from the library. If not, the browser would simply move on to the next string in the field, which would probably be a regular URL.

Furthermore, the URN proposal specifies a cross-platform solution that X3D vendors can use to store URN binding information. This is based on the recommended practice set forth by the Universal Media Working Group (see http://www.web3d.org/WorkingGroups/media/proposals/urn.html).

X3D Extension Proposals

At the time of this writing, several X3D core extension proposals were under consideration by the X3D design team. These documents propose formal extensions to the "core" X3D architecture, meaning these technologies aren't suggested as required technology in the main X3D specification. Instead, they represent major extensions that are likely to be implemented by a variety of vendors.

X3D Multitexture Approach

Rob Glidden of Quadramix (http://www.quadramix.com/) and Sun Microsystems (http://www.sun.com) have offered a proposal for multiple textures in X3D. Among the operations that could be performed with more than one texture are blending, bump mapping, and reflection mapping.

Every owner of a 2D bitmap graphics program like Photoshop or Paint Shop Pro is aware that there are several ways to blend or combine one image with another. Rob's Multitexture Proposal proposes addition, multiplication, and linear function. Why ask the X3D rendering engine to do this when you can just as easily do it beforehand? Animation. Rob's choices for the blending options are intended to be the ones that look best when you use animation to vary one or both images.

Bump mapping has been used for a long time in the raytracing community. When you apply an image (usually a greyscale image) to a surface as a bump map, you instruct the rendering engine to look at the value in the bump map image that corresponds to each point on the surface and raise or lower that point depending on whether the value for that point is light or dark. This will give the effect of a bumpy surface and is also a way to create interesting geometry very cheaply. For example, you could specify a cube as your geometry, specify a bump map and the appropriate scaling, and end up with an island featuring mountains and canyons.

Regular texturing affects the diffuse coloring of a surface, and bump mapping affects the height (in the direction of the normal) of the surface. Reflection mapping affects the shininess of a surface. Just like bump mapping, you take a greyscale file and apply it to the surface. For each point in the file, the lighter the point in the map, the shinier the surface will be.

It's unclear whether the Core Profile will have any of these features, but they are certainly candidates for other profiles, for example, a (presently unspecified) High Fidelity Rendering Profile. Having the idea in mind now that these features might be added to X3D later will certainly help the designers of the Core Profile avoid design constraints that would prevent features like these from being added down the road.

X3D ParticleSet Proposal

Rob Glidden has also proposed a particle set construct for X3D that will allow X3D to fairly easily render fire, smoke, fireworks, waterfalls, trees, clouds, explosions, flocks, cloth, and other animated graphics effects.

Algorithmic animation is an emerging technology that's just recently started to be used extensively in 3D graphics for movies. This would enable our 3D worlds on the Web to take advantage of this emerging technology and would additionally provide a way for students and animators to use X3D to try out some of their ideas cheaply.

It's also possible to use these algorithms for single "particles," especially when you want to add some constrained random appearance to the animation.

This may be a candidate for a hypothetical High Fidelity Animation Profile.

NURBS

NURBS is a cryptic acronym that stands for Non-Uniform Rational B-Splines. If that's clear as mud, try this: Have you ever used a 2D "drawing" program that has Bezier curves? Then you know that Bezier curves let you get nearly any kind of curve you want by specifying a very small number of points. NURBS do the same thing: they let you specify very complex and interesting 3D surfaces with a small number of data points (see Chapter 3, "Entering the Third Dimension," to learn more about curved surfaces and NURBS). That's especially attractive in X3D and other 3D web technologies because it dramatically increases the bang per byte transferred over the user's net connection

Holger Grahn of blaxxun has proposed a NURBS extension, not for X3D—though it could easily fit into X3D—but for VRML97. What's more, he's written it in to the blaxxun Contact browser, and ParallelGraphics has done an independent implementation of his NURBS nodes in the Cortona browser. Virtock Technologies has written support for the NURBS nodes into their Spazz3D modeler (http://www.spazz3d.com/), and other modelers and browsers will no doubt be following.

It is widely held among X3D contributors that NURBS is a done deal. Although VRML specification designers had originally considered NURBS and rejected them as being impractical on today's hardware (as Chapter 20, "Why X3D?"), nothing convinces people faster than working code.

And the Winner Is...

On September 27–29, 1999, there was a 3-day retreat for the X3D design team hosted by 3DLabs in San Jose, California, USA. At that retreat X3D designers reviewed all major proposals and contributions and arrived at a rough consensus as to what nodes would be in the X3D Core Profile and what nodes would be out (see Table 21.5). Before you look at the two lists, however, keep two things in mind:

1. At the time of this writing, consensus is forming but hasn't quite formed yet on the fields of the nodes that are "in" and what the precise use and function of these nodes will be.

2. While the lists contain node names, remember that X3D may not even have nodes in the way VRML does. We're talking about areas of functionality.

The "In" list is much more solid than the "Out" list. It wouldn't be a bit surprising, for example, to see TextureCoordinate and some limited audio show up on the "In" list in the final product. Many items on the "Out" list are pretty firm, however, including the geometry primitives, ElevationGrid, Extrusion, SpotLight, MovieTexture, and Fog.

Table 21.5   X3D Core Profile

Out	*In*
AudioClip	Anchor
Billboard	Appearance
Box	Background
Collision	Color
ColorInterpolator	CoordinateInterpolator
Cone	DirectionalLight
Coordinate	Group
Cylinder	ImageTexture
CylinderSensor	Inline
ElevationGrid	IndexedFaceSet
Extrusion	IndexedLineSet
Fog	Material
FontStyle	NavigationInfo
ImageTexture	OrientationInterpolator
LOD	PointSet
MovieTexture	PositionInterpolator

Out	*In*
PixelTexture	ScalarInterpolator
PlaneSensor	Shape
PointLight	Transform
ProximitySensor	TimeSensor
Script	TouchSensor
Sound	Viewpoint
Sphere	WorldInfo
SphereSensor	
SpotLight	
Switch	
Text	
TextureCoordinate	
TextureTransform	
VisibilitySensor	

There are many more aspects of X3D on which consensus is forming (e.g., extensibility, color and lighting model) but haven't yet solidified. Reading the various proposals now on the table can give you an idea of where X3D is headed on those issues (http://www.web3d.org/x3d.htm).

Summary

X3D is happening. What's more, it is driven by a set of requirements that are based not only on the latest technical developments, but also on the needs of specific application domains and well-informed estimates of market needs.

The architectural framework for the design appears to be remarkably clear. There will be a number of components, some with different levels of capability, grouped into profiles. Two profiles have been clearly identified:

- A **Core Profile** that everything else plugs into
- A **VRML97 Compatibility Profile** that preserves the value of existing VRML97 assets

The Core Profile will specify not a language, but a set of objects, methods, and interfaces that can be implemented in Java, XML, something that looks like VRML, or a compressed binary format that the author never sees except as her modeler shows the 3D representations she's creating.

It's likely that the VRML97 Compatibility Profile will ship with (or very shortly after) the Core Profile. Other profiles, which we've neglected in this discussion but which have been suggested in some of the proposals, will almost certainly ship later.

Core X3D will undoubtedly meet its goal of small size. Chris Marrin has reported that he's already compiled a core version of Blendo that weighs in at under 200K, even with a full VRML-style color and lighting model. The Shout demo, meanwhile, is so small that it almost seems impossible.

Following is a complete list of URLs referenced in this chapter:

X3D Task Group   http://www.web3d.org/x3d.html

Web3D Consortium   http://www.web3d.org/

"Core X3D" book web site   http://www.CoreX3D.com/

Web3D Gallery X3D Area   http://www.web3dgallery.com/x3d/

Web3D Consortium Working and Task Groups   http://www.web3d.org/WorkingGroups/

3DXML White Paper   http://www.web3d.org/WorkingGroups/dbwork/ancona/home.html

Shout3D   http://www.shout3d.com/

Shout Interactive   http://www.shoutinteractive.com/

blaxxun, Inc.   http://www.blaxxun.com/

Cybertown   http://www.cybertown.com/

External Authoring Interface (EAI) Working Group   http://www.web3d.org/WorkingGroups/vrml-eai/

DRaW Computing Associates, Inc.   http://www.drawcomp.com/

OpenWorlds   http://www.openworlds.com/

newObjectivity   http://www.newobjectivity.com/

Lucid Actual   http://www.biorococo.com/

Jamal   http://www.web3d.org/TaskGroups/x3d/lucidActual/jamal/Jamal.html

Universal Media Working Group   http://www.web3d.org/WorkingGroups/media/

URN Recommended Practice Proposal   http://www.web3d.org/WorkingGroups/media/proposals/urn.html

Quadramix   http://www.quadramix.com/

Spazz3D   http://www.spazz3d.com/

WEAVING X3D INTO WEB PAGES

Topics in This Chapter

- Introducing X3D Markup Language (X3DML)
- X3DML fundamentals
- Examining the X3D Document Type Definition (DTD)

Chapter 22

As described in Chapter 21, "X3D Overview," X3D changes the VRML specification from a set of defined nodes and fields to an interface definition language (IDL). This approach enables multiple bindings of the X3D specification. These bindings are grammars that provide the actual contents of an X3D document. In X3D, VRML nodesets are bound to an XML grammar currently defined as an XML Document Type Definition (DTD) in accordance with the XML 1.0 specification. In the material that follows, this application language is referred to as X3D Markup Language or simply *X3DML*.

This chapter provides an overview of the concepts of XML as applied in X3D to help you understand how X3DML is woven into a Web page. X3DML enables you to create 3D worlds using tags and attributes that are similar to HTML, can be integrated with HTML, and can take advantage of the quickly growing set of tools for creating, publishing, maintaining, and integrating XML application languages. General background concepts and examples are presented first, followed by a detailed description of the XML syntax needed to thoroughly understand the X3DML DTD.

Warning

At the time of this writing, X3D was under development. Because it was undergoing rapid design changes, a complete DTD was not available and so is not presented in this chapter. An express goal of the X3D effort, however, is to provide an XML binding for the VRML abstract syntax. To this end, background information related to this goal, and various approaches and issues it involves, are described in this chapter. For updates to this constantly evolving material, vist the Core Web3D Web site at http://www.CoreWeb3D.com/.

The material in this chapter assumes that you are familiar with both VRML and XML. To learn about VRML, you can turn to Part 2 of this book. For details about XML, you can vist the World Wide Web Consortium's XML Web site at http://www.w3.org/XML/ or refer to any of the various online XML resources listed in Appendix E, "X3D Resources."

Why Use Markup?

In application languages, data and scripts are treated equally in the file as long as they are well-formed nodes. This simplifies the middleware. The client is a consumer of well-formed nodes validatible by standard means where necessary. Lexical unification enables shared resources that simplify the framework. This simplification enables contract-based systems for frameworks to interoperate. The key to business on the Web was (and still is) the dependable interoperation of the Web framework of application languages. To define these, XML provides well-respected concepts from the parent language, Standard Generalized Markup Language (SGML), known as Document Type Definitions (DTDs). To increase the flexibility and range of applicability, XML also introduces XML schemas and namespaces.

> *"SGML was made to protect information from people like us...."*
> Dr. Charles Goldfarb, addressing a group of professional systems developers

While much of this is emerging technology on the Web, it is based on well-researched and thoroughly developed technologies from the SGML community. These systems have been under development for over three decades. They have been used for some of the largest and most complex engineering enterprises to successfully manage the requirements for designing and building systems whose life cycles are in excess of thirty years. The success of the system results from the initial requirement that the formats be as independent as possible of the implementation. In systems that are origin sensitive, this is notable.

The focus of XML is different. With XML, the range of the life cycle of the information is not the dominant reason to use it, although that is still enhanced; it is the ability to cheaply and easily make information systems that interoperate easily because the formats are of the same lexical ancestry. From packet to purse, the information is easier to handle if the parser is common.

If business systems don't interoperate naturally and easily, humans who rely on such systems won't either. The most important business decision the procurement specialist can make today is the decision to support standards-based innovation. XML-based applications languages are a key standard. The tools to develop interfaces, database tables, n-dimensional trees, complex documents for negotiation of processes and calculated data, and more can be obtained at minimal expense through the use of XML because the description is portable, light, regular, easy to generate and modify, and sharable. *Not all information is free, but it is shared.*

There are many published books that cover SGML and XML in detail, including the Charles Goldfarb Series from Prentice Hall. In this chapter, we'll focus our attention on the background and application of XML as an X3D binding.

What Is XML?

The most widely used language on the Web today is HyperText Markup Language, or HTML. HTML is an application of its parent standard, ISO 8879, the Standard Generalized Markup Language, or SGML.

In 1996–97, work was initiated in the World Wide Web Consortium (W3C) to create a subset of ISO 8879 SGML for use by Web applications. The result was the Extensible Markup Language (XML), which specifies SGML features that Web markup applications share. XML has quickly become the most widely and rapidly implemented of the W3C recommended practices (visit the W3C at http://www.w3.org/ for details related to the XML and SGML) .

SGML is a metalanguage, meaning that it is a specification used to construct other languages. By specification, SGML selects a set of lexical symbols and layers them into a description of an application language. This is then used to create hierarchical descriptions of documents whose namespace is amenable to tree-based descriptions.

XML 1.0 both simplifies and extends the SGML standard. XML is a conformant subset of ISO 8879. By adding the concepts of well-formedness, simplifying the tagging requirements, and freezing the features of the system declaration, the related standards developed for XML extend SGML successfully. Families of XML standards are being developed which are themselves XML applications.

This notion of application languages is important to understand because several well-intentioned texts incorrectly refer to HTML as a "subset of SGML," which it is not. A subset of a standard is a subset of the features of the standard, not an application of the features of the standard. HTML is an application of the features of SGML. For brevity, we will refer to such application languages simply as "markup languages."

Markup languages have their origin in the GenCode efforts of the late 1960s in which publishers were devising a means to exchange working files among large publishing houses. The term "GenCode" or "Generic Coding" refers to a design by which a simple set of codes are inserted into text to designate the text as being a paragraph, table element, list, and so forth. The original version of HTML was an example of the GenCode approach.

The term "markup" was adopted because the gencodes were used much as a layout editor would use marks on production galleys of manuscripts. The term Generalized Markup Language (GML) was used by Goldfarb, Mosher, and Lorie at IBM for the system they created for computerized legal publishing. The GenCode and IBM efforts merged under the leadership of Dr. Charles Goldfarb and emerged as the international standard now known as the Standard Generalized Markup Language (SGML).

Why Create X3DML?

When the VRML Consortium Next Generation (NG) design team met at the 1998 VRML Symposium summit, a goal of VRML-NG became development of an XML tagset for VRML. Given the rapid adoption by Web vendors of

XML as a transport format of choice for content, the quickly emerging tools that could be applied to any XML application, and the opportunity to make 3D more accessible and easier to learn for a wider audience of authors (particularly those whose primary language was HTML), the opportunity to create a 3D graphics language using markup technology was recognized as a benefit to the Web3D community and market.

The VRML97 design is a well-formed, lean, and lexically stingy format. The XML format cannot be said to improve it from that point of view. Mapping VRML to XML provides content makers with more options in the tools with which they build complex content. XML provides excellent opportunities for tools to be developed by freeware, shareware, and commercial software communities. Because it is also the responsibility of a consortium to create business opportunities for its members, a binding of VRML97 to an XML format was proposed. As stated in the VRML-NG design requirements:

> **The X3D XML tagset is a lightweight 3D media file format supporting an API and runtime that is highly interoperable with 2D Web standards and well suited for present-day Web developers with minimal to moderate 3D experience, but is designed to be extended into the full X3D specification.**

- **Components and Profiles.** The XML tagset for X3D shall be grouped into functional component groups, and profiles shall be defined for particular collections of components.

- **Useful for HTML programmers.** The XML tagset for X3D shall be designed in such a way as to be understandable to HTML programmers without extensive 3D training.

- **Enable Page Integration.** The XML tagset for X3D shall enable integration of 3D content with the rest of the XML document.

- **Mapping to X3D format.** There shall be a direct mapping from the XML tagset for X3D to the X3D file format.

Prior to this meeting, discussions had been held both on the wwwVRML email list and within the VRML Enterprise Working Group about the potential for applying XML to 3D languages. The formalization of this as a goal brought several private efforts to the surface and engaged individuals and companies with XML expertise to work on the X3D project.

X3DML Fundamentals

VRML97, as you may recall from Part 2 of this book, is defined as a set of nodes and fields. X3DML provides a set of XML general entities and element type declarations for creating an XML-compliant coding of the X3D graphics language. In this section, we will examine how the definition of the X3DML binding differs from that of the VRML97 binding and discuss some of the important issues of designing the X3DML DTD (and how these affect the information in the X3DML content). In addition, we'll look at some examples of different approaches to binding an XML application language to VRML.

To understand how the definition of the XML binding differs from the definition of the VRML97 binding, let's look at a simple X3D object expressed in both grammars. A detailed description of the DTD syntax and language features is provided later. For now, however, it is useful to note the look and feel of the two bindings as illustrated in Table 22.1

In the example in Table 22.1, you may notice that the XML and VRML definitions look very similar. In particular:

- **Both definitions are hierarchical.** They define a tree of nodes, or named objects.
- **Both name object characteristics** such as the node name (Billboard) and node elements (axisOfRotation, bboxCenter, and bboxSize).
- **Both definitions provide default values** for these characteristics.

While semantically these two definitions declare the same object, there are subtle differences that illustrate the different approaches to declaring XML element types and VRML nodes. Specifically:

- **X3DML is an application of a metalanguage;** VRML97 is not. VRML97 is specified by one parent standard. X3DML is specified by both the ISO draft for the next generation of VRML and the W3C specification for XML. Note the use of <!ELEMENT and <!ATTLIST. These are names provided by the XML 1.0 specification per ISO 8879 SGML to declare that the values within declare XML Element and Attribute Types.
- **An XML Element Type Definition can explicitly define a tree of elements and the members of the tree.** In the example, the elements in the tree are a named group, or parameter entity (see

Table 22.1 X3DML and VRML97 Grammar	

	Definition	Instance
X	`<!ELEMENT Billboard %Children; >`	`<billboard`
M	`<!ATTLIST Billboard`	`DEF="GalaxyLounge"`
L	`axisOfRotation CDATA "(0 1 0)"`	`axisOfRotation="(0.0 1.0 0.0)" >`
	`bboxCenter CDATA "(0 0 0)"`	
	`bboxSize CDATA "(−1 −1 −1)"`	*...children elements here...*
	`DEF ID #IMPLIED`	
	`USE IDREF #IMPLIED >`	`</billboard>`
V	`Billboard {`	`DEF GalaxyLounge Billboard{`
R	`eventIn MFNode addChildren`	`axisOfRotation 0.0 1.0 0.0`
M	`eventIn MFNode removeChildren`	*... children nodes here...*
L	`exposedField SFVec3f axisOfRotation 0 1 0 #`	
9	`exposedField MFNode children []`	`}`
7	`field SFVec3f bboxCenter 0 0 0 # (∞)`	
	`field SFVec3f bboxSize −1 −1 −1 # (0,∞) or −1, −1, −1`	
	`}`	

below). A VRML node indicates that a tree of nodes can exist and that these are added or removed.

- **The VRML97 datatypes (e.g., exposedField) are included in the VRML definition.** The XML Element Type only provides XML datatypes for the lexical description of the document (e.g., CDATA).

- **The DEF/USE attributes of the XML Element Type are explicitly defined in the DTD as a characteristic.** In VRML97, they are included in the specification as a documented characteristic of that language.

Now that you have a feel for the look of the two bindings, we will examine the trade-offs in the design of the X3DML DTD. There are three related questions to ask in any DTD design:

1. How much information must be explicit in the markup language versus that which can be unambiguously determined from the

language specification (that is, from the comments and other explanatory text)?

2. How much information does the author need to do his job versus what the software needs to do its job? In other words, given the first item in this list, how much information can be safely defaulted?

3. How much information must be explicitly stated in the file to ensure that the intent of the author and the specification designer can be maintained and reused, particularly if the software used to create it is obsolete or unavailable?

The first question is related to the commonality of implementation. Anything required by specification and not stated in the file must be provided by the implementation, and the implementation must conform. The danger here is in the interpretation by the implementor of the explanatory texts. It is often difficult, if not downright excruciating, to document the semantics of a design without resorting to a programming example. As a result, a file with precisely the same content can render and behave differently on two different implementations. Note that no language design can completely solve this problem. Conformance testing of implementations is also required (to address this issue, the U.S. National Institute of Standards and Technologies (NIST) is currently creating a suite of conformance tests for X3D; visit the X3D Web site at http://www.web3d.org/x3d.html for details).

The second question is related to capability. Languages such as XML enable the application-language designer to provide default values that the implementation must support either by hardcoding these values into the implementation or by getting them from a DTD or schema. A further danger is that unless an identical DTD or schema is used by all implementors, or defaults are misinterpreted or even augmented in code, it is possible for vendor-specific features to be implemented silently. Anything that is not stated in the specification and not provided in the file supports a nonstandard feature that the author must use wisely or not at all.

The third question is the hardest to answer because it requires the language designer to make educated guesses about the evolution of technology in the future. If the designer makes a conservative bet, *all* of the information specified is preserved but the file grows larger, can be hard to read, and can be expensive to author without powerful tools. If the designer makes a liberal bet, the information is easier to create and handle, but it is possible that future technology will only be able to incompletely process the file and the intent of the author, as well as the investment in creating the information, can be lost.

With these issues in mind prior to beginning the X3D effort, members of the VRML Consortium Enterprise Working Group (including Len Bullard, the author of this chapter) created mappings of the VRML97 nodes to an XML DTD. Three DTDs were created by different members as possible approaches to this mapping. To understand the trade-offs in moving to a markup design, these prototypes can be compared.

Tables 22.2 through 22.4 each contain an XML version of a VRML97 Transform node definition, followed by a corresponding instance example. The first, seen in Table 22.2, is a direct mapping to the original VRML97 node that Len Bullard of Intergraph Public Safety created as part of a prototype for a geometry profile. Events and datatypes are not included. The advantages of this approach are that it is easy to translate, easy for the human to read, and easy to implement in a GUI. The disadvantage is that over a long life cycle significant information is lost.

Table 22.3 contains the Transform node provided by Clay Graham of newObjectivity. Note that the interfaces and datatypes are similarly undefined when compared to Len's example in Table 22.2. The Transform node is "empty" in the sense that it does not contain other nodes in a hierarchy. The advantage of this approach is that it maps more directly to the concept

Table 22.2 Direct Mapping of VRML97 Transform

Definition	*Instance*
<!ELEMENT Transform (viewpoint | transform | shape | group | worldinfo | pointlight | spotlight | directionallight | inline | use)+ >	<Transform id="NameOfTransform" bboxcenter="0 0 0" bboxsize="4 4 4" translation="10 5 0" rotation="0 0 0 1"
<!ATTLIST Transform	scale="0.5 0.5 0.5"
id ID #REQUIRED	scaleOrientation="0 0 1 0" center=
bboxcenter CDATA #IMPLIED	"0 0 0" >
bboxsize CDATA #IMPLIED	...
translation CDATA #IMPLIED	</Transform>
rotation CDATA #IMPLIED	
scale CDATA #IMPLIED	
scaleOrientation CDATA #IMPLIED	
center CDATA #IMPLIED >	

Table 22.3 Object Mapping of VRML97 Transform	
Definition	*Instance*
<!ELEMENT Transform EMPTY >	<Transform ID="myID" Transform="0 1 0" scale="0.5 0.5 0.5" >

<!ATTLIST Transform
  ID ID #IMPLIED
  transform CDATA #IMPLIED
scale CDATA #IMPLIED
  rotation CDATA #IMPLIED
  center CDATA #IMPLIED >	

of the transform as a field value of an object instead of an object itself. Although this is good object-oriented design, it raised issues with respect to the implementation of the VRML browser that were not shared as design goals by all of the development community.

Finally, Table 22.4 contains an example from Daniel Lipkin (of *Oracle Corporation* at the time). From the perspective of completeness of specification, this is the best design, because data types and containment are defined. Daniel does this by including the abstraction level of the original VRML specification: nodes contain nodes and fields. He uses XML attributes to specify the nodetype names (Daniel's original mapping has a field parameter entity that is expanded in place for simplicity of presentation in this example).

Table 22.4 Abstract Mapping of VRML97 Transform	
Definition	*Instance*

<!ELEMENT node (sffield | sfnode | mffield | mfnode)° >
<!ATTLIST node
    type CDATA #REQUIRED
    def ID #IMPLIED >
	<node type="Transform">
	  <sffield name="translation">
	    <vec3f x="10" y="-6" z="0"/>
	  </sffield>
	  <mfnode name="children">
	    <node type="DownArrow"
	        def="Next1">
	  </node></mfnode></node>

The advantage of this abstraction is explicitness. Over a long life cycle, no information is lost. This kind of abstraction is used in many XML specifications (such as XML schemas). The disadvantage is the difficulty of composing in this form without good editor support. However, the other approaches shown in Tables 22.2 and 22.3 can be mapped to this one without loss of information; therefore, it is the most complete representation of the original VRML property set.

The VRML97 standard is a concise property set that is used for one language. It does not require the node/field abstraction to be expressed in the content format.

Note

There is a phrase coined by David Cooper of Antech Corporation during the U.S. Navy MID project: "More Meta Than Thou," or MMTT for short. It describes the tendency of designers and design groups to look for and include higher levels of abstraction in the application language design. The choice of the layer of abstraction that the DTD represents is critical to making trade-offs of efficiency and making the information more robust with respect to reuse and management for long life cycles.

The X3DML DTD states no assumptions about adding or removing children, because this mixes the implementation of the language, which can manipulate a data set, with the declaration of the data set. VRML97 nodes are more concise, but they explicitly declare that the implementation must provide an interface for adding or removing children to implicitly indicate that the nodes have children nodes and fields. Essentially, VRML97 presumes an object-oriented implementation, whereas XML does not.

The implementation of related standards for X3DML and more integration with other emerging XML markup languages is likely. A primary reason for this is the existence of different and powerful models that can manipulate the contents of the languages using the same scripting languages and interfaces.

A standard Application Programming Interface (API) for manipulating the information represented by XML application languages is recommended by the W3C, the organization that created XML. The Document Object Model (DOM) will enable the X3DML author to use the same scripting skills acquired for Dynamic HTML (DHTML). X3DML does not preclude other

APIs from being created for X3DML content. For example, take the Simple API for XML (SAX). Where DOM implementations create an in-memory representation of XML objects that can then be manipulated using the DOM API, SAX parses the XML file and responds immediately to events (that is, the named values in the file) through callbacks. SAX is considered an "event-oriented" API. The choice of the API depends on the goals of the implementation, but the existence of both models testifies to the power of the markup approach to enable flexible implementation choices.

Introduction to the X3DML Vocabulary

XML application languages are vocabularies. A vocabulary is a set of names and rules for using names to describe a universe, which is sometimes called a domain of discourse. In more simplistic terms, a vocabulary names the things we talk about and enables us to use those in sentences. To formally declare a vocabulary, we must provide names for the things described by the vocabulary. To rigorously declare a vocabulary, we must also provide rules that govern the order of the names used in a valid sentence in that vocabulary.

Describing a vocabulary requires us first to name the things a vocabulary has. An XML vocabulary is currently defined by a Document Type Definition consisting of a Document Type Declaration and markup declarations. Markup declarations declare a tree of nodes. In creating the X3D Document Type Definitions, for most cases nodes have been mapped to child elements and fields have been mapped to XML attribute lists.

Just as a person doesn't need the dictionary to make up sentences, an XML user does not need to know all of those rules to speak XML. When we speak to each other, we understand each other because we have agreed on how to make sentences. This concept is carried into XML as well-formedness. For a VRML author, this is already an assumed state. VRML is self-descriptive. X3DML is defined by a DTD, but unlike SGML, XML extends markup applications with the concept of a well-formed file. Many of the simplifications made in creating the XML subset were made to enable XML files to be self-descriptive.

X3DML Document Type Definition (DTD)

Because XML is self-descriptive, most X3DML authors will never have to be deeply aware of the X3D Document Type Definition (DTD) unless they are configuring an XML editor to work with the X3DML application language, creating transforms using languages such as Extensible Stylesheet Language Transformations (XSLT), or creating X3DML dynamically. In all of these cases, the X3DML DTD provides the rules for creating valid instances of X3DML and a means to determine if an instance received or sent is valid. It is important to understand the difference between a *well-formed* instance and a *valid* instance:

- **Well-formed** describes a document that lexically conforms to the XML 1.0 specification. This includes things such as: all begin tags have end tags, EMPTY tags without end tags must end with the /> characters, an XML Declaration begins the instance, a root element is required, and so on.

- **Valid** describes a document that is in accordance with the content models of a specific Document Type Definition. For example, within the X3D element, an instance can optionally have zero or one header element. It must have one and only one scene element. These are just two of the many X3D DTD rules that a X3D document must comform with in order to be considered "valid."

By discriminating between the concepts of well-formedness and validity, XML opens up markup languages to a wider range of applications. It is much easier and more efficient to use XML for smaller, dynamic applications if it is not required that each instance reference a DTD, or that a DTD even exist. Therefore, it becomes the system designer's prerogative to choose where, when, how, or whether to use validation. Validation of correct-by-construction instances is redundant; however, when using structurally unaware editing tools, such as the Windows NotePad or Professsional File Editor, the DTD combined with a parser is a fast and effective mechanism for ferreting out small errors. In addition, many markup editors are DTD aware; they use the DTD to style the editing interface such that any instance made with that editor is automatically correct by construction.

XML's parent standard, ISO 8879-SGML, requires all documents to be valid, which in turn requires all SGML documents to have a DTD. XML relaxes this constraint by saying that all XML documents must be well-formed, but that validity, the state of corresponding without deviation to a DTD, is a local rule and not enforced. As a result, not all XML documents are required to have DTDs. Because early X3D adopters are likely to be using authoring tools such as IBM's Java-based Xeena XML editor (see the accompanying note), some basics of using the X3DML DTD are provided below. Later, a more detailed description of XML DTDs is provided if you want to learn more about them to understand their use in advanced applications.

Note

Xeena is a visual, Java-based XML editing tool created by IBM. Xeena is available free of charge from IBM's alphaWorks site at http://www. alphaWorks.ibm.com/tech/xeena/. Xeena can be used to author, edit, and validate X3D scenes using the Web3D Consortium's freely available X3D DTD (visit the X3D Web site at http://www.web3d.org/x3d.html to learn more about Xeena and the X3D DTD).

The basic unit of construction in XML is the *element type definition*. An element type definition has:

- **A generic identifier,** informally a tag name. In the following example, the tag name is "Billboard":

```
<!ELEMENT Billboard
```

- **A content model.** This is a set of of tag names and *entity* names plus symbols used to indicate whether the elements can be repeated (and in what order they can occur). In the following example, the content is a *parameter entity* (parameter entities are named groups in the DTD that are expanded in place when referenced):

```
<!ELEMENT Billboard %Children; >
```

- **An attribute type definition list.** Attributes are characteristics of the element and are similar to VRML fields. Following is an attribute type definition list for the example Billboard element:

```
<!ATTLIST Billboard
        axisOfRotation CDATA "(0 1 0)"
        bboxCenter     CDATA "(0 0 0)"
        bboxSize       CDATA "(-1 -1 -1)"
        DEF ID         #IMPLIED
        USE IDREF      #IMPLIED >
```

The X3DML DTD declares *parameter entities*, element types, and attribute types to define a tree structure. In the example shown, parameter entities are included as content for other element type defininitions. Attribute types define the characteristics of the element type of the same name. Following is a fragment of the X3DML DTD current as of the time of this writing (although it will almost certainly change over time, as this technology is under active development by the Web3D Consortium):

```
<?xml version='1.0' encoding='UTF-8' ?>
<!DOCTYPE X3D [
<!ENTITY % SceneNodes "( %GroupingNodes; | %BindableNodes; |
   %BehaviorLeafNodes;  |     %LightNodes;     WorldInfo       |
   PROTO )*,   ROUTE* " >
<!ELEMENT X3D  ( Header? , Scene ) >
<!ELEMENT Header ( #PCDATA ) >
<!ELEMENT Scene ( %SceneNodes; ) >

<!ELEMENT Billboard %Children; >
 <!ATTLIST Billboard
         axisOfRotation CDATA "(0 1 0)"
         bboxCenter     CDATA "(0 0 0)"
         bboxSize       CDATA "(-1 -1 -1)"
         DEF ID      #IMPLIED
         USE IDREF   #IMPLIED>
<!ELEMENT WorldInfo EMPTY >
<!ATTLIST WorldInfo
          info  CDATA #IMPLIED
          title CDATA #IMPLIED
          DEF ID      #IMPLIED
          USE IDREF   #IMPLIED>
```

To read a DTD, you must find the root of the tree and follow the names as they are defined in each branch. Because a DTD is modularized using named parameter entities, you'll usually need to expand these to find out the actual tree contents. To make this concept more concrete, let's walk down a branch from the root in the above fragment showing where entities have been used, and expand them in place to show the actual element type definitions.

First, as with all XML documents, an *XML Declaration* declares the version and encoding of the document—in this case, XML version 1.0 and the UTF-8 encoding:

```
<?xml version='1.0' encoding='UTF-8' ?>
```

Next comes the *Document Type Declaration*, which names the element type in the DTD that is the root of the tree:

```
<!DOCTYPE X3D [
```

The content for the X3D element is defined next. In this case, the X3D element type consists of an optional Header element and a Scene element.

```
<!ELEMENT X3D  ( Header? , Scene ) >
```

Following from left to right, the next branch is the Header element type definition. The Header element can contain text (#PCDATA). #PCDATA is an XML keyword (short for *parsed character data*) indicating that the contents may contain both text and markup. Since no element definitions are included in the content model, the content of the Header element is text only. This branch stops at the text definition:

```
<!ELEMENT Header ( #PCDATA ) >
```

At the Scene element type, we find that a parameter entity name, SceneNodes, is used to define the contents of the Scene element. A parameter entity names a string that is included by name wherever it is referenced:

```
<!ELEMENT Scene ( %SceneNodes; ) >
```

Take a closer look at the entity definition for SceneNodes. You should notice that it also has parameter entities in its contents (e.g., LightNodes) as well as element types (e.g., WorldInfo):

```
<!ENTITY % SceneNodes "( %GroupingNodes; | %BindableNodes; |
    %BehaviorLeafNodes; | %LightNodes;  WorldInfo | PROTO )*,
    ROUTE* " >
```

Keeping these concepts in mind, then, the first expansion of the scene nodes element type

```
<!ELEMENT Scene ( %SceneNodes; ) >
```

gives us the following:

```
<!ELEMENT    Scene  (%GroupingNodes; |    %BindableNodes; |
    %BehaviorLeafNodes; | %LightNodes; | WorldInfo | PROTO )*,
    ROUTE*  ) >
```

Each entity is expanded until the definition consists of element and attribute type declarations. Following is an example of a fully expanded element type:

```
<!ELEMENT Billboard (ColorInterpolator | CoordinateInterpolator    |
CylinderSensor | NormalInterpolator | OrientationInterpolator    |
PlaneSensor    | PositionInterpolator    | ProximitySensor    |
ScalarInterpolator | Script | SphereSensor | TimeSensor | TouchSensor
```

```
| Background | Fog | NavigationInfo | Viewpoint | Anchor | Billboard |
Collision | Group | Inline | LOD | Switch | Transform | Shape | Sound
| WorldInfo | DirectionalLight | SpotLight | PointLight)*>
```

X3DML also includes XML EMPTY element types. An EMPTY element has only attribute values for content and does not contain other elements or text. For example:

```
<!ELEMENT WorldInfo EMPTY >
<!ATTLIST WorldInfo
  info CDATA #IMPLIED
  title CDATA #IMPLIED
  DEF ID #IMPLIED
  USE IDREF #IMPLIED >
```

A well-formed X3DML example is:

```
<?xml version="1.0" encoding="UTF-8" ?>
<X3D>
   <Header>Information the browser can ignore or use goes here.</Header>
   <Scene>
    <WorldInfo info="[My description, copyright information, etc.]"
        title="Title of My World" />
    <Background skyColor="[0.0 0.0 1.0]" />
    <NavigationInfo headlight="true" avatarSize="[0.25 1.6 0.75 ]"
    type="[WALK]"   />
    <Viewpoint  DEF="Opening"
        orientation="(0.0 0.0 1.0 0.0)" fieldOfView="0.785398"
        description="Opening Viewpoint" bind="true" position="(0.0 0.0
        5.0)"/>
     <Group DEF="mySphere" bboxCenter="(0.0 0.0 0.0)"
        bboxSize="(-1.0 -1.0 -1.0)">
        <Shape >
            <Sphere  DEF="MyWorld" radius="1.0"/>
        </Shape>
      </Group>
   </Scene>
</X3D>
```

This file will be displayed as a bland-looking sphere floating in a sea of blue. It may not look like much, but it's a triumph in terms of expressing VRML with XML, and it illustrates in fact the essence of X3D.

DEF/USE: Use of ID/IDREF

As you may recall from Chapter 5, "VRML Fundamentals," VRML97 supports DEF names for VRML nodes. VRML's DEF mechanism enables the author to specify that the definition of the named node is reused elsewhere in the content through a corresponding USE statement. In X3DML, DEF/USE is defined by applying the XML token types, ID and IDREF. Attributes whose token type is ID must be unique within the document. The typical application is to use them as the unique identifier of the element, similar to a primary key in a relational database. An attribute whose token type is IDREF must have the value of an ID within the document. The IDREF serves as a pointer to the element, similar to a foreign key in a relational database.

By XML constraint, the value of the USE attribute in an element must be the value of a DEF attribute in the same document. By application semantic constraint, a USE'd attribute means that the contents of the DEF'ed element are copied but are not independent. Any change to the DEF'd element is reflected in all of the copies. The use of ID/IDREF is a stronger constraint in the X3DML definition than in the VRML97 definition, which allows DEF names to occur multiple times but does not specify the result.

As a validation constraint, duplicate DEFs are not allowed within the XML file. Backward compatibility with VRML97 can be provided if conversion processors notify the user of any conflict and request action or if a converted file is validated (from VRML97 to XML/X3D) using the Document Type Definition provided herein. Implementors must ensure that any element that contains a USE element does not have other attributes in the containing element. This is an X3D constraint. It does not affect XML validation.

XML Schemas

It is likely that after the first phase of X3D design is over, the emphasis may shift from using XML DTDs to XML Schemas. XML schemas are a more powerful and flexible means of defining XML application languages. Why aren't DTDs adequate?

DTDs are often used to create the user interface for building the document. A DTD designed to correctly define a large class of documents may be too cumbersome to use. That is, the writer is given so many options, it takes a lot of time and resources to figure out which options apply in which situations. Any forms designer recognizes the problem: too many controls on one page make the interface crowded and unintuitive.

Defining, documenting, and developing software that could handle such combinations proves to be a massive and expensive task. While pseudomodularity techniques such as parameter entities can be applied to the task of managing the document type definition, not enough can be done to reduce the complexity of the software required to support it. Unlike relational databases, whose indexes and tables are relatively simple structures to manage and aggregate, hierarchical trees of names/nodes have bewildering potential sets of complex structures.

To use such a DTD well, a DTD designer often customizes it. This is done by:

- **Separating the DTD into multiple DTDs**
- **Editing the content models**
- **Editing parameter entities that define content models while leaving the names in the content models the same**
- **Creating conditional sections**
- **Creating a library of entities that can be dynamically combined to create a short lifecycle but efficient DTD to match the requirements of a local process**

The process of customizing a DTD results in one of two kinds of products:

1. **Proper subset**—the DTD is smaller, but any document it defines is valid by the original document type definition
2. **Improper subset**—some documents it defines are not valid by the original document type definition

Creating these subsets takes time and resources, yet even then there are limits to what can be done with a DTD when defining a document:

- **The frequency models** (*, +, ?, none) **are limited to none, one, or infinity.** You cannot specify a range limit for nodes in the instance, such as "only ten elements of this type can occur in this list," except by cumbersome means.
- **The content models are closed.** You cannot add or delete types at runtime unless you dynamically generate the DTD, and in that case,

it is not a true contract or record of authority (persistent and referenceable by direct name).

- **DTDs specify a very limited set of data types,** e.g., CDATA, NMTOKENs, etc. Database designers find that a more comprehensive set is needed for many operations, such as Date, Currency, etc. Further, there is no means outside the element and attribute declarations for the user to define new data types. Using markup, essentially all types are really strings with some special spelling considerations; these have to be coerced if used in a different system to enable efficient processing.

- **DTDs are in a different syntax than the document instance.** You need a completely different processing model and user interface to create and maintain them.

- **DTDs cannot take advantage of true classing features,** such as inheritance or aggregation. Modularization within a DTD is limited to string macros (parameter entities, or "PEs").

DTDs can be modularized using SGML techniques, and this works as long as the names for the modules are registered and the DTD applied is correct for the process. If you have to choose, lots of little DTDs are better than a monolith. Even with modularization, SGML DTDs are not powerful enough.

Because these problems were known, much work was already underway in the SGML communities that created the HyTime and DSSSL standards as well as the Text Encoding Initiative in the mid to late 1980s and early 1990s. However, when XML became a work item for the W3C, the efforts to improve markup schemas became part of the effort to put SGML on the Web.

As part of this work, new designs for schemas began to emerge to take advantage of XML's adaptations of well-formedness and restricted lexical features. From these designs, a W3C working group merged the different concepts into the current draft recommendation for XML Schemas.

There are significant differences between XML DTDs and XML Schemas. For example:

1. **XML schemas are written in the instance syntax.** The advantage is a common parser, and the same APIs can be used to access, change, or delete the information in the schema. Thus, the overall framework for the XML applications is smaller, and the

schema can be considered a dynamic part of the overall system. For instance, schema information can be accessed using the DOM API to get information to create graphical user interfaces. While the use of DTDs to create GUIs was common for SGML applications, it was difficult and not doable using scripting techniques common to Web applications. XML schemas are an evolutionary step on the path of XML-enabled Web browsers to truly universal clients.

2. **XML schemas have two parts.** Part 1 describes the structures used to create schemas. These enable the developer to create element and attribute definitions for trees similar to DTDs. Beyond DTDs, more robust means of creating content models and reusable groups are provided. These include archetypes for creating named groups that replace DTD parameter entities. Content models can be closed, as they are in an XML DTD. However, they can also be open, such that any content can be added; or they can be refinable, such that some content can be added but other content remains restricted. Ranges can be defined. In a DTD, the only ranges are none, one, or many. In a schema, the designer can state, for example, that a certain element occurs precisely five times.

3. **Part two of the XML schema draft recommendation includes data types.** Where SGML data types are limited to essentially strings, XML data types include most of those known to the programming and relational database communities, such as integers, double-precision numbers, etc.

Overall, the designer can more precisely define the content of the document using the XML schema. The application of these is not yet precisely defined. Because XML schemas are XML documents, it is possible, for example, to use XML namespaces and create superschemas that reuse parts of other schemas. Also, because of the greater variety of data types, it is possible to use XML schemas at runtime to check data types. Such applications are in the speculative stage of development, and there are many problems and issues to be resolved before they will appear in commercial applications. For these reasons, XML schemas are considered by some to be beyond the bleeding edge, and as of this writing, no submissions for X3DML using the draft XML schema have been made.

Another issue that emerged with regard to X3DML DTDs and schemas is how to map PROTOs and EXTERNPROTOs from VRML97. Of the VRML97 productions, the PROTO is the most objectlike. It provides the ability to create new named productions by combining existing productions. In this way, it is like a DTD or schema in XML. Unlike an XML DTD or schema, however, it also provides a way to define an interface to the PROTO so that events can be routed to it from interpolators and scripts. It is more like a declaration of an object in an object-oriented programming language than an element in a markup language. Because it enables the creation of new productions, it also duplicates the role of the schema or DTD, as noted above. Thus, PROTOS have been the problem child of the X3D effort, given that they most explicitly express the intent of the VRML97 designers that VRML is a model for an object-oriented implementation.

Several approaches have been proposed for mapping the PROTO and EXTERNPROTO productions to XML, but none have completely satisfied all of the requirements, particularly where a runtime environment and a well-formed, context-free parse are needed. The solutions have ranged from breaking up the PROTO into several elements to creating a new X3D-centric schema language which is more objectlike. The current XML Schema proposals from the W3C are designed to meet more relational database application requirements than object requirements. As of this writing, there is not a consensus on the final approach.

Note

The World Wide Web Consortium (W3C) does not write or maintain standards. It creates recommendations that must be approved by the W3C Director. Because international standards have the force of law and are ratified by countries, consortium products should not be cited as standards. As of this writing, the XML Schema recommendation is still a draft and continues to be changed. As such, the use of schemas in X3DML is highly experimental.

Adding X3D/XML to Your Web Page

In Chapter 6, "Weaving VRML into Web Pages," you learned how to stitch VRML content into Web pages using HTML's OBJECT and EMBED tags. This technique is also being adopted by early implementors of X3D. In many cases, a parameterized OBJECT or APPLET tag is used as a standalone element with a reference to the external file. For example, following is a tag based on the Shout implementation:

```
<applet CODEBASE="../codedir"
        CODE="applets/myApplet.class"
        ARCHIVE="my3DClasses.zip"
        WIDTH="200"
        HEIGHT="200">
<param name="src" value="myworld.x3d">
<param name="headlightOn" value="true">
</applet>
```

This method includes values for the Java applet class associated with the Shout file and the display. This parameter list can be much longer and include values to be passed to the runtime engine to tune its performance, values for zipping and unzipping the content and the runtime components, and so forth.

It is likely that early adopters of the X3DML tagset may use these means as well. However, because X3DML is an XML application language, XML-specific means are emerging for mixing XML vocabularies in so-called aggregate or compound documents. The most specific means is XML namespaces. The examples that follow are from the Microsoft Internet Explorer Version 5.0 (IE5.0) implementations of namespaces. Mileage may vary. Note that the means for using namespaces applies the OBJECT tag to indicate the component which will handle instances of tags in the associated namespace.

Namespaces

Namespaces are defined to enable an author to use tags from different application languages in the same document. A namespace essentially prefixes an element type name (tag name) with a Uniform Resource Identifier (URI) so that the name is unique. Remember, parameter entities are a means to modularize a DTD, not an XML document. Herein, the term "aggregation" is used to refer to the practice of using elements defined in different DTDs in the same document.

Document aggregation is a simple idea. It is similar to creating a report or view using multiple record sets in relational systems. The problem with this approach is name collisions. It is always possible, and in fact, highly probable, that two designers will use the same name for two different things. While manual or automated means can be used to sort these out, this isn't practical for production and fast exchange. Further, for formal processes that depend on a record of authority, this isn't always legal.

The application to the Internet makes the problem harder by requiring these names to be universal not only to the local document, but to *all of the Internet*. This requirement is impractical in extreme or arbitrary cases. However, the Internet already provides a systemic solution to the problems of universal namespaces: domain name registries map to URIs. The familiar http path construction is, for practical applications, a universal name. So the solution is to use this as a means to identify local namescopes. A URI is considered identical to another URI if they have exactly the same characters.

There are several problems, however. URIs allow characters that are not legal names in XML, they must be declared locally in the instance, and the result must scope beyond the document:

- **Scope**—a range within which a name is guaranteed to be unique
- **Universal Name**—a name whose scope is larger than the document in which it is used
- **Qualified Name**—a name whose scope is bound by a separately declared unique name
- **Namespace**—a qualified range for a collection of names (a namespace is qualified by naming it with a URI). A namespace is not a set; it may contain duplicates.

To compare this with existing technology, in a relational system the query designer qualifies the names of fields by prefixing the name with the name of the table. In cases where they need a more convenient name, they alias that name (name it something else). For example, in an SQL query, you might see:

```
myTable.ThisField AS myField, yourTable.ThisField AS yourField
```

The solution for markup applications is the same. A means to prefix a generic identifier or attribute name is provided. In the following, we provide examples of the Vector Markup Language (VML), a 2D graphics markup language currently implemented in Microsoft IE5.0. It is possible that future versions of browsers will enable you to integrate X3DML components and content using these techniques.

The XML specification reserves a name: *xmlns*, which is used as an attribute to declare a namespace prefix. Because characters can appear in

URIs which are not legal in XML names, an alias is declared for use as a prefix to a local element or attribute name. These are separated by a colon (:). First, a name is qualified by an attribute declaration using the reserved namespace qualifier (the QName), xmlns:

```
xmlns:v="urn:schemas-microsoft-com:vml">
```

This statement binds the "local" symbol to the "urn:schemas-microsoft-com:vml" name. That name is assumed by specification to be unique. To give a scope to this qualified name, it is declared within an element used in the document (not the DTD), typically the root element:

```
<html xmlns:v="urn:schemas-microsoft-com:vml">
```

The "local" name is now bound within the html element. This means that the scope of the binding is the html element and its contents (other elements, attributes, and their values within the letter tree of nodes).

Implementors should be aware that the right-hand side, the URN, is the name which is bound and used as the real prefix for scoping. The left-hand side, v, is an alias for the prefix.

An object tag is used to associate the component to the object ID:

```
<object id="VMLRender"
    classid="CLSID:10072CEC-8CC1-11D1-986E-00A0C955B42E">
</object>
```

The id of the object is bound to a style declaration:

```
<style>
    v\:* { behavior: url(#VMLRender); }
</style>
```

Now when authors want to use VML tags to embed graphics inside the HTML document, they use element types from the VML specification plus the declared prefix alias.

```
<v:oval style='width:120pt; height:80pt;' fillcolor="red">
    <v:shadow on="t" type="perspective" origin=".5,.5"
        offset="0,0" matrix=",-92680f,,,,-95367431641e-17"/>
</v:oval>
<v:rect style='width:120pt;height:80pt;' fillcolor="red">
    <v:textbox>My Shape is an Oval.</v:textbox>
</v:rect>
```

The result is the image seen in Figure 22-1, which will appear in the HTML document as if it were created by an external image but is instead a

Figure 22-1   A simple vector graphic created with Vector Markup Language (VML).

vector graphic. Some day soon this capacity will extend to animated 3D images.

Namespace Scoping

All unprefixed elements also belong to the namespace. Namespace scopes are overridden by declarations deeper in the tree. To illustrate the use of name scoping, in the following example letter, greeting, and body belong to the local scope. Logo belongs to myCompany, and image (img) belongs to HTML. A blank namespace declaration declares there is no default namespace, unless of course it is overridden deeper in the element. So the closing and the contained signature do not default, and politeness is scoped by politePolice:

```
<letter id='myletter' xmlns:local='http://www.claude.org/schema'
            xmlns:myCompany='http://www.claude.org/logos'>
 <local:greeting id='g001' >Hello Claude!</local:greeting>
 <body>It is good to know how rich you are, Cousin!</body>
 <closing xmlns="" >
  <politeness xmlns="http://www.politePolice.org/schema' >
  Sincerely,
  </politeness>
  <signature>Cousin Claude</signature>
 </closing>
 <myCompany:logo>
  <img src="logo.gif"
     xmlns:html='http://www.w3c.org/TR/REC-html40' />
 </myCompany:logo>
</letter>
```

The same idea works for attributes, although the default namespace does not apply to attribute names. To ensure uniqueness of attribute names, no element can have two attributes whose expanded names (name, namespace name, element name) are identical:

```
<letter id='myletter' xmlns:local='http://www.claude.org/schema'>
 <address number="600" local:street="Rue de Ville"
   local:city="Calais"
 </address>
</letter>
```

If a namespace is declared using a default value in an external, be aware that a nonvalidating XML parser is not required to recognize that. For that reason, declare namespaces directly in the instance or in a default value in the internal subset of the DTD.

Note

All the XML namespace specification says is that the name is unique. It does not specify that a DTD exists for that name or that a schema can be found at the other end of the URI. This has been hotly debated, but the reality is that there are many other means to create a unique name, and many other resources that might be identified by the URI, such as Java applets. For that reason, the specification is silent about using the URI as a value for hyperlinking to a resource or what that resource can be, although the applications are obvious. It is likely that the XML Schemas specification will formalize the means for discovering the schema, if one exists, for a namespace.

Summary of Namespaces

Namespaces enable authors to combine fragments of instances from different documents that are defined by different schema. The result is a single document that is friendly to the resources of connecting computers across a network, able to contain parts from different sources (thereby enhancing reuse of information), and still compatible with SGML. The downside: as of yet, there are no formal means to validate aggregate documents in XML, and the problem with ID/IDREFs is not solved. Under a single DTD or schema, it is possible to restrict some combinations of content that formal policies of organizations can be enforced and caught when the document is validated. This is a tougher problem with aggregates precisely because the semantics expressed by the policies are not necessarily shared or expressed abstractly. So the quick solutions are systemic: it becomes an authoring and quality assurance problem.

While this may be changed with XML schemas so that a validation process is formalized, some designers do not consider it a problem given that the process which aggregates the document follows the authoring; so presumably the pieces are correct by construction. Resolution of ID/IDREFs by post-processing and revalidating is not considered a hard problem and can be dealt with by translation. In short, the advantages of aggregation outweigh the disadvantages of revalidating or using trusted sources and post-processing.

Document Type Definitions (DTDs) in Detail

This section provides a more detailed description of XML DTDs. XML 1.0 declares symbols and rules for any XML document. A DTD declares the symbols and rules in your document. Using a DTD you can:

- **Prove a document is of the type you need**
- **Quickly find errors** in the structure of documents, including ones that are hard to spot using just your eyeballs
- **Specify default values** for named things
- **Use the information in the DTD to create and modify other applications,** such as editors. By this technique, you can create documents that are correct by construction; after that, you don't need the DTD again until you modify the document or the editor.

If all you ever need is a map for your neighborhood, you probably don't need more than one map. You learn all the symbols on that map, the rules for reading that map, keep that map handy, and after a while know the neighborhood so well you seldom use the map. Markup applications are like that. If you have been using HTML for a while, you can probably type the names of tags in faster than you can look them up. At this point, you have a favorite subset of these tags that you use for any document, and unless you have to do something new, you never consult a help file or document that describes HTML tags.

You are confident; you are serene. Then something happens. Usually it is the new guy they hired who is assigned to write a document for your group, or it is another group, maybe a business partner, that sends you a document. Or you send a document to someone and they call you to tell you it isn't what they asked for. You are asked to review the document, make necessary changes, and then put it on the local Web site or redeliver it. You open it up and...IT'S A BIG MESS!

This leads us to the first reason you care: A DTD or schema is a rigorous description of the names, the types of names, and the order in which names can occur in a document. Because a DTD is rigorously defined and described, you can use it like a broom to clean up the document, but only if you use the right broom.

Of course, that means you need to know the kind of broom and what it is named. Here is the name of the HTML DTD:

```
<!DOCTYPE HTML PUBLIC "-//W3C//DTD HTML 3.2//EN">
```

Because XML names have names, the name of this is *Document Type Declaration*. Of course, this is just the name, the "handle" on the broom. To actually do any cleaning, we need the rest of the broom, but let's just look at the handle for now. It consists of:

- **<**—which we have seen before and know indicates the start of the name.

- **!**—this is new and indicates that a special name, a definition, follows.

- **DOCTYPE**—this is a name for another kind of definition, the document type.

- **HTML**—this is the name of the element that is the root of the document tree.

- **PUBLIC**—this is a reserved symbol; it indicates that the rest of the broom is in the closet where anyone can get it and use it (the DTD is on public record).

- **"-//W3C//DTD HTML 3.2//EN"**—this is the name of the broom in the closet (an external identifier) composed of the organization, the version of the document type, and the language it is in (English). Think of this string as the name of the public record of the DTD.

Notice that some of the concepts we have learned so far are exemplified here. We have an ordered set of symbols, some special local symbols, and a name that formally identifies the thing we need, the document type. So, we have a means to establish the broom's identity. But what about its location? We could go to the mythical Formal Registry Of All Names (should one be in your universe) and get the location. But look at this alternative to the external identifier:

```
<!DOCTYPE HTML SYSTEM "C:/mydir/dtds/html32.dtd">
```

It looks the same, except now we have a special symbol, SYSTEM, which indicates that the thing we want is on the local system, a path which identifies precisely where the thing is, and a local name (the file name). We know the location of the directory where the DTD is and the name the local system uses to identify it. Most enlightened administrators of systems use this version of the Document Type Declaration in documents so they can refer to a local copy of the DTD. It is faster, and we can cheat by customizing the local copy to meet local rules.

But we said a DTD is a Document Type Declaration, didn't we? No. The broom is a DTD and it has a name: *Document Type Definition*. Time to get the DTD out of the closet and clean up the mess. We need to understand:

- **What a Document Type Definition Does**—A DTD formally and rigorously describes a grammar for a class of documents.

- **What a Document Type Definition Defines**—A DTD defines the rules for valid documents of a named class.

- **How to Use a Document Type Definition**—This depends on what you need to do with it, which may depend on the politics of your locale.

What a Document Type Definition Does

Earlier, we discussed Document Type Definitions as a means to define an XML vocabulary. In this section, we describe the parts of an XML DTD in detail. A DTD has:

- **Document Type Declaration** ("Doctype")
- **Markup Declarations** (a tree of Nodes)

We have already covered the Doctype. *Markup Declarations* declare a tree of nodes. The types of these nodes have names. They are:

- **Processing Instructions**
- **Element Type Declarations**

- **Attribute List Declarations**
- **Empty Element Declarations**
- **Entity Declarations** (parameter and general)
- **Character References**
- **Notation Declarations**
- **Comments**
- **CDATA Sections** (Character Data)
- **Conditional Sections**
- **Special Declarations**

What a Document Type Definition Defines

Again, most X3DML authors will not need to be familiar with the XML concepts of a DTD in detail. Still, it is useful for more advanced users to see how XML DTDs work and what their components are.

We will look at the basics so that you can become familiar with the components of DTDs. Listing 22.1 contains an example of a complete Document Type Definition and a sample document with labeled parts. Because XML application languages use the same constructs, these are not X3DML examples. A trivial example is provided so that you can contrast this DTD with the X3DML DTD and understand what is common.

Note

This example includes the most used features of DTDs as well as some not yet used by X3DML.

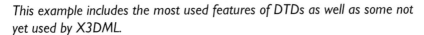

Listing 22.1   DTD example

```
              XML Declaration:  <?xml version='1.0' encoding='UTF-8' ?>
   Document Type Declaration:  <!DOCTYPE greetings [
        Notation Declaration:  <!NOTATION vrml SYSTEM "x3d.dll" >
Parameter Entity Declaration:  <!ENTITY % greeting "nice | notnice" >
  General Entity Declaration:  <!ENTITY myCousinsName "Claude" >
       Character Declaration:  <!ENTITY amp "&#38;" >

    Element Type Declaration:  <!ELEMENT greetings (%greeting;)+ >
```

```
                                <!ELEMENT greeting (#PCDATA) >
Attribute List Declaration:     <!ATTLIST greeting
                                id        ID    #REQUIRED
                                lang      CDATA #IMPLIED >
  Element Type Declaration:     <!ELEMENT nice (#PCDATA) >
  Element Type Declaration:     <!ELEMENT notNice (#PCDATA) >
                                ]>

                   Comment:     <!-- One Claude is an idiot and my cousin.  The
                                other Claude is rich and my cousin.
                                Should I be nice? -->

             Document Root:     <greetings>
                  Elements:       <greeting id='gr001' lang='english'>
                                    <nice>
                                      Hello, &myCousinsName; &amp; how are you?
                                    </nice>
                                    <notNice>
                                      Get Lost, &myCousinsName;!
                                    </notNice>
                                  </greeting>
                Close Root:     </greetings>
```

Starting from the top, let's look at the contents of the DTD example. Since we have seen the XML Declaration earlier, we move on to the Document Type Declaration.

Document Type Declaration

Notice that the following document type declaration does not include the keywords, or DTD name:

```
<!DOCTYPE greetings [ definitions and declarations ] >
```

It includes the name of the element that must be the root of the vocabulary tree, and more importantly, it includes the actual definitions of the tree inside the square bracket symbols, [ ]. Element definitions inside the Document Type Declaration are called an *internal subset* to distinguish them from definitions that can be included using a PUBLIC name or a SYSTEM identifier. That set of definitions is known as an *external subset*. Some document DTDs have both, and the XML specification has rules for which take precedence in case of duplicate definitions.

Notation Declaration

```
<!NOTATION vrml SYSTEM "x3d.dll" >
```

A Notation Declaration names unparsed entities, formats of elements that have Notation attributes, or the applications for processing instructions. These may be a different syntax for information such as a graphic format. A notation names the type and optionally may include information about where on the local system a processor for that data type may be found (e.g., in lieu of a system registered helper). Many DTDs contain a standard set of Notation Declarations even if the notation is not used in the document and even if a processor is not available on the local system. Consider that the DTD specifies the rules for a class of documents, and this makes a lot of sense. The notations declare all of the kinds of different information types a document of this class may contain.

Parameter Entity Declaration

```
<!ENTITY % greeting "nice | notnice" >
```

Entity Declarations name chunks of text that are substituted anywhere a reference to the name is found. Parameter Entity Declarations name chunks that are used in DTDs. Because you can name the chunk, and the named chunk can include other named chunks, PEs are used for pseudomodularization and DTD maintenance. PEs can only be used in the Document Type Declaration. Note that in the example DTD, the Greeting element declaration includes a PE named "greeting" in the content model (between the parentheses). During parsing, the entity is expanded such that the PE contents are substituted. So:

```
<!ELEMENT greetings (%greeting;)+ >
```

becomes:

```
<!ELEMENT greetings (nice | notNice)+ >
```

Note the use of the percent symbol (%) when the entity is declared. Note the use of the percent symbol when the entity is used in a DTD. They are separated by white space in the declaration but NOT when used as a name (the most common mistake when using parameter entities). There are some tricky bits to keep up with when using PEs. Ensure that they don't end with ordering indicators such as (|) or (,), which can cause the resulting expansion to be malformed.

General Entity Declaration

```
<!ENTITY myCousinsName "Claude" >
```

A general entity is used to declare chunks of text to be reused in documents, in contrast to a parameter entity that is used to declare chunks of text to be reused in DTDs. Note the use of the ampersand symbol (&) plus the name when the entity is used in the document. Note also that, unlike the parameter entity, the ampersand is not used when the entity is declared (the most common mistake when declaring general entities).

The example given above is for an *internal entity*. The content is given in the declaration. For sharable information or information that might be in a different notation, an *external entity* is available. An external entity contains the entity name, a SYSTEM identifier giving the local location name of the entity, and, optionally, a PUBLIC identifier, which is a universal name typically identifying the specification for the entity format.

```
<!ENTITY myWorld SYSTEM "http://myPage/myWorld.wrl"
         PUBLIC "-/W3D/VRML//EN"   >
```

The external entity declaration may contain an *NDATA* keyword that identifies it as an external unparsed entity (non-XML), followed by a name which must match the name of a declared Notation.

```
<!ENTITY myWorld SYSTEM "http://myPage/myWorld.wrl" NDATA wrl  >
```

Character Declaration

```
<!ENTITY amp "&#38;" >
```

Character declarations are used to name a character that is either reserved as a special character (e.g., the ampersand and the greater than and less than symbols) or is part of a character set that may not be supported by the system. For example, a copyright symbol is not found on a standard QWERTY keyboard, so the character declaration can be used to include it in a document. When used in a document, the name is called a *character reference*, and it isn't a testimony to my cousin's smarts; it is the declared name put where you want the character to appear. Lists of character declarations can usually be found in the appendix of most HTML reference documents.

XML reserves a set of character declarations that do NOT have to be declared for compatibility with HTML. However, an enlightened DTD designer declares them anyway.

Element Type Declaration

```
<!ELEMENT greetings (nice | notNice)+ >
```

Element type declarations are the most important definition to learn. Elements are the start and end tags that make up most of the logical structures—trees of nodes—in XML. As with a Backus-Naur Format (BNF) syntax and regular expression syntax, the productions can be very complex.

Element type declarations:

- **Name the element type**
- **Encode the tree of element types** and other nodes that can be contained within the node tree, as well as specifying their order and the number of times they can occur. In XML doctrine, contained nodes are the *children* of the node they are contained by.

The element type declaration in the example declares an element type named greetings which contains one to an infinite (+) number of nice OR (|) notNice elements.

Two kinds of new symbols are introduced:

- **Ordering Indicators**—(|) Choice, aka, OR; (,) Sequence
- **Frequency Indicators**—(+) One or more; (*) Zero or more; (?) 0 or one; (none) one

Here are some examples:

```
(foo | bar)—Foo OR Bar.  Only one
(foo | bar)?—Foo OR Bar. One or none
(foo | bar)+—Foo OR Bar. One or many
(foo | bar)*—For OR Bar. Zero or many
(foo, bar)—Foo AND Bar.  Both once
(foo* | bar*)—Foo OR Bar. Either or none many times in any order
```

You can build up complex conditions for groups of these, which can make the tree arbitrarily complex. Further, since an element type named in a content model also includes all of the element types in its definition, the tree can be very deep. To make things more interesting, element types can include themselves and do recursion deep enough to make Gödel, Escher, and Bach weep with self-referential joy (und herz und mund und that und leben).

There is a special case node type that can be contained in the content model of an element type. It is called *Parsed Character Data,* and the name

Tip

Since most element type declarations consist of patterns that are repeated in other element type declarations, parameter entities are used extensively to ease maintenance of the DTD by modularization. However, on parse, they are expanded in place. Note that heavily modularized DTDs are hard to read and understand.

used to represent it in the DTD is *#PCDATA.* PCDATA is essentially what we think of as text. This is straightforward, but for some applications it is necessary to put markup inside text. When doing this, it is possible to create an ambiguous condition in which it is difficult for an XML processor to keep track of where text and markup begins and ends.

An XML processor cannot "look ahead" to find out where the next matching end tag is, and since text is a node type, it makes errors. The technical way of saying this is that XML element type definitions are deterministic finite-state automatons; but hey, even Claude knows that is too hard to remember, so just remember *mixed-content model,* meaning that markup is mixed with text. The mixed-content model is best shown by example. In the following HTML, the image tag (<img>) is in the middle of a paragraph of text.

```
<p>Claude, you are such an <img src="idiot.jpg" />!!!
    Go to <a href='hell.rtf'>The Devil</a>!</p>
```

Because of the potential ambiguity, there is a special way to write mixed-content models—for example:

```
<!ELEMENT p (#PCDATA | img | a)* >
```

The PCDATA keyword is first, followed by elements separated by OR indicators and closed with the Optional flag.

Attribute List Declaration

```
<!ATTLIST greeting id ID #REQUIRED language CDATA #IMPLIED >
```

Attribute lists are value-pair assignments on an element. Essentially, they declare information about the element, such as its unique identifier, default values, or any other information which the element should carry as metadata but not typical content. HTML designers have stretched the use of attributes to include such things as script function calls. Attribute declarations cannot be repeated in an attribute list.

There are three basic parts:

- **Attribute Name**—the name by which the attribute is called in the document.
- **Attribute Type**—one of three kinds: strings, tokens, and enumerated types.
- **Attribute Default Value**—a token or quoted string literal used as the default value.

The token types are:

- **CDATA**—a reserved name indicating character data, the string type.
- **ID**—a token type for a unique identifier. The value for an ID type must be unique within the namespace scope of the root element of the document (usually within the file).
- **IDREF**—must have the value of an ID in the scope of the root element. This serves as if it were a foreign key in a relational database. In many applications where relational data is exported as XML documents, ID/IDREF(s) are used to model key relationships.
- **IDREFS**—IDREF groups. Useful for modeling *n*-way relationships.
- **ENTITY**—a name of an unparsed entity, which must have been declared in the DTD.
- **ENTITIES**—a group of entity names.
- **NMTOKEN**—a name. It must conform to the XML rules for creating names. Note that in cases where an aggregate document is created, ID/IDREF(s) can potentially collide. That is, even if each part of the aggregate is validated, the aggregate in total is not. In this case, NMTOKEN(s) may be preferred, as they maintain the value as a

well-formed name which, although weaker than validation, is preferred to CDATA. This really depends on the implementation, because in the process of creating the aggregate, the program or person responsible for aggregating data should resolve name collisions.

- **NMTOKENS**—a group of name tokens.

The enumerated types:

- **Notation Types**—must be the name of a Notation declared in the DTD. Used to interpret the content of the element to which the attribute pertains.
- **Enumeration**—a list of NMTOKEN names separated by OR symbols, a choice; typically has a default value specified following the enumeration.

The default values:

- **#IMPLIED or #REQUIRED**—these are reserved names to declare that any instance of the attribute in the element must have a value that is explicitly given (#REQUIRED) or is provided by the system (#IMPLIED). Note that #IMPLIED does not mean "optional."
- **#FIXED**—the default specified in the quoted literal of the attribute declaration is always applied, aka, hardwired. While useful, this default type requires that the DTD be read prior to processing or that the values be hardwired in the application. In cases of well-formed or trusted source processing, the DTD is not used. In cases where the values are hardwired in the application, it is equivalent to using a #IMPLIED type.
- **Attribute Value**—defaults can be specified by ending the attribute declaration with a quoted string containing the value. In the case of an enumeration, it must be a member of the enumerated set.

EMPTY Element Types

```
<!ELEMENT headOfClaude EMPTY >
<!ATTLIST headOfClaude
          id  ID #REQUIRED
          idiotSmile IDREF #IMPLIED >
```

An element which has only attributes and no content or end tag is an EMPTY element. These are often used for tags, such as image tags, which reference a picture but have no displayable content. These may be start tags followed immediately by end tags:

```
<headOfClaude id="claude001" ></headOfClaude>
```

or may use the special closing symbol where it is not necessary to declare it. To keep the requirement that all documents be well-formed but not require a DTD to determine if an element is empty by design, the /> symbol is used to end the empty element:

```
<headOfClaude id="claude001" idiotSmile="smile001' />
```

XML Comments

```
<!-- One Claude is an idiot & my cousin. The other Claude is
rich and my cousin. Should I be nice? -->
```

Comments are easy. They enable you to put in notes about anything, but typically they are used to label or document the semantics of some part of the markup declarations. As shown in the example, enter the <!-- and the --> begin and end symbols, and then you can enter any text you need without the requirement to put escaping symbols (character entities) within the text. Note the ampersand in the example above. There are two restrictions:

1. **Do not use the -- symbol** within the comment.
2. **Comments cannot nest** or be put inside other markup declarations. This is different from SGML, which allows this.

CDATA Sections

```
<![CDATA[<foo>MyFooContent</foo>]]>
```

These are not shown in the example DTD. CDATA sections are similar to comments in that they can contained reserved symbols, including markup as shown. However, unlike comments, which may not be passed to the XML processor, CDATA sections are passed and, therefore, can be displayed; hence, they are used principally to escape markup. *Another example would be to include scripts that contain greater-than or less-than symbols.* CDATA sections cannot nest.

Conditional Sections

While not shown in the DTD example, conditional sections are a means to make parts of the DTD optional. The keyword indicates whether the contents of the section are included in or excluded from the DTD logical structure (that is, are part of the declared document type in use). Conditional sections can be declared only in the external subset (outside and before the square brackets and content inside the DOCTYPE declaration). These can be nested.

Conditional sections resemble CDATA sections with different keywords, IGNORE or INCLUDE.

```
<![IGNORE[<!ELEMENT reviewComment (name, note) >]]>
```

or

```
<![INCLUDE[<!ELEMENT reviewComment (name, note) >]]>
```

For clarity, the keyword is often replaced with a parameter entity to name the state indicated by the inclusion or exclusion. For example, a document may be in different states of organizational processes, and within those processes, the required contents may vary. This can be indicated by naming these states and using it as the name of a parameter entity with the keyword.

```
<!ENTITY % draft 'INCLUDE' >
<!ENTITY % final 'IGNORE' >
<![%final; [<!ELEMENT body (title, p) >]]>
<![%draft; [<!ELEMENT body (title, p, reviewComment) >]]>
```

When the draft PE is used in the DTD, review comment element types are included. When the final PE is used, review comments are ignored.

Special Declarations

There are processing instructions and attributes which are defined as part of the XML specification and declared in documents to enable special processing.

- **Standalone Document Declaration**—declares whether there are external entity declarations. If "yes," there are no external declarations. If "no," there are or may be:

```
<?xml version='1.0' standalone='yes' ?>
```

- **Whitespace Handling**—An attribute that when attached to an element declares that whitespace is preserved in that element when it is passed to a processor. The enumerated values are 'default' (use the processor default modes) or 'preserve' (pass the white space):

```
<!ATTLIST foo  xml:space (default | preserve) 'preserve' >
```

- **Language Identification**—used to identify the natural or formal language in which the content is written. Values for the attribute are defined in IETF RFC 1766. The attribute is scoped by the element to which it is attached:

```
<!— French — >
<!ATTLIST greeting  xml:lang  NMTOKEN 'fr'>
```

A Longer View

It has been said that the major failing of VRML97 has been content that did not perform well within the limits of the VRML97 technology. A different view is that even where the limits were respected, the content created with that technology could not be sustained. VRML implementations have varied widely, have not enabled fidelity of presentation across platforms, and have thereby created a crisis of confidence in the VRML marketplace. There is no advantage in using a standard if implementations of that standard do not enable the content to be sustained, regardless of the performance issues.

The trends in creating, maintaining, and publishing information for the last three decades have been driven by the prevalence of digital tools and the concomitant need to ensure that the evolution and limits of these tools do not inhibit the lifespan of that information. As this is written, the restrictions of time, location, and functionality that characterized the age of print are being removed, yet the challenge of ensuring that the information will survive the technology used to create it remain. Our tools are enabling the processes to become more efficient, faster, and more widespread, but our tools can also limit the time our information lasts by coupling it too tightly to the requirements of any given digital environment.

As Teilhard de Chardin speculated, the trend in evolution is to integrate higher levels of information. While it may be impossible to create information that will last forever, a wise designer hedges the bet by applying the technology supported by the greatest number of other technologies. This can bring down cost, ease the burden of integration, and, with enlightened language design, do the best job of sustaining information against time and evolution. On the Internet, the dominant presentation technology is based on markup. The future of markup is XML.

X3DML is a language designed to integrate easily with other languages, to precisely describe the types of information needed for creating animated 3D worlds, and, within the constraints of current technology, to be free of the impediments of given tool implementations. It matters little that we are able to create more powerful representations if we cannot sustain what is created. X3DML is being designed to broaden the tools available to authors and to ensure that what they create will last by putting that information into a form that is used by more tools, more implementors, and more authors. The commitment to X3DML is the commitment to the longer view of the content creator, who only thrives when content is considered more valuable than the tools used to produce it.

Summary

In X3D, VRML nodesets are bound to an XML grammar currently defined as an XML Document Type Definition (DTD). In application languages, data and scripts are treated equally in the file as long as they are well-formed nodes. This simplifies the middleware. The client is a consumer of well-formed nodes that are validatible where necessary. Lexical unification enables shared resources that simplify the framework. To define these markup languages, XML provides well-respected concepts from the parent-language Document Type Definitions (DTDs), XML schemas, and namespaces.

XML is the transport format of choice for Web content. An XMLized version of VRML makes 3D more accessible and easier to learn, particularly to those authors whose primary language is HTML. This binding provides a set of XML general entities and element type declarations for creating an XML 3D graphics language. We have reviewed the concepts and techniques of XML language design and how these are being applied to create the XML VRML binding, which we refer to as the X3D Markup Language (X3DML) vocabulary. An XML vocabulary is a tree of nodes. In creating the X3D Document Type Definitions, nodes have been mapped to child elements and fields have been mapped to XML attribute lists for most cases.

It is likely that in the year 2000 the X3DML vocabulary will be rewritten using new XML techniques, such as XML schemas which enable the vocabulary to be declared in instance syntax. At that time, namespaces that enable mixing of elements from different vocabularies in documents will be added. This will simplify modularization, extend the language, and facilitate smoother integration with XHTML. With the completion of this work, X3D will be able to support more complex and much longer-lasting content development.

Following is a complete list of URLs referenced in this chapter:

Core Web3D web site   http://www.CoreWeb3D.com

World Wide Web Consortium's XML Web site
   http://www.w3.org/XML/

World Wide Web Consortium   http://www.w3.org/

XEENA   http://www.alphaWorks.ibm.com/xeena

X3D Task Group   http://www.web3d.org/x3d.html

Appendix A

VRML Browsers

This appendix lists several of the most popular VRML browsers. Here you'll find vendor-specific information related to platform support, custom features, OBJECT element CLASS ID attributes, and EMBED element custom parameters. For direct links to these and other VRML browsers, visit http://www.Web3DGallery.com/vrml/browsers/.

Contact, by blaxxun

Home page: http://www.blaxxun.com/products/contact/

Developer: http://www.blaxxun.com/developer/

Platforms supported: Windows 95, Windows 98, Windows NT, and Windows 2000 (available as a Web browser plug-in compatible with current browsers from Netscape and Microsoft).

Major Custom Features: Multiuser VRML worlds, NURBS, Universal Media

Class ID:
```
<OBJECT CLASSID="clsid:4B6E3013-6E45-11D0-9309-0020AFE05CC8">
```

Contact is a multiuser VRML browser created by blaxxun.

Contact <EMBED> Attributes

usage: **<EMBED ... *attribute="value"*>**

Attribute	Value	Description
VRML-DASHBOARD	TRUE	Turns on dashboard controls
	FALSE	Turns off dashboard controls

Cortona, by ParallelGraphics

Home page: http://www.parallelgraphics.com/htm/en/prod/

Developer: http://www.parallelgraphics.com/htm/en/prod/

Platforms supported: Microsoft Windows 95/98, Windows NT, and Windows 2000. Internet Explorer 3.02 or higher (4.01 recommended) or Netscape Navigator 3.01 or higher (4.0+ recommended).

Major Custom Features: NURBS, Real Audio and Real Video, Flash, multiuser worlds

Class ID:

<OBJECT CLASSID="clsid:86A88967-7A20-11D2-8EDA-00600818EDB1">

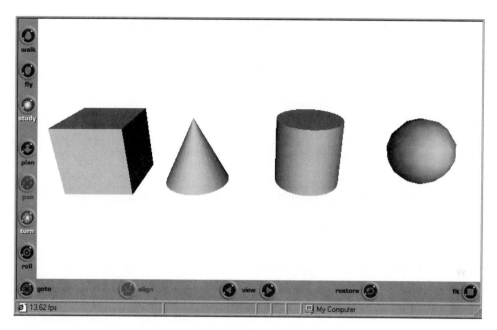

Cortona, by ParallelGraphics.

Cortona <EMBED> Attributes

usage: <EMBED ... *attribute="value"***>**

Attribute	*Value*	*Description*
VRML-DASHBOARD	TRUE	Turns on dashboard controls
	FALSE	Turns off dashboard controls
VRML-BACKGROUND-COLOR	#rrggbb	Specifies world background color using hexadecimal values in the form RED, GREEN, BLUE.

Cosmo Player, by Cosmo Software

Home page: http://www.cosmosoftware.com/

Developer: http://www.cosmosoftware.com/support/

Platforms supported: Windows 3.1, 95, 98, NT, SGI IRIX, 2000, Power Macintosh with Mac OS 7.6.1 or later, Netscape 4.04 or later.

Class ID:

<OBJECT CLASSID="06646724-bcf3-11d0-9518-00c04fc2dd79">

Cosmo Player is now owned by Computer Associates (http://www.cai.com).

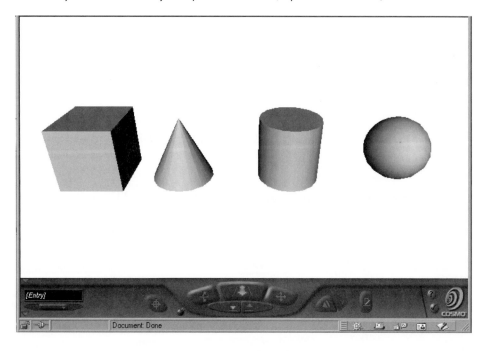

| Cosmo Player <EMBED> Attributes | | |

usage: **<EMBED ...** *attribute="value"***>**

Attribute	*Value*	*Description*
VRML-DASHBOARD	TRUE	Turns on dashboard controls
	FALSE	Turns off dashboard controls
VRML-BACKGROUND-COLOR	#rrggbb	Specifies world background color using hexadecimal values in the form RED, GREEN, BLUE.

VRML 2.0 Viewer, by Microsoft

Home page: http://www.microsoft.com/vrml/

Developer: http://www.microsoft.com/vrml/toolbar/

Platforms supported: Windows 95, 98, NT, and 2000 (Internet Explorer 3.0, 3.01, 3.02, or 4.0 versions)

Class ID:

<OBJECT CLASSID="clsid:90A7533D-88FE-11D0-9DBE-0000C0411FC3">

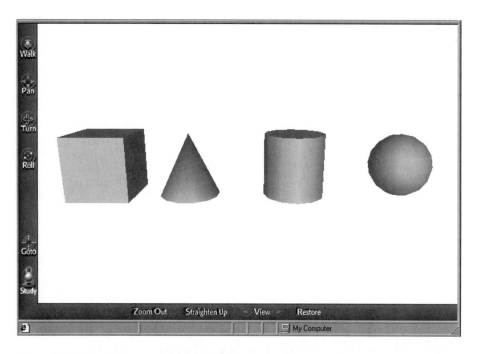

Microsoft's VRML 2.0 Viewer is based on Intervista WorldView.

Microsoft's VRML 2.0 Viewer and Intervista WorldView <EMBED> Attributes

usage: <EMBED ... *attribute*=*"value"*>

Attribute	*Value*	*Description*
VRML_DASHBOARD (or SGI_DASHBOARD)	TRUE	Turns on horizontal and vertical toolbars
	FALSE	Turns off horizontal and vertical toolbars
VRML_IMAGEQUALITY (or SGI_IMAGEQUALITY)	BEST SMOOTH SMOOTHEST	Sets image quality to "Smooth" Sets image quality to "Flat" Sets image quality to "Wireframe"
VRML_POPMENU (or SGI_POPMENU)	TRUE	Enables right mouse button menu.

Attribute	Value	Description
	FALSE	Disables right mouse button menu.
VRML_SPLASHSCREEN	TRUE	Displays splash screen at startup
(or SGI_SPLASHSCREEN)	FALSE	Prevents splash screen from appearing at startup
WorldView 2.1 supports all of the above, plus the following:		
VRML_ DITHERING	TRUE	Turns on dithering
	FALSE	Turns off dithering
VRML_FULLCOLOR	TRUE	Turns on Full Color mode
	FALSE	Turns off Full Color mode

WorldView, by Intervista

Home page	http://www.intervista.com/worldview/
Developer:	http://www.intervista.com/support/worldview/dev/

Platforms supported: WorldView 2.1 for Microsoft Internet Explorer (Windows 95 and NT), WorldView 2.0 for Netscape Navigator (Windows 95 and NT), WorldView 2.0 for Macintosh for Netscape Navigator

Class ID:
<OBJECT CLASSID="clsid:b4d99696-acb2-11d1-a635-00609753e802">

See previous table for custom <EMBED> attributes.

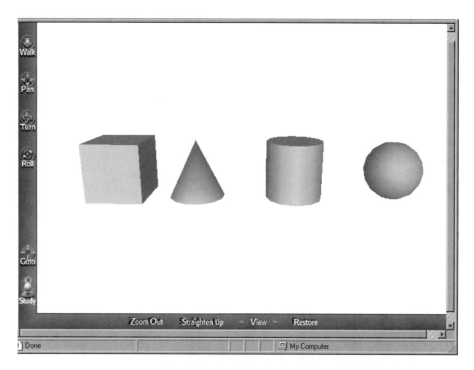

Microsoft's VRML 2.0 Viewer is based on Intervista WorldView. WorldView, like Cosmo-Player, is now owned by Computer Associates (http://www.cai.com).

Appendix B

VRML Resources

This appendix lists a number of valuable online resources for VRML users and developers. For direct links to these and other resources, visit the Core Web3D web site at http://www.CoreWeb3D.com/.

Core Web3D Book Site (http://www.CoreWeb3D.com/)
The online site for this book. From the Core Web3D Web site, you can download the source code listings found in the pages of this book, jump directly to URLs found in each chapter and appendix, and read errata and revision information.

comp.lang.vrml FAQ (http://home.hiwaay.net/~crispen/vrmlworks/faq/)
A compilation of Frequently Asked Questions (FAQ) generated by the comp.lang.vrml newsgroup. Compiled and maintained by Core Web3D contributing author Bob Crispen, this FAQ is available through the VRMLworks site (see below).

comp.lang.vrml Newsgroup (news:comp.lang.vrml)
The computer-language newsgroup dedicated to VRML. Like the www-vrml Mailing List (see below), the comp.lang.vrml newsgroup is an electronic forum through which a wide variety of VRML development questions and answers are exchanged. (As a newsgroup, however, comp.lang.vrml requires a news reader.)

Focus on Web3D (http://web3d.about.com/)
A wealth of Web3D-related information compiled and maintained by guide Sandy Ressler. Originally a VRML-specific site, Focus on Web3D is now a regularly updated resource dedicated to all popular forms of Internet-based 3D. It includes links to VRML authoring tools, a VRML browser comparison chart, VRML tutorials, and much, much more.

Humanoid Animation (H-Anim) Specification (http://www.h-anim.org)
The VRML Humanoid Animation (H-Anim) specification describes a standard for VRML representation of humanoids. It was developed by the Web3D Consortium's H-Anim Working Group, which is co-chaired by Core Web3D contributing author Bernie Roehl.

Macintosh Web3D (http://www.MacWeb3D.org/)
A Web3D resource targeted specifically at the Macintosh community. The Macintosh Web3D site (more commonly known as MacWeb3D) showcases content, tools, resources, and news for the Macintosh VRML user.

PNG Support in VRML Browsers (http://www.cdrom.com/pub/png/pngvrml.html)
A detailed summary of Portable Network Graphics (PNG) support provided by various VRML browsers.

PROTO Repository (http://www.vrml-content.org/)
Freely available VRML prototypes (custom, reusable VRML nodes), with sample source code of each.

Universal Media (http://www.web3d.org/WorkingGroups/media/)
Freely available textures, sounds, and 3D objects for use in VRML worlds. May be used as usual, or as part of the Web3D Consortium's Universal Media system to eliminate download time for such content. Developed by the Web3D Consortium's Universal Media Working Group, which is chaired by Core Web3D author Aaron E. Walsh.

VRML Detector (http://cic.nist.gov/vrml/vbdetect.html)
Comprehensive VRML browser detectors ("sniffers") that can determine whether visitors to your VRML pages are properly equipped (detects today's most popular VRML browsers). Supports Netscape Navigator and Internet Explorer (JavaScript and VBScript detector source code supplied).

VRML Repository (http://www.web3d.org/vrml/)

Comprehensive VRML resource site hosted by the Web3D Consortium (see below). Provides access to a wide variety of VRML tools, browsers, content, development guides, and tutorials. Billed as an impartial community resource for VRML resource dissemination, the VRML Repository includes links to commercial products, shareware, and freeware.

VRML97 Field Data Types and Event Reference (http://www. web3d.org/technicalinfo/specifications/vrml97/part1/fieldsRef.html)

The section of the VRML97 Specification that describes the data types supported by VRML fields (such as SFBool, SFColor, MFString, and so forth), as well as the syntax and general semantics of events. This is a direct link to Part 5, "Field and Event Reference," of the VRML Specification (see below).

VRML97 Specification (http://www.web3d.org/technicalinfo/ specifications/vrml97/index.htm/

The official specification for VRML97, the international standard (ISO/IEC 14772-1997) for 3D on the Internet. The VRML97 specification is a technical document that describes VRML and its capabilities in detail. Because it is very technical in nature, it may be difficult to comprehend if you are new to VRML (see the VRML97 Specification Annotated Reference below).

VRML97 Specification Annotated Reference (http://www.best.com/ ~rikk/Book/)

An ideal companion to the VRML97 specification (see above), this online annotated reference manual describes the VRML97 specification in great detail. Written by VRML architects Rikk Carey and Gavin Bell, the VRML97 Specification Annotated Reference includes a number of source code examples.

VRMLworks (http://home.hiwaay.net/~crispen/vrmlworks/)

Developed and maintained by Core Web3D contributing author Bob Crispen, the VRMLworks leads visitors through a range of VRML topics (from choosing and installing a VRML browser, to building VRML worlds, and points in-between). Includes online tutorials, the comp.lang.vrml FAQ (see above), and a bounty of links to tools, resources, and content.

Web3D Consortium (http://www.web3d.org/)

As the standards-setting organization responsible for developing VRML and X3D, the Web3D Consortium (formerly the VRML Consortium) consists of approximately 50 high-technology companies that contribute to the design, development, and marketing of Web3D. Specifications, resources, technical documents, press releases, symposia, mailing lists, and working groups are provided through this site. Links to various VRML-related sites are also provided.

Web3D Consortium Groups (http://www.web3d.org/WorkingGroups/)
A master list of all Working Groups and Task Groups chartered by the Web3D Consortium (see above). Because these groups are open to the public, you can subscribe to the email lists through which they communicate (look for subscription information on the main page of the group that you'd like to join).

Web3D Gallery (http://www.web3dgallery.com/)
An online gallery of Web3D content, including all of the VRML sites listed in this book. Showcases VRML, Java 3D, MPEG-4/BIFS, X3D, and other forms of Web3D content. The VRML area of the Web3D Gallery includes links to a variety of VRML development tools, tutorials, and resources.

www-vrml Mailing List (mailto: www-vrml@web3d.org)
The main VRML email list hosted by the Web3D Consortium (see above). Also known as the "Big List." VRML developers of all levels—from beginner to expert—communicate through www-vrml on a wide variety of VRML-related topics. To join, send an email to majordomo@web3d.org. The subject of your email should be blank (empty), and the body should contain the text "subscribe www-vrml" (no quotes).

Appendix C

Java 3D Resources

This appendix lists a number of online resources for Java 3D users and developers. For direct links to these and other resources, visit the Core Web3D site at http://www.CoreWeb3D.com/.

Core Web3D Book Site (http://www.CoreWeb3D.com/)
The online site for this book. From the Core Web3D Web site, you can download the source code listings found in the pages of this book, jump directly to URLs found in each chapter and appendix, and read errata and revision information.

Core Java 3D Book Site (http://www.CoreJava3D.com/)
The online site for Core Java 3D, the forthcoming companion book to Core Web3D. As a reader of Core Web3D, you can download several Java 3D chapters from the Core Java 3D Web site that are not available to the general public.

Java Web Site (http://java.sun.com/)
The official home of Java, the technology on top of which Java 3D is built (see Java 3D Web Site below). Contains valuable resources for Java developers at all levels, including API specifications and implementations, tutorials, articles, specifications, tools, news, and much more.

Java 3D Web Site (http://java.sun.com/products/java-media/3D/)
The official home of Java 3D, a member of Sun's Java Media family. Includes Java 3D API specifications and implementations, loaders, tutorials, articles, white papers, guides, presentations, development tools, success stories, early access technology previews, and more.

Java 3D Mailing List (mailto: java3d-interest@java.sun.com)
The main Java 3D email list hosted by Sun Microsystems. Java 3D developers at all levels—from beginner to expert—communicate through java3d-interest about a wide variety of related topics. To join, send an email to listserv@java.sun.com. The subject of your email should be blank (empty), and the body should contain the text "subscribe java3d-interest YOUR NAME" (no quotes). For example: `subscribe java3d-interest John Doe`

comp.lang.java.3d Newsgroup (news: comp.lang.java.3d)
The computer-language newsgroup dedicated to 3D programming with Java. Discussion on this list is not limited strictly to the Java 3D API, although Java 3D topics account for the majority of traffic. Like the Java 3D Mailing List (see above), the comp.lang.java.3d newsgroup is an electronic forum through which a wide variety of Java 3D development questions and answers are exchanged. (As a newsgroup, however, comp.lang.java.3d requires a news reader.)

Java 3D Community (http://www.j3d.org/)
The Java 3D Community is a site created for members of the Java 3D community to share information related to Java 3D. Developed and maintained by Stephen Pietrowicz and Core Web3D contributing author Justin Couch, the Java 3D Community was established at the time this book went to print and promises to become a hub of Java 3D-related information. Site areas include the Java 3D FAQ (see below), tutorials, utilities, books, and news.

Java 3D FAQ (http://www.j3d.org/faq/)
The Java 3D FAQ provides answers to a number of common Java 3D questions generated by the Java 3D Mailing List (see above) and the comp.lang.java.3d Newsgroup (see above). The Java 3D FAQ is arranged into seven primary topics: Introduction to Java 3D, Java 3D Information, Running Java 3D, Java 3D and VRML, How Do I..., Video Hardware, and Programming Questions. The Java 3D FAQ is compiled and maintained by Stephen Pietrowicz and Core Web3D contributing author Justin Couch.

Java 3D Loader Archive (http://www.billday.com/Java3DArchive/)
The Java 3D Loader Archive acts as a clearinghouse of information on Java 3D loaders and shapes. At the time of this writing, the site listed 20 Java 3D loaders as well as 11 Java 3D shapes (including Ellipsoid, Torus, Spring, Möbius Strip, Knot, and Shell).

VRML-Java3D Working Group (http://www.web3d.org/Working-Groups/vrml-java3d/)
The Web3D Consortium VRML-Java3D working group, whose charter is to further the relationship between VRML and Java 3D (see Web3D Consortium). Here you will find the latest versions of the Java 3D VRML97 loader and viewer, for which the complete source code is freely available.

Focus on Web3D (http://web3d.about.com/)
A wealth of Web3D-related information compiled and maintained by guide Sandy Ressler. Originally a VRML-specific site, Focus on Web3D is now a regularly updated resource dedicated to all popular forms of Internet-based 3D, including Java 3D.

Universal Media (http://www.web3d.org/WorkingGroups/media/)
Freely available textures, sounds, and 3D objects for use in Java 3D worlds. May be used as usual, or as part of the Web3D Consortium's Universal Media system to eliminate download time for such content. Developed by the Web3D Consortium's Universal Media Working Group, which is chaired by Core Web3D author Aaron E. Walsh.

Web3D Consortium (http://www.web3d.org/)
As the standards-setting organization responsible for developing VRML and X3D, the Web3D Consortium (formerly the VRML Consortium) consists of approximately 50 high-technology companies that contribute to the design, development, and marketing of Web3D. Host of the VRML-Java3D Working Group (see above).

Web3D Gallery (http://www.web3dgallery.com/)
An online gallery of Web3D content, including all of the Java 3D sites listed in this book. Showcases VRML, Java 3D, MPEG-4/BIFS, X3D, and other forms of Web3D content. The Java area of the Web3D Gallery includes links to a variety of Java 3D development tools, tutorials, and resources.

Appendix D

MPEG-4 Resources

This appendix lists a number of online resources for MPEG-4/BIFS users and developers, followed by the references cited in Part 4 of this book. Because MPEG-4/BIFS is based on the VRML97 format, you should refer to Appendix B, "VRML Resources," for a comprehensive listing of online VRML resources (only a few are listed here). For direct links to these and other resources, visit the Core Web3D Web site at http://www.CoreWeb3D.com/.

Core Web3D Book Site (http://www.CoreWeb3D.com/)
The online site for this book. From the Core Web3D Web site, you can download the source code listings found in the pages of this book, jump directly to URLs found in each chapter and appendix, and read errata and revision information.

MPEG Web Site (http://www.cselt.it/mpeg/)
The official MPEG Web site. This site contains a wealth of information on all MPEG standards, including articles, slides, Frequently Asked Questions (FAQ), and links to various MPEG resources.

MPEG-4 Web Site (http://www.cselt.it/mpeg/standards/mpeg-4/mpeg-4.htm)
Home page for the MPEG-4 standard for multimedia applications. Here you'll find an overview of the MPEG-4 standard, which is also available from the main MPEG Web site (see above).

VRML-MPEG4 Task Group (http://www.web3d.org/WorkingGroups/vrml-mpeg4/)

As an official Web3D Consortium Task Group, VRML-MPEG4 is chartered to develop opportunities for integration and interoperation of VRML and MPEG-4 (see Web3D Consortium below).

VRML97 Specification (http://www.web3d.org/technicalinfo/specifications/vrml97/index.htm/)

The official specification for VRML97, the international standard (ISO/IEC 14772-1997) for 3D on the Internet, upon which MPEG-4/BIFS is built. The VRML97 specification is a technical document that describes VRML and its capabilities in detail. Because it is very technical in nature, it may be difficult to comprehend if you are new to VRML (see the VRML97 Specification Annotated Reference below).

VRML97 Specification Annotated Reference (http://www.best.com/~rikk/Book/)

An ideal companion to the VRML97 specification (see above), this online annotated reference manual describes the VRML97 specification in great detail. Written by VRML architects Rikk Carey and Gavin Bell, the VRML97 Specification Annotated Reference includes a number of source code examples.

Web3D Consortium (http://www.web3d.org/)

As the standards-setting organization responsible for developing VRML and X3D, the Web3D Consortium (formerly the VRML Consortium) consists of approximately 50 high technology companies that contribute to the design, development, and marketing of Web3D. Specifications, resources, technical documents, press releases, symposia, mailing lists, and working groups are provided through this site. Links to various VRML-related sites are also provided.

Web3D Consortium Groups (http://www.web3d.org/WorkingGroups/)

A master list of all working groups and task groups chartered by the Web3D Consortium (see above). Because these groups are open to the public, you can subscribe to the email lists through which they communicate (look for subscription information on the main page of the group that you would like to join).

Web3D Gallery (http://www.web3dgallery.com/)

An online gallery of Web3D content, including all of the MPEG sites listed in this book. Showcases VRML, Java 3D, MPEG-4/BIFS, X3D, and other forms of Web3D content. The MPEG area of the Web3D Gallery includes links to a variety of MPEG-4 development tools, tutorials, and resources.

The following sites and publications are referenced in Part 4 of this book:

1. ISO/IEC 14772-1, The Virtual Reality Modeling Language (VRML), 1997, http://www.web3d.org/vrml/
2. ISO/IEC 14496-2, *Coding of Audio-Visual Objects: Video*, October 1998
3. ISO/IEC 14496-3, *Coding of Audio-Visual Objects: Audio*, October 1998
4. ISO/IEC 14496-1, *Coding of Audio-Visual Objects: Systems*, October 1998. For a detailed description of BIFS version 1, object descriptor mechanism, and timing issues.
5. ISO/IEC 14496-2, *Coding of Audio-Visual Objects: Video*, October 1998. For an in-depth description of visual bitstreams: MPEG-4 video, facial animation, and 2D meshes animation.
6. MPEG Web site: http://www.cselt.it/mpeg
7. MPEG-4 Synthetic Audio Web site http://sound.media.mit.edu/mpeg4/
8. Audio coding Web site: http://www.tnt.uni-hannover.de/project/mpeg/audio
9. Structured audio coding Web site: http://sound.media.mit.edu/mpeg4
10. MPEG-4 Systems Web site: http://garuda.imag.fr/MPEG4
11. Natural video coding Web site: http://bs.hhi.de/mpeg-video/
12. Synthetic visual coding Web site: http://www.es.com/mpeg4-snhc
13. MPEG-4 Industry Forum Web site: http://www.mphif.org
14. ISO/IEC 14496-1 FPDAM1, *Coding of Audio-Visual Objects: Systems, Part 2: Advanced BIFS*, October 1999. This is a preliminary document for BIFS version 2 that was standardized in December 1999.
15. ISO/IEC 14496-1 FPDAM1, *Coding of Audio-Visual Objects: Systems, Part 3: MPEG-J*, October 1999. A preliminary document for MPEG-J that was standardized in December 1999.

In-depth information on MPEG-4 and MPEG-7 can be found in the May and June 1998 issues of *IEEE Proceedings* as well as the following publications:

16. Rob Koenen, "MPEG-4 multimedia of our time," *IEEE Spectrum*, vol. 36, no. 2 February 1999. An overview of the capabilities of MPEG-4 with focus on the needs of our time.

17. Julien Signès, "MPEG-4's binary format for scene description," SPIE Tutorial Issue on the MPEG-4 Standard, *Image Communication*. An excellent introduction to BIFS protocols.

18. P. van Beek, A. M. Tekalp, N. Zhuang, I. Celasun, and M. Xia, "Hierarchical 2D mesh representation, tracking and compression for object-based video," *IEEE Trans. on Circuits and Systems for Video Technology*, vol. 9, no. 2, Special Issue on Synthetic/Natural Hybrid Video Coding, pp. 353–369, March 1999. In-depth information on mesh 2D objects and their applications.

19. A. M. Tekalp, P. van Beek, C. Toklu, and B. Günsel, "2D Mesh-based visual object representation for interactive synthetic/natural digital video," *Proceedings of the IEEE*, vol. 86, no. 6, pp. 1029–1051, Special Issue on Multimedia Signal Processing, June 1998. In-depth information on mesh 2D objects and their applications.

20. C. Herpel and A. Eleftheriadis, "MPEG-4 systems: elementary stream management," *Image Communication Journal*, Tutorial Issue on the MPEG-4 Standard, vol. 15, issue 3, Oct. 1999. This article provides in-depth information on how the elementary streams are related to each other in various scenarios.

21. Atul Puri and Tsuhan Chen, in *Advances in Multimedia: Standards, Systems, and Networks*, Marcel Dekker, New York, 1999. In-depth information on MPEG-4 and MPEG-7.

22. Sharp's Internet ViewCam, the first MPEG-4 video camcorder. Information at http://www.sharp-usa.com/internetviewcam/

23. *ENST MPEG-4 tools*. http://www.enst.fr/~dufourd/mpeg-4

24. *La Boutique Bleue*. France Télécom. 1998. http://www.lorraine.region.francetelecom.fr. The first example of BIFS-Command content available on the Internet. This virtual shop enables you to play with all the features of France Télécom's pagers and phones. A must-see.

25. ISO/IEC 10646-1, *Universal Character Set*. 1993. For information on Unicode and UTF-8.

Information on signal and image processing and compensation:

26. R. C. Gonzales and R. E. Wood. *Digital Image Processing*. Reading, MA: Addison-Wesley, 1992.

27. H. Held and T. R. Marshall. *Data Compression*, New York: John Wiley & Sons, 3d ed., 1991.
28. A. K. Jain. *Fundamentals of Digital Image Processing*. Englewood Cliffs, NJ: Prentice Hall, 1989.
29. S. K. Mitra and J. K. Kaiser, eds. *Handbook for Digital Signal Processing*. New York: John Wiley & Sons, 1993.
30. M. Nelson. *The Data Compression Book*. M&T Books, 1991.
31. W. K. Pratt. *Digital Image Processing*. Wiley-Interscience, 1978.
32. Khalid Sayood. *Introduction to Data Compression*. Morgan Kaufmann Publishers, 1996.
33. J. A. Storer. *Data Compression—Method and Theory*. Computer Science Press, 1988.
34. C. E. Shannon. "A mathematical theory of communication." *Bell System Technical Journal*, 27:379–423, 623–656, 1948.

Some articles on arithmetic coding:

35. G. G. Langdon, Jr. "An introduction to arithmetic coding." *IBM Journal of Research and Development*, 28:135–149, March 1984.
36. J. J. Rissanen and G. G. Langdon. "Arithmetic coding." *IBM Journal of Research and Development*, 23(2):149–162, March 1979.
37. I. H. Witten, R. Neal, and J. G. Cleary. "Arithmetic coding for data compression." *Communications of the ACM*, 30:520–540, June 1997.

The following references are related to computer graphics techniques and other standards:

38. ISO/IEC 10646-1, Universal Character Set. 1993. For information on Unicode and UTF-8.
39. Foley et al, *Computer Graphics: Principles and Practice*, 2nd ed. Addison-Wesley, July 1997.
40. Alan Watt and Mark Watt. Advanced Animation and Rendering Techniques: Theory and Practice. Addison-Wesley, 1992.

Appendix E

X3D Resources

This appendix lists a number of online resources related to Extensible 3D (X3D), the next generation of VRML. Links to Extensible Markup Language (XML) are also provided because of the close relationship that X3D has with XML. For direct links to these and other resources, visit the Core Web3D Web site at http://www.CoreWeb3D.com/.

Core Web3D Book Site (http://www.CoreWeb3D.com/)
The online site for this book. From the Core Web3D Web site, you can download the source code listings found in the pages of this book, jump directly to URLs found in each chapter and appendix, and read errata and revision information.

Core X3D Book Site (http://www.CoreX3D.com/)
The online site for Core X3D, the forthcoming companion book to Core Web3D. As a reader of Core Web3D you can download several X3D chapters from the Core X3D Web site that are not available to the general public.

Focus on Web3D (http://web3d.about.com/)
A wealth of Web3D-related information compiled and maintained by guide Sandy Ressler. Originally a VRML-specific site, Focus on Web3D is now a regularly updated resource dedicated to all popular forms of Internet-based 3D including X3D.

Macintosh Web3D (http://www.MacWeb3D.org/)
A Web3D resource targeted specifically at the Macintosh community. The Macintosh Web3D site (more commonly known as MacWeb3D) showcases content, tools, resources, and news for the Macintosh VRML and X3D user.

Universal Media (http://www.web3d.org/WorkingGroups/media/)
Freely available textures, sounds, and 3D objects for use in X3D worlds. May be used as usual or as part of the Web3D Consortium's Universal Media system to eliminate download time for such content. Developed by the Web3D Consortium's Universal Media Working Group, which is chaired by Core Web3D author Aaron E. Walsh.

Web3D Consortium (http://www.web3d.org/)
As the standards-setting organization responsible for developing VRML and X3D, the Web3D Consortium (formerly the VRML Consortium) consists of approximately 50 high-technology companies that contribute to the design, development, and marketing of Web3D. Specifications, resources, technical documents, press releases, symposia, mailing lists, and working groups are provided through this site. Links to various X3D resources are also provided.

Web3D Consortium Groups (http://www.web3d.org/WorkingGroups/)
A master list of all Working Groups and Task Groups chartered by the Web3D Consortium (see above), including the X3D Task Group. Because these groups are open to the public, you can subscribe to the email lists through which they communicate (look for subscription information on the main page of the group that you'd like to join).

Web3D Gallery (http://www.web3dgallery.com/)
An online gallery of Web3D content, including all of the X3D sites listed in this book. Showcases VRML, Java 3D, MPEG-4/BIFS, X3D, and other forms of Web3D content. The X3D area of the Web3D Gallery includes links to a variety of X3D development tools, tutorials, and resources.

www-vrml Mailing List (mailto: www-vrml@web3d.org)
The main VRML email list hosted by the Web3D Consortium (see above). Because X3D is the next generation of VRML, this list is often used to discuss X3D (developers of all levels communicate through www-vrml on a wide variety of VRML and X3D topics). To join, send an email to majordomo@web3d.org. The subject of your email should be blank (empty), and the body should contain the text "subscribe www-vrml" (no quotes).

X3D FAQ (http://www.web3d.org/TaskGroups/x3d/faq/)
A compilation of Frequently Asked Questions (FAQ) generated by the X3D design and development process. Compiled and maintained by Martin Reddy.

X3D Specification (http://www.web3d.org/technicalinfo/specifications/specifications.htm)
The Web3D Consortium specification site for X3D. At the time of this writing, a draft X3D specification was available, with a final specification due in early 2000. The X3D specification is a technical document that describes X3D and its capabilities in detail. Because X3D is the next generation of VRML, the X3D specification bears a close resemblance to the VRML97 specification (see Appendix B, "VRML Resources").

X3D Task Group (http://www.web3d.org/x3d.html)
Home of the Web3D Consortium X3D Task Group. Links to a wide variety of resources and materials related to the design and development of X3D are available through this site, including the official X3D specification, preliminary specification proposals, surveys, meeting minutes, sample XML tagsets, code examples, development tools, timelines, mailing lists, and more.

XML Home Page (http://www.w3.org/XML/)
The World Wide Web Consortium (W3C) Extensible Markup Language (XML) home page. As the official site through which XML is developed and promoted by the W3C, this site includes the XML specification, related events and publications, software, working groups and forums, and more.

XML.com (http://www.xml.com/)
A commercial Web site dedicated to teaching developers how to learn and use XML. As a collaborative partnership between Seybold Publications and an affiliate of O'Reilly & Associates, this site includes an annotated version of the XML specification, newsletters, guides, tutorials, and a variety of other resources related to XML.

XML.org (http://www.xml.org/)
A self-supporting community resource chartered to provide developers with a credible source of timely and accurate XML information. XML.org serves as a reference for XML vocabularies, DTDs, schemas, and namespaces. Includes news, events, and other resources related to XML.

Appendix F

Other 3D Technologies for the Web

VRML, Java 3D, MPEG-4, and X3D are far from being the only 3D technologies for the Web, although they're arguably the most significant. Both VRML and MPEG-4 are already ISO/IEC international standards, and X3D should become an international standard after the final specification is produced. Java 3D's opportunity for standardization, meanwhile, is closely tied to Java's potential standardization.

There are, however, many other forms of 3D for the Web. Following are just a few of these technologies (assembled from a discussion started by Cindy Ballreich on the www-vrml discussion list and a number of sites compiled by Core Web3D contributing author Bob Crispen). These and many more can be found on the 3D Engines list at http://cg.cs.tu-berlin.de/~ki/engines.html. 3D Engines has been around as nearly as long as the Web itself, and it features a comprehensive listing of many different forms of 3D (a variety of software, hardware, Web-based, and stand-alone 3D technologies can be found here).

Smaller, more focused lists of 3D technologies for the Web can be found at the Web3D Gallery (http://www.web3dgallery.com/), VRMLworks (http://home.hiwaay.net/~crispen/vrmlworks/), and Focus on Web3D (http://web3d.about.com/). Focus on Web3D also offers a comparison of several Internet 3D technologies (http://web3d.about.com/library/blw3dcomp.htm) as well as a complete list at (http://web3d.about.com/msubw3d.htm).

3D Dreams (http://www.doitin3d.com/)
Also known as Spike. A plug-in for Macromedia's Director that can be viewed with a small Shockwave plug-in. If you visit a site that contains Spike content, the plug-in downloads automatically.

3D Groove (http://www.3dgroove.com/)
A proprietary Web browser plug-in focused primarily on streaming ads.

Active Worlds (http://www.activeworlds.com/)
The first 3D technology on the Web to support shared virtual worlds, avatars, and chat. The tight control over the proprietary format and authoring tools has meant that there are no alternate sources, but there is an upside to proprietary formats: you're never in doubt as to whether your world ought to work properly.

Alice (http://www.alice.org/)
Designed for those new to computer graphics and animation, Alice stresses animation over rendering. Although Alice's rendering isn't nearly as good as VRML's, the creators of this technology claim that it's much easier to animate using their toolkit (which features the Python language).

Anfy3D (http://www.anfyteam.com/panfy3d.html)
A pure Java Web browser plug-in with a large variety of specialized applets. The popular Spazz3D VRML modeler (http://www.spazz3d.com/) also exports to Anfy3D.

Bang Space (http://this.is/bang/)
A open source virtual environment based on Lambda MOO/Java3D.

blaxxun 3D (http://www.blaxxun.com/)
A pure Java (no plug-in) 3D technology that supports a functional subset of VRML97. blaxxun 3D formed the basis of blaxxun's X3D proposal.

Brilliant Digital Entertainment (B3D) (http://www.b3d.com/)
Proprietary Web browser plug-in. Works with 3DStudio MAX.

Cortona (http://www.parallelgraphics.com/htm/en/)
This popular VRML browser also supports proprietary technology developed by ParallelGraphics.

Cult3D (http://www.cult3d.com/)
A proprietary Web browser plug-in that supports a large number of platforms.

Flatland (3DML) http://www.flatland.com/
The Flatland Rover plug-in is very lightweight and uses 3D Markup Language (3DML), based on HTML, which is intended to make authoring simple.

GEL (http://www.gel3d.org/)
An open source application that uses QuickDraw for rendering.

Hypercosm (http://www.hypercosm.com/)
Uses the OMAR language and claims a very small file size.

IPIX (http://www.ipix.com)
A popular proprietary technology that is used to create 360° "photo bubble" panoramas.

MetaStream (http://www.metastream.com/)
A popular streaming 3D technology developed by MetaCreations and Intel.

Neo3D (http://www.neo3d.com/)
A proprietary 3D component generation system based on Microsoft's COM (Component Object Model).

NeMo (http://www.nemo.com)
Real-time 3D development and delivery system for interactive behaviors.

OpenInventor (http://www.tgs.com/)
The ancestor of VRML, OpenInventor is still going strong under the aegis of Template Graphics Software (TGS). The TGS viewer features support for stereo vision.

OpenSpace 3D (http://www.virtus.com/).
Macromedia Director plug-in features streaming and geometry compression.

QuickTime VR (QTVR) (http://www.apple.com/quicktime/)
Apple's QTVR was one of the first 3D technologies for the Web. Based on the QuickTime movie format, QTVR is used to create 360-degree panoramic scenes.

Pulse (http://www.pulse3d.com/)
Proprietary Web browser plug-in that supports streaming and geometry compression.

Shout3D (http://www.shout3d.com/)
As a pure Java (no plug-in) 3D applet created by Shout Interactive, Shout3D is the application upon which the Shout proposal for X3D was based. Shout3D supports a functional subset of the VRML97 standard.

Superscape (http://www.superscape.com/)
A pioneer in 3D on the Web, Superscape's viewer supports both VRML and a proprietary format.

Vecta3D/LightSpace3D (http://www.ideaworks3d.com/main/)
Macromedia Flash plug-in that supports streaming 3D.

Web Glide (http://www.webglide.com)
A proprietary 3D format and technology selected by Real Networks to serve as the basis for 3D in forthcoming versions of Real's player.

Wild Tangent (http://www.wildtangent.com/)
Proprietary Web browser plug-in that provides direct access to Microsoft's Direct3D API.

WorldUp (http://www.sense8.com)
Based on Sense8's World Toolkit (WTK) format, WorldUp offers high-performance 3D.

ZAP (http://www.tgs.com/P3/)
Proprietary Web browser plug-in developed by Template Graphics Software (TGS).

Index